CorelDRAW! 5 MADE EASY:
The Basics and Beyond

CorelDRAW! 5 MADE EASY:
The Basics and Beyond

Martin Matthews
Carole Boggs Matthews

Osborne **McGraw-Hill**
Berkeley New York St. Louis San Francisco
Auckland Bogotá Hamburg London Madrid
Mexico City Milan Montreal New Delhi Panama City
Paris São Paulo Singapore Sydney
Tokyo Toronto

Osborne **McGraw-Hill**
2600 Tenth Street
Berkeley, California 94710
U.S.A.

For information on translations or book distributors outside of the U.S.A., please write to Osborne **McGraw-Hill** at the above address.

CorelDRAW! 5 Made Easy: The Basics and Beyond

Copyright © 1994 by Martin Matthews and Carole Boggs Matthews. All rights reserved. Printed in the United States of America. Except as permitted under the Copyright Act of 1976, no part of this publication may be reproduced or distributed in any form or by any means, or stored in a database or retrieval system, without the prior written permission of the publisher, with the exception that the program listings may be entered, stored, and executed in a computer system, but they may not be reproduced for publication.

1234567890 DOC 9987654

ISBN 0-07-882066-9

Publisher
Lawrence Levitsky

Acquisitions Editor
Scott Rogers

Project Editor
Wendy Rinaldi

Computer Designer
Peter F. Hancik

Quality Control Specialist
Joe Scuderi

Illustrator
Marla Shelasky

Cover Designer
Davison Designs

Interior Designer
Marla Shelasky

Information has been obtained by Osborne **McGraw-Hill** from sources believed to be reliable. However, because of the possibility of human or mechanical error by our sources, Osborne **McGraw-Hill**, or others, Osborne **McGraw-Hill** does not guarantee the accuracy, adequacy, or completeness of any information and is not responsible for any errors or omissions or the results obtained from use of such information.

About the Authors ...

Martin S. Matthews and Carole Boggs Matthews are the authors of numerous best-selling books, including **Using Pagemaker 5 for Windows**, **Pagemaker 4 for the Macintosh**, and two previous editions of **CorelDRAW! Made Easy**. Other topics they have written about include Windows Networking, Excel, Q&A, and Paradox. Both authors have over 20 years of computer experience.

CONTENTS at a GLANCE

I	**Introducing CorelDRAW! 5**	
1	Getting Acquainted with CorelDRAW!	3
2	Drawing and Working with Lines and Curves	37
3	Drawing and Working with Rectangles and Ellipses	75
4	Adding Text	95
5	Selecting, Moving, and Arranging Objects	135
6	Defining the Outline Pen	173
7	Defining Outline and Fill Color	207
II	**Using Advanced Features of CorelDRAW! 5**	
8	Transforming Objects	257
9	Shaping Lines, Curves, Rectangles, and Ellipses	293
10	Shaping and Editing Text	339
11	Cutting, Copying, Pasting, and Object Linking and Embedding (OLE)	365
12	Printing and Processing Your Images	393
13	Creating Special Effects	437
14	Combining CorelDRAW! Features	495

III Using CorelVENTURA
- 15 Getting Acquainted with CorelVENTURA **525**
- 16 Importing Text and Using Style Sheets **541**
- 17 Using Frames and Importing Graphics **577**
- 18 Integrating CorelDRAW! and CorelVENTURA **601**

IV Using Other Corel 5 Components
- 19 Using CorelCHART **633**
- 20 Introducing CorelPHOTO-PAINT **663**
- 21 Introducing CorelMOVE **689**
- 22 Introducing CorelSHOW **713**
- 23 Tracing Bitmap Images **727**

V Appendixes
- A Installing CorelDRAW! 5 .... **751**
- B Importing and Exporting Files **759**
-    Index **775**

TABLE of CONTENTS

Acknowledgments xxiii
Introduction xxv

I ▬ Introducing CorelDRAW! 5

1 ▬ Getting Acquainted with CorelDRAW! 3
    The CorelDRAW! 5 Package 4
    Starting CorelDRAW! 5
    The CorelDRAW! Screen 7
    CorelDRAW! Menus 10
    Dialog Boxes 13
        Roll-up Windows 16
    Ribbon Bar Buttons 17
    The CorelDRAW! Toolbox 18
        Drawing Tools 19
        Editing Tools 21
        Tools for Customizing the CorelDRAW!
            Screen 22
    Using Magnification and View Selection 23
        The Zoom-In Tool 24
        The Zoom-Out Tool 27

Viewing at Actual Size	28
Viewing a Selected Object	29
Fitting a Graphic in a Window	30
Viewing an Entire Page	32
Quitting CorelDRAW!	33

2 ▰ Drawing and Working with Lines and Curves 37

Freehand Versus Bézier Mode	38
Drawing Straight Lines	38
Using the Status Line to Improve Precision	39
Erasing Portions of a Line	41
Constraining a Line to an Angle	41
Clearing the Screen	42
Drawing Multisegment Lines	43
Drawing a Polygon	44
Straight Lines in Bézier Mode	44
Drawing Single Lines in Bézier Mode	45
Drawing a Polygon in Bézier Mode	46
Drawing Curves in Freehand Mode	47
Erasing Portions of a Curve	48
Drawing Multisegment Curves	49
Closing an Open Path	49
Full Color Versus Wireframe Modes	50
Drawing Curves in Bézier Mode	51
The Dimension Lines Feature	55
Setting the Drawing Scale	55
Using Dimension Lines	56
Using Callouts	58
Increasing Precision	60
Setting the Grid and Displaying Rulers	60
Joining Lines and Curves Automatically	62
Adjusting the AutoJoin Threshold	63
Creating a Drawing Using Lines, Curves, and Polygons	65
Saving Your Work	69
Retrieving a File	71

3 ▰ Drawing and Working with Rectangles and Ellipses 75

Drawing a Rectangle	76
Drawing a Rectangle from Any Corner	76

Drawing a Rectangle from the Center Outward	78
Drawing a Square	78
Drawing a Square from Any Corner	79
Practicing with the Grid	80
Creating a Drawing Using Rectangles and Squares	82
Drawing an Ellipse	85
Using the Rim as a Starting Point for an Ellipse	85
Drawing an Ellipse from the Center Outward	86
Drawing a Circle	87
Using the Rim as a Starting Point for a Circle	87
Creating a Drawing Using Ellipses and Circles	88

4 Adding Text — 95

Entering Text	96
Selecting the Text Tool	96
Artistic and Paragraph Text	97
Selecting an Insertion Point	98
Edit Text Dialog Box	99
Using the Keyboard and Mouse	101
Entering Text	101
Entering Text in the Edit Text Dialog Box	102
Using the Keyboard to Move Around	102
Using the Mouse	103
Entering Text Directly on the Printable Page Area	103
Aligning Text	105
Left Alignment	105
Center Alignment	106
Right Alignment	106
No Alignment	106
Selecting a Type Size	108
Selecting a Font	109
Different Fonts	109
Selecting a Style	112
Adjusting Text Spacing	114
Adjusting and Comparing Spacing	117
Working with Paragraphs	117
Extracting Text from CorelDRAW!	120

        Merging, Importing, and Pasting Text into
           CorelDRAW! 123
        Putting Text in Columns 124
        Paragraph Attributes 124
        Using the Spelling Checker 126
        Thesaurus 128
        Find and Replace 129
    Using the Symbol Library 130
    Entering Special Characters 131

5 ▄▄▄ Selecting, Moving, and Arranging Objects 135

    Selecting and Deselecting Objects 136
        Single Objects 137
        Multiple Objects 140
        Selecting All Objects in a Graphic 143
        Cycling Through Objects 143
    Moving Objects 145
        Moving a Single Object 146
        Moving Multiple Objects 147
        Moving at a 90-Degree Angle 147
        Moving Objects with the Keyboard (Nudge) 149
        Positioning an Object Using Precise
           Measurements 149
        Copying an Object While Moving It 151
    Arranging Objects 153
        Reordering Superimposed Objects 153
        Grouping and Ungrouping Objects 156
        Combining and Breaking Objects Apart 157
        Aligning Objects 160
    Layers 164
        Layer Features 165
    Weld, Intersection, and Trim 168

6 ▄▄▄ Defining the Outline Pen 173

    Defining Outline Pen Attributes 174
    Using the Outline Pen 174
        Creating Objects with Default Attributes 176
        Customizing Outline Pen Defaults 182
        Selecting a Preset Outline Pen Width 184

  Editing Outline Pen Attributes of Existing
   Objects 185
 Outline Pen Hints 202
  Defining an Outline Pen for Text 202
  Varying Your Calligraphic Style 203
  Copying Outline Styles 204

7 ▰▰▰ Defining Outline and Fill Color 207

 Defining an Object's Outline Color Attributes 209
 Outlining with Spot Color 210
  Setting New Outline Color Defaults 210
  Assigning Spot Color Outlines 213
  Setting New Spot Color Outline Pen Defaults 215
  Using the Pen Roll-Up for Outline Color 217
 Outlining with PostScript Halftone Screen Patterns 218
  Selecting Halftone Screen Patterns 218
 Outlining with Process Color 220
  Defining a New Color and Adding It to the
   Custom Palettes 223
 Outlining with Black, White, or Gray 225
 Copying Outline Color and Pen Styles 227
 Defining Fill Color Attributes 228
 Filling an Object with Uniform Spot Color 229
 Filling an Object with PostScript Halftone Screen
  Patterns 234
 Custom Fountain Fills 237
  Defining Linear Fountain Fills 237
  Defining Radial Fountain Fills 241
  Defining Conical and Square Fountain Fills 245
 Bitmap and Vector Fill Patterns 246
  Using Bitmap Fill Patterns 246
 PostScript Texture Fills 252
 Fill Roll-Up 253
 Fill Tool Hints 253
  Copying Fill Styles 253
  Using Fountain Steps to Enhance Previews and
   Printing 254

II — Using Advanced Features of CorelDRAW! 5

8 — Transforming Objects ... 257
- The Transform Roll-Up ... 258
- Sizing an Object ... 259
  - Sizing Horizontally ... 260
  - Sizing Vertically ... 262
  - Sizing with the Transform Roll-Up ... 265
- Scaling an Object ... 267
  - Precise Scaling with the Transform Roll-Up ... 269
  - Sizing and Scaling from the Center ... 270
- Creating a Mirror Image ... 271
  - Creating a Diagonal Mirror Image ... 273
  - Mirroring an Object with the Transform Roll-Up ... 274
- Rotating an Object ... 275
  - Rotating with the Transform Roll-Up ... 281
- Skewing an Object ... 282
  - Skewing with the Transform Roll-Up ... 285
- Repeating a Transformation ... 286
- *CorelDRAW! in Action: Redlake* ... 291

9 — Shaping Lines, Curves, Rectangles, and Ellipses ... 293
- About the Shape Tool ... 294
- Shaping Lines and Curves ... 294
  - Selecting Lines and Curves with the Shape Tool ... 295
  - Selecting Nodes of a Line or Curve ... 297
  - Moving Nodes and Control Points ... 301
  - Editing Nodes ... 307
  - Working with the Node Edit Roll-Up ... 307
- Shaping Rectangles and Squares ... 326
  - Rounding the Corners of a Rectangle ... 326
  - Stretched, Rotated, or Skewed Rectangles and Squares ... 328
  - Converting a Rectangle to a Curve Object ... 329
- Shaping Ellipses and Circles ... 330
  - Creating an Open Arc ... 330
  - Creating a Pie Wedge ... 331

   Converting Ellipses and Circles to Curve
    Objects 332
  CorelDRAW! in Action: Leimaker in Moonlight *337*

10   Shaping and Editing Text 339

 Editing Attributes for a Text String 340
 Selecting and Editing Text with the Shape Tool 342
 The Character Attributes Dialog Box 344
  Reviewing the Dialog Box 345
  Editing Font and Style 346
  Editing Type Size 347
  Horizontal and Vertical Shift 348
  Creating Superscripts and Subscripts 349
  Editing Character Angle 349
 Kerning Text Interactively 350
  Kerning Single Characters 351
  Kerning Multiple Characters 353
 Adjusting Spacing Interactively 354
  Adjusting Inter-Character Spacing 354
  Adjusting Inter-Word Spacing 356
  Adjusting Inter-Line Spacing 357
 Reshaping Characters 358
 CorelDRAW! in Action: Mogensen *363*

11   Cutting, Copying, Pasting, and Object Linking and Embedding (OLE) 365

 About the Windows Clipboard 366
 Copy, Cut, Duplicate, Clone, or Delete 367
 Copying and Pasting Objects 367
  Copying and Pasting Objects Within a
   Picture 368
  Copying and Pasting Between Pictures 369
 Cutting and Pasting Objects 370
  Cutting and Pasting Within a Picture 371
  Cutting and Pasting Between Pictures 372
 Working with Different Applications 373
  Clipboard Memory Limits 374
  Transferring Objects to Other Applications 375
  Transferring Objects from Other Applications 376
  Object Linking and Embedding 376

Duplicating and Cloning Objects	380
Cloning an Object	384
Copying an Object's Attributes	385
CorelDRAW! in Action: Cobra	*391*

12 ▰ Printing and Processing Your Images 393

Output Devices	394
Preparing to Print	396
Printer Installation and Setup	396
Printer Timeouts	398
Disabling the Print Manager	399
The Print Setup Dialog Box	400
The Print Dialog Box	400
Selecting the Print Command	402
Checking Printer Setup	404
Number of Copies	404
Pages	404
Printing Only Selected Objects	404
Tiling a Graphic	406
Scaling an Image	408
Fitting an Image to the Page	409
Printing to a File	410
Using Print Options	412
Printing File Information with a Graphic	412
Color Separations, Crop Marks, and Registration Marks	415
Film Negative Format	421
Fountain Fill Steps	422
Flatness Setting for PostScript	423
Screen Frequency for PostScript	424
Using Type 1 Fonts with PostScript	425
Hardware-Specific Tips	426
PostScript Printers and Controllers	426
HP LaserJet Printers and Compatibles	428
HP DeskJet and PaintJet	428
Genuine HP and Other Plotters	428
Dot-Matrix Printers	428
Complex Artwork on PostScript Printers	429
Downloadable PostScript Error Handler	429
Printing PostScript Textures	430
Printing Complex Curve Objects	431

	Printing Fountain Fills	431
	300 DPI Printers Versus High-Resolution Imagesetters	432
	CorelDRAW! in Action: Imagination	*435*

13 ▬ Creating Special Effects 437

Using an Envelope		441
	Creating and Duplicating Text	443
	Straight Line Envelope	443
	Single Arc Envelope	445
	Two Curves Envelope	446
	Using CTRL and SHIFT with Envelopes	446
	Unconstrained Envelope	448
	Adding a New Envelope	450
	Create From	451
	Clearing an Envelope	453
Creating Perspective Effects		453
	Using One- or Two-Point Perspective	453
	Using the Vanishing Point	455
	Adding a New Perspective	456
	Copy Perspective From	457
	Clearing a Perspective	457
Blending Objects		459
	Blending Two Objects	459
	Rotating the Blended Objects	460
Extruding Objects		464
	Extrude Roll-Up Window	466
	Extrusion Presets	467
	Type and Depth	468
	Clearing an Extrusion	471
	3-D Rotation	472
	Shading and Coloring	473
	Applying Extrusions to Open Paths	476
Using Contours		476
Using PowerLines		479
	Applying PowerLines to an Object	480
	Varying the Nib	482
	Using Pressure Lines	483
Using Lens		485
Using PowerClip		488
CorelDRAW! in Action: Exploded Desk		*493*

14 Combining CorelDRAW! Features — 495
Integrating Clip-Art and Line Art — 496
Creating the Headline — 497
Entering Remaining Text — 498
Adding Clip-Art — 499
Fitting Text to a Path — 501
Fit Text To Path Roll-Up — 502
Using Fit Text To Path — 504
Achieving Special Effects with Text and Graphics — 512
CorelDRAW! in Action: Entrance — *521*

III Using CorelVENTURA

15 Getting Acquainted with CorelVENTURA — 525
Frames, Tags, Chapters, and Publications — 526
Frames — 526
Tags — 527
Chapters and Publications — 528
The CorelVENTURA Screen — 529
Rulers — 529
CorelVENTURA Menus — 530
File Menu — 530
Edit Menu — 532
View Menu — 532
Layout Menu — 533
Format Menu — 533
Table Menu — 533
Tools Menu — 534
The CorelVENTURA Ribbon — 534
CorelVENTURA Toolbox — 534
Zoom Tool — 536
Frame Tool/Shape Tool — 536
Text Tool — 537
Tag Base Text Tool — 537
Drawing Tool — 537
Page Controls — 538
Status Line — 538

16 Importing Text and Using Style Sheets — 541
Creating a CorelVENTURA Chapter — 542

	Selecting a Style Sheet	543
	Setting Chapter Attributes	546
	Setting Frame Attributes	550
Importing Text Files		555
Using Style Tags		558
	Formatting the Body Text Tag	559

17 Using Frames and Importing Graphics — 577
- Using Frames — 578
  - Using the Frame Tool — 578
  - Frame Tags — 581
- Working With Graphics — 582
  - Importing Graphics — 582
  - Sizing, Scaling, and Cropping Graphics — 583
  - Box Text — 586
- Other Text Frames — 589
  - Captions — 589
  - Generated Tags — 591
  - Repeating Frames — 593
  - Headers and Footers — 594
  - Footnotes — 597

18 Integrating CorelDRAW! and CorelVENTURA — 601
- Designing a Publication — 602
  - Chapter Layout — 603
  - Choosing a Font — 604
  - Chapter Layout — 610
  - Frame Attributes — 610
  - Using the Story Editor — 611
- Importing Graphics with Corel MOSAIC — 613
  - Editing Graphics in CorelDRAW! — 615
  - Adding Chapters to a Publication — 618
- Working with Tables — 619
  - Creating a Table — 619
  - Importing Tables with CorelQUERY — 623

IV Using Other Corel 5 Components

19 Using CorelCHART — 633
- Charting Basics — 634

Starting CorelCHART 636
Creating a New Chart 638
Using the Data Manager 639
    Entering Data with the Data Manager 640
    Importing Data with the Data Manager 642
    Using OLE 643
Customizing Charts 643
    Formatting Text 643
    Changing the Bars 644
    Adding a Legend 644
    Adding Labels 645
    Graphics 647
Modifying Chart Elements 651
Creating Chart Templates 652
Chart Types 653
    Bar Charts 653
    Line Charts 655
    Area Charts 655
    Pie Charts 656
    3-D Riser Charts 657
    3-D Surface Charts 658
    3-D Scatter Charts 658
    Scatter Charts 658
    Polar Charts 658
    Radar Charts 659
    Bubble Charts 659
    High/Low/Open/Close Charts 659
    Spectral Mapped Charts 660
    Gantt Charts 660
    Histograms 660
    Table Charts 661
    Pictographs 661

20 Introducing CorelPHOTO-PAINT 663
CorelPHOTO-PAINT Overview 664
    Getting Started with CorelPHOTO-PAINT 664
    CorelPHOTO-PAINT Screen Elements 666
Using CorelPHOTO-PAINT Features 674
    Making Selections 674
    Working with Objects 676
    Masks and Filters 679

Retouching Images	684
Drawing Tools	686

21 Introducing CorelMOVE 689

Animation Basics	690
Getting Started with CorelMOVE	691
CorelMOVE Screen	692
CorelMOVE Menus	692
Preferences Dialog Box	692
Animation Information Dialog Box	694
CorelMOVE Toolbox	694
Path Tool	695
Actor Tool	697
Prop Tool	701
Sound Tool	701
Cue Tool	701
CorelMOVE Control Panel	704
Playback Controls	704
Opening a CorelMOVE Animation	705
Timelines Roll-Up	706
Library Roll-Up	708
Cel Sequencer Roll-Up	709

22 Introducing CorelSHOW 713

CorelSHOW Overview	714
Getting Started with CorelSHOW	714
CorelSHOW Screen Elements	715
CorelSHOW Modes	717
CorelSHOW Toolbox	717
The Ribbon Bar	719
Text Ribbon Bar	724
Previewing a Presentation	724
Pop-up Menu	725
CorelSHOW Runtime Player	725

23 Tracing Bitmap Images 727

Creating a Bitmap Image	728
Importing a Bitmap Image	728
AutoTracing an Imported Bitmap	730
Tracing Manually	734

    Tracing with CorelTRACE 738
        Preparing to Use CorelTRACE 738
        Loading CorelTRACE 739
        Opening Files to Trace 741
        Tracing a Bitmap with CorelTRACE 742
        Customizing Your Tracing Options 744

V Appendixes

A Installing CorelDRAW! 5 751
    System Requirements 752
    Installing the Software 754
        Creating a Directory 756

B Importing and Exporting Files 759
    Bitmap Versus Object-Oriented Graphics 760
        Using Help for Importing and Exporting 764
    Importing: An Overview 765
        Bringing in a File 766
        Importing Bitmap Graphics 766
        Importing Object-Oriented Graphics 767
    Exporting: An Overview 768
        Preparing for Exporting 768
        The Export Dialog Box 769
    Exporting to Bitmap Graphics Formats 770
        Specifying a Bitmap Graphics Resolution 771
    Exporting to Object-Oriented Graphics Formats 772
        Exporting to an EPS Format 772

Index 775

ACKNOWLEDGMENTS

A number of people provided much appreciated assistance for this edition of **CorelDRAW! Made Easy**. The original authors, Emil and Sybil Ihrig of VersaTech Associates are not only ever-present through their tremendous initial work but they also did a superb job of technically reviewing this edition, adding not only to the accuracy of the work but also a number of tips, notes, and cautions. Erik Poulsen is responsible for the excellent work on the CorelVENTURA chapters and John Cronan is responsible for updating the CorelCHART, CorelPHOTO-PAINT, and CorelMOVE chapters. The acquisitions team assembled by Osborne/McGraw-Hill was superbly lead by Scott Rogers with invaluable and long-suffering support from Kelly Vogel. The Osborne editorial team was lead by Wendy Rinaldi who not only made sure the book was very readable but also provided a foundation of common sense and understanding in the maelstrom of nonfunctional software and impossible schedules. All of these people put out a considerable amount of effort in a short period of time along with more than a little of themselves to produce an excellent product. Their effort and the results are greatly appreciated.

INTRODUCTION

Since its initial release in January of 1989, CorelDRAW! has become the most talked-about graphics software package for IBM-compatible PCs. It is easy to understand why the program has received many major industry awards and so much favorable attention. Quite simply, no other drawing package offers so many powerful drawing, text-handling, autotracing, color separation, and special effects capabilities in a single package. CorelDRAW! 5 continues this tradition by adding a greatly enhanced CorelVENTURA to its already significant desktop publishing capabilities as well as a large number of enhancements to its existing applications and utilities.

About This Book

CorelDRAW! 5 Made Easy is a step-by-step training guide to CorelDRAW! that leads you from elementary skills to more complex ones. Each chapter contains hands-on exercises that are richly and clearly illustrated so that you can match the results on your computer screen.

This book makes few assumptions about your graphics experience or computer background. If you have never used a mouse or worked with a drawing package, you can begin with the exercises in the early chapters and move forward as you master each skill. On the other hand, if you have experience in desktop publishing, graphic design, or technical illustration, you can concentrate on the chapters that cover more advanced features or features that are new to you. Even the basic chapters contain exercises that stimulate your creativity, so it is worth your while to browse through each chapter in order to gain new knowledge and ideas.

How This Book Is Organized

CorelDRAW! 5 Made Easy is designed to let you learn by doing, regardless of whether you are a new, intermediate, or advanced user of CorelDRAW!. You begin to draw right away and as the book proceeds, you continue to build on the skills you have learned in previous chapters.

The organization of this book is based on the philosophy that knowing how to perform a particular task is more important than simply knowing the location of a tool or menu command. The body of the book, therefore, contains step-by-step exercises that begin with basic drawing skills and then progress to advanced skills that combine multiple techniques.

The organization of each chapter will help you quickly locate any information that you need to learn. Each section within a chapter begins with an overview of a particular skill and its importance in the context of other CorelDRAW! functions. In most chapters, every section contains one or more hands-on exercises that allow you to practice the skill being taught.

Conventions Used in This Book

CorelDRAW! 5 Made Easy uses several conventions designed to help you locate information quickly. The most important of these are

- ✦ Terms essential to the operation of CorelDRAW! or the understanding of this book appear in *italics* the first time they are introduced.
- ✦ The first time an icon or tool in the CorelDRAW! toolbox or interface is discussed, it often appears as a small graphic in the margin beside the text.
- ✦ You can locate the steps of any exercise quickly by looking for the numbered paragraphs that are indented from the left margin.
- ✦ Keypress names appear in small capital letters, which set them off from the regular text, for example, ENTER.
- ✦ Text or information that you must enter using the keyboard appears in **boldface**.

Part 1

INTRODUCING

CorelDRAW! 5

GETTING ACQUAINTED with CorelDRAW!

Welcome

to CorelDRAW!. You have selected one of the most innovative and advanced graphics tools available for the PC. CorelDRAW! will sharpen your creative edge by allowing you to edit any line, shape, or character with ease and precision; fit text to a curve; autotrace existing artwork; create custom color separations and moving animation presentations; produce desktop publishing documents; and accomplish many other tasks. You can combine

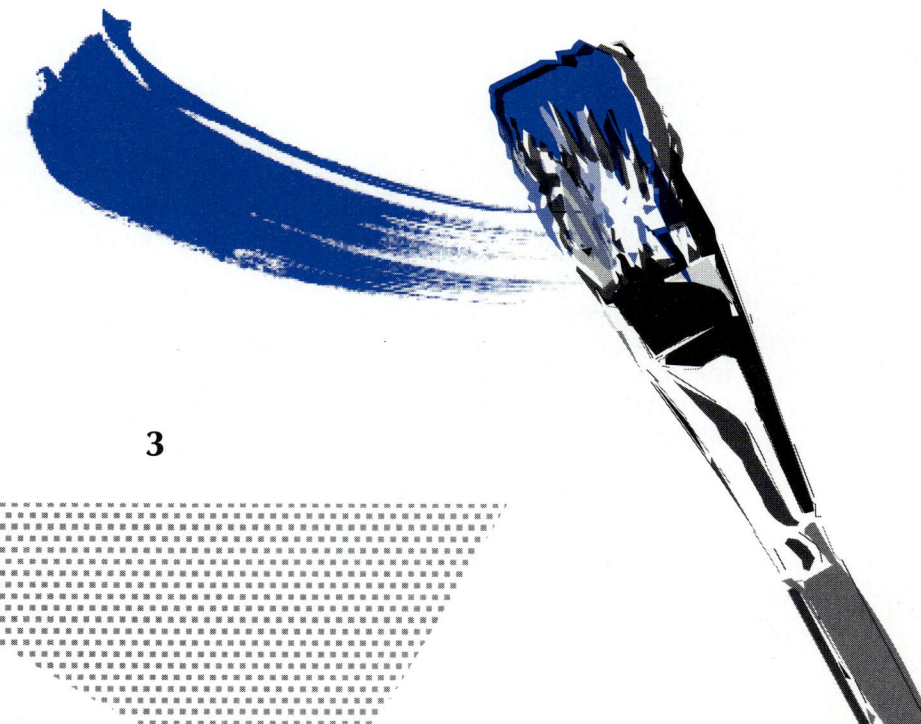

CorelDRAW!'s features to achieve many different special effects, such as placing a line of text or an object in perspective; folding, contouring, rotating, or extruding a line of text or an object; blending two lines of text or two objects; and creating mirror images, masks, and 3-D simulations. CorelDRAW! makes these and other capabilities work for you at speeds far surpassing those of other graphics programs.

The CorelDRAW! 5 Package

When you buy the CorelDRAW! 5 package you get much more than a program for drawing and illustration. There are actually six major products or applications within the CorelDRAW! package in addition to four utilities. These products and their functions are

Product	Function
CorelDRAW!	Drawing and illustration with text handling
CorelVENTURA	Page layout and document composition with text and graphics
CorelPHOTO-PAINT	Painting and photo retouching with image enhancement
CorelCHART	Charting or graphing entered or imported data
CorelSHOW	Creating presentations using other Corel objects
CorelMOVE	Creating animated presentations
CorelTRACE	Converting bitmapped images to vector graphics
CorelMOSAIC	Storing, organizing, compressing, and accessing graphic images
CorelQUERY	Retrieving data from databases and tables
CorelCAPTURE	Capturing screen images

Although you can do page layout in both CorelDRAW! and CorelVENTURA, the two are aimed at very different types of documents. CorelDRAW! is meant to be used for one- or two-page, highly visual pieces such as flyers, posters, and small brochures. Ventura, on the other hand, is meant for longer, heavily textual documents, such as newsletters, magazines, books, and catalogs. This doesn't mean that you can't do a brochure in Ventura or a newsletter in CorelDRAW!; it is just that you should consider the graphics handling strength of CorelDRAW! and the text handling strength of Ventura when you select the tool you want to do a job.

Getting Acquainted with CorelDRAW!

In addition to the products and utilities, CorelDRAW! 5 also includes over 850 fonts and over 22,000 pieces of clip-art to support your creative and technical endeavors. Your software also contains many symbols that you can use as you would text characters as well as 100 high resolution photographs and a library of animations and cartoon figures to use in CorelMOVE.

This book will show you how to use and master each of the Corel products in a hands-on approach that you can follow along on your computer. Therefore, if you haven't installed CorelDRAW!, turn to Appendix A now before continuing with this chapter.

Starting CorelDRAW!

To start CorelDRAW!, first turn on your computer. Next, you may or may not need to start Windows. If Windows does not automatically appear when you start your computer, use the first instruction below for that purpose. If you already have Windows up on your screen, skip to the paragraph following the first step.

1. Type **win** and press ENTER to start Windows. After an introductory screen and a few seconds, the Program Manager window appears on the screen, a sample of which is shown in Figure 1-1.

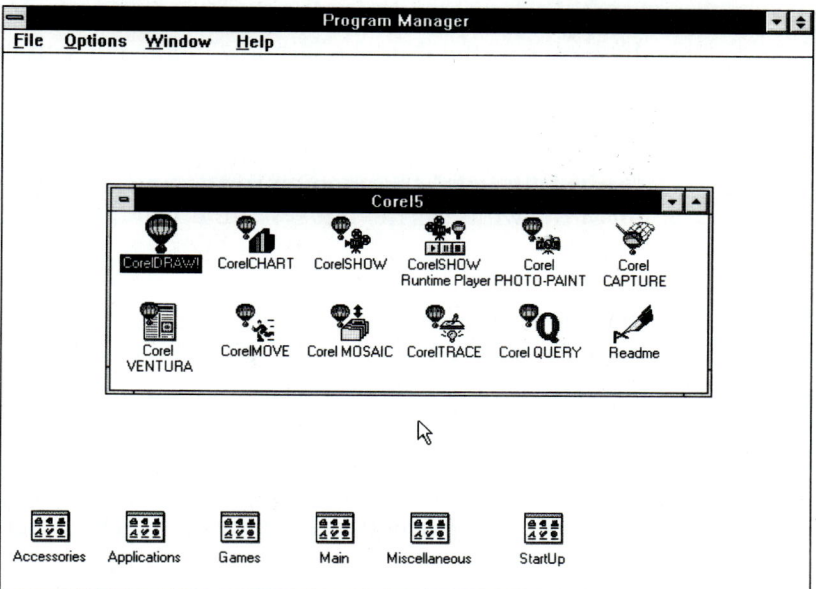

Program Manager window with Corel5 group window open
Figure 1-1.

CorelDRAW! 5 Made Easy

Corel5

Depending on how you or someone else last left Corel on your computer, the Corel5 window may be open, as shown in Figure 1-1, or you may see an icon at the bottom of the Program Manager window. If you don't see an open window with the title "Corel5," look for an icon with that name, like the one on the left.

2. If you don't see either the Corel5 window or icon, open the Window menu by *clicking* on Window in the menu bar of the Program Manager window (with your mouse, place the mouse pointer on top of the word "Window" and press and release the left mouse button). The Window menu should open and look like this:

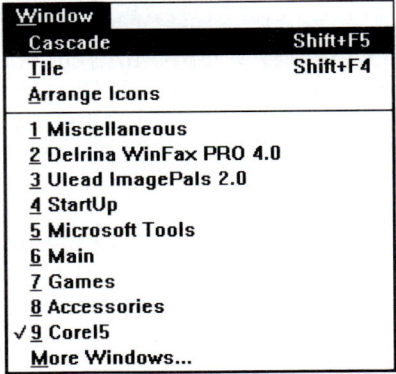

3. If you see "Corel5" in the Window menu, click on it (place the mouse pointer on top of the phrase "Corel5" and press and release the left mouse button). Your Corel5 group window should open.

4. If you don't see "Corel5" and you do see "More Windows," click on "More Windows" and then on the downward pointing arrow to display all of the windows in your system. If you now see "Corel5," click on it.

Caution: If you still don't see "Corel5" in the Window menu, you need to turn to Appendix A and install CorelDRAW!. Do that now and then return here.

5. If Corel5 is an icon, open it now by *double-clicking* on the Corel5 group icon (place the mouse pointer on the icon and press and release the left mouse button twice in rapid succession). The Corel5 group window should open.

6. With the Corel5 group window open, start CorelDRAW! by double-clicking on the CorelDRAW! application icon (place the mouse

Getting Acquainted with CorelDRAW!

pointer on the icon and press and release the left mouse button twice in rapid succession).

After a moment, a copyright and information screen is displayed, then the CorelDRAW! screen appears.

The CorelDRAW! Screen

You will see references to the various screen components of CorelDRAW! many times throughout this book. Take a moment now to familiarize yourself with these terms and their functions within the program. Figure 1-2 shows the location of each screen component.

Window Border   The Window border marks the boundaries of the CorelDRAW! window. By placing your mouse pointer on and dragging the border, you can change the size of the window either vertically or horizontally, or, when you point on a corner, you can change both dimensions.

Title Bar   The title bar, at the top of the CorelDRAW! window, shows the name of the program you are working in and the name of the currently loaded image. All files in CorelDRAW! format have the file extension .CDR

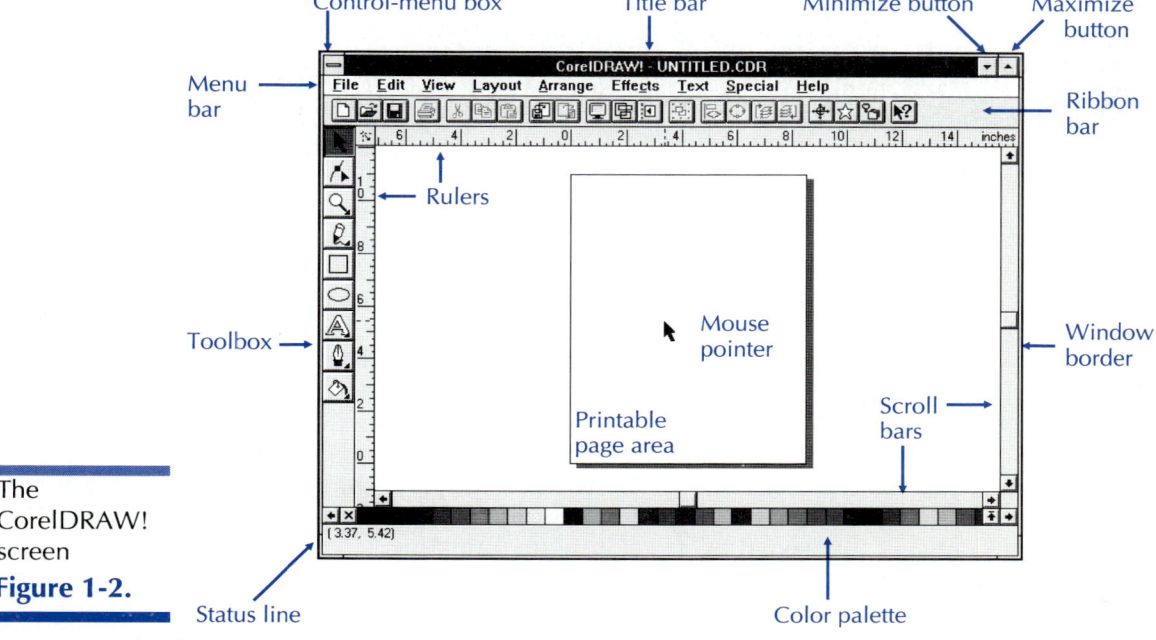

The CorelDRAW! screen
Figure 1-2.

directly after the filename. When you first load CorelDRAW!, the screen hasn't been saved yet, so the title bar reads "UNTITLED.CDR."

Minimize Button   The minimize button is in the title bar at the upper-right corner of your screen, the second button from the right. Click on this button to return to the Corel5 group icon. When running as an icon within Windows, CorelDRAW! frees up memory that you can use to run another application. To restore CorelDRAW! to its previous size, position the mouse over the icon and double-click.

Maximize Button   If you want to make the CorelDRAW! window fill the entire screen, click on the maximize button located to the right of the minimize button. This button then turns into the restore button, as shown in the margin. You can return the CorelDRAW! window to its previous size by clicking on the restore button once more.

Control-Menu Box   You can use the Control-menu box as another easy way to move, minimize, maximize, or otherwise change the size of the CorelDRAW! program window. To use the Control-menu box, simply click on the small bar inside the box, or press ALT-SPACEBAR, and the Control menu will appear. Select the command you want by clicking on it. When you have finished, click anywhere outside the Control menu to close it. The Control menu is a Windows feature that is not heavily needed by CorelDRAW!.

Menu Bar   The menu bar contains nine menus that you open or pull down by clicking on one of the menu names. See the section "CorelDRAW! Menus" later in this chapter for a brief summary of the command options in each menu.

Ribbon Bar   The ribbon bar, immediately below the menu bar, contains a set of buttons that allow you to carry out a number of menu commands with a single click on a button. See the section "Ribbon Bar Buttons" later in this chapter for an explanation of each button. The ribbon bar may be turned off to provide a larger drawing area by choosing Preferences from the Special menu, clicking on the View tab, and then clicking on Show Ribbon Bar.

Printable Page Area   You create your images in the printable page area. The exact size of the page depends on the printer or other output device that you installed when you set up Microsoft Windows, as well as on the settings you choose through the Page Setup command in the Layout menu. When you first load CorelDRAW!, the screen displays the total printable page area. Once you learn about magnification later in this chapter, you can adjust the area of the page that is visible at any one time.

Getting Acquainted with CorelDRAW!

Scroll Bars   The scroll bars are most useful when you are looking at a magnified view of the page. Use the horizontal scroll bar to move to the left or right of the currently visible area of the page; use the vertical scroll bar to move to an area of the page that is above or below the currently visible area.

Rulers   The horizontal and vertical rulers that appear in Figure 1-2 might not be on your screen. These are optional and must be specifically turned on by selecting Rulers from the View menu. A dashed line in each ruler shows you where the mouse pointer is. You can see such lines at about 3.5 on the horizontal ruler and about 5.5 on the vertical ruler. These are the same as the coordinates in the status line. The rulers allow you to judge the relative sizes and placements of objects quickly and accurately.

Toolbox   The toolbox contains tools that carry out the most important and powerful drawing and editing functions in CorelDRAW!. Click on a tool icon to select it. The tool icon now appears on dark gray background. Other changes to the screen or to a selected object may also occur, depending on which tool you have selected. For a brief explanation of the function of each tool, see the section, "The CorelDRAW! Toolbox," later in this chapter. The toolbox can be left fixed on the left side of the CorelDRAW! window or can be made into a floating window that you can drag around the screen. By having the toolbox float, you allow your drawing to take up the extra half-inch of the screen that was occupied by the toolbox. Chapter 3 will show you how to do this.

Color Palette   The color palette at the bottom of the CorelDRAW! window in Figure 1-2 allows you to apply shades of gray on a monochrome screen or shades of gray and colors on a color monitor. Like the rulers, the color palette can be turned on or off in the View menu and you can also select the type of colors you want displayed. In CorelDRAW!, shading and color can be applied to either a character's or an object's outline, or its body.

Status Line   The status line, which in CorelDRAW! 5 appears by default at the bottom of the screen, contains a rich source of information about the image you have on your screen. When you first load CorelDRAW!, this line contains only a pair of numbers: the coordinates of the mouse pointer. When you are drawing or editing images, however, it displays information such as number, type, and dimensions of objects you select and the distance you travel when moving these objects. The exact nature of the information displayed depends on what you are doing at the time. The status line is an invaluable aid to technical illustration or to any work that requires precision. The status line may be moved up to its old position above the horizontal ruler, reduced to a single line of text, or turned off altogether to provide a larger drawing area by choosing Preferences from the Special menu, clicking on the View tab, and then clicking on the appropriate Status Line options.

With a basic understanding of the screen elements, you can get around the CorelDRAW! window easily. The next four sections of this chapter explore the primary interface elements—menus, dialog boxes, buttons, and tools—in greater depth.

CorelDRAW! Menus

When you open or *pull down* a menu, some commands appear in boldface, while others appear dimmer, in gray. You can select any command that appears in boldface, but commands in gray are not available to you at the moment. Commands become available for selection depending on the objects you are working with and the actions you perform on them.

You'll learn to use the menus by working with particular functions of CorelDRAW!, but the following sections will briefly describe the major purposes of each. Open each menu by clicking on it and look at the menu as you are reading about it.

The File Menu The File menu allows you to start a new drawing, to save a drawing as a *file* on a disk, and to reopen a drawing you have previously saved. You can also import and export parts or all of a drawing, open the Mosaic roll-up window, print a drawing, and determine the color profile of your monitor, scanner, and printer as well as exit from CorelDRAW!. The four most recent files you have worked with are listed at the bottom of the menu and can be easily opened by double-clicking on the filename.

The Edit Menu The Edit menu allows you to undo, redo, or repeat the last action you performed; to cut, copy, and paste objects or images; to delete, duplicate, or *clone* (duplicate where the copy also receives any modifications made to the original) objects; to copy or change styles of objects and text; to select all the objects in a drawing; and to insert objects from and manage links with other applications.

The View Menu The View menu has one very clear function: to help you customize the user interface and make the CorelDRAW! screen work the way you do. Use the commands in this menu to display or hide the rulers and color palette, to have the toolbox fixed or floating, to select the roll-up windows to display, to set the screen for wireframe or full-screen previews of your images, to determine how you want bitmaps and colors displayed; and to refresh or redraw the window.

Getting Acquainted with CorelDRAW!

The View and other menus contain options that open "roll-ups," which is short for "roll-up window." A roll-up window is a dialog box that remains on the screen either at its normal size or "rolled up" with just its title bar showing. Roll-up windows will be fully discussed in the next major section, "Dialog Boxes."

The Layout Menu   The Layout menu allows you to control the layout of pages. You can insert or delete pages, go from one page to another, set margins and page sizes, and work with layers that allow you to construct your drawing in multiple overlays. You can manage styles and the scale assigned to drawings and set attributes for the grid and for guidelines. Finally, you can turn on or off the property of an object *snapping to* the grid, guidelines, or another object as you move the first object.

The Arrange Menu   The Arrange menu deals with the relative placement of objects within an image. Select the commands in this menu to align or order a selected object or group of objects; to combine, group, ungroup, or break apart selected objects; and to weld, intersect, trim, or separate objects. You can also convert text to curves. You will find more details about the Arrange menu commands in Chapter 5.

The Effects Menu   The Effects menu allows you to open a number of roll-ups with which you can create special effects with text and objects that transform their images. Among the roll-ups available are Transform, which allows you to distort the image in specific ways; Envelope, where you can place text or an object in an envelope and then shape that envelope to make the object appear to be in perspective; Blend, which allows you to combine two lines of text or two objects; Extrude and Contour, which give a 3-dimensional effect to an image; PowerLine, which draws lines that look like they were created with traditional artist tools; and Lens, which creates the effects of looking at an object through a lens, as in magnification. Also with the Effects menu, you can remove (*clear*) a transformation, add or clear a perspective on an object, and copy or clone the effects from one object to another. Special effects are discussed in more detail in Chapter 13.

The Text Menu   The Text menu provides features for formatting and handling text, including changing the character, frame, and paragraph attributes; finding and replacing text; checking spelling; and locating synonyms. Alternatively, you can open a text roll-up with many of these same features in it. You can also fit text to a path, straighten it back out, or align it to a baseline. If you are doing a lot of typing, you can enter shortcuts in the PowerType dialog box to, among other things, automatically capitalize the first letter of a sentence, correct two initial capital letters, and replace something you type, like "cd," with a word you have specified, like

"CorelDRAW!." Finally, you can open an Edit Text dialog box with the currently selected text and change both the text and its character and paragraph attributes.

The Special Menu   The Special menu is used for miscellaneous functions not found in other menus. If you have a drawing tablet, the special menu allows you to turn on an onscreen keyboard that you can use with the tablet. The Special menu provides for the fine-tuning of many different program parameters using the Preferences option. These options are discussed throughout the book. The Special menu provides the means for opening the Symbol and Presets roll-ups, where you can select text symbols and *presets* (frequently used actions that have been recorded and stored). The Special menu also allows you to create patterns out of a selected object, line endings or arrows that can be attached to the end of a line, and symbols from a selected object. Finally, you can extract text as an ASCII string for editing, and then merge it back into a drawing.

The Help Menu   The Help menu allows you to access a wealth of online help features, including a tutorial. Through the Contents button you can choose help topics that cover the screen, menus, tools, and keyboard shortcuts and that also explain how to perform certain functions, as you can see in Figure 1-3. You can also get a quick look at how to use the comprehensive Help feature by selecting How To Use Help from the Help menu of the Contents dialog box.

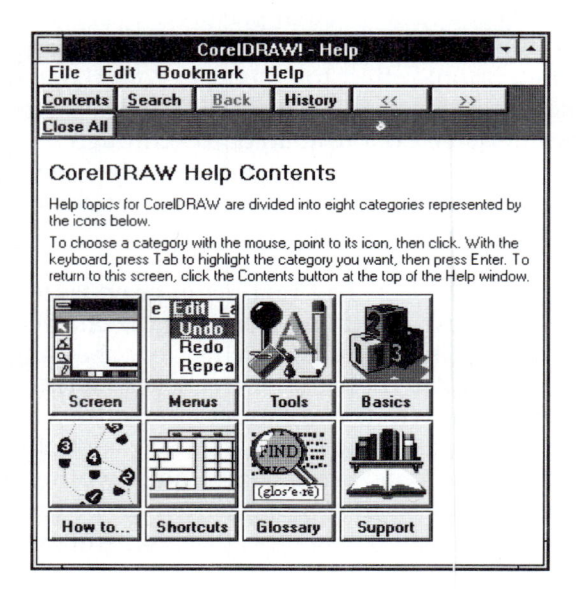

CorelDRAW! Help contents
Figure 1-3.

Getting Acquainted with CorelDRAW!

By selecting Search For Help On from the Help menu, you can type in a word or choose one from a list and you will be shown all topics matching your search criteria.

The final option on the Help menu, About CorelDRAW!, displays information on the current version of CorelDRAW! and other useful information on the number of objects and groups that are open, and on the available disk space on your C drive.

There are other ways in which you can get help. First, by pressing F1, the Help Contents option shown in Figure 1-3 is displayed, giving you the same eight categories of help that are available directly from the menu. Other methods—pressing and holding down SHIFT while pressing F1, choosing Screen/Menu Help from the Help menu, or clicking on the far right button in the Ribbon bar—all provide the same *context-sensitive* help, where the mouse pointer changes to a question mark and arrow.

You can then click this question mark on a menu command or screen item, and a help window will be displayed providing information on that particular subject.

Dialog Boxes

Some menu commands are automatic: Click on them, and CorelDRAW! performs the action immediately. Other commands are followed by three dots (an ellipsis), indicating that you must enter additional information before CorelDRAW! can execute the command. You enter this additional information through dialog boxes that pop up on the screen when you click on the command. This section introduces you to the look and feel of typical dialog boxes. Also, much of what is said here applies to roll-up windows, which are very similar to dialog boxes.

Dialog boxes contain several kinds of controls and other ways for you to enter information. Compare the following descriptions with the dialog box elements in Figures 1-4 and 1-5 to familiarize yourself with operations in a dialog box. Look at Figure 1-4 first.

Option Buttons   Round option buttons like those in Figure 1-4 present you with mutually exclusive choices. In a group of option buttons, you can select only one at a time. When you click on an option button to select it, the interior becomes dark.

Check Boxes   Square check boxes offer you choices that are not mutually exclusive, so you can select more than one option simultaneously. Check boxes, which are shown in Figure 1-4, behave like light switches: you turn them on or off when you click to select or deselect them. When you turn on

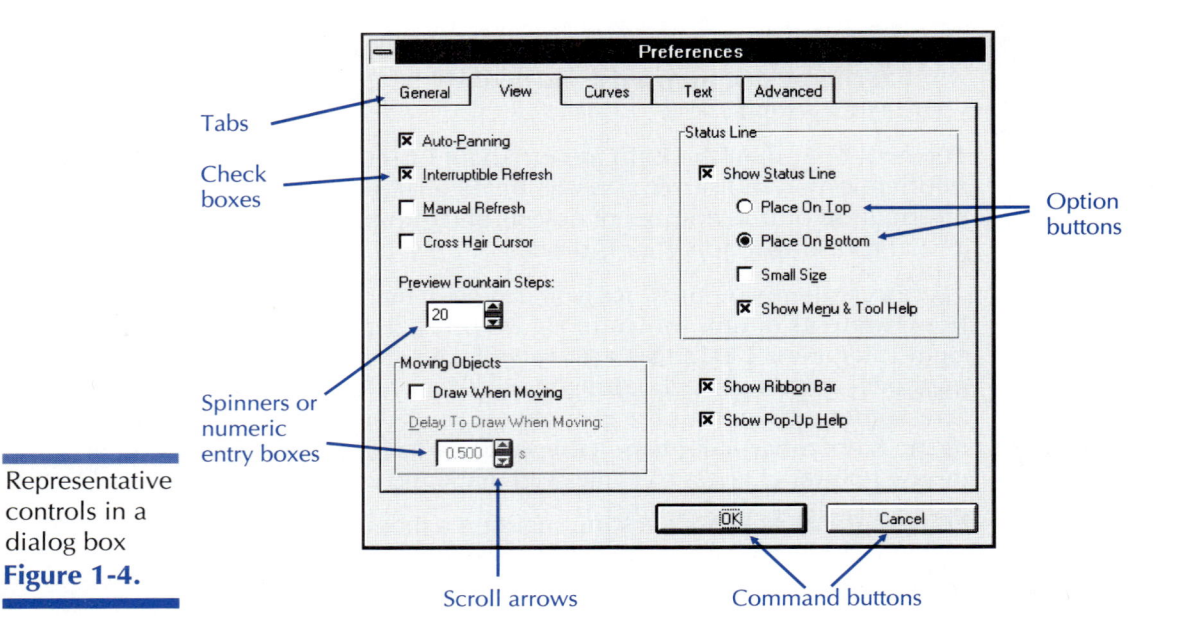

CorelDRAW! 5 Made Easy

Representative controls in a dialog box
Figure 1-4.

Tabs — Check boxes — Spinners or numeric entry boxes — Scroll arrows — Option buttons — Command buttons

or enable an option in a check box, an X fills it. When you turn off or disable the option, the X disappears.

Command Buttons   The larger buttons in a dialog box are command buttons, which are shown in Figure 1-4. When selected, a command button is highlighted temporarily, and usually CorelDRAW! performs the command instantly. When you click on a command button that has a label followed by an ellipsis, you open another dialog box that is nested within it.

Spinner, or Numeric Entry Box   A rectangle that contains numeric entries and that has a pair of up and down scroll arrows is a spinner, or a numeric entry box (shown in Figure 1-4). You can change the numeric values in four ways. To increase or decrease the value by a single increment, click on the up or down arrow, respectively. To increase or decrease the value by a large amount, press and hold the mouse button over one of the scroll arrows or position the mouse pointer between the arrows and then drag the mouse up or down to change the number. You can also double-click on the value itself to select it and then type in a new number.

Tabs   Some dialog boxes, like the one shown in Figure 1-4, actually contain several dialog boxes in one. You select which dialog box you want to work on by clicking on one of the tabs at the top of the dialog box. The

Getting Acquainted with CorelDRAW!

dialog box contents changes according to which dialog box has been selected.

Drop-Down List Box   Rectangles with a downward pointing arrow on the right are drop-down list boxes, as shown in Figure 1-5. By clicking on the arrow, a list drops down (or in a few cases, pops up) from which you can select an option. When a drop-down list is opened, you can choose an option by clicking on it or by typing enough letters to uniquely select the option.

Text box   Text boxes, like the one shown in Figure 1-5, are used in some dialog boxes to enter strings of text. Depending on the dialog box involved, text strings might represent filenames, path names, or text to appear in an image. To enter new text where none exists, click in the text box and type the text. To edit an existing text string, click on the string, then use the keyboard to erase or add text. You will become familiar with the specific keys to use as you learn about each type of text box.

List Box   List boxes list the names of choices available to the user, such as filenames, directory and drive names, or typestyle names. Click on a name in the list box to select it. List boxes (see Figure 1-5) are open all the time but are otherwise similar to drop-down list boxes.

Many list boxes and drop-down list boxes have scroll bars on their right side in order to display more of the list than is initially displayed. You can use the scroll bar to access the portions of the list that are outside of the currently visible area. To move up or down one name at a time, click on the up or down arrows on the scroll bar. To move up or down continuously,

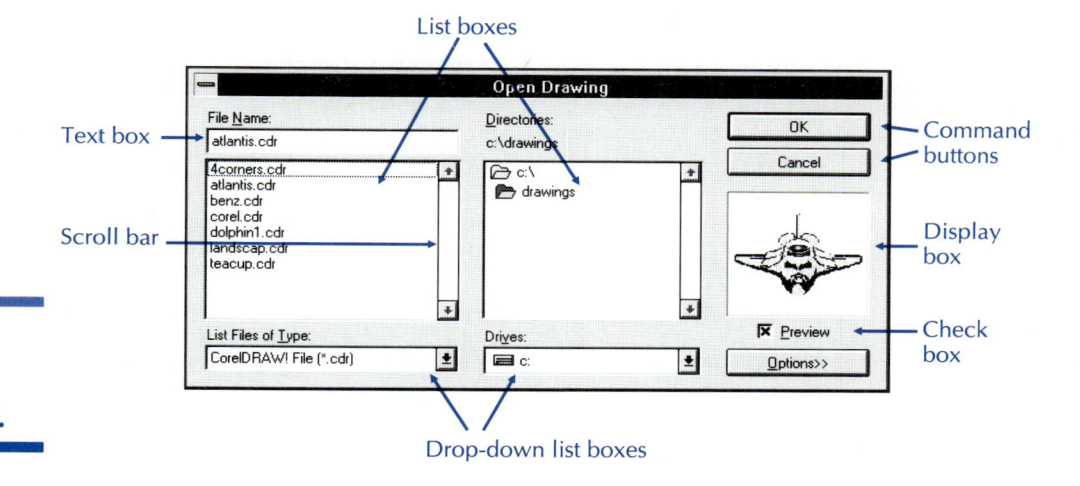

Additional dialog box controls
Figure 1-5.

press and hold the mouse button over the up or down arrow of the scroll bar. Alternatively, you can click on the scroll bar itself, drag the scroll box, or press PGUP or PGDN to move up or down the list box in large increments.

Display Box   Some dialog boxes, such as the one shown in Figure 1-5, contain *display boxes* that show you your current selection. You cannot perform any action in the display box; instead, its contents change as you change your selections in the dialog box.

Some options in a dialog box may appear dim or gray, indicating that you cannot select them at the moment. There may also be a command button within a dialog box that appears in boldface or has a bold outline around it. This command button represents the default selection. You can simply press ENTER to activate that selection. The OK command button is normally the default. The OK button accepts and processes the entries you make in the dialog box. You can leave most dialog boxes without changing any settings by clicking on the Cancel button or pressing ESC.

You will learn more about operating within dialog boxes and about specific dialog boxes as you read the other chapters in this book.

Roll-up Windows

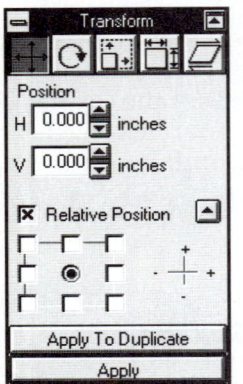

Roll-up windows are a special form of dialog box that you can keep on the screen to allow faster access to the features provided in the window. Once you've chosen a roll-up from a menu, you can choose any of the offered features and watch them take effect while the roll-up stays open on the screen. You can also move the roll-up by dragging its title bar. After you've completed a task, you then have the choice of either keeping the roll-up on the screen in its full size or rolling it up to its minimized size by clicking on the arrow in the upper-right corner, as shown here:

More than one roll-up can be kept on your screen at a time. A convenient way to display one or more minimized roll-ups is to choose the Arrange or Arrange All option from the roll-up's Control menu, which is located in the upper-left corner of the roll-up window. When chosen, Arrange (which is for one roll-up) or Arrange All (which is for multiple roll-ups) moves the minimized windows into a single column starting in the upper-right or upper-left corner of the full CorelDRAW! window.

You can also remove any roll-up from the screen by double-clicking its Control-menu box, or by selecting Close from its Control menu.

Getting Acquainted with CorelDRAW!

Ribbon Bar Buttons

As handy as menu options are, some require as many as three or four steps to carry them out. For that reason, CorelDRAW! 5 has added a ribbon bar with 21 buttons on it that carry out 21 different menu options by simply clicking on a button. The ribbon bar is shown here and the buttons and the functions they perform are described in Table 1-1.

Button	Function Performed
	Create a new drawing
	Open a drawing
	Save active drawing
	Print active drawing
	Cut selection to clipboard
	Copy selection to clipboard
	Paste contents of clipboard
	Import text or object
	Export selection to another format
	Display drawing in full-screen preview
	Display drawing as a wireframe
	Snap selection to guidelines
	Group selected objects

Ribbon Bar Buttons and Their Functions
Table 1-1.

Button	Function Performed
	Open the Align dialog box
	Convert text to curves
	Move selection to the top layer
	Move selection to the bottom layer
	Open the Transform roll-up
	Open the Symbol roll-up
	Open the Mosaic roll-up
	Initiate context sensitive help

Ribbon Bar Buttons and Their Functions (*continued*)
Table 1-1.

The CorelDRAW! Toolbox

One of the features that makes CorelDRAW! so easy to work with is the economy of the screen. The number of tools in the CorelDRAW! toolbox (see Figure 1-6) is deceptively small. Several of the tools have more than one function, and nested submenus *flyout* when you select them. This method of organization reduces screen clutter and keeps related functions together.

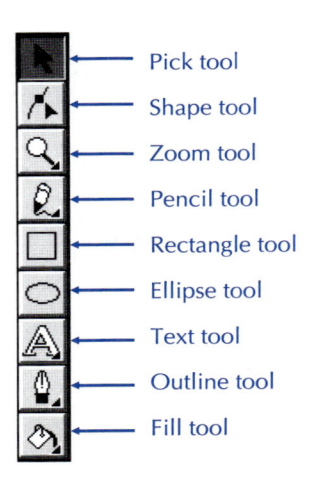

- Pick tool
- Shape tool
- Zoom tool
- Pencil tool
- Rectangle tool
- Ellipse tool
- Text tool
- Outline tool
- Fill tool

CorelDRAW! toolbox icons
Figure 1-6.

Getting Acquainted with CorelDRAW!

The tools in the CorelDRAW! toolbox perform three different kinds of functions. Some allow you to draw objects, others let you edit the objects you have drawn, and a third group permits you to alter the appearance of the screen so that you can work more efficiently. This section describes each tool briefly in the context of its respective function.

Drawing Tools

CorelDRAW! allows you to create or work with nine different types of objects, as shown in Figure 1-7. Because you use the same tools and techniques for some of the objects, however, there are actually only five different *classes* of objects. These classes, and the kinds of objects you can design in each, are

- Lines, curves, and polygons
- Rectangles and squares
- Ellipses and circles
- Text
- Bitmap (pixel-based) images imported from a scanner or paint program

Does nine seem like a small number? Professional artists and graphic designers know that basic geometrical shapes are the building blocks on which more elaborate images are constructed. After you "build" an object using one of the drawing tools, you can use one or more of the editing tools in the CorelDRAW! toolbox to reshape, rearrange, color, and outline it.

The four creating tools—the Pencil tool, the Rectangle tool, the Ellipse tool, and the Text tool—are all you need to create eight of the nine object types in

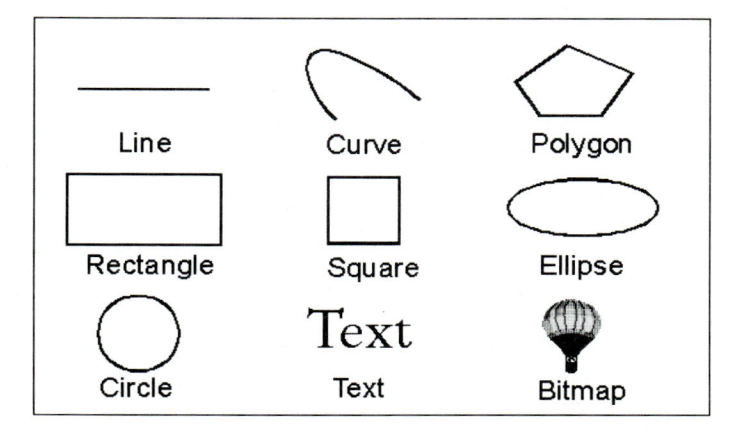

The nine types of objects
Figure 1-7.

CorelDRAW!. You work with the last object type, a bitmap image, after importing it. (See Chapters 7 and 23 for a fuller discussion of this subject.)

The Pencil Tool   The Pencil tool is the most basic drawing tool in the CorelDRAW! toolbox. This single tool allows you to create lines, curves, curved objects, and polygons. The Pencil tool can be changed from a single-mode freehand drawing instrument to a more sophisticated multimode instrument using Bézier lines and curves, or to one of four Dimension Lines modes. Freehand mode is the default and is used for less precise work. Bézier mode is selected from the flyout menu. Click on the Pencil tool, hold the mouse button down, and six icons, one for each drawing mode, are displayed, as shown on the left. Bézier mode is used for smooth, precise curves, which remain so even when magnified or distorted. The four Dimension Lines modes are used to place lines that show dimensions between two objects or locations or identify an object, as you would use in technical drawings.

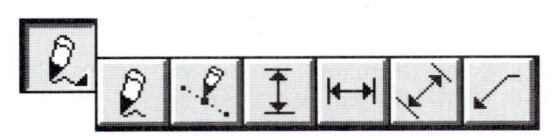

Chapter 2 guides you through a series of exercises that teach you the basic CorelDRAW! skills for using this tool in all five modes.

To select the Pencil tool, press F5 or click on the Pencil icon once, and then move the mouse pointer into the white space on the page. When you select this tool, the mouse pointer becomes a crosshair, the Pencil tool icon becomes highlighted, and the message "Drawing in Freehand Mode...," "Drawing in Bézier Mode...," "Creating Linear Dimension...," or "Creating Callout" appears in the status line.

The Rectangle Tool   The Rectangle tool lets you draw rectangles and squares. You'll create your own rectangles and squares in Chapter 3. To round the corners of a rectangle, however, you need to use the Shape tool, one of the editing tools in the CorelDRAW! toolbox.

To select the Rectangle tool, press F6 or click on the Rectangle icon once, and then move the mouse pointer into the white space on the page. The Rectangle icon becomes highlighted, the mouse pointer becomes a crosshair, and the message "Rectangle..." appears in the status line.

The Ellipse Tool   The Ellipse tool allows you to create ellipses and perfect circles. You will learn more about using the Ellipse tool in Chapter 3.

To select the Ellipse tool, press F7 or click on the Ellipse icon once, and then move the mouse pointer into the white space on the page. The Ellipse icon becomes highlighted, the mouse pointer becomes a crosshair, and the message "Ellipse..." appears in the status line.

Getting Acquainted with CorelDRAW!

The Text Tool The Text tool contains a flyout menu with two icons for choosing between artistic text and paragraph text. Artistic text is a simple string of characters as might appear on a poster. Paragraph text is longer and has more spacing attributes; the text in a brochure is an example of paragraph text. Either form of the text tool gives you access to the many Corel Systems fonts and to thousands of other commercial fonts as well. Besides alphabetic characters, CorelDRAW! includes an extensive symbol library that you can also access with the Text tool. Chapter 4 teaches you how to enter text in CorelDRAW!.

To select the Artistic Text tool, press F8 or click on the Text icon once, and then move the pointer into the white space on the page. The Text icon becomes highlighted, the mouse pointer becomes a crosshair, and the message "Text..." appears in the status line.

If you "scribbled" on the page while trying out any of the drawing tools, clear the screen before proceeding. To do this, click on the File menu and select the New command. The following dialog box appears:

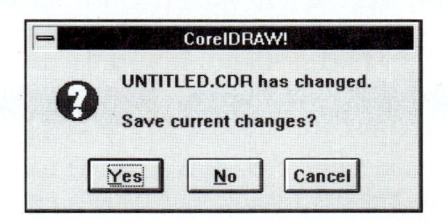

Select the No command button to exit the message box and clear the screen.

Editing Tools

Once you have created objects on a page with the drawing or text tools, you use a different group of tools to move, arrange, shape, and manipulate the objects. The editing tools include the Pick tool, the Shape tool, the Outline tool, and the Fill tool.

The Pick Tool The Pick tool is really two tools in one, varying according to the mode. In the *select mode,* you can select objects in order to move, arrange, group, or combine them. In the *transformation mode,* you can use the Pick tool to rotate, skew, stretch, reflect, move, or scale a selected object. This tool does not let you change the basic shape of an object, however. Chapters 5 and 8 introduce you to all the functions of the Pick tool.

The Shape Tool The Shape tool allows you to modify the shape of an object. Use this tool to smooth or distort any shape, add rounded corners to rectangles, convert a circle into a wedge or arc, modify a curve, or kern individual characters in a text string. You can select the Shape tool by clicking on it or by pressing F10. Chapters 9 and 10 cover the basics of using this tool.

The Outline Tool   The Outline tool, like the Pick tool, functions in more than one way. Use the Outline tool and its associated flyout menu to choose a standard or custom outline color or to create a custom outline "pen" for a selected object. Chapters 6 and 7 instruct you in the use of this tool.

The Fill Tool   Use the Fill tool and its associated flyout menu to select a standard or custom fill color for selected objects or text. As you'll learn in Chapter 7, your options include custom colors, POSTSCRIPT screens, patterns, fountain and texture fills, and POSTSCRIPT textures.

Tools for Customizing the CorelDRAW! Screen

The third group of tools helps you customize the CorelDRAW! interface so that it works the way you do. Only one of these tools, the Zoom tool, is visible in the CorelDRAW! toolbox. The Zoom tool and its associated flyout menu let you control just how much of your picture you will view at one time. Use this tool when you need to work on a smaller area in fine detail, or when you need to zoom in or out of a picture.

When you start CorelDRAW! or open a new file, full-page view is the default view of the page on the screen. This view has obvious limitations if you need to edit images or do fine detail work. The Zoom tool can customize the viewing area of your screen any way you wish. As you become familiar with this tool, you will experience greater drawing convenience and ease in editing.

The Zoom tool resembles a small magnifying glass and is really a view adjustment tool, because it allows you to zoom in or out of the viewing area in a variety of different ways. Because the Zoom tool gives you complete control over the content of the viewing area, it can enhance every object you draw and increases the usefulness of every tool in the CorelDRAW! toolbox.

The Zoom tool is really six separate tools. When you select this tool, a flyout menu appears, giving you six tools for adjusting your viewing area, as shown here:

Getting Acquainted with CorelDRAW!

Zoom-In The Zoom-In tool allows you to zoom in on any area of a drawing that you select by drawing a rectangle with the Zoom-In tool around the area you want.

Zoom-Out The Zoom-Out tool either zooms out of your current image by a factor of two or, if your screen currently shows a zoom-in view, returns you to the previous view.

Actual Size The Actual Size tool lets you see your drawing in the actual size it will be printed.

Selected Object The Selected Object tool zooms in on the selected objects in your drawing so they and they alone fill the drawing area.

Fit-in-Window The Fit-in-Window tool lets you see all of the current drawing—everything you have placed on the page—in the current CorelDRAW! window.

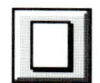

Show Page The Show Page tool returns you to the default full-page view of your graphic.

Using Magnification and View Selection

Adjusting the view on your screen (in particular, adjusting the magnification) is critical to being able to draw with precision. Therefore the remainder of this chapter is spent learning to use the various tools within the zoom tool to change the view presented on the screen.

In order to have something to magnify, open any piece of clip-art that you wish. The file USA_T.CMX was used here. It was imported off the first CD-ROM with the path shown here (your drive may be different):

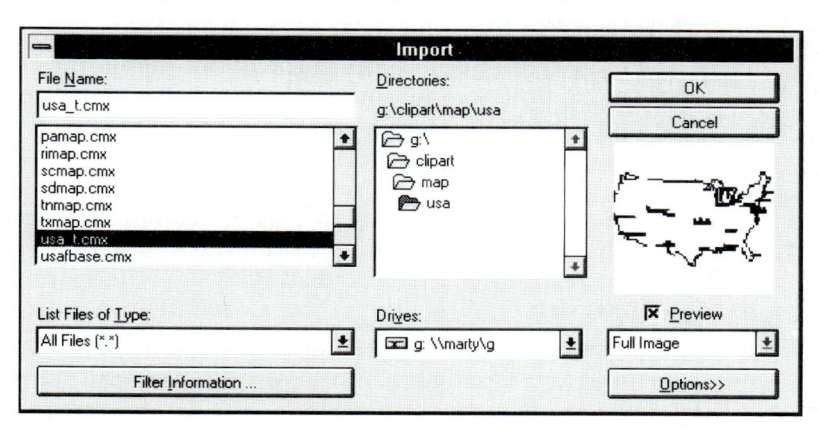

When you have a picture on your screen, perform these steps:

1. Select the Zoom tool by positioning the mouse pointer over the Zoom tool in the toolbox and clicking once. The menu containing the six viewing options flies out slightly below and to the right of the Zoom tool.

2. Select a tool from the flyout menu using either the mouse or your keyboard. To select a tool using the mouse, simply click on it, or drag the mouse pointer until you highlight the tool and then release the mouse button. To select a tool using the keyboard, you must use individual function keys for each of the Zoom tools. (The Actual Size and Selected Object tools are not available through the keyboard.) The function keys and the Zoom tools they activate are

   - F2 **Zoom-In**
   - F3 **Zoom-Out**
   - F4 **Fit-in-Window**
   - SHIFT-F4 **Show Page**

All six of the Zoom tools except the Zoom-In tool perform their functions automatically when you select them. The following sections discuss each Zoom tool and present hands-on exercises for you to practice using them.

The Zoom-In Tool

The Zoom-In tool looks like the main Zoom tool, except that it is smaller and contains a plus sign. The Zoom-In tool is the most versatile of the six Zoom tools because it lets you define precisely how much of your picture you want to view at once. It is invaluable for drawing fine details or editing small areas of a picture.

Defining the Viewing Area

Unlike the other Zoom tools in the flyout menu, the Zoom-In tool does not perform its function automatically. You have to define the zoom-in area through a series of four general steps. Try this yourself now on the map or the piece of clip-art you are using:

1. Select the Zoom-In tool by first activating the Zoom tool and then selecting the Zoom-In tool from the flyout menu or by pressing F2. The mouse pointer changes to an image of a magnifying glass containing a plus sign.

2. Position the mouse pointer at any corner of the area you want to magnify; usually it is most convenient to start at the upper-left corner.

Getting Acquainted with CorelDRAW!

3. Press and hold the mouse button at that corner and then drag the mouse diagonally toward the opposite corner of the area on which you want to zoom in. A dotted rectangle (a *marquee*) will follow your mouse pointer and "lasso" the zoom-in area, as in the example in Figure 1-8.

4. When you have surrounded the area on which you want to zoom in, release the mouse button. The screen redraws, as in Figure 1-9, and the viewing window now contains a close-up view of only the objects you selected.

You can zoom in on successively finer areas of the screen using the Zoom-In tool. You must reselect the Zoom-In tool each time you wish to magnify further, however, for as soon as the screen is redrawn, CorelDRAW! automatically returns to the Pick tool. Simply select the Zoom-In tool again and select another area, as shown in Figure 1-10. The number of times you can zoom in depends on the type of monitor and display adapter you use. Try zooming in on progressively smaller areas; eventually, you reach a point where you are unable to zoom in any further. When this occurs, you have reached the maximum magnification possible for your monitor and display adapter. At that point, 1 pixel on the screen represents approximately 1/1000 of an inch. You must use another Zoom tool first before you can use the Zoom-In tool again.

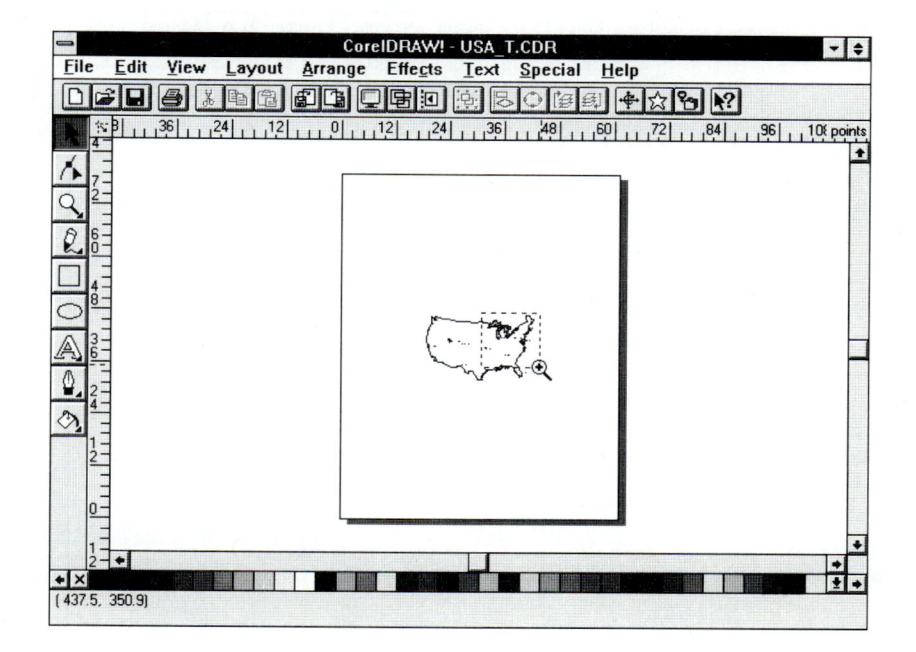

Selecting an area with the marquee

Figure 1-8.

CorelDRAW! 5 Made Easy

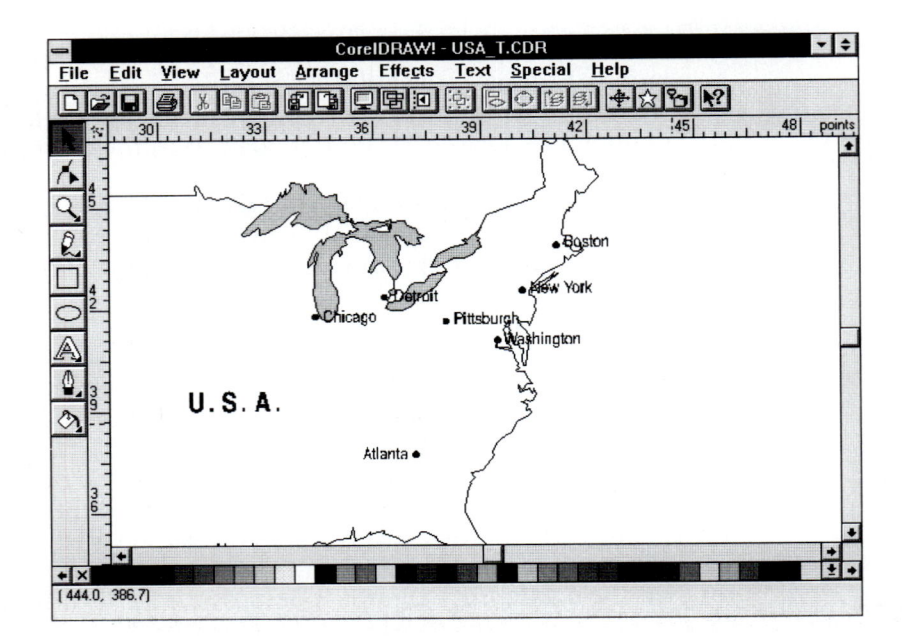

A close-up view of the selected area
Figure 1-9.

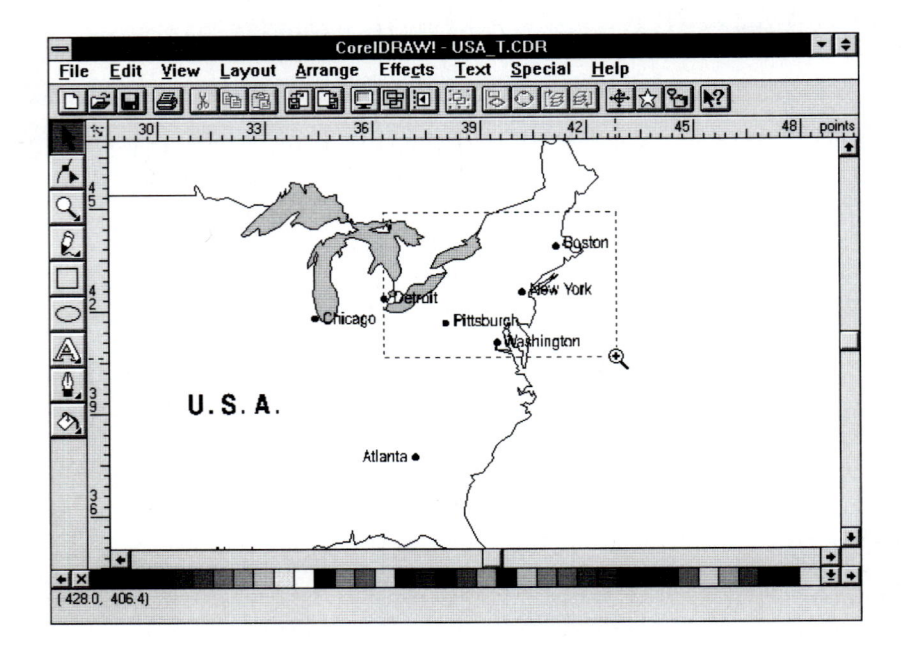

Zooming in a second time
Figure 1-10.

Tip: You can set the right mouse button to zoom in, by a factor of two, on any point you select. Do this by choosing Preferences in the Special menu, then click on the General tab. From the Right Mouse Button drop-down list box, you can select one of the five options. Click on 2X Zoom and then on OK again in the Preferences dialog box. After setting the mouse button, a single click of the right button will zoom in, while a double-click will zoom out. The area where you click will be at the center of the new screen.

The Zoom-Out Tool

The Zoom-Out tool looks like the main Zoom tool, except that it is a little smaller and contains a minus sign. As soon as you select this tool, it defines the zoom-out area for you automatically in one of two ways:

- If you are currently in an actual size, a fit-in-window, or in show page viewing magnification, selecting the Zoom-Out tool causes your current viewing area to zoom out (expand) by a factor of two.

- If you are currently in a zoom-in viewing magnification, selecting the Zoom-Out tool causes you to return to the previously selected view. You can therefore use the Zoom-Out tool to back out of successive zoom-ins one step at a time.

The maximum zoom-out you can achieve is a view that allows you to see one side of a 48 by 48-inch drawing.

To use the Zoom-Out tool, select the Zoom tool, and click on the Zoom-Out tool or press F3. The mouse pointer does not change shape when you select this tool, but the screen redraws according to the preceding rules.

In the following simple exercise, you will practice using the Zoom-Out tool on the map or clip-art that you opened and used above. (Your screen should be at one greater stage of magnification than that shown in Figure 1-10.)

1. Select the Zoom tool and then click on the Zoom-Out tool or press F3. The screen redraws to the previous level of magnification, as shown in Figure 1-9.
2. Select the Zoom-Out tool again. Your screen should now look like Figure 1-8, which is at full-page view where you started.
3. Select the Zoom-Out tool a third time. You can still see the full page, but it now appears at half size, as in Figure 1-11.

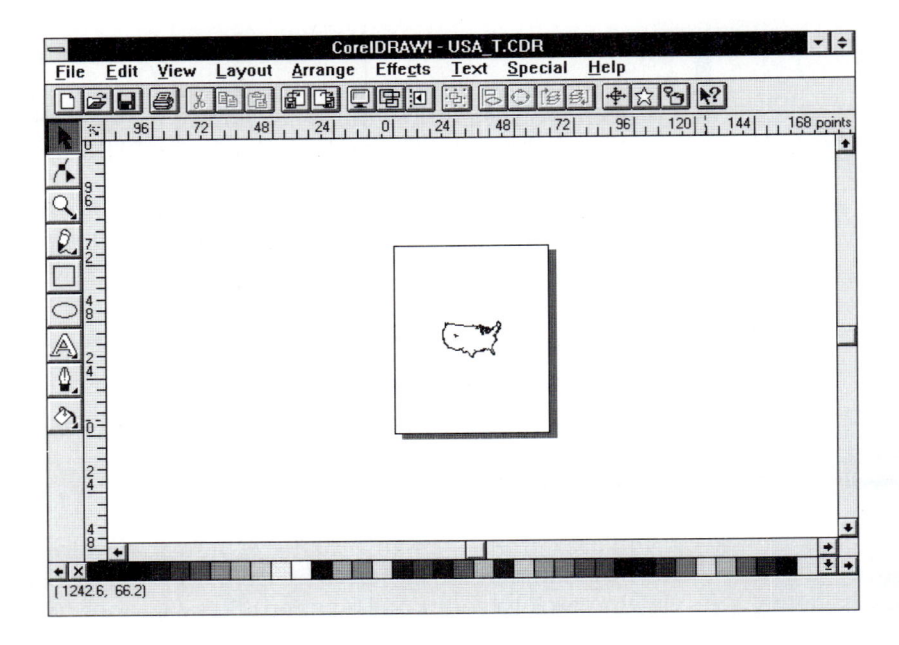

Zooming out to a 50 percent page view
Figure 1-11.

4. Select the Zoom-Out tool a final time. This time, you zoom out only a little further. You cannot zoom out further than this.

You have seen how the Zoom-In and Zoom-Out tools work well together when you are interested in editing a picture in minute detail. In the next section, you will learn how to achieve the kind of view that is useful when you want to print your image.

Viewing at Actual Size

When you want to see approximately how large your image will look when printed, use the Actual Size tool in the Zoom flyout menu. At a 1:1 viewing magnification, 1 inch on your screen corresponds to about 1 inch on the printed page. The amount of the page you see at this magnification may vary, depending on the way Microsoft Windows works with your monitor.

To achieve actual size viewing magnification, select the Zoom tool and click on the **1:1** tool. You can practice using this tool on the map that you used earlier.

1. Select the Actual Size (1:1) tool. The screen redraws to display an area of your image similar to Figure 1-12. The actual area may vary because of the variety of monitors and display adapters available. At this viewing magnification, your text still appears small.

Getting Acquainted with CorelDRAW!

Viewing an image at actual size
Figure 1-12.

2. Select the Zoom-Out tool. Since you were in a 1:1 view previously, you zoom out by a factor of 2.

The next two sections show you how to fit either a selected part of or an entire image within the viewing window. This is a different from a specific level of magnification.

Viewing a Selected Object

Often you want to look at just one part of an object. As you have already seen, you can lasso that part with the Zoom-in tool and display it that way. With CorelDRAW! 5, though, you can also select an object and zoom-in on just that selected object with the Selected Zoom tool. This is simpler than lassoing and is useful for odd-shaped objects.

See how this works with the map or piece of clip-art on your screen by following these instructions (the image on your screen should be zoomed out to show some or all of the page edges):

1. Click on the map or the object on your screen to select it. The object should have eight *selection boxes* around it.

2. Click on the Zoom tool to open the flyout menu and then click on the Selected Zoom tool. The object on your screen should enlarge until it just fills the viewing window, as you can see in Figure 1-13.

3. Clear the screen by selecting New from the File menu.

Fitting a Graphic in a Window

When the pictures you draw extend all the way to the edge of the page, they already fit within the viewing window. The Fit-in-Window tool is not of much use to you in such cases. When some blank space exists, however, you can use the Fit-in-Window tool to view everything you have drawn, but no more. This can be especially useful for small designs, such as logos.

To select the Fit-in-Window tool, first select the Zoom tool, then click on the Fit-in-Window tool or press F4. The screen redraws to fill the entire viewing area with the graphic image. Practice using this tool on one of the sample CorelDRAW! files in the following exercise.

1. Import another clip-art file. PELICAN3.CMX from the \CLIPART\BIRD\ directory on the first CD-ROM is used here. Note that there is some blank or "white" space at both the bottom and top of the page, as seen in Figure 1-14.

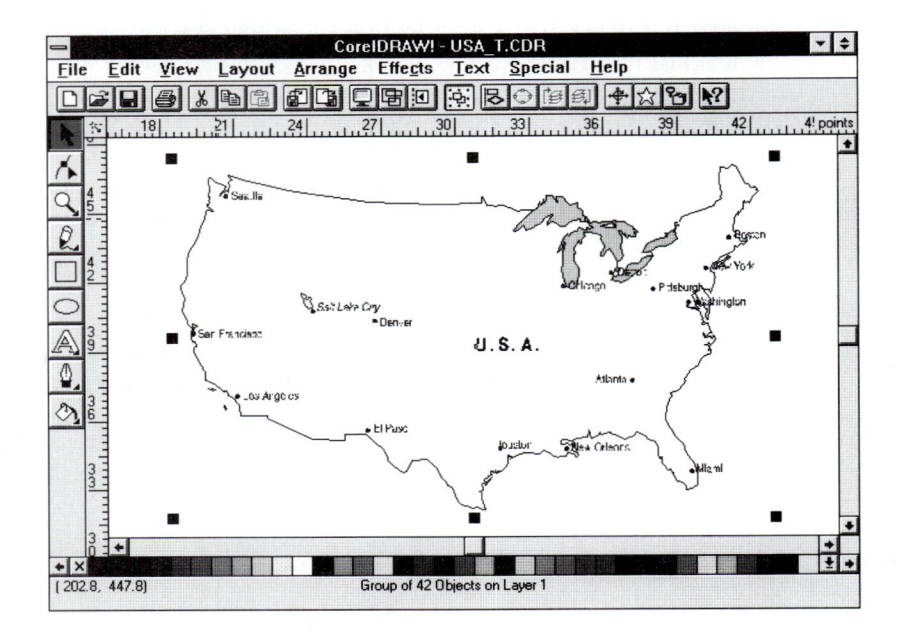

The selected object fills the window

Figure 1-13.

Getting Acquainted with CorelDRAW!

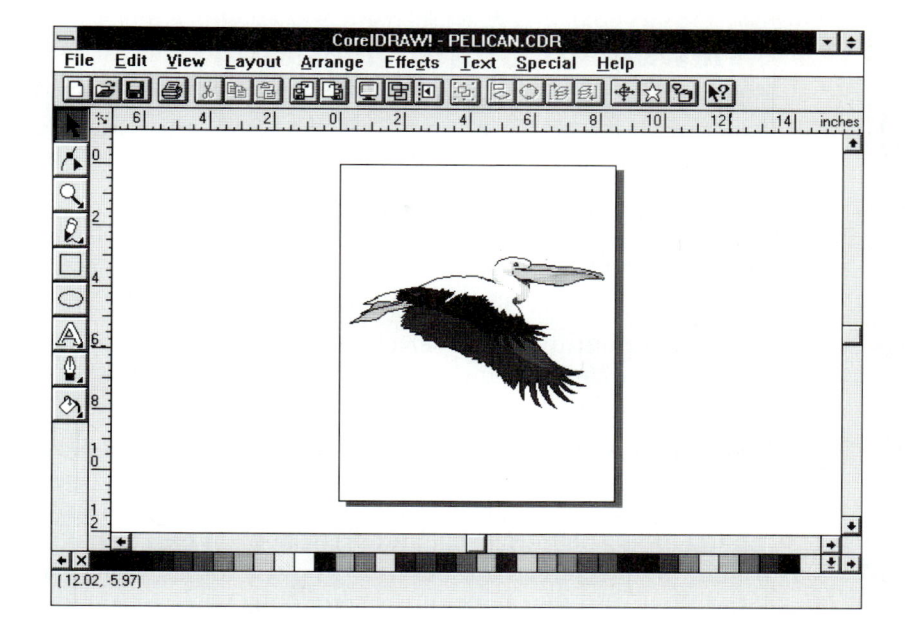

Image with unused blank space at top and bottom
Figure 1-14.

2. Select the fit-in-window view by selecting the Zoom tool and clicking on the Fit-in-Window tool. Now you see only the pelican, as shown in Figure 1-15.

Fitting the image within the viewing area
Figure 1-15.

Viewing an Entire Page

The full-page view is the default view when you load CorelDRAW! or open a picture. It is easy to return to this view from any other view you have selected. Simply select the Zoom tool and click on the Show Page tool or press SHIFT-F4.

You have now mastered all of the view selection tools, but there is still another method, called *panning,* that you can use to control your viewing area.

Use the Zoom-In tool to select a small portion of the pelican. That portion will fill the viewing area, and even though you see only the selected part, the whole drawing has been expanded.

Regardless of which view you are in, you can always move beyond your current viewing area to see what lies beyond it. This operation is called panning and moves the image around on the screen so you can see different parts of it. The horizontal and vertical scroll bars at the bottom and right sides of your screen are the tools you use to pan a picture. Figure 1-16 shows the three different parts of the scroll bars you can use for panning.

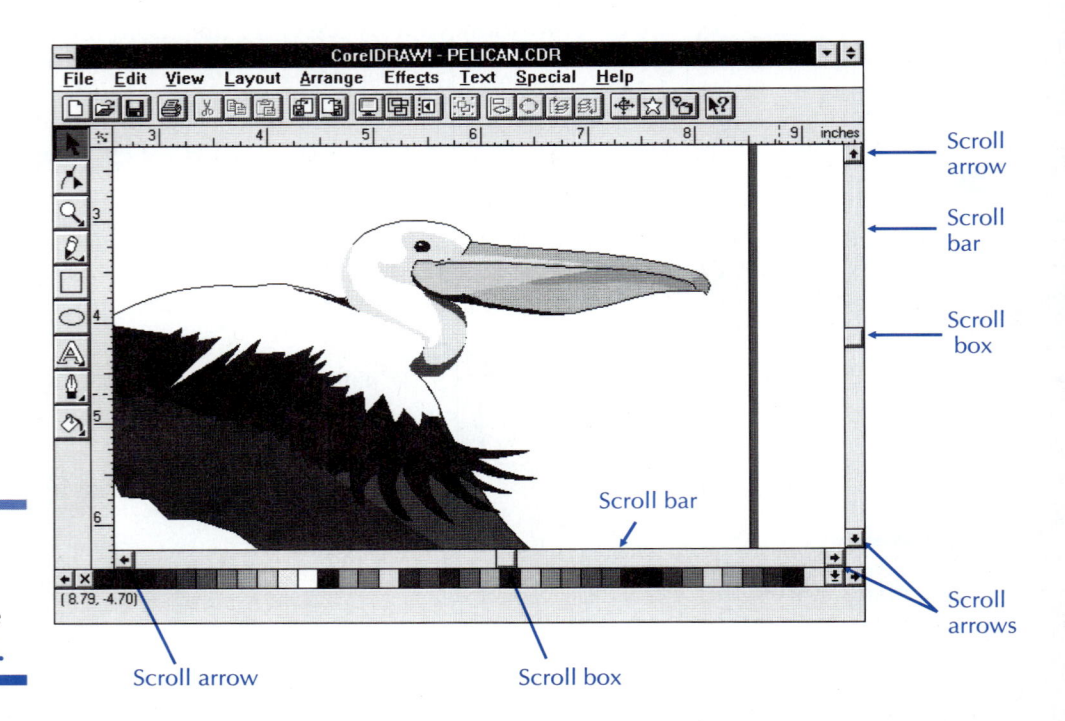

Using the parts of the scroll bar to pan a picture
Figure 1-16.

Getting Acquainted with CorelDRAW!

- To pan in small increments, click on a scroll arrow. The size of the increment varies, depending on your monitor and display adapter combination. If you click on the right horizontal scroll arrow, the image in the viewing window appears to move to the left. If you click on the left horizontal arrow, the image appears to move to the right. This is an excellent method to use when you need to edit an image in fine detail.

- To pan in large increments, click on the scroll bar on either side of the scroll box, located in the middle of the horizontal and vertical scroll bars. Once again, the image appears to move in the opposite direction from where you clicked. This method has only limited usefulness for editing, because the movement of the screen is rather jumpy and unpredictable.

- To control the exact distance that you pan, position the mouse pointer over the scroll box and drag it across the scroll bar in the direction that you want to pan. Release the mouse button when you reach the desired area.

Now that you are familiar with all of the Zoom tools and with the scroll bars, you have complete control over the portion of your picture that you display at any one time. In Chapters 5 and 8, you will put this new skill to work to help you select, arrange, and move objects and text.

Quitting CorelDRAW!

Now that you are familiar with the screen components, exit CorelDRAW! and return to the Program Manager. You can use the mouse, the keyboard and mouse, or the keyboard alone to quit CorelDRAW!.

Using the mouse, double-click on the Control-menu box in the upper-left corner, or display the File menu by moving the mouse pointer to the File menu name and then click once. Then, select the Exit command by clicking on it once.

Using both mouse and keyboard, display the File menu by clicking on the menu name. Then, with the File menu displayed, press X.

Using the keyboard alone, you can either press ALT-F to display the File menu and then press X, or press ALT-F4.

Tip: If you have attempted to draw during this session, you will get a message like: "UNTITLED.CDR has changed, Save current changes?" Click on the No command button to abandon your changes.

If you are like most CorelDRAW! users, you will want to begin drawing immediately. This book encourages you to draw. In Chapter 2 you will use the Pencil tool to begin drawing lines and curves.

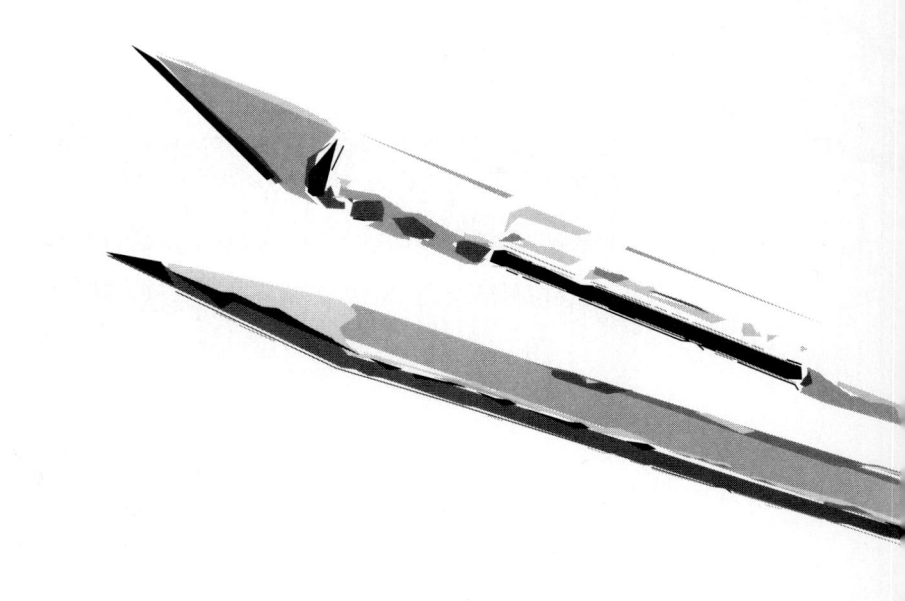

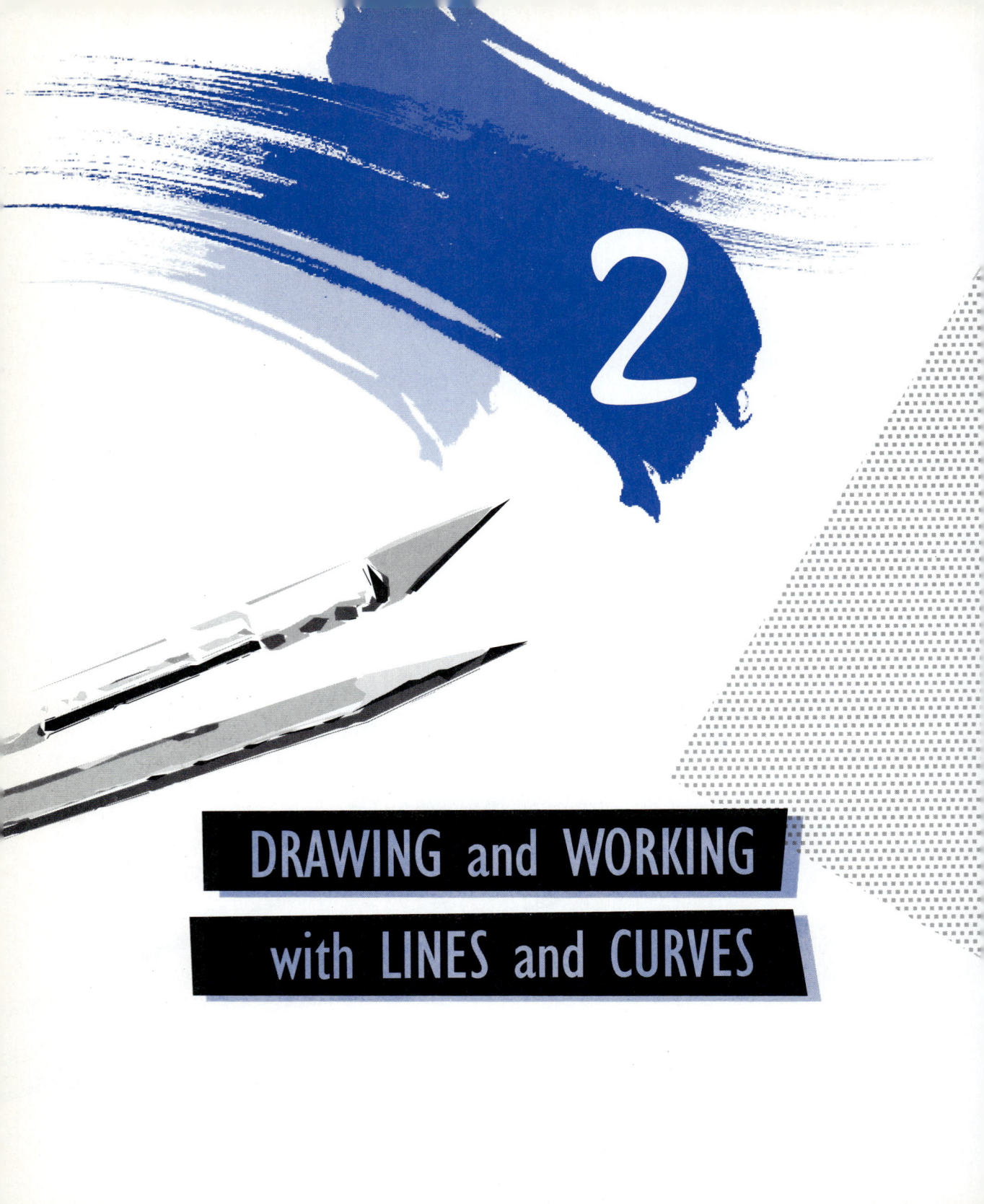

2

DRAWING and WORKING with LINES and CURVES

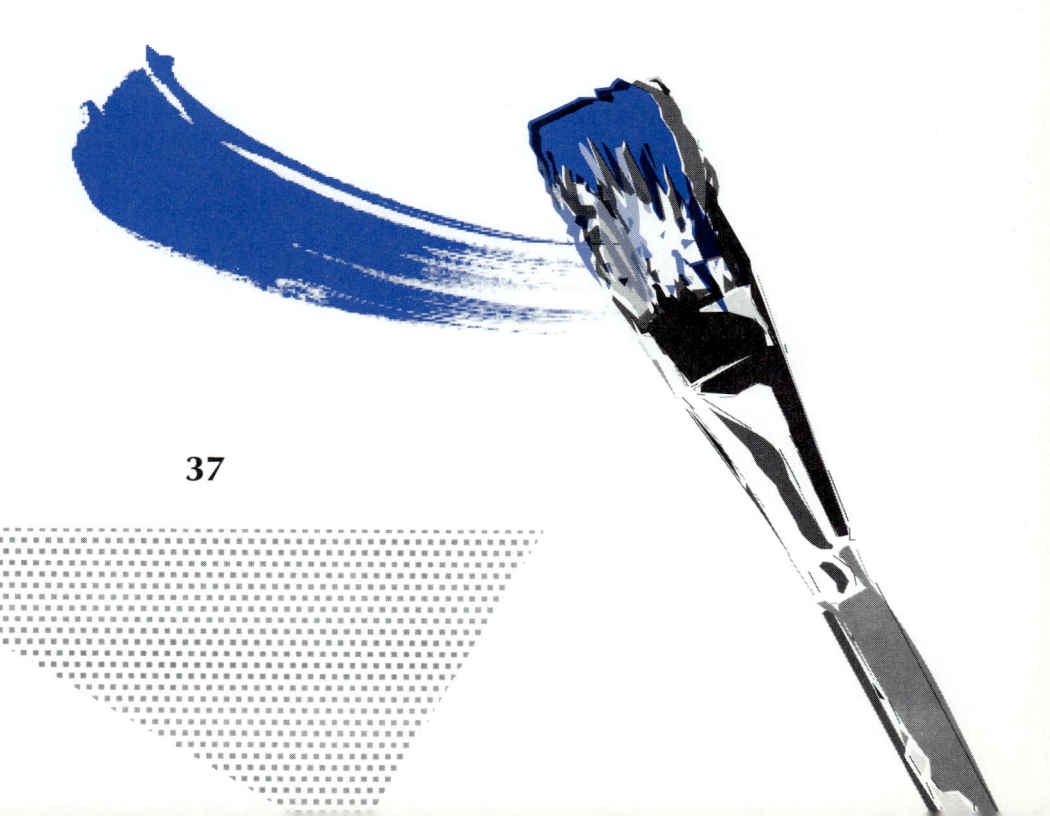

The Pencil tool is the most versatile tool in the CorelDRAW! toolbox. By using this tool in two of its four modes, you can create both straight and curved lines, and from these simple building blocks you can construct an almost infinite variety of polygons and irregular shapes. The third mode, Dimension Lines, allows you to place vertical, horizontal, and angular lines that display dimensions of objects or other lines on a page. The fourth mode allows callouts to be placed on drawings. Work through the exercises in this chapter to become thoroughly familiar with this most basic CorelDRAW! tool.

Freehand Versus Bézier Mode

The Pencil tool has two modes of drawing: Freehand mode, where curves mirror the movements of your hand on a mouse, and Bézier (pronounced "bay-z-air") mode, where curves are precisely placed between two or more points you identify. Drawing straight lines is very similar in the two modes, but drawing curves is very different. In the remaining sections of this chapter, Freehand mode, the default, will be discussed first, and then Bézier mode. Dimension Lines and Callout modes are discussed after the first two drawing modes.

Drawing Straight Lines

In the language of the CorelDRAW! interface, *line* refers to any straight line, while *curve* refers to curved lines, irregular lines, and closed objects you create with such lines. Drawing a straight line requires that you work with the mouse in a different way than when you draw a curved or irregular line. To draw a straight line in CorelDRAW! follow these steps:

1. Load CorelDRAW! if it isn't running already.
2. Position the mouse pointer over the Pencil tool icon and click once. The pointer changes to a crosshair as you move it off the icon, and the Feehand tool icon becomes darkened.
3. Position the crosshair pointer where you want a line to begin. This can be anywhere inside the printable page area.
4. Press *and immediately release (click)* the left mouse button, and then move the crosshair pointer toward the point where you want to end the line. A straight line appears and extends as far as you move the crosshair pointer, as shown here. You can move the line in any direction, or make the segment longer or shorter.
5. When you have established the length and direction you want, complete the line by clicking and releasing the mouse button. As shown

Drawing and Working with Lines and Curves 39

here, a small square *node* appears at each end of the line to show that the line is complete and can be selected for further work.

6. Press DEL to clear the line from the screen.

Tip: When you begin to draw a line, be sure to release the mouse button immediately after you press it. If you continue to hold down the mouse button while moving the crosshair pointer, you create a curve instead of a straight line.

Using the Status Line to Improve Precision

Chapter 1 introduced you briefly to the status line and its potential for helping you draw with precision and accuracy. In the next exercise, pay attention to the useful information that appears on the status line.

1. With the Freehand tool still selected, begin another line by clicking the mouse button at a point about halfway down the left side of the page. The coordinates on the left side of the status line should be *about* 1.0, 5.5 (absolute precision is not important).

2. Move the mouse toward the right side of the page. Don't click a second time yet.

3. Notice that as soon as you clicked once and began to move the mouse, a message appeared on the status line, as shown here:

```
(6.54, -5.50)      DX: 5.56 DY: 0.00 inches Distance: 5.56 Angle: 0.0 degrees
                   Start: (0.99, -5.50) End: (6.54, -5.50)
```

Look more closely at the status line. It includes information about the line you are drawing. The codes in the status line and their meanings are discussed next. (Your measurements may be different. Also, the measurements may be set as millimeters, inches, picas, or points. If your screen does not show the same measurement units as this book, you can change the setting in the Layout menu by choosing Grid & Scale Setup and then Grid Frequency. Set both the horizontal and vertical measurements to inches.)

dx The *dx* code refers to the *x*-coordinate or horizontal location of your line on the page relative to the starting point. The number following this code identifies how far your line has traveled (in other words, its distance) from that starting point along the x or horizontal axis. A positive number (one with no minus sign in front of it) indicates that you are extending the line to the right of the starting point, while a negative number indicates the reverse.

dy The *dy* code refers to the *y*-coordinate or vertical location of your line on the page relative to the starting point. The number following this code identifies how far your line has traveled (in other words, its distance) above or below that starting point along the y or vertical axis. A positive number indicates that you are extending the line above the starting point, while a negative number indicates that you are extending it below the starting point.

inches The unit of measurement for the current *dx* and *dy* position indicators appears on the status line as well. The CorelDRAW! default is inches, but you can change it to millimeters or picas and points using the Grid & Scale Setup command in the Layout menu. You'll gain experience with the grid later in this chapter.

distance The number following this text indicates the length of your line relative to the starting point.

angle The number following this text indicates the angle of the line relative to an imaginary compass, where 0 degrees is at the 3 o'clock position, 90 degrees is at the 12 o'clock position, 180 degrees is at the 9 o'clock position, and –90 degrees is at the 6 o'clock position.

Start and End The pairs of numbers following each of these items represent the coordinates of the start and end points of the line.

Continue the preceding exercise with these steps:

1. Choose an end point for the line and click again to freeze the line in place. Note that the status line indicators disappear as soon as you complete the line.
2. Press DEL to delete the line before going further.

As you may have noticed, information appears on the status line only when you are performing some action on an object. This information makes CorelDRAW! especially powerful for applications requiring great precision, such as technical illustration.

Erasing Portions of a Line

In the following exercise, you'll practice erasing part of a line that you have extended but not completed. You can always backtrack and shorten a line in CorelDRAW!, as long as you have not clicked a second time to complete it.

1. With the Freehand tool still selected, choose a starting point for another line.
2. Move the pointer downward and to the right until the *dx* indicator reads about 5.00 inches and the *dy* indicator reads about –1.00 inches, as shown in Figure 2-1.
3. Without clicking the mouse button a second time, shorten the line until the *dx* indicator reads 4.00 inches. Notice that the line you have drawn behaves flexibly and becomes shorter as you move the mouse backward.
4. Click a second time to freeze the line at about *dx* 4.00 inches.
5. Before going any further, delete the line by pressing DEL.

Constraining a Line to an Angle

You need not rely on the status line alone to control the precision of your drawing. You can also use the CTRL key while drawing to *constrain* (force) a line to an angle in increments of 15 degrees. In the following exercise, you'll create a series of seven straight lines this way.

1. With the Freehand tool still selected, *press and hold* CTRL and click the mouse button to choose a starting point for the line.

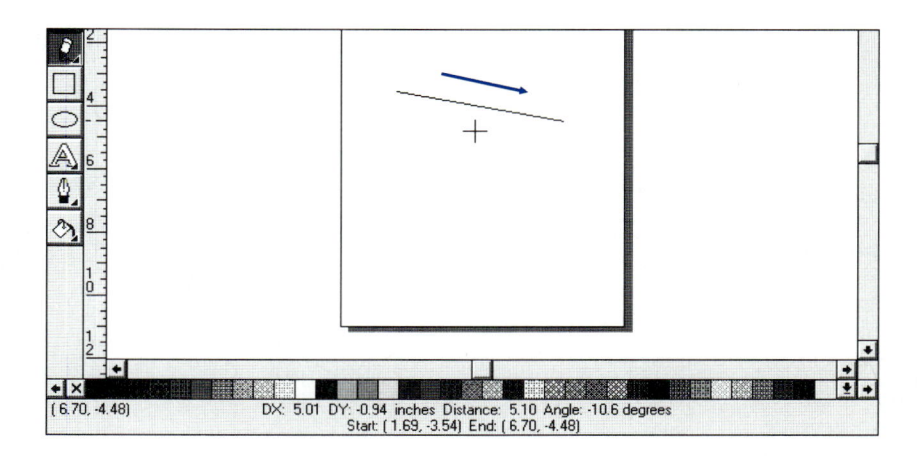

Extending a line using the status line indicator
Figure 2-1.

2. Release the mouse button, but continue holding CTRL as you extend the line outward and downward from the starting point. Try moving the line to different angles in a clockwise direction. As the angle indicator in the status line shows, the line does not move smoothly but instead "jumps" in increments of 15 degrees.

3. Now, extend the line straight outward, so that the angle indicator on the status line reads 0 degrees. While still holding down CTRL, click the mouse button a second time to freeze the line at this angle.

4. Release CTRL. (Remember always to release the mouse button *before* you release CTRL. If you release CTRL first, the line doesn't necessarily align to an angle.)

5. Draw six more lines in the same way, each sharing a common starting point. Extend the second line at an angle of 15 degrees, the third at an angle of 30 degrees, the fourth at an angle of 45 degrees, the fifth at an angle of 60 degrees, the sixth at an angle of 75 degrees, and the seventh at an angle of 90 degrees. When you are finished, your lines should match the pattern shown in Figure 2-2.

Clearing the Screen

Before going any further, clear the screen of the lines you have created so far.

1. Click on the File menu to pull it down.
2. Select the New command.
3. A message box appears with this message: "UNTITLED.CDR has changed, Save current changes?"
4. Click on the No command button to exit the message box and clear the screen.

The Pick tool in the tool box is highlighted by default, just as when you first loaded CorelDRAW!.

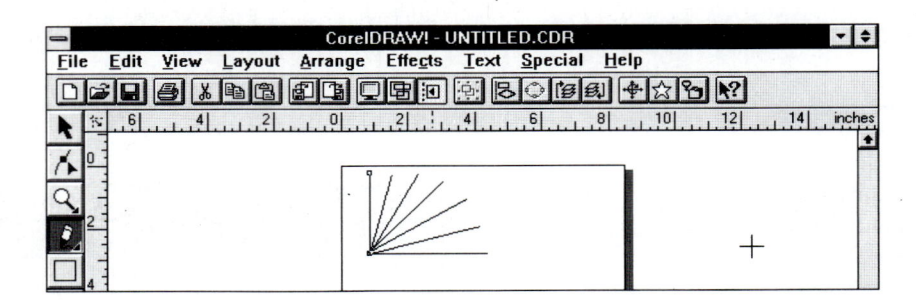

Constraining lines to angles in 15-degree increments
Figure 2-2.

Drawing Multisegment Lines

With CorelDRAW!, you can easily draw several straight lines in sequence so that each begins where the previous one left off. Use this technique both for drawing open-ended line figures and for constructing polygons. In the present exercise, you will construct a series of peaks and valleys.

1. Select the Freehand tool using a shortcut—press the F5 function key. Then click to choose a line starting point. Extend a line upward and to the right.
2. When you reach the desired end point for the line, freeze it in place with a *double click* rather than a single click of the mouse button.
3. Move the mouse downward and to the right, without clicking again. The flexible line follows the crosshair pointer automatically.
4. Double-click again to freeze the second line in place.
5. Continue zigzagging in this way until you have created several peaks and valleys similar to those in Figure 2-3.
6. When you reach the last valley, click once instead of twice to end the multisegment line.
7. Press DEL to clear the screen before proceeding.

Tip: After the final click, if you make a mistake drawing, you can erase the last line segment you completed in one of two ways. You either press ALT-BACKSPACE to delete individual line segments, or select the Undo Curve Append command in the Edit menu. (You can also recreate deleted line segments with Redo Curve Append.) Don't press DEL when drawing a multisegment line, or you will erase all of the segments you have drawn so far.

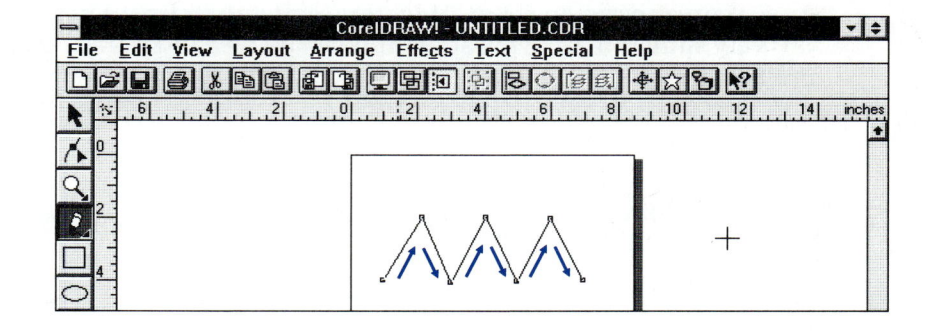

Drawing multisegment lines
Figure 2-3.

Drawing a Polygon

A *polygon* is a closed two-dimensional figure bounded by straight lines. You create polygons in CorelDRAW! by drawing multisegment lines and then connecting the end point to the starting point. In the following exercise, you'll create a polygon figure like the one shown here:

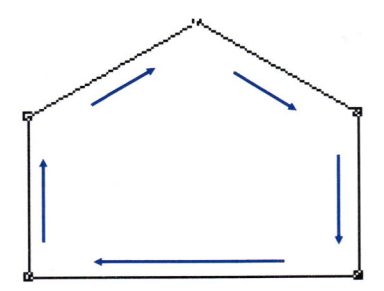

1. Draw the first line, double-clicking at the line end point so that you can continue drawing without interruption.
2. Draw four additional lines in the same way, following the pattern shown above. End the last line segment with a single click at the point where the first line segment began.

Did your last line segment "snap" to the beginning of the first? Or does a small gap remain between them? If you can still see a small gap, don't worry. In the section "Joining Lines and Curves Automatically," later in this chapter, you'll learn how to adjust the level of sensitivity at which one line will join automatically to another. If your lines did snap together to form an enclosed polygon, it may fill with a solid black color if the standard defaults are set. For now, clear the screen and begin the next exercise.

Straight Lines in Bézier Mode

The Bézier mode of drawing identifies end points or nodes and places lines or curves between them. Therefore, drawing straight lines in Bézier mode is very similar to drawing straight lines in Freehand mode. Try it next and see for yourself.

To use Bézier mode:

1. Select Bézier mode by pointing on the Pencil tool and pressing and holding the mouse button down until the Pencil flyout menu appears, like this:

Drawing and Working with Lines and Curves

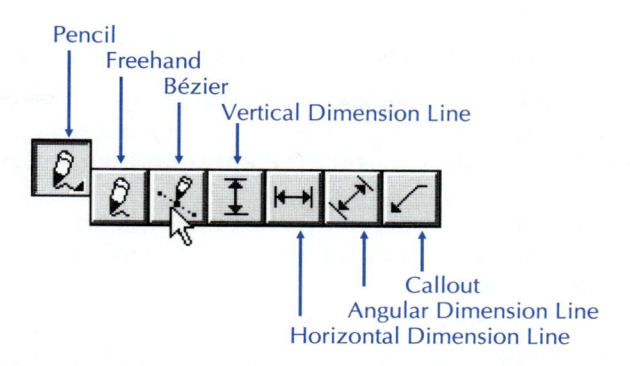

Pencil
Freehand
Bézier
Vertical Dimension Line
Callout
Angular Dimension Line
Horizontal Dimension Line

2. Click on the Bézier tool, the second from the left of the six icons on the flyout menu.

Your status line should now include the words "Drawing in Bézier Mode..."

Drawing Single Lines in Bézier Mode

Now draw a single line segment as you did earlier in Freehand mode.

1. Click on a starting point in the middle left of the page, immediately release the mouse button (if you hold down the mouse button, CorelDRAW! will think you are drawing a curve), and move the mouse pointer to the upper right of the page.

    Notice that the starting point is a solid black square. This starting point is a node, a point on a line that is used to define the line. When you start the line, the starting point is selected and is therefore black. Also, there is no line connecting the starting point and the mouse pointer and no information in the status line except the coordinates of the mouse pointer. A line does not appear and there is no information in the status line because a Bézier line is not defined until you have placed at least two nodes.

2. Click on an end node. A straight line is drawn between the two nodes, as shown below. Information now appears in the status line: "Curve on Layer 1" and "Number of nodes:2." The line segment is called a "curve."

Drawing a Polygon in Bézier Mode

Unlike Freehand mode, you can continue to add line segments after clicking on an end node only once in Bézier mode. Do that next to build a polygon (your screen should still be as you left it after drawing the first Bézier line segment).

1. Click on two more nodes, first one straight down toward the lower right and the other toward the lower left. Lines will be added connecting the nodes.

2. Position the mouse pointer on top of the original starting node and click one final time. The result is a four-sided polygon like the one shown in Figure 2-4. If your sides join to form a polygon (that is, not an open shape), and you are using a fill pattern (as shown in the figure), your polygon will fill with the pattern defined as the default, such as a solid black color. Chapter 7 discusses this in more detail.

As you can see, there are many mechanical similarities between Freehand and Bézier drawing of straight lines. The results are virtually the same, but the screen looks very different during the creation of the lines. For straight lines there is little reason to use Bézier over Freehand.

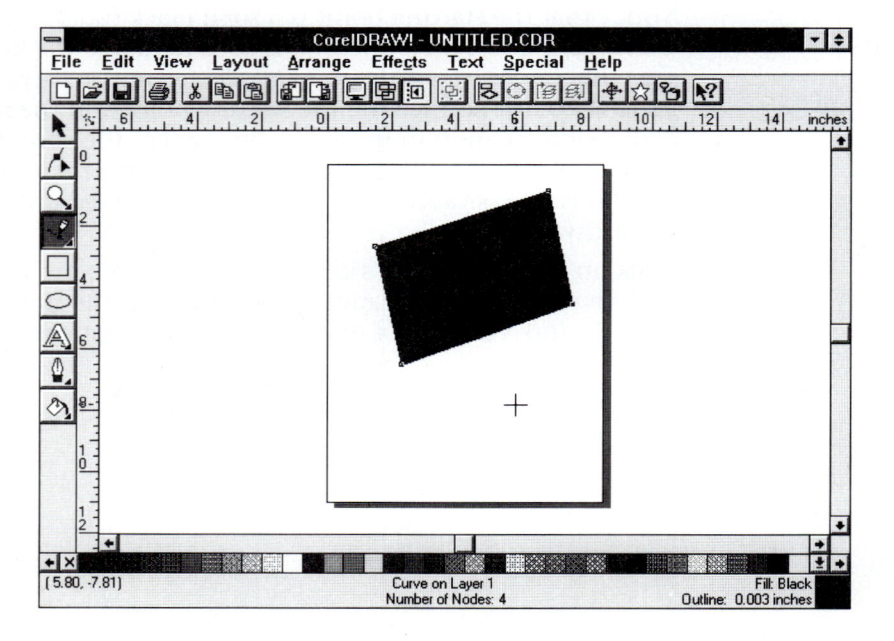

Bézier polygon
Figure 2-4.

Drawing and Working with Lines and Curves

Tip: As in Freehand, in Bézier mode you can move the mouse pointer in any direction, including backward, over the path already traveled to "erase" the object before clicking on a node. After clicking on a node you can use Undo (either ALT-BACKSPACE or choose Undo from the Edit menu) to erase the previous line (or curve) segment. If you want to delete the entire object (line or polygon) while it is still selected (you can see all of the nodes), press DEL.

Tip: If you want to draw two or more Bézier line segments that are not connected, press the SPACEBAR twice, then draw your second line.

3. Press DEL to clear your drawing. To return to Freehand mode, click on the Bézier Pencil tool and hold the mouse button until the flyout menu appears.

Now you can either release the mouse button and click on the Freehand tool or continue holding the mouse button down and drag the mouse pointer to the Freehand tool, and then release the mouse button. You are returned to your drawing, in Freehand mode, ready to begin working with curves.

Drawing Curves in Freehand Mode

The Freehand tool has a twofold purpose in CorelDRAW!: you can use it to draw curved or irregular lines as well as straight lines. This section introduces you to the basics of drawing a simple curve, closing the path of a curve to form a closed curve object, and erasing unwanted portions of a curve as you draw.

To draw a simple curve:

1. Select the Freehand tool if it is not still selected.
2. Position the crosshair pointer at the point on the page where you want a curve to begin and then *press and hold* the mouse button. The Start and End coordinates appear on the status line.
3. Continue to hold the mouse button and *drag* the mouse along the path where you want the curve to continue. Follow the example in Figure 2-5.
4. Upon completing the curve, release the mouse button. The curve disappears momentarily while CorelDRAW! calculates exactly where it should go. Then the curve reappears with many small square nodes, as in Figure 2-5. Note that when you have finished, the words "Curve on Layer 1" and the number of nodes appears in the middle of the status

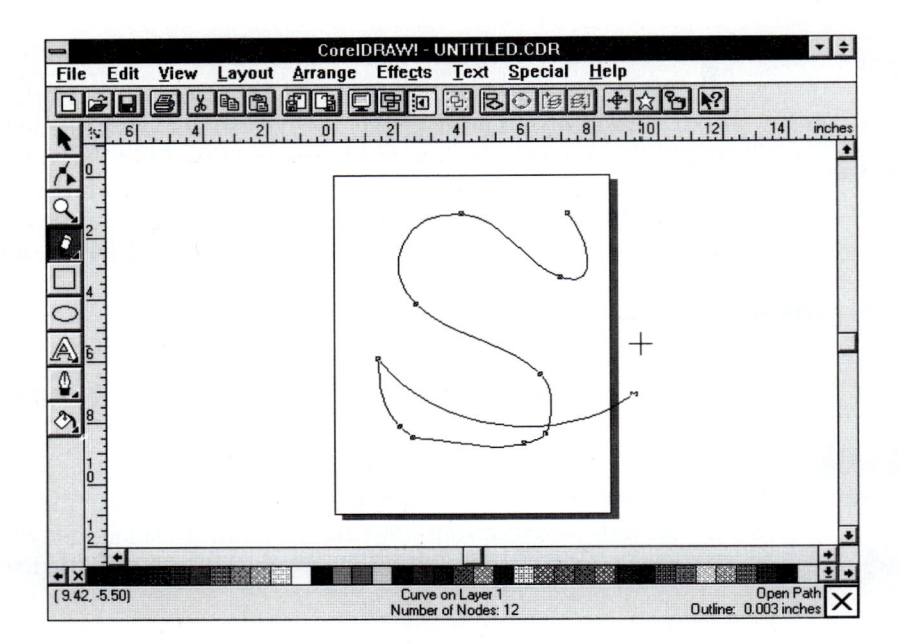

Drawing a curve
Figure 2-5.

line, and the message "Open Path" appears at the right side of the status line. "Open Path" indicates that you have drawn a curved line, not a closed figure.

5. Press DEL or select the Undo command in the Edit menu to clear the curve you have just drawn.

Tip: To draw a straight line, click and release the mouse button. To draw a curve, press and hold the mouse button and drag the mouse along the desired path.

Erasing Portions of a Curve

Should you make a mistake while drawing a curve, you can backtrack and erase what you have drawn, as long as you have not yet released the mouse button. You use SHIFT to erase the portion of a curve that you no longer want.

1. Begin another curve by pressing and holding the mouse button over the point at which you want the curve to start.
2. Drag the mouse as desired. Do not release the mouse button yet.

3. While still holding down the mouse button, press and hold SHIFT and backtrack over as much of the curve as you wish to erase.

4. After you have erased a portion of the curve, release SHIFT and continue to draw by dragging the mouse in the desired direction.

5. Release the mouse button to finalize the curve. Delete the curve by pressing DEL.

Drawing Multisegment Curves

Just as you drew multisegment lines, you can also draw multisegment curves. You can join two successive curves together automatically if the starting point of the second curve is within a few pixels of the end point of the first curve.

1. Select a starting point for the first curve and begin dragging the mouse.
2. Complete the curve by releasing the mouse button. Do not move the mouse pointer from the point at which your first curve ends.
3. Draw the second curve and complete it. The second curve should "snap" to the first.

If the two curved lines didn't snap together, you moved the pointer farther than five pixels away before starting the second curve. Don't worry about it at this point. CorelDRAW! has a default value of five pixels distance for automatic joining of lines and curves. In the "Joining Lines and Curves Automatically" section of this chapter, you will learn how to adjust the sensitivity of this AutoJoin feature.

Closing an Open Path

When you drew your first curve, the message "Open Path" appeared at the right side of the status line. This message indicates that your curved line is not a closed object and, therefore, that you cannot fill it with a color or pattern (see Chapter 7). You can create a closed curve object with the Freehand tool, however. Refer to Figure 2-6 to create a closed outline of any shape for this exercise. You'll draw this shape as a single curve.

1. Before beginning the exercise, select New from the File menu to clear the screen. When a message box appears and asks whether you want to save your changes, select No.

    You may at this point want to set an option to fill a closed shape with a color or pattern. To do this you can select the Fill icon and click on the black color square. A Uniform Fill dialog box will be displayed. Ensure that a check mark is next to the Graphic option and click on OK. If you want more information, see Chapter 7.

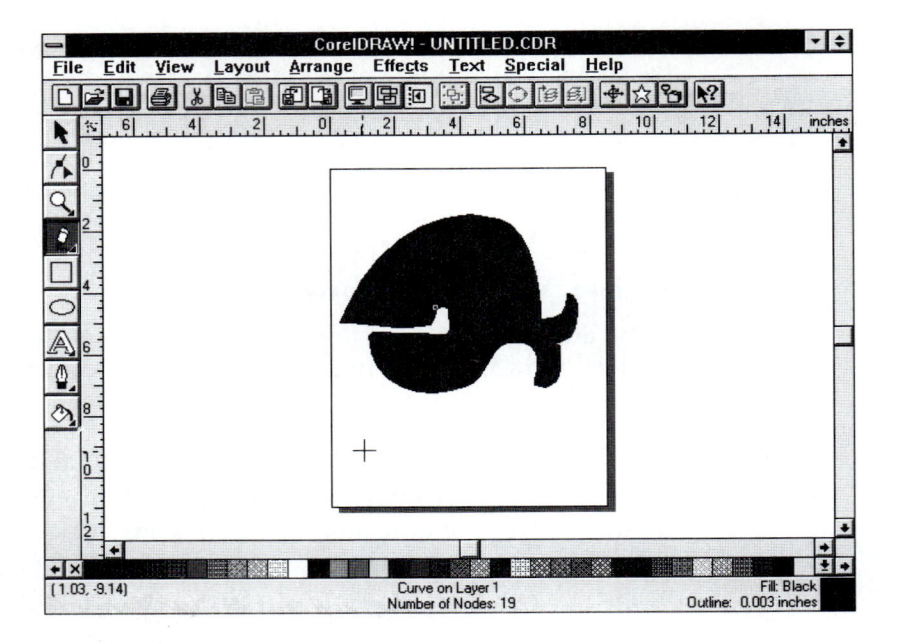

Drawing a closed curve object
Figure 2-6.

2. Select the Freehand tool.
3. Start the curve wherever you wish.
4. Continue dragging the mouse to create the closed shape. Your drawing doesn't have to look exactly like the one in Figure 2-6. If you make a mistake, press SHIFT and backtrack to erase the portions of the curve that you do not want.
5. When you return to the point at which you began, make sure you are over your starting point and then release the mouse button. After a second the object reappears as a solid black shape.

Note that the message in the middle of the status line now reads "Curve" and the number of nodes. At the right side of the status line, the message "Fill:Black" appears, followed by a representation of a solid black color. This indicates that you now have a closed curve object and that it is filled with the default color, black.

Full Color Versus Wireframe Modes

In the last exercise and in the two previous polygon exercises, it was noted that the polygon would fill with solid black color when and if the polygon was closed and if the default settings were still in effect. You can see the full color of an object as you are working on it. Occasionally you may wish to

Drawing and Working with Lines and Curves 51

work in *Wireframe mode,* where you can see only an object's outline and therefore not its color. Although by default all work is done in full color mode, you can switch to Wireframe mode when it is beneficial to work with an object's outline. You do this by choosing Wireframe from the View menu. You can return to full color mode by again choosing Wireframe to turn it off. Try this with the current drawing.

Drawing Curves in Bézier Mode

If you are like most people, drawing smooth curves in Freehand mode is very difficult, if not impossible. Of course, as you'll see in Chapter 9, CorelDRAW!'s Shape tool allows you to clean up messy artwork very quickly. As an alternative, though, the Bézier mode of drawing allows you to draw smooth curves to start with—after a little practice.

The principle of Bézier drawing is that you place a node, set a pair of control points that determine the slope and height or depth of the curve, and then place the next node. The method is to place the crosshair where you want a node, press and hold the mouse button while you drag the control points until you are satisfied with their positioning, release the mouse button, and go on and do the same thing for the next node. When you have two or more nodes, curves appear between them reflecting your settings. This is very different from Freehand mode drawing and will take some getting used to. Dragging the mouse with the button depressed moves the control points in two dimensions and only indirectly identifies the path of the curve. Understanding how to handle control points, though, will help you use the Shape tool in Chapter 9.

The only way to really understand Bézier drawing is to try it.

1. Clear your screen by selecting New from the File menu and choosing No in answer to the Save Changes message.
2. Momentarily hold the mouse button while clicking on the Pencil tool to open the flyout menu, and then select the Bézier mode icon.
3. Move the mouse pointer to where you want to start the curve and press and hold the left mouse button.
4. Move the mouse in any direction while continuing to hold the left mouse button, and you should see the *control points* appear—two small black boxes and dashed lines connecting them to the larger node, as shown here:

There are three principles involved in moving the mouse to set the control points:

- Begin by dragging a control point in the direction that you want the curve to leave the node.
- Drag the control point away from the node to increase the height or depth of the curve, and drag the control point toward the node to decrease the height or depth.
- Rotate the control points about the node to change the slope of the curve. The slope follows the rotational increment of the control point.

5. Drag the control point out away from the node toward 2 o'clock and swing it in an arc about the node. Notice how the two points move in opposite directions. Continue to hold the left mouse button.

6. Drag the control point in toward the node until it is about a half inch away from the node and swing it until the control point that you clicked on is pointing at 2 o'clock. Your node should look like this:

7. Release the mouse button and move the mouse pointer to where you want the second node to be—about two inches to the right and in line with the first node.

8. Again press and hold the left mouse button to set the node.

9. Drag the control point toward 5 o'clock so it is about a half inch away from the node.

10. Release the mouse button. A curve segment is drawn between the two nodes that should look like this:

Drawing and Working with Lines and Curves

11. Move the mouse pointer and press and hold the mouse button to set a third node about one inch below and in the middle of the first two nodes.
12. Drag the control point so it is about a quarter of an inch to the left of the node, at 9 o'clock.
13. Release the mouse button. A second curve segment will appear, as shown here:

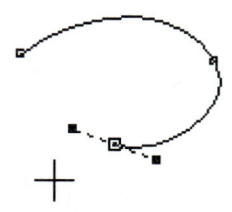

14. Move the mouse pointer until it is on top of the first node you set and press and hold the mouse button.
15. Drag the control points until they are about a half inch away from the node and the top control point is aimed at 12 o'clock, like this:

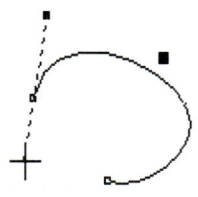

16. Release the mouse button. A third curve segment appears, completing a curved triangle, which will be filled with solid black in full color mode.

Note: If your curved triangle does not fill with solid black, it is probably because you need to turn off Wireframe mode in the View menu.

Practice drawing other Bézier objects. Notice how moving the control points both in and out from the node and in an arc around the node can radically change the curve segment to its left (behind the node) and, to a lesser extent, the curve segment to the right (ahead of the node). Also, notice how the number of nodes can affect the finished object. As a general rule, the fewer nodes the better, but there are some minimums.

A continuous curve like a circle should have a node every 120 degrees or three nodes on a circle like this:

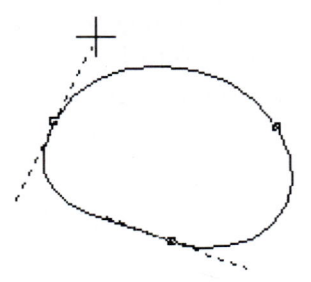

A curve that changes direction, such as a sine wave, needs a node for every two changes in direction, as shown here:

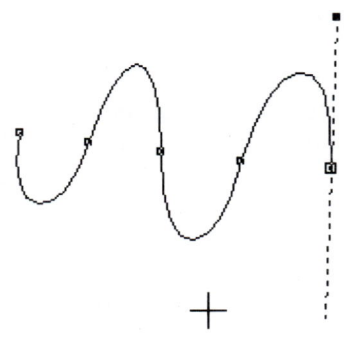

A curve that changes direction in a sharp point (called a cusp) needs a node for every change in direction, like this:

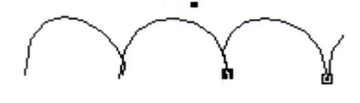

Clear the screen by selecting New from the File menu and responding No when asked to save the changes.

Drawing and Working with Lines and Curves

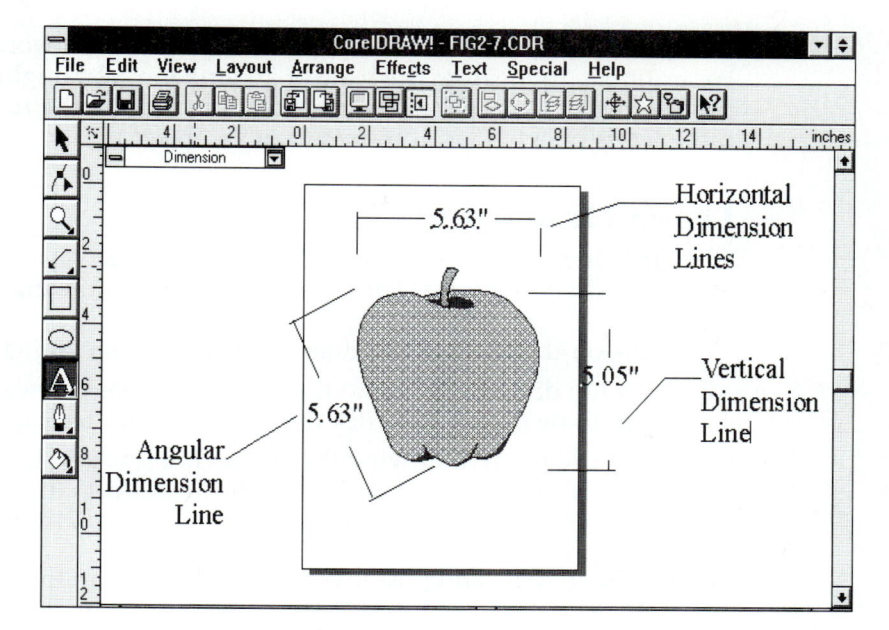

Examples of the Vertical, Horizontal, and Angular Dimension tools
Figure 2-7.

The Dimension Lines Feature

Dimension lines can be used to display measurements, sizes of objects, or distances between them, as you might need in technical drawings, for example.

CorelDRAW! offers three dimension line tools:

Vertical   Horizontal   Angular

Figure 2-7 shows examples of how these three tools may be used.

Setting the Drawing Scale

The drawing scale is set in the top part of the Grid & Scale Layout menu, Scale dialog box, as shown here:

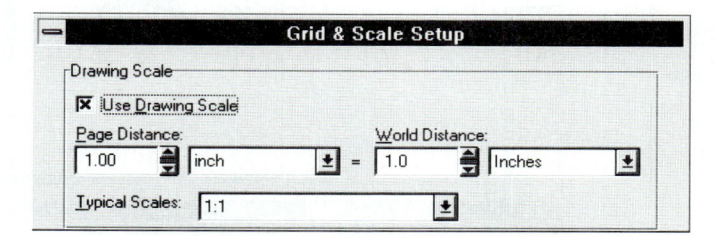

In it you equate a number of units on the page to "real world" equivalents. For example, to measure the scale of an airplane, you might set inches on a page equivalent to feet of an airplane (the world), or the number of millimeters on a blueprint to meters of an object.

Using Dimension Lines

Since the three dimension line tools operate similarly, you will experiment with just two of the tools. There are three steps to drawing a dimension line:

1. Click on the point of the drawing where the measurement is to begin.
2. Drag the dimension line to the location where you want the ending point to be placed and click the mouse button to place it.
3. Move the pointer, moving the dimension line and the label rectangle, to where you want the dimension line extended and the label placed and click the mouse button to place the line and label.

To see how to draw and position a dimension line, follow these steps:

1. Select the Freehand tool and draw a box or circle, something like what is shown in Figure 2-8, which shows the completed drawings with 2-dimension lines. You measure this drawing first with the Vertical Dimension tool.

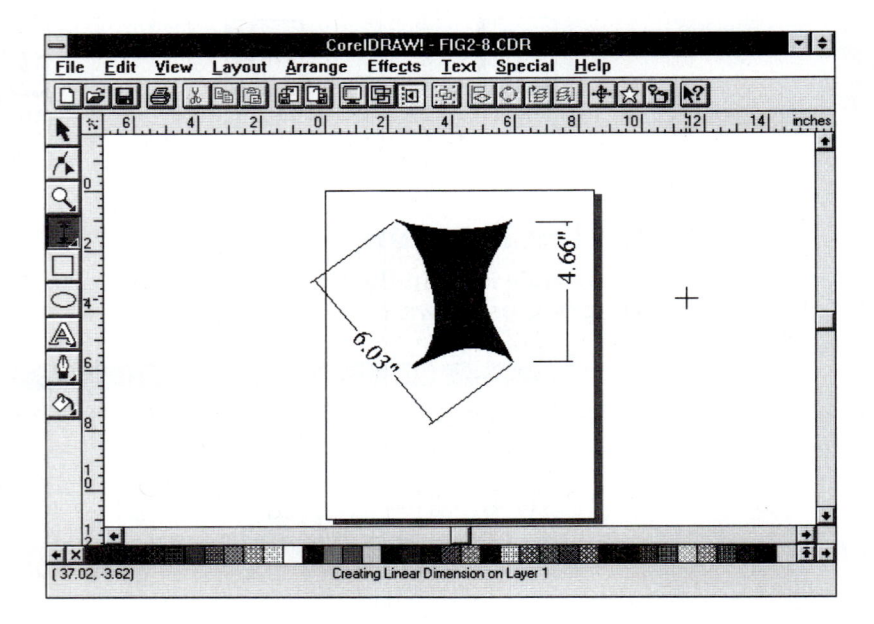

Drawing measured with 2-dimension lines

Figure 2-8.

Drawing and Working with Lines and Curves

2. Hold the mouse while clicking on the Pencil tool to open the flyout menu. Select the Vertical Dimension tool, which is the first dimension line with the vertical line.

3. Move the mouse pointer to the right of the top of the drawing and click the left mouse button to anchor the beginning point, as shown here:

4. Experiment with moving the dimension line by moving the mouse pointer left and right, up and down. Move the pointer off the page as well. You'll see how the vertical dimension line can be positioned left or right, shortened, or lengthened by moving the pointer.

    When you have seen what to expect in the vertical line movement, move the mouse pointer to the bottom of the drawing, directly under the beginning point, and click the mouse button.

5. Experiment again by moving the vertical line to the right and left. See how you can position it in exact locations. A small rectangle surrounds the pointer as you move it. This identifies the location of the dimension label.

Pull the line to the right slightly and place the pointer somewhere near the top of the vertical line, then click the mouse button. The position of the pointer indicates where the dimension is to be placed on the line.

Figure 2-8, displayed earlier, shows what your screen may look like (your font and point size may differ). You can see the dimension label has been placed approximately where you clicked the final time.

Tip: You can change the format and placement of the dimension label by changing the settings in the Dimension roll-up. You can automatically center the label on the vertical line, and you can print it horizontally rather than vertically as it is in Figure 2-8. By pressing Alt-F2, the Dimension roll-up is displayed. From the roll-up you also can choose a default display pattern for how the dimension will be printed.

Tip: The units of measurement are the same as those set for the horizontal rulers. To change these, reset the Horizontal Grid Frequency setting in the Grid & Scale Setup dialog box found on the Layout menu.

Try this second method of placing a dimension line. You are going to measure the distance from the upper-left to the lower-right of the drawing with an angular dimension line.

1. Pressing on the Dimension tool, select the Angular Dimension tool from the flyout. Place the mouse pointer on the top left of the drawing and click the mouse button as before to begin the measurement.
2. Move the pointer diagonally to the bottom right of the drawing and click the mouse button to identify the end point.
3. Move the pointer to the left dragging the dimension line away from the drawing, as shown in Figure 2-8. Move the rectangle near the center of the diagonal line and click the mouse button to place the dimension label.

Figure 2-8 again shows an example and how the resulting lines differ. Depending on the requirements of the drawings, you can use vertical, horizontal or angular Dimension tools to produce a dimension line shaped the way you need it.

Tip: The dimension label is printed according to the default font and point size. To change the default, select the label and then display the Text roll-up dialog box from the Text menu and reset the default values.

Tip: When drawing with the Angular Dimension Line, you can constrain the lines to 15 degree increments by holding down CTRL simultaneously.

Using Callouts

The last tool on the Pencil toolbar is for creating callouts. A *callout* is used to identify or emphasize an area or point on a drawing, as shown here:

Drawing and Working with Lines and Curves

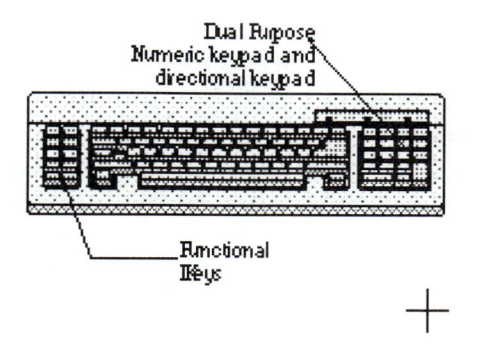

Using the figure just drawn with the dimension lines, you will create two callouts: the first is a 2-segment line that requires three clicks of the mouse button. The second is a 1-segment line requiring one single click and one double click. Figure 2-9 shows the results.

1. Click and hold the Pencil icon (Angular Dimension mode). Then select the Callout tool, the rightmost icon.
2. To identify the starting point, click on the lower-right corner of the drawing. Move the pointer down slightly and to the right and click again. This ends the first line segment. Move the pointer to the right until you are satisfied with the second line segment and click again. At

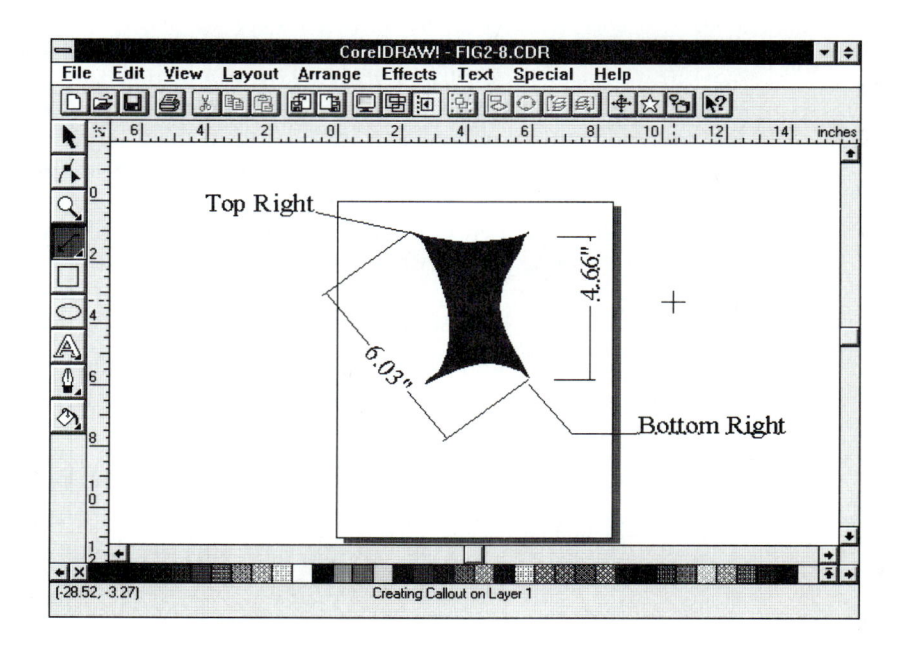

Drawing with callouts
Figure 2-9.

this point the pointer turns into an I-beam icon for entering text for the callout. Type **Bottom Right**.

The process is very similar to that for creating a one segment line, except that a double click replaces the last two clicks.

3. Move the pointer to the top left of the drawing and click once to anchor the line and begin the line segment. Move the line up to the left and double-click when the line is the length you want. Type **Top Left**. Your drawing should look something like Figure 2-9.

Select New from the File menu to prepare for the next section on how to increase precision.

Increasing Precision

In addition to the mouse pointer coordinates and the other line and curve data displayed in the status line, CorelDRAW! has three features that aid in precision drawing. These are an adjustable grid that underlies the drawing surface and assists in aligning points and objects, a pair of rulers to give you a visual reference to where you are, and the ability to place nonprinting guidelines on the page for purposes of alignment.

The grid, the guidelines, and objects can optionally be given a magnet-like property that causes points or objects that are placed near them to be drawn to them. These are called Snap To Grid, Snap To Guidelines, and Snap To Objects. The Snap To property can be turned on and off, like the rulers, through the Layout menu. You can also turn Snap To Grid on and off by pressing CTRL-Y. In addition, the Layout menu provides access to Setup dialog boxes for grids and guidelines. The Grid & Scale Setup dialog box allows you to display the grid on the screen (as a series of faint dots) and, when it is displayed, to determine the horizontal and vertical spacing of the grid. The Grid & Scale Setup dialog box also allows you to turn the Snap To Grid property on and off by clicking on its check box. With the Guidelines Setup dialog box, you can place guidelines with a very high degree of precision. You can also place guidelines by dragging them out of either ruler and placing them by visually aligning them in the opposite ruler.

This section shows you how to use the rulers and the grid to draw with greater precision. Guidelines will be used and discussed further in a later section.

Setting the Grid and Displaying Rulers

You will next make several changes to the settings for the grid and turn on the Snap To property. Then you will turn on the display of both the grid and the rulers.

Drawing and Working with Lines and Curves

1. Select the New command from the File menu to clear the screen of the shape you drew in the last exercise. Don't save any changes.
2. Select the Grid & Scale Setup command from the Layout menu. The dialog box in Figure 2-10 appears. The settings in your software may be different from the ones in the figure.

   The top part of the dialog box shows the Drawing Scale which you have already seen. It allows you to set measurement equivalents for dimension lines. The Grid Frequency controls the distance between grid lines. The Grid Origin establishes where the grid, relative to the lower-left corner of the page, originates.
3. Adjust both horizontal and vertical grid frequencies to 16.00 per inch, if necessary. To change the value in the numeric entry box, press and hold the mouse button over the up or down scroll arrow until the number changes to 16.00. Alternatively, you can click on the numeric value itself and type in the new number. To change the unit of measurement in the rectangular units box, just click on it and select the word "inch."
4. Click on Show Grid to turn on its display and then adjust the Grid Origin, if necessary, so the vertical position of the lower-left corner is at 11 inches. (Some versions of CorelDRAW! use the upper-left corner as the point of reference, in which case a vertical position of 0 is correct.) Check that the horizontal position is set at 0.0.
5. Look at the Snap To Grid check box. If no check mark appears in front of it, select it to make the grid active. If a check mark already appears in front of it, you don't need to do anything. Click on OK to save these settings and close the dialog box.

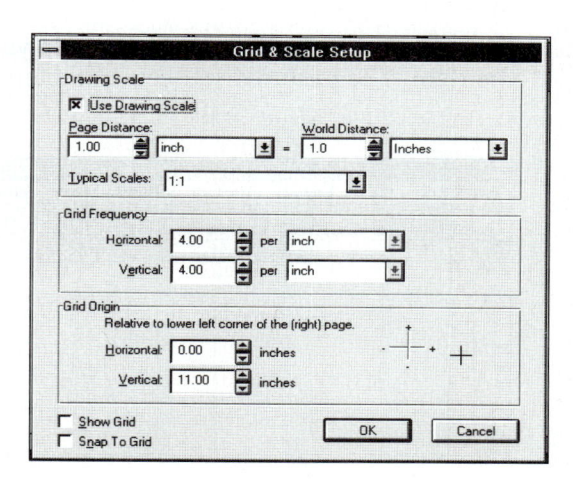

Grid & Scale Setup dialog box
Figure 2-10.

6. Reopen the Layout menu and notice that the Snap To Grid option now has a check mark next to it, showing the feature is turned on.

7. If there is not already a check mark by it, choose the Rulers command from the View menu. Since you have set the grid size to inches, the rulers will also display in inches, as in Figure 2-11. Notice that the zero point for both the horizontal and vertical rulers begins at the upper-left corner of the page area, as shown in the figure. This is a convenient way to set the rulers so that you can measure everything relative to that corner.

Joining Lines and Curves Automatically

CorelDRAW! has a feature called AutoJoin that causes lines and curves to "snap" together automatically when their end points are separated by a preset number of *pixels* (the smallest element on a screen—the "dots" with which everything is built). You can adjust the threshold number of pixels, AutoJoin, through the Curves tab on the Preferences command in the Special menu.

Literal joining of two end points is important because CorelDRAW! classifies an object as being either open or closed. If an object is open, you cannot fill it with a color or shade. Try out the AutoJoin feature and then change the AutoJoin threshold and see the effect with these steps:

1. Select the Freehand tool, then move the crosshair pointer to a point 1 inch to the right of the zero point on the horizontal ruler and 2 inches below the zero point on the vertical ruler. Notice that as you move the mouse, dotted "shadow" lines in each ruler show you the exact location of your pointer.

2. Click once at this point to begin drawing a line. The parameters in the status line appear.

3. Using the rulers and status line to help you, extend the line 4 inches to the right. The *dx* and distance parameters on the status line should read

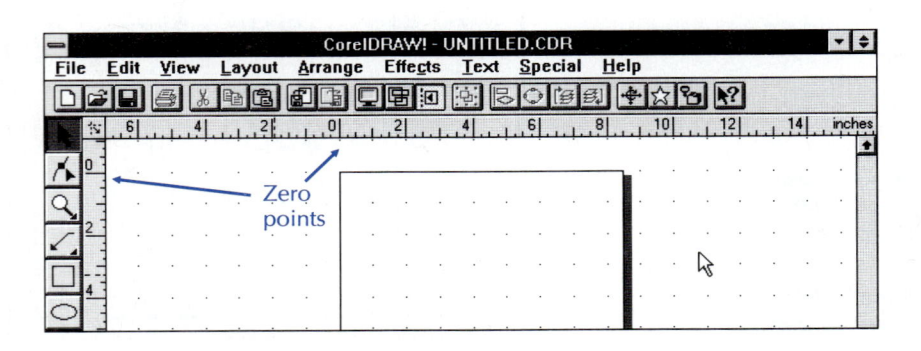

Displaying the rulers

Figure 2-11.

Drawing and Working with Lines and Curves

4.0 inches. Click a second time to freeze the line in position. Notice how both the grid display and the grid's Snap To feature help you do this.

4. Move the crosshair pointer exactly 1/4 inch to the right of the end point of the line. Use the rulers to help you.

5. Press and hold the mouse button at this point and drag the mouse to form a squiggling curve, as shown here:

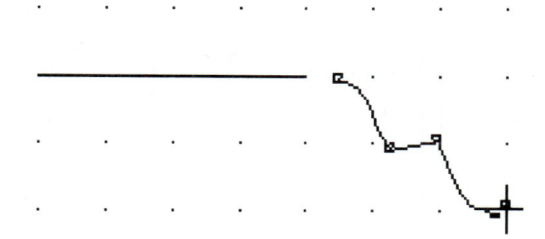

6. Release the mouse button to complete the curve. If you began the curve 1/4 inch or more to the right of the line end point, the curve remains separate from the line and does not snap to it. In order to make a curve snap to a line automatically at this distance, you'll need to adjust the AutoJoin threshold value in the Preferences dialog box. (You'll become familiar with this process in the next section.)

Adjusting the AutoJoin Threshold

The AutoJoin feature determines how far apart (in pixels) two Freehand or Bézier lines or curves have to be for them to join together automatically. If the setting in the Preferences-Curves dialog box is a small number, such as 3 or less, lines snap together only if you draw with a very exact hand. Use this lower setting when you want to *prevent* lines from joining accidentally. If your technique is less precise, you can set the AutoJoin threshold value to a number higher than 5 pixels so that lines will snap together even if you don't have a steady hand.

1. Select the Curves tab from the Preferences command in the Special menu. The Preferences-Curves dialog box in Figure 2-12 appears. The default setting for most of the features in this dialog box is 5 pixels. You'll use some of the other settings later on, when you learn skills for which these settings are useful. For now, concern yourself only with the AutoJoin setting.

2. Set the AutoJoin value to 10 pixels by clicking several times on the up scroll arrow.

3. Select OK to save the new value and return to the drawing.

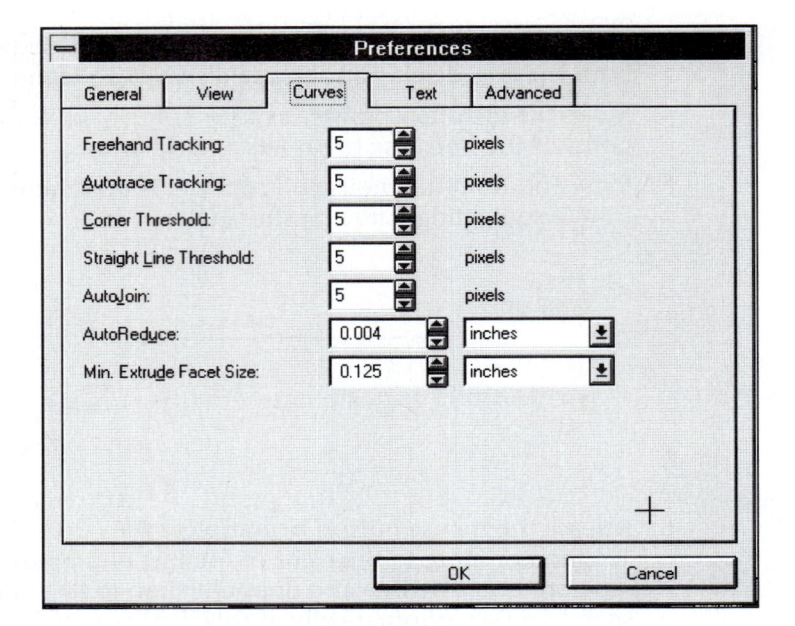

AutoJoin in the Preferences-Curves dialog box

Figure 2-12.

4. Now you can redraw the line and make the curve snap to it. With the Freehand tool selected, redraw a straight line as you did in steps 1 through 3 of the previous section, except move the line down four inches on the vertical ruler.

5. Move the crosshair to a point 1/4 inch to the right of the end point of the line and then press and hold the mouse button to begin drawing a curve.

6. Drag the mouse and draw the squiggling curve as you did in step 5 of the previous section.

7. Release the mouse button. This time, the curve joins automatically to the line, as shown in Figure 2-13.

8. Select New from the File menu to clear the screen before going further.

The AutoJoin feature has other uses besides allowing you to connect lines and curves. You can also use it to accomplish the following:

♦ Join lines to lines or curves to curves

♦ Add a curve or line to the end of an existing curve, line, or object that you have selected

♦ Create closed curve objects and polygons by starting and ending a curve (or a series of line segments) at the same point

Drawing and Working with Lines and Curves

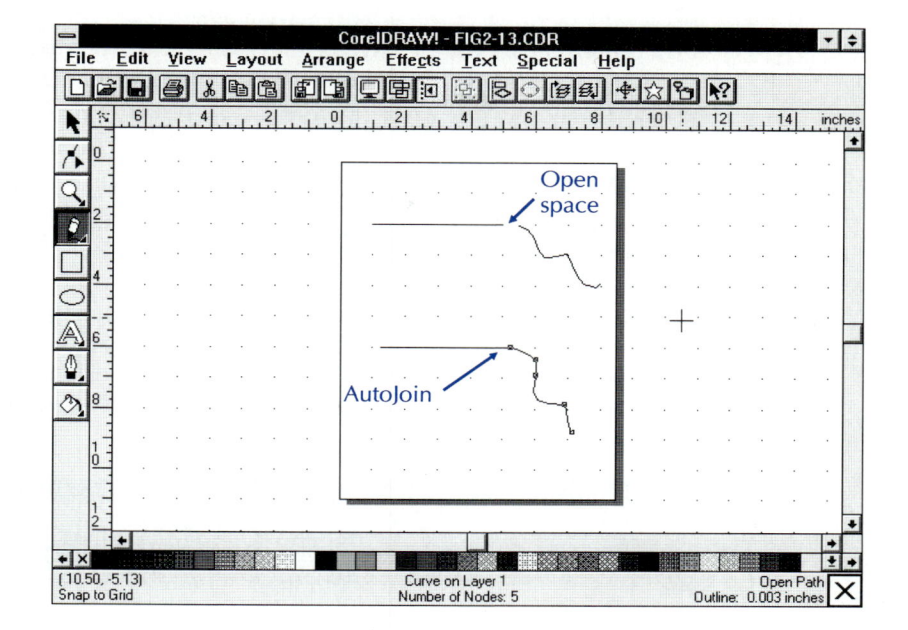

Before and after: Curve snapping to a line (AutoJoin value high)
Figure 2-13.

Creating a Drawing Using Lines, Curves, and Polygons

You have learned how to create all of the simple objects—line, curve, closed curve, and polygon—that you can make with the Pencil tool. In this exercise, you'll bring together all of the skills you have learned by drawing a kite that consists of lines, curves, and a polygon. Use Figures 2-14 through 2-17 as a guide to help you position the start and end points of the lines and curves.

1. Turn on the rulers and show the grid (if they do not appear onscreen already) by selecting Rulers from the View menu and Show Grid from the Grid & Scale Setup dialog box reached from the Layout menu.
2. Also from the Layout menu, select Snap To Guidelines (if not already selected). From the View menu select Wireframe. You have now turned on all of CorelDRAW!'s precision enhancement features.

   Guidelines, nonprinting lines placed on a drawing by either dragging on a ruler or via a dialog box, are used like the grid to align objects in a drawing. Guidelines have two major benefits over the grid: they can be placed anywhere, not just on a ruler mark, and, since they are continuous dotted lines, they provide a better visual reference than the grid dots. When a guideline is near a grid line, the guideline always takes priority. This allows you to place a guideline very near a grid line and have objects on a drawing aligned to the guideline, whereas turning on Snap To Grid will not move objects already on the drawing.

Since the drawing you are doing here uses only major ruler coordinates, you could very easily do it without guidelines. Use the guidelines anyway to see how they work and to use them as a visual reference.

3. With any tool and from any point on the horizontal ruler at the top of the drawing area, drag a horizontal guideline down to 7 inches below the zero point on the vertical ruler. (Move the mouse pointer to the horizontal ruler; press and hold the left mouse button while moving the mouse pointer, along with the dotted line that appears, down to 7 inches; then release the mouse button.) You'll see that the Snap To Grid helps you align the guideline. Your screen should look like this as you are dragging the guideline:

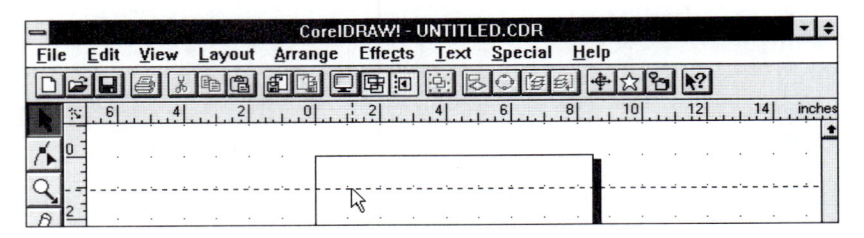

4. As you did in step 3, drag two more horizontal guidelines down to 3 inches and 1 inch below the zero point on the vertical ruler.

If you misplace a guideline, move the mouse pointer to it, press and drag the left mouse button and a four-headed arrow appears. Drag the line into proper position. You can drag a guideline off the page to get rid of it. Also, you can double-click on a guideline and get the Guideline Setup dialog box. From there you can move a guideline precisely or delete it.

5. Again as in step 3, drag three vertical guidelines to the right from the vertical ruler and place them at 6, 4, and 2 inches to the right of the zero point on the horizontal ruler.

When you are done placing all of the guidelines, your screen should look like the one shown in Figure 2-14.

6. Select the Freehand tool. Your first task will be to form a triangular shape, as shown in Figure 2-15.

7. Move to a point 2 inches to the right of the zero point on the horizontal ruler and 3 inches below the zero point on the vertical ruler and then click once to start a line.

8. Extend the line upward and to the right until you reach a point 4 inches to the right of the horizontal zero point and 1 inch below the vertical zero point. Use the status line information to help you.

Drawing and Working with Lines and Curves

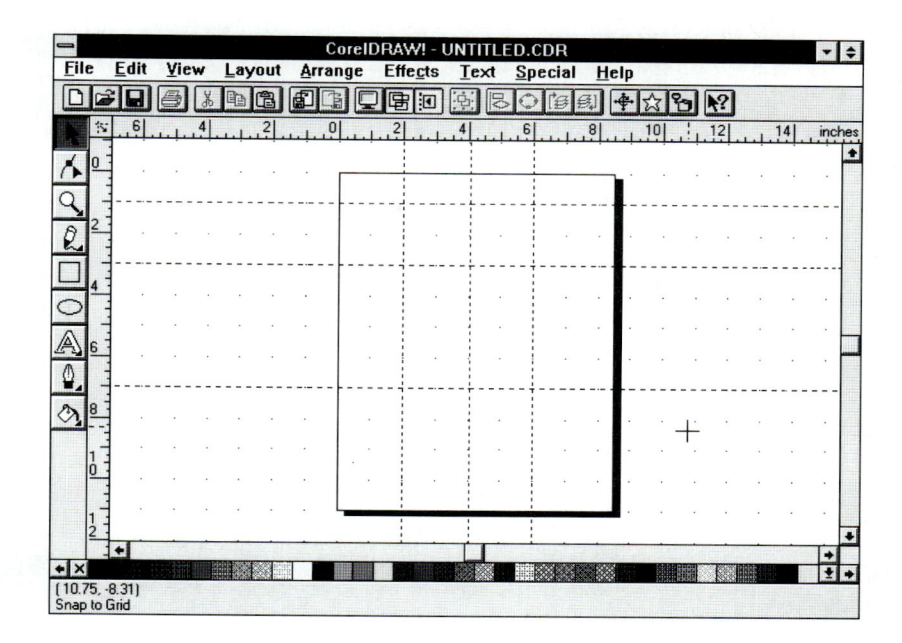

Guidelines in place
Figure 2-14.

Double-click and release the mouse button at this point. With the intersections of the guidelines at each of these points, the lines you are drawing jump to these points if you get anywhere near them.

9. Extend the next line segment downward and to the right until you reach a point 6 inches to the right of the horizontal zero point and 3 inches below the vertical zero point. Double-click at this point to add another line segment.

10. Extend another line segment horizontally to the left until you reach the starting point. Double-click at this point. The last line segment will connect to the first line segment and form a triangle, as shown in Figure 2-15.

11. From this point, extend another line segment downward and to the right until you reach a point 4 inches to the right of the horizontal zero point and 7 inches below the vertical zero point. Double-click at this point to complete this segment.

12. Now, extend a segment upward to the lower-right corner of the original triangle, as in Figure 2-16. Click just once to finish the line and complete the basic kite shape.

13. Next, add a vertical crosspiece to the kite. Since this line must be absolutely vertical, begin by pressing and holding CTRL and then clicking once at the top of the kite.

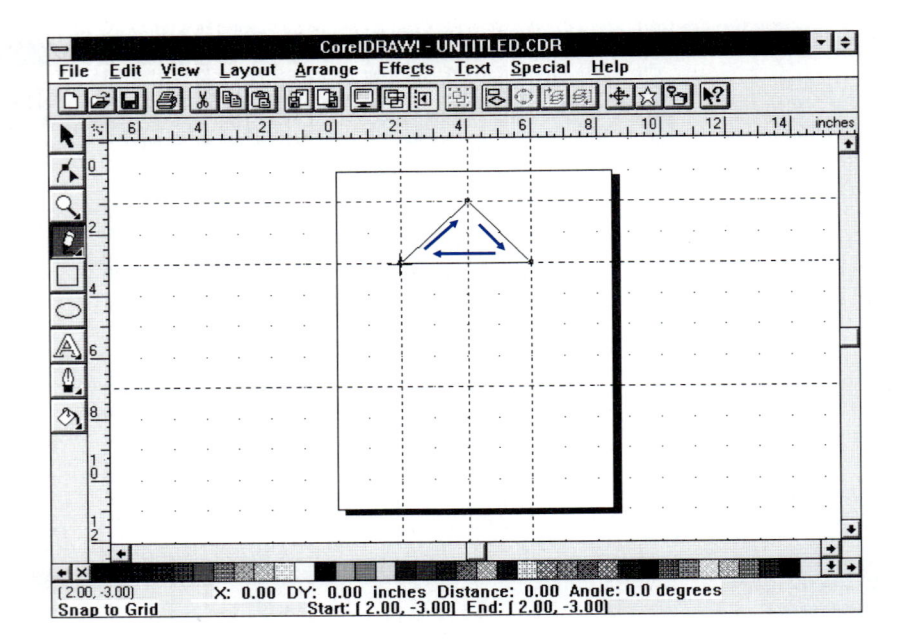

Drawing a kite: the first three line segments
Figure 2-15.

14. While holding CTRL, extend this new line to the base of the kite, as shown in Figure 2-17 of the completed kite, and then click once. Release CTRL. You are next going to attach a curve to this line.

15. To attach a curve to the line, press and hold the mouse button and then draw a kite tail similar to the one in Figure 2-17. Release the mouse button to complete the curve.

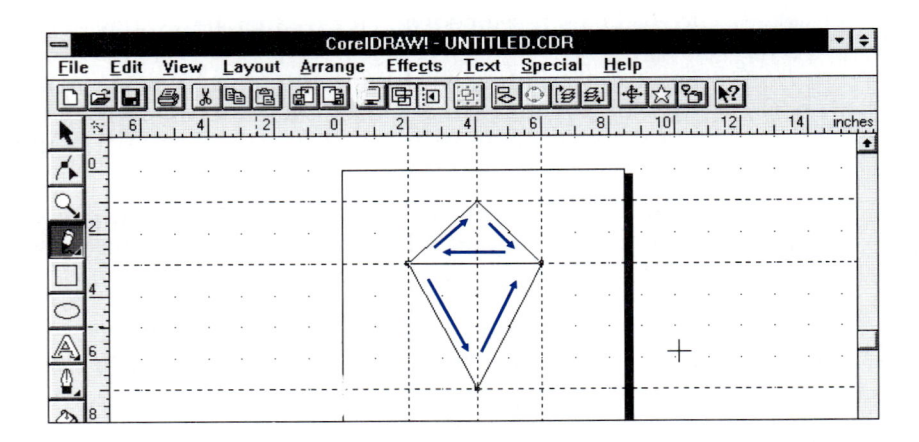

Completing the basic kite shape
Figure 2-16.

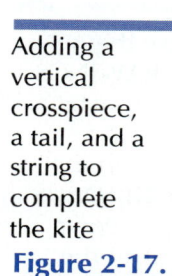

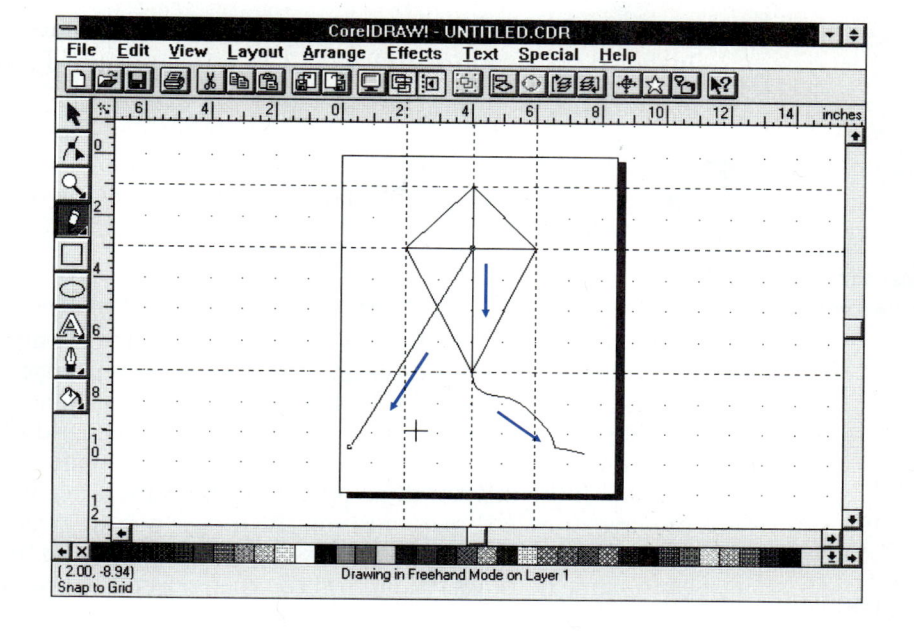

Adding a vertical crosspiece, a tail, and a string to complete the kite
Figure 2-17.

16. Finally, add a string to the kite. While pressing and holding CTRL, click on the point at which the crosspieces meet and extend a line diagonally downward and to the left until you reach the margin of the printable page area. Use Figure 2-17 as a guide. Click once to complete the line. Release CTRL.
17. Your kite should now look similar to the one in Figure 2-17. Leave the kite on your screen for the concluding section of this chapter.
18. To remove the grid lines (for further exercises Chapter 3), turn off the grid by selecting Grid & Scale Setup from the Layout menu. Click on Show Grid. The check mark will be removed. Click on OK.

Saving Your Work

As you work on your own drawings, save your work frequently during a session. If you don't save often enough, you could lose an image in the event of an unexpected power or hardware failure.

In order to save a new drawing, you must establish a filename for it. To save the kite you just drew, follow these steps:

1. Select the Save As command from the File menu to display the Save Drawing dialog box shown in Figure 2-18. The Directories indicator should show that you are in the C:\COREL50\DRAW directory of your

hard drive. (Path names may vary, depending on how and where you installed the software. In Figure 2-18, directory \CDRAW is used instead of \COREL50.)

> **Tip:** A shortcut step to displaying the Save Drawing dialog box is to click on the Save icon.

2. If the path is different from what you want or if you want to save the drawing in a different drive and/or directory, for example, C:\DRAWINGS as suggested in Appendix A, change to the correct drive and directory by double-clicking on the correct entries in the Drives and Directories list boxes. When you double-click, the selected path name will appear in the list box. If the drive or directory name you want is not visible in the Drives or Directories list boxes, position the mouse pointer over the up or down arrow in the scroll bar, then press and hold the mouse button until the path name becomes visible. You can then select the drive or directory name.

3. Name the drawing by clicking in the File Name text entry box and then typing the desired name of your file. Delete the default characters if they are not what you want. Use no more than eight characters; CorelDRAW! adds the .CDR extension for you when you select the OK command button. In this case, type **kite**.

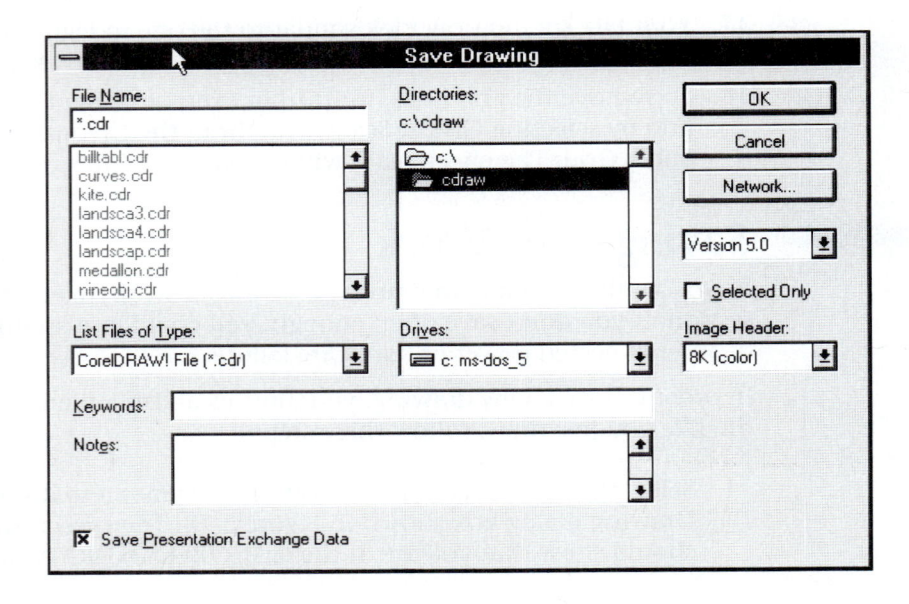

Save Drawing dialog box
Figure 2-18.

Drawing and Working with Lines and Curves

4. Save the file by clicking on the OK command button or pressing ENTER. CorelDRAW! adds the extension .CDR to the file. You exit the Save File dialog box and return to your drawing. Notice that the title bar now contains the name of your drawing, KITE.CDR.

5. Select New from the File menu to clear the screen before continuing. Since you have just saved a picture, the Save Changes warning box doesn't appear.

The foregoing procedure applies only the first time you save a drawing. To save a drawing that has already been saved, select the Save command from the File menu, or click on the Save icon, or press CTRL-S.

Retrieving a File

To open a drawing that you have saved, use the following procedure. In this exercise, you'll open the KITE.CDR file you just saved.

1. Select Open from the File menu. The Open Drawing dialog box appears, as in Figure 2-19. Its layout is very similar to the Save Drawing dialog box.

Tip: A shortcut step to displaying the Open Drawing dialog box is to click on the Open icon.

2. If you saved your file in a directory other than the default directory (the DRAW directory), select the drive and/or directory name from the Directories list box. Use the scroll bar if necessary.

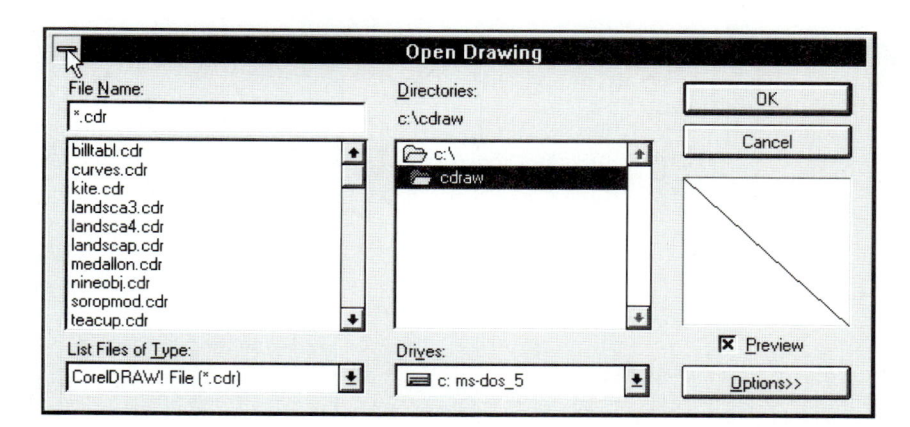

Open Drawing dialog box
Figure 2-19.

3. If you can't see the file KITE.CDR in the File Name list box, position the mouse pointer over the down arrow in the scroll bar and then press and hold it until the filename becomes visible.

4. Click once on the filename, KITE.CDR. The name appears in reverse video (white lettering on black or colored background—depending on the color options set) and displays in the File Name text box. Also, you will see a miniature of the drawing in the Preview box.

5. To open the file, select the OK command or press ENTER. You may see a Conflicting Styles dialog box telling you that the styles in KITE.CDR are different from those in CORELDRW.CDT and asking whether you want the CorelDRAW! styles to prevail. For now, click on NO.

    After a moment, the file displays in the window and its name appears in the title bar.

6. Exit CorelDRAW! by pressing ALT-F4, or by selecting Exit from the File menu.

Tip: There's a shortcut to opening a file once you are in the Open Drawing dialog box. Instead of clicking once on the filename and then clicking on OK, you can simply double-click on the filename.

That's all there is to it. You have created a complete drawing using the various modes of the Pencil tool, saved it, and loaded it again. Along the way, you have learned how to do Freehand and Bézier drawing of both lines and curves and to use the dimension lines, callouts, rulers, grid, guidelines, and status line to help you work.

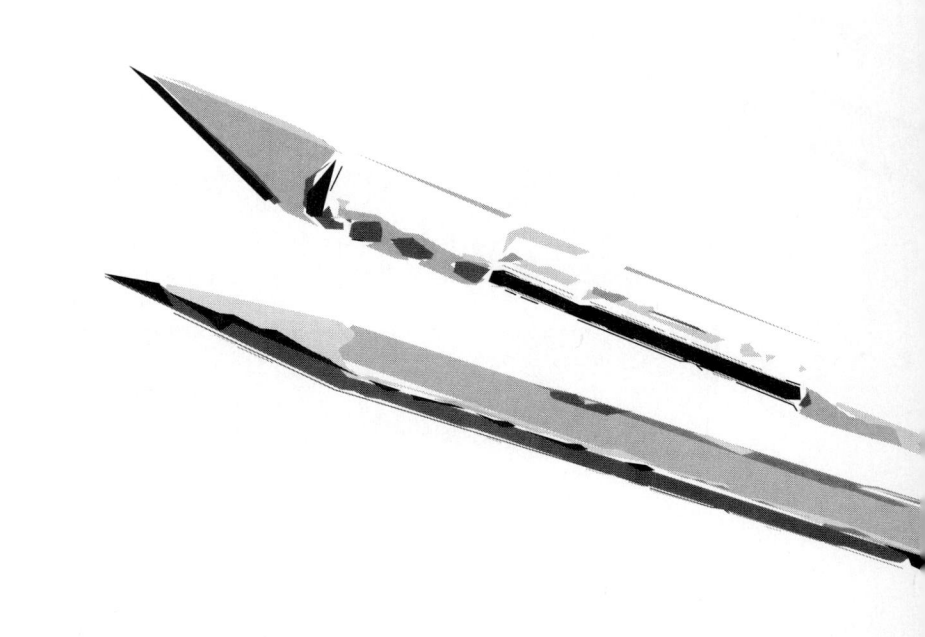

3

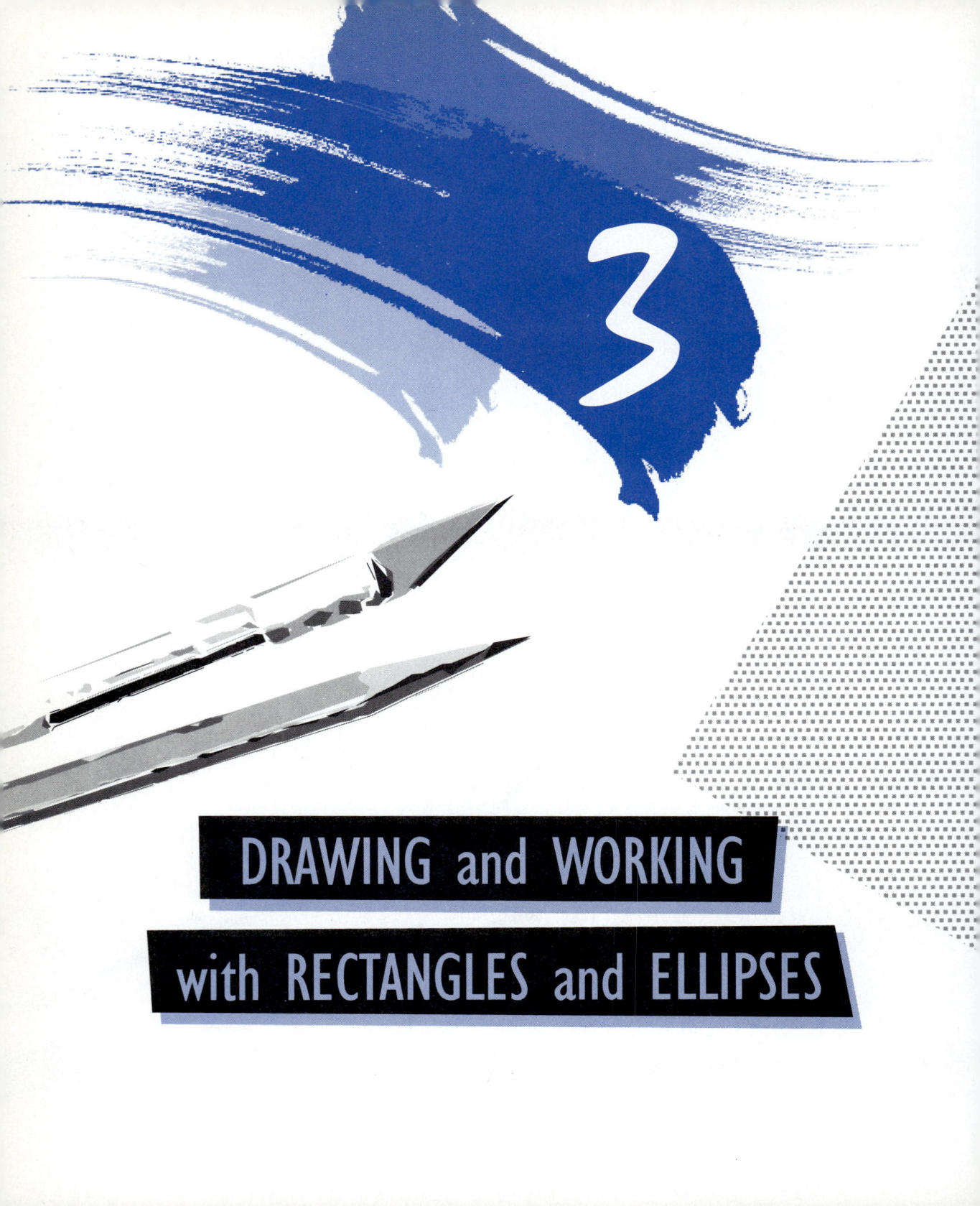

DRAWING and WORKING with RECTANGLES and ELLIPSES

Rectangles

and ellipses are basic shapes that underlie many complex forms in nature or created by man. In this chapter you will use the Rectangle tool to create rectangles and squares and the Ellipse tool to create ellipses and circles. As you work your way through the exercises in later chapters, you will apply a host of CorelDRAW! special effects, fills, and shaping techniques to rectangles and ellipses to make them come alive.

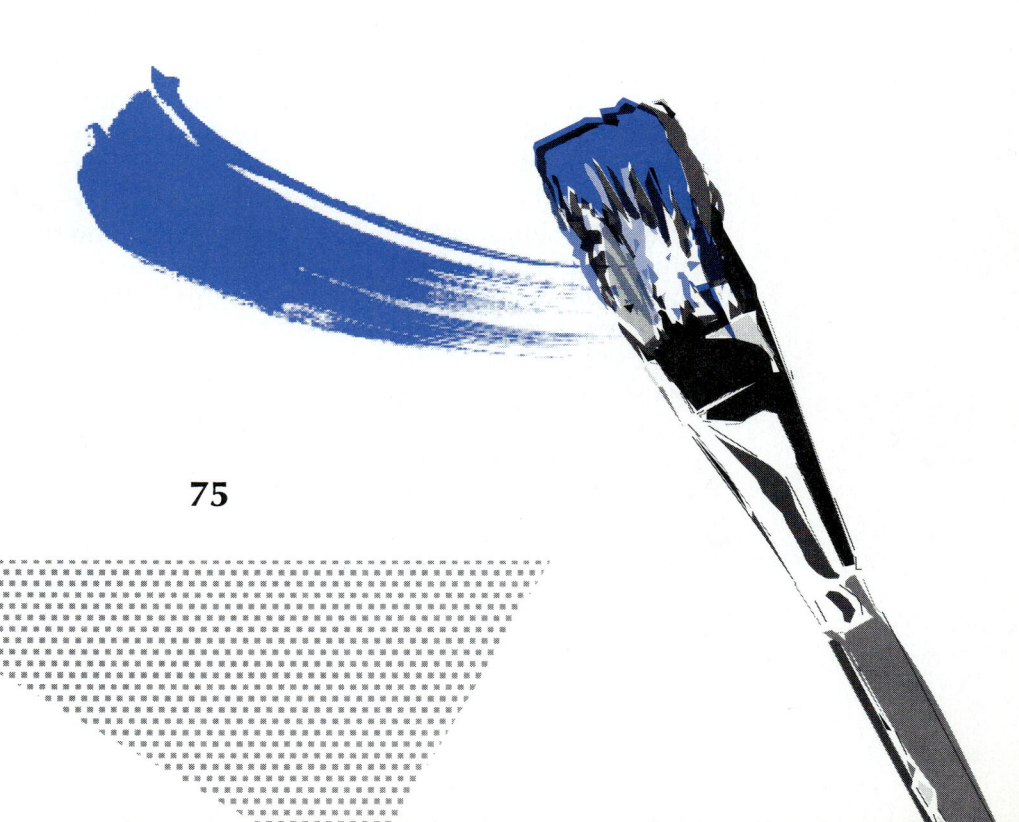

Drawing a Rectangle

Using the Rectangle tool in the CorelDRAW! toolbox, you can initiate a rectangle from any of its four corners, as well as from the center outward. Having this degree of freedom and control over the placement of rectangles saves you time and effort when you lay out your illustrations.

Drawing a Rectangle from Any Corner

You can start a rectangle from any of its four corners. The corner that represents the starting point always remains fixed as you draw; the rest of the outline expands or contracts as you move the pointer diagonally. This flexibility in choosing a starting point allows you to place a rectangle more quickly and precisely within a drawing. Perform the following exercise to become familiar with how CorelDRAW! reacts when you use different corners as starting points.

1. Load CorelDRAW! if you are not running it already.
2. Click on the View menu and make sure there is a check mark beside Rulers and Wireframe. If not, click on the item to insert one.
3. Choose Preferences from the Special menu and click on View. If Show Status Line does not have an X in its check box, click on it to turn it on. Then click on Place On Top to move the status line from its default position at the bottom of the screen to its alternate position above the horizontal ruler. A lot of attention is placed on the status line in this chapter and placing it this way gives you a chance to try the alternate position. Click on OK.
4. Choose Toolbox from the View menu and then click on Floating to undock the toolbar and allow it to be moved around the screen. Once again, this gives you a chance to try an alternate arrangement for the toolbox. The figures and illustrations in this chapter reflect this alternative arrangement. If you don't like it, feel free to return to the default settings by reversing steps 3 and 4.
5. Select the Rectangle tool by placing the mouse pointer over the Rectangle icon and clicking once, and then moving the pointer out of the toolbox and to the right. The mouse pointer changes to a crosshair, the Rectangle icon is selected, and the status line shows "Rectangle on Layer 1."
6. Position the pointer anywhere on the printable page area, press and hold the left mouse button, and drag the mouse downward and to the

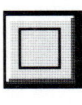

Drawing and Working with Rectangles and Ellipses

right along a diagonal path, as shown in Figure 3-1. The Width and Height indicators in the status line will change as you move the pointer.

7. Experiment with different widths and heights until you achieve the shape you want. You can easily modify the shape of the rectangle by redirecting the movement of the mouse. Notice that the upper-left corner, which was your starting point, remains fixed.

8. When the rectangle is the size and shape you want, release the mouse button. This action freezes the rectangle in place, and a node will appear at each of the four corners. The status line displays the messages "Rectangle on Layer 1" and "Fill: Black" followed by a black square, as in Figure 3-2. The "Fill: Black" message indicates that the rectangle has a default interior color of black. If you do not have Wireframe selected in the View menu, the rectangle you made will be black. You will learn more about fills in Chapter 7.

9. Press and hold the mouse button at a new starting point and then move the pointer along a diagonal path downward and to the left. Release the mouse button when the rectangle has the dimensions you want. Practice making several rectangles by starting at different corners.

10. While the last rectangle is still selected—has nodes at the corners—select Delete from the Edit menu or press DEL to remove it.

11. Clear the whole page by choosing New from the File menu and clicking on No in answer to the "Save current changes?" question. Another way to clear the page is to click on Select All in the Edit Menu and then press DEL.

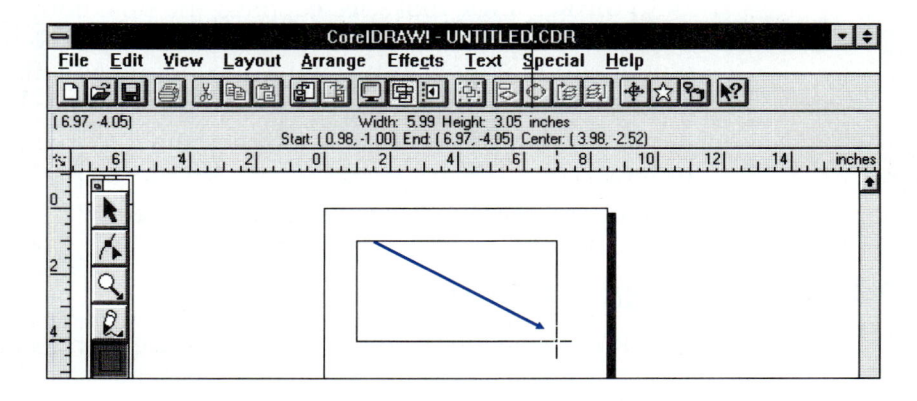

Drawing a rectangle
Figure 3-1.

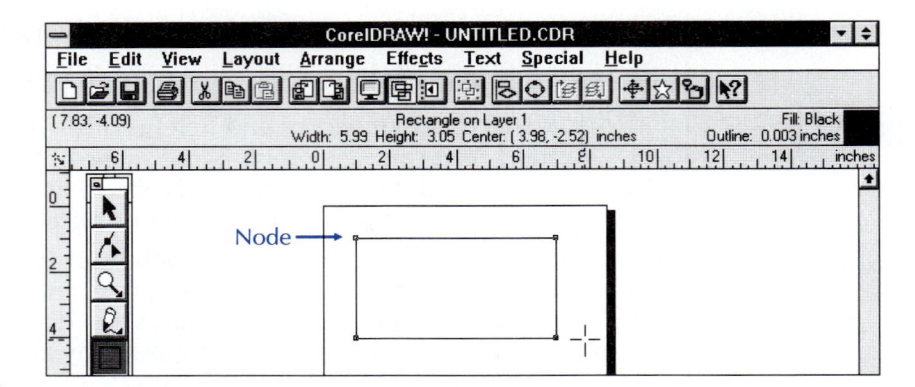

Completing a rectangle
Figure 3-2.

The type of information appearing in the status line reflects the kind of object you are drawing. When you create a line, the status line displays the *x* and *y* coordinates, the distance (*dx,dy*) traveled, and the angle of the line. When you create a rectangle, the status line displays the width, height, start, end, and center. After the mouse button is released, the start and end are no longer shown.

Drawing a Rectangle from the Center Outward

CorelDRAW! allows you to draw a rectangle from the center outward. Using this technique, you can place rectangular shapes more precisely within a graphic, without having to pay close attention to rulers or grid spacing. The width and height indicators display the exact dimensions of the rectangle as you draw. Draw a rectangle now, using the center as its starting point.

1. With the Rectangle tool selected, press and hold both SHIFT and the mouse button at the desired starting point. Keep both SHIFT and the mouse button pressed as you move the mouse. As with any rectangle, you can draw in any direction, as you see in Figure 3-3.
2. Release the mouse button first and then the SHIFT key to complete the rectangle.
3. Press DEL to clear the rectangle from the screen.

Drawing a Square

In CorelDRAW!, you use the same tool to produce both rectangles and perfect squares. The technique is similar, except that you use the CTRL key to constrain a rectangle to a square.

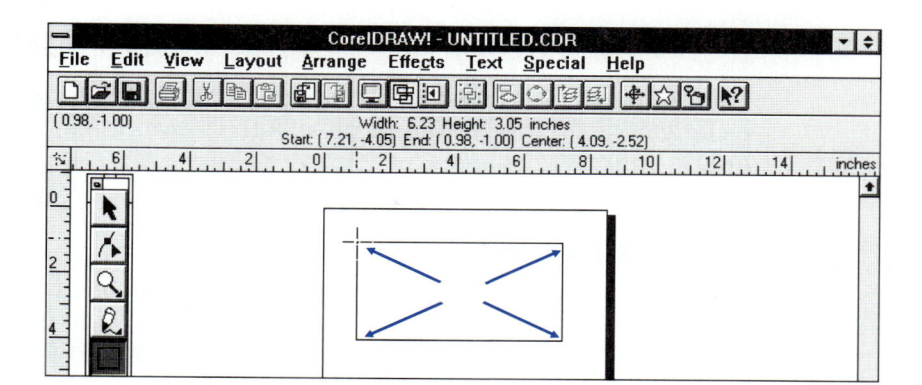

Drawing and Working with Rectangles and Ellipses 79

Drawing a rectangle from the center outward
Figure 3-3.

Drawing a Square from Any Corner

Follow these steps to draw a square. As with a rectangle, you can use any corner as your starting point.

1. With the Rectangle tool selected, position the pointer where you want to begin the square.

2. Press and hold both CTRL and the mouse button and then draw diagonally in any direction. Note that the status line indicators show that the width and height of the shape are equal, as in Figure 3-4.

3. To complete the square, release the mouse button first, and then release CTRL. If you release CTRL first, you might draw a rectangle with unequal sides rather than a square.

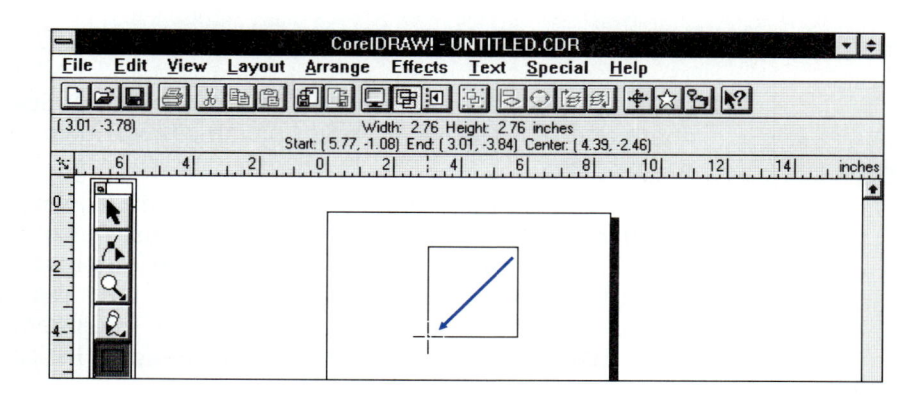

Drawing a square
Figure 3-4.

4. Press DEL to clear the square from the screen.

You can draw a square using the center as the starting point just as you did a rectangle. To do this, you must press both CTRL and SHIFT, as well as the mouse button.

Practicing with the Grid

If your work includes design-oriented applications, such as technical illustrations, architectural renderings, or graphic design, you might sometimes find it necessary to align geometrical shapes horizontally or vertically in fixed increments. In this section, you can practice aligning rectangles and squares *while* drawing them. Later in this chapter you will be introduced to techniques for aligning shapes *after* you have drawn them.

Tip: As you learned in the previous chapter, the grid in CorelDRAW! can either be invisible or a pattern of dots on the screen. Objects are aligned to the grid because of the Snap To feature, which is similar to a magnetic attraction.

One way to align objects while drawing is to take advantage of the Grid & Scale Setup and Snap To commands in the Layout menu. The process of aligning new objects to a grid consists of four steps:

- Adjusting the grid spacing
- Displaying the grid
- Displaying the rulers
- Enabling the Snap To Grid feature

Follow these steps to practice using the grid:

1. Pull down the Layout menu and choose the Grid & Scale Setup command. The Grid & Scale Setup dialog box shown in Figure 3-5 will display.
2. Adjust both the Horizontal and Vertical Grid Frequency values to 2.00 per inch. To do this, press and hold the mouse button over the lower scroll arrow until the number "2.00" appears. Alternatively, you can drag across the current value and type **2.00**. Press TAB twice to go from Horizontal to Vertical. If the selected unit of measurement is something other than inches, click on the unit's drop-down list and choose "inch."

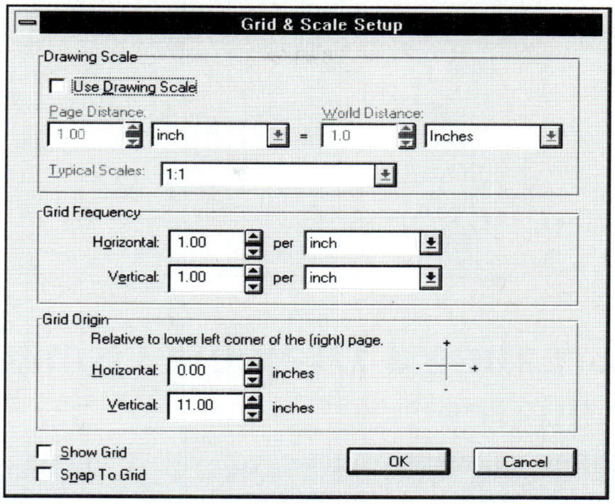

Drawing and Working with Rectangles and Ellipses

Adjusting Grid Frequency
Figure 3-5.

With Snap To Grid turned on, you can align and place objects automatically on the grid, and a message appears to that effect in the lower-left corner of the status line.

3. If they are not already checked, click on Show Grid and Snap To Grid, then click on OK to save these settings, and exit the dialog box.
4. If you didn't do it above, turn on the rulers and the Wireframe Drawing mode by selecting both the Rulers and Wireframe commands in the View menu. Check marks will appear next to both commands, indicating that they are now active.
5. Next, select the Rectangle tool and position the pointer at the 1-inch mark on both the horizontal and vertical rulers. Even if you place the pointer inexactly, the corner of the rectangle will align perfectly to the 1-inch marks when you begin to draw. This is the Snap To feature in operation.
6. Press and hold the mouse button and draw a rectangle 4 inches wide and 3 inches high.
7. Draw a second rectangle the same size as the first, beginning at a point 1/2 inch to the right and 1/2 inch below the starting point of the first. The extension of the mouse pointer in the rulers—a dotted line—should align exactly with the 1/2-inch marks on both rulers. The grid setting prevents you from "missing the mark."
8. Draw a third rectangle from a starting point 1/2 inch below and 1/2 inch to the right of the starting point of the second. Your three rectangles should align like the ones in Figure 3-6.
9. Select New from the File menu to clear all of the rectangles from the screen. When the "Save Current Changes?" message box appears, select No.

Now that you have practiced drawing all possible types of rectangles, you are ready to build a drawing with rectangular and freehand elements.

Drawing rectangles at 1/2-inch intervals
Figure 3-6.

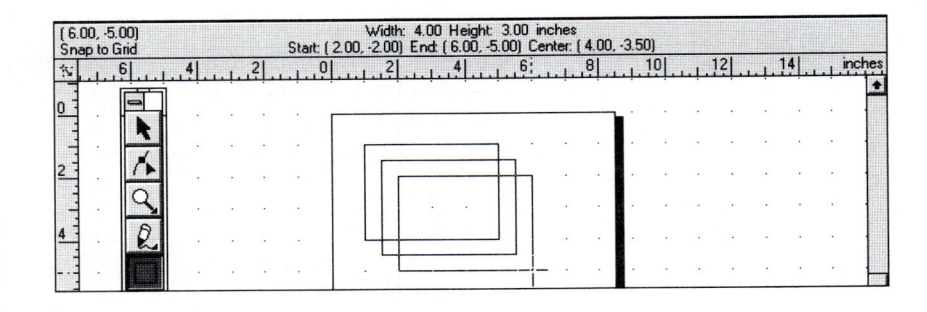

Creating a Drawing Using Rectangles and Squares

In the following exercise, you will integrate all the skills you have learned so far by creating a teacup that includes rectangles, squares, and freehand drawing elements. In the process, you will also learn how to adjust the relative smoothness of curved lines you draw with the Freehand tool. The adjustment involves a feature called Freehand Tracking, which controls how closely CorelDRAW! follows the movements of your mouse pointer when you draw curves.

To prepare for this exercise, select the Grid & Scale Setup command from the Layout menu and adjust both the Horizontal and Vertical Grid Frequency to 8.00 per inch. Both Show Grid and Snap To Grid should still be selected, and Rulers should be turned on. Refer to the steps in the preceding section if necessary.

When you are ready to create the drawing, proceed through the following steps, using the numbers in Figure 3-7 as a guide. If you wish, use the rulers as an aid in laying out your work.

1. Draw a rectangle (1) to represent the body of the teacup. It should be higher than it is wide.

2. Position your pointer at the right side of this rectangle and attach a rectangular handle (2) to the body of the teacup. The handle should touch the edge of the teacup but not overlap it; the grid settings you have chosen will prevent overlapping.

3. Draw a smaller rectangle (3) inside the one you just created (2) to make the opening in the handle.

4. Now select the Freehand tool and add a straight line (4) to the base of the teacup. (Freehand mode should be selected, not Bézier. If you need to change the drawing mode, click on and hold the Pencil tool until the

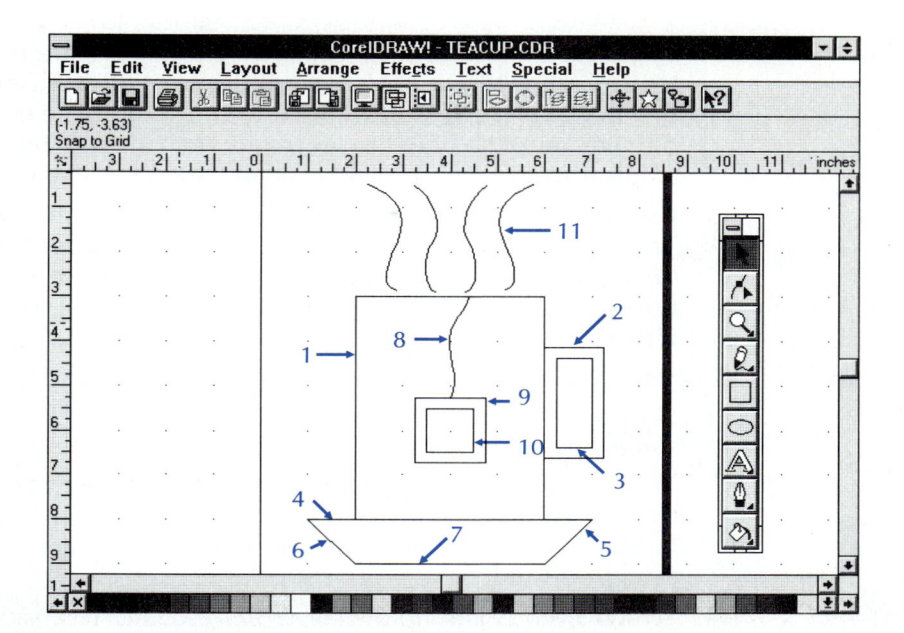

Drawing and Working with Rectangles and Ellipses 83

Drawing a teacup using rectangles, squares, and freehand elements
Figure 3-7.

flyout menu appears, then click on the leftmost icon.) This represents the top of the saucer. Remember to press and hold CTRL while drawing to ensure that the line remains perfectly horizontal; use the information in the status line if you need guidance.

5. Extend diagonal lines (5) and (6) down from each end of the top of the saucer. Check the status line indicators as you draw. The angle for the diagonal line to the left (6) should read -45 degrees, while the angle for the diagonal line to the right (5) should read -135 degrees. Again, press and hold CTRL while drawing the line to ensure that the line remains on a 15-degree increment. Also, be sure to make both lines the same length. Each line snaps to the saucer base to form a multisegment line, as you learned in Chapter 2.

6. Now add another straight line (7) to form the bottom of the saucer. Remember to constrain the line using CTRL. The saucer base snaps to the other line segments to form a single object, a polygon.

7. With the Freehand tool still selected, press and hold the mouse button and draw a curve (8) to represent the string of a tea bag. Does your string appear excessively jagged? If it does, you can adjust the Freehand Tracking setting in the next set of steps.

8. Before adjusting the Freehand Tracking value, erase the tea bag string you have just drawn by selecting Undo from the Edit menu.

9. Select the Curves tab from the Preferences option in the Special menu to display the dialog box shown in Figure 3-8. You used this same dialog box in Chapter 2 to adjust the AutoJoin values. The default value in the numeric entry box next to Freehand Tracking is 5, but you are going to adjust it to a higher number to make smoother curves.

10. Using the scroll arrow, adjust the sensitivity level in the Freehand Tracking option to 10 pixels. This is the highest number possible and causes CorelDRAW! to smooth your curved lines as you draw. Lower numbers, on the other hand, cause the Pencil tool to track every little dip and rise as you move the mouse.

11. Select OK to exit the dialog box and save your setting.

12. Now draw the tea bag string a second time. Your curve should be somewhat smoother now, more like the one in Figure 3-7.

13. Next, attach a tag to the string. Select the Rectangle tool again, position the pointer about 3/4 inch below the bottom of the string, press and hold CTRL and SHIFT simultaneously, and draw a square (9) from the center outward.

14. To add a center label to the tag, create a square (10) inside the first square. Select one of the corners as the starting point for this smaller square.

15. To add a finishing touch to your drawing, create some steam (11) by selecting the Freehand tool and drawing some curves. Since you have set Freehand Tracking to a higher number of pixels, you can create more effective "steam."

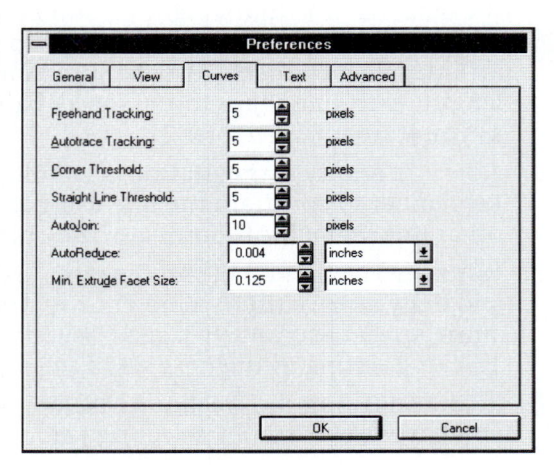

Adjusting the Freehand Tracking value for smoother curves

Figure 3-8.

Drawing and Working with Rectangles and Ellipses 85

16. Finally, save your drawing. Select the Save As command from the File menu and, after you select the directory you want to use, type **teacup**. When you click on the OK command button, CorelDRAW! adds the extension .CDR automatically.
17. Choose New from the File menu to clear the screen and prepare for a new drawing.

Drawing an Ellipse

The Ellipse tool in CorelDRAW! allows you to create both ellipses and perfect circles. Follow the exercises in this section to create ellipses and circles of many different shapes and sizes. In later chapters, you will expand your skills and apply a rich variety of special effects and shaping techniques to these basic geometrical forms.

CorelDRAW! allows you to start an ellipse from any point on the rim or to draw an ellipse from the center point outward by using the SHIFT key. This second method allows you to place ellipses precisely within a graphic.

Using the Rim as a Starting Point for an Ellipse

You can initiate an ellipse from any point on its rim. This flexibility in choosing your starting point allows you to position an ellipse within a drawing without sacrificing precision. Although you cannot use a corner as a starting point for ellipses and circles, you can still use the width and height indicators as guides.

CorelDRAW! gives you an additional visual cue when you are drawing ellipses and circles. If your starting point is on the upper half of the rim, CorelDRAW! places the node at the uppermost point of the ellipse; if your starting point is on the lower half of the rim, CorelDRAW! places the node at the bottommost point of the ellipse. Perform the following exercises to become familiar with how CorelDRAW! reacts when you choose different points on the rim as starting points for an ellipse.

1. Click on the Ellipse tool and position the pointer anywhere on the printable page area, press and hold the mouse button, and drag the mouse downward and to the right along a diagonal path, as shown in Figure 3-9. The indicators on the status line display the width and height of the ellipse.
2. When the ellipse is the shape you want, release the mouse button. This action completes the ellipse and freezes it in place. As in Figure 3-10, a single node appears at the uppermost point of the ellipse, and the status

Drawing an ellipse from top to bottom
Figure 3-9.

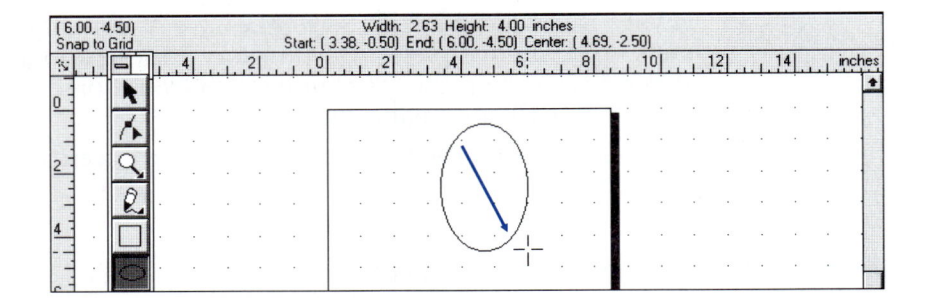

line changes to display the messages "Ellipse on Layer 1" and "Fill: Black" followed by a solid black rectangle. Press DEL to clear the page.

3. Choose a new starting point and draw an ellipse from bottom to top. Press and hold the mouse button at a desired starting point anywhere on the bottom half of the rim and then move the pointer upward in a diagonal direction.

4. When the ellipse has the dimensions you want, release the mouse button. Note that the node is now at the bottom of the ellipse.

5. Press DEL to clear this ellipse from the screen.

Drawing an Ellipse from the Center Outward

CorelDRAW! allows you to draw an ellipse from the center outward, just as you did with rectangles and squares. This feature offers you a more interactive method of working, without sacrificing precision. The width and height indicators continue to display the exact dimensions of the ellipse as you draw. Practice drawing an ellipse using the center as a starting point with these steps:

1. With the Ellipse tool selected, press and hold both SHIFT and the mouse button at the desired starting point. Keep both SHIFT and the mouse

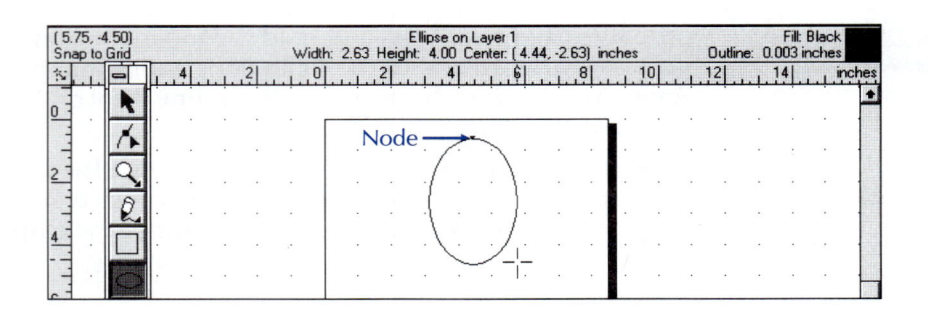

A completed ellipse showing the node at the top
Figure 3-10.

Drawing and Working with Rectangles and Ellipses

Drawing an ellipse from the center outward
Figure 3-11.

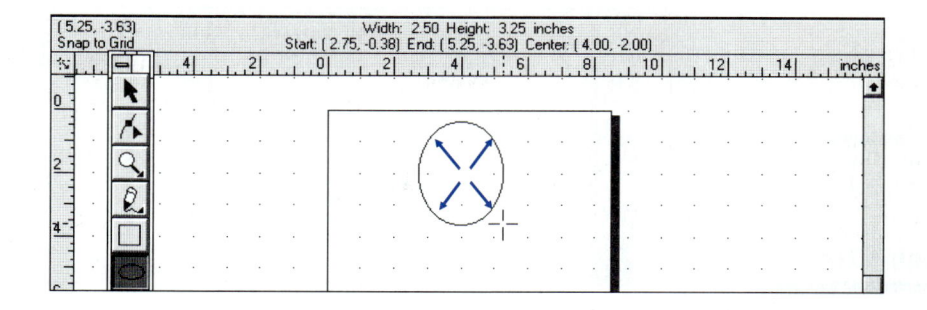

button depressed as you move the mouse. As with any ellipse, you can draw in whichever direction you choose, as you see in Figure 3-11, in which an ellipse was drawn from its center outward.

2. Release the mouse button and then release SHIFT to complete the ellipse. Be sure to release the mouse button before you release SHIFT, or the ellipse may "snap" away from the center point you have chosen, and your center point will be treated as a rim point.

3. Clear the ellipse from the screen by pressing DEL.

Drawing a Circle

In CorelDRAW! you use a single tool to produce both ellipses and perfect circles, just as you use the same tool to produce rectangles and squares. The technique is similar: you use CTRL to constrain an ellipse to a circle. As with ellipses, you can choose either the rim or the center of the circle as a starting point.

Using the Rim as a Starting Point for a Circle

Perform the following exercise to create a perfect circle, starting from the circle's rim:

1. With the Ellipse tool selected, position the pointer at a desired starting point.
2. Press and hold both CTRL and the mouse button and draw diagonally in any direction. As you can see in Figure 3-12, the status line indicators show that both the width and the height of the shape are equal.
3. To complete the circle, release the mouse button and then CTRL. Be sure to release the mouse button *before* you release CTRL, or your circle may turn into an ordinary ellipse of unequal height and width.
4. Clear the circle from the screen by pressing DEL.

Drawing a circle using CTRL

Figure 3-12.

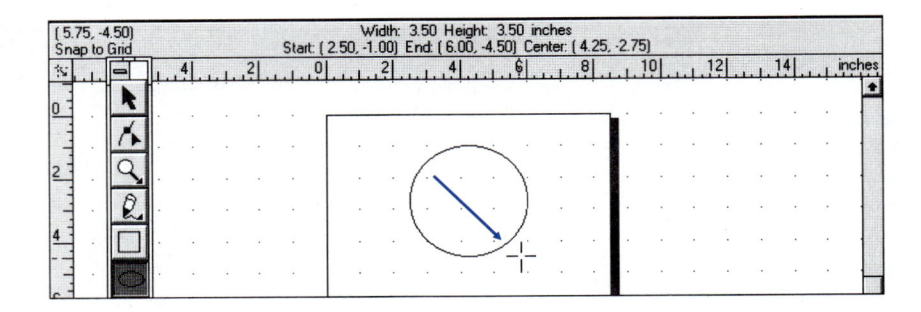

Because of the way CorelDRAW! works, you are actually creating an imaginary rectangle when you draw an ellipse or circle. That is why the status line indicator for a perfect circle displays width and height instead of diameter. The ellipse or circle fits inside the rectangle, as you will see more clearly when you begin to select objects later in Chapter 5.

As is true with other objects, you can draw a circle using the center as a starting point by pressing SHIFT.

Now that you have created some circles and ellipses using all of the available techniques, you can integrate these shapes into an original drawing. Continue with the next section to consolidate your skills.

Creating a Drawing Using Ellipses and Circles

A high Freehand Tracking setting lets you draw smoother curves. A high AutoJoin setting causes lines and curves to snap together even when their end points are a few pixels apart.

The following exercise brings together all the skills you have learned so far. You will create a drawing (of a house and its environment) that will include ellipses, circles, rectangles, squares, and freehand drawing elements. The grid can assist you with some of the geometrical elements of the drawing; other elements you can draw freehand. Since this drawing will be wider than it is high, you will also learn how to adjust the page format from *portrait* (the default vertical format) to *landscape* (horizontal format). The first few steps get you into the habit of anticipating and preparing for your drawing needs before you actually begin to draw, so that you can draw quickly and without interruption. Use the numbers in Figure 3-13 as a guide in performing this exercise.

1. To prepare for the geometrical portion of the drawing, select the Grid & Scale Setup command from the Layout menu and adjust both the Horizontal and Vertical Grid Frequencies to 4.00 per inch. If you need help, refer to the "Practicing with the Grid" section of this chapter.

2. Change the page setup so that your page is wider than it is long. To do this, select the Page Setup command from the Layout menu. When the Page Setup dialog box in Figure 3-14 appears, click on the Landscape

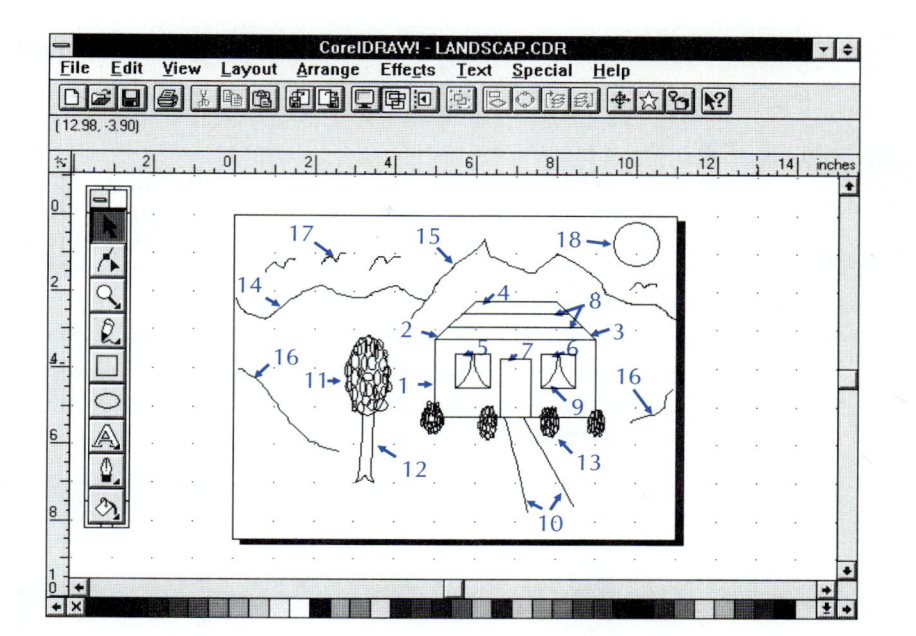

Drawing and Working with Rectangles and Ellipses

A drawing using ellipses, circles, rectangles, and freehand elements

Figure 3-13.

option button to set the orientation to landscape. Exit by selecting the OK command button.

3. Select the Curves tab from the Preferences command in the Special menu and set both the Freehand Tracking and the AutoJoin options to

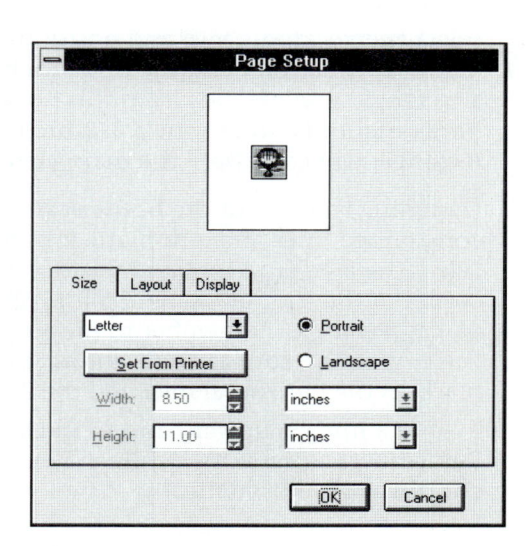

Page Setup dialog box

Figure 3-14.

10 pixels, if they are not already. Click on the OK command button twice to exit both dialog boxes.

Tip: When you changed the page setup from portrait to landscape, the vertical ruler went back to its default of zero being in the lower-left corner. (You may remember that you moved the vertical zero to the upper-left corner in Chapter 2.) Change this again for this drawing, to provide a more normal reference.

4. Move the mouse pointer to the icon at the intersection of the vertical and horizontal rulers. Click and hold the mouse button and drag the ruler crosshair to the upper-left corner of the page, as shown here:

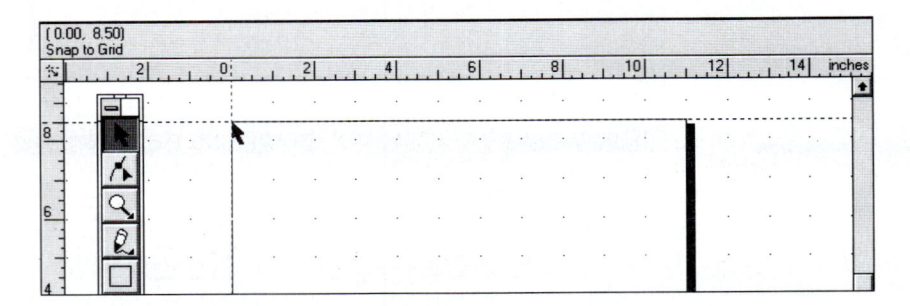

Notice that the lines snap to the corner grid point. Release the mouse button, and the zero point on the rulers will be opposite the upper-left corner of the page.

5. Select the Rectangle tool and position the pointer at the 5-inch mark on the horizontal ruler and the 3 1/2-inch mark on the vertical ruler. Draw a rectangle that extends from this point to the 9-inch mark on the horizontal ruler and to the 5 1/2-inch mark on the vertical ruler. This rectangle will constitute the main element of the house (1).

6. Designing the roof of the house requires three steps involving constrained lines and automatic joining of lines to form a polygon. Select the Freehand tool and position your pointer at the upper-left corner of the "house." Extend a line (2) upward and to the right at a 45-degree angle. Remember to press CTRL while drawing to constrain this line to the correct angle automatically. End the line at the 6-inch mark on the horizontal ruler and the 2 1/2-inch mark on the vertical ruler.

7. Extend a line (3) upward and to the left at a 135-degree angle. Remember to press CTRL while drawing to constrain this line to the control angle automatically. When you reach the 8-inch mark on the

horizontal ruler and the 2 1/2-inch mark on the vertical ruler, end the line with a double-click so you can continue with another line segment.

8. While continuing to hold CTRL, extend a horizontal line (4) back to the first diagonal line (2) and single-click to end it. The two line segments should snap together and form a polygon that constitutes the "roof" of the house.

9. You will need smaller grid increments when drawing the next few objects. Select the Grid Setup command from the Layout menu again and set both the Horizontal and Vertical Grid Frequencies to 8.00 per inch. Select OK to save this setting and return to your drawing.

10. Create two square windows for the house. To create the first window, select the Rectangle tool and begin a square (5) near the left side of the house, a little below the "roof." Practice drawing a square from the center outward using the CTRL-SHIFT key combination. Notice the dimensions of your square just before you complete it, so that you can draw a square of the same size in the next step. If you do not like the first square you draw, press DEL immediately to erase it and try again.

11. Create a second square window (6) near the right side of the house. Make sure this square is the same size as the first and that it begins and ends on the same horizontal plane. The grid settings should help you place it correctly.

12. Make a rectangular door (7) for the house about halfway between the two windows. Use the rulers to help guide your movement. If you make a mistake, press DEL or select Undo in the Edit menu to delete the rectangle and try again.

Tip: Change both the horizontal and vertical grid frequencies to 6.00 in the Grid Setup dialog box since you are trying to divide an inch into three equal parts in the next step.

13. To create planes of shingles for the roof, select the Pencil tool, press and hold CTRL and draw two perfectly horizontal lines (8) across the roof.

14. Add asymmetrical curtains for the house by drawing some diagonal freehand curves (9) inside the windows. Remember to press and hold the mouse button as you draw to create curves instead of lines.

15. Draw a freehand sidewalk (10) that widens as it approaches the foreground of your picture.

16. Select the Ellipse tool and draw an elongated ellipse (11) to the left of the house. This represents the foliage of a poplar tree.

17. Select the Freehand tool and form the trunk of the poplar by adding some freehand vertical curves (12) beneath it. If you wish, you can add some small lines to the "foliage" of the poplar.
18. Select the Ellipse tool again and draw a series of "bushes" (13) immediately in front of the house. Use ellipses for the outlines of the bushes; create detail in the bushes by inserting a few ellipses and circles inside each one. Insert more ellipses to create a denser bush. (You can practice this technique on the poplar tree, too.)
19. Select the Freehand tool and create a mountain (14) behind and to the left of the house. Use curved instead of straight lines. Your mountain doesn't have to look exactly like the one in the figure.
20. Before creating the second mountain, select the Curves tab from the Preferences command in the Special menu and set Freehand Tracking to 1 pixel. This will make the outlines of your subsequent freehand curves more jagged. Select OK twice to exit the dialog boxes and save the new setting.
21. Draw the second mountain (15) behind the house. Notice that the outline of this mountain looks rougher than the outline of the first mountain.
22. Continue by using freehand curves to add a little landscaping (16) beneath the mountain and, if desired, a few birds (17).
23. Select the Ellipse tool and create a sun (18) by drawing a circle from the center outward at the upper-right corner of the picture.
24. Save your drawing by selecting the Save As command from the File menu. When the Save As dialog box appears, select the correct directory, type **landscap**, and click on OK. CorelDRAW! adds the .CDR extension automatically.
25. Finally, if you want to leave CorelDRAW! for a while, choose Exit from the File menu to return to Windows. If you want to go on to Chapter 4 without leaving CorelDRAW!, choose New from the File menu to clear the screen.

Congratulations! You have mastered the Rectangle and Ellipse tools and created another masterpiece with CorelDRAW!.

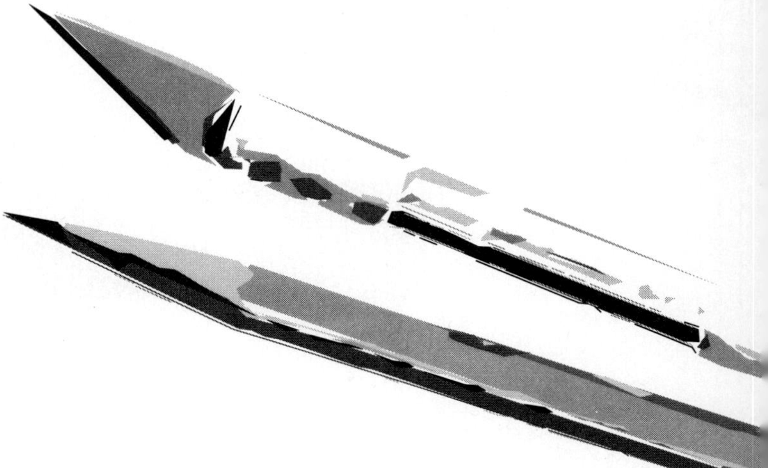

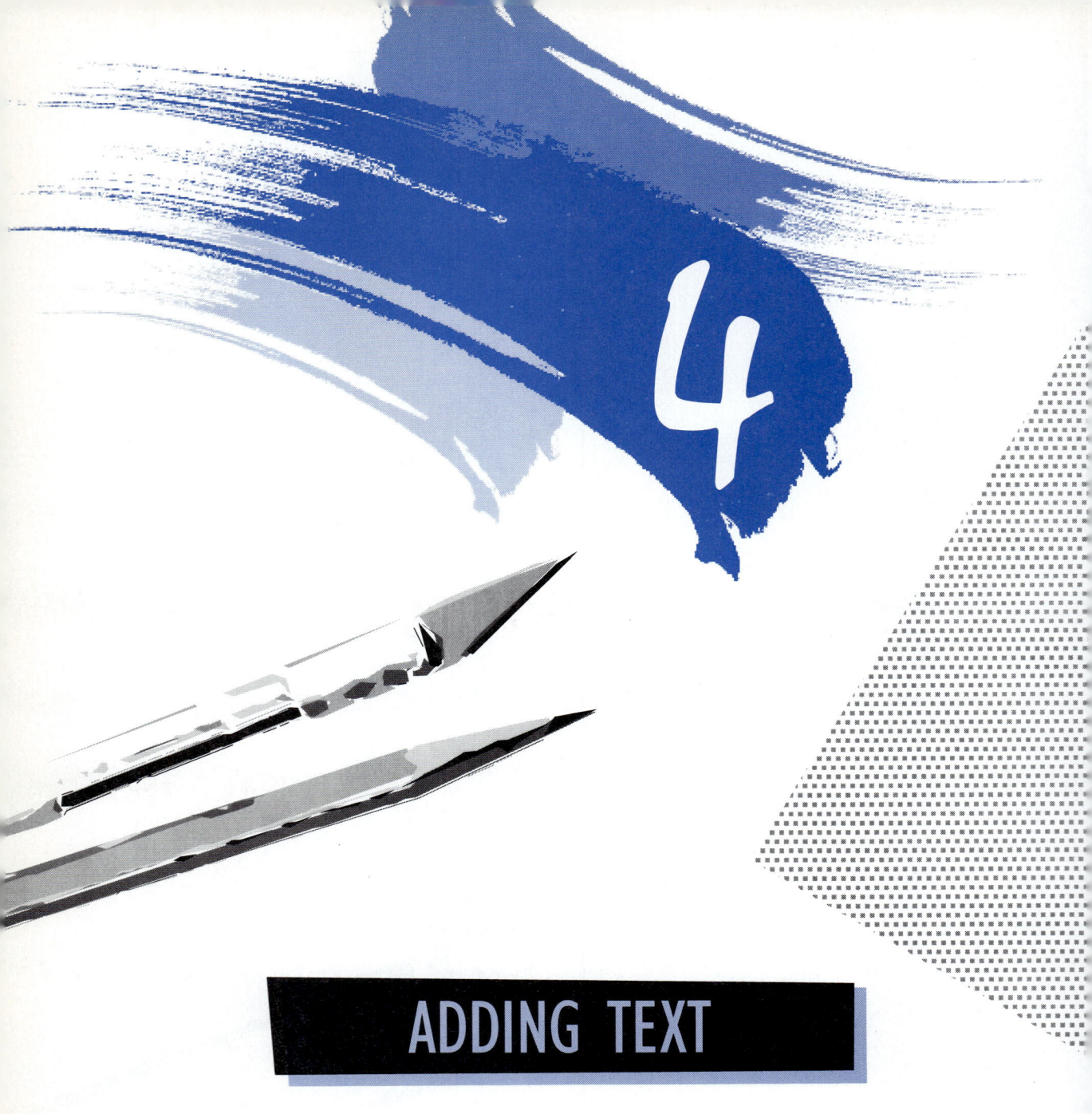

4

ADDING TEXT

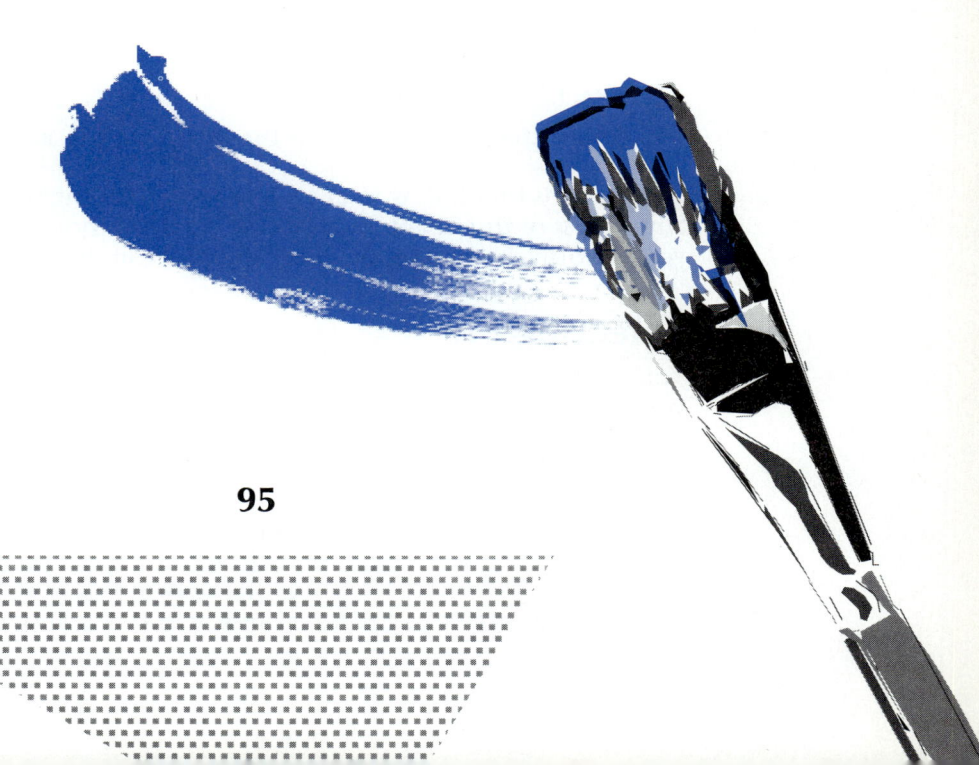

The advanced text-handling features of CorelDRAW! let you turn text into a work of art. You can rotate, skew, reshape, and edit a character or text *string* (a group of characters) just as you would any other object. You can perform these feats with the extensive library of fonts provided with CorelDRAW! or available from other manufacturers. The fonts provided with CorelDRAW! either are or look similar to standard industry fonts and will print on any Windows-compatible printer. Since the Corel fonts are in the Windows standard TrueType format you can use them with all your Windows applications—a real bonus!

In this chapter, you will learn how to insert text into a drawing and select the font, style, point size, alignment, and spacing attributes of your text. You will also learn how to enter special foreign language or symbol characters. After you have completed the exercises in this chapter, you will be ready to tackle more advanced techniques for reshaping your text in Chapter 10.

Entering Text

The Text tool, the last of the four basic drawing tools in CorelDRAW!, is represented by the letter "A." You use the Text tool to insert text into your pictures, just as you use the Ellipse or Rectangle tool to insert geometrical objects. The process of inserting text into a drawing can involve up to eight steps:

1. Select the Text tool.
2. Choose between artistic text and paragraph text.
3. Select an insertion point.
4. Enter text.
5. Choose the size of your text.
6. Set the alignment for the text.
7. Select a font and style.
8. Adjust the spacing between the letters, words, and lines of your text.

The sections that follow treat each of the preceding steps in greater detail. Since most of this chapter consists of exercises, however, the order in which you perform these steps may vary slightly from this list.

Selecting the Text Tool

You use the Text tool in CorelDRAW! to enter new text on a page. When you first load CorelDRAW!, the Pick tool is highlighted; in order to enter text, you must activate the Text tool. In the following brief exercise, you will first adjust the page format and then activate the Text tool.

1. If the printable page area is in portrait format (vertical instead of horizontal), select Page Setup from the Layout menu and select Landscape format. If you did the drawing exercise at the end of Chapter 3, the printable page area is already in landscape format. This is because

Adding Text

CorelDRAW! always "remembers" the page setup you used the last time you created a new drawing.

2. For the same reason, open the View menu and choose Wireframe to turn off that feature.
3. Select the Text tool by positioning the mouse pointer over the tool. Then press and momentarily hold down the mouse button. A two-icon flyout menu appears, as shown here:

The icons represent the two uses of the Text tool: to enter artistic text and to enter paragraph text.

The Artistic text entry tool on the left, which is the default, allows you to enter text in Artistic mode. The Paragraph text entry tool on the right allows you to enter text in Paragraph mode. The distinction between the two modes is explained in the next section.

4. Select Artistic text entry mode by clicking on the left icon. The mouse pointer turns into a crosshair.

Artistic and Paragraph Text

Artistic text is designed for shorter text strings, such as titles, captions, and notes, that can be up to 8,000 characters long. *Paragraph* text is designed for larger blocks of text, such as copy for a brochure. Paragraph text is added in *frames* where each frame is a file that can have up to 850 paragraphs and each paragraph can have up to 8,000 characters.

To enter artistic text, you simply click the Artistic Text tool at the point on the page where you want text to begin. For a paragraph, you drag a *frame,* a box to contain the text, from where you want text to start to where you want text to end. Frames can be linked so that a paragraph text file will flow from frame to frame.

Paragraph text provides many of the attributes of word processing. Text will automatically wrap at the end of a line; text can be justified (aligned on the left and right), as well as left-aligned, right-aligned, and centered; text can be cut and pasted to and from the Clipboard; you can adjust the space between paragraphs in addition to adjusting the space between characters, words, and lines; and you can create up to eight columns with a *gutter* (space between columns) that you define. Bulleted lists can be created using any of the symbols included with CorelDRAW! as bullets. Also, you can import text files created with a word processor, such as Word for Windows or WordPerfect.

Although CorelDRAW! handles paragraphs well and for smaller documents it is a good way to work with paragraphs, longer paragraph text is the primary domain of Ventura. While there is a gray area where either program can do the job, if you have over four pages of paragraph text, Ventura is normally the better choice.

Selecting an Insertion Point

The *insertion point* is the point on the printable page where you want a new text string to begin. In CorelDRAW!, you can enter text directly on the page, or you can type it in a special dialog box, where you also select its attributes. To select an insertion point and prepare for the other exercises in this chapter, follow these steps:

1. Open the Grid & Scale Setup dialog box from the Layout menu and make sure that Snap To Grid and Show Grid are on, and set both the Horizontal and Vertical Grid Frequencies to 2.00 per inch. If your screen does not already display rulers, also select Rulers from the View menu.

2. Position the mouse pointer at the top center of the page area at 5 1/2 inches horizontal and 1/2 inch vertical (zero should be at the top of your page), click once, and type **CorelDRAW!**. Select the Edit Text option from the Text menu, or use the shortcut key combination CTRL-SHIFT-T. The Edit Text dialog box displays, as shown in Figure 4-1.

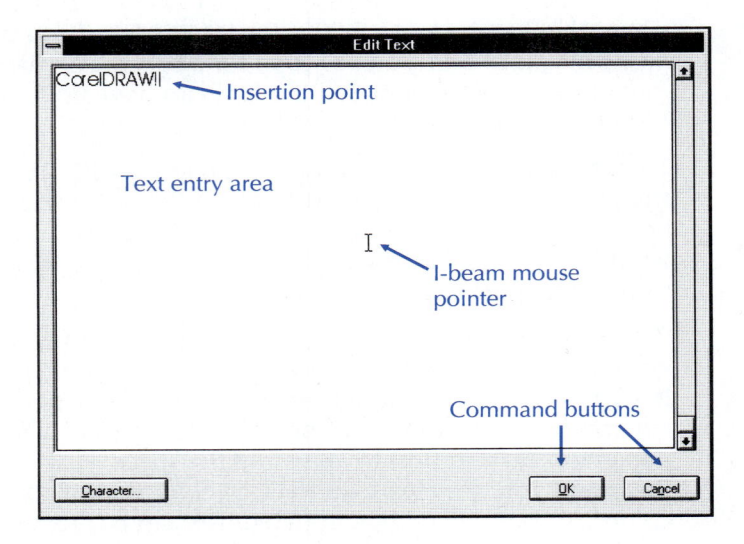

Edit Text dialog box
Figure 4-1.

Adding Text

Edit Text Dialog Box

Using the Edit Text dialog box, you can enter text and then customize it in many different ways. Take a moment to become familiar with the layout of this dialog box and the way the keyboard functions within it.

The following paragraphs describe the components of the Edit Text dialog box and its respective functions. Figure 4-1 shows the major components. While this discussion is for artistic text, the Edit Text dialog box is the same for paragraph text.

Insertion Point   An insertion point appears in the text entry area at the right end of the text string when you first open this dialog box. You can type or edit your text string, or series of characters, in this window. You can move the insertion point anywhere within the text string by using the arrow keys (including HOME and END) or by clicking the I-beam mouse pointer where you want the insertion point.

Command Buttons   The Character command button opens a dialog box, discussed next, that allows you to set character attributes. Both OK and Cancel close the Edit Text dialog box and either saves the work you have done in the dialog box and displays it onscreen or allows you to exit the Edit Text dialog box without saving any changes that have been made.

Character Dialog Box

Clicking on the Character command button in the Edit Text dialog box opens the Character Attributes dialog box shown in Figure 4-2. The Character Attributes dialog box allows you to do character formatting using the elements described in the following paragraphs. You can open the Character Attributes dialog box by selecting it from the Edit Text dialog box, by choosing it directly from the Text menu or by double-clicking on a text node with the Shape tool (although the dialog box adds the shift and angle controls when opened this way).

Fonts List Box   The Fonts list box contains the names of all the fonts from which you can choose, including those provided by CorelDRAW! and any you may have from other sources.

Type Size Selection Box   Use the type size selection box to choose the size for the text you enter. The default setting for this attribute is 24 points, but you can change this value by using the scroll arrows at the right side of the selection box. (See "Selecting a Type Size" later in this chapter.)

Type Size Units Drop-Down List Box   Click on the arrow in the type size units box to change the unit of measuring type sizes from points (the default) to inches, millimeters, picas, or points.

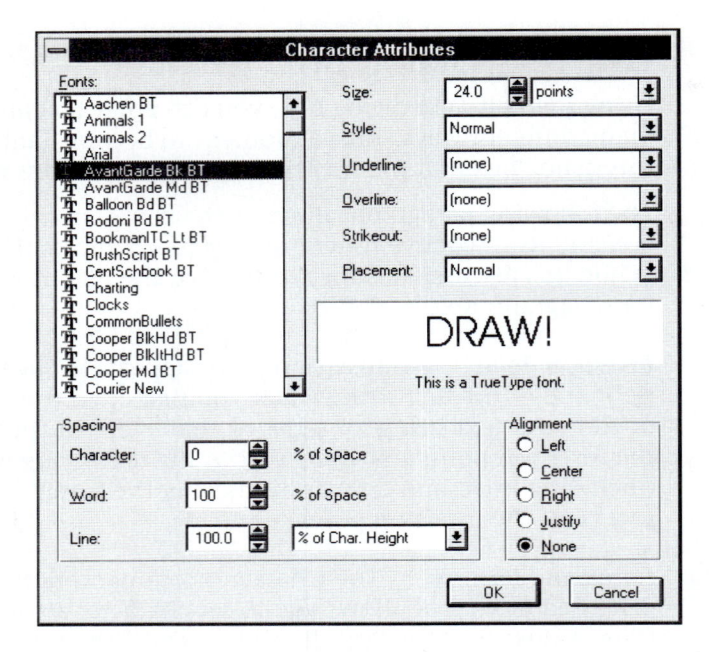

Character
Attributes
dialog box
Figure 4-2.

Style Drop-Down List Box Once you choose a font, use the Style list box to specify the style in which you want the font to appear. In CorelDRAW!, *font* refers to an entire character set that shares the same basic design (for example, Arial), regardless of the size (for example, 10 points) or weight (for example, bold or italic). A *style* is narrower in scope. One style includes only a single weight (normal, bold, italic, or bold-italic) for a particular font. Although there are four possible styles for any font, some fonts are not available in all four styles, and the unavailable styles are therefore dimmed.

Underline, Overline, and Strikeout Drop-Down List Boxes The Underline, Overline, and Strikeout drop-down list boxes let you add a single or double line of various thicknesses below, above, or through the middle of selected text.

Placement Drop-Down List Box Use the Placement drop-down list box to subscript or superscript selected text.

Sample Characters Display Box When you select a font, the Sample Characters display box will display in that font as much of your text as fits in the box. This gives you a true WYSIWYG example of the font. Additionally, CorelDRAW! adds a statement below the display box that indicates whether the font is a TrueType font supported by Windows 3.1 or a font created by another source, such as Adobe Type Manager.

Adding Text

Alignment Option Buttons   Use the alignment option buttons to align your text relative to the insertion point. The default setting for artistic text is unaligned. The choices of left, center, right, justify (right and left), or none are fully described under "Aligning Text" later in this chapter.

Character, Word, and Line Spacing Selection Boxes   The Spacing selection boxes allow you to specify the spacing between characters, words, and lines. See the "Adjusting Text Spacing" section in this chapter for detailed instructions on how to adjust spacing.

Using the Keyboard and Mouse

You can use both the mouse and the keyboard to move among the attributes in the Character dialog box. If you are using a mouse to move around in this dialog box, you can select an attribute in four different ways: by clicking on an option or command button; by scrolling with a scroll bar or scroll arrow; by clicking in a selection box; or by choosing from a drop-down list box. You work with option or command buttons to choose alignment and to close the dialog box; with scroll bars or scroll arrows to choose fonts; with a selection box to choose from different font sizes and the spacing of text; and with drop-down list boxes to choose styles, size, units, types of lines, and placement of text.

If you prefer to use the keyboard in the Character dialog box, you can select most attributes using TAB, SHIFT-TAB, and the arrow keys on your numeric pad. When you first enter the dialog box, the highlight appears in the upper left—the list of fonts. To move to the next attribute, press TAB, or press ALT along with the appropriate underlined letter. Continuing to press TAB moves you from one attribute to the next, while SHIFT-TAB moves you between attributes in the reverse order.

Now you are familiar with the Edit Text and Character dialog boxes as they appear with artistic text. The only difference with paragraph text is that a Paragraph dialog box is available. This will be discussed in later sections in this chapter. In the following sections you will learn how to set artistic text attributes for yourself.

Entering Text

Text can be entered either directly on the printable page area in the CorelDRAW! window or in the text entry area in the Edit Text dialog box. In the next section, you will become acquainted with the use of the text entry area, followed by some of the unique properties of direct entry, including the use of the Text roll-up. The exercises on text entry and manipulation will use both methods to let you see for yourself when to use one over the other.

Entering Text in the Edit Text Dialog Box

When you first open the Edit Text dialog box, the text entry area is automatically selected, as you can see by the insertion point in Figure 4-1. If you are not in the text entry area press CTRL-SHIFT-T now to return there. To enter text, simply begin typing. For this exercise, enter text in the following way:

1. Type **CorelDRAW!** at the insertion point if it's not there already.
2. Press ENTER to begin a new line, type **Made**, and press ENTER again.
3. On the third line, type **Easy**.

Your text entry area should now look like this:

```
-                        Text
CorelDRAW!
Made         I
Easy|
```

Using the Keyboard to Move Around

The way you use your keyboard to move around in the CorelDRAW! text entry area may differ from the way you use it in a word processor. Whenever you have several lines of text in the text entry area, you can use the following keyboard commands:

- Press ENTER to start a new line within the text entry area and begin entering text into it. The window will hold as many lines of text as you generate, as long as you do not exceed the 8,000-character limit.
- Press the DOWN ARROW key to move the insertion point down one line. (This does not apply if you are already on the last line of text.)
- Press PGDN to move the insertion point down to the right end of the last line of text.
- Press the UP ARROW key to move the insertion point up one line. (This has no effect if you are already on the top line of text.)
- Press PGUP to move the insertion point up to the first line of text.
- Press HOME to move the insertion point to the beginning of the current line.

Adding Text

- Press END to move the insertion point to the end of the current line.
- Press the RIGHT ARROW key to move the insertion point one letter at a time to the right.
- Press the LEFT ARROW key to move the insertion point one letter at a time to the left.
- Press BACKSPACE to delete the character immediately preceding the insertion point.
- Press DEL to delete the character immediately following the insertion point.

Using the Mouse

You can also perform some text entry operations using the mouse:

- Use the scroll bar at the right side of the text entry area to locate a line of text that is not currently visible.
- If you want to insert text at a given point, click at that point.
- To select one or more characters in a text string, position the insertion point at the first character you want to select and then drag the mouse across the desired characters. The characters appear highlighted, as shown here:

- You can delete a text string that you have selected in this way by pressing DEL.

Continue to experiment with the keyboard controls and the mouse until you feel comfortable with them. Entering text directly on the printable page area, you will find, uses the same text editing techniques.

Entering Text Directly on the Printable Page Area

CorelDRAW! allows you to type both artistic and paragraph text directly on the printable page area with the attributes that you choose. The mechanics of entering the text here are the same as entering it in the text entry area of the Edit Text dialog box: you establish the insertion point by clicking the mouse, and you use the same navigating and editing keys as you do in the text entry area (HOME, END, BACKSPACE, DEL, and the arrow keys).

To change the attributes of the text you enter, you can use the Edit Text dialog box, directly open the Character dialog box from the Text menu or press its shortcut key CTRL-T, or use the Text roll-up that lets you access the more common attributes. The following exercise repeats the previous text entry, but this time directly in the printable page area:

1. Close the Edit Text Edit dialog box by clicking on the OK button.
2. Choose New from the File menu and click on No when asked if you want to save the changes to the current file, "Untitled.CDR." A blank page appears.
3. Open the Text menu and choose Text Roll-Up, or, using the keyboard, press CTRL-F2. The Text roll-up appears on your screen, as shown here:

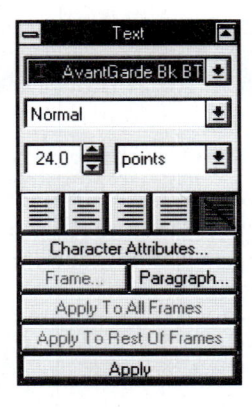

The Text roll-up lets you choose the font, type style, size, units, and alignment. The Character Attribute button is used to open the Character Attributes dialog box you saw previously so you can change other character attributes such as superscript and subscript. The dimmed Frame button is used only with paragraph text. The Paragraph button opens the Paragraph dialog box. For any of your choices to take effect you must choose one of the Apply buttons after changing the attributes. Apply To All Frames and Apply To Rest Of Frames are only available with paragraph text.

Tip: You can use both the mouse and the TAB key to switch among the Text roll-up attributes, but the mouse works the best. Some of the attribute buttons do not allow you to easily see whether they are active.

Adding Text

1. Select the Artistic Text tool and place the insertion point at 5 1/2 inches horizontal and 1 inch vertical.
2. Type **CorelDRAW!**, press ENTER, type **Made**, press ENTER, and finally, type **Easy** and press ENTER.

   You should be looking at the same text entry that you made earlier in the text entry area. Select Edit Text from the Text menu to verify this. When you are satisfied that it's the same, return to the printable page area by clicking the Cancel or OK button.

   As you probably noticed, the Text roll-up is taking up some of the printable page.
3. Roll up the Text roll-up by clicking on the up arrow in the upper-right corner.

Now that you have a feel for both the text entry area and direct-entry ways of adding text, the following exercises will guide you through text attribute usage.

Aligning Text

The next exercise involves deciding how you want to align the text. You have five choices available on the Text roll-up with either artistic or paragraph text: Left, Center, Right, Justified, and None.

Left Alignment

Left is the default alignment setting. When you choose this setting, text will align on the page as though the initial insertion point were the left margin.

1. You will need to reopen the Text roll-up by either clicking on the down arrow of the "rolled-up" title bar, or choosing Text Roll-Up from the Text menu. If the Left button (leftmost icon in the row under the font size, which turns on left alignment) is not selected, use the mouse to select it by positioning the mouse pointer over the icon and clicking once. The Left button darkens when you select it.
2. Select Apply from the Text roll-up. The text that you entered displays on the page in the default font, left-aligned at the 5 1/2-inch mark, as in Figure 4-3. The text string has a default fill of black like other closed objects in CorelDRAW!.
3. Leave this text on the page and select another insertion point, at the 3-inch vertical mark and the 5 1/2-inch horizontal mark, just below the first text string.

Note: The type size in Figures 4-3 and 4-4 looks larger than what appears on your screen. The size has been increased from the default 24 points to 40 points so you can better see the text and the effects of alignment selections. You will do the same on your screen when you use the Size attribute.

Center Alignment

When you select Center alignment, the initial insertion point becomes the midpoint of any string you type. Perform these steps to compare center alignment with left alignment:

1. Type **CorelDRAW!** on one line, **Made** on the next, and **Easy** on the third line, as you did in the last section.
2. Using the mouse, change to center alignment by clicking on the Center icon (second from the Left button) and clicking once.
3. Select Apply. The text you entered appears in the default font, center-aligned with respect to the 5 1/2-inch mark.
4. Leave this text on the page. Select a third insertion point, this time at the 5-inch vertical mark and the 5 1/2-inch horizontal mark, just below the center-aligned text.

Right Alignment

When you select Right alignment, the text aligns on the page area as though the initial insertion point were the right margin. Perform these steps to compare right alignment with left and center alignment:

1. Again type **CorelDRAW! Made Easy** on three lines as you did in the previous exercises.
2. Using the mouse, change to right alignment by clicking on the Right button (middle alignment icon) and clicking once.
3. Select Apply. The text you entered appears in the default font, right-aligned with respect to the 5 1/2-inch mark.
4. Leave this text on the page. Select a fourth insertion point, this time at the 7-inch vertical and 5 1/2-inch horizontal mark.

No Alignment

When you select no alignment, text displays on the page exactly as you enter it. This selection is useful when you want to add unusual spacing at the

Adding Text

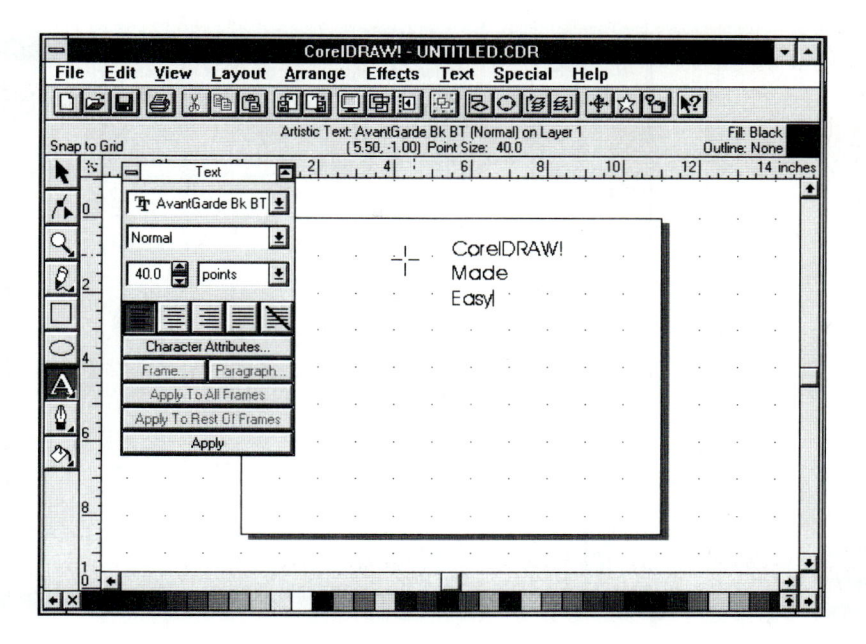

Left-justified text
Figure 4-3.

beginning of a line in a text string. Perform these steps to compare text with no alignment to text with left, center, and right alignment:

1. Type **CorelDRAW!** and press ENTER.
2. On the second line, indent two spaces, type **Made**, and press ENTER again.
3. On the third line, indent four spaces and type **Easy**.
4. Using the mouse, change the alignment to None by clicking on the rightmost alignment button.
5. Select Apply. The text that you entered appears in the default font, with the spacing exactly as you typed it. Your page should now look like Figure 4-4.
6. Clear the page of text by selecting New from the File menu. Do not save the changes. Notice the Text roll-up remains on the screen.

Justified text, which is aligned on both the left and right and created by the second from the Right button, is applicable only to paragraphs for which you have not pressed ENTER at the end of each line. With text such as you have entered here, justified alignment will look just like left alignment because you press ENTER at the end of each line.

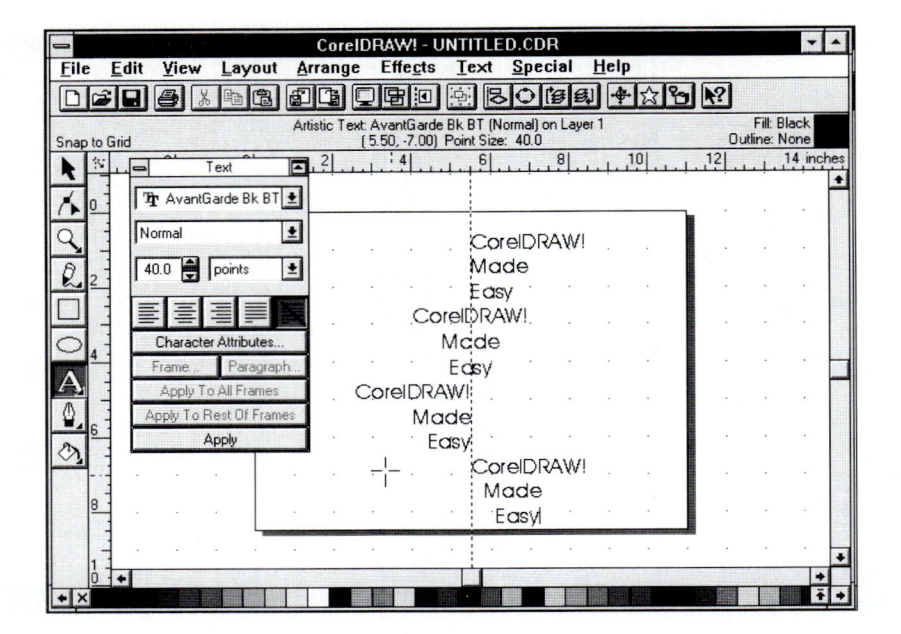

Center, right, and unaligned text added
Figure 4-4.

Selecting a Type Size

Normally, you will select alignment and font settings for a text string before you specify the type size, which is measured in points (72 points make up an inch). For this exercise, however, you will want to see results on the full page in a larger size than the default value of 24 points.

To change the default type size from 24 to 100 points using the mouse, follow these steps:

1. Position the pointer over the upper scroll arrow next to the Size box in the Text roll-up and depress and hold the mouse button. As you hold the mouse button down, the numerical value in the Size box increases.
2. Release the mouse button when the value in the Size box reaches 100.0.
3. Click on Apply. The Text Attributes dialog box will be displayed, as shown here:

Adding Text

> **Text Attributes**
>
> There is no text object currently selected. To which types of new objects will the default apply?
>
> ☒ Artistic Text
> ☒ Paragraph Text
>
> [OK] [Cancel]

4. Click on the Paragraph Text check box to turn it off; only Artistic Text should be selected. Click on OK. The default for artistic text is now 100 points, and the default for paragraph text remains at 24 points.

Selecting a Font

So far, you have used only the default font in CorelDRAW!. In this section, you will have the opportunity to experiment with some of the different fonts and styles supplied with your software.

Different Fonts

Many books and trade magazines offer guidelines for selecting an appropriate font. A thorough discussion of the subject is beyond the scope of this book; however, when choosing the font to use in a CorelDRAW! graphic, you should consider the tone and purpose of your work, as well as your intended audience. As an example, consider the two fonts shown here:

Brush Script
Futura Book

You probably would not choose an elaborate, script font such as Brush Script for a graphic that you would present to a meeting of civil engineers; a font such as Futura Book might prove a better choice.

Note: The discussion of fonts in this and the following chapters talks about fonts that may or may not be available to you depending on what fonts you have loaded on your system. All of the fonts discussed are included in the Corel package. Feel free to substitute other similar fonts if you do not have the specific fonts discussed here.

Practice selecting fonts in the following exercise (the Text roll-up should still be open on your screen).

1. With nothing selected and a new drawing on your screen, change the point size in the Text roll-up to 60 points by pressing and holding the mouse button while pointing on the upward pointing arrow.
2. Click on the Left alignment button in the Text roll-up and then click on Apply.
3. Click on OK to apply these attributes to both artistic and paragraph text that you will enter.
4. Select the Artistic Text tool and then, by clicking, place an insertion point at the 3-inch mark on the horizontal ruler and 1 inch on the vertical ruler.
5. Type **AvantGarde**. Press and hold SHIFT while pressing HOME to select the text you just typed.
6. Select the AdvantGarde Bk font from the Font drop-down list box. You select a font by:
   a. Clicking on the drop-down arrow on the right end of the font drop-down list box;
   b. Using the scroll bar to scroll the list of fonts until you see the font you want;
   c. Clicking on the font you want.
7. Click on Apply. In your printable page area, you will see the AvantGarde text string with the selected attributes, as shown next:

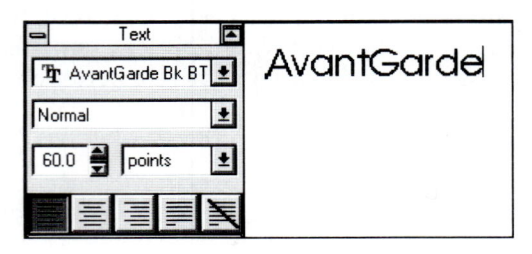

Adding Text

8. Select another insertion point at the 3-inch mark on the horizontal ruler and the 2 1/2-inch mark on the vertical ruler.
9. Type **Balloon** and press SHIFT-HOME to select the text.
10. Select the Balloon Bd font in the Fonts drop-down list box and click on Apply. You will see the Balloon text string beneath the AvantGarde text string, like this:

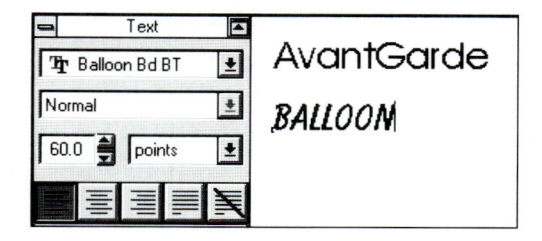

The Balloon font uses only uppercase characters.

11. Select a third insertion point at the 3-inch mark on the horizontal ruler and the 4-inch mark on the vertical ruler.
12. Type **Franklin Gothic** and press SHIFT-HOME to select the text.
13. Select the FrnkGoth ITC Hv font from the drop-down list box and click on Apply. Your text strings should look like this:

14. Select a fourth insertion point at the 3-inch mark on the horizontal ruler and the 5 1/2-inch mark on the vertical ruler.
15. Type **Animals** and press SHIFT-HOME to select the text.
16. Select Animals from the font drop-down list box and click on Apply. Notice that nonalphabetic symbols, rather than letters, appear in the sample characters window as you can see next. This font, like many others that come with CorelDRAW!, consists of symbols rather than letters.

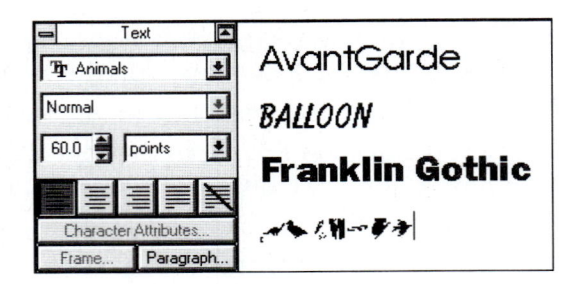

Note: Even though you have entered all of the text strings at the same point size, some appear larger than others. Each font has its own characteristic width and height.

17. Clear the screen by selecting New from the File menu. Do not save any changes.
18. Practice trying out different fonts. When you are ready for the next section, clear the screen by selecting New from the File menu. You will learn how to select different styles that are available for some fonts.

Selecting a Style

While you were experimenting with fonts in the foregoing exercise, you may have noticed that not all styles were offered for some fonts. This is because some fonts have only one or two styles available, while others have three or four.

Perform the following exercise to practice selecting available type styles for the CorelDRAW! fonts. This exercise uses the direct entry method and the Text roll-up. The instructions are less descriptive since you should now have the tools to easily move through the menus.

1. With a new drawing and nothing selected on your screen, in the Text roll-up change the font to Times New Roman, the text size to 75 points, the alignment to center, and click on Apply. In the Text Attributes dialog box, confirm that only Artistic Text is checked and then click on OK.
2. Select the Artistic Text tool and then choose an insertion point that is at the 5 1/2-inch mark on the horizontal ruler and the 1-inch mark on the vertical ruler.

Adding Text

3. Type **Times New Roman**. This provides an example of the font in Normal style as you can see here:

Times New Roman

4. Select another insertion point at the 5 1/2-inch horizontal and 2 1/2 inch vertical ruler marks.
5. Type **Times New Roman**, highlight the text by dragging across it with the mouse, and select the Normal-Italic style from the style drop-down list box.
6. Click on Apply to display the resulting italic text on the page, like this:

Times New Roman
Times New Roman

7. Select two more insertion points at 5 1/2 inch horizontal and at 4 and 5 1/2 inch respectively on the vertical ruler.
8. Type **Times New Roman** at each of the insertion points. Instead of highlighting either of the text strings by dragging or with the keyboard (SHIFT-HOME), you will use the Pick tool.

   Chapter 5 provides an in-depth discussion on the use of the Pick tool, but it's necessary at this point to introduce the text-selecting properties of the tool.

   For CorelDRAW! to change the attributes of a text string, the string must be selected. In simple cases, where there is only one string, some attributes can be changed without you doing the selecting because CorelDRAW! "knows" which text to change. As you increase the number of text strings, you must highlight the text by dragging; or, if CorelDRAW! does not accept the attribute change, select it with the Pick tool.

9. Select the Pick tool and click the mouse pointer on a letter in the first of the two new text strings you just typed. The words "Times New Roman" become surrounded by eight selection markers. The full use of these boxes is discussed in Chapter 5, but for the purposes here, they identify the text as being selected.

The Pick tool is used to select, move, or arrange objects or text.

> **Caution:** Double-clicking on text with the Pick tool invokes the Rotate and Skew feature. If you accidentally do this, just click on the text again to get the selection boxes back.

10. In the Text roll-up, select Bold in the style drop-down list box and click on Apply. The third text sample becomes bold.
11. Click on the last text string to select it, select Bold-Italic in the style drop-down list box, and click on Apply to display the resulting text on the page. Click on a blank portion of the screen to remove the highlighting. The text strings on your screen should now look like this:

Times New Roman
Times New Roman
Times New Roman
Times New Roman

12. Select New from the File menu to clear the screen before continuing with another exercise.

Take a few moments to practice selecting styles for other fonts. When you have finished, continue with the next section to learn how to adjust spacing when you enter a new text string.

Adjusting Text Spacing

The settings for spacing in the Character Attributes dialog box allow you to control the space between characters, words, and lines of text and gives you considerable control over how text looks.

In this chapter, you are working with attributes only as you enter text. However, CorelDRAW! also allows you to adjust text spacing *interactively*. This means that even after text displays on the page, you can change the spacing of one character, several characters, or an entire text string without going back to the dialog box. You will learn more about how to change spacing attributes for existing text in Chapter 10.

Adding Text

Setting Up the Exercise

In the following exercise, you will have the opportunity to review what you have learned thus far about setting text attributes.

If you have forgotten how to perform any of these functions, go back to the relevant section and review it.

1. With a new drawing and nothing selected on your screen, in the Text roll-up, change the font to Garmd ITC Bk (Garamond ITC Book), the style to Normal, the text size to 50 points, the alignment to center, and click on Apply. In the Text Attributes dialog box click on OK.
2. Select the Artistic Text tool if it is not selected already and select an insertion point near the top of the page at 5 1/2-inches on the horizontal ruler and 1 1/2-inches on the vertical ruler.
3. Enter four lines of text in the printable page area. Type your name on the first line, your address on the second, your city, state, and ZIP code on the third, and your telephone number on the fourth. It should look like Figure 4-5, except that the actual text in your printable page area will be your name and address, as you have entered them.
4. Click on the Character Attributes button in the Text roll-up. The Character Attributes dialog box opens. This is the same dialog box that you opened from the Edit Text dialog box. It can also be opened directly from the Text menu or with the keyboard shortcut CTRL-T.

Initial text with Garamond ITC Book, Normal style, center alignment, 50 points

Figure 4-5.

Spacing Options

The three options for adjusting spacing in the Character Attributes dialog box are Character, Word, and Line. You will not change them at this point in the exercise, but take a moment to become familiar with the options.

Character   The Character option controls spacing between each pair of characters within each word of the text. The default value is 0 percent of the normal space for a given font and size. In other words, as a default, CorelDRAW! uses only the normal spacing between characters that has been designed into a font unless you change that value. This measurement is relative, rather than absolute, so that your spacing will stay constant as you scale your text or change the font. You can adjust the value of inter-character spacing in increments of whole percentage points using the scroll arrows or you can type in a value.

Word   The Word option controls spacing between each word of the text that you enter. The default value is 100 percent of a space "character" (pressing the SPACEBAR once) in a given font and size. You can adjust the value of inter-word spacing in increments of whole percentage points using the scroll arrows or by typing in a value.

Line   When your text contains more than one line, the Line option controls the amount of space between each line. In the printing industry, this type of spacing is also known as *leading*. The default value is 100 percent of the type size, which means that if your text size is 10 points, the total amount of space between two lines is exactly 10 points. You can adjust inter-line spacing in increments of 1/10 of 1 percent.

You can adjust the spacing values in two ways: by scrolling with the mouse or by using the keyboard.

To adjust values using the mouse only:

1. Position the mouse pointer on the up or down scroll arrow. If you want to increase the value, position it on the up arrow; if you want to decrease the value, position it on the down arrow.
2. Press and hold the mouse button until the value you want displays in the adjoining box and then release the mouse button.

To adjust values using the keyboard:

1. Use TAB or SHIFT-TAB to go from item to item in the dialog box. When you reach one of the spacing number boxes, the entire number will be highlighted. This means that if you type a new number, you will completely replace the original number.

2. Type in the value you want. To go to the next setting, press TAB or SHIFT-TAB.

Leave the spacing options at their default settings for now and click on OK to exit the Character Attributes dialog box. Your text string has the default settings of 100 percent spacing between words and lines and no extra spacing between characters. If your screen still has the select boxes around your text, click on a blank area of the screen and they will disappear.

Adjusting and Comparing Spacing

Now that you are acquainted with the way spacing works, you will create another text string, identical to the first except that its spacing values differ. You can then visually compare the results of your spacing adjustments.

1. With the Artistic Text tool, select an insertion point at the 5 1/2-inch mark on the horizontal ruler and the 5-inch mark on the vertical ruler, just beneath the last line of text on the page.
2. Type your name, street address, city, state, and ZIP, and telephone number on four separate lines.
3. Click on the Pick tool to highlight the new text. From the Text roll-up, click on the Character Attributes button to open the Character Attributes dialog box.
4. This time, adjust the spacing in the Character number box to 50 percent, Word to 200 percent, and Line to 130 percent. This means that the additional space between characters will equal half of the normal space, the space between words will equal twice the normal space, and the space between lines will equal 1.3 times the height of the font itself.
5. Click on OK to save these settings and then click on Apply to transfer the effect of the settings to the selected text. Click off the printable page area in any white area to remove the selection boxes. The second text string now displays the new settings as you can see in Figure 4-6.
6. Select New from the File menu to clear the screen. Do not save any changes.

Working with Paragraphs

So far in this chapter, all of your work has been in Artistic Text mode. This is fine for titles, captions, and other pieces of text that are only a few short lines. If you are creating a brochure, a flyer, or other documents where you need large blocks of text, you should use Paragraph mode. Paragraph mode

Comparison of default and custom spacing attributes
Figure 4-6.

offers several features that are valuable for large blocks of text and are not available in Artistic Text mode. Among these features are

- An increase in the character limit from a single 8,000 character paragraph, to 850 8,000 character paragraphs
- Automatic word wrap at the end of each line
- Variable line length controlled by a frame, or bounding box, whose dimensions and attributes can be changed
- Justified (full left and right) alignment
- The ability to define up to eight columns with variable column widths and inter-column (gutter) spacing
- The ability to paste text into the text entry area or onto the page from the Windows Clipboard
- The ability to import text created with a word processor
- Adjustable inter-paragraph spacing
- The ability to control text hyphenation

As with artistic text, paragraph text can be entered directly on the printable page area, or you can open the Edit Text dialog box and use the text entry area.

Try out Paragraph mode now with these steps:

1. With an empty printable page area and nothing selected, open the Text roll-up if it isn't already and select Bookman ITC Light as the font,

Adding Text

Normal style, 25 points for the size, justified for the alignment, and click on Apply. In the Text Attributes dialog box, make sure Paragraph Text is selected and click on OK. Click on the roll-up arrow on the right in the Text roll-up's title bar.

2. Select the Paragraph Text tool (the rightmost icon in the Text tool flyout menu) and place the mouse pointer at 1 inch on the horizontal ruler and 1/2 inch on the vertical ruler.
3. Press and hold the mouse button while dragging the mouse pointer to 10 inches on the horizontal ruler and 8 inches on the vertical ruler, as shown in Figure 4-7, and then release the mouse button.

   The frame dimensions of the paragraph will be set. After you release the mouse button, the insertion point appears at the beginning of the frame. Though the printable page area does not show that you are in Paragraph mode, the status line will display "Text on Layer 1."
4. Type several paragraphs, such as those shown following this step. It doesn't matter what you type as long as you have two or more paragraphs about as long as those shown. Press ENTER only at the end of each paragraph (except the last) and let CorelDRAW! automatically wrap the text at the end of each line.

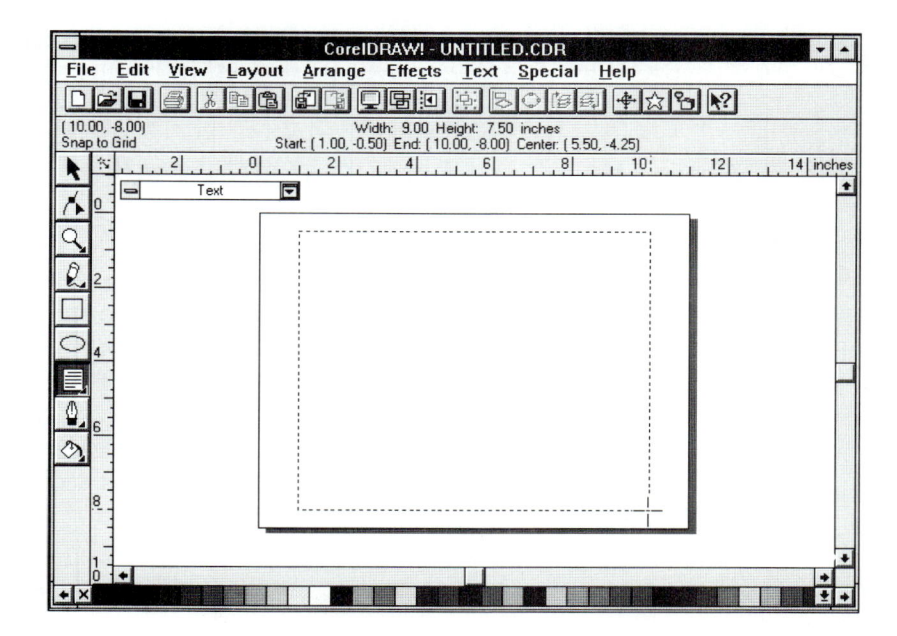

Forming the Paragraph mode bounding box or frame
Figure 4-7.

Here are two sample paragraphs you can type:

CorelDRAW!'s paragraph mode, first available in version 2.0, provides many features that are valuable for entering large blocks of text. Among these features are: an increase in the character limit, automatic wordwrap at the end of each line, a line length that is controlled by the size of the frame, full (both left and right) justification, text hyphenation, and the ability to define up to eight columns.

Paragraph mode also allows you to paste text from the Windows Clipboard, import text files created with a word processor, and adjust the inter-paragraph spacing. Paragraph mode is used in building brochures, flyers, and other documents where large blocks of text are needed.

5. Select both paragraphs by pressing CTRL-SHIFT-HOME.
6. Open the Text roll-up, click on the Paragraph button, change Line spacing to 120 percent and After Paragraph spacing to 200 percent. (You'll learn more about the Paragraph dialog box under "Paragraph Attributes," later in this chapter.)
7. Click on OK to close the dialog box and then click on Apply to transfer the settings to the waiting paragraphs. Press END to remove the highlight. The text will appear within the frame, as shown in Figure 4-8.

   To preserve the typing you have done, save this file.
8. From the File menu select Save As, if necessary, change to the DRAWINGS directory, type **paratext** in the filename text box, and press ENTER or click on OK.

Extracting Text from CorelDRAW!

CorelDRAW! includes a feature that allows you to extract text from CorelDRAW! in a format that is usable in a word processing program. You can modify the text in the word processor and then merge the text back into CorelDRAW!, automatically reattaching all of the formatting, such as font, size, and style, that was originally attached to the text. (In the word processing program you will not see any of the formatting.)

In this section you will extract the paragraph text you entered, bring that text into a word processor, modify it, save it, save it again as a plain text file, and place it on the Windows Clipboard. In the next section, you will bring each of these files back into CorelDRAW!.

Adding Text

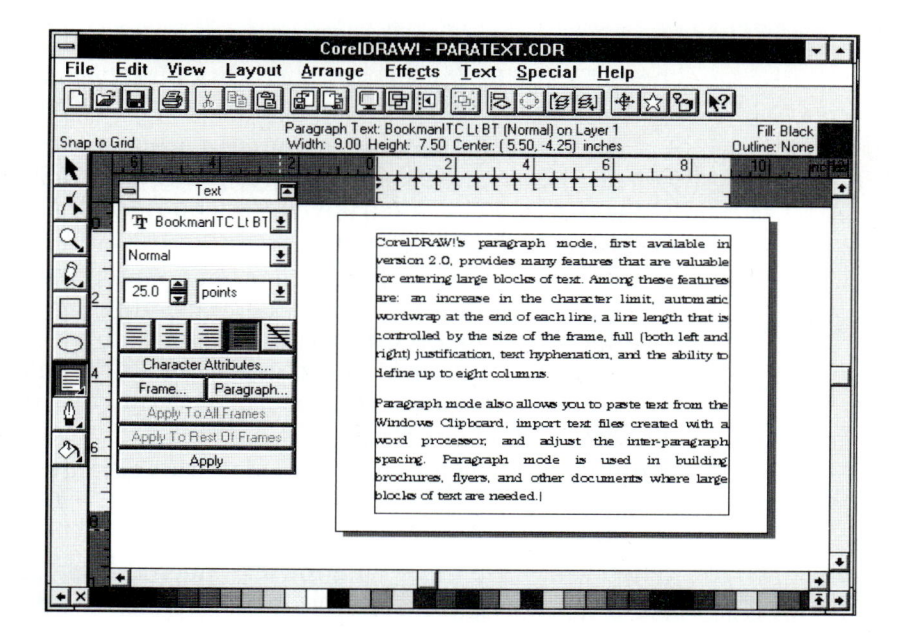

Paragraph text as it is displayed on the page
Figure 4-8.

Start by extracting the text from CorelDRAW!. The text you typed should still be on the screen, as shown in Figure 4-8. To extract it, you must select it with the Pick tool.

1. Select the Pick tool to select the text.
2. From the Special menu, select Extract. The Extract dialog box will open.
3. Make sure the DRAWINGS or another suitable directory is selected, type **extrpara** in the File Name text box, and click on OK.

   You have now written an ASCII text file containing the paragraphs you entered. In the following steps you will switch out of CorelDRAW! without closing it, open Windows Write, and edit that file. (Almost any word processor could be used in place of Windows Write.)

4. Open the Control menu in the upper-left corner of the CorelDRAW! window and select Switch To.
5. From the Task list, double-click on Program Manager. The Program Manager window will open.
6. Open the Accessories group (if necessary) and double-click on Write. The Write word processing program will open.
7. Select Open from the File menu. In the Directories list box, locate the DRAWINGS directory, to which you extracted the EXTRPARA.TXT file. If you installed CorelDRAW! according to the instructions in Appendix

A, this is C:\DRAWINGS. In the List File of Type drop-down list box, choose Text Files (*.TXT) and then click on *extrpara.txt* in the File Name list box. The filename is displayed in the File Name entry box. Click on OK.

8. A dialog box will open asking, "Do you want to convert this file to Write format?" Click on No Conversion to preserve the ASCII text format. The text you entered in CorelDRAW! will appear on the Windows Write screen, as shown in Figure 4-9.

    The first two lines and the last four lines of text (the last line is blank) are reserved for CorelDRAW! to use in merging the text back in. It is, therefore, very important that you do not change these six lines or the paragraph codes in front of each paragraph, or CorelDRAW! will not be able to merge this file. You can change all other parts of the file except the first two and last two lines.

9. Modify any of the text you entered. In this exercise, it doesn't matter what you modify, as long as you can recognize the change when you get back to CorelDRAW!.

10. When you finish modifying the text, open the File menu and save the file under its original filename, EXTRPARA.TXT. This is the file that will be used to merge back into your CorelDRAW! PARATEXT.CDR file.

    Now that you have saved the merge file, you can remove the first two and last four lines as well as the paragraph codes to make another text file that you can import into CorelDRAW!. Also, you will copy the remaining text to the Windows Clipboard and paste it into CorelDRAW!.

11. Delete the first two and last four lines of the file as well as the paragraph codes so you only have the text you entered (select the text by dragging over them with the mouse and press DEL).

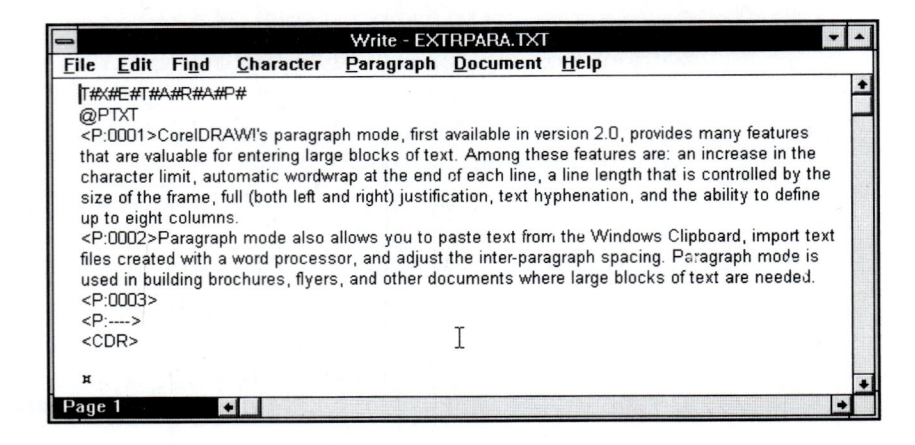

Paragraph text in Windows Write

Figure 4-9.

Adding Text

12. From the File menu, select Save As, type **test.txt**, and click on OK. This is the file you will import.
13. Select all of the text you entered and have now modified by dragging over it with the mouse, and then from the Edit menu select Copy. This places a copy of the text on the Windows Clipboard.
14. Double-click on the Control menu to close Windows Write, and then open the Program Manager's Control menu and select Switch To.
15. Double-click on CorelDRAW! to switch to that program. CorelDRAW! will reappear on the screen.

Merging, Importing, and Pasting Text into CorelDRAW!

You now have four copies of the text you entered: the original file you saved in PARATEXT.CDR, the modified merge file EXTRPARA.TXT, the clean text file TEST.TXT, and finally, the copy on the Windows Clipboard. Use each of the last three of these copies to see how CorelDRAW! merges, imports, and pastes text from outside CorelDRAW!.

1. From the Special menu, select Merge-Back. The Merge-Back dialog box will open.
2. Double-click on EXTRPARA.TXT in the File Name list box. After a moment you will see the revised text displayed on the page. The copy of PARATEXT.CDR in memory has now been revised with the changes you made in Windows Write. All of the formatting in the original file has been maintained. If you had some graphic elements in the file, they would also remain unchanged. Only the words and their positions have changed.
3. Select New from the File menu to clear your screen. Save the revised file if you wish.
4. Select the Paragraph Text tool and draw a paragraph bounding box from 1 inch on the horizontal and 1/2 inch on the vertical ruler to 10 inches on the horizontal and 8 inches on the vertical ruler.
5. Open the File menu, click on Import, make sure you are in the correct directory, and then double-click on TEST.TXT. The revised text will be brought into the paragraph frame.
6. Click on Cancel to throw away the imported text.
7. The frame that you established in step 4 returns to the screen.
8. Press CTRL-V or choose Paste from the Edit menu. Once again the revised text will come into the paragraph frame, this time from the Windows Clipboard. The only difference is that now there is a carriage return at the end of each line.

You have now seen how you get text out of CorelDRAW! and how you can bring text back into CorelDRAW! in three different ways. Now look at how you can use columns in CorelDRAW!.

Putting Text in Columns

Many brochures, flyers, and other documents appropriate for CorelDRAW! put text into multiple columns instead of one wider column in an effort to make the text easier to read. Try it here. You should still have the revised paragraphs you pasted into the paragraph frame on your screen.

1. Press CTRL-SHIFT-HOME to select both of your paragraphs.
2. Open your Text roll-up if it isn't already and then click on Frame. The Frame Attributes dialog box will open, as shown here:

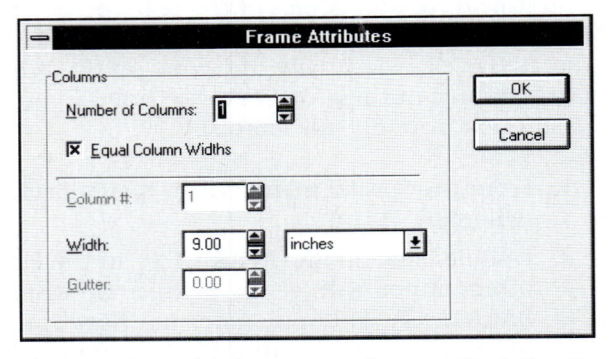

3. Type **2** for the number of columns, make sure that the Equal Column Widths check box is checked, then drag across the Width number box, type **4.25**, press TAB twice to move to the Gutter number box, and type **.5** to make the space between columns 1/2 inch.
4. Click on OK to close the Frame Attributes dialog box and click on Apply Two Frame. After a moment the text will appear in a two-column format, as shown in Figure 4-10.

Paragraph Attributes

Paragraph attributes can also be set using the Paragraph dialog box shown in Figure 4-11. You open this dialog box using the Paragraph button in the Text roll-up, the Paragraph option in the Text menu, or the Paragraph command button in the Edit Text dialog box. With the Paragraph dialog box you can adjust spacing, alignment, hyphenation, tabs (left, right, center, and decimal), indents, and the symbol and its attributes used for bulleted lists.

Adding Text

Text in two-column format
Figure 4-10.

Paragraph Spacing

The spacing options in the Paragraph dialog box are the same as those in the Character Attributes dialog box except for the Before and After Paragraph options. If you are in Paragraph mode, and you have more than one paragraph, the Before and After Paragraph options control the amount of space between each pair of paragraphs. The default values are 100 percent of the type size Before Paragraph and 0 percent After Paragraph. If your text size is 10 points, the space between paragraphs will be 10 points. You can adjust the inter-paragraph spacing by increments of 1/10 of 1 percent.

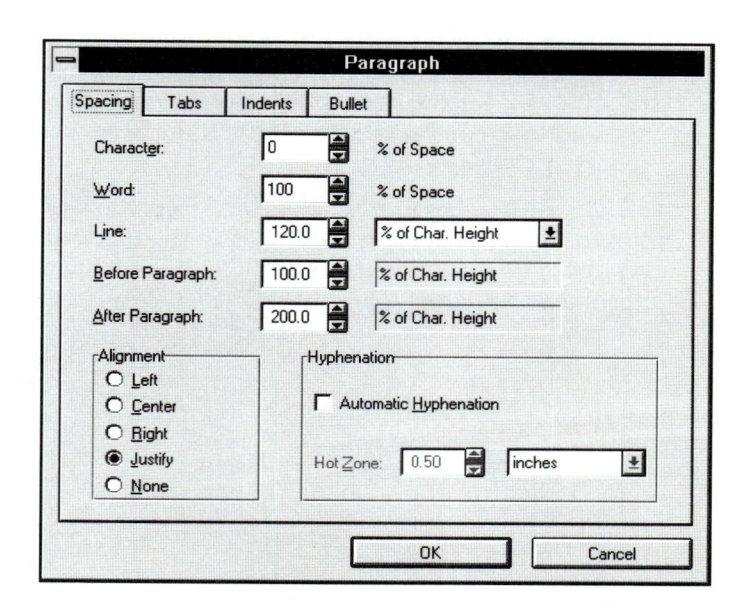

Paragraph dialog box
Figure 4-11.

Hyphenation

When enabled by clicking on the Automatic Hyphenation check box in the Paragraph dialog box, CorelDRAW! will hyphenate words at the end of a line if three conditions occur: they begin before the left edge of the hot zone, they continue beyond the right edge of the frame, and a valid hyphenation break occurs within the zone. The *hot zone* extends from the right side of the paragraph text frame toward the left, according to the distance listed in the Hot Zone box. The unit of distance in the hot zone is the same as that currently entered in the units box. If a word begins in the hot zone and continues beyond the frame's right edge, it will wrap to the beginning of the next line.

Using the two columns of paragraph text that are still selected on your screen, try CorelDRAW!'s hyphenation capability with these steps:

1. Click on Paragraph in the Text roll-up to open the Paragraph dialog box.
2. Click on the Automatic Hyphenation check box. Leave the default 0.50 inches Hot Zone, click on OK, and again on Apply.
3. Roll up the Text roll-up and then click on the Fit-in-Window (second from the right) tool in the Zoom tool flyout menu. You can now see the hyphens that have been added as shown in Figure 4-12.

Using the Spelling Checker

CorelDRAW! allows you to spell check text in either Artistic or Paragraph Text mode. To use the spelling checker you can either highlight the text to check, which can be one word or an entire block of text, or you can type a word in the Unknown Word text entry box of the Spell Check dialog box. You open the Spell Check dialog box by choosing Spell Checker from the Text menu. If you then click on the Range>> command button, the dialog box expands as shown in Figure 4-13.

Selecting the Pick tool will highlight your entire text selection.

Clicking on the Begin Check button starts the spell checking. If a word is found that is not among the words in the dictionary, it will appear in the Unknown Word entry box. CorelDRAW! will automatically offer spelling alternatives which will appear in the Change To text box and in the list beneath it if there are more than one. If you select one of the alternatives in the list, that word moves up to the Change To text box. You can choose

Adding Text

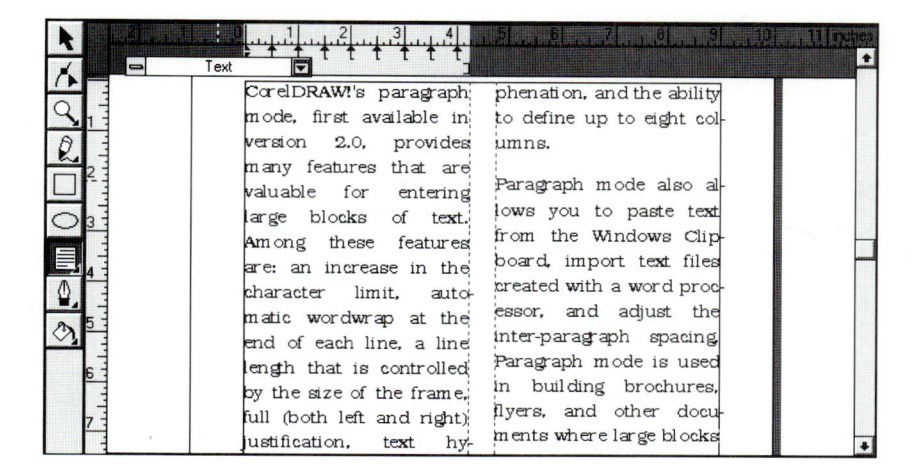

Paragraph text after it has been hyphenated
Figure 4-12.

between replacing this particular occurrence or all occurrences of the word by clicking on either Change or Change All. If you don't want to replace the word with any of the suggested alternatives, you can ignore either one or all occurrences of the word by clicking on either Skip or Skip All. Finally, you can manually enter a word into the Change To text entry box.

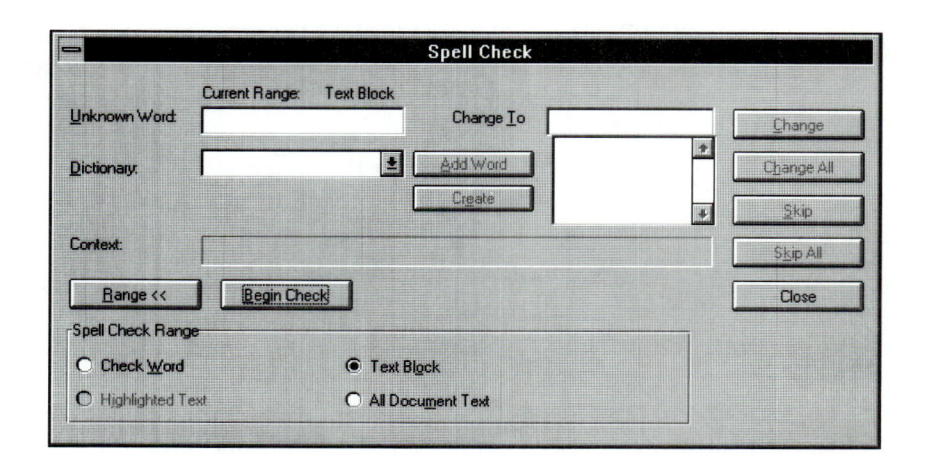

Expanded Spell Check dialog box
Figure 4-13.

Check the spelling of the two paragraphs you currently have on your screen with these instructions:

1. Select the Pick tool to select the paragraphs and then choose Spell Checker from the Text menu. The Spell Check dialog box will open.

2. Click on Begin Check. The spelling checker will begin checking the paragraphs. If nothing else, it will stop on the word "CorelDRAW!'s" as you can see here:

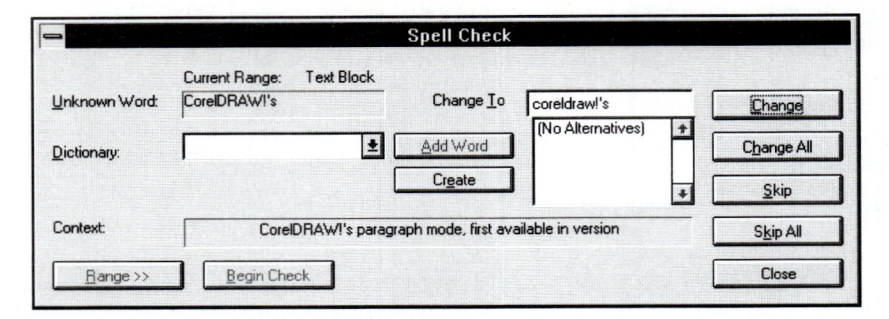

If you use the word "CorelDRAW!'s" very much you may want to add that word to your personal dictionary. Do that next by continuing with these steps:

3. Click on Create and type a filename like **mydictry** in the Name entry box and click on OK to create your personal dictionary. The name you gave to the dictionary appears in the Dictionary drop-down list box.

4. Click on the Add Word button. The word is added to MYDICTRY and the spell checking continues until it stops on the word "wordwrap." The word "word-wrap" appears in the Change To text box as the suggested alternative.

5. Click on Change to accept the suggested alternative. Again the spell checking continues until it reaches "inter-paragraph" where it stops but does not offer an alternative.

6. Click on Skip. If no other words are found, a message appears "Spell check complete." Click on OK to close the Spell Check dialog box and return to your paragraph text.

Thesaurus

CorelDRAW!'s Thesaurus provides synonyms and definitions for selected (or manually entered) words. Simply highlight a word using the Text tool and open the Thesaurus from the Text menu. Or, open the Thesaurus and enter a word in the Looked UP text entry area and click on Look Up. In either case,

Adding Text

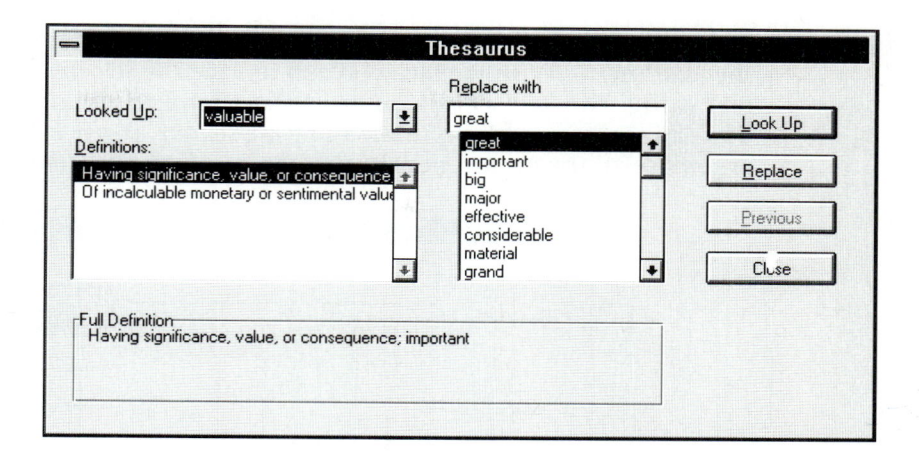

Thesaurus dialog box
Figure 4-14.

CorelDRAW! offers various definitions and synonyms. If you decide to replace the word you looked up, highlight the word and click on the Replace button.

If you highlight the word "valuable" in your paragraph text and open the Thesaurus, the dialog box will look like Figure 4-14. You can then select a synonym like "important" and click on Replace or select a different definition and get a different set of synonyms from which to choose. If you don't want any of the synonyms, click on Close.

Find and Replace

Find and Replace are two additional features to help you edit your text. The Find dialog box, shown next, is opened by choosing Find from the Text menu. A text string up to 100 characters long can be entered in the Find text box. Clicking on Find Next will move the highlight from its current location in the text to the next occurrence of the text string you entered. When the end of the document is reached, you will be prompted whether you want the search to continue from the beginning of the paragraph text. The Match Case option is used when you want an exact match, including upper- and lowercase, of a text string.

The Replace dialog box, shown next, is similar to Find and is also found on the Text menu. With Replace you can replace the selected text with another text string. The Replace option can also match the case of the search string. You can replace single occurrences of the search string, with confirmation, or replace all the occurrences in the paragraph text without confirmation.

Using the Symbol Library

CorelDRAW! includes a library of over 5,000 symbols that are stored and retrieved like characters in a font using the Text tool. The symbols are simple, but effective, drawings that are stored as vector images (unlike most clip art, which is stored as bitmap images). As a result, the symbols can be enlarged, stretched, rotated, and edited like any other CorelDRAW! object without any loss in the quality of the image. Also, they take very little room to store. To use the symbols, you must install them on your hard disk. CorelDRAW!'s Install program will do this for you, as discussed in Appendix A.

The symbols are organized into a number of categories; for example, Animals, Common Bullets, Sign Language, and Windings. These categories are like fonts. You first select a category, and then from that category you select a particular symbol. The number of symbols in a category varies from 30 to over 200, with the average around 80. Corel includes with CorelDRAW! a catalog of all of the symbols, giving each a number within a category. If you know this number, once you have selected a category you can enter the number and get the symbol. Also, as you will see in a moment, you can select a symbol from a display box once you have decided on a category.

Try this feature now by selecting several symbols.

1. Click on the Symbols icon from the ribbon bar (third icon from the right). The Symbols roll-up opens, as shown in Figure 4-15.
2. Click on several categories in the drop-down list box at the top of the roll-up.

Adding Text

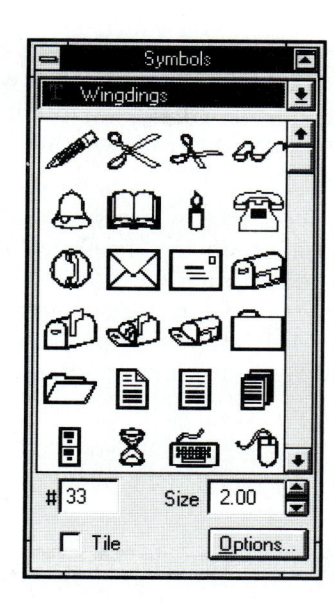

Symbols roll-up
Figure 4-15.

3. Use the scroll arrows below the Sample window to see additional symbols in the Computers category.

   Repeat steps 2 and 3 to look at a number of symbols. Notice below the scroll arrows, there is a Size number box where you can specify the initial size of a symbol when it is placed on the page.

In future chapters you will see how you can also size symbols that have already been placed on the page.

4. Change the size to 1 inch and then drag a symbol onto the printed-page area.
5. Drag several more symbols at various sizes onto the printed page area.

The Symbol Library provides a good source of quick art that can be used for many purposes.

Entering Special Characters

CorelDRAW! includes several different proprietary character sets beyond the standard alphabet and characters that appear on your computer keyboard. You can enter special characters either on the drawing page or in the text entry area of the Edit Text dialog box, and you can adjust alignment, type size, and spacing for these special characters, just as you can for alphabetic characters.

A complete listing of the contents of each character set appears on the Character Reference Chart provided with your software. Also, some of the character sets are available as symbols in the Symbol Library. Each of the fonts is a category in the list box, and each of the characters is a symbol.

No matter which of the character sets you are using, characters above ASCII 126 are not accessible by pressing a single key on your keyboard. To type one of these special characters, press and hold ALT and then type the appropriate number on your numeric keypad. Be sure to include the 0 that precedes each number. For example, to type an ellipsis (. . .) in the standard character set, type **0133**. Always refer to your CorelDRAW! Character Reference Chart when you are entering special characters.

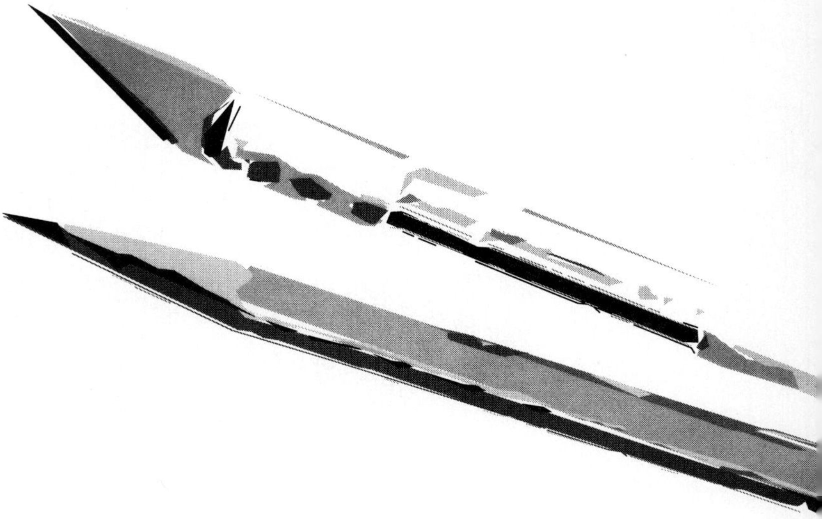

SELECTING, MOVING, and ARRANGING OBJECTS

In order to change the appearance or position of any object or text string, you must first select it. Once you have selected an object, you can move and rearrange it; stretch, scale, rotate, or skew it; give it a custom outline; or fill it with a color or pattern. Learning how to select an object is therefore an important prerequisite to mastering most of the skills in CorelDRAW!. Though you were introduced to the basics of text selection in Chapter 4, this chapter shows you the full capabilities of object and text selection.

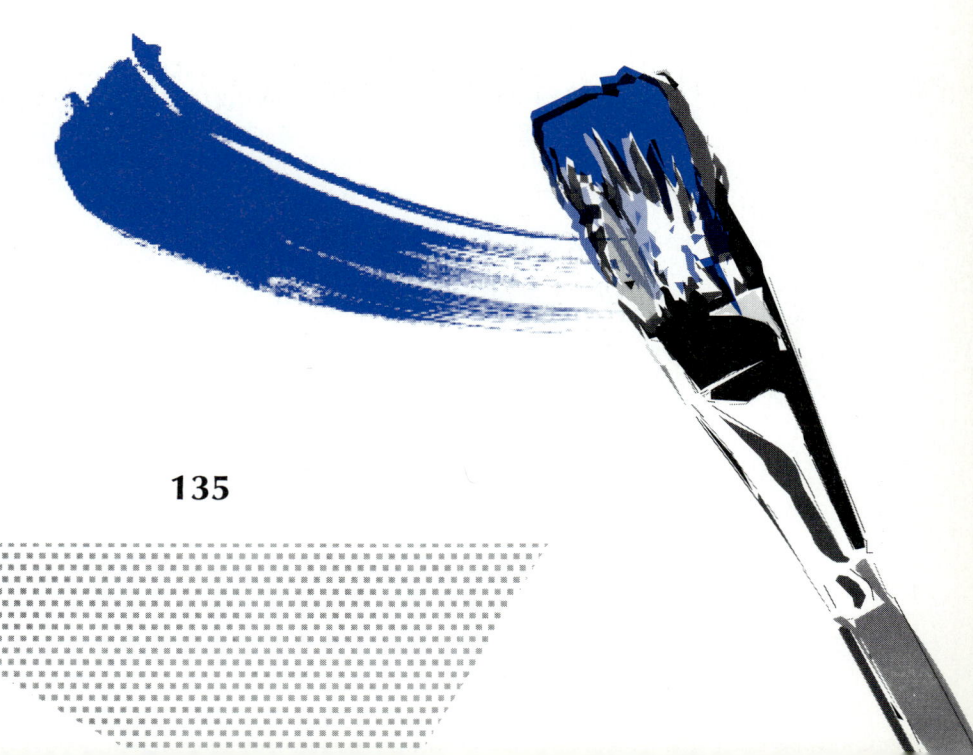

You use the Pick tool, the first tool in the CorelDRAW! toolbox, to select objects and text. When you first load CorelDRAW!, the Pick tool is automatically active and remains active until you choose a different tool. If you are already working with one of the other tools, you can activate the Pick tool by clicking on the Pick tool icon in the toolbox.

Tip: Pressing the SPACEBAR once is an alternative way to reactivate the Pick tool when you are using one of the other tools. This shortcut allows you to switch back and forth between tools quickly. To reactivate the tool you were working with before you selected the Pick tool, press the SPACEBAR again. Use this shortcut when you want to draw objects, immediately move, rearrange, or transform them, and then continue drawing.

The Pick tool performs more than one function; it has both a select mode and a transformation mode. The select mode includes all those functions—selecting, moving, and arranging—that do not require you to change the size or structure of the object. The transformation mode allows you to stretch, scale, rotate, skew, or reflect objects. This chapter covers the functions of the select mode; Chapter 8 will acquaint you with the use of the Pick tool in the transformation mode.

Selecting and Deselecting Objects

You can select objects only when the Pick tool is active. This tool is always active when you first open a drawing, when you begin a new drawing, and immediately after you save your work. To activate the Pick tool when you're using the Shape tool or one of the drawing tools, you either press the SPACEBAR or click on the Pick tool icon once.

Once the Pick tool is active, you can select one or more objects by:

- Clicking on the outline of an object.
- Holding down SHIFT while clicking on the outlines of several objects.
- *Lassoing* several objects by drawing an imaginary line around them with the Pick tool.

The technique you choose depends on the number of objects you are selecting, the placement of the objects within the graphic, and whether it's more convenient to select objects with the mouse or with the keyboard shortcuts.

Selecting, Moving, and Arranging Objects

The CorelDRAW! screen gives you three visual cues to let you know that an object is selected. First, a *selection box,* consisting of eight small rectangles called *handles,* surrounds the object. These markers allow you to stretch and scale the object, as you'll learn in Chapter 8. Second, one or more tiny hollow nodes appear on the outline of the object or group of objects. The number of nodes displayed depends on the type and number of objects selected. The nodes are the means by which you can change an object's shape, as you'll learn in Chapters 9 and 10. Finally, the status line tells you the type of object you have selected (rectangle, ellipse, curve, and so on) or the number of objects you have selected if you have selected more than one.

Single Objects

Any time you activate the Pick tool while working on a graphic, the Pick tool automatically selects the last object you were working on with another tool. If you want to select a different object, simply click once anywhere on the new object's *outline.* Clicking on the inside of a rectangle or ellipse, or on an open space inside a letter, has no effect. Also, you must click on a point unique to that object; it cannot share that point with the outline of any other object. Only if an object is the same type and size as another object on top of it will it have no unique selection point available. For information on how to select superimposed objects without unique selection points, see the "Cycling Through Objects" section of this chapter.

To *deselect* an object or text string so that the tools or menu commands you use no longer affect it, click in any open area on the page. Alternatively, you can select a different object and thereby automatically deselect the previously selected object.

In the following exercise, you will practice selecting and deselecting objects in a piece of clip-art. You will use the SPACEBAR to select objects that you have just drawn and the mouse to select other objects.

1. From the \CLIPART\ANIMAL\ subdirectory on the first CD-ROM, import the DOLPHIN1.CMX file. If you do not have this available to you, open any simple black and white piece of clip-art you have. Save this as DOLPHIN1.CDR. Note that when the drawing is displayed on the screen, the Pick tool is already active, as shown in Figure 5-1.

Note: Anyone from the Pacific Northwest or who has seen the movie "Free Willy" will recognize that this is not a dolphin but an Orca, or Killer whale. In deference to its filename, though, it will continue to be called a dolphin.

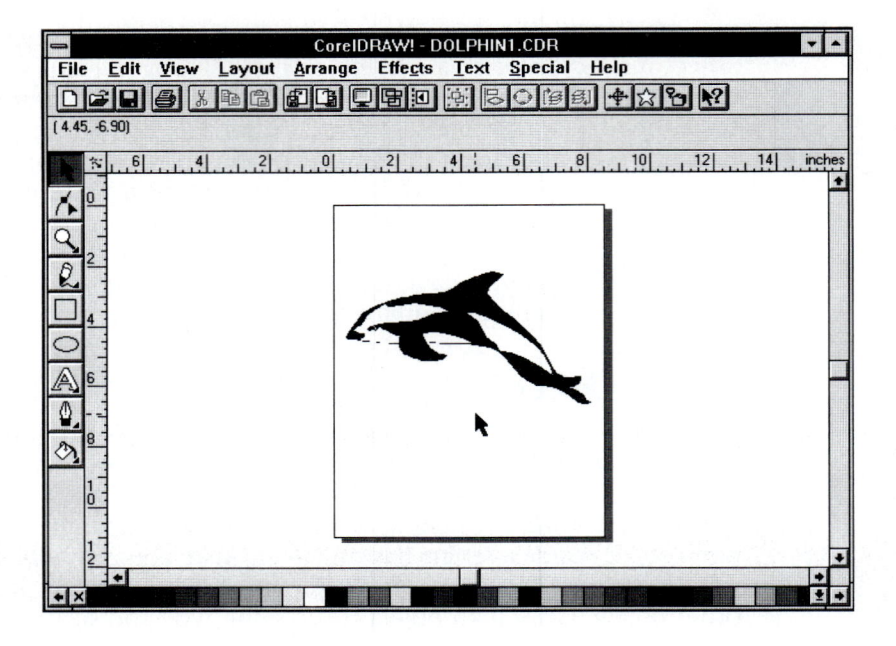

DOLPHIN1.CMX as it comes in with the Pick tool selected
Figure 5-1.

2. To work with this drawing, turn on Wireframe mode in the View menu and turn off Rulers to give you more room. Also, in the Layout menu, turn off Snap To Grid if it is turned on.

3. Select the Zoom tool and then select the Fit-in-Page (second from the right) from the flyout menu.. The screen redraws to show a screen similar to what you see in Figure 5-2.

4. Select the Freehand tool and use it to draw a very simple little fish in the lower-left corner of the drawing. Be sure to connect the starting point to the end point, so that the curve representing the fish becomes a closed path that you can fill later.

5. As soon as the fish appears, press the SPACEBAR to activate the Pick tool. Since the fish is the last object you drew, CorelDRAW! automatically selects it. A selection box surrounds the fish, and the status line indicates "Curve on Layer 1," as in Figure 5-3.

6. Click on the outline of the fish again. Black two-way arrows replace the handles of the selection box as you can see here:

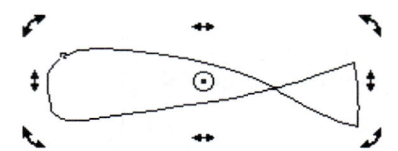

Selecting, Moving, and Arranging Objects

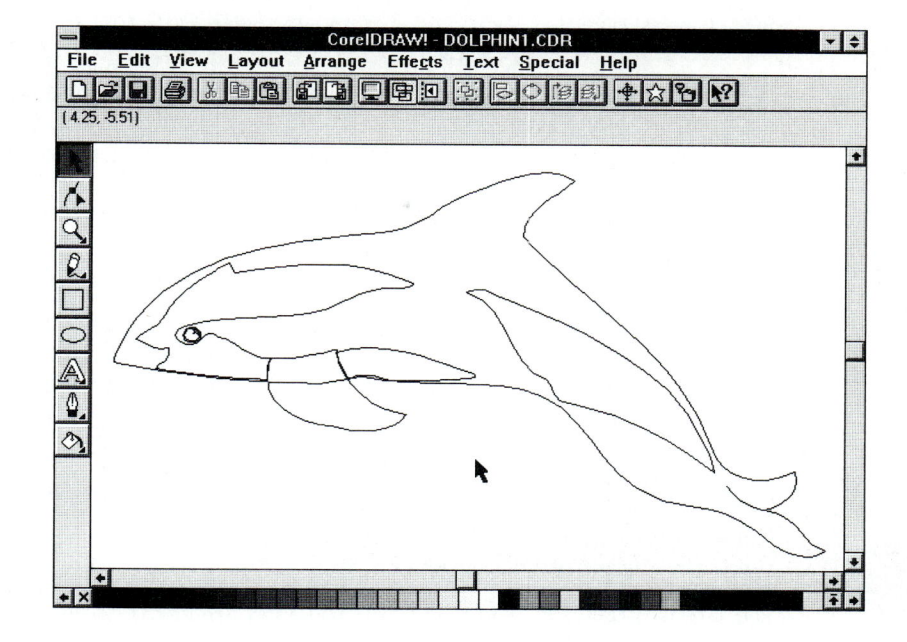

Figure 5-2.
Magnifying the wireframe dolphin in file DOLPHIN1.CDR

Your second click has enabled the rotate and skew functions of the Pick tool.

7. Click on the fish's outline again to toggle back to the select mode.

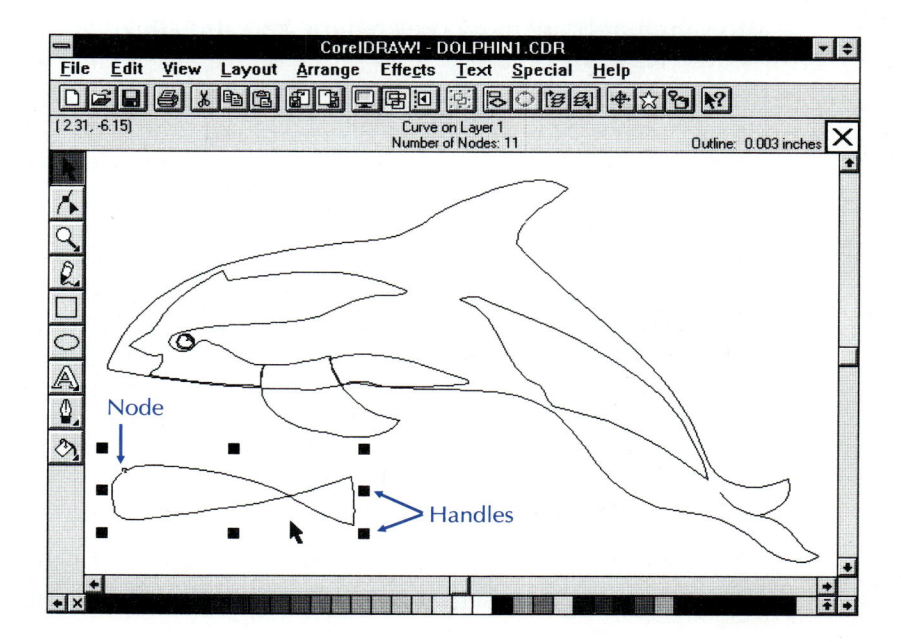

Figure 5-3.
Using the SPACEBAR to select the last object drawn

Multiple Objects

It's often more convenient to perform an operation on several objects simultaneously than to perform the same operation on a series of objects individually. Assume, for example, that you want to move the dolphin and the fish together to another location within the drawing. Since these are two separate objects, moving each object individually would be tedious and might lead to inaccurate placement.

CorelDRAW! gives you three alternative solutions to this type of problem. The first solution, *jointly selecting* the objects, is appropriate when you want to keep multiple objects together only temporarily, without merging them into a single entity. For example, you might want to fill a certain number of objects in a drawing with the same color or pattern or move them all by the same distance. You can jointly select several objects by clicking on them while holding down the SHIFT key, by drawing a marquee around them, or by using the Select All command in the Edit menu. Your choice of technique depends on both the number of objects you want to select and their location within the graphic.

If the multiple objects you want to select are components of a larger object and should remain together at all times, you might choose to *group* them, as you will learn to do later in this chapter. CorelDRAW! will still remember that a grouped object is made up of separate smaller objects. If the multiple objects belong together and contain many curves, you can choose to *combine* them into a single object. Combining objects, unlike grouping them, reduces the amount of memory they require and also allows you to reshape the entire resulting object.

You will learn more about the uses of grouping and combining multiple objects in the "Arranging Objects" portion of this chapter. The following group of sections lets you practice common methods of selecting multiple objects.

Selecting with the SHIFT key

When you want to select a few objects at a time, you can conveniently select them one after another by clicking on them while holding down the SHIFT key. The SHIFT key method is especially useful when the objects you want to select are not next to one another within the graphic. In the next exercise, you will practice selecting multiple objects using the following method:

- Select the first object by clicking on its outline.
- Depress and hold SHIFT and select the next object.
- Continue selecting objects in this way, holding down SHIFT continuously.
- When you have selected all desired objects, release SHIFT.

Selecting, Moving, and Arranging Objects 141

To deselect one or more of the objects you have selected in this way, hold down SHIFT and click again on that object's outline. This action affects only that object; other objects in the group remain selected. To deselect all of the selected objects simultaneously, click on any free space.

Each time you select another object using SHIFT, the selection box expands to surround all the objects you have selected so far. Objects that you did not select also may fall within the boundaries of the selection box, making it difficult for you to see just which objects you have selected. The following exercise shows how you can use the status line information and the preview window as aids in selecting multiple objects with SHIFT. The dolphin and the fish should still be on your screen.

1. If the screen is not already maximized, use the maximize button to enlarge the size of the working area. Also, select the Zoom tool, and then select the Fit-in-Window from the flyout menu.
2. Click on the fish if it is not already selected. A selection box surrounds the object, and the status line indicates that you have selected a curve.
3. Depress and hold SHIFT and click anywhere on the outlines of the dolphin. The message in the status line changes to "2 Objects Selected on Layer 1," and the selection box shown in Figure 5-4 surrounds both objects.

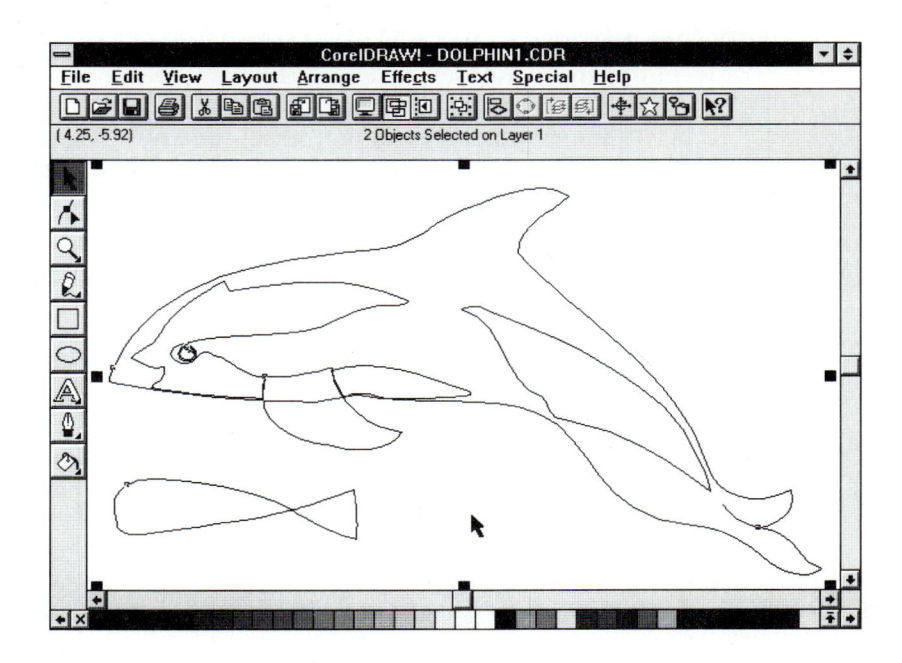

Selecting nonadjacent objects using SHIFT
Figure 5-4.

Selecting with the Marquee

If you need to select a large number of objects at once, using the mouse and SHIFT can be tedious. A shortcut is to draw a marquee around all of the desired objects with the Pick tool. The method for using a marquee is as follows:

- Position the mouse pointer just above and to the left of the first object you want to select. (You can begin from any corner of the group of objects, but the upper-left corner is usually most convenient.)
- Depress the mouse button and drag the mouse diagonally in the direction of the other objects you want to select. A dotted rectangle (the marquee) follows the pointer. Make sure that each object you want to select falls completely within this rectangle or CorelDRAW! will not select it.
- When you have enclosed the last object you want to select within the marquee, release the mouse button. The selection box appears, encompassing all of the objects within the selected area.

If you want to exclude some of the objects that fall within the selected area, you can deselect them using SHIFT. Lasso the entire group of objects first, depress and hold SHIFT, and click on a particular object's outline to deselect that object. You can also use the status line and preview window as "quality control" aids to guide you in selecting exactly the objects you want.

Perform the following exercise to gain skill at selecting objects quickly with the marquee. Use the Zoom tool for magnification, the status line for information, and the preview window to make the selection process more efficient. Use SHIFT to fine-tune your selection and add or subtract objects to or from the group you selected with the marquee.

1. Select the Zoom tool and then select the Show Page tool from the flyout menu. Click on any white space outside of the fish and dolphin to deselect them.
2. Position the mouse pointer above and to the left of the dolphin. Drag the mouse downward and to the right until the marquee surrounds both the dolphin and the fish, like this:

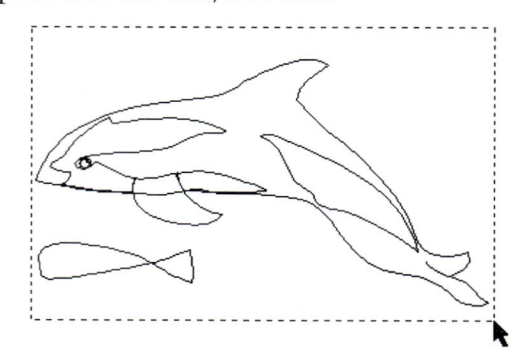

Selecting, Moving, and Arranging Objects

3. Release the mouse button. The selection box appears, and the status line indicates that two objects are selected.
4. Depress and hold SHIFT and then click once anywhere on the outline of the fish. CorelDRAW! deselects it, and the status line shows that only the group of objects that make up the dolphin is selected.
5. Click on any white space to deselect the dolphin.

Selecting All Objects in a Graphic

If you want to perform an operation on all the objects in a graphic, you can select them by drawing a marquee. A quicker way to select all objects is simply to invoke the Select All command in the Edit menu. Using this command, you can be sure that you haven't left out any objects.

You now know several methods for selecting single and multiple objects. Most of the time, selecting objects is a straightforward process in CorelDRAW!. But what if your graphic contains many small objects or you want to select an object that may have several other layers of objects on top of it? The next section makes that process easy for you.

Cycling Through Objects

The object selection techniques you have learned so far in this chapter are adequate for many applications. However, when working with complex drawings containing many objects or superimposed objects, you may find it more convenient to cycle through the objects using TAB. The following steps summarize this technique:

- Select an object near or on top of the object you want to select.
- Press TAB. CorelDRAW! deselects the first object and selects the next object in the drawing. The "next" object is the one that was drawn just prior to the currently selected object. Each time you press TAB, CorelDRAW! cycles backward to another object. If you press TAB often enough, you eventually select the first object again, and the cycle begins once more.

The following sections show you two different situations in which you might choose to cycle through objects in a drawing. The first section provides an example of objects that have other objects superimposed on them. The second section demonstrates how to locate and select small objects in a complex drawing.

Cycling Through Superimposed Objects

You may recall that in order to select an object in CorelDRAW!, you must click on a unique point on its outline, a point not shared by any other object. This limitation does not exist when you have separate objects, because you can usually see separate outlines. The only exception is when two or more objects are the same size and shape and overlay one another exactly.

Why might you choose to create two identical overlapping objects? You can achieve desirable and interesting design effects by varying the color and thickness of the outlines and fills used in each object. In Chapters 6 and 7, you will learn more about outlines and fill colors. For now, you need only know that to select the object in the background, you first select the top object and then press TAB to select the object behind it. If there are more than two objects you simply keep pressing TAB to select them. The status line will give you clues as to which object is selected.

Cycling Through Many Objects

There is another, more common use for TAB when selecting objects in CorelDRAW!. Clip-art, technical illustrations, and other complex drawings often contain many small objects close together. Even in magnified view, trying to select one or more of these with the mouse can be difficult at best. To ease the process, you can select one object and then press TAB repeatedly until the minute detail you are looking for is selected. CorelDRAW! cycles backward through the objects, selecting them in the reverse order to which you drew them. To cycle forward through the objects in a drawing, press SHIFT-TAB. Perform the following brief exercise to gain a clearer understanding of how the TAB key method of selection works. The dolphin and fish should still be on your screen in Wireframe, full-page view.

1. Select Fit-in-Window view from the Zoom fly-out menu. Also, choose Wireframe from the View menu to turn it off so you can see the fill patterns.
2. Click on the Dolphin to select it. The status line shows you that it is a group of six separate objects.
3. Press TAB. The fish you drew will be selected. Press TAB again and you will reselect the dolphin. You can see how TAB cycles through objects.
4. With the dolphin selected, choose Ungroup from the Arrange menu. This breaks apart the dolphin into its six components. (You will learn more about the Group and Ungroup commands later in this chapter.)
5. Press TAB several times. On the first TAB, you will again go to the fish you drew. On the second and successive TABs, you will start cycling through the components of the dolphin. TAB all the way through the dolphin until you get to the fish again.

Selecting, Moving, and Arranging Objects

6. Press SHIFT-TAB several times. Now CorelDRAW! selects objects in the opposite order. See if you can identify all six components by a combination of the selection-box handles and the information in the status line. For example, Figure 5-5 shows that the white of the dolphin's eye has been selected—you know this by the fill color and the selection box.

Now you are familiar with all of the available techniques for selecting any number of objects. In the next portion of this chapter, you will move selected objects to other areas within the drawing.

Moving Objects

Once you have selected an object, you can move it by positioning the pointer over any point on its *outline* (not on the selection box) and then dragging the mouse along with the object to the desired location. The status line provides you with precise, real-time information about the distance you are traveling, the *x* and *y* components of that distance, and the angle of movement. You can achieve precision worthy of the most demanding technical illustrations if you choose to work with the status line and grid.

Factors such as the number of objects you want to move, whether you want to constrain movement to a 90-degree angle, and whether you want to make a copy of the object determine your choice of technique.

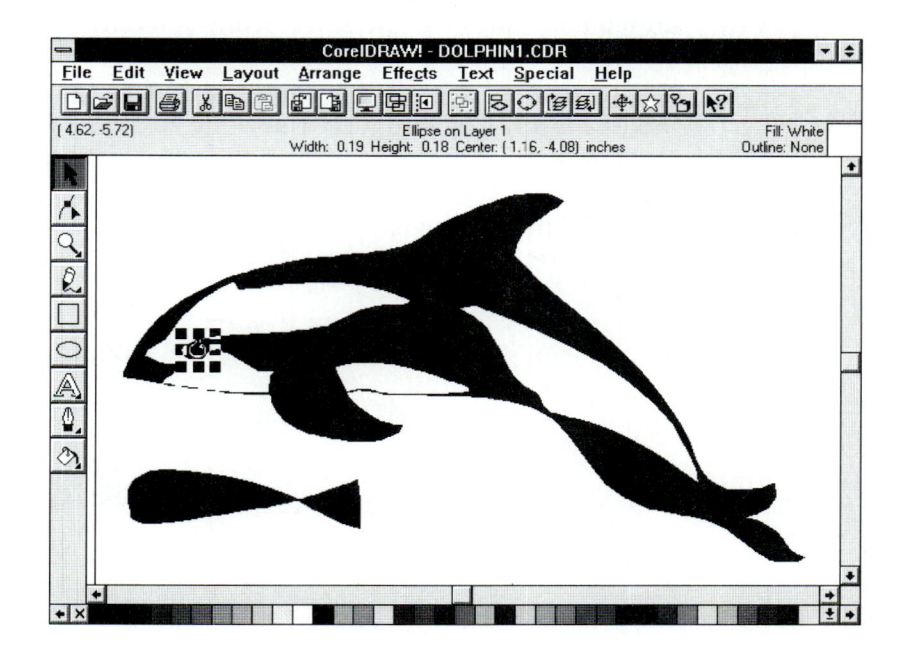

Using TAB to select just the white of the dolphin's eye
Figure 5-5.

Moving a Single Object

The appearance of an object undergoes several changes during the process of moving it. Try the following exercise to dissect the dolphin and become familiar with those changes. The dolphin and fish should still be on your screen with the fish selected.

1. Delete the fish by making sure it is the only object selected and then pressing DEL. (If you happen to delete one of the components of the dolphin in error, immediately press CTRL-Z or choose Undo from the Edit menu.)
2. Click on the Show Page tool in the Zoom fly-out menu and choose Wireframe from the View menu to turn it back on.
3. Click on part of the dolphin to select it—for example the outline of the white areas.
4. Move the mouse pointer to any point on the outline of the selected part of the dolphin, press and hold the mouse button, and begin dragging the mouse downward to separate the component you selected from the rest of the dolphin. The screen does not change immediately, because CorelDRAW! has a built-in, three-pixel safety zone; you must drag the mouse at least three pixels away from the starting point before the object begins to "move." As soon as you pass the three-pixel safety zone, the mouse pointer changes to a four-way arrow, and a dotted replica of the selection box follows the pointer, as shown in Figure 5-6. This dotted box represents the object while you are moving it; as you can see in the figure, the object itself seems to remain in its original position.
5. When you have dragged the dotted box below the dolphin, release the mouse button. The outline of the white areas disappears from its original position and reappears in the new location.
6. Press TAB to select the next object and drag it below the dolphin. Continue that process until all six components are separated as shown here:

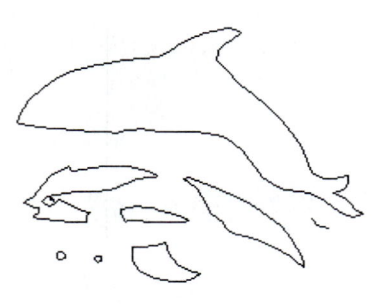

Selecting, Moving, and Arranging Objects

Dragging the dotted move box to move an object
Figure 5-6.

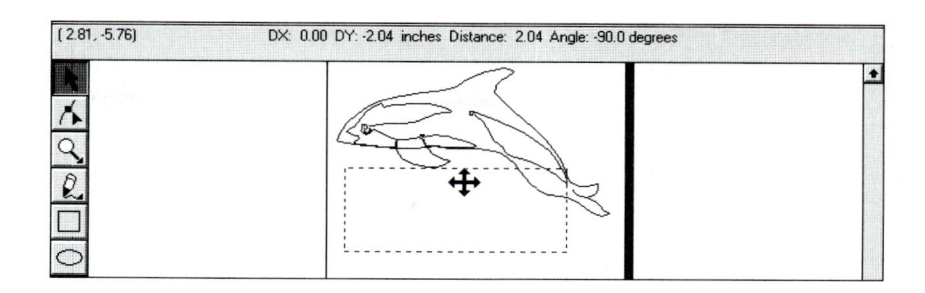

These are the basic steps involved in moving an object, but CorelDRAW! offers you additional refinements for moving multiple objects, constraining an object to move at a 90-degree angle, and retaining a copy of an object while moving it.

Moving Multiple Objects

The technique for moving multiple, selected objects differs very little from the way you move single objects. When more than one object is selected, you simply press and hold the mouse button on the outline of *any one* of the objects within the selected group. The entire group moves together as you drag the mouse, as you can see in this simple exercise.

1. Select Fit-in-Window view and draw a marquee to lasso the two components of the dolphin's eye. The status line should indicate that two objects are selected.
2. Position the mouse pointer over either of the outlines in the eye, and then drag the mouse until the dotted move box is back in the main outline of the dolphin, as shown in Figure 5-7.
3. Release the mouse button. The eye components disappear from their original location and reappear in the new location.

Moving at a 90-Degree Angle

The techniques you have learned so far in this chapter apply to moving objects in any direction. But what if the nature of your drawing requires that you move objects straight up or down, or directly to the right or left? You could, of course, use the coordinates information in the status line to reposition the object precisely. But CorelDRAW! also offers you a more intuitive method of moving objects at an exact 90-degree angle using CTRL. This is a convenient method for obtaining precision without slowing your drawing pace. Perform the following exercise to practice constraining the movement of objects vertically or horizontally.

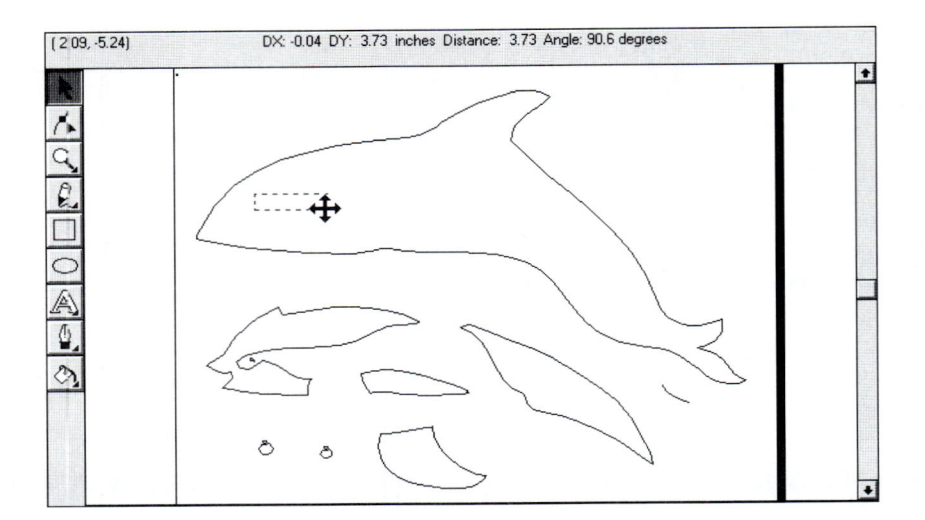

Moving multiple objects to a new location
Figure 5-7.

1. Select one of the eye components, press and hold CTRL, and then drag the component to the right. Even if you don't have a steady hand, the component remains at exactly the same horizontal level of the drawing. The information on the status line verifies the steadiness of your movement: the *dy* indicator remains at zero and the angle indicator either remains at zero or at 180 degrees, depending on which component you choose, as in the following illustration:

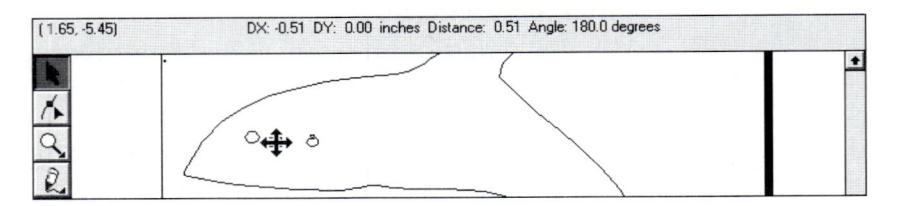

   Release the mouse button first and then release CTRL to reposition the component at the new location. If you release CTRL first, the selected object is no longer constrained and can move up or down relative to the starting point.

2. Press and hold CTRL and the mouse button a second time. This time, drag the eye component above its current location. The component remains in the same vertical level, and the *dx* indicator remains at zero. This time the angle indicator displays 90 degrees:

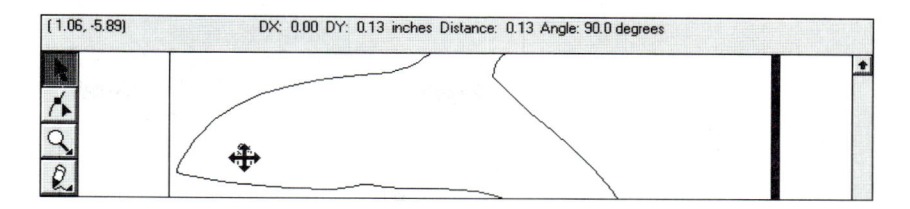

Moving Objects with the Keyboard (Nudge)

As you moved objects in the preceding exercises, you probably found that it was difficult to move an object in very small increments with any precision—most people repeatedly overshoot the mark.

CorelDRAW! has a feature called Nudge, which allows you to use the arrow keys on your keyboard to move the selected object(s) by as little as 0.001 inch. The amount by which you move an object each time you press an arrow key, and the unit of measure, are determined in the Preferences dialog box reached from the Special menu. The default increment is 0.10 inch. Also, since you only have arrow keys pointing in 90-degree increments, nudging is always constrained to 90-degree increments. Follow these steps to practice nudging by positioning the black part of the eye within the white part.

1. Look at the status line and determine whether you have the black part of the eye selected by looking at the fill indicator on the right. If it doesn't say "Black," press TAB until you have selected the black part.
2. Open the Preferences dialog box from the Special menu and set the Nudge increment in the General tab to 0.01 inch. Click on OK to return to the drawing.
3. Press the arrow keys as necessary to move the black part of the eye until it is centered in the white part. When you think you have it aligned, turn off Wireframe in the View menu to see the black part in the white.

Practice this on your own for several minutes. Nudging can be very useful.

Positioning an Object Using Precise Measurements

If you wish to position an object an exact measured distance from its current location, or at a specific location using coordinates, use the Position button in the Transform roll-up that you open from the Effects menu. The Transform roll-up has five buttons across the top; the leftmost button allows you to enter horizontal and vertical measurements with which to position the selected object(s), as shown here:

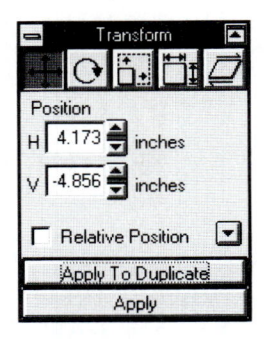

To move the object to the right horizontally or up vertically, enter a positive number; to move it to the left or down, enter a negative number. If the Relative Position check box is not checked, the horizontal and vertical measurements are absolute coordinates on the grid formed by the rulers. With Relative Position checked, the measurements are the distance you want to move the object from its current location. The down arrow in the lower right of the roll-up expands the roll-up to include a set of node check boxes that specify which part of the object you are moving is aligned to measurements entered, as shown here:

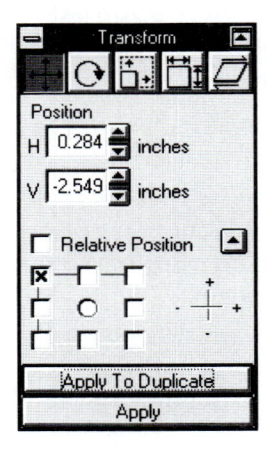

Follow these steps to move an object to precise coordinates (some part of the dolphin should still be selected):

1. Select Rulers in the View menu if they are not already on and use the crosshair in the upper left of the ruler guides to reset the ruler origins, so that 0 appears on the upper-left corner of the page.
2. Select Transform Roll-Up from the Effects menu. The Relative Position check box should not be selected.

Selecting, Moving, and Arranging Objects

3. Click on the down arrow to expand the roll-up and click on the center node, indicating that the center of the object should be aligned to the measurements you will enter.

Note: The "node box" represents the parts of the object that are used to align, i.e., if you clicked the upper-left box, the upper-left "corner" of the ellipse would align on the coordinates.

4. Press TAB to cycle through the components of the dolphin until you reach the object that represents the main black area of the dolphin.
5. Enter 4.25 in the Horizontal coordinate box and –2.5 in the Vertical coordinate box. Click on Apply. The black area will be relocated so that its center is aligned with the coordinates.

   You can also leave the original object in place and move a copy to the specific location by clicking on the Apply To Duplicate button.

Tip: You can get the position of the center or of any node around an object by selecting the object and opening the Transform roll-up in Position mode. You can also watch that position change as you "nudge" an object or after you have moved it with the mouse.

6. Select New from the File menu and answer No to "Save current changes?" Also double-click the Transform roll-up's Control-menu box to close it.

Copying an Object While Moving It

You may recall that while you are moving an object, it seems to remain in place and you appear to be moving only a dotted rectangular substitute. CorelDRAW! lets you take this feature a step further: you can make an identical copy of the object as you move it. The copy remains at the initial location while you move the original to a new location. This handy technique has interesting design possibilities, as you can discover for yourself by performing the next exercise.

1. Select Page Setup from the Layout menu and click on Landscape and then on OK. Also select the Grid & Scale Setup command from the Layout menu, set both the Horizontal and Vertical Grid Frequency to 2.0 per inch, set Vertical Grid Origin to 8.5 inches, and turn on Show

Grid and Snap To Grid. Click on OK. Then, from the View menu, turn on the Rulers option if it is off and turn off Wireframe if it is on.

2. Select the Text tool and then select an insertion point at the 1-inch mark on both the horizontal and vertical rulers. Type **Arrow** in lowercase with a capital "A". Select the word by selecting the Pick tool, open the Text roll-up (in the Text menu), and set the text attributes to Bookman normal (or any font and style you choose) and 100 points. Click on Apply and close the Text roll-up.

3. Press and hold the mouse button over the outline of any letter and begin to drag downward and to the right. Since you have set grid spacing in large units, the dotted move box travels and snaps in visibly discrete increments.

4. Continue holding down the mouse button. When the upper-left corner of the dotted move box snaps to a point 1/2 inch below and to the right of the starting point (about midway down and across the letter "A"), press and release the + key in the numeric keypad. At the left of the status line, the message "Leave Original" appears, as shown in Figure 5-8. The + key in CorelDRAW! is also called the Leave Original key.

5. Release the mouse button. An exact copy of the object appears at the starting point, and the original appears at the new location. (If nothing happens, press and release the + key more rapidly.)

6. Make four more copies of the text string in the same way, using the + key or right mouse button, and moving the text object in 1/2-inch increments downward and to the right. You should now have a total of six identical text strings.

7. Change the direction in which you move the text object. Make five additional copies as you move the text object downward and to the left in 1/2-inch increments. When you are finished, 11 identical text strings form an arrowhead shape. Your screen should look like Figure 5-9.

8. Select Save As from the File menu and save this drawing under the name ARROW1.CDR.

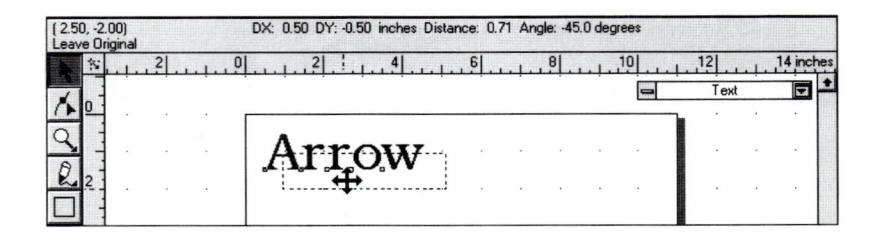

Copying an object while moving it
Figure 5-8.

Selecting, Moving, and Arranging Objects 153

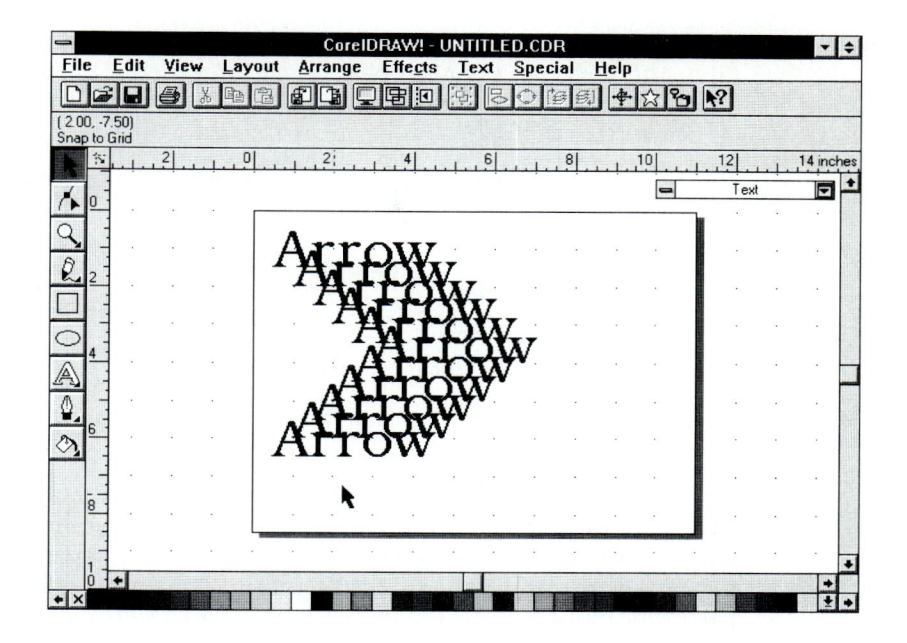

Completed arrow design
Figure 5-9.

Using the preceding exercise as an example, you can probably think up additional design ideas for copying single or multiple objects as you move them. Go on to the next sections of this chapter to discover ways of changing the relative order of objects within a drawing.

Arranging Objects

In CorelDRAW!, you can align objects relative to one another, change the order of superimposed objects, and group and combine separate objects. All of these techniques are ways of arranging objects on the page. The Arrange menu contains all of the commands you will use in this chapter, plus a few others that are discussed in later chapters. The next four sections demonstrate the most common methods of arranging selected objects.

Reordering Superimposed Objects

When you draw a series of objects, CorelDRAW! always places the object you drew *last* on top of all of the other objects. If you could look at the ARROW1.CDR file in 3-D, for example, you would see that the first text string you created is beneath all of the others you subsequently copied.

You can change the order of objects at any time by applying one of five commands in the Order option of the Arrange menu to a selected object or group of objects. The five commands—To Front, To Back, Forward One, Back One, and Reverse Order—appear on a flyout menu, as shown here:

```
Arrange
  Align...              Ctrl+A
  Order                          To Front       Shift+PgUp
                                 To Back        Shift+PgDn
  Group                 Ctrl+G   Forward One    Ctrl+PgUp
  Ungroup               Ctrl+U   Back One       Ctrl+PgDn
  Combine               Ctrl+L   Reverse Order
  Break Apart           Ctrl+K
  Weld
  Intersection
  Trim
  Separate
  Convert To Curves     Ctrl+Q
```

The To Front, To Back, Forward One, and Back One commands rearrange the selected objects *relative* to the other objects on the page, but they do not rearrange objects within a selected group. The Reverse Order command, on the other hand, rearranges the objects *within* a selected group, but it does not alter the relationship between the selected objects and the other objects in the drawing. Practice working with these commands now using a new piece of clip-art, the CD-ROM file PANDA_B.CMX. If this is not available to you, use any piece of simple clip-art you have available.

1. Select the Import command from the File menu and import the file PANDA_B.CMX in the \CLIPART\ANIMAL\ subdirectory on the first CD-ROM.
2. Click anywhere on the drawing. When the drawing is selected, you'll see it's a group of eight objects.
3. Choose the Ungroup command in the Arrange menu to allow rearrangement of the individual objects.
4. Select (lasso) the eyes, nose, and mouth of the panda as shown here:

Selecting, Moving, and Arranging Objects 155

Be sure to include all of the eyes, nose, and mouth but not the ears or hind paw. You have selected everything you want if you have selected four objects.

5. Press F2 to select the Zoom-In tool and lasso just the face.
6. Pull down the Arrange menu and, from the Order option flyout, select the To Back command. The eyes, nose, and mouth disappear behind the white of the face that had been in the background, as shown in Figure 5-10. When you apply this command to a group of objects, however, the relative order of the objects *within* the group does not change.
7. With the same group of objects still selected, select the To Front command from the Order option flyout on the Arrange menu. Now the objects reappear in their original order, in front of the background objects.
8. Leave these objects selected and select the Back One command from the Order option flyout on the Arrange menu. This command moves the selected objects back behind the first layer beneath them. Since the next layer back is transparent (only an outline), there is no effect in doing this. If you select Back One several more times, you will see that there are two transparent layers, then the eyes disappear under the third layer, and finally the nose and mouth disappear behind the fourth layer.
9. Select the To Front command to return the objects to their original order on the screen. Leave this drawing on the screen for the next exercise.

Using the To Back command on selected objects
Figure 5-10.

Grouping and Ungrouping Objects

Selecting multiple objects with the marquee or SHIFT key is fine if you want to apply certain commands or operations to them on a one-time basis only. However, most drawings contain subsets of objects that belong together, such as the elements of a logo on a business card. If you want the same set of objects to form a single entity at all times, consider *grouping* them instead of merely selecting them.

To group multiple objects, you first select them and then apply the Group command in the Arrange menu. Thereafter, the group responds to any operation collectively. You can move, align, color, and outline them together, without individually selecting each component of the group. However, CorelDRAW! still "knows" that the component objects have separate identities. As a result, you cannot apply the Reverse Order command to a group or reshape the group using the Shape tool. You can also create groups within groups, and then use the Ungroup command to break them down into their component objects again.

In the last exercise, all objects in the PANDA_B.CMX file were selected and then ungrouped. Continue working with this file to become familiar with the basics of grouping and ungrouping objects.

1. The group made up of the parts of the face should still be selected. The status line should display the message "4 Objects Selected on Layer 1," as shown in Figure 5-11.

Grouping multiple objects
Figure 5-11.

Selecting, Moving, and Arranging Objects

2. Select the Group command in the Arrange menu. The status line message changes immediately from "4 Objects Selected on Layer 1" to "Group of 4 Objects on Layer 1."
3. Open the Order option flyout on the Arrange menu and notice that Reverse Order is dim—it isn't available, since the selected objects have been grouped. Select Ungroup and then select the Reverse Order command from the Order option flyout of the Arrange menu. The 4 objects that used to form the group are now reversed in order—what was on top is now on the bottom relative to the other item in the group. You don't really see any change, though, because the only change is *within* the group.
4. Select the Reverse Order command again from the Order option flyout on the Arrange menu. The original order returns.
5. Click on one of the black patches behind the eyes. You will select both black patches as well as both ears. Hold down SHIFT and then click on both eyes to select them. You will have four objects selected: the black objects and the eyes.
6. Select Reverse Order and now the eyes disappear behind the black patches. One final time select Reverse Order to restore the original order.
7. Select the Group command from the Arrange menu. The message in the status line changes to "Group of 3 Objects on Layer 1."
8. Press F3 to zoom out and return to a normal screen.
9. Press and hold the mouse button at any point along the outline of any of the selected objects and drag the mouse with the selected objects to the bottom of the page. The entire group moves together and relocates when you release the mouse button, as shown in Figure 5-12.
10. Practice moving the group around, ungrouping, forming new groups, rearranging the groups, and moving various objects in relation to one another.

    Before and after grouping objects and text strings, look at the menus to see how grouping affects which commands you can and cannot select.
11. When you are done, select New from the File menu to clear the screen before proceeding. Do not save any changes to this drawing.

Combining and Breaking Objects Apart

The Arrange menu contains two sets of commands that seem almost identical in content, but are actually two different operations: Group/Ungroup and Combine/Break Apart. Grouping is used when you want to simply "handle" a group of objects as a single object; for example

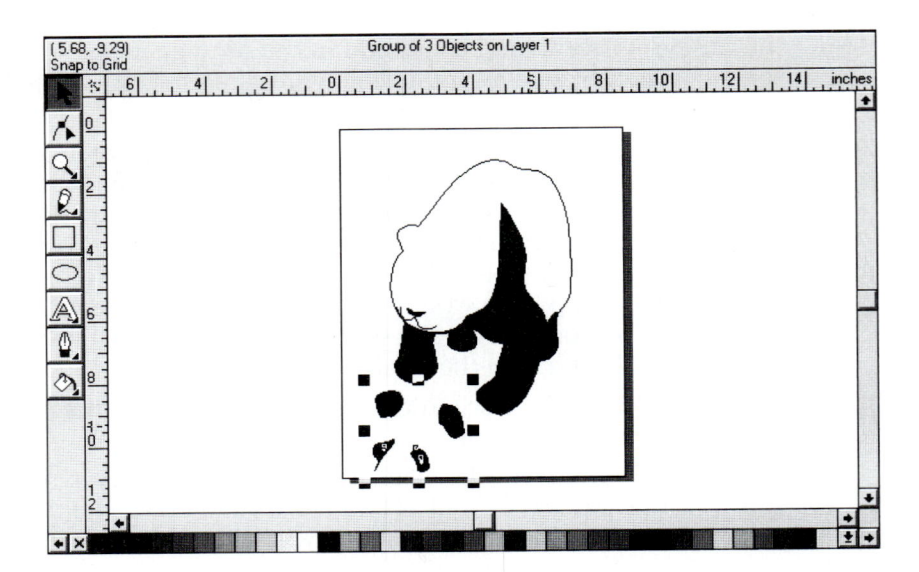

Moving the selected group

Figure 5-12.

when you want to move, copy, or position them. Combining on the other hand, is a more complex operation that is used in the following situations:

♦ When you want multiple objects to become a single object *that you can reshape* with the Shape tool

♦ When the objects contain many nodes and curves and you want to reduce the total amount of memory they consume

♦ When you want to create special effects such as transparent masks, behind which you can place other objects

In these situations, simply grouping objects would not yield the desired results.

Later chapters, especially Chapter 14, contain several examples of creative uses for the Combine command. There is one interesting use of Combine, however, that you can try out in this chapter. If you combine objects with other objects contained within them, the net result is a reverse color effect that makes alternating objects transparent and creates contrast. For a clearer understanding of how this works, try the following exercise.

1. Open the TEACUP.CDR file. The window displays a solid black mass, as shown next, because you haven't yet applied different fill colors or outlines to separate objects. (If your tea cup does not fill with black, it could be for one of two reasons: Wireframe is still turned on in the View

Selecting, Moving, and Arranging Objects

menu or No Fill is the active fill. In the later case, select all of the tea cup and saucer, open the Fill flyout, and click on the black fill.

2. Press SHIFT-F9 to go to Wireframe mode and select both the larger rectangle that forms the outline of the handle and the inner rectangle. Use either the marquee or the SHIFT key method. When you are done, the status line should say "2 Objects Selected on Layer 1."
3. Select the Combine command from the Arrange menu. Press SHIFT-F9 again to turn off Wireframe, and the inside of the inner rectangle becomes transparent, as you can see here:

This "special effect" occurs because the Combine command causes all overlapping areas in a graphic to appear transparent. Notice that the status line now refers to the combined object as a single curve object.

Because of the hollow areas you created when you selected the Combine command, you can now distinguish the handle from the rest of the cup.

4. Save this file under the new name TEACUP2.CDR.
5. Select the newly combined handle, if it is not still selected, and then select the Break Apart command from the Arrange menu. All objects revert to their previous state and become black again.

6. Clear the screen by clicking on the New (leftmost) button in the ribbon bar. Do not save any changes.

Aligning Objects

Earlier in this chapter, you saw how you can move objects precisely using the CTRL key as a substitute for the grid. The Align command in the Arrange menu offers you another quick and easy method for aligning selected objects without having to spend all of your drawing time measuring. To align objects, you simply select the objects, click on the Align command, and then adjust the horizontal and vertical alignment settings in the Align dialog box.

You could try to memorize the abstract effects of all 15 possible settings, but experiencing those settings for yourself might be more meaningful. In the following exercise, you will create a rectangle and pretend it's a billiard table. Then you will add a billiard ball and apply various alignment settings to the ball and the table.

1. Start with the page in landscape orientation with the rulers and grid displayed, the Snap To Grid turned on, the horizontal and vertical grid frequencies set to 16 per inch, the vertical grid origin set to 8.5, and Wireframe mode turned on. Select the Rectangle tool and draw a rectangle 8 inches wide and 4 inches high. This rectangle represents the surface of the billiard table.

2. Use the Zoom to Selected tool in the Zoom flyout menu to magnify the area of the page that contains the rectangle.

3. Select the Ellipse tool, press and hold both SHIFT and CTRL , and draw a perfectly circular "ball" of about 1/2-inch diameter from the center out in the middle of the table.

4. Press the SPACEBAR to switch to the Pick tool and select the ball. Next press SHIFT and select the table, then select the Align command in the Arrange menu. The Align dialog box appears, as shown here:

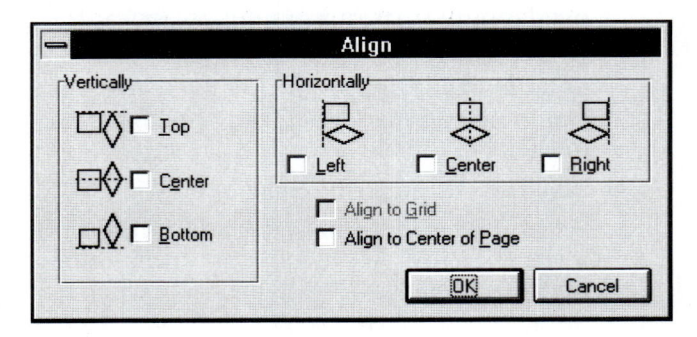

Selecting, Moving, and Arranging Objects

The Align dialog box contains two areas of option buttons. The settings in the upper-right area of the dialog box pertain to the relative *horizontal* alignment of the selected objects, while the settings in the left part of the dialog box pertain to their relative *vertical* alignment. You can set horizontal and vertical alignment independently of each other or mix them, for a total of 15 possible settings. When multiple objects are selected and you choose the Horizontally Left, Horizontally Right, Vertically Top, or Vertically Bottom alignment option, CorelDRAW! repositions all but one of the objects. The object *last selected* remains in place. All other objects are moved to carry out the desired alignment. When you select Horizontally Center or Vertically Center alignment, however, CorelDRAW! repositions all of the selected objects, unless one of them is already in the desired location.

1. Select Horizontally Left in the Align dialog box and then click on the OK command button. The billiard ball reappears in position 1 in Figure 5-13, aligned to the left edge of the table.

   If your screen does not look like Figure 5-13—you can see only half of your table, or your table moved and the ball stayed stationary—then you selected your table first and the ball last. The last object selected stays stationary, and previously selected items are moved the first time you do an alignment.

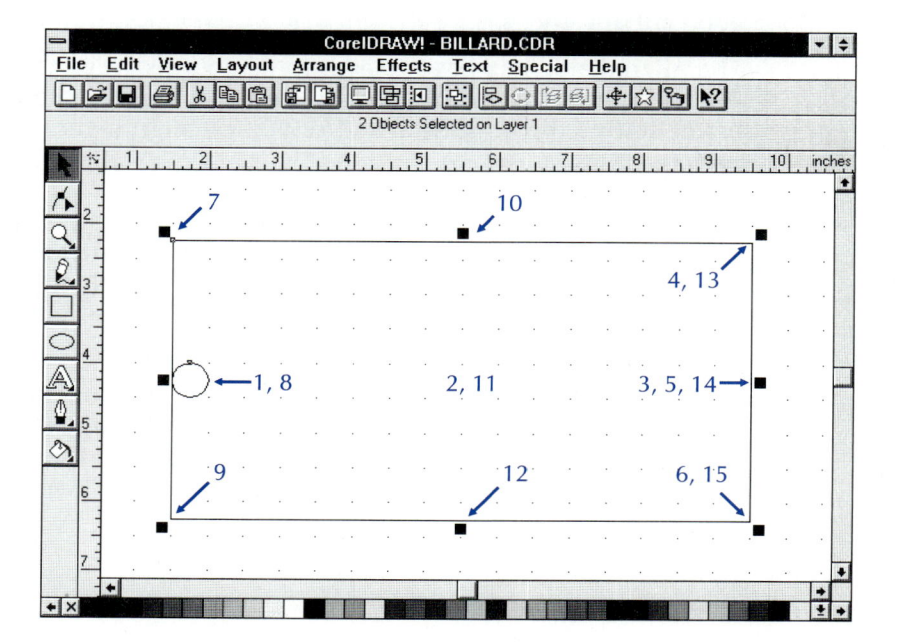

Figure 5-13.
Results of Align dialog box settings

2. Select the Align command repeatedly and choose each of the numbered settings in the following list, one at a time. As you select each setting, check the location of the billiard ball against the corresponding numbers in Figure 5-13.

   (1) Horizontally Left
   (2) Horizontally Center
   (3) Horizontally Right
   (4) Vertically Top
   (5) Vertically Center
   (6) Vertically Bottom
   (7) Horizontally Left-Vertically Top
   (8) Horizontally Left-Vertically Center
   (9) Horizontally Left-Vertically Bottom
   (10) Horizontally Center-Vertically Top
   (11) Horizontally Center-Vertically Center
   (12) Horizontally Center-Vertically Bottom
   (13) Horizontally Right-Vertically Top
   (14) Horizontally Right-Vertically Center
   (15) Horizontally Right-Vertically Bottom

If you do the above alignments having selected the ball first and the table second, you will notice that the ball always moves and the table stays in one place, as you would expect. This is different from earlier versions of CorelDRAW! where the two objects alternated their movement and is a very good enhancement.

The Align dialog box has two additional options, Align to Grid and Align to Center of Page. When either of these options are used, you want to set it before setting the horizontal and/or vertical alignments. Try both of these options now.

1. Open the Align dialog box and click on Align to Center of Page. Notice that the Horizontally Center and Vertically Center alignment have also been selected as a default. Click on OK. The ball returns to the center of the table, and both objects are positioned in the center of the page.
2. From the Zoom menu, select Full Page View.
3. Again select Align to Center of Page from the Align dialog box. Then click on Horizontally Left and Vertically Top and click on OK. The ball moves to the upper-left corner of the table, and the upper-left corner of the table moves to the center of the page, as shown in Figure 5-14.

Selecting, Moving, and Arranging Objects 163

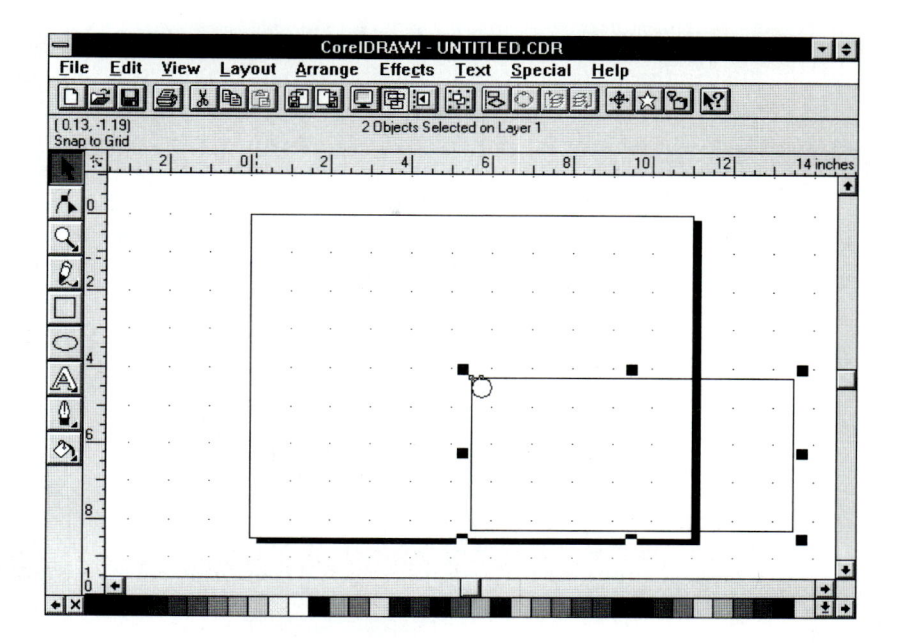

Upper-left corner aligned to center of page
Figure 5-14.

In Align to Center of Page, the objects first position themselves in accordance with the horizontal and vertical alignment instructions, and then the common point of alignment is positioned in the center of the page.

1. Click on anything other than the ball or the table to deselect them both, then click on the table to select only it.
2. In the Grid Setup dialog box reached from the Layout menu, set both Horizontal and Vertical Grid Frequency to 2.
3. Using the arrow keys, nudge the table so that it is away from grid lines in both directions.
4. Open the Align dialog box and click on Horizontally Left and Vertically Top and select Align to Grid. Click on OK. The table will move to the nearest grid point that is up and to the left of the table's original position.

The Align to Grid command does not position objects in relation to each other, but rather it individually aligns objects (all that are selected) in relation to the nearest grid point in the direction specified by the horizontal and vertical alignment commands.

Experiment on your own, perhaps with other objects in drawings you have already created. Other objects may align in a slightly different way, depending on the order in which you select alignment settings.

When you are through practicing using the Align feature, clear the screen using the New button in the ribbon bar. Do not save any changes.

Layers

CorelDRAW! can allow you to create a drawing in different layers. Just as you can stack transparencies on an overhead projector, you can create a drawing in distinct layers so that you can hide certain objects, prevent certain objects from being changed, and control the printing of the drawing layer by layer. This last feature is important in more complex drawings where printing time is a factor.

You probably noticed in the examples throughout this book that the status line displays the current object followed by the words "on Layer 1." This is the layer assigned to all new drawings. You can have as many layers as you want, but new objects are placed only on the active layer.

Layering is controlled by the Layers roll-up window (accessed through the Layout menu or by pressing CTRL-F3), which looks like this:

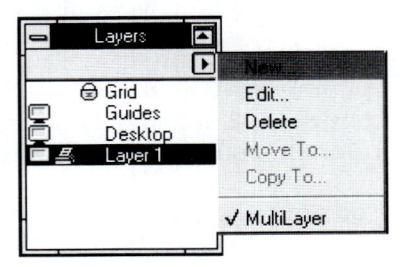

The four layers that appear in the Layers roll-up are CorelDRAW!'s defaults: Grid, Guides, Desktop, and Layer 1. There are three possible icons to the left of each layer: a monitor that says the layer is visible, a printer that tells you the layer is printable, and a padlock that says a layer is locked and you cannot place anything on it. The highlighted Layer 1 is the active layer, and all new objects and text will be on it. A layer becomes active when you select and highlight its name in the Layers roll-up window. The Desktop is active when you have multilayers, as you do in this default setup.

The Guides layer contains any guidelines that you may choose. These are the same guidelines available from the Layout menu, and drawings made on other layers will snap to them. You can also draw on the Guides layer, by making it the active layer. The Grid layer is similar to the Guides layer, except you cannot make the Grid layer the active layer. Consequently, it is a locked layer on which nothing can be drawn. The Grid layer is simply a series of points that can help you draw accurately in other layers.

Selecting, Moving, and Arranging Objects

Layer Features

Clicking on the right-pointing arrow below the title bar of the Layers roll-up opens a flyout menu, which allows you to create a new layer or to edit, delete, copy, or move existing layers. Additionally, you can change the stacking order of your layers or use multilayering to select objects across any layer, except for locked or hidden objects.

Editing a Layer

When you double-click on a layer in the Layers roll-up or choose Edit from the flyout menu, the Edit Layers dialog box opens, as shown here:

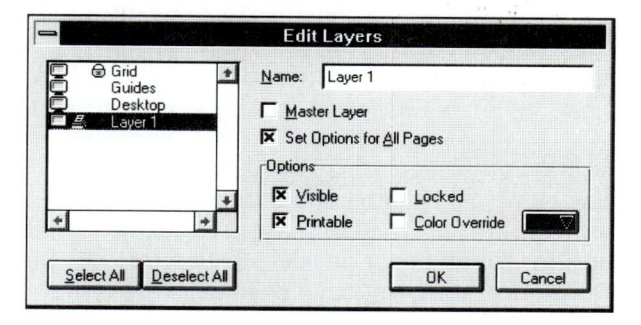

A text box identifies the name of the layer, which you can rename anything you want, using up to 32 characters. The dialog box contains six check boxes. The first allows you to identify a layer as a master layer. If the Set Options for All Pages check box is also checked, all objects on the master layer will be displayed on all pages of the document. Other check boxes allow you to choose whether to make a layer visible or invisible on the screen, an option that is useful when trying to present objects on a complex graphic more clearly. A layer may be printable or unprintable. It may be locked, whereby a layer cannot be accidentally edited. You can also set Color Override, which determines whether you see your object as a color outline or a black solid on the screen. (The default is a black solid.) You can change the color of the outline by clicking on the button next to Color Override. Checking the Set Options for All Pages check box for a layer will cause its objects to be displayed for all pages, whether it is a master layer or not.

Note: The Edit Layers dialog box for Guides or Grid layers contains an added Setup button. Depending on which layer is selected, the Guidelines Setup or Grid Setup dialog box will open when Setup is selected.

Finally, the Edit Layers dialog box allows you select or deselect all of the objects on a layer. This can be very helpful in multilayer drawings.

Creating a Layer
If you choose New from the Layers flyout menu, the New Layer dialog box opens like this:

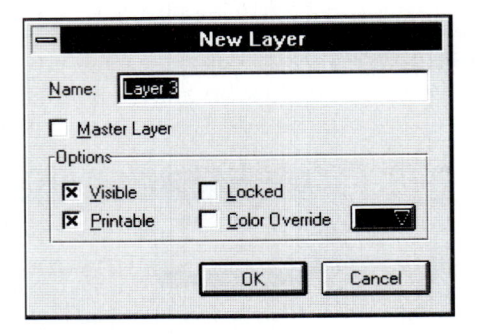

The New Layer dialog box allows you to name the new layer and has the same options as the Edit Layers dialog box, except that you cannot set options for all pages or select or deselect all objects (presumably a new layer would not have any objects on it).

Deleting a Layer
To delete a layer, simply click on the layer name in the Layers roll-up window and then click on the right-pointing arrow. Choose Delete and the layer and all of its objects are deleted. When you delete a layer, the layer below it on the list becomes the active layer.

Moving or Copying Objects or Text from One Layer to Another
The procedures are the same for both moving and copying objects and text from one layer to another. First, you must select the object you want to move or copy. You can tell which layer it is on by the displayed message on the status line. Next, from the Layers roll-up window, click on the right-pointing arrow and choose either Move To or Copy To. A "To?" arrow appears. Finally, click the "To?" arrow on the new layer in the Layers roll-up window where you want the object located.

Multilayering
Generally, in order to select an object, it must be on the active layer. By choosing the MultiLayer option from the Layers roll-up flyout menu, you can select and edit any object regardless of the layer on which it resides. There are two things to note about multilayering. First, locking a layer overrides the MultiLayer option's access to objects on that layer. Second, in

Selecting, Moving, and Arranging Objects

order to perform the moving and copying features, MultiLayer must be active.

Changing the Layer Stacking Order

The order in which the layers are listed in the Layers roll-up window is the same order in which the layers are stacked in your drawing; the top being first and the bottom last. To change the existing order, drag the layer name you want to move from its present location in the scroll box and place it on top of the name of the layer you want it to overlay in your drawing. When you release the mouse button, the list will be rearranged—as will the order of the layers in your drawing. You can get an understanding of layering with the following simple exercise:

1. Your page should be in landscape orientation with Rulers and Wireframe off, Grid off, and Snap-to Grid on.
2. With the Rectangle tool, draw a rectangle roughly three inches square.
3. With the rectangle selected, open the Fill tool at the bottom of the toolbox and click on solid black.
4. With the Ellipse tool, draw an ellipse inside the rectangle and, with the Fill tool, make it white.
5. With the Text tool, type the word **Super** in the ellipse. Use the Text roll-up to adjust the size so it will fit inside the ellipse. You now have a stack of three objects, one on top of the other, all on Layer 1;

6. Open the Layers roll-up from the Layout menu.
7. From the Layers flyout menu, choose New and click on OK in the New Layer dialog box.
8. Click on Layer 1 to return there, click on the rectangle you drew (make sure you have not selected the ellipse), open the Layers flyout menu, choose Move To, and click on Layer 2. The black rectangle now covers the ellipse and text, proving that Layer 2 is on top of Layer 1, as shown next. (Click on Layer 1 to further clinch this proof.)

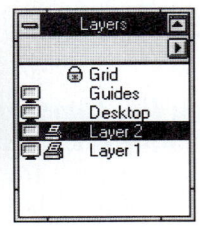

9. In the Layers roll-up window, drag Layer 1 up above Layer 2. CorelDRAW! switches the two layers to restore the original order of your drawing, like this:

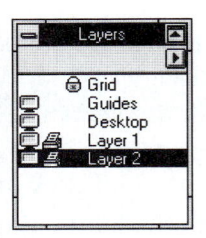

10. Click on the New button and do not save your work. Also, close the Layers roll-up.

Weld, Intersection, and Trim

In addition to Group and Combine, there are three additional ways to join two or more objects into one or more new objects that have a single fill and cannot be broken apart. These are Weld, Intersection, and Trim. Weld joins two or more overlapping objects to create a resulting object with a border that is the sum of the original objects and with overlapping borders removed. Intersection joins two or more overlapping objects to create a resulting object that takes on the border of the intersection of the original objects. Trim creates a new object that is the part of the last selected object that is not common to other overlapping objects. In all three cases, the outline and fill features of the last object selected will be in effect for the new object(s). Try out these additional methods of joining objects with the following exercise:

1. Select Portrait orientation and turn on Wireframe mode.
2. Using the Ellipse tool, draw a circle in the upper-left portion of the page. Fill it with any pattern by clicking on the Fill tool and then clicking on the pattern you want (you won't initially see the fill since you are in Wireframe mode). (Chapter 7 describes the Fill feature in depth.)

Selecting, Moving, and Arranging Objects

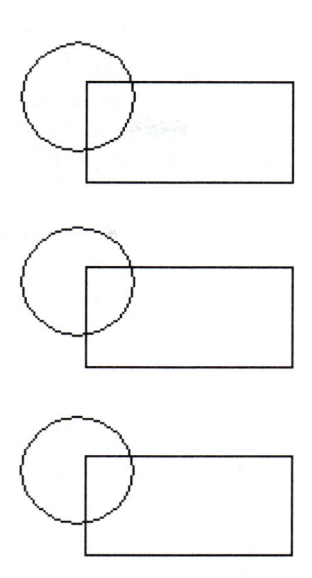

Separate objects ready for joining
Figure 5-15.

3. Using the Rectangle tool, draw a square that overlaps the circle. Fill it with a different pattern.
4. With the Pick tool, lasso both objects to select them. From the Edit menu, choose Copy and then, again from the Edit menu, choose Paste twice. Three copies of the original two objects are now on top of each other with the top copy selected.
5. Drag the selected copy to the bottom of the page and select the second copy (you need to click first on the ellipse and then the rectangle—you can't use marquee selection in this case or you would get both remaining copies) and drag it to the middle of the page. Your page should now look like Figure 5-15.
6. With the Pick tool, click first on the top ellipse, press and hold SHIFT, and then click on the top rectangle.
7. From the Arrange menu select Weld. The outline of the two objects becomes one and the common border is removed, as shown here:

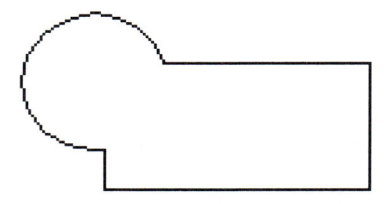

8. With the Pick tool and SHIFT, click on the middle ellipse and then on the middle rectangle.

9. From the Arrange menu select Intersection. Then click on the ellipse and drag it to the left and click on the rectangle and drag it to the right. In the middle is a new object formed by the intersection of the original objects, as you can see next:

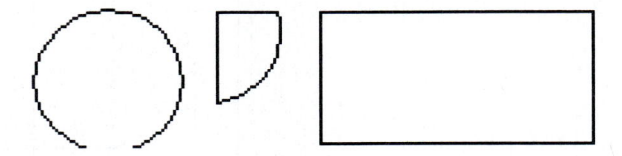

10. Finally, click on the bottom ellipse and then, holding down SHIFT, click on the bottom rectangle.
11. From the Arrange menu select Trim. Drag the ellipse to the left and what was the rectangle to the right. You can see the rectangle has a "bite" taken out of it where the ellipse was overlapping it like this:

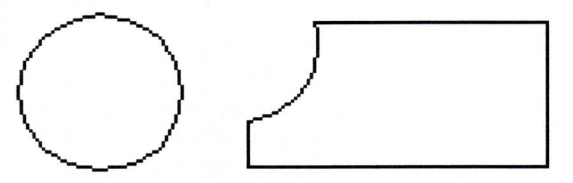

12. Turn off Wireframe in the View menu and you can see that the resulting fill of the newly created object is the fill of the last selected object, as shown in Figure 5-16.
13. Click on New (the work shouldn't remain on the screen for the next chapter).

Now you have had an opportunity to practice all of the functions of the Pick tool that do not require you to change the size or structure of selected objects. In Chapter 8 you will explore the transformation mode of the Pick

Selecting, Moving, and Arranging Objects

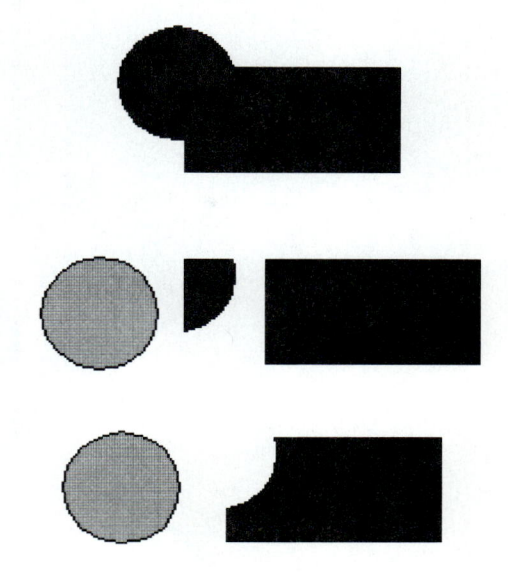

Joined objects take on the fill of the last selected object
Figure 5-16.

tool and learn to stretch, scale, rotate, skew, and mirror a selected object or group of objects. First, though, in Chapters 6 and 7 you will get experience using the Outline and Fill tools and applying color.

6

DEFINING the OUTLINE PEN

In CorelDRAW!, all objects have Outline Pen, outline color, and object fill attributes. In addition, text has its own set of attributes, as you will learn in Chapter 10. All of the objects you created and edited until now have had standard black fills and fixed-width black outlines. In this chapter, however, you will modify outline attributes using the CorelDRAW! Outline Pen.

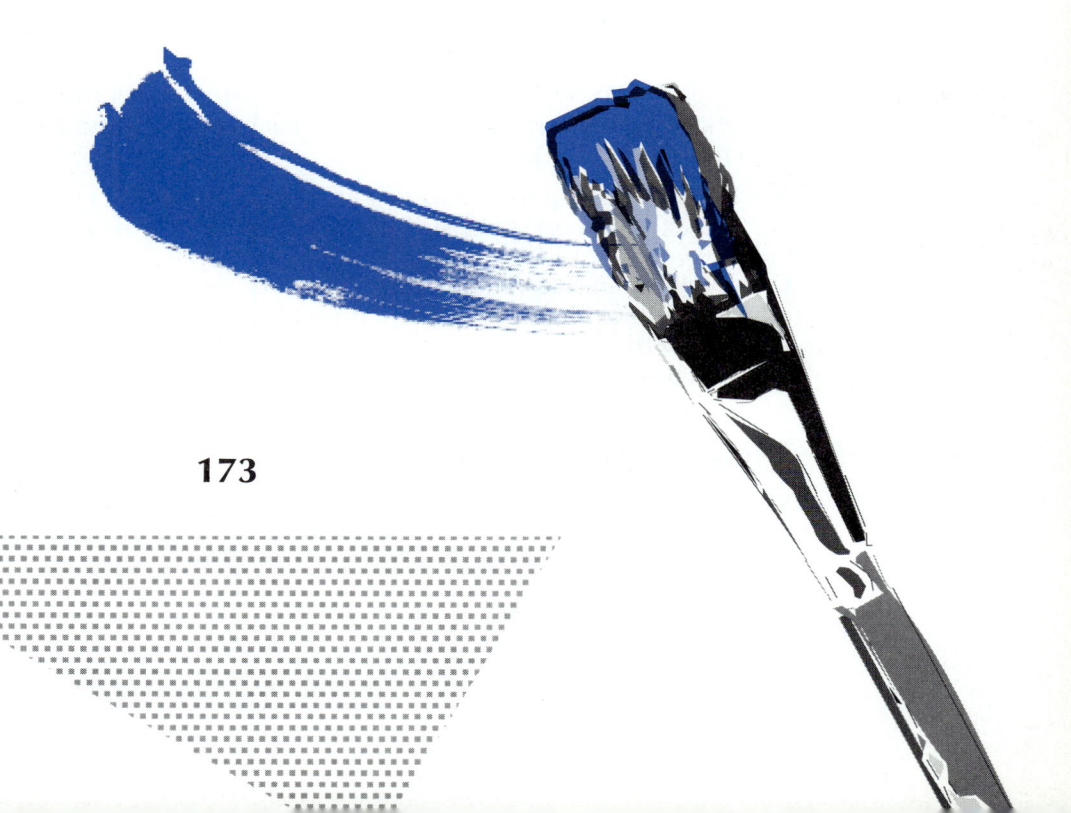

The Outline Pen is actually two tools in one. In order to create an outline for any object, you need to define the *Outline Pen* and the *outline color* in two separate steps. Think of the Outline Pen, which you will explore in this chapter, as a calligraphic pen capable of representing the shape of an almost infinite number of replaceable nibs and of emulating the possible ways you can slant your hand while drawing. The outline color, which you will learn about in Chapter 7, represents the ink and textures that flow from the pen.

When defining an Outline Pen for any object, you can vary the width, line style, corner shape, line ending style, and nib shape of the pen. You can also control the placement of the outline relative to the object's fill color. Only CorelDRAW! allows you so great a degree of control over the shape and appearance of your drawings. With your first try, you can create ornate calligraphic effects and simulate a hand-sketched look electronically.

Defining Outline Pen Attributes

The method you use to define Outline Pen attributes depends on whether you are creating new objects with the current default settings, editing attributes for existing objects, or altering default outline settings. The following list summarizes the available possibilities.

- ♦ To create an object with the current default Outline Pen attributes, select the appropriate drawing tool and draw the object. You can then select the Outline Pen to view the current default outline attributes (optional).

- ♦ To edit Outline Pen attributes for an existing object (including grouped or combined objects), activate the Pick tool, select the object, and then click on the Outline Pen.

- ♦ To begin setting new Outline Pen default attributes, click on the Outline Pen and then on the desired icon without first selecting an object.

Once you have selected the Outline Pen, you can choose between defining a custom Outline Pen or selecting a preset outline width. In the remaining sections of this chapter, you will practice customizing Outline Pen attributes and selecting preset Outline Pen widths for both planned and existing objects.

Using the Outline Pen

You have complete control over the attributes of the Outline Pen in CorelDRAW! thanks to a series of attributes that can be modified. There are three ways to modify these attributes:

- ♦ Directly from the Outline Pen flyout menu, shown in the following illustration. You use the flyout menu to make quick standard changes to an outline. All three ways of changing attributes start with this flyout menu.

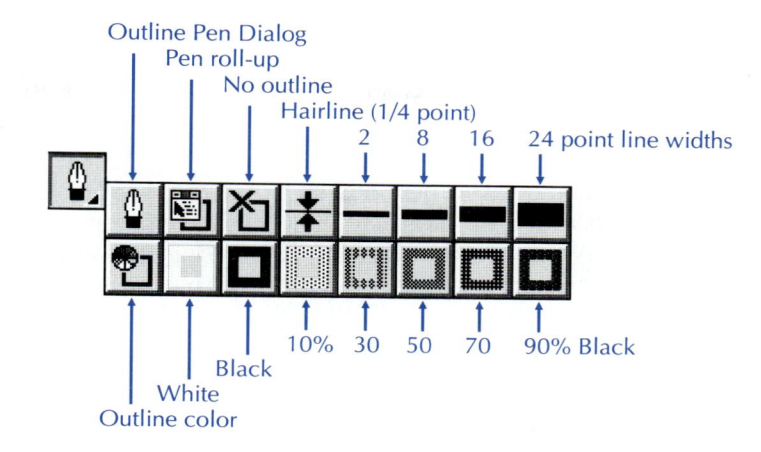

Defining the Outline Pen

```
Outline Pen Dialog
    Pen roll-up
        No outline
            Hairline (1/4 point)
                     2    8   16   24 point line widths
```

```
                  10%  30  50  70  90% Black
              Black
        White
Outline color
```

♦ From a dialog box that allows the attributes to be modified with greater precision. The dialog box is displayed by clicking on the Outline Pen Dialog tool, the first icon on the flyout menu, which is identical in appearance to the Outline Pen icon. By altering the settings in this dialog box, you can vary the outline's placement and width, change the shape of corners and line ending styles, design custom nibs, and create an array of calligraphic effects.

The Pen roll-up window allows you to quickly see the results of your attribute changes without opening the dialog box.

♦ From the Pen roll-up, shown in the next illustration. The Pen roll-up is displayed by clicking on the Outline Pen roll-up icon, next to the Outline Pen Dialog tool. Once the roll-up is accessed, it remains on the screen and can be rolled up or down at will.

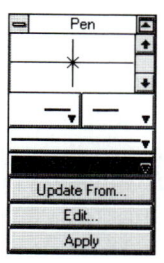

In the following exercises, you will create an object with default Outline Pen attributes and become familiar with the settings in the Outline Pen dialog box and Pen roll-up. Then you will edit Outline Pen attributes for existing objects in the sample files that came packaged with your software. Finally, you will set up new default Outline Pen attributes that will apply to objects you draw later.

If you simply want to specify outline width, without creating a custom Outline Pen, turn to the section "Selecting a Preset Outline Pen Width," later in this chapter. There, you will find out how to alter the width of the Outline Pen quickly, without accessing a dialog box or the roll-up.

Creating Objects with Default Attributes

When you create a new object, CorelDRAW! applies the current default settings to it automatically. You can leave those settings as they are or edit them. When you edit Outline Pen settings for a newly created object, however, your changes apply only to that object. Other objects that you create keep the default Outline Pen attributes until you set new defaults. If you want to change the defaults themselves, refer to the section "Customizing Outline Pen Defaults," later in this chapter.

In the exercise that follows, you will create a text string, select the Outline Pen flyout menu, access the Outline Pen dialog box, and observe the default Outline Pen attributes that are standard with CorelDRAW!.

1. Make sure that the Rulers, Show Grid, and Snap To Grid commands are turned off, select the Zoom tool, and set magnification to actual size (1:1).

2. Activate the Text tool and select an insertion point near the upper-left edge of the page. Type **outline pen.**

3. Open the Edit Text dialog box from the Text menu. Drag the text I-beam pointer over the text to select it.

4. Click on the Character button and set the text attributes to AGaramond, normal style, and 90 points.

    Set Character Spacing to 10 percent. Select the left alignment button , as shown in Figure 6-1, and then select OK on both the Character and Edit Text dialog boxes. Your screen will look like Figure 6-2.

5. Assuming that Wireframe is turned off on the View menu (if it isn't, turn it off), the interior of the text string is black or whatever the default fill color is. For the purposes of this exercise, you want to remove the fill color to clearly view your outline. To do this, click on the X at the left end of the onscreen color palette. (If your text seems to have vanished completely, you will find a solution in the next step.)

Defining the Outline Pen

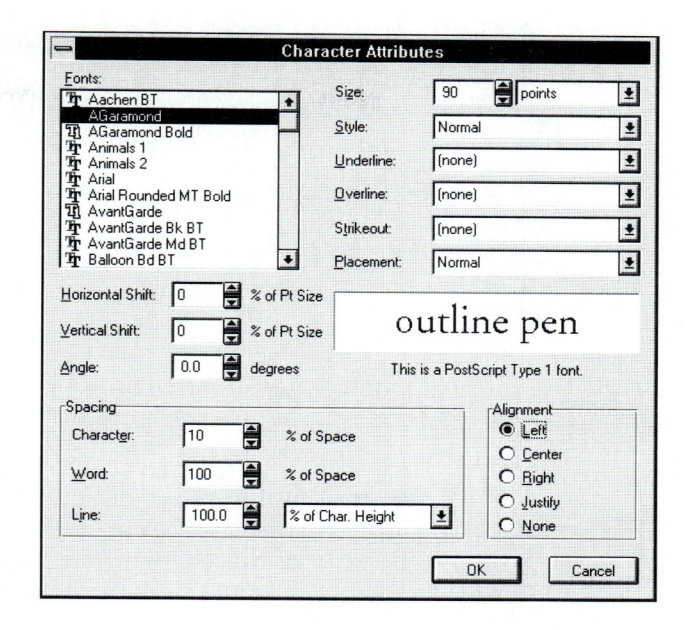

Character settings for the Edit Text dialog box
Figure 6-1.

6. Click on the Outline Pen icon. A flyout menu appears, as shown below. Click on the Hairline icon, fifth from the right. The text will reappear.

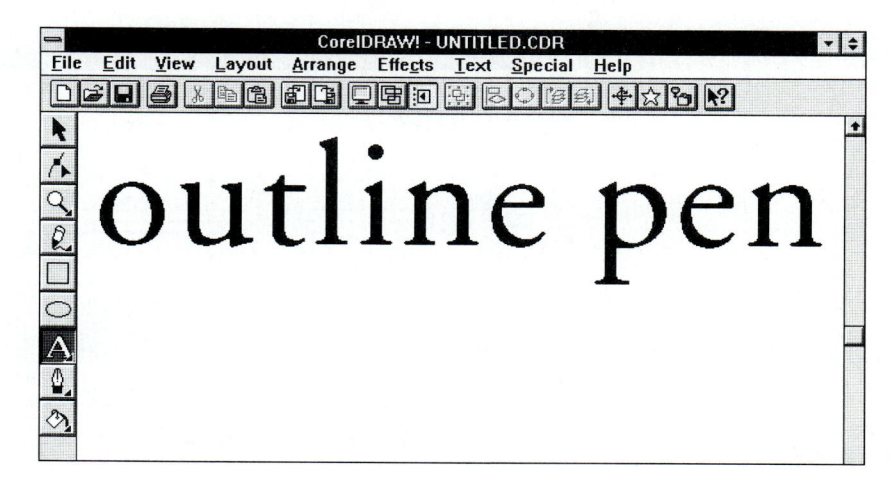

Text after Character settings
Figure 6-2.

Outline text with fill removed
Figure 6-3.

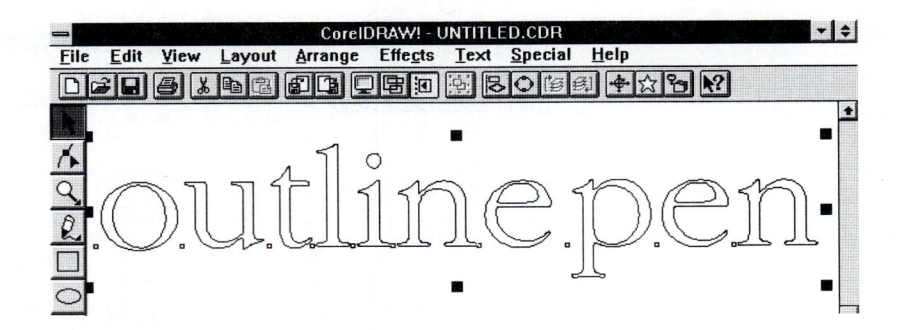

7. Use the Pick tool to size and move the text string so that it looks similar to Figure 6-3.

   The text string redisplays with just the outline. The center is hollow.

   As you just saw, the Outline Pen flyout menu contains two rows of options. The top row consists of controls for the Outline Pen, which you will use throughout this chapter. The second row, which you will work with in Chapter 7, contains controls for the outline fill color. (Clicking on the solid black icon in the second row of this flyout menu would also make text reappear after fill has been removed.)

8. Click again on the Outline Pen. For the moment, ignore all but the first (leftmost) icon in the top row of the flyout menu. The seven icons after the first one allow you either to open the Pen roll-up window or to quickly specify fixed outline widths. You will practice working with outline widths later, in "Selecting a Preset Outline Pen Width." For now, click on the first icon in the top row, the Outline Pen Dialog Tool icon. It looks just like the Outline Pen icon, but it has the more specialized function of allowing you to specify all the possible attributes of the Outline Pen. The Outline Pen dialog box displays, as in Figure 6-4.

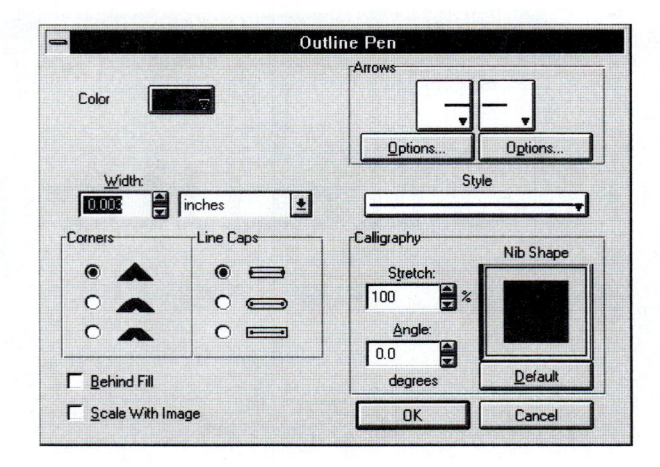

Outline Pen dialog box
Figure 6-4.

Defining the Outline Pen

The Outline Pen dialog box contains controls for nine Outline Pen attributes. The default settings on your screen should match the settings in Figure 6-4, unless you or another user altered them since installing the software. (One setting that is an exception and could differ is Width.) If your dialog box shows different settings, adjust them to match the ones in the figure. Then, take a moment to become familiar with the attributes and how they function.

Color A display box in the upper-left area of the dialog box shows you the current fill color. When you click on the scroll arrow, a color palette is opened that is identical to the normal onscreen palette except for the arrangement of the color choices. At the bottom of the color display box is the More button, which opens the Outline Color dialog box, giving you access to the full range of outline coloring. In Chapter 7 you will learn how these features are used.

Arrows The pair of boxes next to the color display box allow you to select or construct a line ending (such as an arrowhead) to go on either end of a line. These line endings are displayed in a flyout that you can open by clicking on either the left (line-beginning) or right (line-ending) Arrows display box, as shown here:

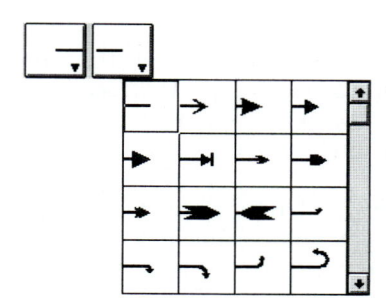

To select a line ending, scroll through the boxes of line endings until you see the one you want. Click on the line ending you want, and it will appear in its respective small Arrows display box.

Tip: To find the beginning of a line (normally the left end) or the end of a line (normally the right end) click on the line with the Shape tool and press HOME to highlight the beginning node. Pressing END will cause the ending node to be highlighted.

Clicking on the Options button for either the line-beginning or line-ending arrow opens a menu that offers the same four options for each. After you have selected a head or tail shape, the options are enabled. Choosing None removes a line ending you previously selected. You can reverse the beginning and ending arrows by choosing Swap. If you want to remove a line ending from the flyout box of line endings, select it and click on Delete From List. Clicking on the Edit option opens the Arrowhead Editor dialog box shown here:

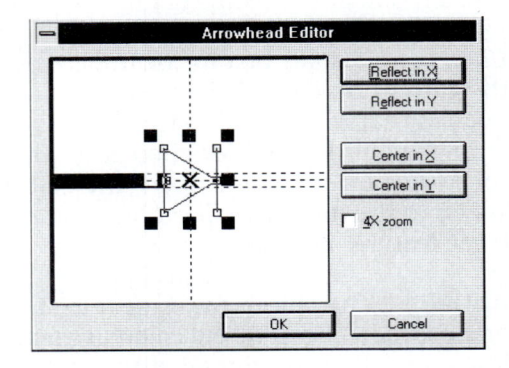

The Arrowhead Editor displays an enlarged arrowhead and allows you to move, scale, and stretch the arrowhead by dragging on it or one of its boundary markers. You can center the arrowhead relative to the X in the middle of the Editor, either horizontally by selecting Center in X or vertically by selecting Center in Y. Also, you can flip or *reflect* the arrowhead relative to the center, either horizontally by selecting Reflect in X or vertically by selecting Reflect in Y. Finally, you can magnify the arrowhead image by clicking on 4X zoom.

Line Width   Under the Color area of the Outline Pen dialog box are two boxes for controlling the current line width. You can change either the specific width number or the unit of measure, from inches to points, for example.

Line Style   A third box, to the right of the line width, shows the current line style. The solid line shown in the box in Figure 6-4 is the default line style. Clicking on the Style display box opens a flyout that allows you to choose from a number of dotted and dashed line styles, as you can see here:

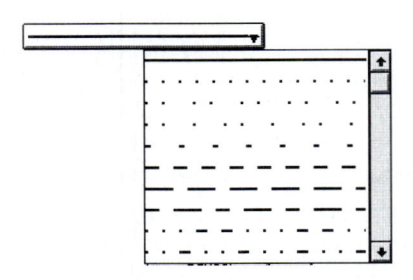

Defining the Outline Pen

To choose a line style, use the scroll bar to display the style you want and click on that line style. You'll be returned to the Outline Pen dialog box, and the line style you choose will now be in the display box.

Corners   The Corners options pertain to objects that tend to have sharp corners: lines, open and closed curve objects, rectangles, and some angular fonts. The three option buttons in this area of the dialog box allow you to choose just how CorelDRAW! shapes those corners. The first (default) option shows a sharp or *miter* corner, where the outer edges of two joining line or curve segments extend until they meet. By altering the Miter Limit setting in the Preferences dialog box, you can control the angle below which CorelDRAW! flattens or bevels the edge of a sharp curve. When you choose the second option button, CorelDRAW! rounds the corners where two lines or curve segments meet. When you choose the third or *bevel* corner option button, corners of joining curve or line segments are flattened. The results of the Corners settings are usually subtle, unless you magnify an object or combine Corners settings with Nib Shape attributes for calligraphic effects.

Line Caps   The Line Caps options apply to lines and open curves, but not to closed path objects such as rectangles, closed curves, or ellipses. These settings determine the ending styles of lines and curves. The first or default option is a *butt line* end style, where the line ends exactly at the end point. The second option gives you *rounded line* end points. When you choose either the second or the third (*square line*) end type, the line extends beyond the end point for a distance equal to half of the line thickness. When you select any of the line end caps, that style applies to both end points of the line or curve. If you have selected dashed lines as your line type for an object, each dash takes on the shape of the line end style you choose.

Calligraphy   The remaining two Outline Pen attributes—Stretch and Angle—help you define a custom pen shape, analogous to the *nib* or point of a calligraphic fountain pen. With default values of 100 percent stretch and 0-degree angle, the pen shape is square, resulting in a plain outline. On their own, these settings will not create calligraphic effects. When you alter them in combination, however, they allow you to outline objects with varying thick and thin strokes at the angle of your choice. You can set the shape of the nib by changing the values in the Stretch and Angle numeric list boxes, or interactively. Using the interactive method, you click and drag the mouse pointer inside the Nib Shape display box, where the pointer changes to a cross. The Stretch and Angle settings are automatically adjusted as you distort the nib shape. You can restore the default square nib by selecting the Default command button below the Nib Shape box. The Corners settings work with the Calligraphy settings to define the appearance of calligraphic strokes, as you will learn in "A Pen Shape for Calligraphic Effects," later in this chapter.

Behind Fill   The Behind Fill check box lets you specify whether the outline of an object should appear in front of or behind the object's fill. The default setting is in front of the fill (empty check box), but if you create objects with thick outlines, you will want to activate Behind Fill. This is especially advisable with text, where thick outlines appearing in front of the fill can obliterate empty spaces and cause text to appear smudged, like this:

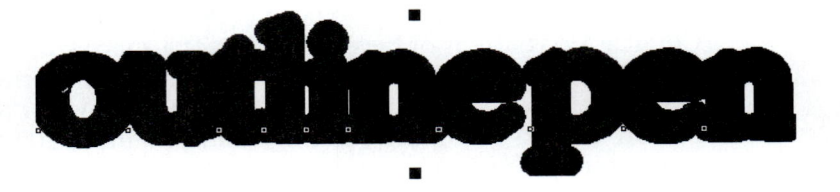

When you place an outline behind the fill, only half of it is visible. The outline therefore appears to be only half as thick as specified.

Scale With Image   When the Scale With Image check box contains an X, the width and angle of the outline change proportionally as you resize, rotate, or skew the object. CorelDRAW! automatically updates the width and angle settings in the Outline Pen dialog box when Scale With Image is active. When the Scale With Image setting is *not* active, the width and angle of an object's outline do not change, no matter how you stretch, scale, rotate, or skew the object. This can lead to some interesting but unintended changes in appearance when you define a calligraphic pen nib for the object, as you will see in the "Scaling the Outline with the Image" section later in this chapter.

Now that you are familiar with the options in the Outline Pen dialog box, exit the dialog box by selecting Cancel. Clear the screen by selecting New from the File menu and clicking on No before going on.

Customizing Outline Pen Defaults

Different artists have different styles, and you may prefer to create most of your objects with Outline Pen styles that differ from the standard settings. If so, perform the exercise in this section to learn how to customize Outline Pen defaults. Objects that you create after changing the default attributes will then conform to the appearance that characterizes your working style.

Creating objects with new Outline Pen defaults is a three-stage process. First, you access the default Outline Pen dialog box. Then you change the Outline

Defining the Outline Pen

Pen attributes. Finally, you create new objects, which automatically adhere to the new default attributes. The dialog box that you use to edit default settings is identical to the Outline Pen dialog box, except for its title and the way you access it.

1. Start with a blank page. (If you are in an existing drawing and want to change default settings, make sure that no object is selected.) Then select the Outline Pen and click on the Outline Pen Dialog Tool icon. Since no object is selected, the dialog box shown here appears.

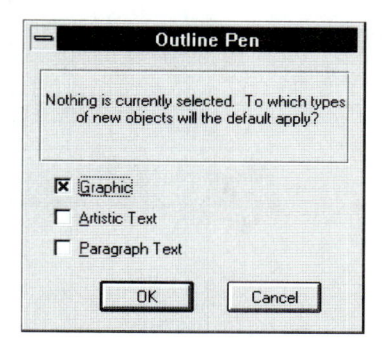

2. Click on the Artistic Text and Paragraph Text check boxes, so that all three have check marks, and then select OK to access the Outline Pen dialog box and have the defaults apply to all new objects. The contents of this dialog box are identical to the contents of the normal Outline Pen dialog box. Only the path of calling up the dialog box without a selected object is different.

CorelDRAW! encourages you to create images according to your unique working habits and style.

3. For now don't change the defaults. As you go through this chapter you will exercise all of the options in this dialog box and become familiar with their effects and what your likes and dislikes are. When you are finished with the chapter, you can come back here and set the defaults to what is right for you.

4. Select Cancel to close the dialog box without change and return to the work area.

It's that easy to alter default settings for the Outline Pen. As with almost every other CorelDRAW! feature, customization is the key word.

On the other hand, if you are involved in technical illustration, or your normal CorelDRAW! tasks are relatively uncomplicated, you may seldom require calligraphy or other special options in the Outline Pen dialog box. The next section shows you how to change the Outline Pen width quickly and interactively, without the use of a dialog box.

Selecting a Preset Outline Pen Width

If width is the Outline Pen attribute you change most frequently, CorelDRAW! offers shortcuts that save you time and keep you out of the Outline Pen dialog box. The first row of the flyout menu that appears when you select the Outline Pen, as shown here, contains five preset outline widths from which you can choose.

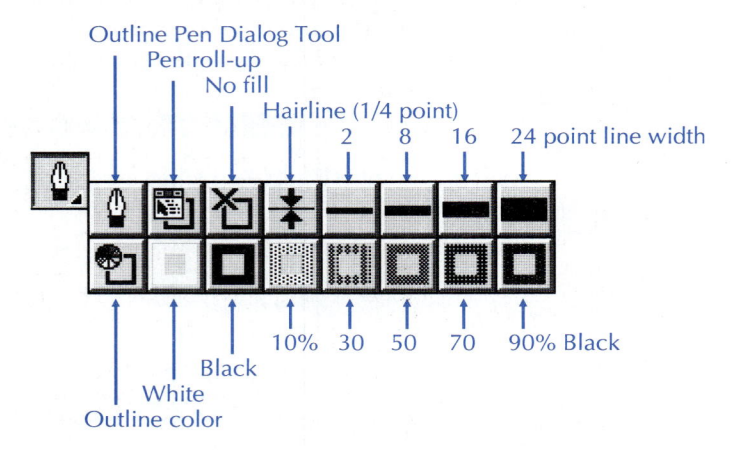

Outline Pen Dialog Tool
Pen roll-up
No fill
Hairline (1/4 point)
2   8   16   24 point line width

10%   30   50   70   90% Black
Black
White
Outline color

You can choose one of these options for a currently selected object, or you can set a fixed line width as a new default. When you choose a preset outline width for a selected object, you apply that width to the selected object only. When you click on one of these options without having first selected an object, however, CorelDRAW! assumes that you want to set the option as a new default width, and the Outline Pen dialog box shown previously pops up. Click on OK to set the selected line width as a new default for objects that you draw in the future. If you meant to select an existing object first, click on the Cancel command button instead.

The second option, next to the Custom Outline Pen icon on the left, is the Pen roll-up, as shown here:

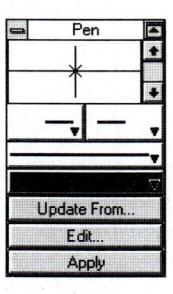

Defining the Outline Pen

The top option in the Pen roll-up allows you to adjust the outline thickness. The default width that should appear is a hairline, shown by a thin line 1/4 point wide, met by two arrows. By clicking on the downward-pointing scroll arrow, you reduce the line thickness to zero, represented by an X through the box, signifying no outline. By clicking on the upward-pointing arrow, you can increase the line width, starting with the hairline, then a line 1 point wide, and then in .01-point increments. Below the outline thickness option are the familiar line ending, line style, and color options. To update the pen attributes from a given object, click on Update From and the pointer will turn into a From arrow, which you use to click on the object. The attributes of the object then update the Outline Pen dialog box. (You then apply these attributes to another selected object.) To open the full Outline Pen dialog box, click on Edit. To apply the attributes you have set in the Pen roll-up to a selected object, click on Apply.

The next icon in the Outline Pen flyout is an X; as in the Pen roll-up window, you can click on this option when you want a selected object to have no outline at all.

The next option, similar to that in the Pen roll-up, represents a hairline (a line 1/4 point wide). The screen, however, does not display a true WYSIWYG representation of an outline this thin.

As shown above, the remaining four options in the flyout menu represent fixed outline widths of 2 (thin), 8 (medium), 16 (med-thick), and 24 (thick) points. Think of these options as "package deals," in which each width selection includes an angle of 0 degrees and a stretch value of 100 percent in the Outline Pen dialog box.

If you have altered any of the other default Outline Pen settings using the Outline Pen dialog box, they are still effective when you select a preset Outline Pen width. For example, if you previously selected the Behind Fill or Scale With Image options as defaults, your outlines will exhibit these attributes even when you select a preset outline width. Since the Angle and Stretch settings are standardized for preset widths, however, you cannot achieve calligraphic effects.

Editing Outline Pen Attributes of Existing Objects

To redefine Outline Pen attributes for an existing (not newly created) object, you must select the object before you access the Outline Pen flyout menu. If you try to access the Outline Pen dialog box without having selected an object, CorelDRAW! assumes that you want to set new defaults for the Outline Pen, and any changes you make in the Outline Pen dialog box will not affect existing objects.

When you define Outline Pen attributes for an existing object that is selected, you are in effect *editing* the object's current outline style. The changes you make apply to that object only and have no effect on the default settings for objects you create later.

If you use the SHIFT method to select multiple objects in order to change their Outline Pen attributes, the Outline Pen dialog box displays the settings for the last object that you selected in the group. If you use the marquee method to select the objects, the dialog box displays the settings for the last object that you drew. Any changes you make will apply to all of the selected objects, however, so be very careful about changing Outline Pen attributes for more than one object at a time.

Each of the following sections concentrates on the effects of editing a specific attribute or related set of attributes in the Outline Pen dialog box. You will work with sample files that best demonstrate how changes to an attribute can alter the overall design and mood of a picture.

Adjusting Line Width

The line width you assign to an object's Outline Pen helps define the balance and weight of that object within a picture. In the following exercise, you will alter the line width for several elements in a text object that you create and then observe how your changes affect it.

1. Open the Outline Pen dialog box and determine whether both the Behind Fill and Scale With Image check boxes are unchecked. If either contains a check mark, click on the box to remove it.
2. Open the Text tool, click anywhere on the page, and type **Hot Tips**. Select the words "Hot Tips" using the Pick tool.
3. From the Text menu select the Text roll-up and set the text to 60 points, ITC Bauhaus, Heavy. Click on Apply.
4. With the text still selected, magnify the area around the words with the Zoom tool. Your screen should now display an area similar to Figure 6-5.

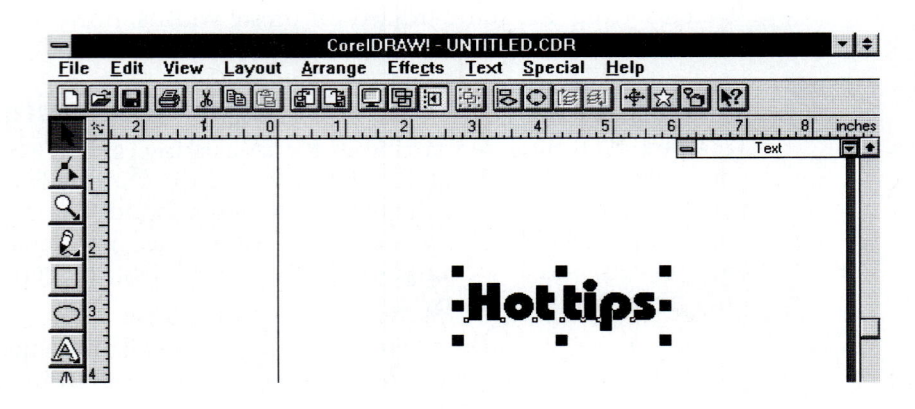

"Hot Tips" test as it starts out

Figure 6-5.

Defining the Outline Pen 187

5. Select the Fill tool and select the light-colored pattern, fourth from the left, bottom roll (the text lightens against the darker background).
6. Select the Outline Pen and click on the line width after the hairline, a 2-point line. Click on the Pick tool. Now, the words "Hot Tips" should look like this:

7. Select the Outline Pen a third time and click on the third line width from the right, an 8-point line. "Hot Tips" should now look like this:

8. Select the Outline Pen again and open the Outline Pen dialog box. Notice that outline width is at 0.111 inch, which is equivalent to 8 points (a point is 1/72 of an inch or 0.014 inch), as shown here. Remember that the default line width is 0.014 inch, which is 1 point.

As you can see, the variation in line width makes a big difference in how an object looks, and you can vary the line width either by selecting one of the established options on the flyout menu or by entering an exact width in the Outline Pen dialog box.

Leave the dialog box open and the "Hot Tips" text on your screen for further use. The next section explores the design possibilities of placing outlines of objects behind or in front of their fills.

Adjusting Placement of Outline and Fill

The Behind Fill setting in the Outline Pen dialog box determines whether the outline of a selected object is placed behind or in front of the object's fill. This attribute is most important when you are working with text. Thick outlines appearing in front of the fill can clog up the open spaces in letters, making the letters appear unclear, as you saw in the 8-point example in the last exercise. In the following exercise, you will adjust outline placement for the letters in the "Hot Tips" text currently displayed.

1. In the Outline Pen dialog box, notice whether the Behind Fill option is selected.
2. If it is not already selected, click on the Behind Fill check box to select it and then select OK to exit the dialog box. The word reappears with a much thinner outline, as shown here:

Actually the outline is just as thick as before, but half of it is hidden behind the fill. You can see this if you watch the screen redraw (unless you have a super-fast computer).

In the next section, you will observe how the Scale With Image setting affects the appearance of resized or transformed objects.

Scaling the Outline with the Image

A wide outline, such as the 8-point width you applied in the last exercise, may be appropriate for large letters, say 75 points and above. If you scale that large type down to 24 points, however, the wide border doesn't look good at all, as you can see here:

The CorelDRAW! Outline Pen dialog box has an option to scale an outline's attributes with the image. If you select Scale With Image by clicking on the check box, an outline's attributes will be appropriately scaled as you change the image. The default, though, is to not scale the attributes, and you are likely to get something that looks like the last illustration.

1. With the "Hot Tips" text still on the screen with an 8-point outline placed behind the fill, use the Text roll-up to scale the image to 24 points. You should get an image on your screen that looks like that shown in the last illustration.
2. Press ALT-BACKSPACE to return the text to its original size.
3. Select the Outline Pen and open the Outline Pen dialog box. If it is not already selected, click on the Scale With Image check box and click on OK.
4. Again, scale the text image to 24 points. Click on Apply. You now get a much more usable image:

Defining the Outline Pen

Hot Tips

5. Clear the image from the screen by selecting New from the File menu; do not save the changes.

Setting Sharp (Miter), Rounded, or Beveled Outline Corners

The effect of changing corner attributes of the Outline Pen is so subtle that it is almost unnoticeable—unless the selected object has a thick outline as well as sharp corners. A thick outline enables you to see the shape of the object change as you cycle through the Corners options. Perform the following exercise to practice altering Corners settings for the letter "E."

1. Select the Text tool, click anywhere on the page, and type **E**.
2. Select the letter "E" with the Pick tool and from the Text roll-up select AvantGarde, Bold, 154 points. Click on Apply.
3. Move the letter "E" to the center of the printable page, magnify the character until it fills the window, select the Outline Pen, and click on the 16-point line width (the second from the right). Next click on the X to the left of the onscreen color palette, to turn off the fill.

When you have completed the preceding steps your screen should look like Figure 6-6. On the screen you see the outline of the letter "E" with

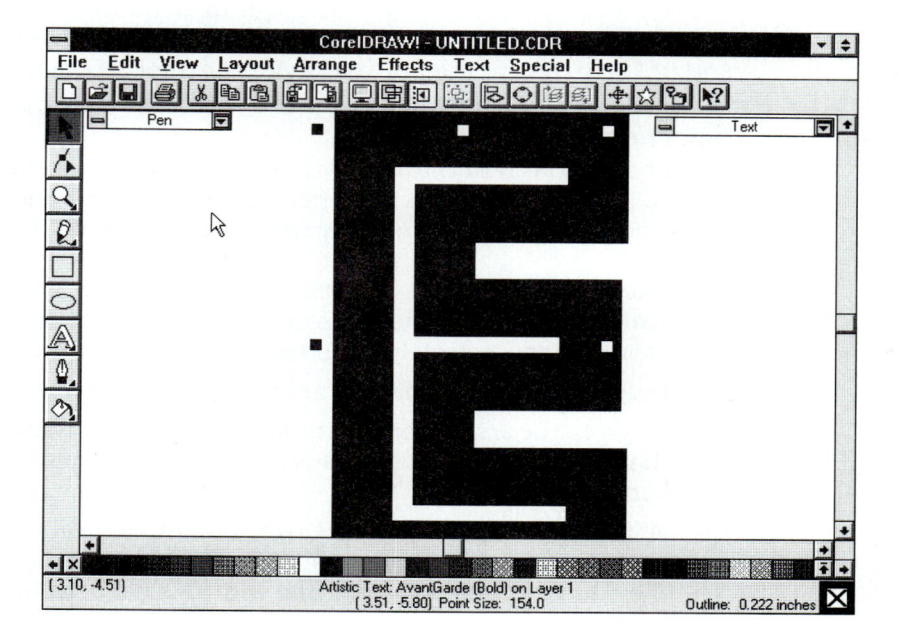

The letter "E" set up to test the types of corners
Figure 6-6.

The letter "E" with (a) sharp or miter, (b) rounded, and (c) beveled corners
Figure 6-7.

a.   b.   c.

12 corners on which to test the three corner styles. The default, the sharp or miter corner, is currently displayed and is shown in Figure 6-7a.

4. Select the Outline Pen, open the Outline Pen dialog box, click on the rounded corner option button, and click on OK. You should see a distinct change in the corners, as shown in Figure 6-7b.

5. Again open the Outline Pen dialog box, select the beveled corner option, and click on OK. Once more, the corners change, as shown in Figure 6-7c.

6. Select New from the File menu to clear the screen. Do not save your changes.

In creating your own drawing, you will find the effects of the Corners options most dramatic when you assign thick outlines to objects that contain at least some cusp nodes. In the next section, you will explore when and how changes to the line end styles can alter an object's appearance.

Selecting Line End Caps

Line end options (*end caps*) apply only to straight lines and open-ended curves. It is difficult to see the difference between line end types unless you create very thick lines or magnify the line a lot—you'll do both here.

1. From the View menu select Rulers. From the Layout menu select Grid & Scale Setup and set the Vertical Grid Origin to 11 inches. From the Layout menu, select Snap To Guidelines if not already selected.

2. Drag vertical guidelines from the ruler on the left to 2 and 4 inches.

3. Magnify the area from 1 inch on the horizontal ruler and 2 inches on the vertical ruler to 5 inches on the horizontal ruler and 4 inches on the vertical ruler.

4. With the Feehand tool, draw two straight, vertical lines down the guidelines from 2 inches to 4 inches. These should be hairline width. If they don't appear to be hairline width, select both lines and then select

Defining the Outline Pen

the hairline width icon from the Outline Pen flyout menu. Deselect these lines by clicking with the Pick tool any place in the work area except on one of the lines.

5. Select the Outline Pen and click on the far right line width, which is 24 points or .333 inch. Click on OK to apply this width to graphic objects.
6. With the Freehand tool, draw three straight, horizontal lines from 2 to 4 inches on the horizontal ruler at 2 1/2, 3, and 3 1/2 inches on the vertical ruler. Your screen should look like Figure 6-8.

   The default line end cap, the *butt* end, is shown in Figure 6-8. The lines end exactly at the termination of the line and are squared off.
7. With the Pick tool select the middle line, open the Outline Pen dialog box, select the middle or rounded line end cap, and click on OK. The line endings on the middle line are now rounded and project beyond the termination of the line, as shown here:
8. Select the bottom horizontal line, open the Outline Pen dialog box, select the bottom or square line end cap, and click on OK. The line

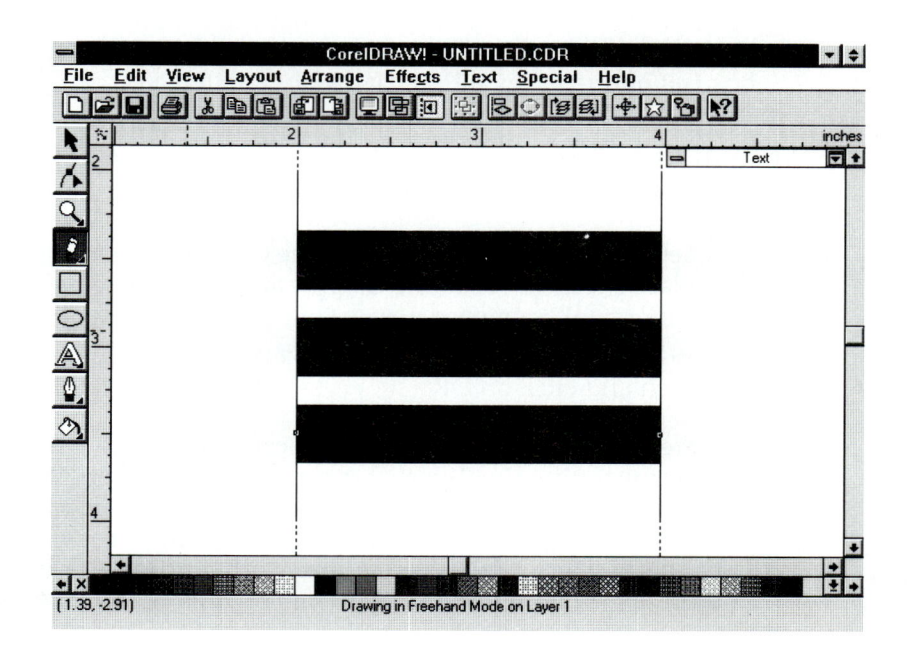

Lines prepared for testing line end caps
Figure 6-8.

endings on the bottom line are now square and project beyond the termination of the line by one-half of the line width. The three line end caps are shown here:

9. Clear the screen by selecting New from the File menu. Don't save the contents.

If an image contains many open-ended curves, selecting rounded line end caps can soften the image, even if the lines are thin. Conversely, you can select butt or square line end styles to give an object a more rough-hewn, sharp appearance.

Using Different Line Styles

So far in this book, all the lines you have drawn, including the lines in the characters you have typed, have been solid lines. CorelDRAW! provides a list box full of line styles and, if that is not enough, you can edit a file named CORELDRAW.DOT and add more.

In the following exercise you'll try out various line styles, look at them in various widths, and apply the different line end caps to them.

1. Select the Outline Pen, click on the Outline Pen Dialog Tool icon, and place check marks in the Graphic and Artistic Text check boxes. Then click on OK to apply a new default line width to these two types of objects.
2. When the Outline Pen dialog box opens, change the line width to 0.020 inch and click on OK.

You are starting with a thicker line because a hairline (1/4 point) is too small for demonstrating the different types of lines. The dots in a dotted line are the same height as the line is wide. Therefore, a dotted hairline has dots that are .003-inch high—three thousandths of an inch! These will print on most laser and PostScript printers, but many other printers cannot print them, and the screen does not display them correctly without magnification.

Defining the Outline Pen

3. Select actual size magnification (1:1) and, with the Pencil tool, draw four straight horizontal lines, each about 3 1/2 inches long, at 4, 4 1/2, 5, and 5 1/2 inches on the vertical ruler.
4. Click on the Text tool, type **Corel** at about 6 1/2 inches on the vertical ruler, select it with the Pick tool, and use the Text roll-up to select Poster Bodoni BT, normal, 60 points, and then click on Apply.
5. While the text is still selected, click on the X at the end of the on-screen palette to turn off the fill. Your screen should look like Figure 6-9.
6. With the Pick tool, click on the second horizontal line, open the Pen roll-up, and click on the third button (line style) from the top. A dashed and dotted line styles list box will open, as shown here:

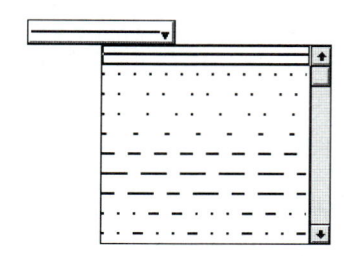

7. Select the second line type from the top. The list box closes, and a normal dotted line appears in the Pen roll-up's line styles field. Click on Apply.
8. Select the third horizontal line and then, from the line styles list box, select the second dashed line (the seventh line type). Click on Apply.

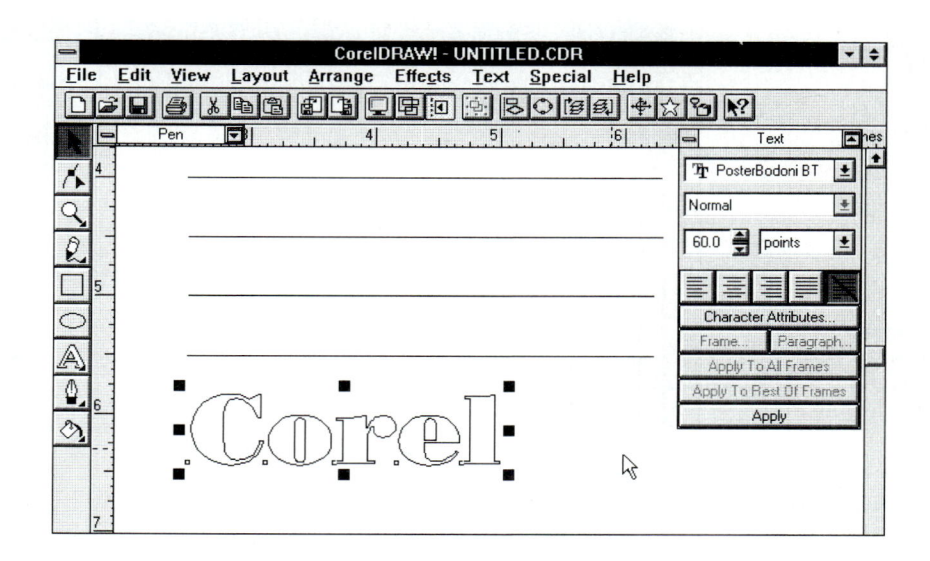

Lines and text prepared for testing line styles
Figure 6-9.

9. Select the fourth horizontal line and, from the line styles list box, select the dash, double-dot line (the tenth line type). Again, click on Apply.
10. Select the text and, from the line styles list box, select the first dotted line and click on Apply. Your screen should now look like Figure 6-10.

    Next, quickly look at how dotted and dashed lines look at various line widths and with various line end caps.
11. With the Pick tool, draw a marquee around the four lines (not the text).
12. From the Outline Pen flyout menu, select various line widths: first 2 points (fourth line width from the right) and then 8 points (third line width from the right). Your lines will look like this:
13. Select New from the File menu and No to clear the work area.

If you want to add more dotted and/or dashed lines, leave CorelDRAW!, bring up an ASCII text editor such as Windows Notepad, and edit the file CORELDRAW.DOT that is in the CUSTOM subdirectory of the directory in which CorelDRAW! was installed. Instructions on adding line types are in the beginning of the file.

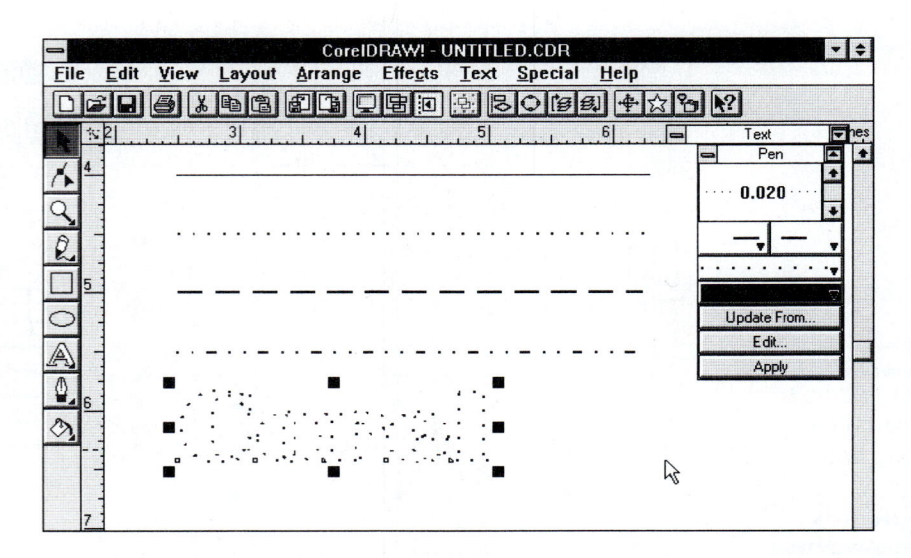

Using various line styles with 1-point lines
Figure 6-10.

Defining the Outline Pen

There is much variety in the styles, widths, and ends you can use with lines. In the next section you will see how to further enhance a line with many different arrowheads and tail feathers.

Adding and Editing Arrowheads

In the earlier section, "Selecting Line End Caps," you saw one technique for ending lines. There are, additionally, a number of arrowhead and tail feather options that you can place on the end of a line. You can also customize an existing arrowhead with the Arrowhead Editor, and add new arrowheads to the arrowhead display boxes. In the next two exercises you will add some arrowheads and tail feathers and customize them using the Outline Pen dialog box, Pen roll-up, and Arrowhead Editor.

1. Select the Outline Pen, click on the fourth line width from the right (2 points), click on Artistic Text and Paragraph Text, and then OK to apply this to all new objects.
2. Draw three horizontal lines about 3 inches long at 2, 3, and 4 inches on the vertical ruler. Be sure to draw the lines from left to right so the left end is the beginning of the line. Set the magnification to actual size. Use the scroll bars to center the three lines on your screen.
3. With the Shape tool, click on the first line and notice that the left end of the line has the larger node, as shown here:

4. Change to the Pick tool. The first line should automatically be selected.
5. From the Outline Pen dialog box, click on the Arrows line-ending (right) display box. An arrowhead selection display box will open.
6. To put an arrowhead on the right end of this line, click on the second arrowhead from the right on the top row.
7. To add some tail feathers on the left end of the line, click on the Arrows line-beginning (left) display box, scroll the set of arrowhead display boxes by pressing the down scroll arrow three times, and then click on the last set of tail feathers on the bottom row, as shown here:

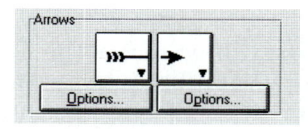

8. Click on OK to return to your drawing, and click on a blank area of the screen. Your arrow should look like this:

9. Use the Pen roll-up to place line endings of your choice on the second and third lines. Click on the next line and then open the Pen roll-up from the Outline Pen roll-up icon if it's not already on your screen. The second field down contains line-beginning (left) and line-ending (right) display boxes identical to those in the Outline Pen dialog box. Click on a box and make your selection, repeat this for the other end, and then click on Apply. (Note that the last line style used in the Pen roll-up was the dotted line. You might want to change this or your lines will become dotted when you click on Apply.) One possible set of choices is shown here:

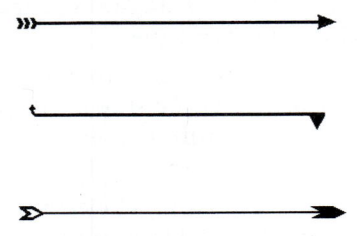

10. With the Pick tool, draw a marquee around the three lines and set the line width, first, to 4 points. Open the Outline Pen dialog box, change the line width to 0.056 inch, and click on OK. (All arrows will be the same since you are also applying the settings last established in the dialog box. You can use the Pen roll-up window's Edit button to open the Outline Pen dialog box, saving mouse movements and keystrokes.) Then set the line width to 8 points (you can use the third icon from the right on the Pen flyout menu). Notice how the size of the line endings changes with the size of the line.
11. Select New from the File menu (and don't save the changes) to clear the work area.

Next, use the Arrowhead Editor to modify an existing arrowhead.

Caution: If you close the Arrowhead Editor after modifying an arrowhead, you will have permanently modified the arrowhead you were working on. You can again modify the arrowhead to try to recreate the original, but you may not get it exactly the way it was.

Defining the Outline Pen   **197**

Tip: To prevent permanently modifying your arrowhead file, leave CorelDRAW!, go to the CUSTOM subdirectory under the directory in which CorelDRAW! is installed, and make a copy of the file that contains the arrowheads—CORELDRW.END. Call the new file CORELDRW.EN1. Then you can modify arrowheads as you wish and, when you are done, you can leave CorelDRAW! once again and copy CORELDRW.EN1 back to CORELDRW.END to restore the original arrowheads.

1. At actual size magnification, draw a horizontal line in the middle of the page.
2. Using the Pen roll-up, click on Edit to open the Outline Pen dialog box. Change to a 4-point (0.056-inch) line width.
3. Select the Arrows line-ending (right) box and click on the second arrowhead from the right on the top row. Click on the Options button and choose the Edit option.
4. By clicking and dragging on the eight boundary markers, you can modify the arrowhead, stretch out both the left and right ends, and reduce the height. In the latter operation it is likely that the arrowhead will get off center vertically. Use the Center in Y command button to correct this. Try Reflect in X to see the effect of this, and use it to return the arrowhead to its original orientation. When you are done, your dialog box should look like this:

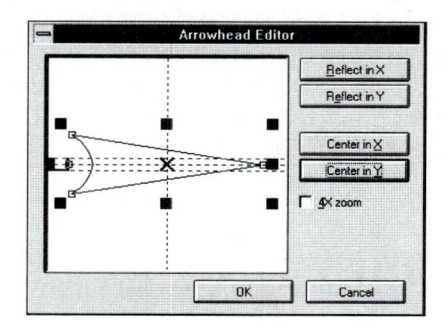

Caution: If you click on OK and close the Arrowhead Editor, you will permanently modify this arrowhead in the Arrows display box. You can come back and move everything back to its original position (see the illustration in the "Arrows" section in the early part of this chapter to see how this should look). But unless you want to do that, choose Cancel to exit the Arrowhead Editor.

5. If you don't mind permanently modifying the second arrowhead, click on OK to close the Editor and return to the Outline Pen dialog box. Then click on OK to return to your drawing, and click Apply in the Pen roll-up. Your arrow should look like this:

6. Select New from the File menu and No to clear the work area.

The Arrowhead Editor is used to stretch, scale, and position an existing arrowhead in relation to the line it will be applied to. If you want to create a new arrowhead, do so in CorelDRAW!, as you would any other object (if you build an arrowhead with multiple objects, select them all and use Combine from the Arrange menu to make one object out of them). Then use the Create Arrow command in the Special menu to save the new arrowhead at the end of the list of arrowheads. It does not matter if you have the relative size of the new arrowhead correct, because you can modify this with the Arrowhead Editor.

In the next section, you will begin working with the pen shapes—Width, Angle, and Stretch— that make calligraphic effects possible in CorelDRAW!.

A Pen Shape for Calligraphic Effects

The Stretch and Angle settings in the Outline Pen dialog box are in a separate enclosed area subtitled "Calligraphy." The Calligraphy option allows you to create variable calligraphic nibs that can be highly effective with freehand drawings and text. If you adjust both the Stretch and Angle settings in various combinations, you can approximate a freehand style of drawing.

In the following exercise, you will experiment with the Nib Shape settings, using some curves you will draw, to achieve both hand-sketched and comic-strip-style looks. You will create three copies of certain drawings and then modify each with different settings.

1. At actual size magnification, and with the rulers turned off, draw an approximation of the objects shown here:

Defining the Outline Pen

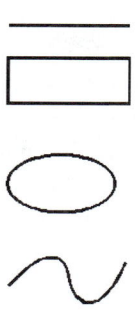

2. With the Pick tool, select the drawings with a marquee box. After selecting all the objects, group them using the Group command in the Arrange menu. Turn off their fill by clicking on the X at the end of the onscreen palette. Open the Outline Pen dialog box and set the Width to .05 inches. Restore the Line Style to a solid line if necessary. Click OK.

3. From the Edit menu select Copy. Then, from the Edit menu select Paste for a second copy of the figures. Drag the highlighted copy to one side of the original. Repeat the Paste operation. Your screen will look something like Figure 6-11. (You may have to decrease your magnification.)

4. Save this image with the File Save As command and the name CURVES.

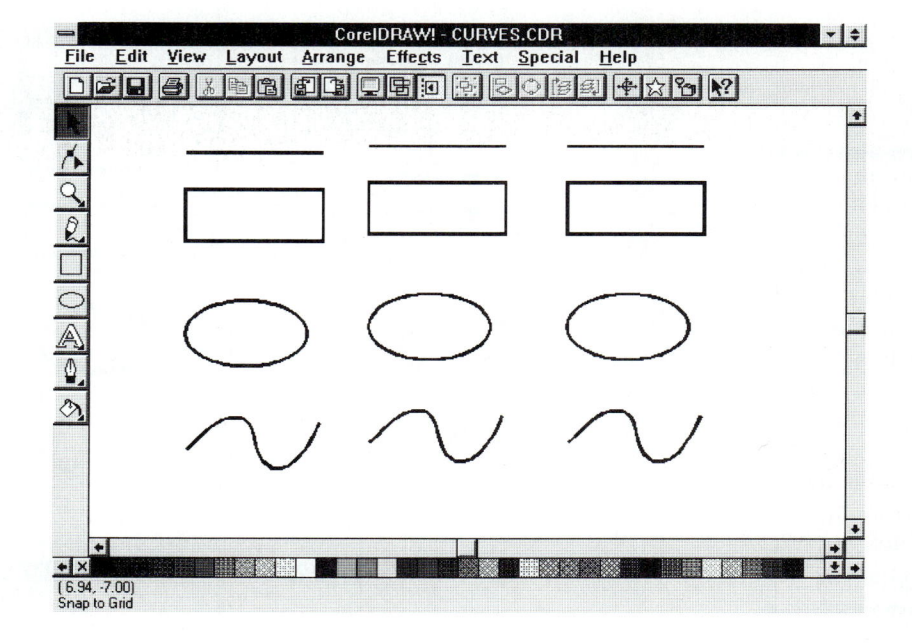

Drawings that will be modified to demonstrate calligraphic effects

Figure 6-11.

5. Select the first group of drawings by clicking on it with the Pick tool. Activate the Outline Pen and open the Outline Pen dialog box. The current Calligraphy settings for this are 100 percent Stretch and 0.0 degrees Angle.

6. Leave the Width value at 0.05 inch, but change the Stretch to 80 percent and the Angle to 10 degrees. This setting translates into a thicker outline and not much slant, with the pen "held" at a 10-degree angle. Click on OK. The effects are shown in outline *a* of Figure 6-12.

7. To vary line thickness, experiment with the Stretch of the nib, expressed as a percentage of the nib width. Keep decreasing the Stretch value all the way to 2 percent, and then select OK. There doesn't seem to be much change.

Tip: It is easier to use the numeric entry boxes to achieve exact Angle and Stretch settings. Interactively using the mouse pointer in the Nib Shape display box is better suited to nibs that can be approximately sized by eye.

As the value in the Stretch numeric entry box decreases, you effectively flatten the nib in one direction; the black symbol representing a pen nib is broad in one dimension and extremely narrow in the other, which makes

Outline *a* shows an Angle of 10 degrees, and Stretch of 80%; *b* an Angle of 80 degrees and Stretch of 10%; *c* an Angle of 10 degrees and Stretch of 10%

Figure 6-12.

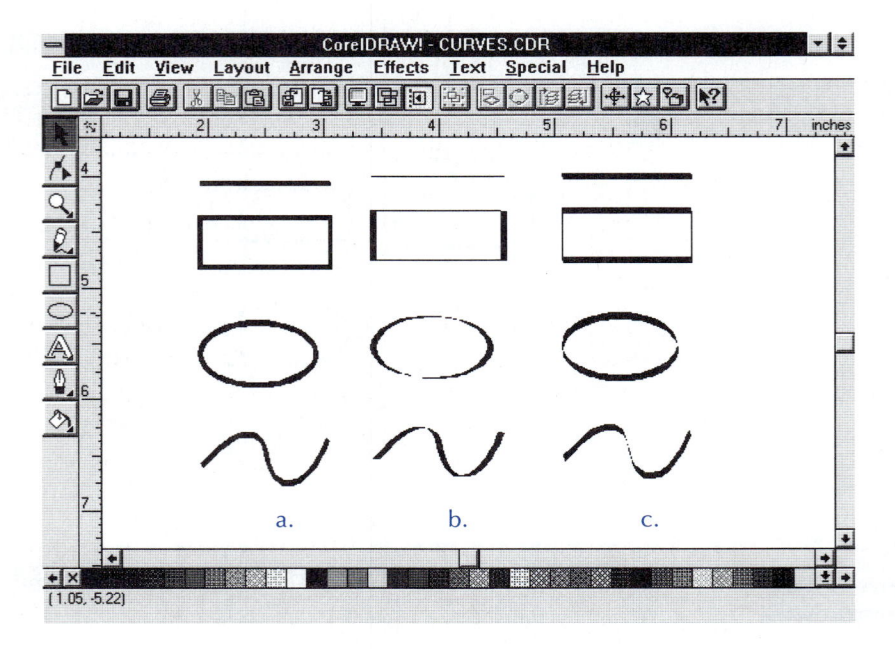

Defining the Outline Pen

more extreme calligraphic effects possible. If you were to increase the Stretch value all the way to 100 percent, the curves of the image would have the same thickness everywhere, and no calligraphic effects could result.

Tip: The Stretch settings represent the relative squareness or roundness of the nib, with 100 percent representing a square nib and 1 percent representing a long and narrow nib. As the Stretch percentage value decreases, the variation in line thickness of a drawn object increases.

1. Select the second group. Access the Outline Pen dialog box once more. Return the Stretch to 10 percent and adjust the Angle of the nib to 80 degrees. You will recall that the Angle setting is analogous to the way you hold a calligraphic pen in your hand (at a 0-degree setting, the Nib Shape display box alters to show you a perfectly vertical nib). Here the angle is quite pronounced.

2. Select OK to exit the dialog box. Now the areas that display the thickest and thinnest lines have shifted (by 70 degrees), as shown in outline *b* of Figure 6-12. Adjusting the Angle value is therefore a convenient way to control where thick and thin lines appear on any selected object.

3. Select the third group. Access the Outline Pen dialog box again and set Width to 0.06 inch, and both Stretch and Angle to 10, and then select OK. The curves are redrawn with a consistently thick outline, much like a cartoon character. See outline *c* of Figure 6-12.

Tip: Click on the Default button. This resets the Stretch and Angle settings to the default values of 100 percent and 0 degrees, respectively—a square nib with no variations in thickness.

4. Experiment with Stretch and Angle settings at this outline width, too. For example, to obtain greater variation in line thickness, set Stretch at a reduced value, such as 4 percent. To change the placement of the thinner segments of the curve, try different Angle settings.

5. Select New from the File menu and answer No to saving the changes to clear the screen.

Chapter 23 gives you more information on how to trace bitmap and scanned images.

The possibilities for creating custom calligraphic nibs should spark your imagination. An interesting use for an image sketched faintly at 0.01-inch width might be as a background illustration in a newsletter, where the text overprints the image without obscuring it totally. You have probably seen applications like this involving outlines of scanned photographs. Chapter 23 will give you more information on how to outline bitmap and scanned images.

Tip: Avoid using 0.00-inch widths unless your draft printer is also the printer you will be using for your final output. As an outline Width setting, 0.00 inch represents the thinnest line your printer is capable of printing. For PostScript printers, this is 1 pixel or 0.03 inch, but for a Linotronic or other high-resolution imagesetter, 0.00 inch could represent something even thinner. Because of the variations among printers, this setting does not truly represent a fixed width, and the screen does not display a WYSIWYG representation of it.

Angle settings are especially useful to help you fine-tune the exact location of thick and thin lines within a drawing. With precise, degree-by-degree control available, you can make sure that thinner areas of a selected curve are positioned exactly where you want them.

Outline Pen Hints

The range of choices available to you makes the Outline Pen one of the richer areas of CorelDRAW!. The following sections contain selected hints for making the most of your choices and coordinating your settings with the type of work you are doing.

Defining an Outline Pen for Text

Do you want text in your drawings to appear normally? Or are you aiming for exaggerated or stylized effects? For a clean-cut look, it's best to create text without an outline, using the X in the Outline Pen flyout menu. When text has a visible outline, some characters appear to be drawn thicker, with the result that spaces within letters (such as in a lowercase "a" or "e") are partially or wholly filled in. This is especially true when you create text in small point sizes.

If your design calls for outlined text, a good way to maintain readability in smaller point sizes is to activate the Behind Fill option in the Outline Pen dialog box. As mentioned earlier, Behind Fill causes the outline to appear half as thick as it really is, because the other half of the outline is hidden behind the object's fill.

In some cases, you may really prefer a slightly smudgy graphic look of text with thick outlines. Let the purpose and design of your illustration be your guide in choosing how to outline text.

Varying Your Calligraphic Style

Unless you have a background in calligraphy, the wealth of Width, Angle, Stretch, and Corners settings available to you in the Outline Pen dialog box can be confusing. The following hints should help put you on the right track if you know the effect you would like to achieve.

Desktop publishers can create faint background illustrations from original artwork or scanned photos and then overprint them with text. The result is a visible but not distracting piece of artwork that enhances the mood of an article or feature. Recommended settings for this kind of graphics effect are Width, 0.03 inch or less; Stretch, 14 percent or less; and a variable Angle according to your tastes. Keep in mind that if you reduce the outline Width setting below 0.02 inch (or 1.2 fractional points), you will not be able to see an accurate representation of the calligraphy on your screen. The outline will still print according to your specifications, however.

Miter corner settings promote an angular look, while rounded corner settings create a smooth appearance.

Illustrators, cartoonists, and other artists seeking a traditional hand-sketched look should set Calligraphy options to achieve the desired variation in line thickness. For finer lines, Outline Pen width should be fairly thin, below 0.05 inch; and for blunter strokes, above 0.06 inch. Stretch should be set to 1 to 2 percent for the maximum variation in line thickness, and closer to 100 percent for minimal variation. The fine-tuning possible with Angle settings permits you to place thicker or thinner lines at exact locations.

For those who are interested in extremely broad calligraphic strokes, consider setting Stretch below 100 percent, removing the fill of an object, and then varying the Angle settings. The example text that follows has a three-dimensional look because it was created at a Width of 0.04 inch, at an Angle of 75 degrees, and with a Stretch of 10 percent:

outline pen

Tip: When the Angle field is 0.0, the pen is vertical. When the Angle is increased, the slant of the pen increases. When the Stretch is 100 percent (the maximum value allowed), the nib shape is a square. When the Stretch is reduced, the nib becomes thinner.

Copying Outline Styles

You can imagine how useful the Copy Attributes From command from the Edit menu can be when you need to copy Outline Pen styles to, or from, even larger blocks of text or groups of objects.

Follow these steps to use the Copy Attributes From command:

1. Have both objects on the screen—those containing the attributes to be copied and those to be copied to.
2. Click with the Pick tool on the object to be copied to.
3. Select Copy Attributes From from the Edit menu. This dialog box is displayed:

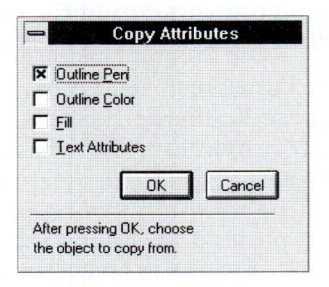

![Copy Attributes dialog box with Outline Pen checked, Outline Color, Fill, and Text Attributes unchecked. OK and Cancel buttons. Text reads: After pressing OK, choose the object to copy from.]

4. Place a check mark beside the Outline Pen option. Click on OK. The pointer turns into an arrow.
5. Move the arrow to the object to copy from and click the pointer. Attributes will be copied to the first selected object from the second.

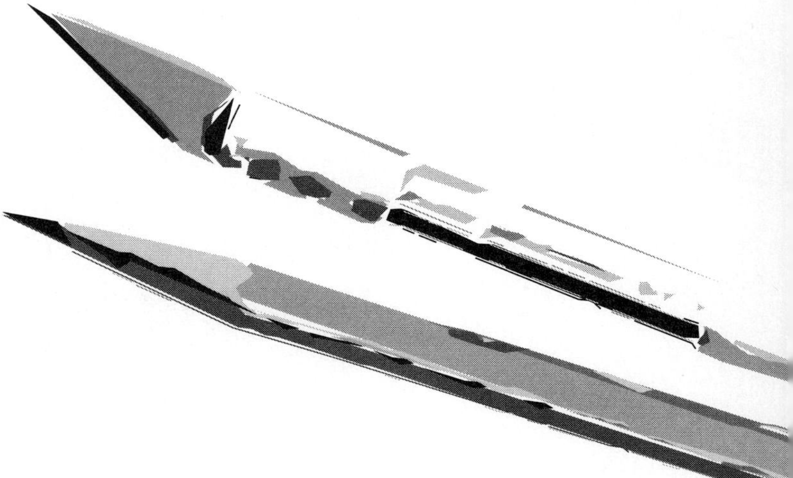

DEFINING OUTLINE and FILL COLOR

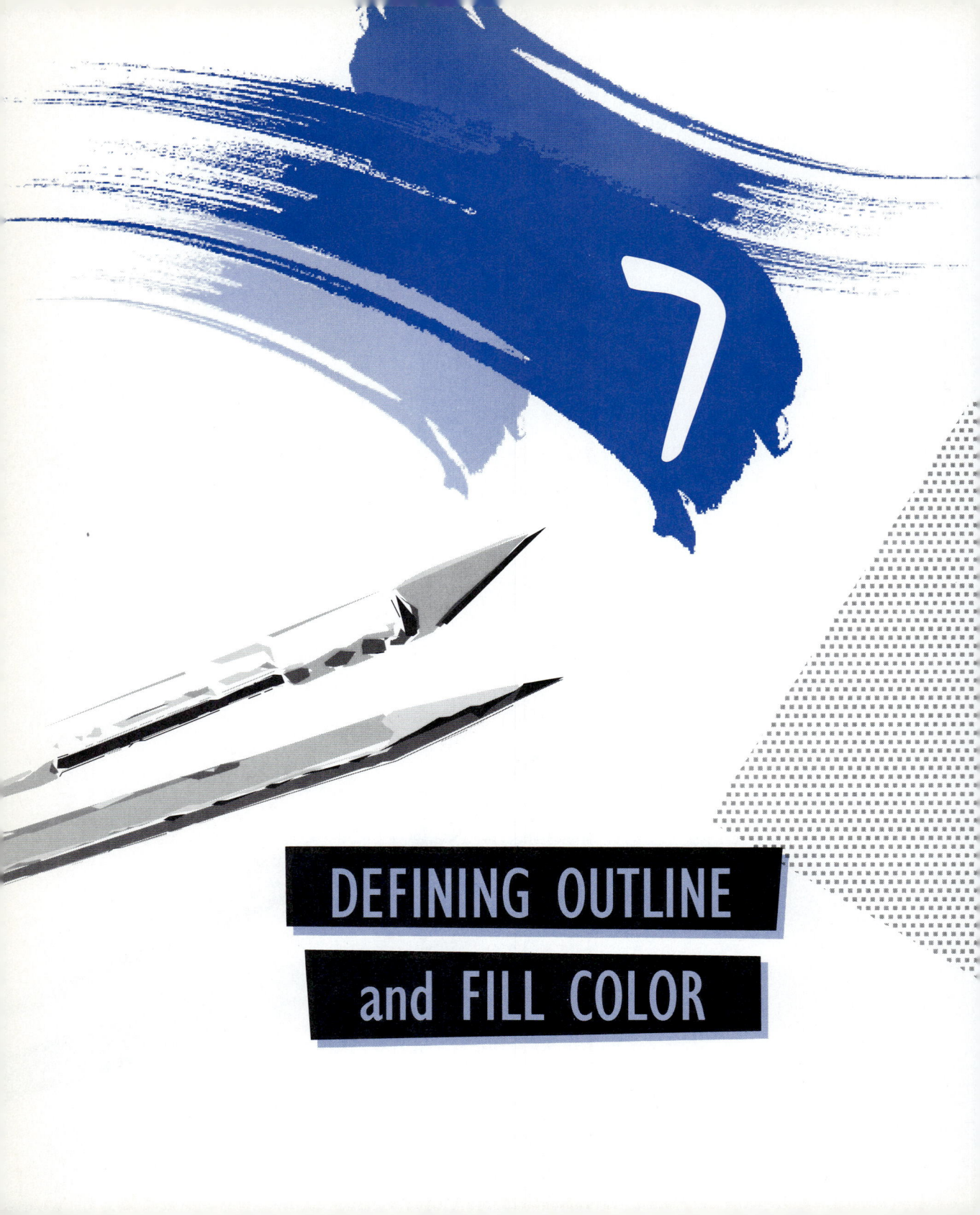

To define an object's outline completely in CorelDRAW!, you must define both the Outline Pen shape and the Outline Color attributes. You learned how to select attributes for the Outline Pen in Chapter 6; in this chapter, you will begin to define Outline Color. As you may recall, the Outline Pen allows you to draw with the characteristic style of a calligraphic pen, using "nibs" of various sizes. Outline Color represents the colors and textures that flow from the pen.

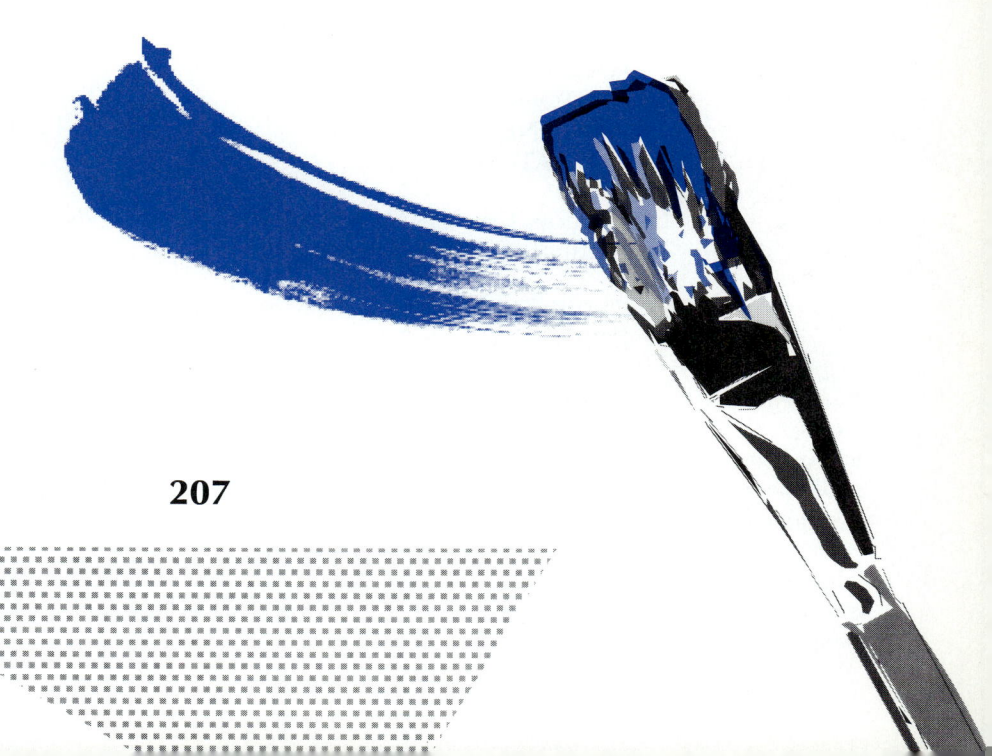

This chapter also introduces you to the CorelDRAW! Fill tool. The Fill tool, as its icon suggests, functions like a paint bucket with a limitless supply of paint, capable of filling the interior of any *leakproof* object. A leakproof object is any object that is a closed path; such objects include everything you create with the Rectangle and Ellipse tools as well as objects created with multiple straight and curved lines in which you made sure to close each intersection. If you draw a curve object in which the two end nodes do not join, the object remains an open path, and you cannot fill it. When you select such an object, the words "Open Path" appear at the right side of the status line. (You can close an open path by joining its end nodes with the Shape tool, as you will learn in Chapter 9.)

Both the Outline and Fill tools offer you a choice between two different color systems—spot color and process color—for assigning color to an object. In the *spot color* system, each color is assigned a unique name or number. Spot color works best for images that contain only a few colors, such as headings in newsletters or single-color objects within black-and-white graphics. The *process color* system, on the other hand, specifies colors in terms of a mix of primary colors or color properties. Process color is more appropriate to use when you plan traditional four-color printing of images that contain a large number of colors.

CorelDRAW! offers four standard color-matching systems used in the printing industry, only one of which is spot color (although FOCOLTONE can simulate spot color):

> FOCOLTONE Colors
> PANTONE Spot Color
> PANTONE Process Color
> TRUMATCH Colors

In addition, CorelDRAW! has five other methods or *models* for specifying color, all of which are process color:

> CMYK (Cyan, Magenta, Yellow, Black) color model
> RGB (Red, Green, Blue) color model
> HSB (Hue, Saturation, Brightness) color model
> Grayscale
> Uniform Colors

You will find more information about color systems and color separation principles in Chapter 12.

Your options for assigning outline and fill colors do not end with the choice of a variety of colors. Unlike a hand-held pen, the CorelDRAW! pen not only dispenses "ink" in all colors of the rainbow, it can lay down an assortment of halftone screens for PostScript printing. In addition, the Fill tool can dispense other types of fills that the Outline Color tool does not provide:

Defining Outline and Fill Color

fountain fills in any combination of colors, two-color and full-color pattern fills from the CorelDRAW! library, texture fills, and 42 different grayscale PostScript texture fills. You will learn more about these types of fills in "Custom Fountain Fills," "Bitmap and Vector Fill Patterns," and "PostScript Texture Fills" later in this chapter.

The exercises in this chapter give you practice in specifying color, gray shades, and PostScript halftone screen patterns for your object outlines and fills. The exercises also give you practice using fountain fills, bitmap fills, vector pattern fills, and PostScript texture fills for objects. The CorelDRAW! window faithfully reproduces your settings, unless you have chosen a PostScript halftone screen or texture fill. Since you cannot preview these types of outlines or fills, you must print out your work on a PostScript printer in order to view it. See Chapter 12 for assistance with printing.

Defining an Object's Outline Color Attributes

You define outline colors in CorelDRAW! using the Outline Color dialog box, shown in Figure 7-1, which you access from the Outline Pen flyout menu. This dialog box allows you to choose a color *model* (the method of defining color) as well as a color, and to select from among several options for other color attributes. The options available in the Outline Color dialog box are determined by the color model or system selected in the Show drop-down list box. You will be using the Outline Color dialog box throughout this chapter; its features will be covered in detail as they are used.

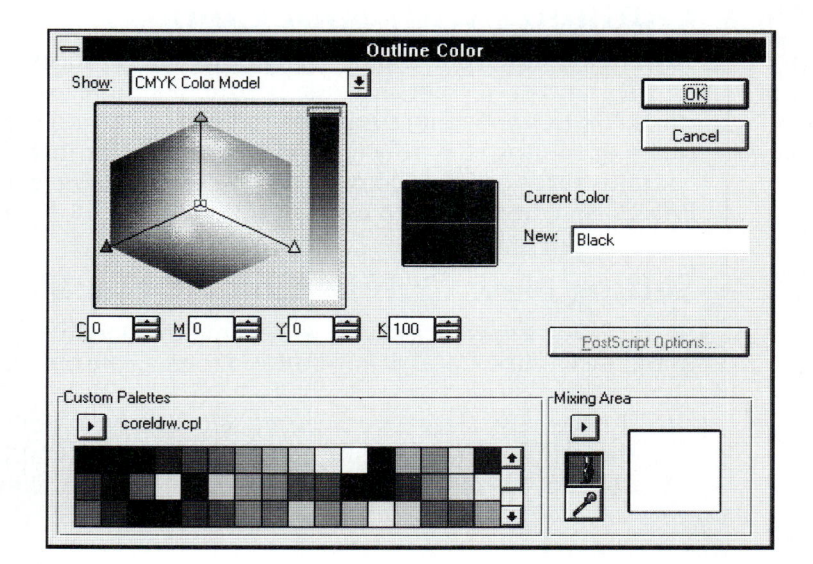

Outline Color dialog box
Figure 7-1.

Tip: If your Outline Color dialog box does not look like Figure 7-1, it has been previously used and left in another mode. You will see how to change this in a moment.

Your first step in defining Outline Color attributes is to determine whether you want to define the attributes for existing objects or for objects not yet rendered. (An existing object can be one that you have just drawn or one that you have saved previously.) When defining Outline Color attributes for an existing object, you are in effect editing its current attributes. The changes you make apply to that object only, not to additional objects you may create later.

On the other hand, when you click on an option in the Outline Pen flyout menu without first selecting an object, CorelDRAW! assumes that you want to change the standard or default attributes for objects that you draw in the future. The object or series of objects that you draw next will automatically incorporate the newly defined Outline Color attributes.

Tip: Always work in full color mode when you alter Outline Color attributes. Wireframe mode does not show you how the selected outline color looks. For most attributes, full color mode lets you see the result of your changes instantly.

Outlining with Spot Color

Use spot color with a PostScript printer since it gives you access to special PostScript halftone screen patterns.

You should base your choice between spot and process color in CorelDRAW! on the number of colors in your picture. If an image contains more than three colors, you would probably find spot color too expensive and time-consuming to produce; choose process color instead. If an image contains three or fewer colors, and you require close color matching, use the PANTONE color model to assign a unique spot color name to each color.

Setting New Outline Color Defaults

In the following exercise, you will define the default Outline Color attributes using the Outline Color dialog box and then create objects with those defaults.

1. If necessary, clear the screen by selecting New from the File menu and then click on the Outline Pen tool. When the Outline Pen flyout menu appears, select the Outline Color icon, the first icon in the second row.

Defining Outline and Fill Color

Outline Color default dialog box
Figure 7-2.

It looks like a color wheel. The dialog box shown in Figure 7-2 appears, asking you which default settings you want to change.

2. Verify that Graphic is selected and click on OK. The Outline Color dialog box is displayed.

3. Select spot color by clicking on the down arrow to the right of the Show drop-down list box and then clicking on PANTONE Spot Colors. The Outline Color dialog box should now look like Figure 7-3. (You may not show the same color selected.)

There are some differences between the Outline Color dialog box with a spot color method selected (as shown in Figure 7-3) and the same dialog box with

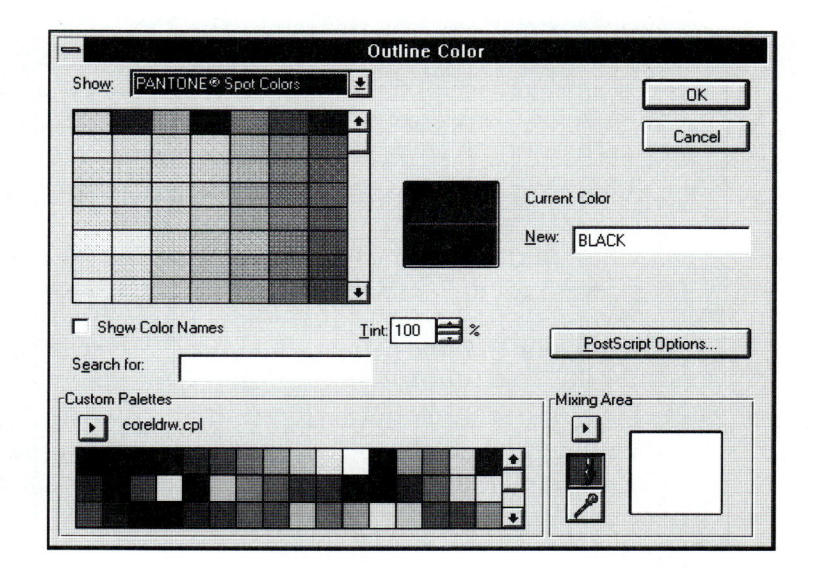

Outline Color dialog box for PANTONE Spot Colors
Figure 7-3.

a process color method selected (as shown in Figure 7-1). These differences are largely a function of the color model and will be covered later in this chapter. Only the spot color dialog box allows you to adjust the percentage of tint and to select a PostScript halftone and its attributes (see "Outlining with PostScript Halftone Screen Patterns" later in this chapter). All versions of the Outline Color dialog box have a small Custom Palette button that opens the menu shown here:

```
n Palettes
  Add Color
  Delete Color...
  New
  Open...
  Save
  Save As...
  Set As Default
```

The Palette menu allows you to add colors to or delete colors from the current palette, and to load a palette from your hard disk or save it to disk.

Once you have made changes in the Outline Color dialog box, those changes will be reflected in its settings the next time you open the dialog box. Therefore, you can make decisions on spot versus process color and the model and palette you want to use when you begin a drawing, and those changes will keep displaying in the dialog box until you change them.

The colors you select using spot color system are from the PANTONE Matching System. Since the colors that appear in the color display box are only approximations, you should use the PANTONE Color Reference Manual to evaluate your choice of colors before printing. In addition, you can specify a percentage of the tint of any spot colors you select. The effect of settings below 100 percent is to render a lighter shade of the selected color on your monitor or color printout.

Continue setting the Outline Color defaults with these steps:

4. Click on the middle color in the top row of the color palette. The selected color, PANTONE Process Black CV, appears in a color display box on the right of the dialog box. The % Tint numeric entry box shows a value of 100 (the default value). The PANTONE identification name for this color displays in the Color Name text box.

5. Click on OK to set the default Outline Color attributes and exit the Outline Color dialog box. New objects that you create will now have the default outline color. Follow the next steps to create a new object.

Defining Outline and Fill Color

6. From the Outline Pen flyout menu select the 2-point width (top row, fourth from the right), click on OK to have it apply to graphic objects, then, at actual size (1:1) magnification, with the Freehand tool draw several curves, as shown in Figure 7-4. (If your closed loop at the bottom is filled with black, open the Fill tool and click on the X to turn off the fill.)

The curves are created with the default outline color and 2-point line width. In the next section you will learn how to change the outline color for existing objects.

Assigning Spot Color Outlines

In the following exercise, you will assign spot colors and shades of gray to the outline of your existing CorelDRAW! objects (created in the previous exercise).

1. Drag a marquee around all of the objects you created in the previous exercise to select them, and choose Group from the Arrange menu.
2. To begin editing the existing Outline Color attributes, click on the Outline Pen and the Custom Outline Color icon, or press SHIFT-F12. The Outline Color dialog box appears.

Tip: If an item is selected, you can immediately open the Outline Color dialog box by pressing the shortcut keys SHIFT-F12.

3. Click on the second color from the right in the top row of the color palette. The PANTONE identification name and number for this color,

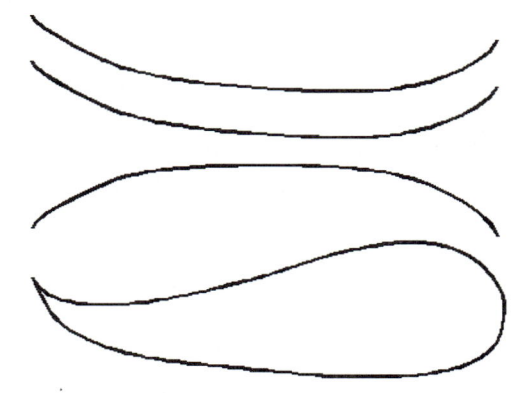

Curved shapes in PANTONE Process Black CV
Figure 7-4.

"PANTONE Red 032 CV," displays in the color name text box. If you have the PANTONE Color Reference Manual, you can compare what you see on the screen with what you see in the manual. There probably is a difference since most color monitors are not perfectly calibrated.

4. Click on OK in the dialog box. Notice that the curves have changed to a red color.
5. Open the Outline Color dialog box again. Once more click on PANTONE Process Black (the middle color in the top row) and set the tint value to 51 percent. The color preview window in the dialog box now displays a 51 percent gray shade in the lower part of the window, which you can compare with the current color in the top of the window.
6. Click on OK. If you have a VGA or Super VGA display card, you will see an actual representation of a 51 percent gray shade in the drawing, as shown in Figure 7-5.
7. Open the Outline Color dialog box once more, reselect PANTONE Red 032 CV (second color from the right in the top row), and then return the tint value to 51 percent. You have just selected a lighter tint of PANTONE Red.
8. Select OK to exit the dialog box with the new Outline Color setting.
9. Save this as CURVES2 and clear the screen by selecting New from the File menu.

Both the Outline Pen shape and color defaults must be set before creating an object. In the next section you will set both defaults and use them with Artistic Text.

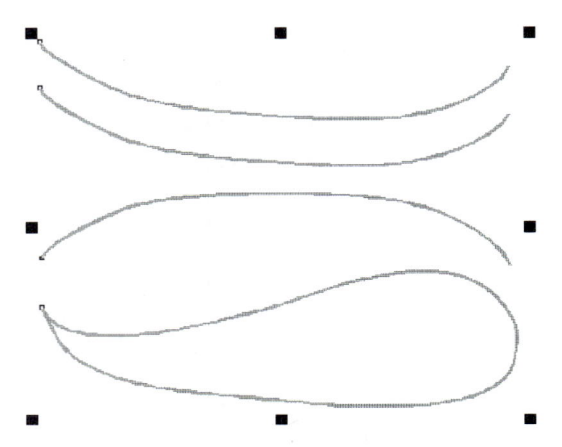

Curves at 51% gray shade
Figure 7-5.

Defining Outline and Fill Color

Setting New Spot Color Outline Pen Defaults

In this exercise, you will change defaults for both the Outline Pen and Spot Outline Color attributes, and then create new objects that exhibit those defaults automatically.

1. Set the display magnification to actual size (1:1).
2. Without creating or selecting any objects, click on the Outline Pen and on the Outline Pen Dialog tool, the leftmost tool in the first row of the flyout menu. A dialog box similar to the one you saw in Figure 7-2 appears, asking whether you want to change default Outline Pen values. Select Artistic Text (you can leave Graphic Text selected in addition) and click on OK to access the Outline Pen dialog box.
3. When the Outline Pen dialog box appears, set the Outline Pen attributes as follows: Width, 0.15 inch; Style, solid line; Corners, sharp (miter); Line Caps, butt (top option); Stretch, 10 percent; Angle,–45 degrees. Do not check either Behind Fill or Scale With Image.
4. Click on the Color button at the top-left section of the dialog box. The color drop-down palette opens, as shown here:

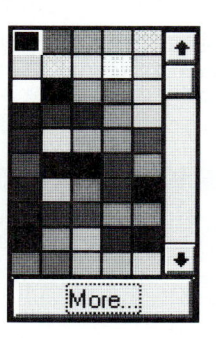

This color palette, although smaller, has the same colors to choose from as the color palette in the Outline Color dialog box.

5. Click on the More button at the bottom of the color palette. The Outline Color dialog box appears.
6. Verify that PANTONE Spot Colors is selected, then choose PANTONE Blue 072 CV color (first box on the right in the top row), and tint value of 100 percent. Select OK twice to save these settings and exit both the Outline Color and Outline Pen dialog boxes.
7. Activate Rulers, make sure Wireframe is off, and then click on the Text tool. Click in the lower-left section of your screen.
8. Open the Text roll-up window from the Text menu and select the following text attributes: no justification, BrushScript BT, normal, 300

points. Click on Apply, type a capital **A**, and select the Pick tool. The letter "A" should be selected. If you followed all the steps up to this point, the text should have a default fill of black. Your screen should look like Figure 7-6, except that the color of the outline is blue. Remember that *all* of the new Outline Pen and Color attributes you have selected apply to the new object automatically.

9. Clear the screen by selecting New from the File menu. Do not save your work.

If you create the same kinds of images regularly in your work, you probably have strong personal preferences for what you would like default outlines to look like. If you wish, start a new drawing on your own, setting up the Outline Pen and Outline Color default attributes that will apply to the basic elements in your drawing. You can edit settings for objects that should have different outline fills by selecting them after you draw them and accessing the appropriate dialog boxes. If you are not satisfied with the results of your Outline Pen or Outline Color attribute settings, you can make adjustments during the drawing process.

You may find selecting a particular spot color from the color palette difficult—it can be hard to find a particular PANTONE color from the more than 700 that are shown. If you have a PANTONE Color Reference Manual or know the PANTONE name or number of a particular color, there is

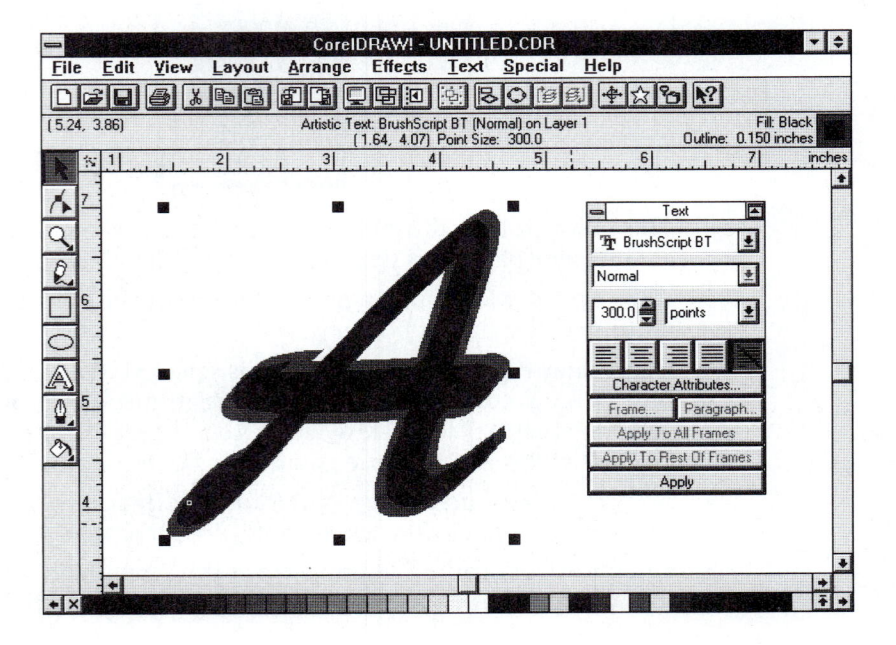

Letter created with new default PANTONE spot color outline
Figure 7-6.

Defining Outline and Fill Color

another way to select a spot color. Select Show Color Names in the Outline Color dialog box, and a list of PANTONE color names, as shown in Figure 7-7, is provided. When you select a color on the list, it is displayed in the color display box to the right of the list. Also, you can enter a few characters of a PANTONE name or number in the Search For box, and that name or number will be highlighted in the list while the color is shown in the display box.

If you click on OK to leave the Outline Color dialog box, you are returned to your drawing. The next time you select the Outline Color icon from the Outline Pen flyout menu, you will get the list of PANTONE colors that you just left (Figure 7-7), not the palette shown in Figure 7-3. If you want to return to the palette when you next select the Outline Color icon, deselect Show color names before leaving the Outline Color dialog box.

Using the Pen Roll-Up for Outline Color

The Pen roll-up, which you'll remember from Chapter 6, opens from the Outline Pen flyout menu (second icon from the left in the top row). It provides two ways to select or change outline color.

The first is the color button (fourth bar up from the bottom), which opens the same color palette you accessed from the Outline Pen dialog box. Clicking on a color in the Pen roll-up palette, and then clicking on Apply,

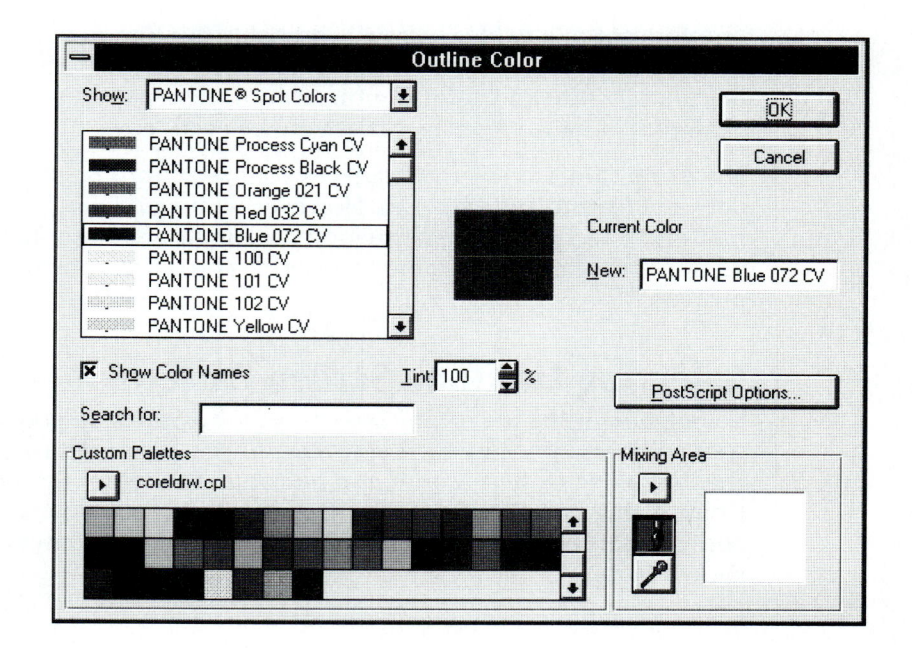

Outline Color dialog box listing spot colors

Figure 7-7.

will apply the color to the outline of the selected object. Clicking on More will access the Outline Color dialog box.

The second method of applying outline color from the Pen roll-up is to click on the Edit button (second from the bottom), which opens the full Outline Pen dialog box. Click on the Color button to open the color palette and then click on More to open the Outline Color dialog box. This is, of course, the same dialog box you get by clicking on the Outline Color icon in the Outline Pen flyout menu, or by pressing SHIFT-F12.

If you own or use a PostScript printer, go on to the next section to learn how to assign a PostScript halftone screen as an outline color. This option is available only when you choose the spot color method, and it takes effect only if you have a PostScript printer. You cannot see it on the screen.

Outlining with PostScript Halftone Screen Patterns

If you work with a PostScript printer, you can elect to fill an outline with a halftone screen pattern of the currently selected spot color. This option is available only when you have selected spot color as your Outline Color method. The CorelDRAW! window displays PostScript halftone screen patterns as solid colors only; to see the patterns, you must print the images on a PostScript printer.

The concept of a *halftone screen* is probably familiar to you already: it is a method of representing continuous tone or color by patterns of dots. Black-and-white and color photographs in newspapers and magazines are examples of halftone images that you see every day.

Since you cannot view the results of your selections on screen, this section does not feature any exercises. However, some guidelines for selecting halftone screen patterns, frequency, and angle are presented in the next section. Chapter 12 has more instructions on printing with PostScript printers.

Selecting Halftone Screen Patterns

To begin defining a halftone screen outline, make sure you have selected the spot color and tint in which you want to print your outline. Then click on the PostScript Options command button at the center right of the Outline Color dialog box. The PostScript Options dialog box opens. This dialog box contains settings for Type, Frequency, and Angle attributes of patterns, as shown here:

Defining Outline and Fill Color

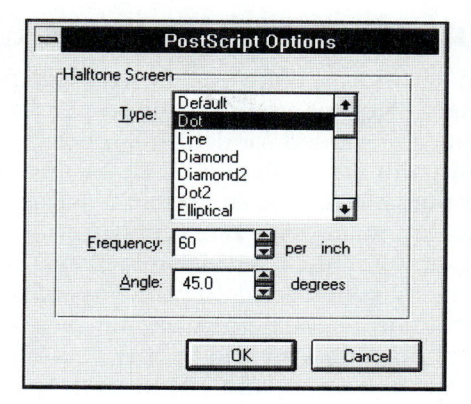

Selecting Halftone Screen Type
The Type option in the PostScript Options dialog box features 15 halftone patterns that are available for your Outline Color work. Your choices are Default, Dot, Line, Diamond, Diamond2, Dot2, Elliptical, Euclidean, Grid, Lines, MicroWaves, OutCircleBlk, OutCircleWhi, Rhomboid, and Star. (Default is a separate, plain or "constant" screen without a pattern in it.) To select a halftone screen type, scroll through the list until you see the name of the desired pattern and click on the name to highlight it.

Selecting Halftone Screen Frequency
The Frequency option in the PostScript Options dialog box allows you to determine how many times per inch the pattern should occur within the outline. The available range is from 0 to 1500 per inch, and the default setting is 60. The number you select depends upon the resolution of your ultimate output device; refer to Chapter 12 for more details on frequency settings for PostScript halftone screens.

Setting Halftone Screen Angle
The third option in the PostScript Options dialog box allows you to specify the angle of the screen pattern when you print it. Keep in mind that the halftone screen angle remains constant, no matter how you transform an object. If you stretch, scale, rotate, or skew an object after assigning it a halftone screen outline, you could alter its appearance significantly. If you do not want this to happen, remember to change the screen angle after performing a transform operation, to match the offset of the transformed object. You will achieve the best results by setting your screen angle at 0, 45, 90, and 180 degrees.

Outlining with Process Color

In the printing industry, color units are used more often than percentages because they are more accurate since there are 255 units in a 100 percent saturation.

With the process color system, you specify color in terms of either a set of primary colors or a set of color properties. CorelDRAW! provides three methods or models for defining process color: CMYK (cyan, magenta, yellow, and black), RGB (red, green, and blue), and HSB (hue, saturation, and brightness). Both CMYK and RGB define a color in terms of the constituent colors in the model, while HSB defines a color in terms of color properties. For example, "Brick Red" is defined as 0 percent cyan, 60 percent magenta, 80 percent yellow, and 20 percent black in the CMYK model. In RGB, it is 204 color units (80 percent) of red, 51 color units (20 percent) of green, and 0 color units of blue; and in HSB, it is 15 degrees of hue, 255 units (100 percent) saturation, and 204 units (80 percent) brightness. You can use any of the three models you are most comfortable with, but CorelDRAW! will convert RGB and HSB to CMYK. Therefore, CMYK will be the primary focus of this book.

You can specify over 16 million colors by using various CMYK percentages. As mentioned previously, you should specify process color instead of spot color when your drawing includes four or more colors and you plan to reproduce it through the four-color printing process.

CMYK is the four-color standard for the printing industry.

CorelDRAW! supports color separation for Process as well as spot color. When you specify color in CMYK terms, your printer generates only four sheets (one each for cyan, magenta, yellow, and black) for every image page, no matter how many colors the image contains. When you specify in spot color terms, on the other hand, the printer generates a separate sheet for every single color used in the drawing. You will learn more about printing Spot and process colors and their separation in Chapter 12.

To specify process colors for an existing object, you select or create the object, click on the Outline Pen, and click again on the Outline Color icon in the flyout menu. When the Outline Color dialog box appears, you select one of the color models to use in defining the color you want. If you pick CMYK, RGB, or HSB, you will be able to create a color by defining a mixture of the constituent colors or color properties, using a dialog box that looks like Figure 7-1. If you pick PANTONE or TRUMATCH Process Colors for the color model, you can select a color from a palette or from a list of names similar to the palette and list you saw with spot color.

For each color model, the Outline Color dialog box looks a little different. The Outline Color dialog boxes for HSB and RGB look, and operate, very much like the one shown in Figure 7-1 for CMYK. In the upper-left corner of the dialog box is a color selector that consists of two objects filled with varying shades of color. By dragging a marker in either object you can define a color. For CMYK and RGB, markers can be moved along three axes in the left-hand object while a singular marker can be moved only up or down in

Defining Outline and Fill Color

the rectangular box. In the CMYK model, the left-hand object defines percentages of cyan, magenta, and yellow while the rectangle defines the percentage of black. In the RGB model, the left-hand object defines percentages of red, green, and blue, which the rectangle also does while keeping the proportion of red, green, and blue the same relative to each other. In the HSB model, the circle defines the hue (it is specified in degrees from 0 to 360 around the circle) and the percentage of saturation (specified by the distance from the center), while the rectangle defines brightness.

Below the visual selector is a set of numeric entry boxes and scroll arrows for selecting the desired percentages or color units of constituent colors or properties. If you are using a process color reference chart, such as the TRUMATCH Colorfinder, you can look for a color in the chart and then enter the percentages or color units that create that color.

In the lower-right corner of the Outline Color dialog box is the mixing area, where you can create new colors by mixing existing ones. The right-pointing arrow opens a menu from which you can load and save custom paint mixes as well as clear the mixing area. The paint brush allows you to add various colors to the mixing area. When colors are added on top of each other they become mixed in proportion to the stroke of the brush. The eye dropper, then, allows you to pick a very specific color out of the mixing area. The color thus chosen is shown in the color selector and in numeric entry boxes below the color selector as shown in Figure 7-8.

In the following exercise, you will specify both the Outline Pen and Process Outline Color for a text string.

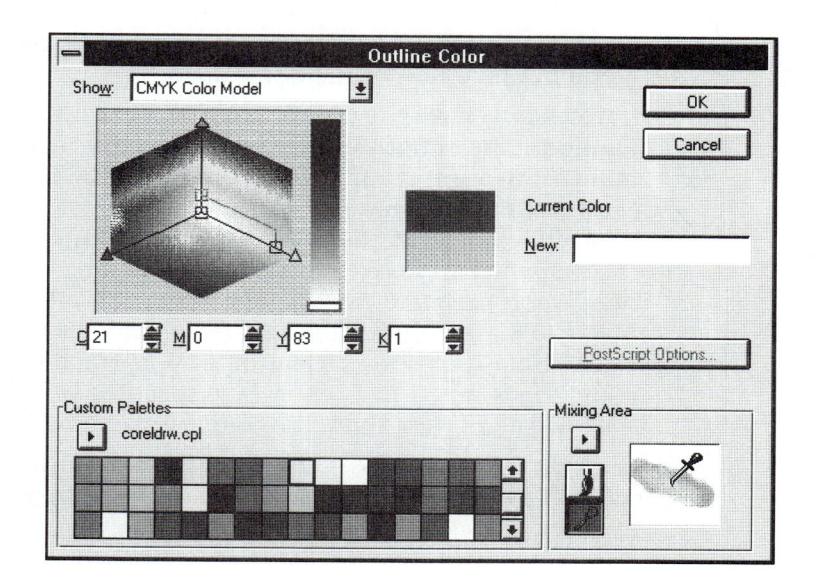

Using the mixing area to create and specify a new color
Figure 7-8.

1. At actual size (1:1) magnification with rulers turned off, select the Text tool, click in the middle of the left side, and type **CorelDRAW!**. Activate the Pick tool to select the text string.
2. Open the Text roll-up and select BrushScript BT Normal, 70-point type. Click on Apply and move or close the roll-up.
3. From the Fill tool flyout menu, click on X to turn off the fill. From the Outline Pen flyout menu, open the Outline Pen dialog box. Select rounded corners, set Width at 0.083 inch (6 points), Stretch at 14 percent, Angle at 0 degrees, and click on OK.

When you are back in the drawing, your screen should look like this:

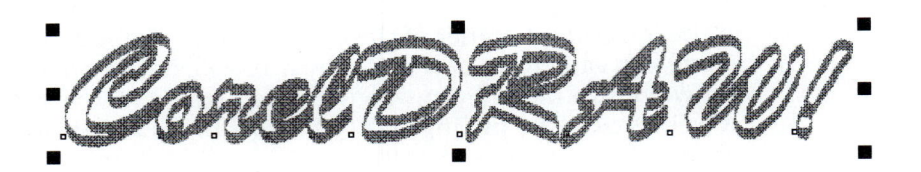

Your settings resulted in a moderately thick text outline, and the calligraphic Nib Shape created an "artistic" look. The rounded corners setting adds a more polished look to the outlines of corners of angular letters. The current color does not do it justice, so you will change it now.

4. With the text string still selected, click on the Outline Pen once more. This time, select the Outline Color icon in the second row of the flyout menu to open the Outline Color dialog box.
5. If necessary, select the CMYK Color Model to switch color selection methods. The options in the dialog box change instantly. Take a moment to again familiarize yourself with the Outline Color dialog box. Move the markers in each of the visual selector boxes and notice how the color changes in the color display box, and how the percentages in the numeric entry boxes change as well. Using the scroll arrows or your mouse and keyboard, set the following color mix: Cyan 40 percent, Magenta 40 percent, Yellow 0 percent, and Black (K) 60 percent. The color display box shows a real-time approximation of changes to the color, as you scroll to or enter each specified value. When you have specified all of the values, the color display box shows a deep navy blue.
6. Click on OK to exit the dialog box. The text string's outline displays as a deep navy blue, providing a contrast to the light background.

Defining Outline and Fill Color

7. Press SHIFT-F12 or click on the Outline Color icon in the Outline Pen flyout menu.
8. Select first RGB and then HSB from the Show drop-down list box and notice that deep navy blue also appears as the defined color in each of these models.

If you click on the same navy blue color (fifth from right, second row) of the color palette at the bottom of the screen, you'll see the name Deep Navy Blue, and that the color percentages are the same. The color is already defined.

Next, define your own color and add it to the custom color palette. Leave the CorelDRAW! text string on your screen and the Outline Color dialog box open. You can use the text string to test your new color.

Defining a New Color and Adding It to the Custom Palettes

The Custom Palettes in the Outline Color dialog box display 94 colors and 10 shades of gray. This is a far cry from the more than 16 million possible colors available with the CMYK model. The color selector in the Outline Color dialog box is Corel's answer to this discrepancy. You have seen how you can define a new color with this color selector when you want to apply it to an object. But if you want to use a color over and over, say a special corporate color you've defined, you will want to add this color to the Outline Color Custom Palettes.

In the following exercise you will define a new color. In the last exercise the color you entered was already on the palette and in the name list. The new color you will define is Deep Royal Blue.

1. Select CMYK Color Model from the Show drop-down list box.
2. Type in the numeric entry boxes, or use the scroll arrows, to define a color mix of 100 percent cyan, 55 percent magenta, 0 percent yellow, and 45 percent black. The color display box will show the color, but the Color Name text entry box is empty because the color is not defined.
3. Click on the Color Name text entry box (identified as New) and type **Deep Royal Blue**. Your dialog box should look like that shown in Figure 7-9. (The squares may appear to be different because of the way the color combinations print in black and white.)
4. Click on OK to return to your drawing and see your new color. More important, clicking on OK defined your new color and added it to the color palette and the name list. See for yourself with the next step.

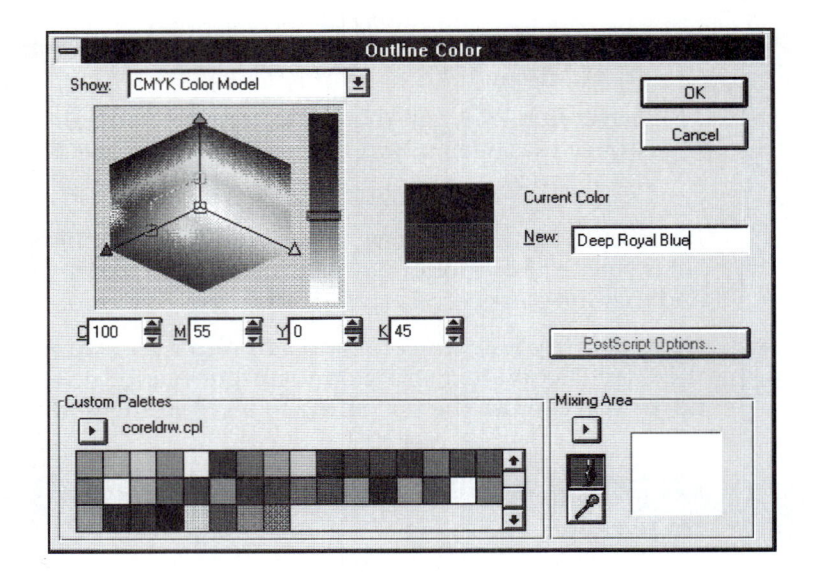

Deep Royal Blue being defined

Figure 7-9.

5. Press SHIFT-F12 to reopen the Outline Color dialog box with your new color highlighted at the bottom of the palette and the name Deep Royal Blue in the Color Name text entry box.

    While it is nice to have a new color in the palette, having it at the end of the list is not very handy. CorelDRAW!, though, allows you to rearrange colors by dragging them around the palette. You can drag a color to any existing location and release the mouse button, and all the existing colors shift to the right and down to accommodate the new color.

6. Point on the new color you just defined (the bottom, rightmost color), press and hold the mouse button while dragging the new color to the top of the palette, and then release the mouse button. Click on the palette's scroll bar above the scroll box and repeat dragging the color up to the top row. On the third repetition, drag the color up to the second row from the top and then over to the fourth color from the right. Now Deep Royal Blue (your new color) is between Deep Navy Blue and Desert Blue, as shown by the pointer in Figure 7-10.

7. Click on OK to close the dialog box and return to the drawing. Leave the text string on your screen to use in the next exercise.

When specifying process colors, you can include as many colors in the picture as you like. When you finally print the image, the results will still be separated into no more than four sheets.

In the next section of this chapter, you will learn a shortcut to specifying Outline Color that will be useful if you usually print to a black-and-white printer.

Defining Outline and Fill Color

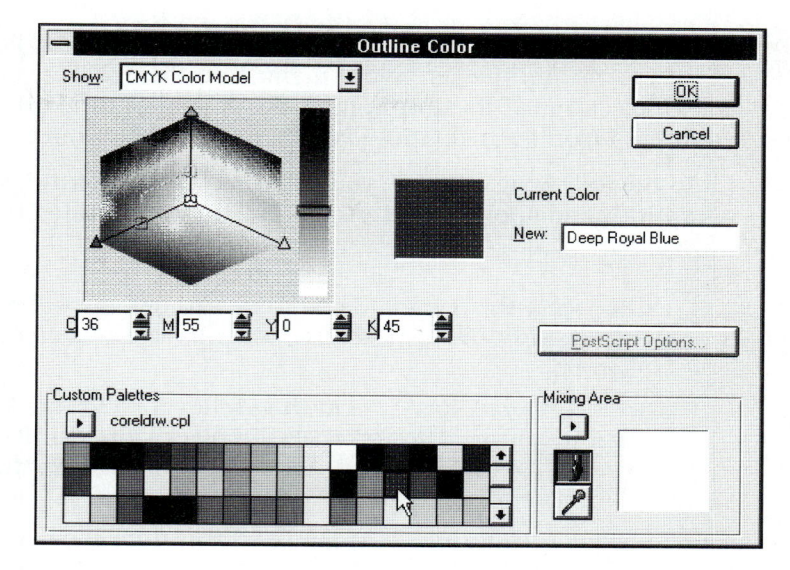

Figure 7-10.
Result of dragging Deep Royal Blue up next to Deep Navy Blue

Outlining with Black, White, or Gray

When you worked with the Outline Pen in Chapter 6, you saw how the first row of the Outline Pen flyout menu contained five preset outline widths that you could select simply by clicking on the desired icon. The arrangement of the second row of the Outline Pen flyout menu is similar. Following the Outline Color icon is a series of seven symbols that let you select a preset outline color (gray shade) quickly, without having to set attributes in a dialog box. As Figure 7-11 shows, the seven outline color options are white, black, and 10, 30, 50, 70, and 90 percent black.

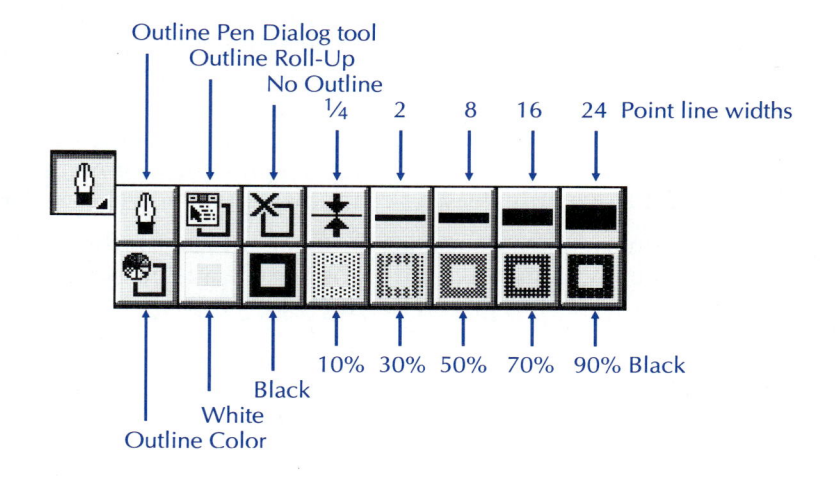

Figure 7-11.
Preset black, white, and gray shades in the Outline Pen flyout

To select a preset Outline Color for an existing object, you select the object, access the Outline Pen flyout menu, and then click on the appropriate icon. To select one of these options as the default outline color, click on the desired icon in the Outline Pen flyout menu without first selecting an object.

In the following exercise, you will select several of the preset Outline Color options and apply them to the text string you created in the previous exercise.

1. Re-create the "CorelDRAW!" text string if you did not leave it on the screen after the last exercise. Magnify the area containing the text as before.
2. Select "CorelDRAW!," and then select the Outline Pen. When the flyout menu appears, click on the solid black icon, third from the left in the second row of the menu. The outline of the text string changes from dark blue to solid black.
3. Select the Outline Pen again and this time click on the 50 percent black outline color, the third symbol from the right in the second row. Now the text outline shows a much lighter color, as you see here:

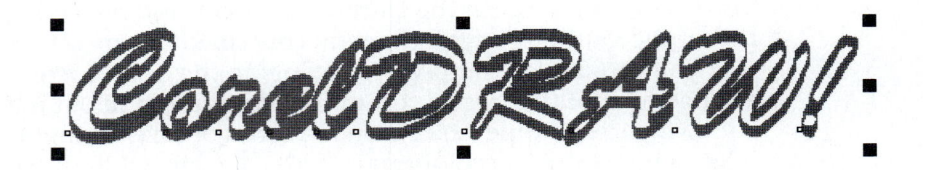

4. Experiment with different preset Outline Color settings. Leave the text string on the screen for the next exercise.

Remember that you are not limited to these preset shades of gray if you use a black-and-white printer. You can use either the spot color or process color system to define other shades of gray. To define shades of gray using the spot color method, access the Outline Color dialog box and set shades of gray by clicking on black and setting % Tint in increments of 1 percent. To define custom shades of gray using the process color method, define a percentage for black only, leaving cyan, magenta, and yellow all at 0 percent.

You can also use the preset shades of gray in the Outline Pen flyout menu in combination with the PostScript halftone screens.

Defining Outline and Fill Color

Copying Outline Color and Pen Styles

In previous chapters, you learned how to use the Copy Attributes From command in the Edit menu to copy text or Outline Pen attributes from one object to another. You use the same command to copy Outline Color attributes between objects, as you will see in the following exercise.

1. With the "CorelDRAW!" text string still on the screen from the previous exercise, zoom out to reduce the size enough to draw a rectangle around the string.
2. With the Rectangle tool, draw a rectangle around the word "CorelDRAW!"; then select the Pick tool and turn off the fill by clicking on the X in the Fill flyout menu. The result is a rectangle around the text string. The rectangle is selected, by default.
3. Select the Copy Attributes From command in the Edit menu. When the Copy Attributes dialog box appears, click on both the Outline Pen and the Outline Color check boxes, and then click on OK. The pointer turns into a thick arrow to use to point to the source object from which to copy its outline attributes.
4. Click on the "CorelDRAW!" text string. The rectangle redisplays to show the same outline thickness and color as the text string, like this:

CorelDRAW!

If your rectangle does not come out as you just saw, it could be that the specifications on your text have been changed. They should be a 6-point line width, with a 50 percent black outline color, and no fill.

5. Clear the screen by selecting the New command and not saving the changes.

For more practice with the Outline Color tool, you can go back to the LANDSCAP.CDR file or any other landscape drawing that you created and edited in earlier chapters. The default outlines and fills or the objects in those files are black, but you can begin to differentiate objects by varying their outlines. You can give custom outlines to interior objects or copy outline styles to multiple objects at one time.

Defining Fill Color Attributes

The Fill tool can only fill "leakproof" objects—those with a closed path.

The final step in completing an object in CorelDRAW! is to define its fill attributes. The Fill tool is similar to the Outline Color tool in that it can dispense spot color, process color, and PostScript halftone screen patterns. In addition, the Fill tool can apply various fountain, pattern, and texture fills.

The Fill tool flyout menu, shown in Figure 7-12, is accessed from the Fill tool icon. The first, or leftmost, icon in the top row of the Fill tool flyout menu is the Uniform Fill icon. This icon opens the Uniform Fill dialog box, which lets you define custom spot and process color fills and PostScript halftone screen patterns. The next icon opens the Fill roll-up window, which gives you access to the color palette and to certain other tools in the Fill flyout menu. The last five icons in the top row of the flyout menu let you access dialog boxes to apply and edit fountain, two-color pattern, full-color pattern, texture, and PostScript texture fills. The first icon of the second row (the X icon) causes an object to have a transparent (or no) fill. The next two icons in the second row let you specify preset fill colors of white and black. The remaining icons in the bottom row let you specify one of four preset shades of gray (10, 30, 50, and 70 percent black) as the fill.

Setting default fill attributes is accomplished in the same manner as outline defaults; settings defined without any objects being selected become the new default fill attributes. Objects you create in the future will be filled with the default fill attributes automatically. When defining fill attributes for an existing object, you are editing that object's current fill. The changes you make apply to that object only, not to additional objects you may create later.

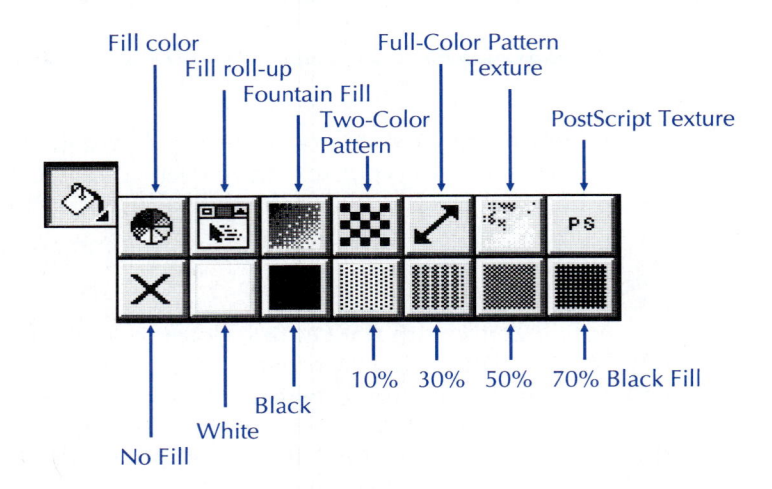

Icons in the Fill tool flyout
Figure 7-12.

Defining Outline and Fill Color

The remaining sections in this chapter offer you practice in working with each dialog box and selecting fill attributes for each of the major types of fills. Whether you are setting fill attributes for selected objects or altering default attributes for objects you haven't drawn yet, the main steps involved are similar.

Filling an Object with Uniform Spot Color

To fill an object with spot color, process color, or a PostScript halftone screen pattern, you use the settings in the Uniform Fill dialog box. This dialog box appears when you click on the Fill Color tool, the first icon in the Fill tool flyout menu. You can also open the Uniform Fill dialog box with the shortcut keys SHIFT-F11. The name "Uniform Fill" distinguishes this type of fill conceptually from fountain, pattern, texture, and PostScript texture fills, which involve multiple hues or patterns rather than a single color. Except for the title, the Uniform Fill dialog box is identical in appearance and function to the Outline Color dialog box you worked with previously.

Tip: You will recall that spot color is the preferred color system when an image contains fewer than four colors or if you want to use PostScript halftone screen patterns. If you do not have a PostScript printer at your disposal and your work does not require spot color or four-color printing, you can use either the spot or process color system to specify fill colors.

As mentioned previously, an object must be a closed path in order for you to fill it. However, a closed path does not assure a solid object. If you combine two or more objects, as you learned to do in Chapter 5, "holes" result where the combined objects overlap. You can then create interesting design effects by surrounding the holes with outline and fill colors. Perform the following exercise to create a logo with transparent text, outline it, and assign a uniform fill spot color to it. You will edit this logo throughout the rest of the chapter as you learn new ways to use the Fill tool flyout menu.

1. To prepare the screen, set magnification to actual size (1:1). In the Grid & Scale Setup dialog box on the Layout menu, activate the Snap To Grid; set both Horizontal and Vertical Grid Frequency units to Picas and the frequency to 1; and set the Vertical Grid Origin to 66 picas. Click on OK. Activate both Wireframe and Rulers from the View menu; because of the grid settings, the rulers display in picas rather than inches.

2. Before beginning to draw, set the default Outline Pen and Outline Color attributes back to the original CorelDRAW! defaults. To do this, click on the Outline Pen Dialog tool in the Outline Pen flyout menu. When the default Outline Pen dialog box appears, select Graphic and Artistic Text

and click on OK. Adjust settings in the Outline Pen dialog box as follows: black color; Width, 0.003 inch; Corners, sharp; Line Caps, butt (topmost); no Arrows; Style, solid line; Angle, 0 degrees; and Stretch, 100 percent. No check boxes should be filled. Click on OK to make these settings the default Outline Pen attributes.

3. Select the Ellipse tool and position the pointer at the 24-pica mark on the horizontal ruler and the 33-pica mark on the vertical ruler. Draw a perfect circle from the center outward, starting from this point, by holding both the SHIFT and CTRL keys down while dragging the mouse. Make the circle 20 picas in diameter or the largest circle you can draw, using the information on the status line to help you. When the circle is drawn, click on Black fill on the onscreen color palette.

4. Activate the Text tool. Select an insertion point near the left edge of the circle, at the 18-pica mark on the horizontal ruler and the 32-pica mark on the vertical ruler. You do not have to position the pointer exactly, because you can align the text and circle later. Type **The World of Corel DRAW!**, one word per line. Then select the text by selecting the Pick tool, open the Text roll-up. Click on the Character Attributes command button. Select the following text attributes: Aachen BT bold (available on CD-ROM), 40 points, and center alignment. Set Character spacing to 20 percent and Line spacing to 80 percent, and then click on OK and on Apply. Next, roll up the Text roll-up. The text appears centered vertically and horizontally within the circle, as shown in Figure 7-13. If the text is not centered perfectly within the circle, then, with the text still selected, drag the text as necessary to center it.

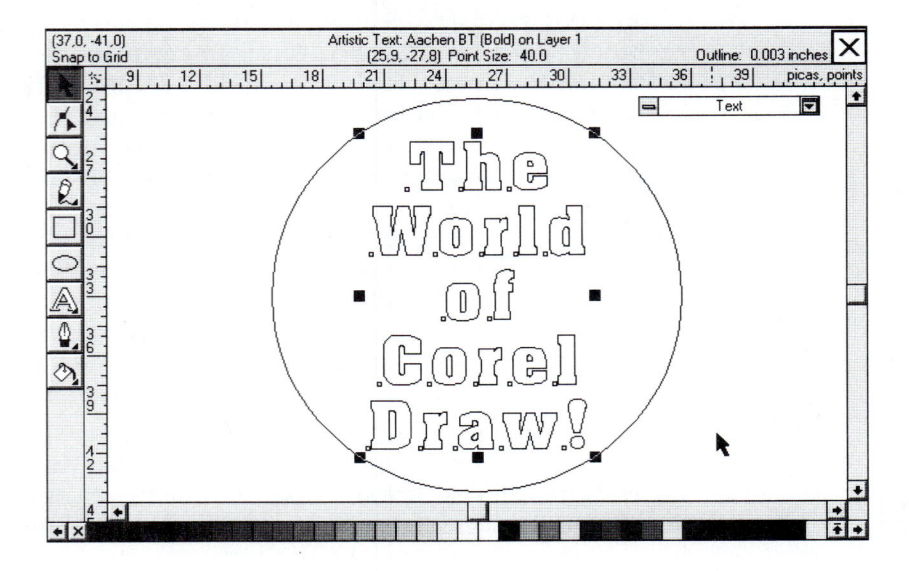

Centering a text string within a circle

Figure 7-13.

Defining Outline and Fill Color

Depending on the type of display and display adapter you have, the diameter of the circle and the point size you can fit in the circle may differ from what is described and shown here. Draw the biggest circle and use the largest type size needed to fill your screen at actual size magnification.

5. Click on both Rulers and Wireframe in the View menu again to deactivate them. You cannot clearly distinguish the text from the circle now, because they have the same outline and fill colors.

6. Select the Preferences command in the Special menu (or press CTRL-J). When the Preferences dialog box appears, adjust both of the numeric settings for the Place Duplicate and Clones option to −2,0 picas and points. Make sure that you make it minus and that you place a comma rather than a period after the 2. Duplicate objects that you create with this setting are offset from the original by the specified amount (in this case, 2 picas below and to the left of the original). Click on OK to exit the dialog box.

7. If necessary, activate the Pick tool, select the circle, and then click on the Duplicate command in the Edit menu. A duplicate of the circle appears below and to the left of the original, and is selected immediately.

8. Change the fill of this duplicate circle to none by clicking on the X at the left of the color palette at the bottom of your screen.

9. Select both the original circle and the text string again using the SHIFT key, and click on the Combine command in the Arrange menu. The message in the status line changes from "2 objects selected" to "Curve on Layer 1." The "Fill:" message at the right side of the status line displays a default fill of black, but the text now appears white, as shown in Figure 7-14. In combining the two objects, you have converted both the circle and the text string to curves. The area behind the text has become not white but transparent.

10. Select the Save command in the File menu. When the Save Drawing dialog box appears, type the name **FILL-1** in the File Name text box and then click on OK.

11. With the combined circle and text still selected, click on the Fill tool and again on the Fill Color tool (you can also press SHIFT-F11). The Uniform Fill dialog box appears. Select PANTONE Spot Colors from the Show drop-down list box, and deselect Show color names if it is selected. Then select the leftmost color in the top row of the palette, PANTONE Process Yellow CV, and set the tint to 55 percent. Your settings should match those in Figure 7-15.

12. Click on OK to exit the dialog box. Now you can see some contrast between the black outline and the fill colors. The text has the same outline style as the circular shape because CorelDRAW! treats the text

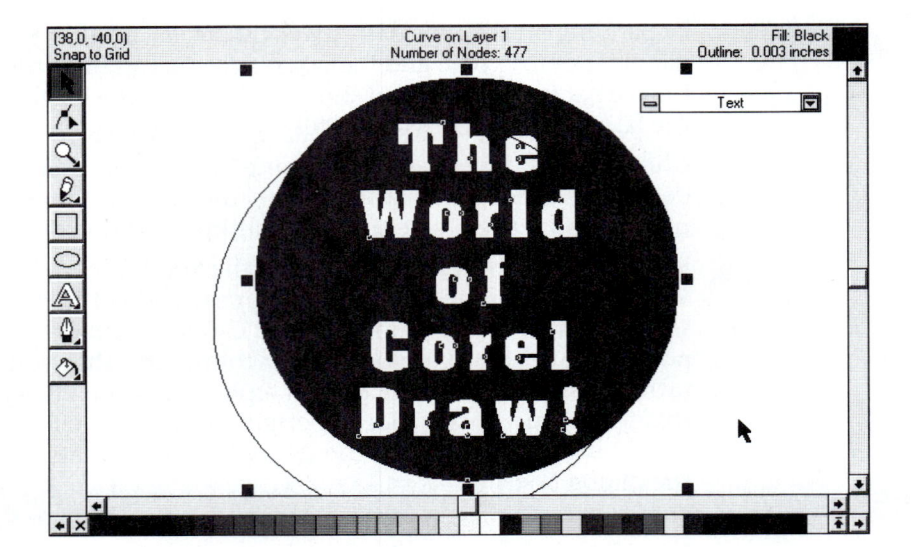

Combining two objects to form a curve object with transparent "holes"
Figure 7-14.

curves as "holes" or edges within the single combined object. The outline is very thin, however, so you will thicken it in the next step.

13. With the curve object still selected, click on the Outline Pen. Access the Outline Pen dialog box by clicking on the Outline Pen Dialog tool (or by pressing F12). Change the Width setting for the Outline Pen to 5.0 points. (Notice not picas & points, just pionts.) Select the Behind Fill

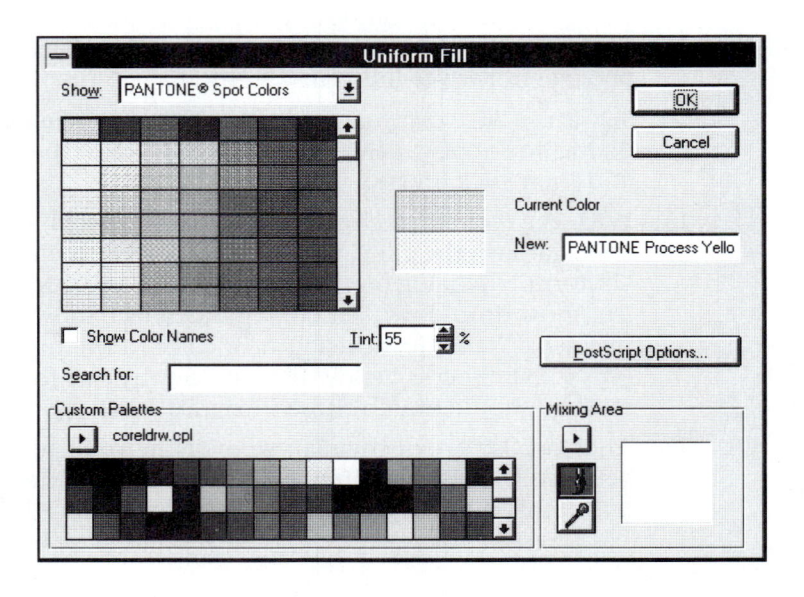

Setting for a spot color uniform fill
Figure 7-15.

Defining Outline and Fill Color

option and then click on OK to apply these settings to the object. Now you see a heavier outline around both the outer rim of the circle and the text, as shown in Figure 7-16. Because you activated the Behind Fill option, the "ink" of the outline doesn't completely clog up the transparent spaces in the text.

14. You are ready to give the finishing touches to the curve object. Press SHIFT-F12 to access the Outline Color dialog box. If not already selected, select PANTONE Spot Colors to be the color model. Select Show color names and type **293** in the Search String text box to select PANTONE 293 CV as the color (a medium blue). Set the tint to 52 percent and click on OK to exit the dialog box.

15. Select the duplicate circle. Press SHIFT-F11 to access the Uniform Fill dialog box. Select Pantone Spot Color and scroll to PANTONE 281 CV (a dark purplish blue), and leave the tint at 100 percent. Click on OK to select this setting and exit the dialog box.

16. The image redisplays to show the background circle creating a dramatic "shadow" effect behind the curve object. The alignment is not quite right yet, however; white space may be visible behind the upper portion of the word "The." To remedy this situation, deactivate the Snap To Grid command and adjust the position of the background circle slightly so that it fills the word "The" completely. Now all of the transparent spaces behind the letters in the curve object have fill behind them.

17. To see this apparent fill more closely, turn on full screen preview by pressing F9. Your screen should look similar to Figure 7-17.

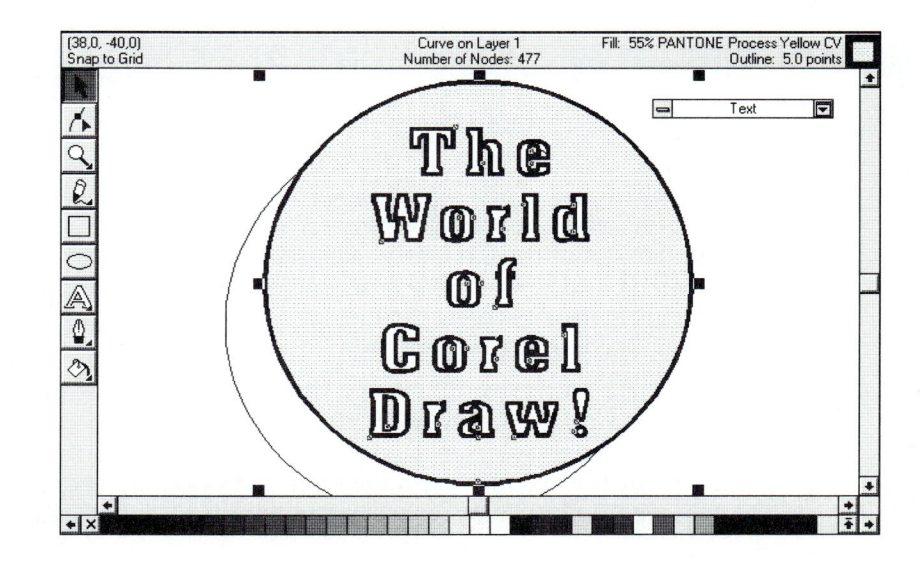

Outline appearing behind fill for clearer text appearance
Figure 7-16.

Apparent fill of transparent areas using a background object
Figure 7-17.

18. Again press F9 to turn off full screen preview and then press CTRL-S to save the changes you have made to this graphic. Leave the graphic on the screen to use in the next exercise.

The kind of object you have just created makes an excellent specimen for outline and fill experiments of all kinds. In the next section, you will add an interesting design effect by specifying a PostScript halftone screen pattern for the background circle in FILL-1.CDR.

Filling an Object with PostScript Halftone Screen Patterns

When you choose the spot color rather than the process color system in the Uniform Fill dialog box, another set of fill specifications becomes available. If you work with a PostScript printer, you can fill an object with a halftone screen pattern of the currently selected spot color. You will recall from your work with Outline Color that the CorelDRAW! preview window displays PostScript halftone screen patterns as a solid color; to see how they actually look, you have to print them on a PostScript printer.

You define a PostScript halftone screen pattern by clicking on the PostScript Options command button at the lower-right side of the Uniform Fill dialog box. You can choose from 15 different screen options, and you can vary the frequency (number of occurrences per inch) and angle of any screen pattern to achieve dramatic differences in the appearance of a spot color fill.

Defining Outline and Fill Color **235**

In the following exercise, you will assign a PostScript halftone screen pattern of a specified angle and frequency to the combined circle-text foreground object in the FILL-1.CDR image and save the altered image under a new name. If you have a PostScript printer, you can print this image with the printing techniques covered in Chapter 12.

1. With FILL-1.CDR still on the screen, select the foreground curve and press SHIFT-F11.
2. When the Uniform Fill dialog box appears, click on the PostScript Options command button on the right side of the dialog box. The PostScript Options dialog box appears.
3. Scroll through the Type list box until the MicroWaves halftone screen type is visible and then select it.
4. Adjust the Frequency setting to 20 per inch. This is a very low frequency (the minimum is 0, the maximum 1500) and will display a dramatic pattern on a 300 dpi PostScript printer.
5. If necessary, use the scroll arrows to adjust the number in the Angle numeric entry box to 45 degrees. This will cause the screen pattern to tilt at a 45-degree angle.
6. When your settings match the ones in Figure 7-18, click on OK to exit the PostScript Options dialog box. Click on OK again to exit the Uniform Fill dialog box and return to the screen image. You will not notice anything different, because the preview window cannot display PostScript patterns.
7. Select the Save As command in the File menu and type **FILL-2** in the File Name text box of the Save Drawing dialog box. Click on OK to save

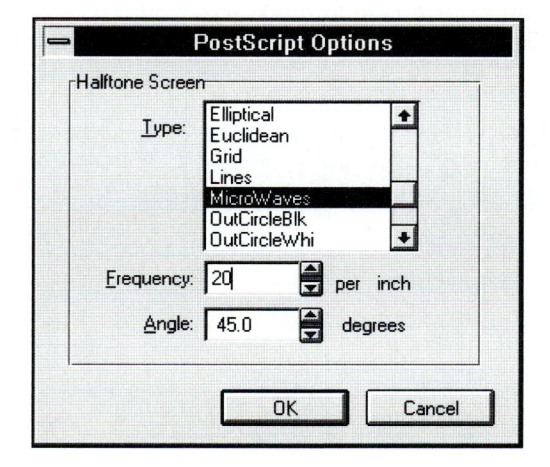

Defining a custom PostScript halftone screen pattern
Figure 7-18.

Printed image of the PostScript halftone screen
Figure 7-19.

the file under this new name. After you complete Chapter 12, you can print this file to see the results of your settings if you have a PostScript printer. Your results should look like Figure 7-19.

When you assign PostScript halftone screen pattern fills to objects, base your choice of frequency on the resolution of the PostScript printer you will use. On any PostScript printer, low frequencies result in more dramatic pattern effects, while high frequencies result in the pattern being hardly visible. The resolution of the printer, not any absolute number, determines what constitutes a low or a high frequency. To achieve the same visual effect on different printers, you should vary the frequency assigned to a screen. For example, you should assign lower screen frequencies when the printer resolution is 300 dpi, higher frequencies for the newer 600 dpi printers, and higher still for imagesetting equipment at resolutions of 1270 dpi and above. Table 7-1 provides information on the number of visible gray levels for each printer resolution at a given screen frequency.

Printer Resolution and Number of Gray Levels Visible for PostScript Halftone Screen Patterns
Table 7-1.

Selected Frequency	Number of Gray Levels		
	300 dpi	**600 dpi**	**1270 dpi**
30 per inch	101	401	1600
60 per inch	26	101	401
100 per inch	10	37	145
120 per inch	7	26	101

Defining Outline and Fill Color

You can specify a PostScript halftone screen pattern as a default fill in the same way that you would specify a normal spot color. The next section will introduce you to one of the most creative types of fills, *fountain fills*, which can be used to effect smooth transitions of two different colors through the interior of an object.

Custom Fountain Fills

When you specify fill colors using the Uniform Fill dialog boxes, you are limited to one color per object. When you select the Fountain Fill icon in the Fill tool flyout menu, however, you can define a fill that blends two different colors or shades of color. If you are familiar with state-of-the-art paint programs or business presentation slides, you have probably seen fountain fills used to make smooth transitions of two different colors or tints. CorelDRAW! makes the color drama of fountain fills available to you through the Fountain Fill dialog box.

By adjusting settings in the Fountain Fill dialog box, you can fill any object with two different colors or tints in such a way that the colors blend evenly from one extreme to the other. CorelDRAW! allows you to create four different types of fountain fills: linear, radial, conical, and square. In a *linear* fountain fill, the color transition occurs in one direction only, determined by the angle that you specify. In a *radial* fountain fill, the blend of start and end colors proceeds concentrically, from the center of the object outward or from the outer rim inward. In a *conical* fill, the blend of colors is made of wedge-shaped steps that radiate in clockwise and counterclockwise directions. In a *square* fill, the blend of colors is in square rings. Whichever type of fountain fill you select, you can specify colors using either the spot color or process color system. If you choose spot color, you can also define PostScript halftone screen patterns to add an extra visual "punch" to your fountain fills.

The following exercises provide practice defining linear, radial, and conical fountain fills using spot color, PostScript halftone screen patterns, and process color.

Defining Linear Fountain Fills

When you specify a linear fountain fill, the start color begins at one edge of the object and the end color appears at the opposite side. In between, the colors blend smoothly along an imaginary line extending from one edge to the other. The direction of the color blend depends on the angle of the fill, over which you have complete control.

You can also control the speed and fineness of the display that defines the fountain fill in the CorelDRAW! window. You do this by choosing Preferences from the Special menu, clicking on Display, and adjusting the Preview Fountain Steps settings. A low setting (2 is the lower limit) causes the fountain fill to display rapidly with a small number of circles. A high value (256 is the upper limit) causes the filled object to redraw very slowly on the screen, but it also results in a very finely graded transition of color. For all output devices except PostScript printers, the Fountain Steps setting also determines the resolution at which the fountain fill will print. You will have the opportunity to practice adjusting this setting and viewing the results on the screen in the "Fill Tool Hints" section of this chapter.

As with other outlines and fills, you can define a linear fountain fill for existing objects or you can set defaults for objects that you have not yet created. The exercises in the next few sections use existing objects as examples.

Spot Color Linear Fountain Fills

Theoretically, you can select any two colors as the start and end colors when you specify a linear fountain fill using the spot color system. In practice, however, it's best to select two tints of the *same* color if you intend to send color separations of the resulting image to a commercial printer. The reason for this has to do with the way spot color is physically reproduced, which makes it difficult to blend two discrete colors evenly.

To open the Fountain Fill dialog box for either future or existing objects, press F11.

In the following exercise, you will define a spot color linear fountain fill for the objects in the FILL-1.CDR file, which you created earlier in the chapter.

1. Open the original FILL-1.CDR file you set up earlier in this chapter (not one of the edited versions). Your screen displays a curve object containing a PANTONE Process Yellow CV spot color at 55 percent tint and a blue PANTONE 293 CV outline at a 52 percent tint. A darker blue (PANTONE 281 CV) fills a circle behind the object.

Tip: To check the current fill colors for an existing object at any time, just select the object, click on the Fill tool, and click on the Uniform Fill icon to display the Uniform Fill dialog box.

2. Adjust the viewing area to fit-in-window magnification.
3. Deselect all objects and reselect the combined circle-text curve object alone.
4. Click on the Fill tool and then on the Fountain Fill icon in the Fill tool flyout (third from the left), or press F11. The Fountain Fill dialog box displays, as shown in Figure 7-20.

Defining Outline and Fill Color

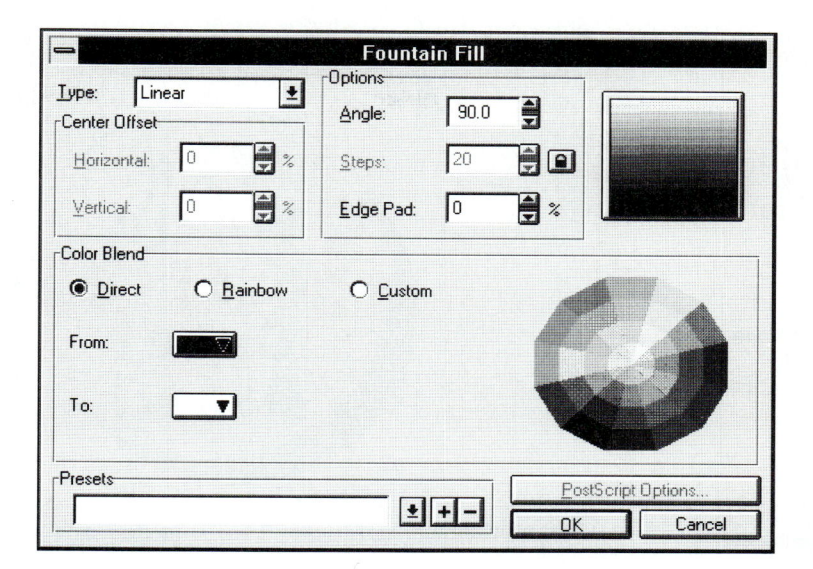

The (default) Fountain Fill dialog box
Figure 7-20.

The Fountain Fill dialog box contains controls for the type of fountain fill (linear, radial, conical, or square); the angle, which determines the direction of the fill; and the From and To colors of the fill. A display box shows the current fill, and other controls for several fill options are available. The default settings are Type, Linear; Angle, 90 degrees; From color, black; and To color, white. These settings would result in a fill that is white at the top, blending gradually into solid black at the bottom.

5. Leave the Type and Angle settings at the defaults. Click on the From color button and then click on More. In the Fountain Fill dialog box, select PANTONE Spot Colors as the model and PANTONE Process Yellow CV (first color in the list) at 100 percent tint. Click on OK.

    Similarly, set the To color to PANTONE Process Yellow CV, but at 0 percent tint, which will look virtually white. Remember that when you define color using the spot color method, both the start and end colors should be different tints of the same color.

6. Click on OK to exit the Fountain Fill dialog box with the new settings. The circle object now shows a darker yellow fill at the bottom, with a gradual transition to white at the top, as shown in Figure 7-21.

7. Access the Fountain Fill dialog box again (F11). This time, change the Angle setting to 45 degrees and then click on OK to exit the dialog box. Now, the combined circle-text redisplays with a fountain fill that is lighter at the upper right and darker at the lower left.

8. For an interesting enhancement, create a fountain fill for the background circle that runs in the opposite direction from the fill for the curve

Spot color linear fountain fill at a 90-degree angle
Figure 7-21.

object. To do this, select the background circle and press F11. When the Fountain Fill dialog box appears, set the From color to PANTONE 281 (use the Search for text box) at a 100 percent tint. Click on OK.

Then set the To color to PANTONE 281 at a 30 percent tint. Change the Angle setting to minus 135 degrees, the exact opposite of the 45-degree setting you chose for the fill of the curve object. This setting will result in a fill running in the exact opposite direction from the fill for the foreground object.

9. Click on OK to exit the dialog box. When the objects are redrawn, you can see that the area behind the letters is a richer color at the upper right than at the lower left. This arrangement adds some visual tension to the mock logo.

10. Select the Save As command from the File menu. When the Save Drawing dialog box appears, type the filename **FILL-3** in the File Name text box, and then click on the OK command button to save the altered picture under this new name.

Tip: If you plan to use a commercial process to reproduce images that contain spot color fountain fills, make sure the start and end colors are two tints of the same color. If you do not plan to reproduce your images by a commercial process, however, this restriction does not apply.

Defining Outline and Fill Color

When you select the spot color method of assigning start and end colors, you can create a fountain fill from black to white by specifying colors as 0 or 100 percent black. Spot color is especially useful for black-and-white linear fountain fills if you are interested in assigning a PostScript halftone screen pattern to the object at the same time. In the next section, you will review the process of specifying a PostScript halftone screen pattern with a linear fountain fill.

Spot Color Linear Fountain Fills with PostScript Halftone Screens

You will recall from your previous work with outline fill colors that the preview window cannot show you how a selected PostScript halftone screen pattern will look when printed. You must actually print the object with such a fill on a PostScript device in order to see the results. The same is true of PostScript halftone screens when you combine them with fountain fills, which is possible when you use the spot color system to specify start and end colors. Here are some tips that should help you achieve a better design on the first try:

- Set the angle of the PostScript halftone screen either at the same angle as the linear fountain fill or at an angle that complements it in a design sense. (You do not want the eye to travel in too many directions at once.) Sometimes, you can determine the best angle only by experimentation; varying the angle of the halftone screen from the angle of the fountain fill can produce unexpected results.

- If you want the halftone screen to be visible when you print it, use a low frequency setting in the PostScript Options dialog box. This is most important if the Fountain Stripes setting in the Preferences dialog box, which controls the fineness of the fountain fill itself, is high.

Go on to the next set of sections to experiment with fountain fills that radiate from the center outward or from the rim inward.

Defining Radial Fountain Fills

When you specify a radial fountain fill, the start color appears all around the outer area of the object and the end color appears at its center, or vice versa. The blending of colors or tints occurs in concentric circles. Because color density in radial fountain fills changes gradually in a circular pattern, a 3-D look is easy to achieve.

You cannot specify an angle when you select a radial fountain fill, but you can control the location of the fill's apparent center. You'll see one way to change the center of a radial fountain fill in this chapter and two others in Chapters 13 and 14.

You can use either spot color or process color to define a radial fountain fill. When you use spot color, you have the additional option of selecting a PostScript halftone screen pattern. The tips contained in the previous section, "Spot Color Linear Fountain Fills with PostScript Halftone Screens," apply to radial fountain fills, too.

You can control both the speed and fineness of the display that defines the fountain fill in full color mode by adjusting the Preview Fountain Steps setting in the Preferences dialog box, as discussed under "Defining Linear Fountain Fills," earlier in this chapter.

As with the linear fountain fill, you can define a radial fountain fill for existing objects or set defaults for objects that you haven't yet created. The exercises in the next few sections use existing objects as examples.

Spot Color Radial Fountain Fills

Here, you will define a black-and-white spot color radial fountain fill for the objects in the FILL-1.CDR file that you created earlier in the chapter.

1. Open the FILL-1.CDR file.
2. Adjust viewing magnification to fit-in-window. Select the combined circle-text and press F11 for the Fountain Fill Dialog box.
3. Set the type to Radial. Click on the From color button and then click on More. Select PANTONE Spot Colors as the color model, PANTONE Process Black with 100 percent tint as the color, and then click on OK to return to the Fountain Fill dialog box. For the To color, also select PANTONE Process Black with 0 percent tint, and click on OK. Then select OK again to exit the Fountain Fill dialog box. The circle-text object redisplays with a brighter area (the 0 percent black of the color range) in its center, as you can see in Figure 7-22. The apparent play of light you achieve with this kind of fill creates a 3-D effect, making the surface of the "globe" appear to curve.

The angle numeric entry box dims and is not accessible when the Radial option is selected.

Select the Save As command in the File menu. When the Save Drawing dialog box appears, type **FILL-4** in the File Name text box and then press ENTER or click on OK.

As long as you choose the spot color method of specifying color, you can select a PostScript halftone screen pattern with a radial fountain fill. The added 3-D effect possible with radial fountain fills can lead to quite dramatic results when you add a halftone screen.

You can change the center of a radial fountain fill to create an off-center highlight for the object. You'll look at one method of doing this next. Two

Defining Outline and Fill Color   **243**

Spot color radial fountain fill with lighter shade at center
Figure 7-22.

other methods for accomplishing this effect are available; both are included among the techniques discussed in Chapter 14.

Edge Padding and Radial Offset

The Fountain Fill dialog box allows you to add edge padding and to offset the center of a radial fill. You may have noticed that when CorelDRAW! creates a fountain fill, it is initially rectangular, filling an object's entire boundary box. When the creation process is complete, the excess is clipped off to fit the shape of the object, for example, the circles in this chapter. As a result, the starting and/or ending bands of the fill may be clipped off. *Edge padding* allows you to increase the percentage of an object's boundary box that is to be occupied by the starting and ending bands up to a maximum of 45 percent. Explore edge padding with the following brief exercise.

1. With FILL-4.CDR still on your screen and the circle-text object still selected, press F11 to open the Fountain Fill dialog box.
2. Type **20** in the Edge Pad numeric entry box and click on OK. Your drawing should look like Figure 7-23. Compare this with Figure 7-22 and you will see the impact of adding 20 percent edge padding.

The other function of the Fountain Fill dialog box is offsetting the center of a radial fill. Look at that next.

1. Again, press F11 to open the Fountain Fill dialog box. (Be sure the Radial button is still selected.)

First and last bands of fountain fill set at 20% of the object
Figure 7-23.

2. Type **20** in both the Horizontal and Vertical numeric entry boxes under Center Offset and click on OK.
3. You should see the center of the radial fountain fill offset to the upper-right corner, as shown in Figure 7-24.
4. Save the current image as FILL-5.

Center of a radial fountain fill offset 20 percent to the right and 20 percent up
Figure 7-24.

Defining Outline and Fill Color

Defining Conical and Square Fountain Fills

When you choose a conical fountain fill, the start color appears in a wedge shape from the outer edge to the center of the object. The end color is also a wedge shape from the outer edge to the center of the object on the side opposite from the start color. The blending of colors radiates in both clockwise and counterclockwise directions from the start color. Figure 7-25 shows a conical fountain fill with a 20 percent horizontal and vertical offset and a 20 degree angular rotation.

Square fountain fills are similar to radial fountain fills except that the bands are square instead of round. The From color is the outermost band and the To the innermost. The corners of the square provide a star effect, as you can see in Figure 7-26.

You can specify an angle and control the location of both a conical and square fill's apparent center when you select a conical fountain fill. A square fill can also have edge padding. You can use either spot or process color to define both conical and square fill as well as PostScript halftone screen patterns. The tips contained in the earlier section, "Spot Color Linear Fountain Fills with PostScript Halftone Screens," apply to both conical and square fountain fills. As with the other fountain fills, you can define conical or square fountain fills for existing objects or set defaults for objects that you haven't yet created.

Conical fountain fill
Figure 7-25.

Square fountain fill
Figure 7-26.

Bitmap and Vector Fill Patterns

CorelDRAW! has two more ways to fill objects: bitmap fill and vector patterns and textures. Bitmap and vector refer to two methods of forming a graphic image in a computer. *Bitmap* images are formed by defining each point (or bit) in an image. *Vector* images are formed by defining the start, end, and characteristics of each line (or vector) in an image. CorelDRAW! comes with a number of bitmap and vector images that can be used to construct fill patterns. You can create your own or modify existing bitmap and vector images and then use them in fill patterns.

Bitmap and vector patterns are formed by repeating an image many times—*tiling*—so that each image is a single tile. CorelDRAW! provides the means of selecting existing bitmap and vector images; of sizing, editing, and offsetting both kinds of images; and of creating, importing, and coloring bitmap images.

Using Bitmap Fill Patterns

Bitmap images are the most numerous and the most easily manipulated, and CorelDRAW! provides greater capability for handling them. Look at bitmap fill patterns with the following exercise.

1. FILL-5.CDR should still be on your screen with the circle-text object selected.

Defining Outline and Fill Color

2. Select the Fill tool and the Two-Color icon that looks like a checkerboard. The Two-Color Pattern dialog box opens.

3. Click on the display box and then on the flyout window's scroll bar to scan through the more than 49 patterns that are included with CorelDRAW!. Then select the Corel image shown here:

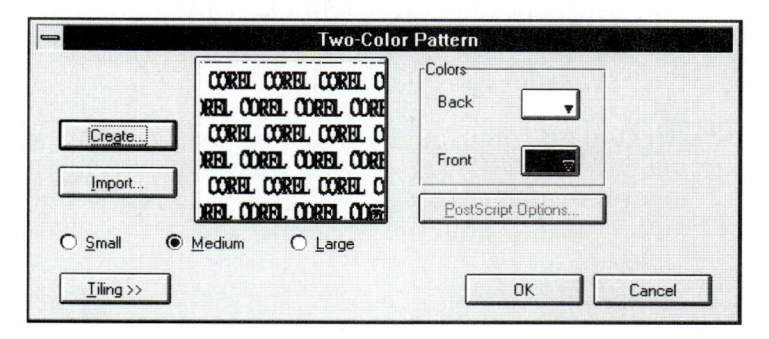

4. First click on Small, then Medium, and then Large to see the difference the three sizes make. Click on Tiling and type in your own sizes in the numeric entry boxes. The height and width do not have to be the same, but for most images you probably want them to be. The maximum size is 15 inches square. (Keep the Medium size.)

   Tile size is the size of each tile or image in the pattern. Different sizes work for different patterns. On some patterns, Small causes the images to look smudged, while on others, Large causes straight lines to have jagged edges. You need to pick the size that is right for the image and for what you are trying to achieve.

   Clicking on either the Front or Back buttons under Colors, or the More buttons, allows you to assign a color to either the foreground (Front)—the word "Corel" in the selected pattern—or the background (Back). The default is a black foreground and white background. The Colors buttons open the color palette, and More opens a color dialog box that is very similar to other color dialog boxes you have used in this chapter. You can choose between spot and process color, choose a color from a palette, specify % Tint (if you are using spot color), and specify a custom process to create a new one, or open an existing one in another file, or another named color. Also, if you are using spot color, you can select a PostScript halftone screen.

5. Click on the Front button and then on More. Keeping the CMYK color model, select 50 percent black and click on OK. In a similar manner, keep the default white for Back, and click on OK to exit the Two-Color Pattern dialog box. You will return to your drawing and see the bitmap pattern provide the fill for the curve object. The text in the curve object

is hard to read because of the lack of contrast among the new fill, the outline of the curve object, and the fill for the duplicate circle. Change the last two to improve the contrast.

6. Select the Outline Pen and select the white icon to change the Outline Color to white.

7. Select the duplicate circle and the Fill tool, and select the black icon to change the circle's fill to black. Your screen should look like Figure 7-27

8. Save your current drawing with the filename FILL-6.

The Import command button in the Two-Color Pattern dialog box opens a file selection dialog box. If you select a file, the image is added to the set of images that you can access in the Two-Color Pattern dialog box. You can offset (stagger) both the horizontal and vertical starting position of each image in the pattern, as well as offset neighboring rows or neighboring columns.

The Create button allows you to create a new bitmap image to use in constructing a fill pattern. When you activate the Create button, the Two-Color Pattern Editor opens, as shown in Figure 7-28. The Two-Color Pattern Editor provides for three different sizes of drawings: 16 pixels ("dots" on your screen) square, 32 pixels square, and 64 pixels square. The more diagonal or curve elements in your image, the larger the size you will need. From a practical standpoint you should use the smallest size possible because

Medium-sized two-color fill pattern
Figure 7-27.

Defining Outline and Fill Color 249

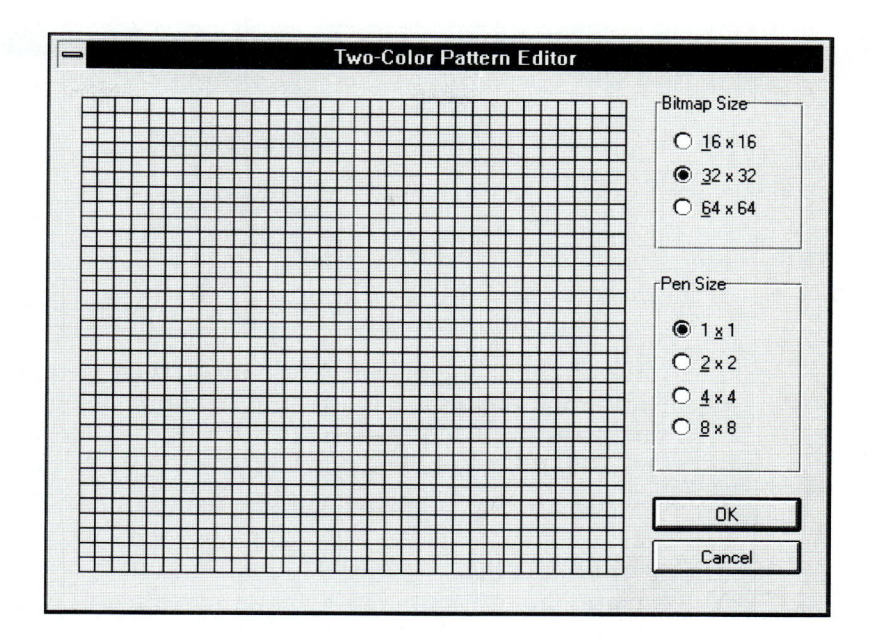

Bitmap Pattern Editor
Figure 7-28.

the larger sizes take longer to draw and take more room on disk. To draw, click the left mouse button to make a pixel black and the right mouse button to make a black pixel white again. If you want to erase an unfinished drawing, change the size, say, from 16 by 16 to 32 by 32. You can then change the size back, and all of the pixels will be clear. When you are done with a drawing, click on OK, and the image will be saved as one of the bitmap images that are available from the Two-Color Pattern dialog box. You can then select it to create a fill pattern.

Using Full-Color Patterns

CorelDRAW! also provides full-color fill patterns. Change the fill in the curve object to a full-color pattern in the following exercise:

1. With FILL-6.CDR still on your screen select the circle-text object. Open the Fill tool flyout menu and select the Full-Color Fill icon. The Full-Color Pattern dialog box will open.

2. The Full-Color Pattern dialog box lets you open disk files with a .PAT extension. Click on the display box to look at the patterns that are available.

3. Select the Corel balloon pattern and click on OK in the display box menu. The balloon pattern will fill the display box as shown here:

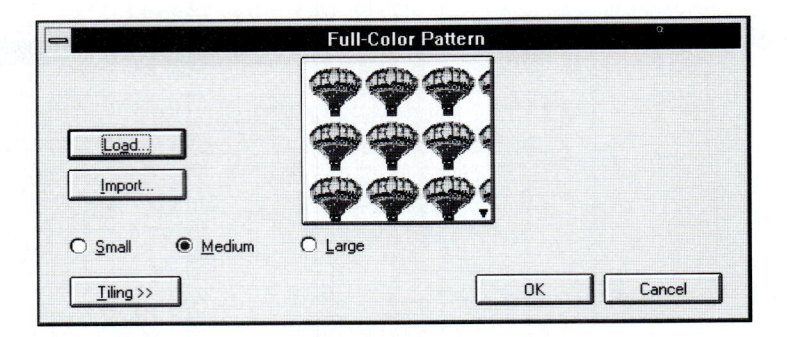

4. Click on the Tiling button, select Small, then Medium, then Large. Notice that the default tile sizes in the numeric entry boxes are not square like two-color patterns are. For now, select Medium and click on OK. Your full-color filled drawing will appear, as shown in Figure 7-29.

5. Save the changed drawing with the name FILL-7.

Using Texture Fills

You can also select from over 100 bitmap texture fills with CorelDRAW!. While two- and full-color fills consist of tiled patterns, textures are created with a mathematical formula. Textures for water, clouds, minerals, and others are available. Each texture can be modified in a number of ways, including by texture number. Each texture has 32,767 texture numbers. To see their effect, change the texture number, then click on the Preview button underneath the preview box.

Full-color pattern fill
Figure 7-29.

Defining Outline and Fill Color

Other parameters, such as color, brightness, contrast, density, and softness can also be modified. The parameters that can be modified depend on the texture selected.

Tip: You can also change texture parameters randomly. Select the Lock icon next to the parameter you wish to modify to change it to the locked position, then click on the Preview button. Each time you click on the Preview button the texture will change.

To select a texture fill, follow these steps:

1. With FILL-7 still on the screen, select the circle-text object.
2. Open the Fill tool flyout and select the Texture Fill icon that looks like clouds. The Texture Fill dialog box will open, as shown in Figure 7-30.
3. Using the scroll bar, select Flames in the Texture List box and click on OK. Your circle-text object will now look like Figure 7-31.

Note: Texture fills require a large amount of memory and a longer time to print. You may need to limit the size and number of texture filled objects in your drawing because of this.

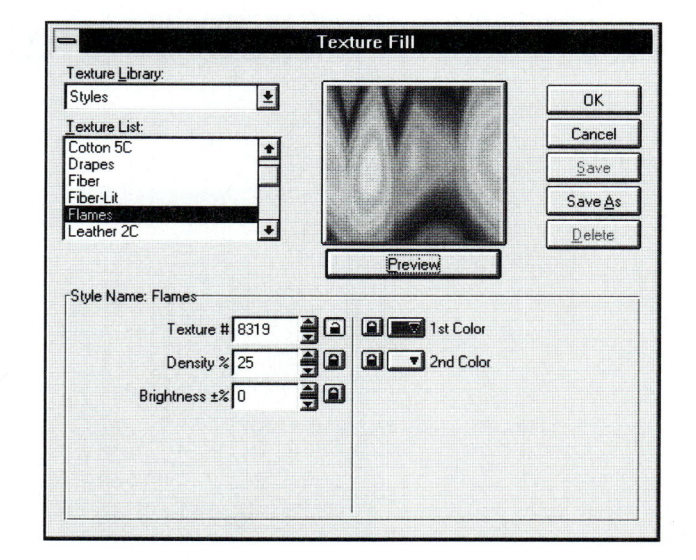

Texture Fill dialog box
Figure 7-30.

Texture fill in art
Figure 7-31.

PostScript Texture Fills

The last icon in the Fill tool flyout is the PostScript Textures icon, which opens the dialog box shown in Figure 7-32. If you print to a PostScript printer, you can fill selected objects with a choice of 42 different PostScript textures. This number is deceptive; although only 42 basic patterns exist, you can alter the parameters for each texture to achieve wide variations in appearance.

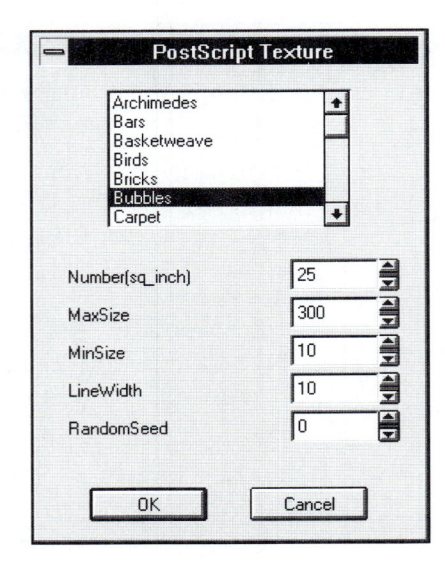

PostScript Texture dialog box
Figure 7-32.

Defining Outline and Fill Color

Chapter 12 contains more information about printing PostScript texture fills.

When you assign a PostScript texture fill to an object, the CorelDRAW! window displays the object with a small gray "PS" pattern on a white background. The Fill designation in the status line, however, indicates the name of the particular texture assigned. Unfortunately, you cannot view these textures until you print them.

Working with PostScript texture fills is an adventure because of the *aleatory*, or chance, characteristics built into the mathematical formulas for the textures. Think of these textures as a way to bring more creative design elements into your drawing, even if your own drawing powers are limited.

Fill Roll-Up

Like many other major functions, fill color has a roll-up window. The Fill roll-up window, shown on the left, is opened by clicking on the Roll-up icon, second from the left in the top row of the Fill flyout menu.

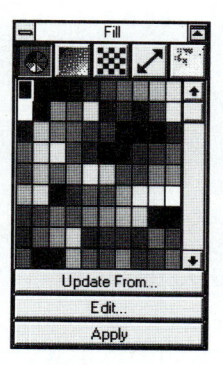

Like other roll-up windows, the Fill roll-up window stays open on your screen until you roll it up or close it. It provides access to the Fill Color, Fountain Fill, Two-Color Pattern, Full-Color Pattern, and Texture Fill dialog boxes. It also allows you to edit the fill of an existing object. To use the Fill roll-up, you first click on one of the five buttons at the top of the roll-up to specify the type of fill you want. Clicking the Edit button, near the bottom of the roll-up, opens the dialog box for the type of fill you have selected. Also, the display area below the five fill-type buttons changes to reflect the type of fill. For uniform fill, this area is the current color palette. For the other types of fill, it provides display boxes and buttons unique to those types.

Fill Tool Hints

Finally, some hints for using the Fill tool are included in this section. These by no means exhaust the many uses to which you can put the Fill tool; rather, they are tips to help you gain speed in your work or to introduce creative effects.

Copying Fill Styles

In previous chapters, you have learned how to use the Copy Attributes From command in the Edit menu to copy text, Outline Pen, or outline fill attributes from one object to another. You can use that same command and its associated dialog box to copy fill styles between objects, too. The following summarizes how to use this feature to best advantage:

1. Select the object or group of objects *to which* you would like to copy the fill attributes of another object.
2. Select the Copy Attributes From command in the Edit menu. When the Copy Attributes dialog box appears, activate the Fill check box by clicking on it. If you want to copy text, Outline Pen, or Outline Color attributes at the same time, activate those check boxes, too.
3. Click on OK to exit the dialog box. The pointer turns into a thick arrow to use to point to the object *from which* you want to copy the fill style.
4. Select the object whose style you want to copy to the selected object. The selected object redisplays with the new fill style.

The entire continuum of fill styles is available to you when you use this command. You can copy spot or process color uniform fills, PostScript halftone screens, preset shades of gray, bitmap fills, or even PostScript textures. Use this command and dialog box as a handy shortcut to defining fill attributes for one or more objects.

Using Fountain Steps to Enhance Previews and Printing

You will recall that the Preferences dialog box (accessible from the Special menu) contains many useful settings to customize the way CorelDRAW! displays your work. One of these settings, Preview Fountain Steps (accessed with the View tab), applies to the use of linear, radial, conical, and square fountain fills.

CorelDRAW! displays a fountain fill by creating a series of concentric circles or squares that begin at the outer edge of the selection box for the object and work their way inward. You have probably noticed this process each time the preview window redraws an object containing a fountain fill. The Preview Fountain Steps setting in the Preferences dialog box lets you determine how many circles CorelDRAW! creates to represent a fountain fill. The number ranges from 2 to 256, with 2 representing 2 circles with coarse outlines, and 256 representing a high number of finely drawn circles. As you can imagine, the window redraws very quickly when Preview Fountain Steps is set to a low number, and extremely slowly when the Preview Fountain Steps setting is high. Further, if you print to a device other than a PostScript printer, the number of circles you select in the Preview Fountain Steps setting represents what will actually print. You can achieve some interesting effects by varying this setting.

Part 2

USING ADVANCED FEATURES
of CorelDRAW! 5

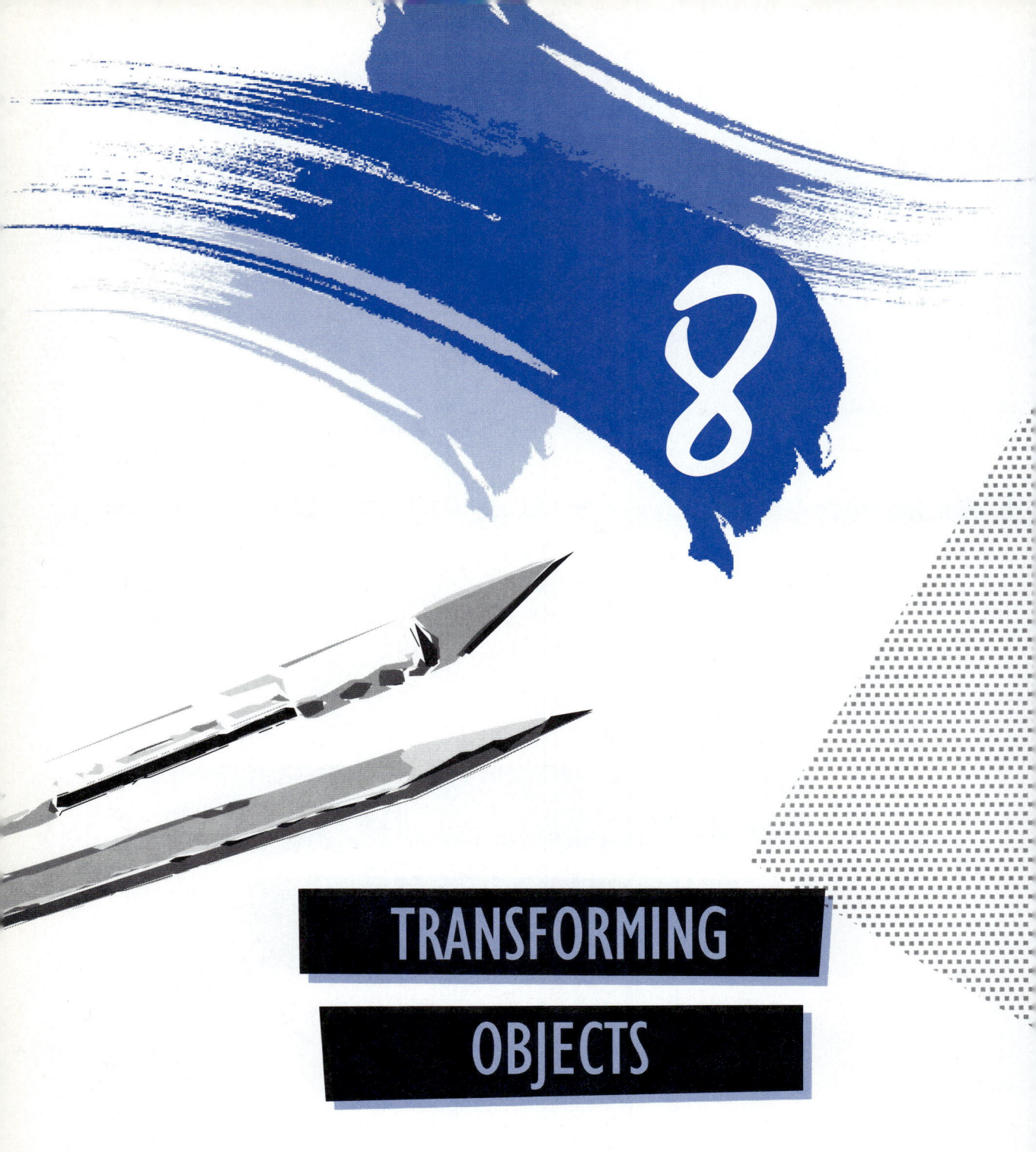

8

TRANSFORMING OBJECTS

In Chapter 5, you learned how to use the Pick tool to select, move, and arrange objects. In this chapter, you will use the Pick tool to transform the size or shape of selected objects.

When you transform an object with the Pick tool, you do not alter its fundamental shape; a rectangle continues to have four corners, and an ellipse remains an oval. (This is not the case when you reshape an object using the Shape tool, which you will learn about in Chapters 9 and 10).

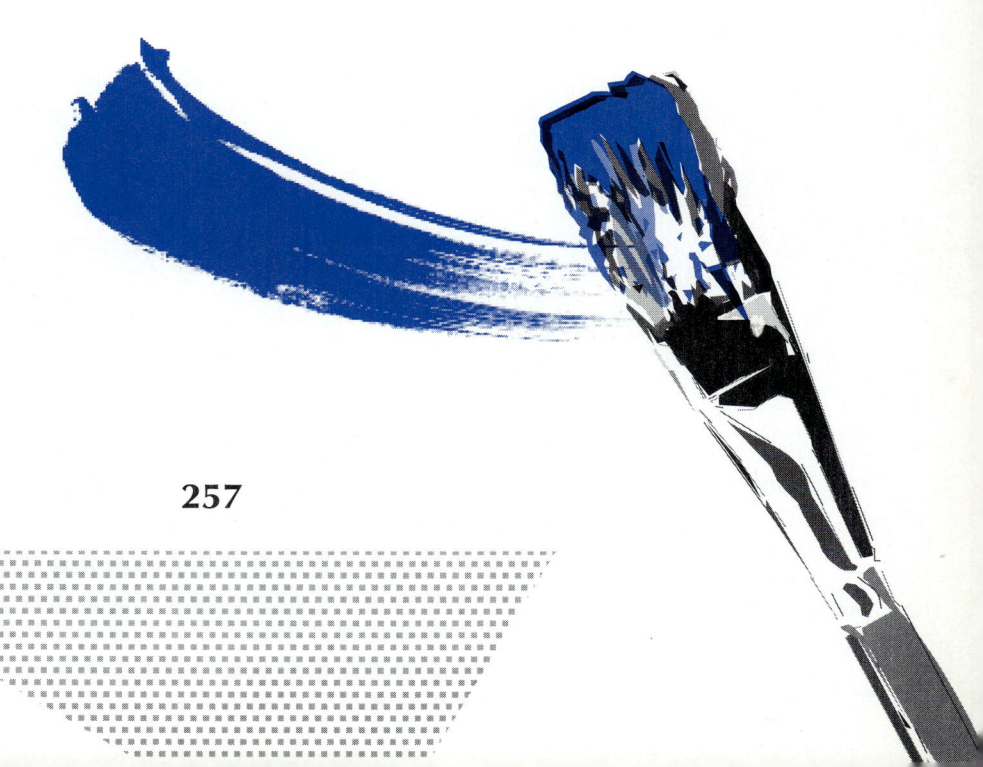

The five basic transformation techniques you will learn in this chapter enable you to size, scale, mirror, rotate, and skew an object in any direction. You will also learn how to retain a copy of the original object, repeat transformations automatically, and return an object to its original format, even if you have transformed it several times.

The exercises in this chapter introduce not only the basic skills that make up the art of transformation, but also the alternative ways you can practice them. CorelDRAW! lets you customize the way you work when transforming objects. If you like to work interactively, you can carry out these functions using the mouse and keyboard alone. For a little extra guidance, you can look to the status line and rulers. And, if you need to render a technical illustration that requires absolute precision, you can select the Transform roll-up from the Effects menu, which is discussed shortly and displayed in Figure 8-1.

Throughout most of this chapter, you will practice each skill using a simple text string that you create in the following section. Although you will practice on this one object, the functions you use—for size, scale and mirror, rotate, and skew—work exactly the same way in CorelDRAW! with multiple selected objects as with single ones. In later exercises, you can practice combining transformation operations with other skills you have learned in previous chapters.

The Transform Roll-Up

Although most of your work will probably be done with the Pick tool, the Transform roll-up allows you greater precision. Use the Transform roll-up to

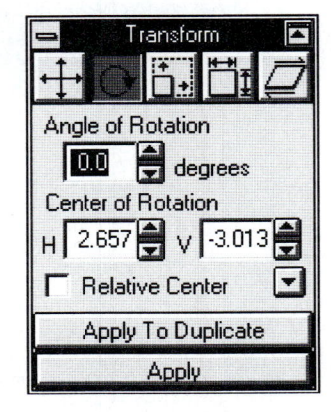

The Transform roll-up used for precision transformations
Figure 8-1.

Transforming Objects

position, rotate, scale, mirror, size, or skew an object by clicking on one of the buttons at the top, as shown here:

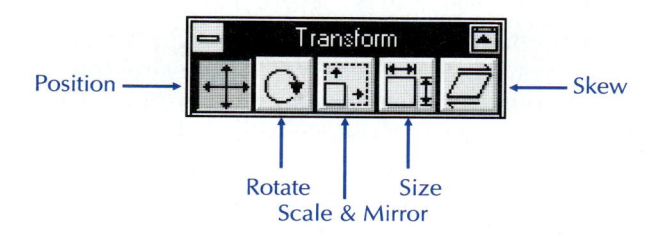

Position — Rotate — Scale & Mirror — Size — Skew

When selected, each button displays a different set of transformation measurements for which you enter the precise amounts for creating a specific transformation. You can then apply the measurement values to a previously selected object, or you can make them apply to a duplicate of a selected object (which will then be created). As each transformation effect is discussed in this chapter, the corresponding Transform roll-up button is also discussed (except for the first button, Position, which is discussed in Chapter 5).

Sizing an Object

As you discovered in Chapter 3, a rectangular selection box, made up of eight black boundary markers, surrounds an object when you select it. These boundary markers, shown in Figure 8-2, have special functions in CorelDRAW!: you use them to size and scale objects. When you *size* an object, you change its *aspect ratio* (the proportion of its width to its height), because you lengthen or shorten it in one direction only. When you *scale* an object, you change the object's length and width at the same time, so the aspect ratio remains the same. To size an object, you must drag one of the four middle boundary markers. To scale an object, you drag one of the four boundary markers in the corners of the selection box.

Selected text object showing boundary markers
Figure 8-2.

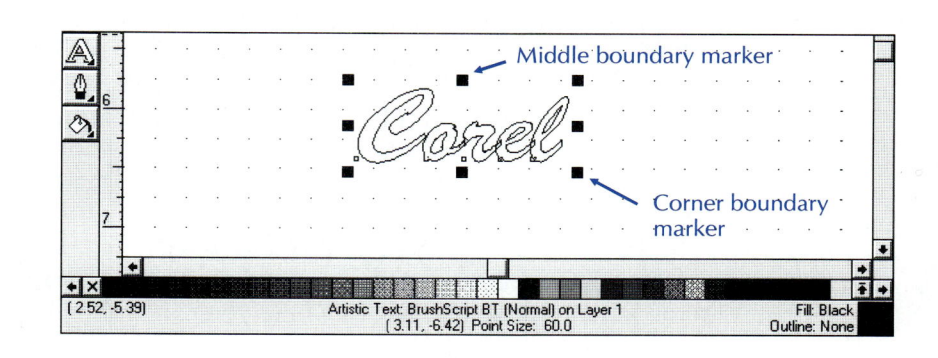

This section covers all of the available techniques for sizing objects, with exercises that will introduce you to both the interactive and menu-assisted methods for sizing and copying objects.

If you prefer to work interactively, bypassing menu commands and dialog boxes, you can size a selected object using the mouse and keyboard alone. You do not sacrifice precision when you work this way, for the status line assists you in setting precise values as you size an object. Practice sizing a text string interactively in the following sections.

Sizing Horizontally

You can size an object in either a horizontal or vertical direction. In the following exercise, you will create a text string and size it toward the right.

1. Make sure your page is in portrait format before you begin. If it is not, choose the Page Setup command from the Layout menu and, from the Size tab, select Letter from the drop-down list box and also select the Portrait button. Click OK. Also from the Layout menu, select Grid & Scale Setup. In the Grid & Scale Setup dialog box, turn off the Show Grid and Snap To Grid options, set the vertical grid origin to 11 inches, and click OK.

2. Make certain Ruler commands in the View menu is selected with a check mark, and that Wireframe is turned off.

3. From the Outline Pen flyout, click on the Hairline icon. Click on Artistic Text and Paragraph Text and then OK to apply the line width to all new objects.

4. From the Fill flyout, click on No Fill (the X). Again click on Artistic Text and Paragraph Text and then OK to apply the fill standard to new object.

5. Select Text Roll-Up from the Text menu or press CTRL-F2. Set the font to BrushScript BT, 60 points; click on the Left justify button and then click on Apply. When the Text Attributes dialog box appears with Artistic Text and Paragraph Text selected, click on OK. You can close the roll-up, or click the roll-up button and leave only the title bar on the screen.

6. Select the Text tool, then select an insertion point at the 1 1/2-inch mark on the horizontal ruler and the 5-inch mark on the vertical ruler. When the insertion point appears, type the text string, **Corel**. The text may appear to have no outline and a gray fill. The standards you set in the Outline Pen and Fill flyouts will appear when the text object is selected with the Pick tool.

7. Select the Zoom tool and choose 1:1 from the flyout menu. Use the scroll bars to move the text to where you can work with it.

Transforming Objects

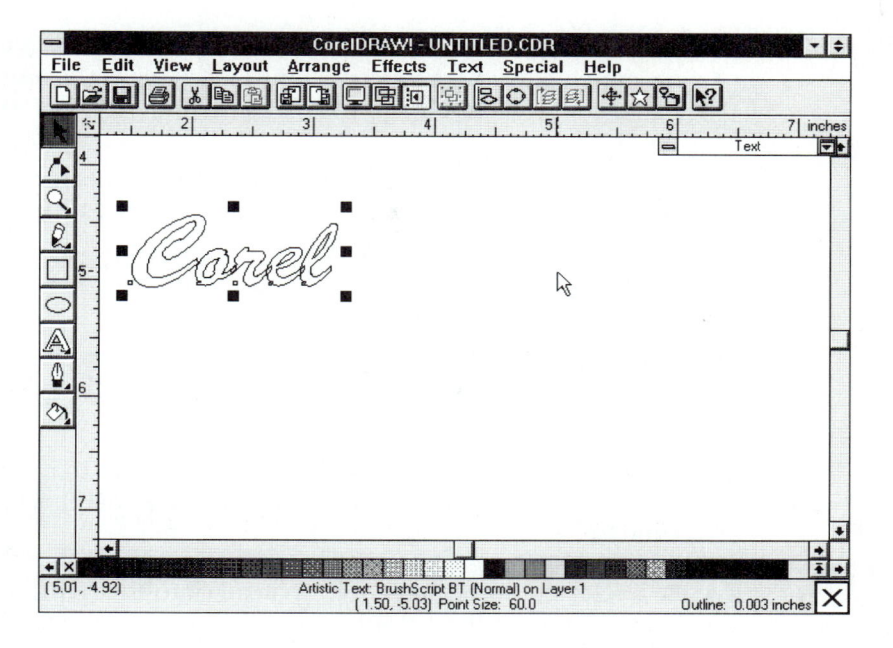

Text roll-up and text string
Figure 8-3.

8. Select the Save As command from the File menu, make sure you are in the directory where you save your drawings, and type **corel.cdr**. (If the text disappears, turn off Wireframe from the View menu.)

9. Press the SPACEBAR to activate the Pick tool. A selection box surrounds the text string immediately, since it was the last object you drew. Your screen should resemble Figure 8-3.

10. Position the pointer directly over the center right boundary marker of the selection box. The mouse pointer changes to a crosshair, as shown here:

11. Depress and hold the mouse and drag the boundary marker to the right. The original object seems to stay in the same place, but a dotted rectangular box follows the pointer, which changes to a two-way horizontal arrow, as shown here:

12. As you drag, the status line displays the message "Y scale:" followed by a numeric value and a percent sign. This value is the amount you are sizing the selected object, shown in increments of 1/10 of a percentage point.

13. After you have sized the object to the desired size, release the mouse button. CorelDRAW! redraws a horizontally sized version of the original object, like the one shown here:

14. Select the Undo command from the Edit menu to return the text string to its original size. The original text string remains selected for the next exercise.

To size a selected object to the left instead of to the right, drag the middle boundary marker at the *left* side of the Selection box. Practice sizing the text string from the left side if you wish, but select Undo after you are finished so that the original text string remains on the screen.

Note: When the mouse pointer is allowed to cross a window border, the object will continue to transform until the pointer is moved back inside the window. This is called Auto-Panning. If you don't like Auto-Panning, you can turn it off in the View tab or the Preferences dialog box reached through the Special menu.

Sizing Vertically

You can also size an object in a vertical direction. The mouse pointer and status line information change to reflect the direction of your size.

1. Select the "Corel" text string if it is not selected already.
2. Position the mouse pointer directly over the top middle boundary marker of the Selection box. The mouse pointer changes to a crosshair.
3. Depress and hold the mouse and drag the boundary marker upward. The original object seems to stay in the same place, but a dotted rectangular box follows the pointer, which changes to a two-way vertical arrow, as shown here:

Transforming Objects

4. As you drag, the status line displays the message "X scale:" followed by a numeric value and a percent sign. This value shows precisely how much you are sizing the selected object in increments of 1/10 of a percent.

5. After you have sized the object to the desired size, release the mouse button. CorelDRAW! redraws a vertically sized version of the original object.

6. Select the Undo Stretch command from the Edit menu to return the text string to its original size.

If you wish, practice sizing the text string downward in a vertical direction. When you are finished, undo your changes to the original object and then proceed with the next exercise.

Sizing in Increments of 100 Percent

In previous chapters, you saw how to use CTRL to constrain your drawing or moving operations to fixed increments or angles. The same holds true when you are sizing a selected object. To size an object in fixed increments of 100 percent, press and hold CTRL as you drag the boundary marker in the desired direction. The status line keeps track of the increments in which you are sizing the object. As always, remember to release the mouse button *before* you release CTRL, or the object may not size in exact increments. In the following exercise, you will triple the width of the original object using CTRL.

1. Select the text string if it is not selected already.

2. Press and hold CTRL and then drag the right middle boundary marker to the right. Notice that the dotted rectangular outline does not follow the two-way arrow pointer continuously; instead, it "snaps" outward only when you have doubled the width of the object, as shown here:

3. When the status line displays the message "Y scale: 300.0%," release the mouse button first and then CTRL . The text string redisplays at triple its original width.
4. Select the Undo command from the Edit menu to revert to the original unsized object.

Retaining a Copy of the Original Object
A useful design technique is to make a copy of the original object as you size it, so that both the original and the sized objects appear on the screen. To retain a copy of the original object, just click the right mouse button once (while depressing the left button) as soon as you begin the sizing, or press the + key on the numeric keypad and the outline box appears. You can choose the technique that is most easy for you.

Note: Pressing the right mouse button while dragging to leave the original does not conflict with the function you assign to the right mouse button in the Preferences dialog box.

You can also retain a copy of the original object when using CTRL. Try this technique now:

1. Select the text string "Corel" if it is not already selected. Position the mouse pointer over the bottom middle boundary marker and begin to drag this marker downward.
2. As soon as the dotted outline box appears, press the + key or press and release the right mouse button once. The message "Leave Original" appears at the left side of the status line.
3. Press and hold CTRL and continue to drag the bottom middle boundary marker downward until the status line reads "Scale: 200.0%."
4. Release the mouse button and then the CTRL key. The screen displays both the original and sized object, as shown here:

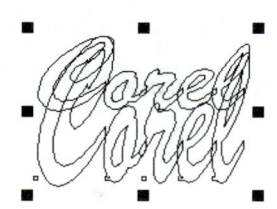

5. Undo your changes to the original text string before continuing.

If the sized object does not appear in the correct proportions, you either failed to press and hold CTRL, or released CTRL before releasing the mouse button. Keep practicing until you feel comfortable with the technique, but remember to undo your changes to be ready for the next exercise.

Sizing with the Transform Roll-Up

If you find the use of the mouse and keyboard controls inconvenient, you can perform all of the possible size operations using the Size option on the Transform roll-up in the Effects menu. The roll-up that opens when you select this command allows you to choose the direction of the size, specify the exact amount of sizing, and retain a copy of the original object.

Sizing an Object

Take another look at the COREL.CDR file that you created in the first part of this chapter. Then try the following exercise to become familiar with the Size roll-up.

1. Select the "Corel" text string and then, from the Effects menu, select the Transform roll-up and click on the Size button (fourth button from the left). The roll-up shown in Figure 8-4 appears (your horizontal and vertical values may differ). The horizontal (H) and vertical (V) controls in the center of the roll-up let you specify the direction and amount of size in increments of .01 inch. The down arrow, when clicked, opens the Relative Position indicators. These indicators allow you to size relative to the current position. The Apply To Duplicate button determines whether you make a copy of the original object as you size it.

2. Set the numeric value for vertical (V) to 1.5 inches, using either the scroll arrow or the keyboard, and then click on Apply. The text string increases in height. Notice, however, that when you size an object using the Size roll-up instead of the mouse, the sized object is centered on the same position as the original. If you want it to appear in another location, click on the object's outline and drag it to the desired location.

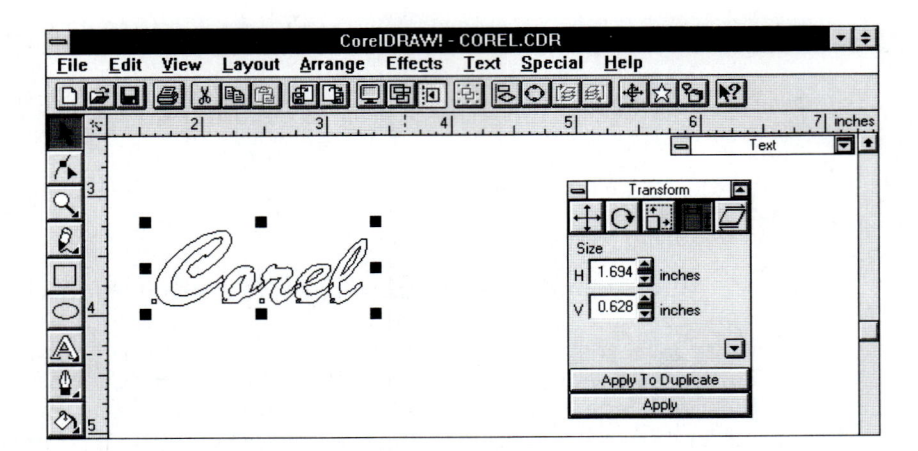

Size roll-up
Figure 8-4.

3. Select the Clear Transformations command from the Effects menu to return the object to its original size. (You can also use Undo in the Edit menu or press CTRL-Z.)

4. While the "Corel" object is selected and the Size option is on the Transform roll-up, set the horizontal value (H) to 2.5 inches, and then select Apply. This time, the text string increases in width.

5. Clear the current transformation by selecting the Clear Transformations command in the Effects menu. This time, you will create a larger size duplicate while retaining the size of the original.

6. Set the vertical (V) value to 1.5 inches and then click on Apply To Duplicate to retain a copy of the original object. CorelDRAW! redisplays the original object against a vertically sized image about 1.5 times the size of the original.

Notice that when you use the Size roll-up for these operations, the sized object is superimposed on the original and both objects share a common point, as shown in Figure 8-5. If you want the sized object to appear above, below, or to the side of the original, first open the Relative Position drop box by clicking on the down arrow (below and to the right of the vertical scale numeric entry box) and then click on the checkbox representing the position the original object will take in relation to its duplicate. Alternatively, you can drag the sized object's outline to the desired location, or you can use the Position button on the Transform roll-up (explained in Chapter 5).

7. To erase the transformed copy of the object so that only the unaltered original remains, select Undo Duplicate from the Edit menu.

Transforming Objects 267

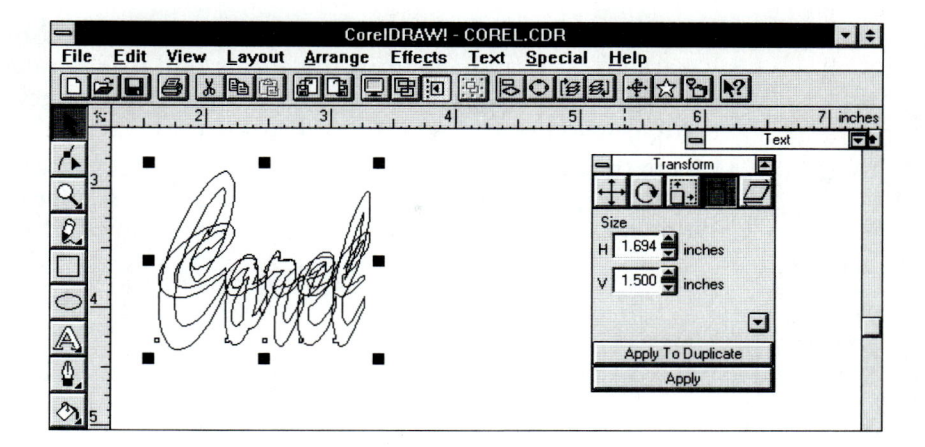

Vertical transformation sharing same center with original
Figure 8-5.

> **Caution:** If you want to erase the copy of the original object after a transformation that leaves the original in place, use Undo Duplicate rather than Clear Transformations. If you use Clear Transformations, the transformed object on the top layer is not erased, but instead becomes an exact copy of the original. The transformation is cleared, but not the object itself. As a result, what looks like one object on the screen is actually two superimposed objects.

8. At this point you can roll up the Transform roll-up and move it to one side. You'll use it again later.

Scaling an Object

As you have just seen, sizing an object involves changing its size in one direction (horizontal or vertical) only. When you *scale* an object, you change its size horizontally and vertically at the same time, thereby maintaining the same proportions and aspect ratio. You can scale an object interactively using the keyboard and mouse, or you can scale an object using the Scale & Mirror option on the Transform roll-up found on the Effects menu. If you prefer to work more spontaneously, you will probably favor the mouse and keyboard controls. Recall that when you size an object, you drag it by one of the *middle* boundary markers. Scaling an object is similar, except that you drag one of the *corner* boundary markers instead.

To practice scaling objects interactively, try this exercise:

1. If it is not selected already, select the "Corel" text string.

2. Position the mouse pointer directly over one of the corner boundary markers. You can scale from any corner but, for the sake of this exercise, use the lower-right corner marker. The pointer changes to a crosshair, just as when you prepared to size an object.

3. Drag the lower-right boundary marker diagonally downward. As you drag, the pointer changes to a four-way arrow, similar to the move arrow, except that it is rotated diagonally, as shown here:

The illustration shows an object increasing in scale from the lower-right corner marker.

The original object appears to stay in the same place, but a dotted outline box follows the scaling pointer. The outline box increases or decreases in size, depending on the direction in which you drag the marker.

Note that the status line displays the message "Scale:" followed by a percentage value. This value tells you precisely how much larger or smaller you are making the object.

4. When the dotted outline box is the size you want the text string to be, release the mouse button. The selected object reappears in a scaled version.

5. Select Clear Transformations in the Effects menu or Undo in the Edit menu to return the object to its original size.

Scaling in Increments of 100 Percent

To scale an object in increments of 100 percent of its size, all you need to do is press and hold CTRL while scaling the object. Just as when you sized objects using CTRL, the dotted outline box does not move smoothly but instead "snaps" at each 100 percent increment. Likewise, the message in the status line changes only when you reach the next 100 percent increment. Remember to release the mouse button *before* you release CTRL, or the increments will not be exact.

Keep in mind, too, that an object scaled to 200 percent of its original size takes up four times the area of the original object, not twice as much, because you are increasing both the height and width of the object by a factor of two.

Transforming Objects

Retaining a Copy While Scaling
To retain a copy of the object in its original location as you scale it, just click the right mouse button (while holding down the left button) as soon as you begin to scale the object or press and release the + key on the numeric keypad. The status line displays the message "Leave Original," just as when you leave a copy while sizing an object.

Precise Scaling with the Transform Roll-Up
If you find the use of the mouse and keyboard controls inconvenient, you can perform all of the scaling operations precisely, using the Scale & Mirror option on the Transform roll-up on the Effects menu. You can specify the amount of scaling desired, retain a copy of the original object, and create mirror images that appear at a diagonal to the original. Work through the following exercise to become familiar with using the Transform roll-up to scale an object.

1. With the COREL.CDR file open and in an actual size viewing magnification, select the "Corel" text string. Open the Transform roll-up and then select the Scale & Mirror button, the middle button, as shown here:

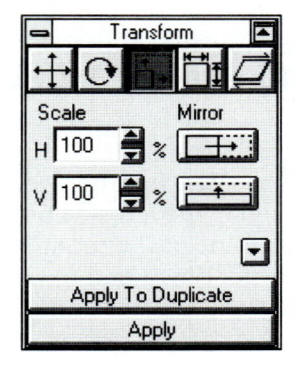

2. To scale an object, you need to set both the horizontal (H) and the vertical (V) values to the same number. Set both of these values to 150 percent, using either the scroll arrow or the keyboard.

3. Click on Apply. The text string increases in both height and width. Notice, however, that a scaled object created with the Scale & Mirror roll-up appears in the same location as the original and has the same center point. If you want the scaled object to appear elsewhere, move it to the desired location.

4. Select the Clear Transformations command from the Effects menu to return the object to its original size.

Retaining a Copy While Using Scale & Mirror

It is easy to make a copy of the original object from the Scale & Mirror roll-up. Simply press Apply To Duplicate before you exit the roll-up.

1. Again make sure the text string "Corel" is selected as well as the Scale & Mirror option (the middle button) of the Tranform roll-up. This time, you will constrain the size of the image to an exact multiple of the original, as you did using CTRL and the mouse. You will also leave a copy of the original object in its original location.

2. Set the vertical and horizontal values to 200 percent and then click on Apply To Duplicate to retain a copy of the original object. CorelDRAW! redisplays the original object along with a scaled text string at two times the size of the original.

3. To erase the transformed copy of the object so that only the unaltered original remains, select the Undo Duplicate command from the Edit menu. If you have moved the copy of the original, select it and press DEL to clear it.

4. Roll up the Transform roll-up and move it to the side for now.

Notice that the scaled object is superimposed on the original. If you want it elsewhere, you must drag it there. Or, you can use the Relative Position drop-down box and click on the check box representing the position of the original object relative to its duplicate.

Sizing and Scaling from the Center

In the previous sizing and scaling exercises using the mouse, the object was modified in one dimension (sizing) or two dimensions (scaling) from a fixed opposite side or sides. In other words, when you dragged the right side of the object to the right, the left side remained fixed and was in the same position as was the right side of the modified object. Similarly, when you dragged the lower-right corner down and to the right, the top and left sides remained fixed and had the same horizontal and vertical position as the modified object.

When you used the Size and Scale & Mirror options and modified an object in one or two dimensions, the opposite sides moved proportionately. That is, with the roll-up, the object was being modified from a fixed center point instead of from a fixed side or sides. When you changed the horizontal and vertical percentages, all four sides changed, leaving the same center point as the original object.

You can also size and scale an object from the center point by pressing SHIFT while dragging with the mouse. This is the same as drawing an ellipse or rectangle from the center by pressing SHIFT while dragging with the Ellipse or Rectangle tool.

Transforming Objects

Recall how you sized and scaled with the mouse originally and see how this changes when you press SHIFT:

1. The COREL.CDR text object should be selected on your page in an actual size view.
2. As you did in an earlier exercise, drag the middle boundary marker on the right side to the right several inches. Notice how the left side remains fixed. Release the mouse button and press CTRL-Z to undo the modification.
3. Press and hold SHIFT while dragging the right middle boundary marker to the right an inch or so. Notice how the left side now moves a proportionate amount—the left and right sides are moving outward in equal amounts. Release the mouse button and press CTRL-Z to undo the modification.
4. Again, as you did before, drag the lower-right corner boundary marker down and to the right several inches. Notice how the left and top sides remain fixed. Release the mouse button and press CTRL-Z to undo the modification.
5. Press and hold SHIFT while dragging the lower-right corner boundary marker down and to the right an inch or so. Notice how the top and left sides are now moving proportionately with the right and bottom sides. Release the mouse button and press CTRL-Z to undo the modification.

> The ability to size or scale an object from the center allows you to more easily fill a regular enclosing space.

Creating a Mirror Image

As you found when sizing and scaling objects, the selection box boundary markers are very useful and easy to use. They are also handy when creating mirror images. The Transform roll-up, another important tool in sizing and scaling, also can be used to create mirror images with its Scale & Mirror option. You will explore both means of creating these visual effects.

Using the middle boundary markers on the selection box, you can create a horizontal or vertical mirror image of an object. You can choose from among several techniques the one most suited to your needs. If, for example, you choose to retain a copy of the original object, you need to use the + key or click the right mouse button. If you choose to make the size of the mirror image an exact multiple of the original, you need to use CTRL after clicking the right mouse button. You can just as easily decide not to copy the original object, or make the mirrored object a custom size. In every case, however, you will drag the *opposite* center boundary marker until it "flips" in the direction in which you want the mirror image to appear.

The following exercise assumes that you want to create a perfect horizontal mirror image of an object, like the one shown here. At the end of the exercise are suggestions for obtaining other results.

In this illustration, the original object is retained, but neither the original nor the mirrored object is sized.

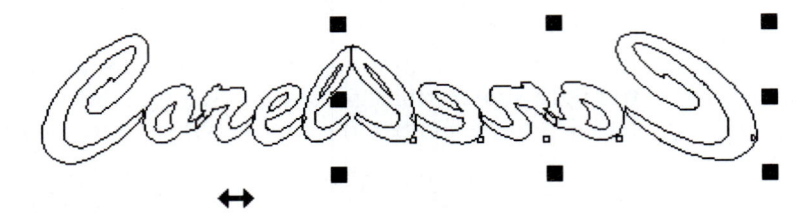

1. Select the text string "Corel" if it isn't selected already.
2. Position the mouse pointer over the left middle boundary marker and begin to drag this marker to the right.
3. As soon as the dotted outline box appears, press the + key or click the right mouse button once. The message "Leave Original" appears at the left side of the status line.
4. Press and hold CTRL and continue to drag the marker to the right. The CTRL key ensures that the size of the mirrored object will be an exact multiple of the original, in this case the identical size (100 percent).
5. When the dotted outline box "snaps" beside the original object and the status line reads "Y scale: 100.0% (Mirrored)," as in Figure 8-6, release the mouse button and then the CTRL key. CorelDRAW! redraws the screen showing both the original and the mirrored object. The mirrored object is selected. If your text strings look different, select Undo Stretch and try the exercise again.
6. Press CTRL-Z for Undo and to return the text string to its original unmirrored state.

You can vary this exercise to achieve different results. For example, to create a vertical mirror image that appears beneath the object, drag the upper middle boundary marker downward. To make the mirror image double or triple the size of the original, keep sizing the mirror object using CTRL. To make the mirror image a custom size, just drag the boundary marker *without* using CTRL. If you want to create a mirror image only, without retaining the original object, do not click the right mouse button or use the + key.

To create a mirror image appearing at a diagonal to the original object, you can use the familiar techniques used in scaling an object.

Transforming Objects

Creating a perfect horizontal mirror image of an object
Figure 8-6.

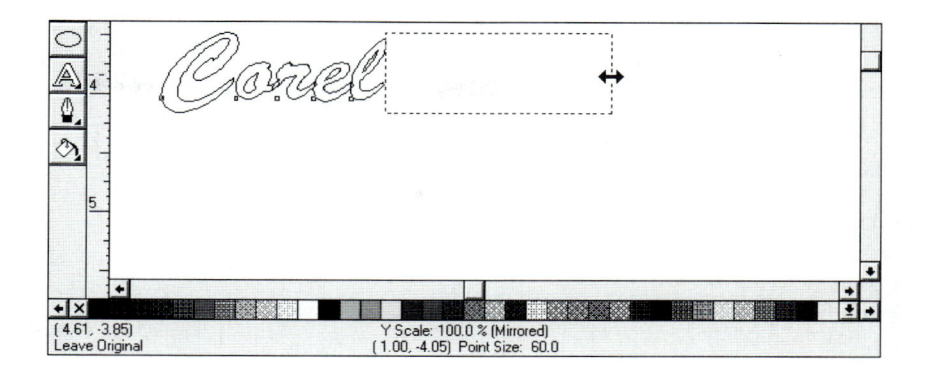

Creating a Diagonal Mirror Image

Using the corner boundary markers on the selection box, you can create a mirror image that appears at a diagonal to the original object. You can choose from among several techniques the one that best suits your needs. If you choose to retain a copy of the original object, you need to click the right mouse button or the + key. If you choose to make the size of the mirror image an exact multiple of the original, you need to use CTRL. You can just as easily decide not to copy the original object or to make the mirrored object a custom size. In every case, however, you drag the *opposite* corner boundary marker until it "flips" in the direction in which you want the mirror image to appear.

The following exercise assumes that you are going to create a perfect diagonal mirror image of an object. In this exercise, the original object remains, but neither the original nor the mirrored object is scaled beyond the original size. At the end of the exercise you will find suggestions for obtaining other results.

1. Select the text string "Corel," if it is not selected already.
2. Position the pointer over the boundary marker in the upper-left corner of the Selection box and begin to drag the marker downward and to the right.
3. As soon as the dotted outline box appears, click the right mouse button or press the + key on your numeric keypad once to leave a copy of the original object. The message "Leave Original" appears at the left side of the status line.
4. Press and hold CTRL and continue dragging the boundary marker until the dotted outline box "snaps" at a diagonal to the original object and the status line reads "Scale: 100.0% (Mirrored)," as shown in Figure 8-7.

Creating a diagonal mirror image of an object while scaling
Figure 8-7.

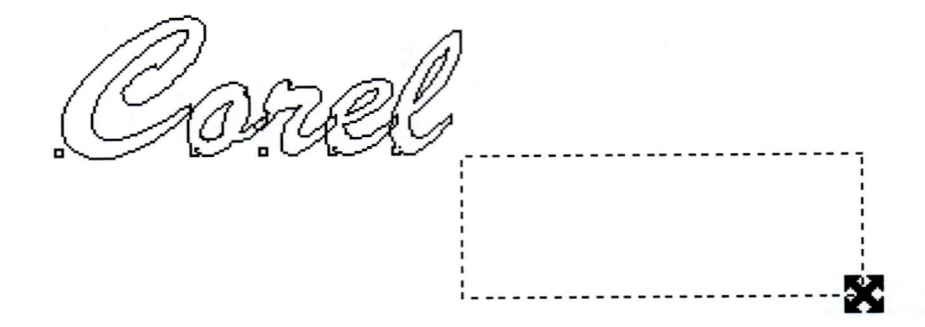

The CTRL key ensures that the size of the mirrored object will be an exact multiple of the original.

5. Release first the mouse button and then the CTRL key. CorelDRAW! redraws the screen showing both the original and the mirrored object. The mirrored object is selected. If your text strings do not appear in this way, try the exercise again.
6. Select Undo Stretch from the Edit menu or press CTRL-Z to return the object to its original unmirrored state.

You can vary this exercise to achieve different results. For example, to place the mirror image at the upper-right corner of the original object, drag from the lower-left corner marker upward. To make the mirror image double or triple the size of the original, keep sizing the mirror object using CTRL. To make the mirror image a custom size, just drag the opposite boundary marker without using CTRL. If you want to create a mirror image only, without retaining the original object, do not click the right mouse button or use the + key.

Mirroring an Object with the Transform Roll-Up

The following exercise shows you how to create a vertical or horizontal mirror image using the Scale & Mirror button on the Transform roll-up instead of the mouse and keyboard. When you create a mirror image, you can choose whether or not to retain a copy of the original object. You should continue working in actual size viewing magnification for this exercise.

1. With the text string in the COREL.CDR file selected, again open the Transform roll-up and make sure the Scale & Mirror roll-up (third icon from the left) is selected.

Transforming Objects

2. Enter 100 % in both the vertical (V) and horizontal (H) scale entry boxes. Click the vertical Mirror button. Click on Apply. The result is as shown here:

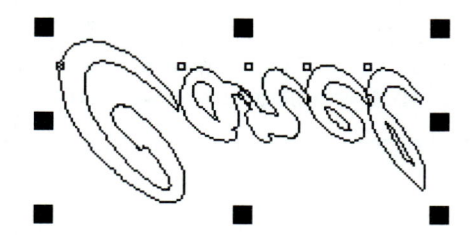

3. Select Clear Transformations from the Effects menu to return the object to its original state.
4. This time, retaining the 100% in both scales boxes, Click on the vertical mirror button to turn it off, and then click on the horizontal Mirror button. Click on Apply. A horizontal mirror image of the original text appears.
5. Select Clear Transformations to return the image to its original state.

You can customize the settings in the Scale & Mirror roll-up to achieve different results.

If you want to merge a copy of the original object with the mirrored version, just click on Apply To Duplicate in the Scale & Mirror roll-up. If you want to make the mirror image larger or smaller than the original, set the scale values accordingly. To get both a horizontal and vertical mirror image, click on both the mirror buttons.

If you want to move the mirror, you can use the Relative Position drop-down box (below and to the right of the vertical scale numeric entry box) and click on the check box representing the position that the mirror object will occupy relative to the original image. That is, if the center check box is selected, the mirror image will appear in the same spot as its original image. If a check box to the side of the center is selected, the mirror image will appear there.

Roll up the Transform roll-up and move it to one side.

Rotating an Object

When you click on an object once using the Pick tool, you can move, arrange, size, or scale it. In addition, the Pick tool can rotate and skew an object. *Rotating* involves turning an object in a clockwise or counterclockwise direction, at an angle that you define. When you *skew* an object, on the other hand, you slant it toward the right, left, top, or bottom in order to create distortion or three-dimensional effects.

As with sizing and scaling, you can rotate an object interactively, using the mouse and keyboard, or you can use the Rotate button on the Transform roll-up in the Effects menu. If you feel more comfortable working with roll-ups than with the mouse and keyboard, you can select the Rotate button after clicking on an object once. To rotate an object interactively, however, you must either click on a selected object a second time, or double-click on an object that you have not yet selected.

Practice entering the interactive rotate/skew mode now, using the text string in the COREL.CDR file.

1. With the COREL.CDR file open and displayed at the actual size viewing magnification, click once on the outline of the text string. The normal selection box with its eight black boundary markers appears.

2. Click on the outline of the text string a second time (be sure the pointer is on the text string or you'll get other results). CorelDRAW! replaces the eight boundary markers with eight two-way arrows, as shown here:

You can drag any one of the corner arrows to rotate the object but, for the sake of this exercise, you will work with the upper-right corner arrow.

3. Position the mouse pointer over the two-way arrow in the upper-right corner of the rotate/skew selection box. When the pointer becomes a crosshair, press and hold the mouse button and drag the mouse in a counterclockwise direction. As soon as you begin to drag, the mouse pointer changes to an arc with arrows at either end. A dotted outline box representing the text string begins to rotate in a counterclockwise direction, as shown in Figure 8-8. Notice that the status line displays the angle of rotation as a positive number.

4. Continue to drag the corner highlighting arrow in a counterclockwise direction until you have rotated the object more than 180 degrees. At that point, the status line begins to display a negative number for the angle of rotation, and the number begins to decrease from 180. Use the number on the status line to inform yourself how far you have rotated a selected object.

Transforming Objects

Rotate an object in a counterclockwise direction
Figure 8-8.

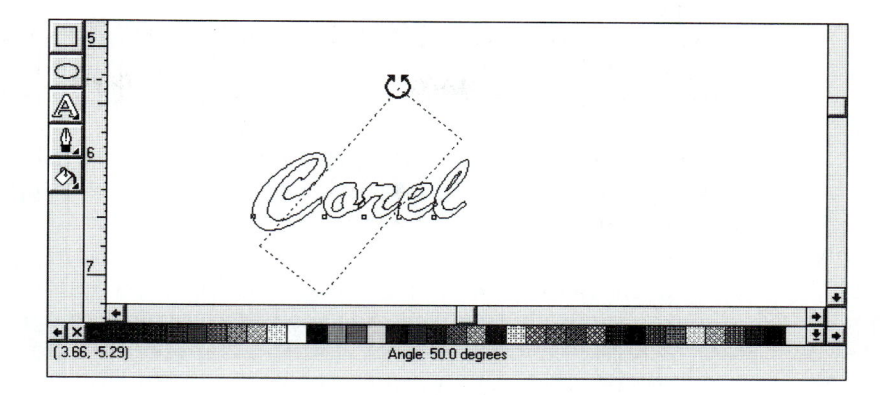

5. Continue rotating the text object until the number becomes positive again. Release the mouse button when the status line indicates an angle of about 17 degrees. CorelDRAW! redisplays the object at the selected angle of rotation.

6. Select the Clear Transformations command from the Effects menu to return the object to its original angle.

7. The text object should again appear selected, with its normal boundary markers. Click on its text outline to redisplay the curved-arrow boundary markers. Drag the highlighting arrow in the upper-right corner again, but in a clockwise direction. The angle indicator on the status line displays a negative number until you rotate the text string more than 180 degrees. At that point, the number becomes positive and begins to decrease from 180 degrees downward.

8. Release the mouse button to redisplay the object at the new angle of rotation.

9. Select the Clear Transformations command from the Effects menu to return the object to its original angle.

Note: You may sometimes rotate an object several times in succession. The angle of rotation displayed in the status line, however, refers to the amount of the current rotation, not to the cumulative angle.

Rotating in Increments of 15 Degrees

As in almost every drawing or editing function of CorelDRAW!, you can use CTRL to constrain movement in the rotation of objects. Simply press and hold CTRL while dragging a corner arrow of the rotate/skew selection box, and the object rotates and "snaps" to successive 15-degree angles. The status line keeps track of the angle of rotation. As always, remember to release the mouse button before you release the CTRL key, or you will not constrain the angle of rotation. You will use the constrain feature in the following exercise.

1. Double-click on the text string if it is not selected already or click once on its outline if it is selected. The two-way arrows appear to show that you are in the rotate/skew mode.

2. Position the pointer over the upper-right corner highlighting arrow until the pointer changes to a crosshair. Press and hold the CTRL key and the mouse button and drag the highlighting arrow in the desired direction. Notice that the dotted rectangular box does not follow the rotation pointer continuously; instead, it "snaps" each time you reach an angle that is a multiple of 15 degrees.

3. When you reach the desired angle, release the mouse button first and then release the CTRL key. The object redisplays at the new angle of rotation.

4. Select Clear Transformations from the Effects menu to return the object to its original angle.

Retaining a Copy While Rotating

If you like to experiment with design, you may find it useful to make a copy of the original object as you rotate it. Figure 8-9 illustrates one design effect you can achieve easily. This text pinwheel, suitable for desktop publishing applications, was created by rotating a text string in increments of 30 degrees and copying the original each time.

A text pinwheel created by repeatedly rotating and retaining a copy of a text string
Figure 8-9.

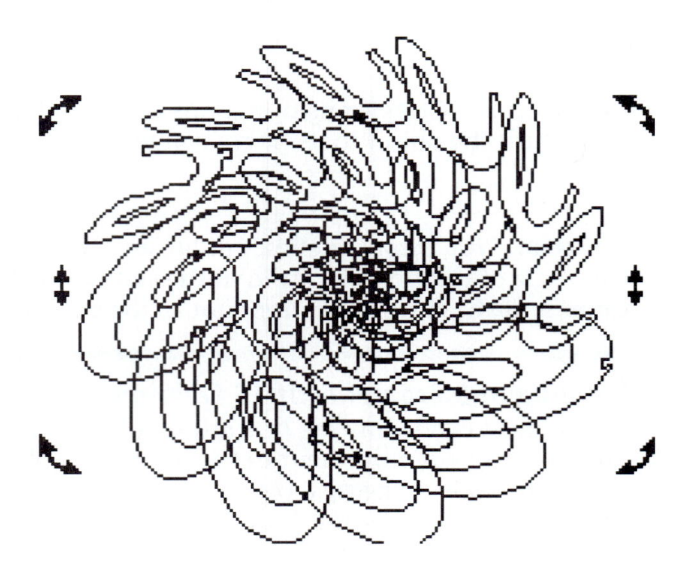

Transforming Objects

You can also retain a copy of the original object using CTRL, but that operation requires a bit more coordination. Try this technique now:

1. With the COREL.CDR file open and in an actual size viewing magnification, click on the text outline "Corel" if it is already selected, or double-click if it is not selected. The rotate/skew highlighting arrows appear. Use the window scroll arrows to move the text object to the center of the screen. Doing this does not change the orientation of your drawing on the page.

2. Position the mouse pointer over the upper-right highlighting arrow marker and begin to drag this marker upward. As soon as the dotted outline box appears, click the right mouse button or press the + key once to leave a copy of the original.

3. Press and hold CTRL and continue dragging the arrow marker upward until the status line reads "angle: 30 degrees."

4. Release the mouse button first and then the CTRL key. The screen displays both the original and the rotated object, as shown here:

5. Continue copying and rotating the text strings four more times at the same angle to create the design shown in Figure 8-9. Then undo your changes to the original text string before going further. Use Undo or press DEL to erase the last rotation, then select the remaining objects one at a time and press DEL for each object. Instead of selecting and deleting each object, it may be easier to use Open in the File menu and again open the original COREL.CDR file.

Changing an Object's Rotation

Look at an object on your screen when it is in rotate/skew mode. In the center of the object is a small dot surrounded by a circle. This graphic aid appears every time you activate the rotate/skew mode and represents the center of rotation of an object. The object turns on this axis as you rotate it. If you want the object to rotate on a different axis, you can alter the center

The center of rotation does not have to be the center of the object.

of rotation freely by dragging the center-of-rotation symbol to the desired location using the mouse. In the following exercise, you will create a simple text design that involves changing the center of a text string's rotation.

1. With the COREL.CDR file open and in an actual size viewing magnification, click on the text outline "Corel" if it is already selected and move it to the center of the display. Click on its outlines again to access the rotate/skew mode.

2. When the rotate/skew selection box appears, position the mouse pointer over the center-of-rotation symbol until it becomes a crosshair. Drag the rotation symbol to the upper-right corner of the rotate/skew selection box, as shown here. Then release the mouse button.

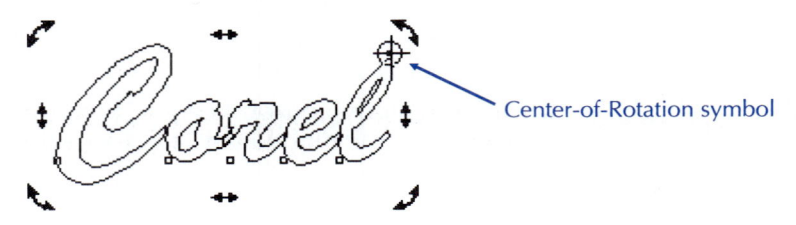

Center-of-Rotation symbol

3. Position the mouse pointer over any one of the corner highlighting arrows and begin dragging the arrow in a clockwise direction. As soon as the dotted outline box appears, click the right mouse button while keeping the left button depressed, or press the + key on your numeric keypad once to leave a copy of the original. Notice that because you have changed the center of rotation, the text string turns on its end rather than on its center point.

4. Press and hold CTRL and continue dragging the marker until the status line shows that you have rotated the text string by –90 degrees.

5. Release the mouse button first, and then the CTRL key. Both the original object and the rotated object display at 90-degree angles to one another.

6. Repeat this process two more times, until you have a text design similar to the one in Figure 8-10. To make all of the text strings behave as though they were one object, click on the Select All command in the Edit menu and group the text strings, using the Group command in the Arrange menu. Now reposition the group to the center of the display.

7. Save this figure as 4CORNERS.CDR.

8. Clear the screen by selecting New from the File menu.

Your new center of rotation does not have to be a highlighting arrow; you can relocate the center anywhere within the Selection box. But a corner or

Transforming Objects 281

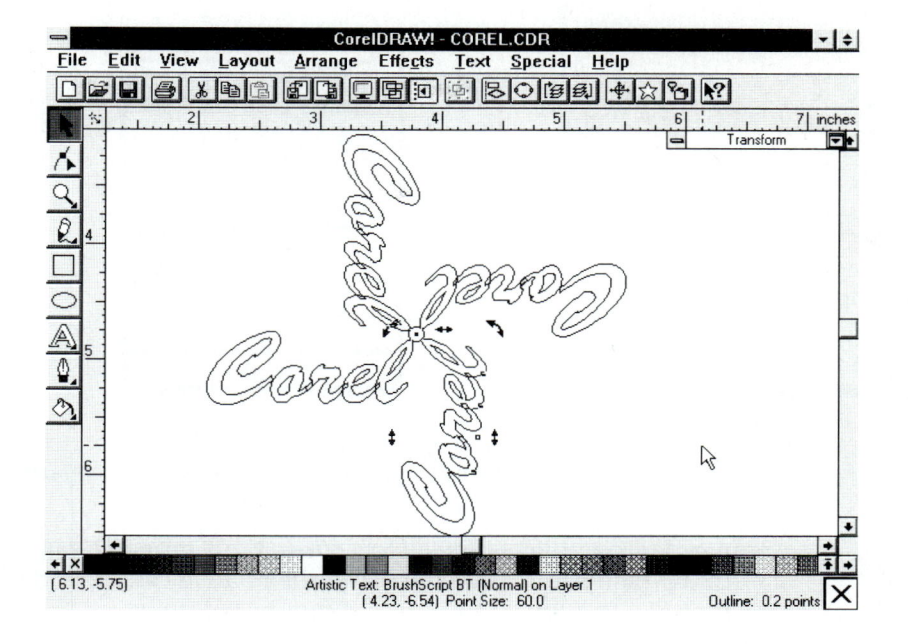

Text design created by rotating and copying an object with an altered center of rotation

Figure 8-10.

boundary of the selected object often proves to be a convenient "handle" when you are performing rotations.

Rotating with the Transform Roll-Up

If you find the use of the keyboard controls inconvenient, you can perform all of the preceding rotation operations with precision using the Rotate button on the Transform menu. You can select this command when either the normal selection box or the rotate/skew selection box is visible around a selected object. Perform the following brief exercise to familiarize yourself with the workings of the Rotate roll-up.

1. Open the COREL.CDR file and set the viewing magnification to 1:1. Place the text where you can work with it. Click once on the text string to select it.

2. Open the Transform roll-up and click on the Rotate button (second from the left). The Rotate roll-up appears, as in Figure 8-11. (Your numbers may differ.)

You can enter a number in the Angle of Rotation numeric entry box either by scrolling in increments of 5 degrees or by clicking on the numeric entry box and typing in a number in increments of 1/10 of a degree.

Rotate button on the Transform roll-up
Figure 8-11.

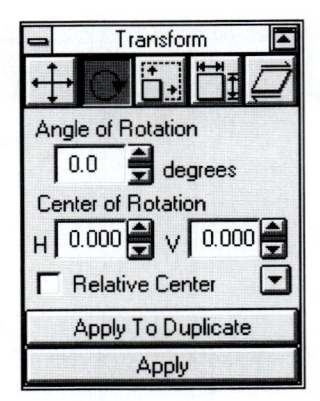

In addition to setting the angle of rotation, you can set the center of rotation to an absolute horizontal or vertical postion, or to a relative position by clicking on the Relative Center check box.

In order to duplicate the effects created in Figure 8-9, but with the Rotate roll-up, you can set the angle and the relative center, and then click on Apply To Duplicate the required number of times.

You cannot skew and rotate an object at the same time.

3. Set Angle of Rotation to 30 degrees. Make sure the horizontal and vertical numeric entry boxes for Center of Rotation both contain 0. Place a check mark in the Relative Center. Click on Apply To Duplicate 5 times. Isn't this a much easier way to produce the Figure 8-9 effects!

4. When you are finished, leave the original image on the screen for the next exercise. Use Undo or press DEL to erase the last rotation, then select the remaining objects one at a time and press DEL for each object. Instead of selecting and deleting each object, it may be easier to use Open in the File menu and again open the original COREL.CDR file.

5. Roll up the Transform roll-up for now.

That's all there is to rotating an object at the angle and axis of your choice. You can leave a copy of the original object while rotating it, just as when you copy an object that you are sizing or scaling. In the next section, you will practice skewing an object to achieve interesting distortion effects.

Skewing an Object

When you skew an object, you slant and distort it at a horizontal or vertical angle, thus warping its appearance. This technique can be useful for creating three-dimensional or surrealistic effects. As with the other techniques you have learned in this chapter, you can skew an object either interactively or by using the controls in the Transform roll-up.

Transforming Objects

1. With the COREL.CDR file open and in an actual size viewing magnification, select the "Corel" text string. Then click a second time anywhere on its outline to enter rotate/skew mode.
2. To begin skewing the object horizontally, position the mouse pointer directly over the upper-middle highlighting arrow and drag it to the right. The mouse pointer changes to two half-arrows pointing in opposite directions, and a dotted outline box slants to the right, the direction you are moving your mouse, as shown in Figure 8-12. The status line keeps track of the current angle of horizontal skew.
3. When you reach the desired skewing angle, release the mouse button. CorelDRAW! redisplays the object as you have skewed it, as shown here:

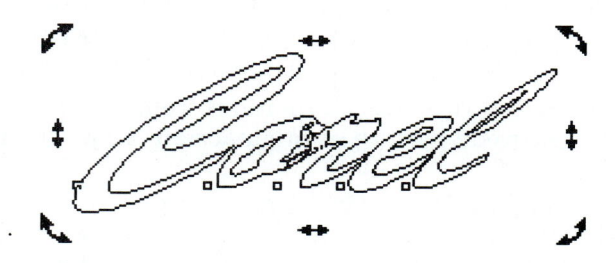

4. Select Clear Transformations from the Effects menu to return the object to its original unskewed state.
5. Practice different angles of horizontal skewing. You can skew an object greater than 85 degrees to the right or left. If you drag one of the middle highlighting arrows along the left or right *side* of the Selection box, you can skew the object in a vertical direction.
6. When you feel comfortable with basic skewing operations, select Clear Transformations from the Effects menu. Leave the text string on the screen for the next exercise.

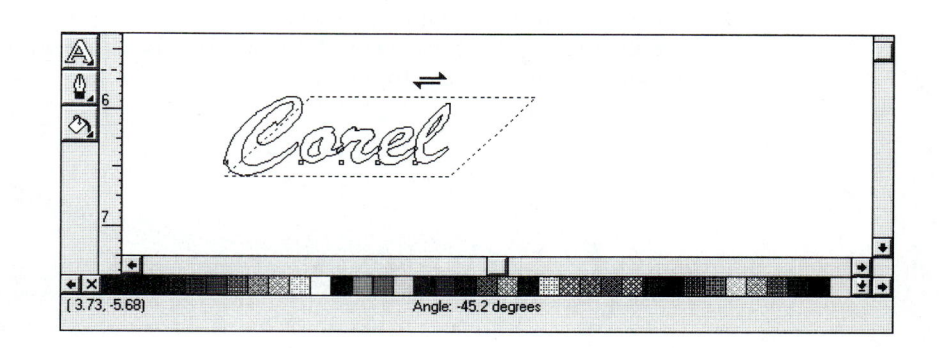

Skewing an object to the right
Figure 8-12.

Skewing in Increments of 15 Degrees

Once again, you can use CTRL to introduce an extra measure of precision to the interactive transformation of objects. When skewing an object, pressing and holding CTRL forces the object to skew in increments of 15 degrees. Try using this constraint feature now.

1. Select the text string "Corel" and enter the rotate/skew mode.
2. Position the mouse pointer over the upper-middle highlighting arrow, press and hold CTRL, and begin dragging the mouse to the right or left, as desired. The mouse pointer changes to the skew pointer, and the dotted outline box "snaps" in the desired direction in increments of 15 degrees.
3. When you reach the desired angle, release the mouse button first and then release the CTRL key. If you release CTRL first, you might not constrain the skewing operation to a 15-degree increment.
4. Select Clear Transformations from the Effects menu to return the skewed object to its original state. Leave the text string on the screen.

Retaining a Copy While Skewing

For an interesting design effect, you can skew an object and then make a copy of the original. As you will see in the following exercise, you can then position the skewed object behind the original to make it seem like a shadow.

1. Select the "Corel" text string and enter rotate/skew mode.
2. Position the mouse pointer over the upper-middle highlighting arrow and begin dragging the arrow to the right. As soon as the dotted outline box appears, click the right mouse button while depressing the left button to leave a copy of the original, or press the + key on your numeric keypad.
3. Press and hold CTRL and continue dragging the marker until the status line shows a skewing angle of –60 degrees.
4. Release the mouse button first and then release the CTRL key. The skewed object, which is selected automatically, appears on top of the copy of the original, as shown here:

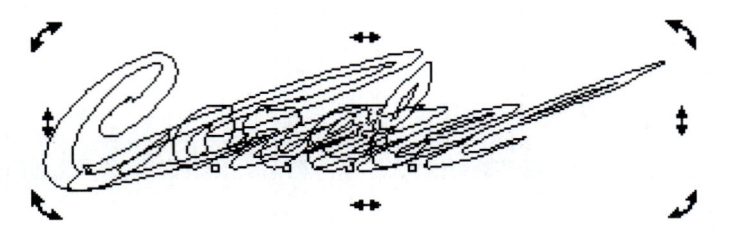

Transforming Objects

5. To place the skewed object behind the unskewed original, click on Order in the Arrange menu and then on To Back in the flyout menu.
6. You can manipulate the skewed object like any other object. Click once on its outline to toggle back to select mode, and then scale it to a larger size by dragging the upper-right corner boundary marker of the Selection box.
7. Click on the black fill option (third option on the second row) of the Fill flyout menu.
8. Now select the original text object. From the Fill flyout menu select a pattern, such as the third from the right, bottom row.
9. Go to the preview window by clicking on Full-Screen Preview in the View menu, or by pressing F9. Your preview should look roughly similar to Figure 8-13. From what you learned about filling objects in Chapter 7, you can refine the appearance of skewed background images to create a clearer "shadow" than this one. To turn the preview screen off, press F9 (the toggle key that turns preview on and off).
10. To remove the transformed copy of the object so that only the unaltered original remains, click on the copy with the Pick tool to select it and press DEL.

Tip: CorelDRAW! has included the option of setting the right mouse button to toggle between the editing window and full-screen preview. If you want to do this, select the Mouse option from Preferences in the Special menu and select Full-Screen Preview.

Skewing with the Transform Roll-Up

If you find the use of keyboard and mouse controls inconvenient, you can perform all of the possible skewing operations using the Skew option on the

Preview of a "shadow" created by skewing and resizing an object
Figure 8-13.

Tranform roll-up in the Effects menu. You can select this command when either the normal selection box or the rotate/skew selection box is visible around a selected object. Perform the following brief exercise to familiarize yourself with using the Skew roll-up to skew an object. The COREL.CDR image should still be on your screen in fit-in-window view.

1. If not so already, set the viewing magnification to 1:1 and click once on the text string to select it.
2. Open the Transform roll-up and select the Skew button (rightmost button). The Skew roll-up appears, as shown here:

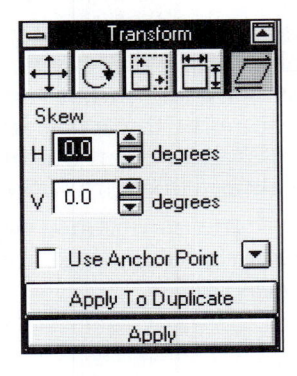

3. First, skew the text object horizontally. Enter a number in the horizontal (H) numeric entry box. You can enter a number either by scrolling in increments of 5 degrees or by clicking on the numeric entry box and typing in a number in increments of 1/10 of a degree. Only values between –75 and 75 degrees are valid.
4. If desired, click on Apply To Duplicate to make a copy of the original object as you rotate it.
5. When you are finished, select Undo Skew to return to the original object and its former angle.
6. Select the text and see that the Skew button on the Transform roll-up is selected once more. This time, enter a number in the vertical (V) numeric entry box. You can adjust this value in the same way that you adjusted the horizontal value in step 3. Click on Apply.
7. When you are finished, select Clear Transformations from the Effects menu to return the original object to its former angle.

A positive number results in skewing to the left; a negative number in skewing to the right.

Repeating a Transformation

CorelDRAW! stores the most recently performed transformation in memory until you quit the current session. You can save design and drawing time by

Transforming Objects

automatically repeating your most recent size, scale, rotate, or skew operation on a different object or set of objects. Just remember that the second object, the one on which you wish to repeat the transformation, must exist on the screen *before* you perform the transformation the first time. If you perform a transformation and then create another object and try to repeat that transformation on it, nothing happens. Perform the following brief exercise to see how this feature can work for you.

1. With the COREL.CDR file open and in actual size viewing magnification, select the Ellipse tool. Now draw a long narrow ellipse to the right of the "Corel" text string at about the 5 1/2-inch mark on the horizontal ruler.

2. Press SPACEBAR to activate the Pick tool. Select the "Corel" text string and then start to drag the lower-right boundary marker downward and to the right. Leave a copy of the original by clicking the right mouse button or by using the + key, as described earlier in this chapter. Then use CTRL to help you scale the text string to 200 percent. Release the mouse button and then the CTRL key.

3. Select the ellipse that you drew next to the text string. Select Repeat Stretch from the Edit menu or press the shortcut keys CTRL-R. This will create a duplicate of the ellipse and scale it to 200%, as described in

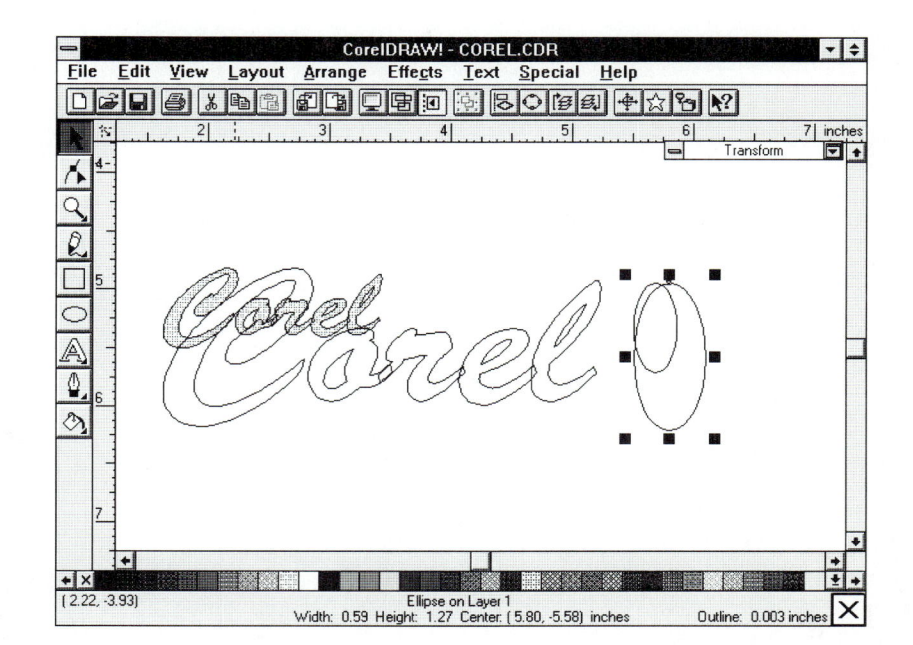

Repeating a transformation on a different object
Figure 8-14.

step 2. If the objects extend beyond your viewing window, adjust viewing magnification to fit-in-window.

4. Select the larger text duplicate and then select No Fill from the Fill flyout menu. Your screen should be similar to Figure 8-14.
5. Select New from the File menu to clear the screen. Do not save any changes to your work.

You have seen how sizing, scaling, rotating, and skewing objects can lead to creative ideas for advanced designs. Continue practicing some of the techniques you have learned and see what original ideas you can come up with on your own. Chapters 13 and 14 will expand on these and other techniques and provide additional stimulation for your imagination.

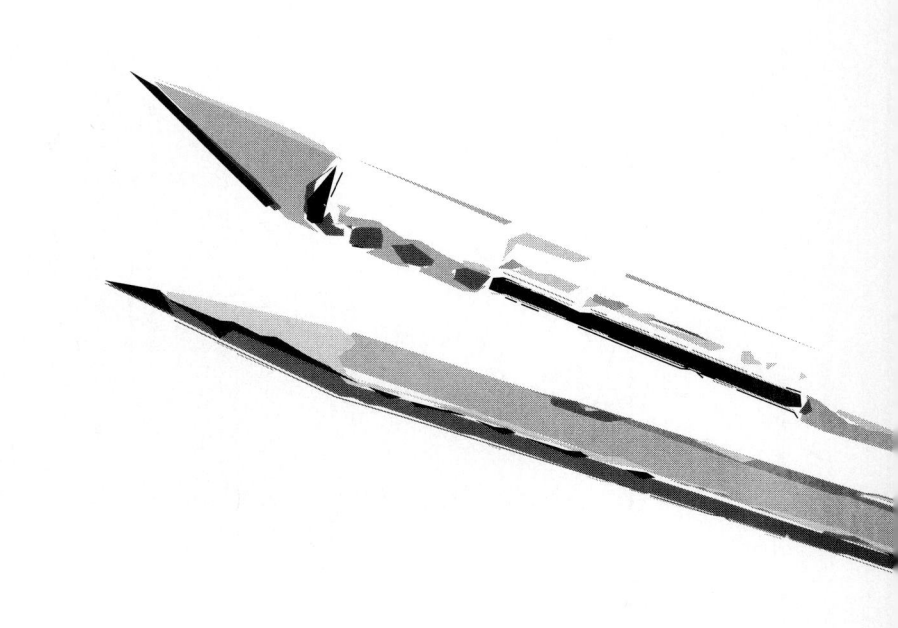

Wm. Mogensen 1992

Transforming Objects

COREL*DRAW! in Action*

WILLIAM MOGENSEN
Redlake

William started this piece by creating two horizontal rectangles: one for the lake, and one for the sky. Fountain fills were then applied to the two rectangles by clicking on the Fill tool, choosing the Fountain Fill icon, then specifying the From and To colors in the Fountain Fill dialog box. For the lower (lake) rectangle, colors were chosen to blend from faded pink to dark brown, helping to create the illusion of the lake receding toward the horizon.

William wanted to give this piece the mood of sunrise or sunset by using varying shades of a few pastel colors. In order to speed up the specification of fills for the various shapes, William created his own palette containing just those colors that he wanted to use throughout the piece. To create the palette he placed two small rectangles off to one side, one at the top and one at the bottom of the screen. He filled one with the lightest shade and the other with the darkest shade, selected both, then created a blend between the extremes using the Blend roll-up with 8 steps specified. To fill a selected shape with a shade from his palette, he chose Copy Attributes From on the Edit menu, checked the Fill box in the Copy Attributes dialog box, then clicked on OK. The mouse pointer then changed to a thick arrow, which he used to click on the desired shade in his palette.

To create each of the three levels of mountains, William selected the Freehand tool, clicked to place the first node, then double-clicked at various other points to create jagged lines between the points. After making three jagged objects, he used the Shape tool for fine-tuning the mountains. He then used the Scale & Mirror command on the Transform roll-up opened from the Effects menu to make a vertical mirror copy of each jagged line (by checking the Apply to Duplicate box in the Scale & Mirror version of the roll-up), and placed these in the lake as reflections.

The cliffs and trees were made similarly, except that William converted the jagged lines to smooth curves. Using the Shape tool he double-clicked on a node to get the Node Edit roll-up, selected all the nodes on the jagged line, then clicked on the To Curve and Smooth buttons.

This piece was in CorelArtShow 4: Page 89, Number 8, File: ENV00042.CDR You may contact William in care of:

>William Mogensen
>10109 Janetta Way
>Shadow Hills, CA 91040
>Voice/Fax: (818) 352-4102

The art on the opposite page was created by and is the property of William Mogensen. It is used with permission.

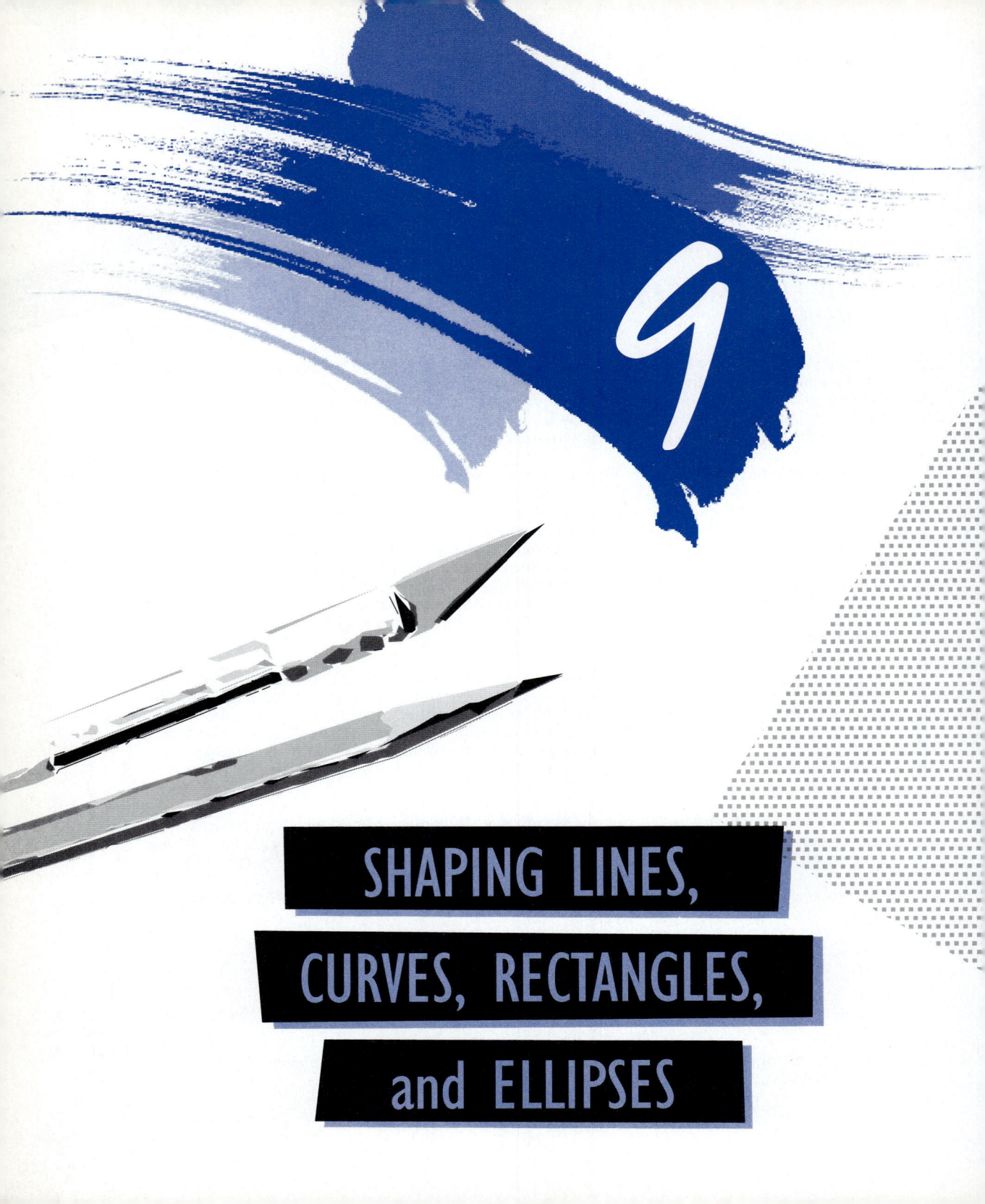

9

SHAPING LINES,
CURVES, RECTANGLES,
and ELLIPSES

The power to reshape any object to the limits of the imagination is at the very heart of CorelDRAW!. Using the Shape tool, you can change any type of object into an image that can showcase your creativity.

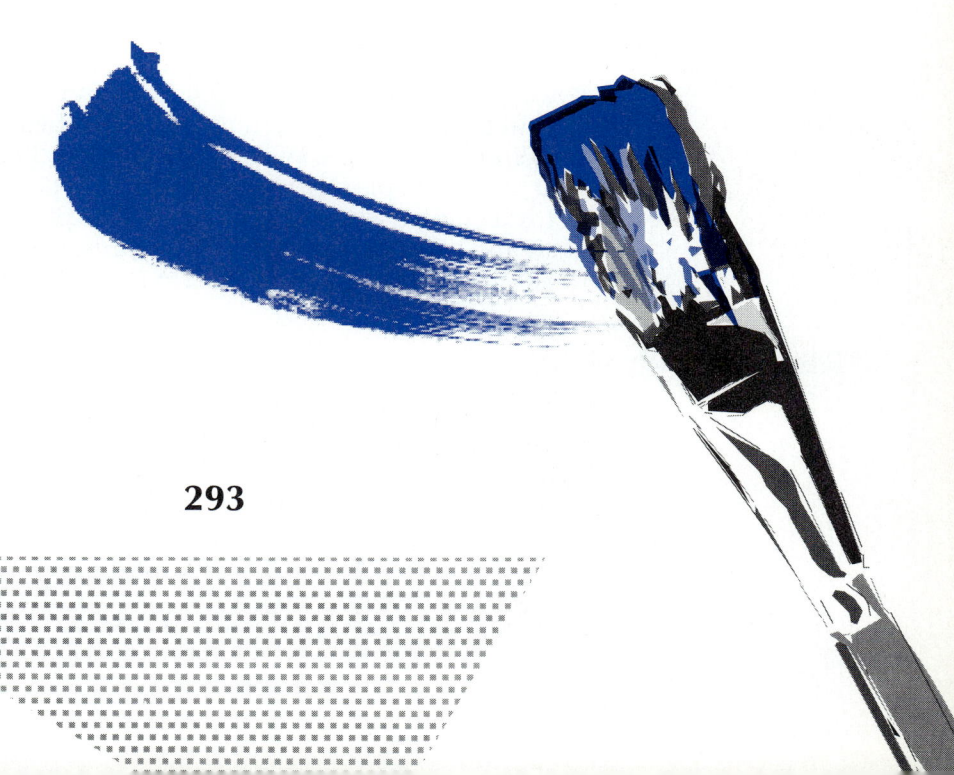

The Shape tool, the second tool in the CorelDRAW! toolbox, allows you to change the underlying shape of an object. Although the Pick tool, in transformation mode, allows you to resize, rotate, or skew an object, it leaves the fundamental shape of the object intact. When you edit an object with the Shape tool, however, it becomes something quite different from what you originally drew.

You can apply the Shape tool to all object types: lines and curves, rectangles and squares, ellipses and circles, text, and pixel-based (bitmap) graphics. Shaping functions for text and bitmap graphics, however, are part of a broader range of editing functions that apply specifically to those object types. You will find information specifically about shaping text in Chapter 10, and about shaping curves to fit traced bitmaps in Chapter 23. This chapter covers techniques for shaping lines, curves, rectangles, and ellipses.

About the Shape Tool

The Shape tool performs several different functions, depending on the kind of object to which it is applied. You take advantage of the most powerful capabilities of the Shape tool when you use it to edit curves, but it has specific effects on other object types as well.

When you are working with lines and curves, the Shape tool is at its most versatile. You can manipulate single curve points (nodes) interactively, move single or multiple curve segments, control the angle of movement, and add or delete curve points in order to exercise greater control over the degree of curvature. You can break apart or join segments of a curve and change one type of node into another. You can even convert curves to straight lines and back again.

When you apply the Shape tool to rectangles and squares, you can round the corners of a rectangle and turn rotated, stretched, or skewed rectangles into near-ellipses and circles. When you apply the Shape tool to ellipses and circles, you can create pie-shaped wedges or arcs. If these shaping options for rectangles and ellipses seem limited, you will be pleased to learn that you can convert any object in CorelDRAW! to curves—and then proceed to apply the most advanced shaping techniques to it.

Shaping Lines and Curves

You may recall that every object in CorelDRAW! has nodes, which appear when you first draw an object and become enlarged when you select the object with the Shape tool. Nodes on a curve (shown in Figure 9-1) are the points through which a curve passes, and each node is associated with the curve segment that immediately precedes it. Control points that appear when you select a single node with the Shape tool determine the curvature of the node and of the curve segments on either side of it. (You will learn more about control points later in this chapter.)

Shaping Lines, Curves, Rectangles, and Ellipses

The Shape tool is at its most powerful when you use it to edit a curve. Ways in which you can reshape a curve include moving, adding, or deleting nodes; changing node shape; breaking nodes apart or joining them together; and manipulating the control points that define the shape of a curve segment.

> You can use the Shape tool to manipulate both nodes and curves.

Your options for shaping straight lines with the Shape tool are much more limited than for curves; lines have no angles of curvature and, therefore, no control points that you can manipulate. When you edit a line segment with the Shape tool, you can only move the nodes to stretch or diminish the length of the line segment. In the course of creating and editing a complex curve object, however, you often need to fuse curve and line segments, change curves into lines, or turn lines into curves. The Shape tool allows you to do all of these things, and so both kinds of freehand objects belong in any discussion of shaping.

The following sections show you how to use the Shape tool to edit specific types of objects. These sections follow the order of the drawing tools in the CorelDRAW! toolbox: lines and curves, rectangles, and ellipses.

Selecting Lines and Curves with the Shape tool

You must select an object with the Shape tool before you can edit it. CorelDRAW! allows you to select only one object with the Shape tool at a

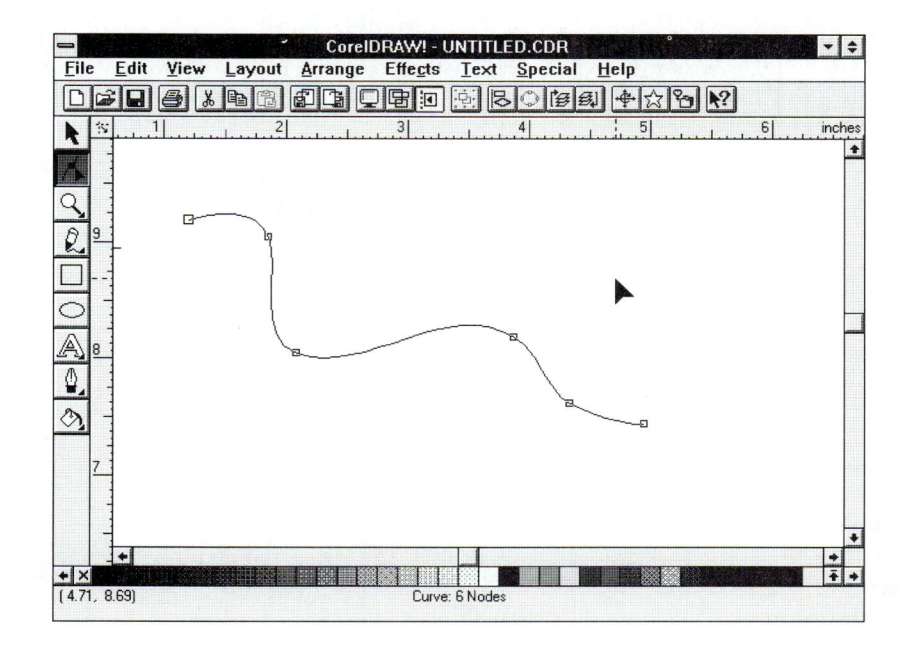

> Displaying the number of nodes in a curve
> **Figure 9-1.**

time. Although the Shape tool affects each type of object in a different way, the basic steps involved in editing are similar with all object types.

In the following exercise you will draw a straight line and a freehand curve and then select each object in turn. Turn off the Snap To Grid option before you begin this exercise.

To select an object for editing, follow these steps:

1. Make certain the rulers are turned on; then, activate your Zoom tool and zoom in on the upper half of the page. Now, select the Freehand tool and draw a straight horizontal line across the top half of the window, as shown in Figure 9-2.
2. Below the line, draw a freehand curve in a horizontal "S" shape. Small nodes appear on the curves.
3. Select the Shape tool.

   The pointer changes to an arrowhead, and the S-curve is automatically selected, because it was the last object you drew. The nodes of the S-curve increase in size, and the status line displays the number of the nodes in the curve, as shown in Figure 9-2. The number of nodes in your curve may differ from the number in the figure. Notice that the node where you started drawing the curve is larger than the others.

   As you have just seen, if the object you want to work with is already selected, its nodes enlarge in size automatically as soon as you select the Shape tool, and the selection box around the object disappears. The number of nodes varies, depending on the object type and (in the case of curves) the way your hand moved when you drew it. If the object

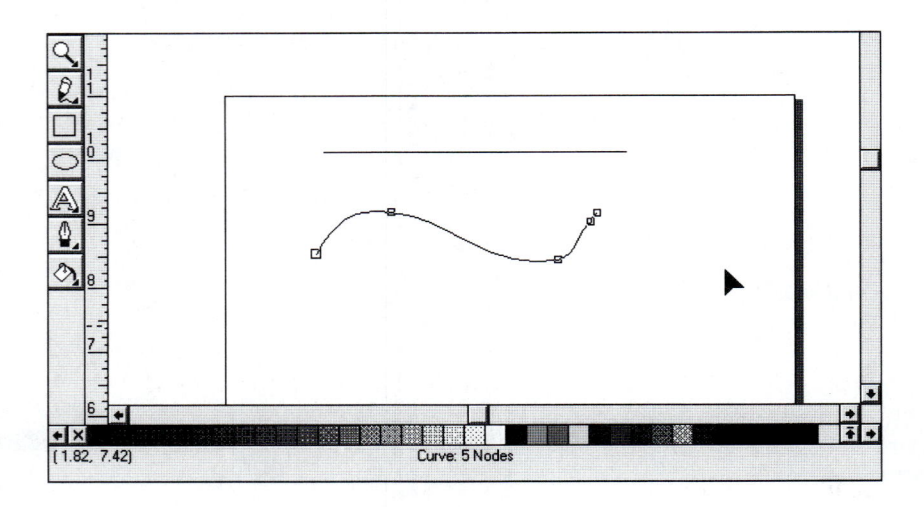

Selecting an object with the Shape tool
Figure 9-2.

Shaping Lines, Curves, Rectangles, and Ellipses

> As far as the Shape tool is concerned, every line has the potential of becoming a curve.

you want to work with is not selected, you can click on any part of the object's outline with the arrowhead pointer. In addition to the enlarged nodes, the status line shows the object type and information about the nodes on the object. If the selected object has multiple nodes, the first node appears larger than the others, as you have seen in the example in Figure 9-2. The first node is the one closest to where you started drawing the object. Often this is the farthest to the left on lines and curves, the one at the top left corner in rectangles, and at the topmost point on ellipses.

4. To deselect the S-curve and select the line, simply click on any point of the line with the Shape tool. Only two nodes appear on the line, one at each end. Again, the node where you started drawing is the larger. The status line displays the message, "Curve: 2 Nodes."

5. Clear the screen by selecting New from the File menu. Do not save your work.

Tip: Activate the Shape tool by clicking on it or by pressing F10. The pointer changes to a thick arrowhead as soon as you move it away from the toolbox and toward the page area.

If multiple objects are selected when you activate the Shape tool, CorelDRAW! automatically deselects all of them, and you must select a single object to edit with the Shape tool. If grouped objects are selected when you activate the shape tool, they also become deselected and your mouse actions have no effect. The only time you can edit more than one object simultaneously is when you *combine* the objects prior to selecting the Shape tool. You will see examples of editing combined objects in the "Shaping Lines and Curves" section of this chapter.

To deselect an object that you are editing with the Shape tool, either click on the outline of a different object or select another tool from the CorelDRAW! toolbox.

Your next step in shaping a selected line or curve is to select one or more of its nodes.

Selecting Nodes of a Line or Curve

Although you can shape only one object at a time, you can select and shape either single or multiple nodes. The shaping options available to you depend on whether you select one node or several. You can reshape a single curve node interactively in one of two ways: by dragging the node itself or by dragging the control points that appear when you select the node. Moving a node stretches and resizes the associated curve segment(s) but does not allow you to change the angle of curvature. Dragging the control points, on the other hand, allows you to change both the angle of curvature at the node and the shape of the associated curve segment(s). When you select multiple nodes, you can move only the nodes, not their control points; as a result, you reshape all of the selected segments in the same way.

In general, you should select single nodes when you need to fine-tune a curve, and multiple nodes when you need to move or reshape several segments in the same way without changing their angle of curvature.

The exercises in the following sections guide you through the available techniques for selecting nodes in preparation for moving or editing them. Along the way, you will become familiar with the different types of nodes that CorelDRAW! generates and how they indicate the shape of a particular curve.

Tip: Nodes of a straight line segment are always cusp nodes and contain no control points. They become important only when you begin adding or deleting nodes or changing a line into a curve. You will concentrate on working with curves in the next few sections.

Selecting and Deselecting Single Nodes and Identifying Node Type

When you click on a single curve node, the status line provides information about the type of node you have selected. The names of the three different types of nodes that CorelDRAW! generates when you draw lines and curves—cusp, smooth, and symmetrical—describe both the curvature at the node and, in the case of curve objects, the way you can shape the node. Straight lines contain only cusp nodes, while curves can contain all three node types.

- ♦ **Cusp nodes** Cusp nodes occur at the end point of a line or curve or at a sharp change of direction in a curve. When you edit the control points of a cusp node, you can alter the curvature of the segment that precedes the node without affecting the segment that follows it.

- ♦ **Smooth nodes** Smooth nodes occur at smooth changes of direction in a curve. When you edit a smooth node, you alter the shape and direction of both the segment preceding and the segment following the node. The curvature of the two segments remains identical in the number of degrees, however.

- ♦ **Symmetrical nodes** Symmetrical nodes occur where the segments preceding and following the node curve in identical ways. (Symmetrical

Shaping Lines, Curves, Rectangles, and Ellipses

nodes occur less frequently than other node types in freehand drawing, but you can change any node type to symmetrical using the Node Edit roll-up, which you will learn about in a moment.) When you edit a symmetrical node, you alter the shape and direction of the curve segments before and after the node in identical ways.

In the following exercise, you will practice selecting and deselecting single nodes.

1. Using the Freehand tool, at actual size (1:1) magnification and with Wireframe (in the View menu) turned on, draw a curve object that looks roughly like Figure 9-3. The object should have sharp curves, gentle curves, and some in between. Don't worry if it doesn't look exactly like Figure 9-3.
2. Select the Shape tool. If the curve object was selected when you clicked on the Shape tool, it should remain selected. If your curve object is not selected, click anywhere on its outline. The status line indicates that this curve object contains 21 nodes (yours may be different).
3. Click on a node at the bottom of the half circle on the selected curve object. The node becomes a black-filled square, and two control points,

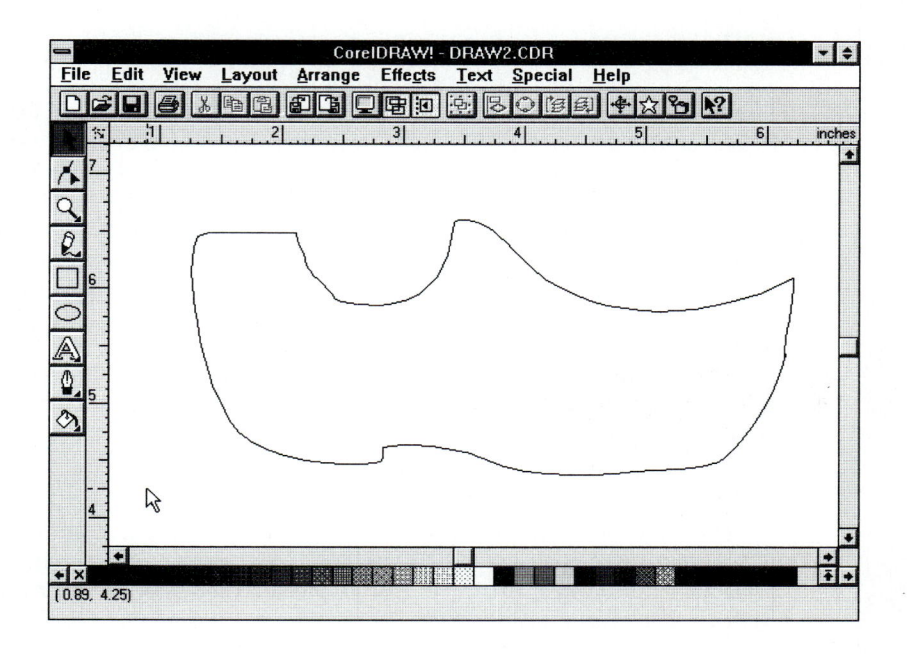

Figure 9-3.
The curve object at 1:1 magnification

tiny black rectangles connected to the node by dotted lines, pop out, as shown here:

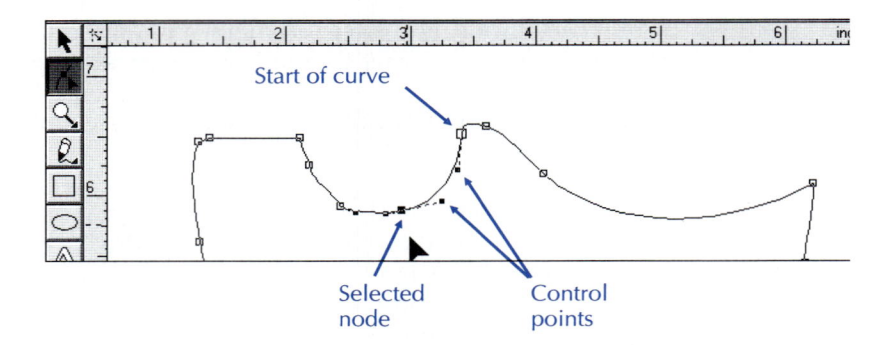

Start of curve

Selected node   *Control points*

(You will also see a control point extending from nodes on either side of the selected node.) The message "Selected Node: Curve Cusp" or "Curve Smooth" appears on the status line, depending on how you drew this curve. Which type of curve does not matter at this point.

4. Click on each node in turn to select it and deselect the previous node. Each time you select a node, control points pop out, and the status line tells you what type of node you have selected. Notice that some of the nodes are cusp nodes, while others are smooth.

5. Leave this object on the screen for the next exercise.

You can always change the node type by using the Node Edit roll-up window, as you will see shortly. But you can also control whether the majority of nodes you generate during the freehand drawing process are smooth or cusped. To generate mostly cusped nodes (and create more jagged curves), select the Curves tab from the Preferences command in the Special menu. Then set the Corner Threshold option in the Preferences-Curves dialog box to 3 pixels or lower. To generate mostly smooth nodes and create smoother curves, set the Corner Threshold option to 8 pixels or higher.

You will become familiar with techniques for moving control points in a moment. First, finish the next section to learn how to select more than one node at a time.

Selecting and Deselecting Multiple Nodes

You select multiple nodes with the Shape tool in the same way that you select multiple objects with the Pick tool, using either SHIFT or the marquee technique. When multiple nodes are selected, you do not have control points to shape your object. You can only move the nodes as a group and

Shaping Lines, Curves, Rectangles, and Ellipses

reshape their associated curve segments by dragging the lines. Review the selection techniques in the following brief exercise.

1. Select the larger-sized node (from the point at which you began drawing). While pressing and holding SHIFT, select a node to the left and to the right of the first node. The nodes turn dark but display no control points, and the status line changes to show the total number of nodes you have selected.

2. Deselect the node farthest to the right in the selected group by holding SHIFT and clicking on the node with the Shape tool. The other nodes remain selected.

3. Deselect all of the selected nodes by releasing SHIFT and clicking on any white space. The curve object itself remains selected for further work with the Shape tool, however.

4. Select the three nodes on the bottom-left side of the object (the heel) by drawing a marquee around them, as shown here:

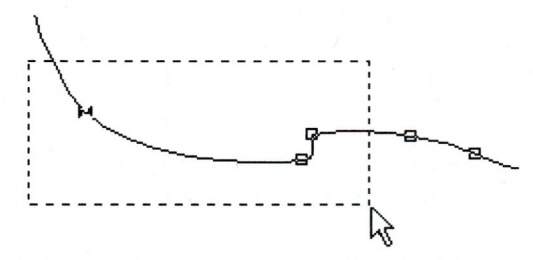

   The selected nodes turn dark after you release the mouse button, and the status line tells you how many nodes you have selected.

5. Deselect one node at a time using SHIFT and the mouse button, or deselect all of the nodes by clicking on any other node or on any white space.

6. When you are finished, clear the screen by selecting New from the File menu. Do not save the changes.

Now that you are familiar with how to select nodes, you are ready to begin editing a curve object. You can edit a curve by moving nodes and control points interactively or by selecting options in the Node Edit roll-up window.

Moving Nodes and Control Points

You can reshape a curve interactively in one of two ways: by moving one or more nodes or by manipulating the control points of a single node. You can move any number of nodes, but in order to work with control points, you can select only one node at a time.

You move nodes when your aim is to stretch, shrink, or move the curve segments on either side of a node. The angle of curvature at selected nodes doesn't change as you move them, because the control points move along with the nodes. The end result of moving nodes is a limited reshaping of the selected area of the curve object.

The type of node you select determines the way control points move.

In general, your best strategy when reshaping curves is to move the nodes first. If just repositioning the nodes does not yield satisfactory results, you can fine-tune the shape of a curve by manipulating the control points of one or more nodes. When you drag control points to reshape a curve, you affect both the angle of curvature at the node and the shape of the curve segment on one or both sides of the node. The effects of this kind of reshaping are much more dramatic.

Try the exercises in each of the following sections to practice moving single or multiple nodes, manipulating control points, and constraining node movement to 90-degree increments.

Moving a Single Node

To move a single node, you simply select the curve and then select and drag the node in the desired direction. In the following exercise, you will draw a waveform curve, select a node, and move the node to reshape the curve.

1. To prepare for the exercise, make sure that the Snap To Grid and Rulers options are turned off. Check to see that all the settings in the Curves tab of the Preferences command in the Special menu are at 5 pixels. (This will result in curves with a fairly even distribution of cusp and smooth nodes.) Set viewing magnification to an actual size (1:1) ratio.

2. Select the Freehand tool and draw a waveform curve similar to the one drawn here: don't be concerned if your curve is shaped a little differently.

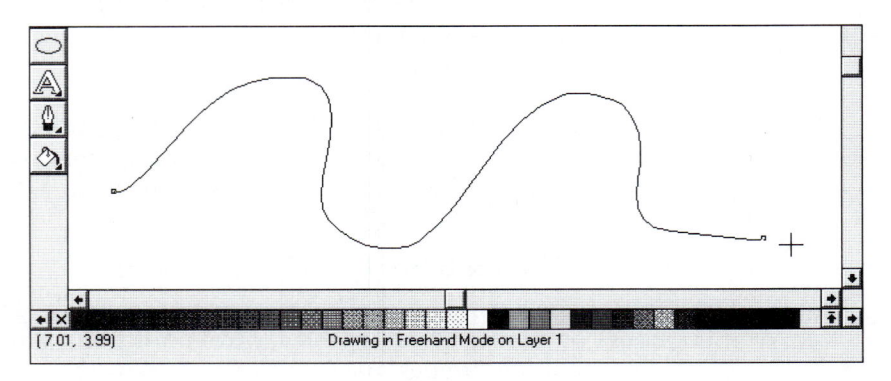

3. Select the Shape tool and then select a node near the crest of one of the curves. Elongate this curve by dragging the node (not the control points) upward and to the right, as shown here:

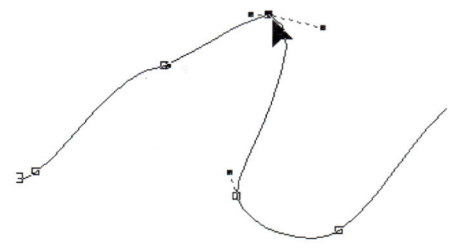

As you begin to move the node, the status line provides information about *dx* and *dy* coordinates, the distance you have traveled, and the angle of movement relative to the starting point. Release the mouse button when you are satisfied with the stretch of your curve.

4. Select Undo from the Edit menu to return the curve to its original shape. Leave this curve on the screen for now. You can use it to move multiple nodes in the next exercise.

Moving Multiple Nodes

There are many cases in which you might choose to move multiple nodes instead of a single node at a time. You might move multiple adjacent nodes, for example, if you need to reposition an entire section of a curve at one time. Or you might select nonadjacent nodes and move them all in the same direction for special design effects. Whatever the case, all you need to do is select the nodes and drag them.

1. Using the mouse button and SHIFT, select one node near the beginning of your waveform curve and one near the end. Again, do not be concerned if the nodes in your curve are in different positions from the nodes in the figure. The process of freehand drawing is so complex that two people rarely produce the same results.

2. Drag one of the nodes upward and to the right. Even though the two selected nodes are separated by several others, they move at the same angle and over the same distance, as shown here:

Selected nodes

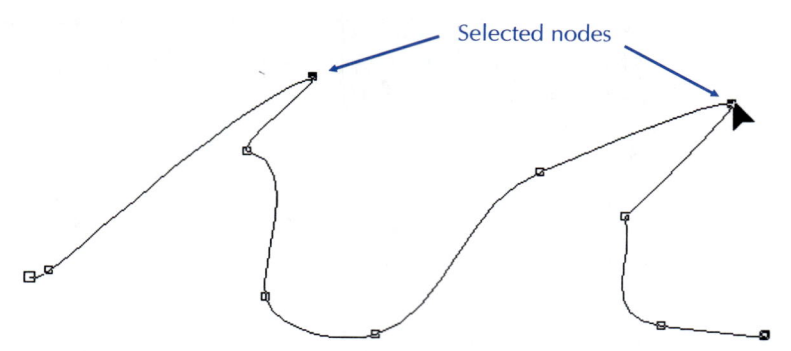

3. Release the mouse button when you are finished. Select Undo from the Edit menu to return the curve object to its former shape.

If you prefer to draft even the most "creative-looking" freehand curves with precision, you may wish to exercise greater control over the angle at which you move nodes. The next section will show you how to move nodes with precision.

Constraining Node Movement to 90-Degree Angles

You have the option of moving nodes and their associated curve segments in increments of 90 degrees relative to your starting point. You use the now familiar CTRL key to achieve this kind of precise movement.

1. Select the same two nodes you worked with in the preceding section, press and hold CTRL, and drag one of the nodes to the right and then up. At first the two nodes do not seem to move at all; then they "snap" at a 90-degree angle from their starting point. The status line in your window reflects this precise angle of movement, as in Figure 9-4.
2. Release the mouse button when you reach the angle you desire. Select New from the File menu to clear the curve from the screen. Do not save your changes.

What if you have moved one or more nodes every which way, but you are still not satisfied with the shape of the curve segments on either side of the node? In the next section you will fine-tune your curves by manipulating the control points of a node.

Moving Control Points

By moving one or both control points of a node, you can control the shape of a curve segment more exactly than if you move just the node itself. The effect of moving control points varies, depending on the type of node—cusp, smooth, or symmetrical. Figure 9-5 (a through d) illustrates this difference.

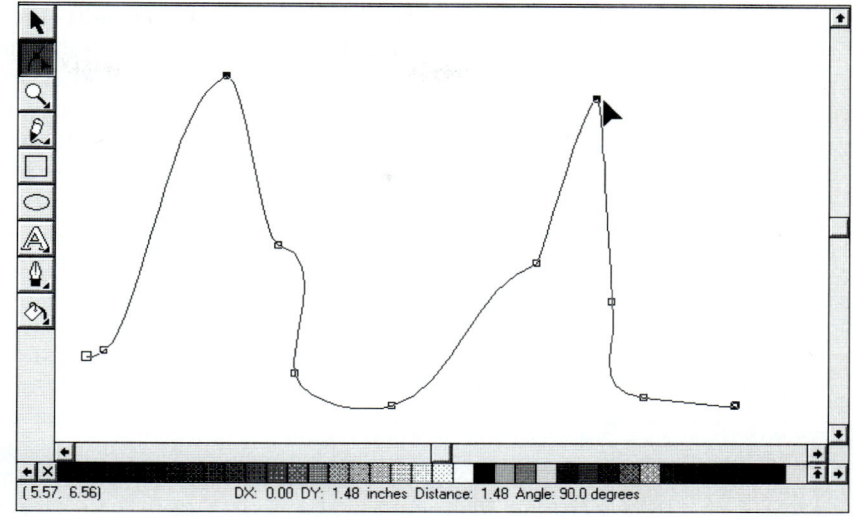

Shaping Lines, Curves, Rectangles, and Ellipses 305

Moving multiple nodes by increments of 90 degrees
Figure 9-4.

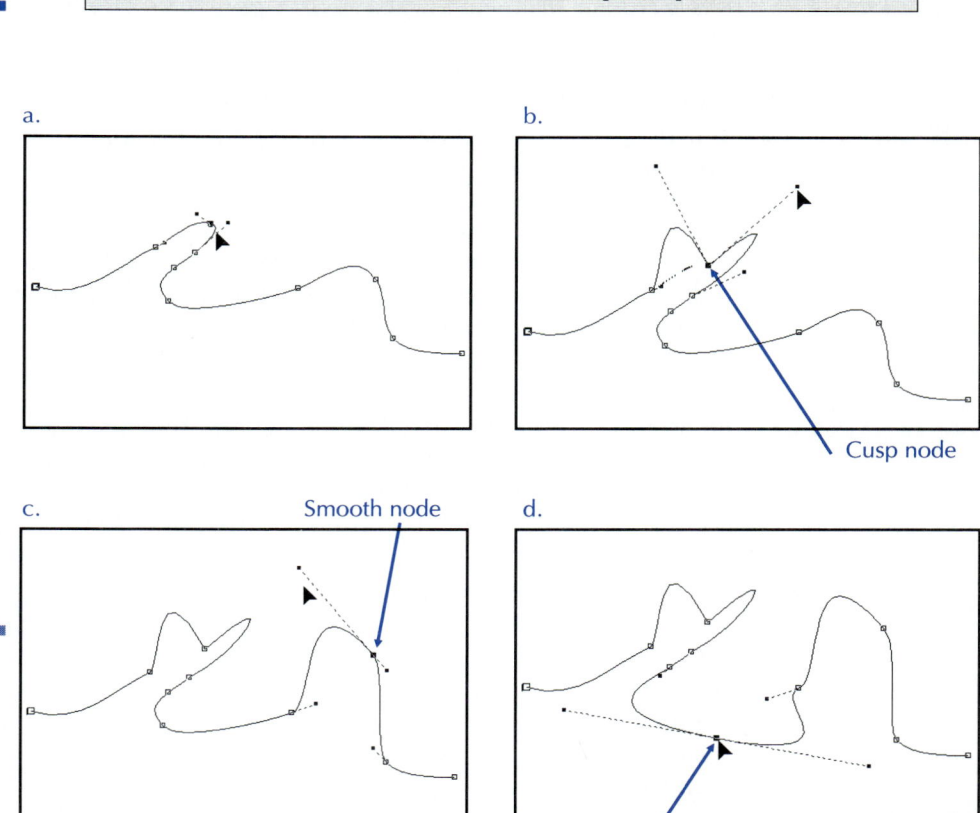

a.

b.
Cusp node

c.
Smooth node

d.
Symmetrical node

Moving control points of a cusp, smooth, and symmetrical node
Figure 9-5.

The control points of cusp nodes are not in a straight-line relationship to one another. This means that you can move one control point and change the shape of one curve segment at a time, without affecting the other associated segment. The control points of smooth nodes, on the other hand, are in a straight line relative to one another. If you move one control point of a smooth node, you affect the curvature of both line segments at once, though not to the same degree. Finally, the control points of a symmetrical node are at an equal distance from the node. When you move one control point of a symmetrical node, the curvature of both associated curve segments changes in exactly the same way. Your waveform curve may not have a symmetrical node; because of the steadiness of hand required, symmetrical nodes rarely occur naturally in freehand drawing. You can practice moving the control points of smooth and cusp nodes, however, by following the steps in the next exercise.

1. Select the Freehand tool and in actual view magnification (1:1) draw a curve similar in shape to the one in Figure 9-5a. Don't be concerned if your curve has a slightly different shape. You should draw part of the curve with a steady hand and another part using more jagged movements. This will result in a more even distribution of node types.

2. With the Shape tool select individual nodes on your waveform curve until you find a cusp node. You will know what type of node you have selected by referring to the status line. Do not use one of the end nodes, however; end nodes have only one control point, because only one curve segment is associated with them. If you can't find a cusp node, redraw the curve to be more jagged, and then try again. Figure 9-5a shows the waveform curve with a cusp node selected and no control points moved.

3. Drag one of the cusp node's control points outward from the node as far as you can without extending it beyond the viewing window. The farther you drag the control point outward, the more angular the curvature of the associated segment becomes. Note also that the curve segment associated with the other control point does not change.

4. Drag the other control point in any direction you choose. The angle of the second curve segment associated with the node changes, independently of the first one. If you have extended both control points independently, you will see a sharp change in curve direction at the node, as in Figure 9-5b.

5. When you have practiced this technique to your satisfaction, find and select a smooth node. Notice that the two control points of this node lie along a straight line.

Shaping Lines, Curves, Rectangles, and Ellipses

6. Drag one of the control points of the smooth node outward from the node, and notice that the other control point is not affected. Now move the control point sideways. The curvature of *both* of the segments associated with the node changes. As shown in the example in Figure 9-5c, however, the two segments do not change in exactly the same way. (The curvature of your curve segments may differ from those in the example, depending on how you drew the curve and moved the control points.)

7. If your waveform curve contains a symmetrical node, select it and move one of the control points outward. Notice that when you move one control point the opposite one moves the same amount. If you do not have a symmetrical node, observe the curvature changes in Figure 9-5d. The curvature of these segments changes by an identical angle.

8. When you have practiced with control points to your satisfaction, activate the Pick tool and press DEL to delete the waveform curve from the screen.

Now you have a working knowledge of all the possible interactive techniques for moving and editing curves. It may sometimes happen, however, that even these techniques are not enough to shape your curve just as you want it. What if you are working with a cusp node and just can't make it smooth enough? Or what if you need an additional node at a certain point to enable you to fit a curve to an exact shape? For these and other node-editing tasks, you can call up the Node Edit roll-up window.

Editing Nodes

Selecting a curve object and moving nodes and control points are interactive operations that you can perform without invoking a command or menu. There are times, however, when you need to *edit* the nodes themselves: to change their shape or to add nodes, delete nodes, join nodes, or break them apart. Editing nodes requires that you use the Node Edit roll-up window that pops up when you double-click on a node or on the curve segment that immediately precedes it.

Working with the Node Edit Roll-Up

To call up the Node Edit roll-up window, double-click on any node or on any curve or line segment. The roll-up can be moved around the work space to keep it away from your work by clicking and holding on the title bar and dragging it to a clear area. It will remain in the window until you close it as you would any window. You can also click on the roll-up arrow and keep only the title bar visible. The Node Edit roll-up is shown in Figure 9-6.

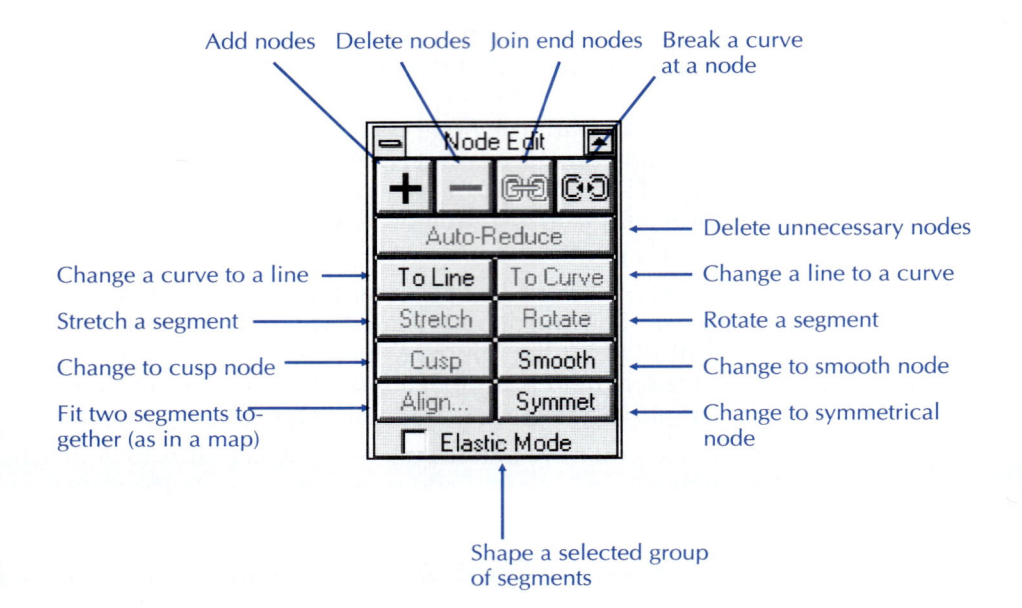

Figure 9-6.
The Node Edit roll-up window

Callouts around the Node Edit roll-up:
- Add nodes
- Delete nodes
- Join end nodes
- Break a curve at a node
- Delete unnecessary nodes
- Change a curve to a line
- Change a line to a curve
- Stretch a segment
- Rotate a segment
- Change to cusp node
- Change to smooth node
- Fit two segments together (as in a map)
- Change to symmetrical node
- Shape a selected group of segments

The commands in the Node Edit roll-up allow you to add or delete selected nodes, join two nodes or break them apart, convert lines to curves and curves to lines, change the node type, or align sets of nodes on two separate subpaths. Not all commands are available to you for every node, however. Some commands appear in gray and are unavailable, depending on the number and type of node(s) you have selected. See the section pertaining to the relevant Node Edit command for more information about why particular commands are not available at certain times. To select commands that are available, click once on the command name.

Except for the Align command, as soon as you select any command from the Node Edit roll-up, CorelDRAW! immediately applies the command to the selected node(s).

Try the exercises in each of the following sections to become familiar with using the commands in the Node Edit roll-up.

Adding a Single Node

If you have moved nodes and manipulated control points to the best of your ability but still cannot achieve the exact shape you want, consider adding one or more nodes where the curvature seems most inadequate. You can add a single node or multiple nodes, depending on how many nodes are selected, but if the node you have selected is the first node of a line or curve, you cannot add a node to it.

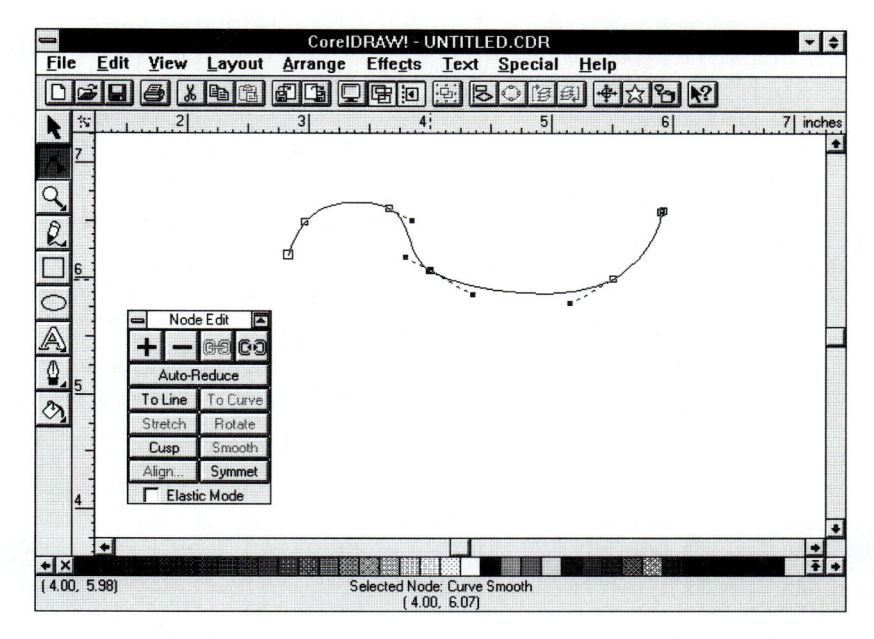

Shaping Lines, Curves, Rectangles, and Ellipses **309**

**The Node Edit roll-up dragged to a convenient working space
Figure 9-7.**

In CorelDRAW! a first node can never have a node or segment preceding it.

The following exercise furnishes the necessary steps to add a single node between two existing nodes. If not already done, set the viewing magnification to actual size (1:1). Make sure that the Snap To Grid is turned off for this and all of the other exercises in the "Editing Nodes" portion of this chapter.

1. Select the Freehand tool and draw a waveform curve similar to the one shown in Figure 9-7. Activate the Shape tool to select the curve for editing. Your curve may contain a different number of nodes than the one in Figure 9-7.

2. Double-click with the Shape tool on either the node or the curve segment immediately in front of the point at which you want to add a node. The Node Edit roll-up appears in your work space. Click on the title bar and drag it to a clear area, as shown in Figure 9-7.

3. Select the Add (+) command from the Node Edit roll-up. A new node appears on the curve or line segment preceding the selected node, as shown here. If you first deselect all of the selected nodes by clicking on any white space, you can move this added node or manipulate its control points just like any other node.

4. After clicking on any white space to deselect selected nodes, leave the current curve on your screen for use in the next exercise.

Tip: Independent of whether the Node Edit roll-up is open, you can add a new node by clicking where you want the node with the Shape tool and pressing + on the numeric keyboard.

Adding Multiple Nodes

Perform the following brief exercise to add several nodes to a curve at one time. The technique is the same as when you add a single node, except that multiple nodes must be selected.

If you add a node to a straight line segment instead of to a curve, and then move the new node, you effectively add a new line segment.

1. You should have a waveform curve on your screen in actual size magnification along with the Node Edit roll-up and the Shape tool, as you left them in the last exercise.

2. Select two or more nodes using either SHIFT or the marquee method. You will add nodes in front of each of these selected nodes. All of the squares that mark the selected nodes blacken, as shown here:

3. Click on the Add (+) command of the Node Edit roll-up. A new node appears in front of each of the selected nodes, as shown here:

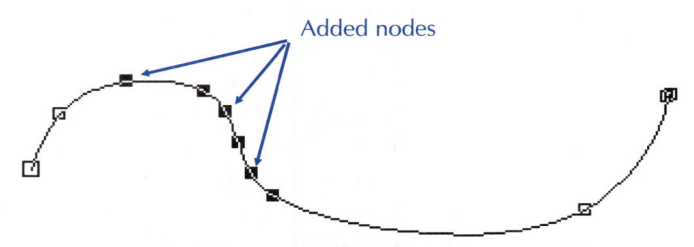

Added nodes

If you deselect all of the currently selected nodes and then select the added nodes individually, you can manipulate their control points to suit your drawing needs.

4. Again, after deselecting the nodes, leave the current curve on your screen for use in the next exercise.

Shaping Lines, Curves, Rectangles, and Ellipses

The counterpart to adding nodes is deleting them. Continue with the next sections to practice deleting one or more nodes from a curve.

Deleting Single and Multiple Nodes

When you draw freehand curves, it is often difficult to control mouse movement completely.

Tip: To draw with less erratic movements, you may want to try using a digital drawing board and pen.

Changing the Freehand Tracking, Corner Threshold, and AutoJoin settings in the Preferences-Curves dialog box may help, but erratic movements while you execute a curve still can produce occasional extraneous nodes. You can smooth out an uneven curve quickly and easily by deleting single or multiple extraneous nodes.

Caution: Always delete nodes with caution. Deleting a node at random, without checking to see if other nodes are nearby, can radically alter the shape of a curve in ways that are not always predictable.

Perform the following exercise to delete nodes from a curve:

1. You should still have a waveform curve on your screen in actual size magnification, and the Node Edit roll-up and Shape tool should be selected as you left them in the last exercise.

2. Using the Shape tool, click on a node that you want to delete, as shown here:

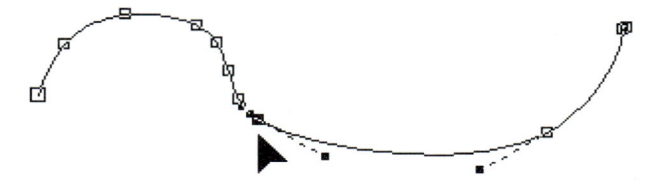

Keep in mind that if you delete one of the end nodes of a curve, you delete the associated curve segment as well. If you delete either node of a straight line, you delete the entire line in the process.

You could at this point select the Delete (–) command from the Node Edit roll-up. CorelDRAW! would delete the node that you selected and redraw the curve without it. The shape of your redrawn curve could be quite different from your original one; just how different it might be depends on the location of the node you selected for deletion.

Tip: As a shortcut to deleting a node, you can select a node and press DEL instead of invoking the Node Edit roll-up.

You can delete multiple nodes as well as single nodes from a curve, as long as all of the nodes you want to delete are selected. To delete multiple nodes follow these steps:

1. Select additional nodes you want to delete, using either SHIFT or the marquee method; three nodes are selected here. Keep in mind that if you delete an end node, you will delete the associated curve segment along with it.

2. Select the Delete (–) command in the Node Edit roll-up. CorelDRAW! immediately deletes the selected nodes from the screen and redraws the curve without them, as shown here:

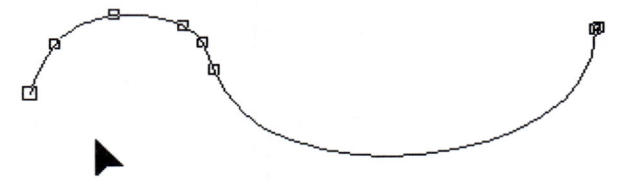

   The shape of the curve can change subtly or dramatically between node positions; the extent of the change depends on the original positions of the selected nodes.

3. Keep the curve for the next example.

You have learned to add and delete nodes when you need to reshape a curve more than the existing nodes allow. Sometimes, though, you may want your

Shaping Lines, Curves, Rectangles, and Ellipses **313**

curve to flatten to the extent that you need to replace a curve segment with a straight line segment. You accomplish this by converting one or more curve segments to straight lines.

Converting a Single Curve Segment to a Straight Line Segment

CorelDRAW! allows you to convert curve segments to line segments. Before you convert a curve to a line, you need to be able to identify whether a selected segment is a curve or a straight line. Some important guidelines to follow are

- A curve segment has two control points; a straight line segment has none.
- When you select the segment or its node, the status line indicates whether the segment is a line or curve.
- The shape of the *selected* node identifies the type of segment that precedes it. A black fill in the selected node signifies a curve segment, while a hollow selected node signifies a straight line segment.

Perform the following exercise to gain experience in converting a single curve segment into a straight line segment.

1. Again, use the curve from the previous example. If your curve has only a couple of nodes left, add a node using the steps you recently learned, so that there is a curve segment that is a good candidate for a straight line.

2. Using the Shape tool, click on a segment or node of a curve that you want to convert to a straight line, as shown here:

3. Now, select the To Line command in the Node Edit roll-up. The two control points related to the selected curve disappear, and the curve segment becomes a straight line segment, as shown here. You can reposition, stretch, or shorten this line segment by using the Shape tool to drag the nodes at either end.

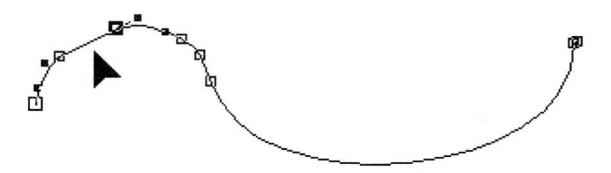

Converting Multiple Curve Segments to Straight Line Segments

If you want a curve object in your drawing to be more angular, you can change its appearance by selecting multiple nodes or curve segments and converting them to straight lines. To convert multiple curve segments to straight line segments, follow these steps:

1. Press ALT-BACKSPACE to undo making the curve segment a line and, if necessary, add a node so that there are at least two curve segments that are good candidates for straight lines.
2. Select the curve segments or nodes you want to convert to straight lines, using either SHIFT or the marquee technique.
3. Select the To Line command in the Node Edit roll-up. The selected curve segments convert to straight lines, and all associated control points are eliminated (straight lines do not include control points). The object becomes much more angular, as shown here. You can now reposition, stretch, or shrink any or all of the line segments by dragging the node(s).

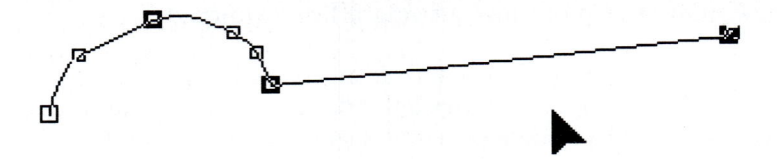

If your object consists of angular line segments but you want to give it much smoother contours, you can convert line segments to curves. The next section shows you how.

Converting Single and Multiple Straight Line Segments to Curve Segments

With CorelDRAW! you can convert straight line segments to curve segments through the Node Edit roll-up. Before you convert a line segment to a curve segment, you need to identify whether a selected segment is a straight line or a curve. If you are uncertain about identifying segments, review the guidelines in the previous section before you proceed. Now try the following exercise:

1. Using the Shape tool, click on one of the straight line segments you just created, or on the *second* (righthand) node of a straight line. (If you select the first (lefthand) node of the line segment, you will not be able to convert it to a curve.) The To Curve button is now available to you, as shown here:

Shaping Lines, Curves, Rectangles, and Ellipses

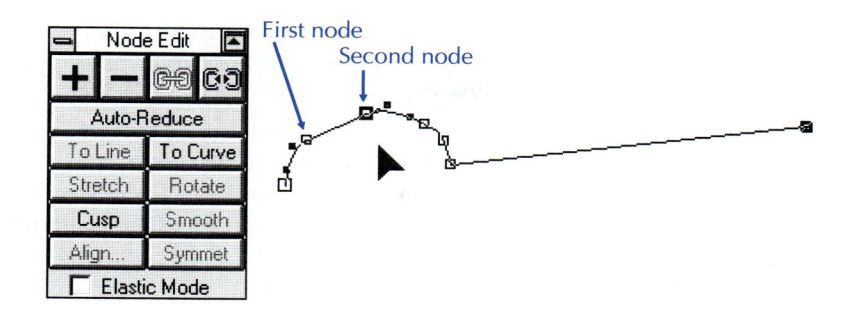

2. Select the To Curve command button in the Node Edit roll-up. CorelDRAW! turns the selected straight line segment into a curve, causing two control points to appear on the line segment. Drag these control points to change the segments to the shape you want.

   You can turn several straight line segments into curve segments at the same time, as long as they are part of the same object. You simply select the several segments and choose the To Curve command in the Node Edit roll-up. The selected straight line segments convert to curve lines. On the surface, the segments do not appear to have changed. However, if you deselect all nodes and then select any one of the converted nodes, two control points appear. You can reshape the peaks and valleys like any other curve.

3. Experiment with converting all the line segments to curves, and prove to yourself that now you really are working with curves.

Another group of commands in the Node Edit roll-up allows you to change the type of single or multiple nodes. These commands—Cusp, Smooth, and Symmetrical—are the subject of the next several sections.

Cusping Single or Multiple Nodes

Cusp nodes are especially useful for rendering an abrupt change in direction at a node.

When you work with a cusp node, you can move either of its control points independently of the other. This makes it possible to independently control the curvature of both of the curve segments that meet at the node, without affecting the other segment.

The following exercise shows you how to turn a single smooth or symmetrical node into a cusped node.

1. Using the Shape tool and the same drawing, click on the node you want to cusp. Select any node except an end node; CorelDRAW! designates all end nodes as cusp nodes.
2. When the Cusp command button is enabled, click on it. The appearance of the curve does not change. However, if you manipulate the control points of this node, as shown here, you will find that you can move one control point without affecting the curve segment on the other side of the node.

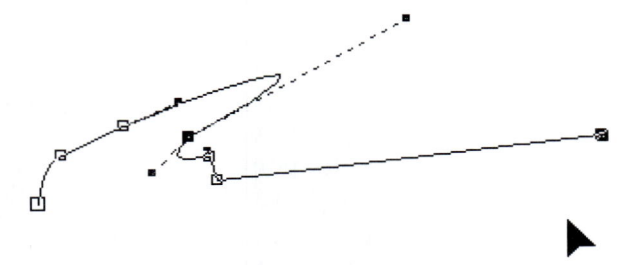

When you want a curve object to have a relatively jagged appearance, but you do not want to turn your curves into straight lines, the next best solution is to change multiple smooth or symmetrical nodes into cusp nodes. You can then shape the cusp nodes to create a more angular appearance for the affected portions of the object.

3. Save your drawing, using File, Save As. You can call it anything you like, for example, CH9TEST. You will use it again in a later exercise.
4. Select New from the File menu to clear the screen.

In the next section, you will become familiar with changing cusped or symmetrical nodes into smooth nodes.

Smoothing Single or Multiple Nodes

In the previous section, you saw that cusp nodes are desirable when you want to create a rougher, more jagged appearance for an object. When you want to make an object's curves smoother, however, you seek out the cusped nodes and turn them into smooth ones.

A smooth node can be defined as a node whose control points always lie along a straight line. A special case exists when a smooth node is located between a straight line and a curve segment, as shown here:

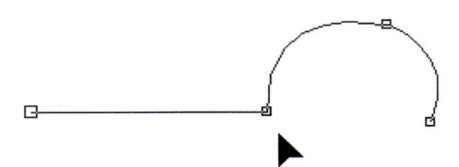

Shaping Lines, Curves, Rectangles, and Ellipses

In such a case, only the side of the node toward the curve segment contains a control point, and you can only move that control point along an imaginary line that follows the extension of the straight line. This restriction maintains the smoothness at the node.

In the next exercise, you will convert a single cusp node that lies at the juncture between a straight line and curve segment into a smooth node.

1. Set viewing magnification to actual size (1:1), select the Pencil tool, and then draw a straight line connected to a curve segment, as shown above. Remember to click at the end of the line segment to attach the curve segment to it automatically.
2. Activate the Shape tool. Your curve object may not include the same number of nodes as the one shown above, but that is not important for the purpose of this exercise.
3. Using the Shape tool, click on the line cusp node next to the curve segment, as shown here:

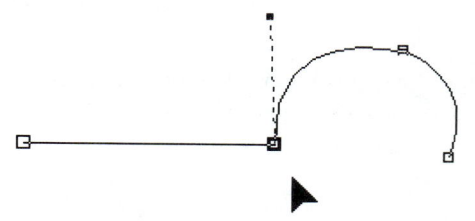

4. In the Node Edit roll-up, click on the Smooth command button. The curve passing through the selected node is smoothed, like the one here, and will remain smooth when you move either the node itself or its control point. The straight line segment does not change, of course.

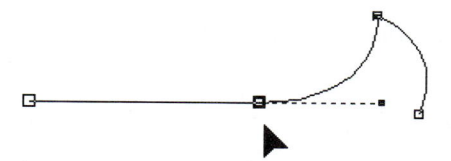

5. Select New from the File menu to clear the screen. Don't bother to save it.

To smooth multiple nodes, you simply select multiple nodes and then repeat the steps for smoothing a single node.

Go on to the next section to learn how you can turn smooth or cusp nodes into symmetrical nodes and how this affects the drawing process.

Making Single or Multiple Nodes Symmetrical

Symmetrical nodes share the same characteristics as smooth nodes, except that the control points on a symmetrical node are equidistant from the node. This means that the curvature is the same on both sides of the symmetrical node. When you move one of the control points, the other control point moves. In effect, symmetry causes the two control points to move as one.

Another important point to remember is that you cannot make a node symmetrical if it connects to a straight line segment. The node must lie between two curve segments in order to qualify for a symmetrical edit.

Perform the following brief exercise to convert a single cusp node to a symmetrical node, using the drawing with a cusp node that you saved earlier.

1. Open the cusp node drawing you saved in the earlier exercise. If its filename (possibly CH9TEST.CDR) appears in the lower part of the File menu, you can open it by clicking on the name.
2. Set viewing magnification to 1:1 and activate the Shape tool to select the curve.
3. Find a cusp node that you want to make symmetrical and then click on it, as shown here:

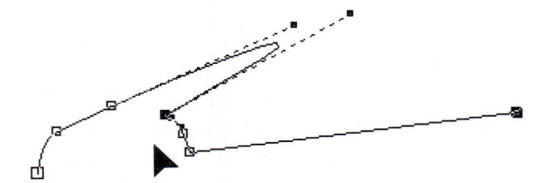

4. Click on the Symmet command button. The selected node is now converted to a symmetrical node, and CorelDRAW! redraws the curve so that it passes through the node symmetrically, as shown here:

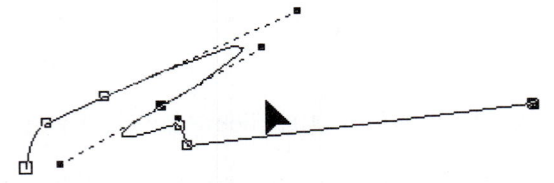

5. Move the control points of this node until you have a satisfactory understanding of how symmetrical nodes work.

Shaping Lines, Curves, Rectangles, and Ellipses

Making multiple nodes symmetrical is just as easy as making single nodes symmetrical. The only difference is that you select more than one node at a time, using either SHIFT or the marquee method.

In the next sections, you will find out how to master the art of breaking nodes apart and joining them together—and why you might choose to do so.

Breaking Curves at Single or Multiple Nodes

Breaking a node involves splitting a curve at a selected node, so that two nodes appear where before there was one. Although you can move the separate sections of a broken node as though they were separate curves, CorelDRAW! does not regard them as separate. These split segments actually constitute different subpaths of the same curve. Breaking a node into separate subpaths gives the impression of spontaneous freehand drawing, yet it allows you to keep separate "drawing strokes" together as one object. Breaking curves at the nodes is also useful when you need to delete a portion of a curve and leave the rest of the curve intact.

Keep in mind that you cannot break a curve at an end node, because there is no segment on the other side of the end point with which to form a separate subpath.

When you break a node, it becomes two unconnected end nodes. You are then free to move either end node and the entire subpath to which it is connected. The two subpaths remain part of the same object, however, as you can see when you select either subpath with the Pick tool. In the following exercise, you will use the curve from the last exercise, break it at a single node, and then observe how CorelDRAW! handles the two resulting subpaths.

1. With the Shape tool, select a node on the side of the curve and click on it, as shown here:

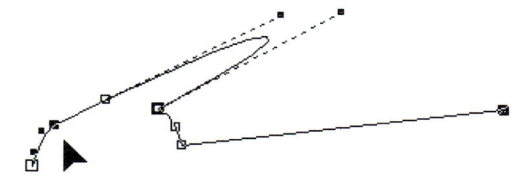

2. Click on the Break command button (rightmost) in the Node Edit roll-up. The single node splits into two nodes. Since they are close together, however, the change is not visible until you begin to move the new end nodes.

3. Move the left end point away from the subpath to the right, as shown here, and then deselect both nodes.

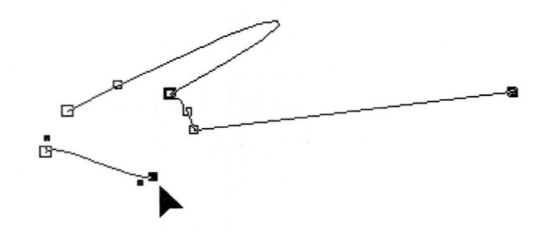

The object itself remains selected for editing, and the status line informs you that the curve now has two subpaths.

4. Press the SPACEBAR to activate the Pick tool. Notice that the Pick tool treats these two subpaths as a single curve object, even though they look like separate curves.

   There may be times when you want to make subpaths into truly separate objects, so that you can manipulate and edit them independently. As the next step shows, CorelDRAW! provides a means for you to turn the subpaths into independent curves.

5. To separate the two subpaths into two truly distinct objects, leave the Pick tool active and then select the Break Apart command from the Arrange menu. This command is available only when multiple subpaths of a single curve object are selected. Deselect both subpaths.

   Now if you click on each subpath with the Pick tool, you will see that each segment would be separately selected.

6. Select New from the File menu to clear the screen. You do not need to resave the cusp node drawing that began this last exercise.

In this brief exercise, you have seen some applications for breaking a curve at a node. For example, you can create two separate objects from a single object, or create separate subpaths that move together as a single object.

Caution: If you break a closed curve object at a node, you will not be able to fill the object with a color or pattern.

When you break a curve at multiple nodes, the result is multiple subpaths, which still remain part of the same object.

The reverse of breaking curves apart is joining them together. In the next section, you will find out when you can and cannot join nodes together, as well as some reasons why you might want to do so.

Joining Nodes

By now, you have probably noticed that the Join command is rarely available for selection in the Node Edit roll-up. You can join nodes only under very specific conditions.

- You can join only two nodes at a time, so only two nodes can be selected.
- The two nodes must be either end nodes of the same object or end nodes of separate subpaths of the same object.
- You cannot join an end node of an open curve to a closed object, such as an ellipse or a rectangle.

When might you want to join two nodes, then? The two chief occasions are when you want to close an open path and when you want to make a single continuous curve from the two separate paths.

Closing an Open Path An open path, as you will recall from your previous freehand drawing experience in CorelDRAW!, is a curve object with end points that do not join and which therefore cannot be filled with a color or pattern. To prevent open paths, you can set the AutoJoin option in the Preferences dialog box to a higher number and thereby make it easier for end nodes to snap together as you draw. There are still times, however, when you might choose to join end points after drawing an open curve. In such cases, use the Join command in the Node Edit roll-up. The following exercise presents a situation in which you could use the Join command to make a drawing process easier.

1. Set magnification to actual size (1:1). Select the Freehand tool and draw a more or less oval curve, but do not finish the curve—stop drawing at a point close to where you started it, as shown here:

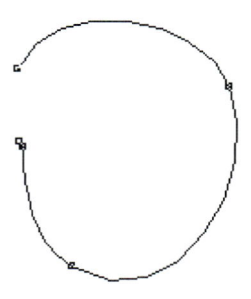

2. Activate the Shape tool to select this curve object and then select both of the end nodes, using the marquee or SHIFT key technique. You can see that the Join command button in the roll-up (second from right in top row) is now available to you, as shown here:

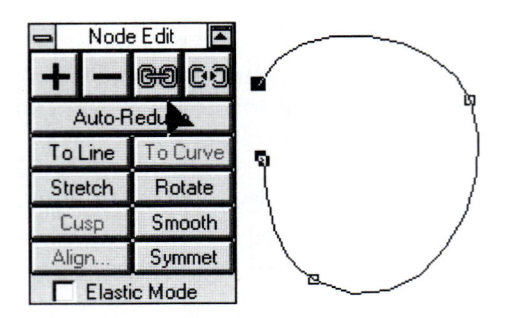

3. Click on the Join command button in the Node Edit roll-up. CorelDRAW! redraws the curve as a closed path. You can then fill this path with a color or pattern, as you learned in Chapter 7.
4. Select New from the File menu to clear the screen. Do not save the drawing.

It is easy to close an open path with the Shape tool. Joining nodes from separate curves, however, is a bit trickier.

Joining Separate Subpaths (Combined Objects)   You can also join two end nodes if they are on two subpaths of the same curve. The two subpaths then become a single, continuous curve segment. A special case exists when you have two separate curve objects (not two subpaths of the same curve) and want to make them into a single curve. Knowing that you cannot join nodes from two separate objects, what do you do? Your best option is to combine the curves using the Pick tool and the Combine command in the Arrange menu. Even though the curves continue to look like separate objects, from the standpoint of CorelDRAW! they become two subpaths of a single curve. You can then join their end nodes to unite the subpaths.

1. Select actual size magnification and, with the Freehand tool, draw four separate curve segments, as shown in Figure 9-8a.
2. With the Pick tool, draw a marquee around all four curve segments to simultaneously select them. If you have a problem with this, choose Select All in the Edit menu.
3. From the Arrange menu, select Combine to make a single broken curve out of the four segments.
4. With the Shape tool, select the curve. Then select one of the three pairs of end points to be joined, double-click on either of the two end points to open the Node Edit roll-up, if it is not already on the screen, and click on the Join button. Select each of the two remaining pairs and click on the Join button for each of them. The result is a single continuous curve, as shown in Figure 9-8b.

Shaping Lines, Curves, Rectangles, and Ellipses

a.

b.

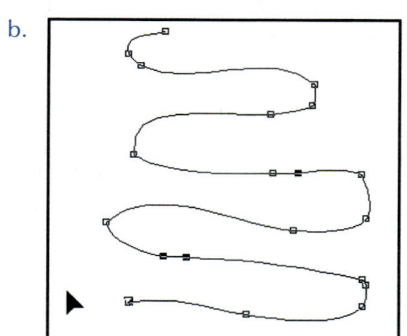

Joining nodes to form a continuous curve
Figure 9-8.

> **Tip:** The only trick to this is to first combine the curve segments with the Pick tool and the Arrange menu before trying to join the segments with the Shape tool.

5. Select New from the File menu; do not save the changes you have made.

Going through this process is a good way to familiarize yourself with all the steps involved in both joining nodes and breaking nodes apart. Perhaps you have some new ideas for using the Join command in some of your own drawings.

Aligning Nodes

If you want two objects to share a common edge, like two pieces in a puzzle, the Align command in the Node Edit roll-up can accomplish it for you. The two objects must first be combined with the Arrange menu, and you must add or delete nodes until there are the same number of nodes in each object in roughly the same location. Once you have completed aligning the two objects, you can break them apart.

Objects can be aligned vertically or horizontally, and they can literally share a common border through the alignment of their control points. If you want to superimpose one object on the other, you align them both horizontally and vertically *and* align their control points. The latter—aligning the objects all three ways—is the default alignment.

You can experiment with the Align command in the Node Edit roll-up in the following exercise.

1. At actual size (1:1) magnification, with the Freehand tool draw two curve objects similar to those shown in Figure 9-9a. (Wireframe should be turned on.)

Tip: Use the SPACEBAR to toggle between the Pick tool and any other tool you are using at the time.

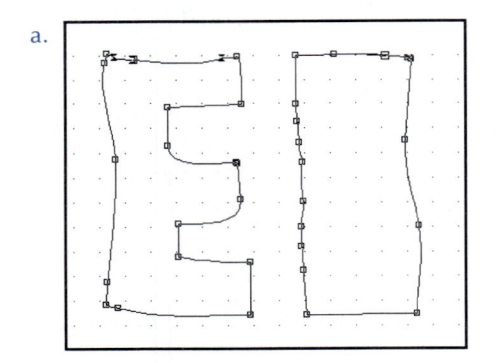

Aligning the nodes of two curve objects
Figure 9-9.

2. With the Pick tool, draw a marquee around both objects to select them. Then, from the Arrange menu, select Combine.
3. With the Shape tool, add or delete nodes until the two objects have the same number of nodes on the "mating" side, in roughly the same position as shown in Figure 9-9a.
4. For each pair of nodes you want to align, perform these steps with the Shape tool in the order given:
    ♦ Select the node to be *realigned* (moved).
    ♦ Press SHIFT and select the node to *align* to (move to).
    ♦ Click on the roll-down arrow to open the Node Edit window.
    ♦ Select Align. The Node Align dialog box will open, as shown here:

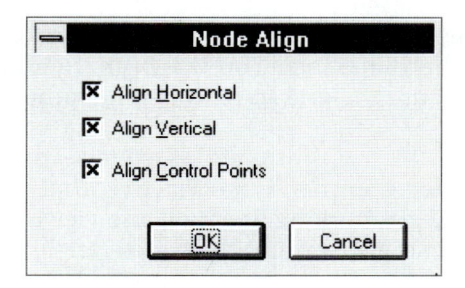

    ♦ Click on OK to accept the default choice of all three options, which will superimpose the nodes and align the control points. You might have to tweak the control points slightly where the moved segment has reversed direction.
    ♦ Deselect the nodes by clicking on any white space before beginning to select the next pair.

    When you have aligned all of the node pairs you want to align, you should have a single curve segment shared by both objects, whose shape is the same as the object to which you aligned, as shown in Figure 9-9b.
5. With the Pick tool, select the combined object and choose Break Apart from the Arrange menu.
6. Click on white space to deselect the combined object and select and drag one of the original objects until you can see the two individual objects again. Now the two objects have a common, although mirror-image, shape on one side, as shown in Figure 9-9c.
7. Select New from the File menu to clear the screen; do not save the changes.
8. You are finished with the Node Edit roll-up for now. Click on its Control-menu box and click on Close.

This concludes your exploration of the techniques for shaping lines and curves. In the remaining sections of this chapter, you will try your hand at shaping rectangular and elliptical objects.

Shaping Rectangles and Squares

For interesting distortions, you can stretch, rotate, or skew rectangles and squares before rounding their corners.

The Shape tool has a specific function when you apply it to rectangles and squares in CorelDRAW!. It rounds the corners of a rectangle, thus creating a whole new shape. The status line keeps track of the radius of the rounded corner as you drag. You can control the degree of rounding interactively, or by using the grid if you want to be exact.

Rounding the Corners of a Rectangle

Complete the following exercise to practice rounding rectangles and squares using the Shape tool. You will begin by rounding corners interactively; later, you will use the grid to perform the same work.

1. For the beginning of this exercise, make sure that the Snap To Grid and Rulers commands are inactive, that Wireframe is turned on, and that you are working in actual size viewing magnification. Then select the Rectangle tool and draw a rectangle of unequal length and width.

2. Activate the Shape tool and select a node at one of the corners of the rectangle. Notice that the status line indicates that the corner radius of this rectangle is 0.00 inches. The corner radius helps you measure the degree to which you have rounded the corners of a rectangle or square with the Shape tool.

3. Position the shaping pointer at this node and begin to drag the corner slowly toward the next nearest corner. As shown here, each corner node separates into two separate nodes, with each node moving farther away from the original corner as you drag. The status line also informs you just how much of a corner radius you are creating. The farther you drag the nodes from the corners, the more the corner radius increases.

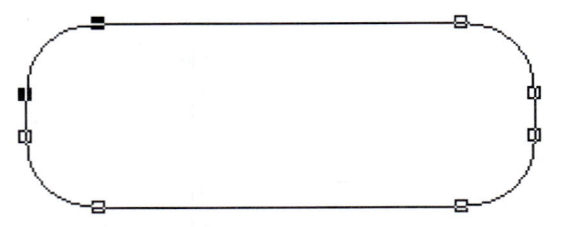

4. Continue dragging the mouse until you reach the logical limit of rounding: when the nodes from adjacent corners meet at the sides of

Shaping Lines, Curves, Rectangles, and Ellipses **327**

the rectangle. At this point, your rounded rectangle has become almost an ellipse, similar to the rectangle shown here:

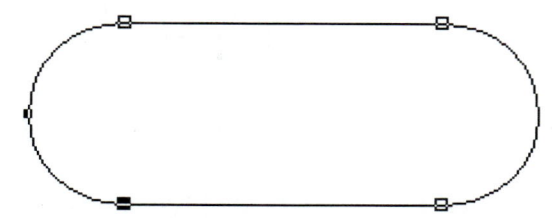

5. Begin dragging the selected node from the middle of the line back to the former corner. As you do so, the corner radius diminishes. You can return the rectangle to its original shape by dragging the nodes all the way back to the corner.

6. Delete the rectangle from the screen, then draw a square and repeat steps 2 through 5. Notice that when you begin with a square and then round the corners to the logical limit, the square becomes a nearly perfect circle rather than an ellipse, as seen here:

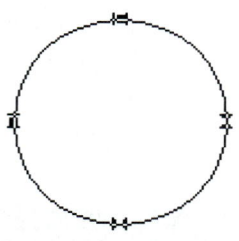

7. Press DEL to clear the screen of the square-turned-circle.

Although the status line information helps you round corners precisely, you can gain even greater precision using the grid and rulers. The next exercise guides you through the process of rounding corners of a rectangle or square with the help of these aids.

1. Open the Grid & Scale Setup dialog box on the Layout menu, set both of the Grid Frequency settings to 4 per inch, turn on Show Grid and Snap To Grid, and click OK. Turn on Rulers if they are not already on.

2. Draw a rectangle 2 inches wide by 1 1/4 inches deep. Activate the Shape tool and select one of the corner nodes of the rectangle.

3. Drag this corner node away from the corner to round the rectangle. This time, the corner radius changes in precise increments of 1/4 inch because of the grid setting.

9

The same thing happens with a square; the radius of the square also changes in increments of 1/4 inch.

4. When you have finished experimenting with the rectangle and the square, select New from the File menu to clear the screen.

In the next section, you will see what can happen when you stretch, rotate, or skew a rectangle or square before attempting to round its corners.

Stretched, Rotated, or Skewed Rectangles and Squares

When you transform a rectangle or square by stretching, rotating, or skewing it with the Pick tool and then round its corners, the value of the corner radius may be distorted. The corner radius indicator on the status line is followed by the word "distorted" in parentheses. As Figure 9-10 shows, the final shape of such a rounded rectangle may also be distorted; in extreme cases it can resemble a skewed flying saucer or rotated ellipse.

Practice this technique on your own and then go on to the next section, where you will find out how to turn a rectangle into a curve so that you can shape it in an infinite number of ways.

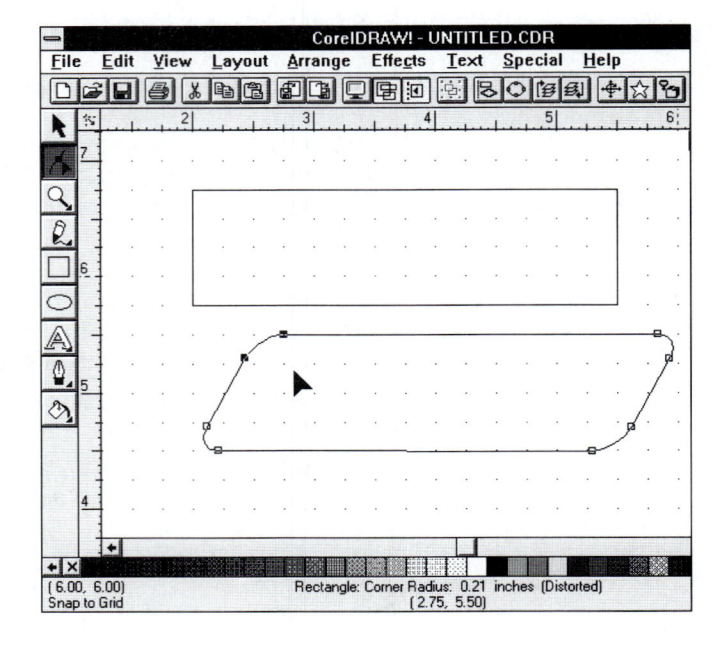

Rounding the corners of a skewed rectangle
Figure 9-10.

Shaping Lines, Curves, Rectangles, and Ellipses

Converting a Rectangle to a Curve Object

If the shaping options for rectangles or squares seem limited to you, don't worry. You can convert any rectangle or square into a curve object and, from that point onward, you can turn a formerly four-cornered object into anything at all. The technique is simple, as you will see in the following brief exercise.

1. Set magnification to actual size (1:1) and make sure Wireframe is turned on in preparation for this exercise.
2. Select the Rectangle tool if it is not selected already and then draw a rectangle of any size or shape.
3. Activate the Pick tool by pressing the SPACEBAR, and select the Convert To Curves command from the Arrange menu. The status line message changes from "Rectangle on Layer 1" to "Curve on Layer 1." Note that the new four-cornered "curve" still has the same number of nodes as when it was a rectangle.
4. Activate the Shape tool and then select and drag one of the nodes in any direction. As the example in Figure 9-11 shows, dragging the node no longer forces the associated line/curve segment to move parallel to the other line segments.
5. Continue warping the shape of this rectangle-turned-curve in a variety of ways. For example, you could add nodes, convert line segments to curves, create symmetrical nodes, or even turn the former rectangle into a candy cane or other hybrid object.
6. The object you have been working on should be selected. If it is not, select it and then press DEL to clear the screen before going on.

Now that you have mastered the art of shaping rectangles and squares, you are ready to apply the Shape tool to ellipses and circles for some quite different effects.

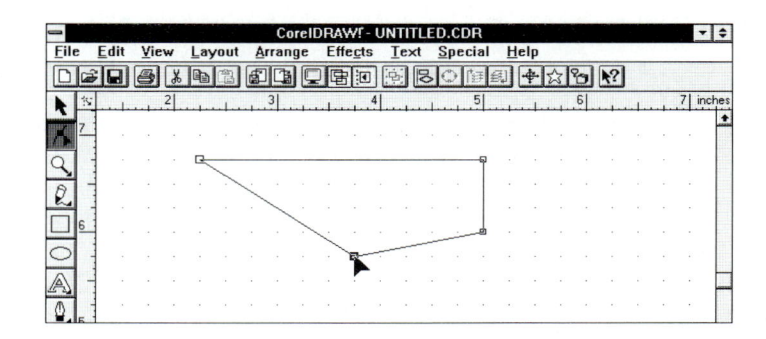

Editing a rectangle that has been converted to curves
Figure 9-11.

Shaping Ellipses and Circles

When you shape ellipses or circles with the Shape tool, you can create either an open arc or a pie wedge. You can even shift back and forth between these two shapes as you draw, depending on whether the tip of the shaping pointer lies inside or outside the ellipse or circle. You also have the option of constraining the angle of an arc or pie wedge to 15-degree increments.

Creating an Open Arc

The status line provides information about the angle of the arc as you draw.

To turn an ellipse or circle into an arc, you position the tip of the shaping pointer just *outside* of the rim at the node and then drag the node in the desired direction. Make certain that the tip of the pointer remains outside the rim of the ellipse as you drag, or you will create a wedge instead of an arc. Practice creating arcs from both ellipses and circles in the following exercise.

1. Turn off the Snap To Grid command if it is active and set the viewing magnification to actual size.
2. Select the Ellipse tool and, by pressing CTRL, draw a perfect circle.
3. Activate the Shape tool to select the circle automatically.
4. Position the tip of the Shape tool exactly at the node, and then drag the node downward slowly, but just outside the rim of the circle, in a clockwise direction. As shown here, the single node separates into two nodes, with the second node following your pointer as you drag. If the circle seems to be turning into a pie wedge instead of an arc, the tip of your mouse pointer is inside the rim of the circle. Move it outside of the rim and try again.

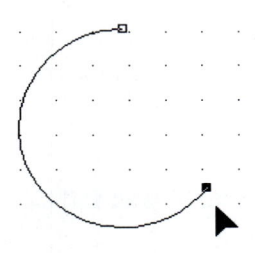

Note that the status line provides information about the angle position of the first and second nodes and about the total angle of the arc. This information is based on a 360-degree wheel, with 0 degrees at 12 o'clock, 90 degrees at 9 o'clock, 180 degrees at 6 o'clock, and 270 degrees at 3 o'clock.

Shaping Lines, Curves, Rectangles, and Ellipses

5. Continue to drag the shaping pointer, but now press and hold the CTRL key as well. The angle of the arc snaps in increments of 15 degrees. Release the mouse button when your arc has the angle you want.
6. Select the Ellipse tool and again draw a perfect circle. Then repeat steps 3, 4, and 5, completing this arc at an approximate 105-degree angle.

Note: If you use an ellipse instead of a circle, the "total angle" information on the status line is followed by the message "distorted" in parentheses. This message occurs because CorelDRAW! bases its calculation of an arc on a perfect circle rather than on an ellipse with different height and width. The angle assignments for arcs created from an ellipse are therefore approximate.

7. Press the SPACEBAR to activate the Pick tool. The newly created arc is selected. Notice that the selection box, like the one shown below, is much larger than the arc itself; in fact, it seems to surround the now invisible but complete original ellipse. The purpose of this large selection box is to make it easy for you to align an arc or wedge concentrically, using the Align command in the Arrange menu. The disadvantage of this large selection box is that when you are selecting objects with the marquee, you must make certain that your marquee surrounds the entire selection box.

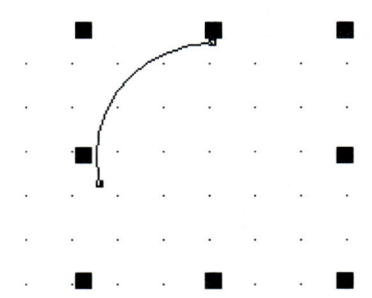

8. Select New from the File menu to clear the screen before going on.

Creating a wedge shape from an ellipse is just as easy as creating an arc, as you will see in the next section.

Creating a Pie Wedge

The only difference between creating an arc and creating a pie wedge is that in the latter case, you position the tip of the shaping pointer *inside* the ellipse or circle as you drag. Perform the following exercise to see the difference for yourself.

1. Set magnification to actual size, select the Ellipse tool, and draw a circle. Activate the Shape tool to select it for editing.

2. Position the tip of the shaping pointer inside the circle exactly at the node, and then begin dragging the node downward in a clockwise direction. The two nodes separate as before, but this time the circle turns into a shape like a pie missing a piece, suitable for pie charts and wedges, as shown here.

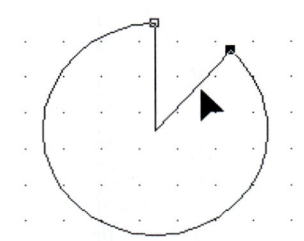

3. Press and hold CTRL and continue dragging the mouse. The angle of the wedge shape now moves in fixed increments of 15 degrees. Release the mouse button when you have obtained the desired angle.

4. Just as you did with the arc, press the SPACEBAR to activate the Pick tool. The wedge is selected. Notice the oversized selection box once more. Make sure to surround this selection box completely whenever you attempt to select a wedge with a narrow total angle.

5. Press DEL to clear the screen.

That's all there is to creating arcs and wedges from ellipses and circles. If these shaping techniques are not flexible enough for you, you can always convert the arc or wedge to a curve object, as you will see in the next section.

Converting Ellipses and Circles to Curve Objects

If the shaping options for ellipses and circles seem limited to you, don't worry. You can convert any ellipse, circle, arc, or wedge into a curve object and, from that point onward, you can add and delete nodes, drag nodes and control points, or change node types. In the following exercise, you will create a wedge from a circle, convert the wedge to curves, and then reshape the new curve object into the body of a baby carriage.

Shaping Lines, Curves, Rectangles, and Ellipses

1. Select the Ellipse tool and draw an ellipse that is wider than it is high, starting from the upper-left area of the rim and moving downward as you drag.

2. Activate the Shape tool and position the arrowhead pointer over the node of the ellipse. Drag the node downward, keeping the tip of the shaping pointer inside the rim, and create a wedge with a total angle of about 240 degrees, as shown here:

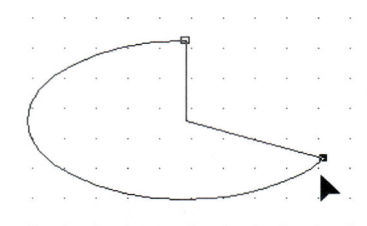

3. Press the SPACEBAR to activate the Pick tool and select the wedge, and then select the Convert To Curves command from the Arrange menu. Notice that because of the shape of the wedge, the new curve object has five nodes, whereas the ellipse had only one node.

4. Reactivate the Shape tool and drag the node farthest to the right upward and outward, as shown here:

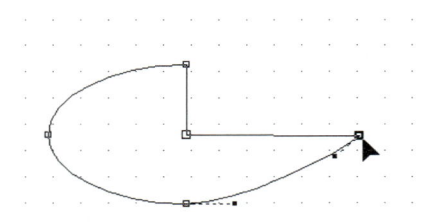

   Since the segment next to this one is a straight line, the selected node has only one control point. Moving this node upward and outward has the effect of stretching the straight line.

5. The curvature of the segment associated with the node you just moved is not adequate to round out the bottom of the "carriage." To remedy this, click on the curve segment (to the left of the selected node) where you want the new node and press + on the numeric keypad. A new node appears between the previously selected node and the one below and to the left of it. It's a smooth node because of the existing curvature, and because the object originated as an ellipse.

6. Select and drag this newly added smooth node downward and to the right, until it forms a nicely rounded bottom to the "carriage" body, as shown here:

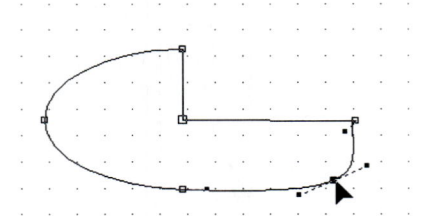

7. Clear the screen by selecting New from the File menu. Do not save the drawing.

Perhaps the example in the preceding exercise will stimulate your imagination to create any number of complex objects from the basic objects available to you through the drawing tools. The Shape tool makes it all possible!

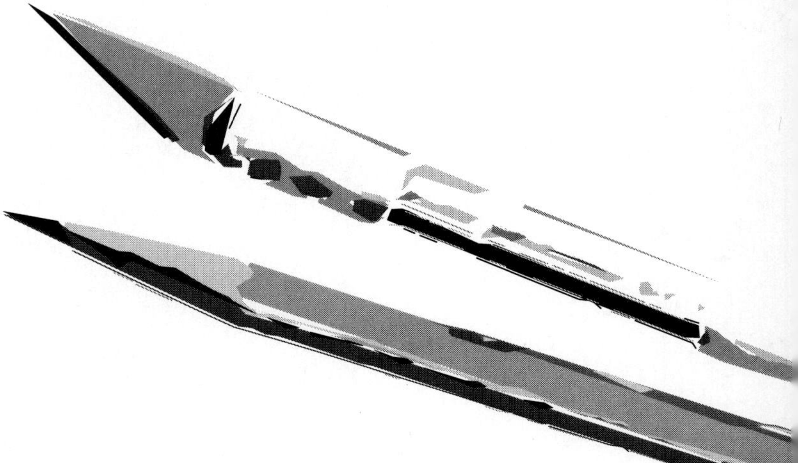

Coming Together in Hawaii

Hui 'ana e Hawai'i - AACI

Shaping Lines, Curves, Rectangles, and Ellipses

CORELDRAW! in Action

CINDY TURNER
Leimaker In Moonlight

Cindy designed this work to be printed on coffee mugs, so one side was created, a mirror copy of it was made, then the moon, stars, and the center leaf were added. Cindy started by importing a scanned pencil drawing of a woman holding a leigh. The bitmap was then traced in CorelDRAW! to create closed shapes which were then filled. Fountain fills were used for the woman's eyelid and the flowers, and uniform fills were used for the rest of the shapes.

The upper leaves were created by first placing points with the Freehand tool for a single leaf. The leaf outline shape was smoothed and refined by adjusting its nodes and control points, then it was filled with a fountain fill. Multiple copies of the leaf were made and changed slightly to differentiate them.

The lower leaves were also created by varying copies of a single leaf. A pointed oval was first created for the leaf outline. Then closed shapes were created for the two halves of the leaf, and a fountain fill was used in each of the two halves to create the illusion of curved surfaces. A center spine shape with a uniform fill covers the junction between the two halves.

Cindy created the moon by making first one circle then duplicating it. She then "opened up" the circle on the left using the Shape tool to get the outside arc. With the Pick tool she moved the second circle against the two ends of the arc. Using the Shape tool she opened up the second circle into the inner arc and aligned the end nodes of the two arcs. The arcs were then selected with the Pick tool and combined into a single object. Again using the Shape tool, she selected the two nodes at one end of the crescent, double-clicked on them, and joined them by clicking on the Join end nodes button on the Node Edit roll-up. This was repeated on the two nodes at the other end of the crescent to complete the moon shape, which was then filled with pale yellow.

This piece was in CorelArtShow 4: Page 64, File: SPC00091.CDR. You may contact Cindy in care of:

> Cindy Turner
> Turner and DeVries
> 701 North Kalaheo Avenue
> Kailua, HI 96734
> (808) 261-2179
> Fax (808) 262-2690

The art on opposite page was created by and is the property of Cindy Turner. It is used with permission.

10

SHAPING and EDITING TEXT

Text can be an important design element, whether you specialize in original art, graphic or industrial design, technical illustration, or desktop publishing. Every choice you make concerning font, style, spacing, alignment, type size, and placement can affect how your intended audience receives your work. You should have the option of editing text attributes at *any* time, not only when you first enter text on a page.

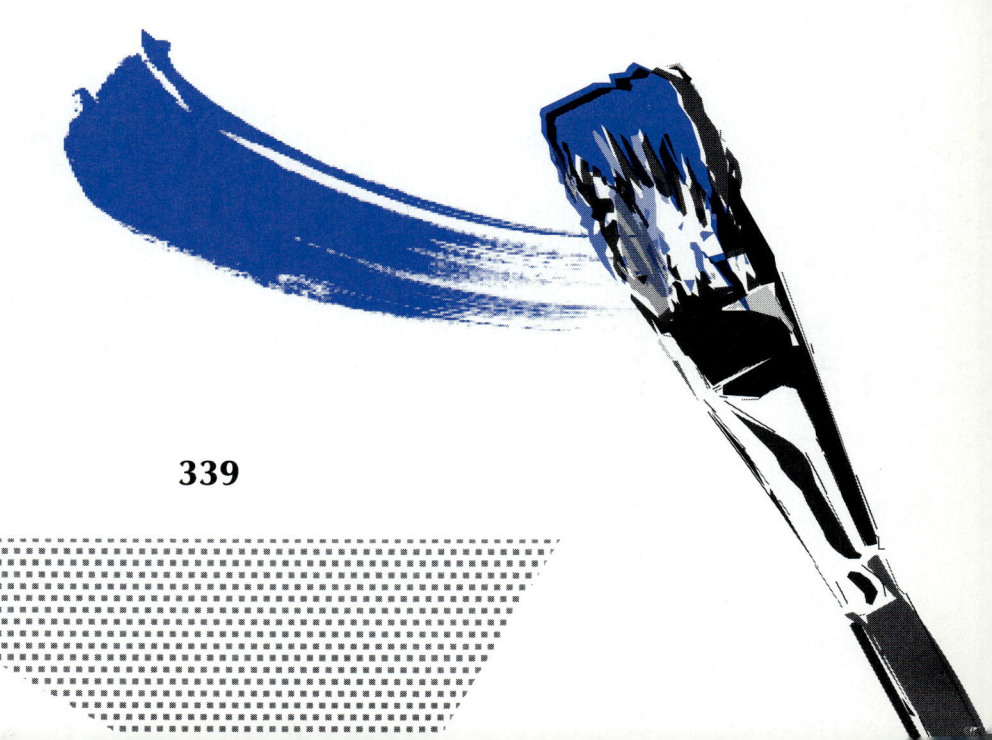

With CorelDRAW!, you do have that option. Using the Pick tool and the Shape tool, you can edit existing text in ways that enhance both its typographic and pictorial value. You already edited text as a graphic element in Chapters 5 and 8 by using the Pick tool to rotate, stretch, scale, skew, and reflect text strings. In this chapter, you will concentrate on editing the *typographical* text attributes (such as font and type size) of individual characters, groups of characters, and complete text strings. You will also learn to customize your text picture even further by converting a text string to a set of curves and then reshaping each curve. The Pick and Shape tools share these editing functions between them.

Editing Attributes for a Text String

Remember the two ways you selected attributes when you first entered a text string—the Text dialog box and the Text roll-up window? You can also use each of these methods to change text attributes that already exist. Do this by clicking in the text string with the Pick tool and then selecting either Edit Text or Text Roll-Up from the Text menu. The changes you make will apply to every character in the text string. To change attributes for selected characters within a text string, you need to use the Shape tool, as described in the section later in this chapter entitled "Selecting and Editing with the Shape tool."

In the first exercise, you will create a short text string that you can use in many different exercises throughout this chapter. Then, you will select the text string and change some of its attributes.

1. Set your viewing magnification to actual size. Turn the Rulers, Wireframe, Show Grid, and Snap To Grid commands off for this portion of the chapter. The figures and illustrations in this chapter show the status line at the top of the window, but you can have it at the bottom if you wish.

2. Open the Outline Pen tool and select no outline as the default for Artistic and Paragraph Text. Similarly, open the Fill tool and select solid black as the default for Artistic and Paragraph text.

3. Select the Text tool and then place an insertion point midway down the left edge of your viewing window. Type the following text string on three separate lines:

    **Doing
    what comes
    naturally**

4. Select the Pick tool which selects the text and then open the Text roll-up.

Shaping and Editing Text

5. Change the text attributes to Cooper Black Italic Headline (CooperBlkItHd BT), 65 points, and center alignment; then select Apply and roll up the Text roll-up.

Note: While you don't have to use the fonts described here, the effects in this chapter are dependent on the particular fonts mentioned, which are available on the first CD-ROM that comes with CorelDRAW!. To access these fonts, first press ALT-TAB to get to the Program Manager and then select Fonts from the Control Panel; next, click on Add, select your CD-ROM drive, and click on the Fonts directory, the TTF subdirectory, and the letter of the alphabet for the font you want; finally, select the font and click on OK to download the font. Press ALT-TAB again to return to CorelDRAW!.

6. Because you have changed the alignment, some of the text may not appear within viewing range. If this is the case, select the Pick tool and drag the text until it fits within the viewing window, as shown in Figure 10-1.

7. Deselect the text string and save your work in a file named DOINWHAT.CDR. Leave the text on the screen for the next exercise.

Changing font, style, justification, and type size
Figure 10-1.

You can change attributes for a text string as often as desired. However, as long as you use the Pick tool to select text, any attribute changes you make will affect the entire text string. If your work requires highly stylized text designs, where attributes must be decided on a character-by-character basis, you need to use the Shape tool.

> **Note:** You can also select and change the font, style, size, and spacing of single characters by selecting the character with the text tool. The text tool, though, does not allow you to change the shape of a character and is not as handy for character-by-character editing.

Selecting and Editing Text with the Shape tool

When the Shape tool is active, you can select any number of characters within a text string and edit their typographical attributes. Depending on how you prefer to work, you can edit attributes either interactively or by means of the Text dialog box, the Text roll-up, or the Character command in the Text menu. Some of these attributes—specifically, font, style, and type size—overlap within the two dialog boxes and the roll-up. Or, you can move letters and adjust spacing and kerning interactively, without using menu commands, roll-ups, or dialog boxes. If all these adjustments fail to give your text the desired look, you can gain more editing control by converting text to curves and then manipulating the nodes and control points.

Before you can edit text attributes on a character-by-character basis, you must first use the Shape tool to select the text string in which the characters are located. This is similar to selecting a curve object as a prerequisite to selecting one or more of its nodes. After you select a text string, you can select a specific character, multiple adjacent or nonadjacent characters, or all characters in the text string. Practice selecting different combinations of characters in the following exercise.

1. Open the DOINWHAT.CDR text file that you created in the last exercise, if it is not open already.

2. Activate the Shape tool and, if the text is not already selected, click once on the outline of any character in the text string. A square node appears at the base of each letter in the text string, and vertical and horizontal arrow symbols appear at the lower-left and lower-right corners of the text string, respectively:

naturally

You will become acquainted with the meaning of these symbols in a moment. For now, it is enough to recognize that this change in the text string's appearance indicates that you have selected it for editing with the Shape tool. The status line shows that you have selected all 23 characters.

3. Select a single character in the text string, the letter "n" in "naturally." Do this by clicking *once* on the node of this character. The status line now contains the message "1 character(s) selected," and the node at the bottom left of the letter turns black, like this:

naturally

4. Deselect the letter "n" by clicking anywhere outside the text string. Notice that the string itself remains selected.
5. Select the initial letter of each word. Click once on the node for the "D" in "Doing." Then press and hold the SHIFT key and click on the node for the initial letter of each of the other words. Check the status line to keep track of the number of characters you select.
6. To deselect these characters, either click on any white space, or press and hold SHIFT and click on each selected character node one by one.
7. Select the entire word "Doing" by lassoing its nodes with a marquee:

Doing

Your marquee does not have to surround the characters completely, as long as it surrounds the nodes. All the nodes of this word become highlighted after you release the mouse button.

8. Deselect these characters and then draw a marquee that surrounds all of the text string. All of the characters are now selected for editing.

9. Deselect all of the characters by clicking on any white space. Leave the text on the screen, with the text string selected for editing with the Shape tool, but with no individual characters selected.

You may be wondering, "Why should I bother to select all the characters with the Shape tool, when I could activate the Pick tool and change attributes for the entire text string?" You can control some attributes that way, but the Character Attributes dialog box with the Shape tool offers you three more options for altering the appearance of text. Read on to find out how those additional attributes can enhance the design of text in CorelDRAW!.

The Character Attributes Dialog Box

Practically the only thing you can't do with the Character Attributes dialog box is change the characters themselves.

When you use the Character Attributes dialog box with the Shape tool, you can control other characteristics of selected characters besides font, style, point size, and spacing. You can tilt characters at any angle and shift them up, down, or sideways. In this section, you will learn how to access this dialog box with the Shape tool and work with each of the controls in it. As you work through the exercises, you will learn about useful applications for each type of attribute. By the end of the section, you will alter the design of the DOINWHAT.CDR text string substantially.

You can access the Character Attributes dialog box either by double-clicking on a selected character node or by going through the Text menu or the Text roll-up. Any attributes that you alter in this dialog box apply only to the characters you have selected. Make sure, then, that you have selected all of the characters you want to edit before accessing the Character Attributes dialog box.

1. With the Shape tool active, select the node in front of the letter "n" in "naturally."
2. Access the Character Attributes dialog box in the way that is most convenient for your working habits. If you prefer to use menu commands, select the Character option from the Text menu. If you like using the mouse best, double-click on any of the selected nodes. Or if your Text roll-up is handy, open it and click on the Character Attributes button. The Character Attributes dialog box shown in Figure 10-2 appears.

Take a moment to become familiar with the options available to you in this dialog box when the Shape tool is active, and with the significance of each attribute.

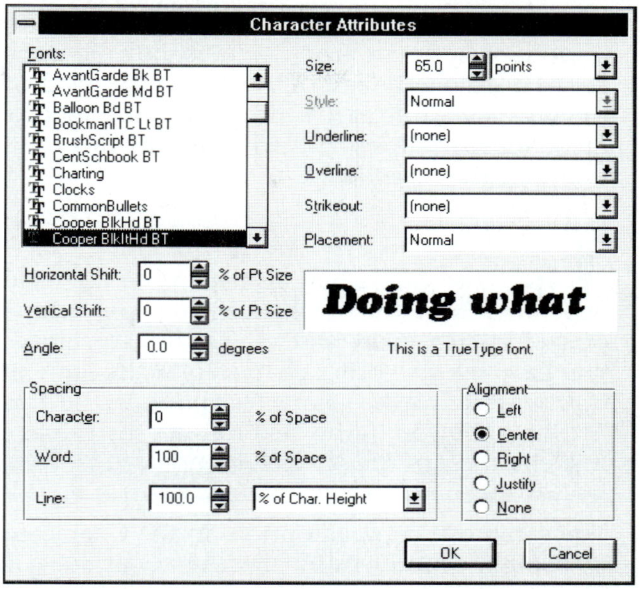

Shaping and Editing Text

Character Attributes dialog box
Figure 10-2.

Reviewing the Dialog Box

The baseline is the imaginary straight line to which text is normally anchored and with which it aligns.

The options in the Character Attributes dialog box, shown in Figure 10-2, allow you to control ten different types of text attributes: font, style, type size and its unit of measure, lines (under, over, and through text), text placement (superscript and subscript), horizontal shift, vertical shift, character angle, spacing, and alignment. You are familiar with the first four and last two attributes, but the concepts behind horizontal and vertical shifts, character angle, superscript, and subscript may be new to you. If so, browse through this section to find out more about these attributes.

Horizontal Shift   The Horizontal Shift option controls the distance, in percentage of point size, by which selected characters shift to the right or left of their original location. This distance varies, depending on the font of the selected characters.

Vertical Shift   The Vertical Shift option controls the distance by which selected characters shift above or below their starting location (baseline). CorelDRAW! expresses this distance as a percentage of the point size of the selected characters. This distance is therefore variable, too.

Character Angle   The Character Angle option allows you to tilt the selected characters in any direction and at any angle. You can turn characters upside down, sideways, or anywhere in between.

Superscript and Subscript   The Superscript and Subscript options, available from the Placement drop-down list box, let you place selected characters above or below the rest of the text, respectively. Superscript text aligns with the imaginary line at the top of surrounding text (for example, the "2" in E = mc^2). Subscript text aligns with the baseline of surrounding text (for example, the "2" in H_2O).

Tip: The values that display in the Character Attributes dialog box depend on how you open the dialog box. If you open it by double-clicking on a character, you will see the settings assigned to that character, even if you have selected other characters at the same time. If you open the dialog box by selecting the Character option in the Text menu or the Character Attributes button in the Text roll-up, the values displayed correspond to the first character in the selected group.

You can move between options in the Character Attributes dialog box either by using the mouse or by pressing TAB or SHIFT-TAB and the arrow keys. Of course, using the mouse is much simpler!

In the next five sections, you will have the opportunity to redesign text imaginatively, using many of the options in the Character Attributes dialog box.

Editing Font and Style

In the following exercise, you will assign a different font and/or style to each letter in the word "naturally." You selected the first letter of the word before entering the dialog box, so you will alter the letter "n" first of all.

1. Select the Aachen font in the Font list box and then select OK. Your text string redisplays on the screen, but now the letter "n" looks quite different from the surrounding letters.

2. Double-click on the character node of the "n" once more. When the dialog box appears this time, it shows the current font of the *selected* character or characters. (See the tip in the previous section.) Press ESC or select Cancel to exit the dialog box without making a change.

3. Select each of the other letters in the word "naturally" in turn. Assign fonts and styles to them in the following order: Park Avenue normal, Franklin Gothic Heavy italic, Cooper Black Headlines normal, Revue normal, Times New Roman normal, University normal, Futura bold italic, and Brush Script normal. When you are finished, the word "naturally" displays an interesting patchwork of fonts:

4. Save the changes you have made by pressing CTRL-S, and leave your work on the screen for the next exercise.

Go on to the next section and apply different point sizes to the letters whose fonts and styles you have already altered.

Editing Type Size

When you changed fonts for each letter in the word "naturally," you left the type sizes unaltered, yet the letters do not appear to be the same size. You have probably guessed by now that different fonts have different heights and widths for the same point size. The point size is a consistent way to measure the size of characters only *within* a given font.

In the following exercise, you will make the letters in "naturally" closer to one another in actual or physical size.

1. Using the Shape tool again, double-click on the character node of the first letter "a" in "naturally." When the Character Attributes dialog box appears, change the point size for this letter to 110 and then select OK. Even though you have substantially increased its point size, this letter only now approximates the height of its neighbors. Point size is measured from the baseline of one line to the baseline above it and is not necessarily a measure of the actual type. You may need to scroll your screen downward to see the word "naturally," since the baseline-to-baseline distance has increased.
2. In the same way, select the first letter "l" and change its type size to 75 points.
3. Finally, select the letter "y" and change its point size to 90. Now, all of the letters seem more uniform in height and size:

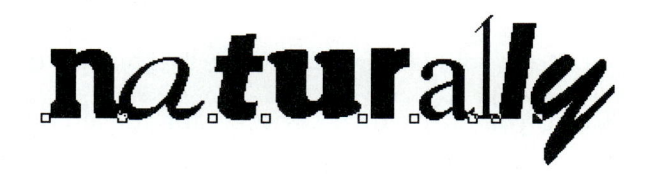

4. Save your work by pressing CTRL-S, leaving the text string on screen.

To edit the word "naturally" so that it conveys a sense of a more natural state, you can shift some of the characters up or down relative to the baseline and move others sideways. In the next exercise, you will practice moving individual characters.

Horizontal and Vertical Shift

When you shift selected characters horizontally, you move them to the right or left of their starting positions, causing them to overlap with other characters on the same line. You can use this technique to convey a sense of being rushed or crowded, or simply to adjust spacing between letters precisely. When you shift characters vertically, they fall above or below the baseline, which can create a feeling of spontaneity or excitement.

In the next exercise, you will shift some of the characters in the word "naturally" to enhance the sense of spontaneity and naturalness in the text.

1. Activate the Shape tool, if it isn't already, and then double-click on the character node for the letter "n" in the word "naturally" to enter the Character Attributes dialog box. Set Horizontal Shift to –25 percent of the point size and then select OK. Because you set the value to a negative number, the letter shifts to the left of its original position.

2. Select the character node for the next letter "a" and set Vertical Shift to 20 percent of point size. When you select OK, the position of the letter shifts above the baseline.

3. Select the following letters in turn, changing the shift settings for each. Change the Vertical Shift of the "r" to –25 percent, the Vertical Shift of the second "l" to 10 percent, and both the Horizontal Shift and Vertical Shift of the "y" to 25 percent. Notice that a negative value for Vertical Shift causes the selected character, "r," to reposition itself below the baseline. The resulting text should now look like this:

4. Save your changes and leave this text on the screen.

So far, you have edited attributes for one letter at a time. In the next section, you will select a group of characters and practice positioning them as superscripts and subscripts.

Creating Superscripts and Subscripts

Perform the following exercise to create superscripts and subscripts.

1. With the Shape tool select the character nodes of all of the letters in the word "comes" except the letter "c." Double-click on the node in front of "o" to access the Character Attributes dialog box.

2. Click on the Placement down arrow, select Superscript, and then click on OK. The selected letters have become small and appear as a superscript to the letter "c," like this:

3. Select the Undo command in the Edit menu to return the selected characters to their original position.

4. Select the same characters again and return to the Character Attributes dialog box by double-clicking on the "o" node. This time, choose Subscript in the Placement drop-down list box. When you select OK, the letters display as a subscript to the letter "c."

5. Press ALT-BACKSPACE or CTRL-Z to return the selected characters to their original position.

In the next section, you will practice tilting the characters in the word "naturally" to different angles.

Editing Character Angle

You can tilt selected characters at any angle using the Character Angle setting in the Character Attributes dialog box. Values between 0 and 180 degrees indicate that you are tilting the characters *above* an imaginary horizon, in a counterclockwise direction. Values between 0 and –180 degrees indicate that you are tilting the characters *below* an imaginary horizon, in a clockwise direction. At a 180-degree angle, the characters are upside down. Practice adjusting character angle in the following exercise.

1. With the Shape tool active, press and hold SHIFT while selecting the character nodes of the letter "n," the letter "u," and the letter "y" in the word "naturally." Double-click on one of these nodes to access the Character Attributes dialog box. Set Character Angle to –15 degrees and then select OK. The selected characters now appear tilted toward the right.

naturally (tilted display)

2. Deselect these three letters and select the letter "t," the second letter "a," and the second letter "l." Double-click on one of these nodes to access the Character Attributes dialog box. Set Character Angle to 15 degrees and then select OK. These characters appear tilted toward the left. The word "naturally" now seems to fly off in all directions:

naturally (tilted display)

3. Save your changes and then select New from the File menu to clear the screen.

This concludes the tutorial on the use of the settings in the Character Attributes dialog box. No doubt you have come up with a few creative ideas of your own while practicing on these exercises. When you are ready to proceed, continue through the next portion of this chapter, where you will learn some convenient ways to kern text and adjust spacing interactively.

Kerning Text Interactively

Kerning, simply defined, is the art of adjusting the space between individual pairs of letters for greater readability. There are many possible letter-pair combinations in the 26 letters of the English alphabet, but most font manufacturers provide automatic kerning for only a few hundred commonly used pairs. Occasionally you will see too much or too little space between adjacent letters. You can kern these letter pairs manually by moving one of the letters subtly to the right or left.

Using kerning as a design element can enhance the power of your message. For instance, you will draw more attention to your text when you kern letters to create special effects, such as expanded letter spacing in selected words of a magazine or newspaper headline.

The exercises in this section offer more extreme examples of kerning than you are likely to find in most text, but they will help you become familiar with the concept of kerning. Follow the steps in each exercise to learn how

Shaping and Editing Text

to kern single or multiple characters. Integrated within the exercises is information on using constraint and alignment techniques to kern more easily and precisely.

Kerning Single Characters

The following exercise lets you practice adjusting spacing between any two text characters. As you work through the steps, you will learn how to ensure that characters align properly with the surrounding text after you move them. Before starting the exercise, adjust viewing magnification to actual size and turn on Rulers. In the Grid & Scale Setup, turn on Show Grid, set both the Horizontal and Vertical Grid Frequency to 8 per inch; and set the Vertical Grid Origin to 11 inches. Click on OK. Retain these settings for both exercises on kerning.

1. Select the Text tool and then select a text insertion point at the 1 1/2-inch mark on the horizontal ruler and the 4 1/2-inch mark on the vertical ruler.

2. Type the word **K e rning** in upper- and lowercase letters. Leave a space after the "K" and another after the "e." Press ENTER to begin a new line and type the word **T e x t** on the second line. Leave one space after the first "T," one space after the "e," and two spaces after the letter "x."

3. Select the Pick tool and open the Text roll-up if it isn't already. Set the font to Garamond bold, the type size to 72 points, and the justification to None, and click on Apply. Roll up the Text roll-up.

4. After the text string appears, as in Figure 10-3, select the Shape tool. Since the text string was the last object you created, the Shape tool selects it automatically. A node appears next to each character in the text string; vertical and horizontal spacing control handles appear at each end of the last line of the text string.

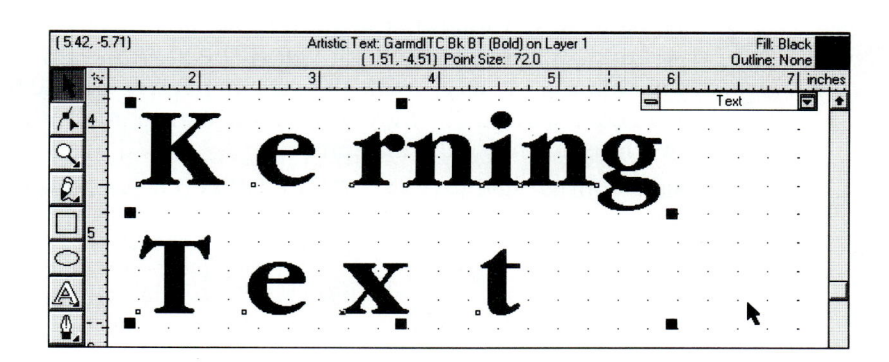

Text in need of kerning
Figure 10-3.

You need to bring the letter "e" in "Kerning" much closer to the "K" and the letters "rning" closer to the "e." You do this by dragging the "e" and the "rning" with the Shape tool. Since you don't want to change the vertical positioning, you can prevent this by pressing CTRL while you drag. Make sure Snap To Grid is turned off or you will not be able to get the exact positioning described in the following steps.

> **Tip:** You can press and hold CTRL while moving the characters, thereby constraining the text to the nearest baseline. Be sure to release the mouse button before you release CTRL to maintain proper alignment.

1. Press and hold CTRL and then press and hold the left mouse button on the node in front of the letter "e." When you begin to move the mouse, the pointer turns into a four-headed arrow. Drag the letter to the left until its node is on the tip of the foot of the "K," as shown in the following illustration. A dotted outline of the letter follows the pointer as you drag. When you release the mouse button, the letter itself appears in this location.

2. If the "e" is not aligned as you want it, snap this letter back to its original position by selecting the Straighten Text command in the Text menu, and then repeat step 16.

   The Straighten Text command erases any previous kerning information, so use it only when you want to return text to its original location. If you forgot to press CTRL while dragging the "e," you can select the Align To Baseline command, also in the Text menu. When you accidentally position a character above or below the baseline, this command forces the character to align with the baseline again. Unlike the Straighten Text command, the Align To Baseline command does not erase any previous kerning information.

3. Save your kerned text as KERN1.CDR and leave it on the screen for the next exercise.

Shaping and Editing Text

Tip: If you require a high degree of precision in the placement of kerned text, zoom in on the character(s) you want to move.

Kerning Multiple Characters

In practice, your most common use for moving and kerning multiple characters within a text string will be to move the remaining characters of a word closer to another letter that you have already kerned. However, you can select and reposition any group of characters, including nonadjacent characters, to another location in the same way.

1. With the KERN1.CDR file displayed in an actual size viewing magnification and the Shape tool active, draw a marquee around the letters "rning."

2. Press and hold CTRL, and then point on the node for the letter "r" and drag the mouse to the left until the pointer is beginning to touch the "e." All the letters in the selected group follow, as shown in the following illustration. If the selected characters do not line up with the adjoining text when you release the mouse button, review step 2 in the previous exercise. You may want to use both the Align To Baseline and Straighten Text commands. Deselect the letters "rning" when you have them in the desired location.

3. Use SHIFT to select the "e" and the second "t" in "Text." Click on the node in front of the letter "e" and drag it to the left until the pointer is on the tip of the foot (or serif) of the "T," as shown here:

Both selected letters should move together across the screen without disturbing the "x." After you release the mouse button, the letters "e" and "t" will appear as shown here:

4. As you can see, the letters "x" and "t" still are not close enough to the "e." Experiment by moving these two letters on your screen until the text string appears normal.

5. Save your changes to the file by pressing CTRL-S. Then select New from the File menu to clear the screen.

Kerning is not the only text attribute that you can adjust interactively with the Shape tool. In the next section, you will learn how to adjust spacing between characters, words, and lines for an entire selected text string.

Adjusting Spacing Interactively

There are two ways to edit inter-character, inter-word, and inter-line spacing of existing text in CorelDRAW!. The first way, as you will recall, is to select the text string with the Pick tool and then open the Character Attributes dialog box using any of the methods discussed previously. Using the dialog box, you can numerically set the spacing you need. You enjoy the advantage of precision but experience the disadvantage of not seeing what you are doing until you are done doing it.

If you prefer to work more spontaneously, CorelDRAW! offers you an interactive method of spacing as well. This method involves selecting the text string with the Shape tool and then dragging one of the two stylized arrows that appear at the text string's lower boundary. Keep in mind, however, that you adjust spacing for *all* of the characters in the text string when you use this technique. To adjust spacing between two individual characters, see the previous "Kerning Single Characters" section of this chapter.

To alter inter-character spacing interactively, drag the horizontal arrow at the lower-right boundary of the text string. To alter inter-word spacing, drag the same arrow while holding down CTRL. And to alter inter-line spacing, drag the vertical arrow at the lower-left boundary of the text string.

Adjusting Inter-Character Spacing

In the following exercise, you will create a text string and adjust the inter-character spacing, observing the changes in the CorelDRAW! window as you work.

Shaping and Editing Text

1. Set viewing magnification to actual size, then activate the Text tool and select an insertion point near the upper-left corner of your viewing window.
2. Type **Running out of** on the first line of the text entry window and **space** on the second. Click on the Pick tool and open the Text roll-up. Set text attributes to Arial normal, 60 points, left aligned, and then select Apply. The text displays in your viewing window. If the text string is not centered in the window, select the text string and center it.
3. Activate the Shape tool. Each character node appears, and stylized vertical and horizontal arrows appear at the lower-left and lower-right boundaries of the text object, as shown in Figure 10-4.
4. Position the shaping pointer directly over the horizontal arrow at the lower-right boundary of the text object, until the pointer turns into a crosshair. Then, drag this arrow to the right. Notice that, as in the example in Figure 10-5, the characters do not seem to move immediately; instead, you see a dotted outline following the two-way arrow pointer. As you drag, the status line displays the message "Inter-Character," followed by information about the horizontal distance by which you are increasing the size of the text boundary.
5. When the right boundary of the text string (represented by the dotted outline) reaches the desired point, release the mouse button. The text repositions itself to align with that boundary, and the space between each character increases proportionately, as shown here:

Running out of

6. If you would like to know the exact inter-character spacing measurement you have obtained, select the text string with the Pick

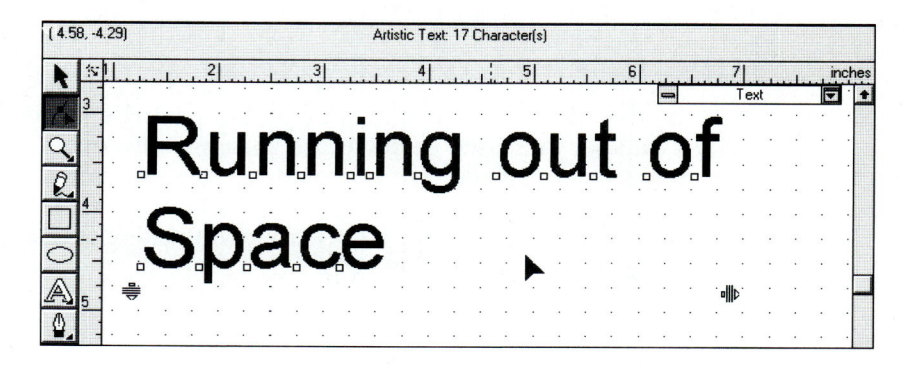

Displaying the spacing adjustment arrows
Figure 10-4.

Adjusting inter-character spacing
Figure 10-5.

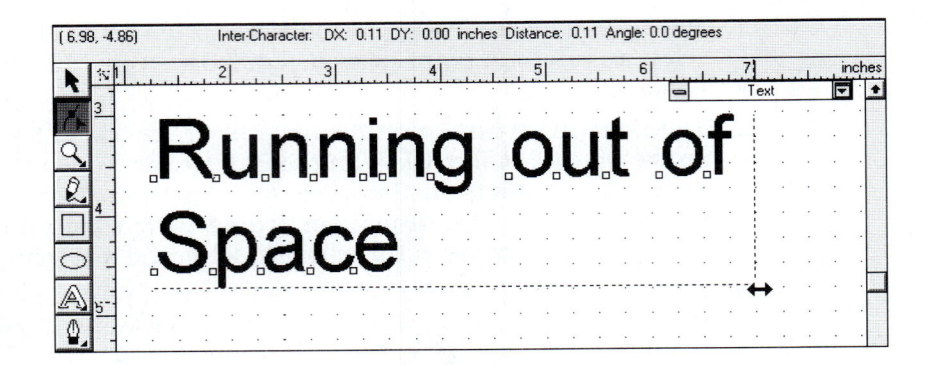

tool and access the Character Attributes dialog box. This is a good way to check for precision.

7. Select the Undo command from the Edit menu to return the text to its former position. Then reselect the Shape tool and *decrease* the space between characters by dragging the horizontal arrow to the left instead of the right. If you decrease the space drastically, letters may even overlap, like this:

8. Select Undo once more to return the characters to their original positions. Leave this text on the screen for now.

Adjusting inter-character spacing is useful when you want to fit text into a defined space in a drawing, without changing the point size or other attributes. Go on to the next section to practice changing inter-word spacing independently of the spacing between characters.

Adjusting Inter-Word Spacing

Suppose that you don't need to change the spacing between letters, but your design calls for increased or decreased spacing between words. To adjust inter-word spacing interactively, you drag the same horizontal arrow that you used for inter-character spacing. The difference is that you also hold down CTRL at the same time. Try the following exercise, using the text string you created in the previous section.

Shaping and Editing Text

1. With the Shape tool active and the text string selected, position the pointer over the horizontal arrow until the pointer turns into a crosshair. Then press and hold CTRL and drag the two-way arrow pointer to the right. The status line displays the message "Inter-Word," followed by the horizontal distance by which you are stretching the text boundary.

2. When the outline that you are dragging has the desired width, release the mouse button first and then CTRL. (If you release CTRL first, you will adjust the inter-character rather than the inter-word spacing.) The text redisplays with increased space between each word, as shown here:

   Running   out   of

3. Press CTRL-Z or select the Undo command in the Edit menu to return the text to its original inter-word spacing.

4. Try decreasing the amount of inter-word spacing by dragging the horizontal arrow to the left instead of the right. When you are finished experimenting, select the Undo command once more. Leave this text on the screen for the next exercise.

You can change the spacing between lines of a text string, as well as between words or characters. The next section gives you hands-on practice in editing inter-line spacing.

Adjusting Inter-Line Spacing

To edit inter-line spacing with the Shape tool, you drag the vertical arrow located at the lower left of the text boundary. Try increasing and decreasing the space between lines now, using the same text string you have been working with for the past two sections. Note that if your text string contains only one line, dragging the vertical arrow has no effect.

1. With the Shape tool active and the text string selected, position the mouse pointer directly over the vertical arrow that appears at the lower-left text boundary and drag this arrow downward. The mouse pointer turns into a two-way vertical arrow. Simultaneously, the status line displays the message "Inter-Line," followed by the vertical distance measurement, which tells you how much you have increased the size of the text boundary.

2. When you have increased the boundary by the desired size, release the mouse button. The text repositions itself to fit the new boundary. As

shown here, only the spacing between lines changes, not the length or size of the text itself:

Running out of

Space

3. To see the precise amount of inter-line spacing that you have added, press the SPACEBAR or activate the Pick tool and then open the Character Attribute dialog box. When you are finished, select Undo from the Edit menu to return the text string to its former inter-line spacing.
4. Reduce the inter-line spacing of the text string by dragging the vertical arrow upward instead of downward. When you are finished, select Undo to return the text to its former spacing.
5. Select New from the File menu and click on No when asked if you want to save current changes, to clear the screen before beginning the next section.

By now, you have explored all of the possible text attributes that you can change using the Pick and Shape tools. If, however, you need to give your text an even more customized look, you have the option of converting text to a curved object and then editing its nodes.

Reshaping Characters

To give messages extra flair, you might need stylized text characters that just don't exist in standard fonts. CorelDRAW! can help you create such "text pictures" easily. All you have to do is select text attributes that approximate the effect you want to achieve and then convert the text string to curves. You can then reshape the text using the Pick and Shape tools.

The following exercise contains a simple step-by-step example of how to create stylized text pictures. Carry out the steps and give your own imagination a boost!

1. To prepare for this exercise, turn off Rulers, Snap To Grid, and Show Grid, and set the viewing magnification to actual size.

Shaping and Editing Text

"Snake" text: Garamond bold italic, 120 points
Figure 10-6.

Snake

A *drop cap* is an initial capital letter that stretches below the baseline of the remaining text.

2. Activate the Text tool and select an insertion point in the upper left of your working area.
3. Type **Snake** in upper- and lowercase letters and open the Text roll-up. Test each of the fonts in the Fonts list box against the sample display character. The capital "S" of the Garamond font bears a fairly strong resemblance to a snake, so set text attributes to Garamond bold italic, 120 points, and left alignment. Click on Apply to display your text on the page, as shown in Figure 10-6.
4. Activate the Shape tool and double-click on the node for the letter "S" to open the Character Attributes dialog box.
5. Your aim is to increase the size of the letter "S" and make it a *drop cap*. To achieve this, set the type size for the letter "S" to 220 points and set Vertical Shift to –20 percent of type size. Select OK to make these changes take effect. Your text should now look like this:

Snake

6. Activate the Pick tool (or press the SPACEBAR) to select the entire text string, and then click on the Convert To Curves option in the Arrange menu. The text redisplays with many little nodes, indicating that it has become a curve object. If you activate the Shape tool again, the status line displays the message, "Curve: 238 nodes on 8 subpaths." This message indicates that CorelDRAW! now considers this text string to be one object with eight combined segments.
7. Activate the Pick tool again and select the Break Apart command in the Arrange menu. Each letter is now a separate object.

Note: The spaces inside the "a," "k," and "e" fill in because the letters are formed by two objects that you just broke apart. When the two objects are combined, their common area becomes transparent, causing the space. Remember the teacup handle example in Chapter 5. If you want the spaces to reappear, select the characters with the Pick tool and choose **Combine** from the **Arrange** menu.

8. Deselect all of the letters and then click on the letter "S" with the Pick tool. Stretch the letter vertically by dragging the middle boundary markers on the upper and lower sides of the selection box. Your goal is to elongate the letter, thereby enhancing the "snake-like" appearance. You may need to scroll your screen to see all of the "S."

9. Now, activate the Shape tool and manipulate the nodes of the "S" so that you achieve the general look of the following illustration. Make some areas of the "snake" narrower and others broader. You will want to reshape and move the snake's head, too. Make the "tail" of the snake narrower, as well.

10. You can try to match the results here exactly or develop your own creative enhancements utilizing all of the skills you have learned up to this point in the book. When you are satisfied with the appearance of the snake, save the image under the filename SNAKE.CDR.

11. Select **New** from the **File** menu to clear the screen.

As you can see, the possibilities for creating custom characters for text are virtually endless. If you find yourself fired up with new ideas for your own projects, experiment until you design a word picture that best enhances your message.

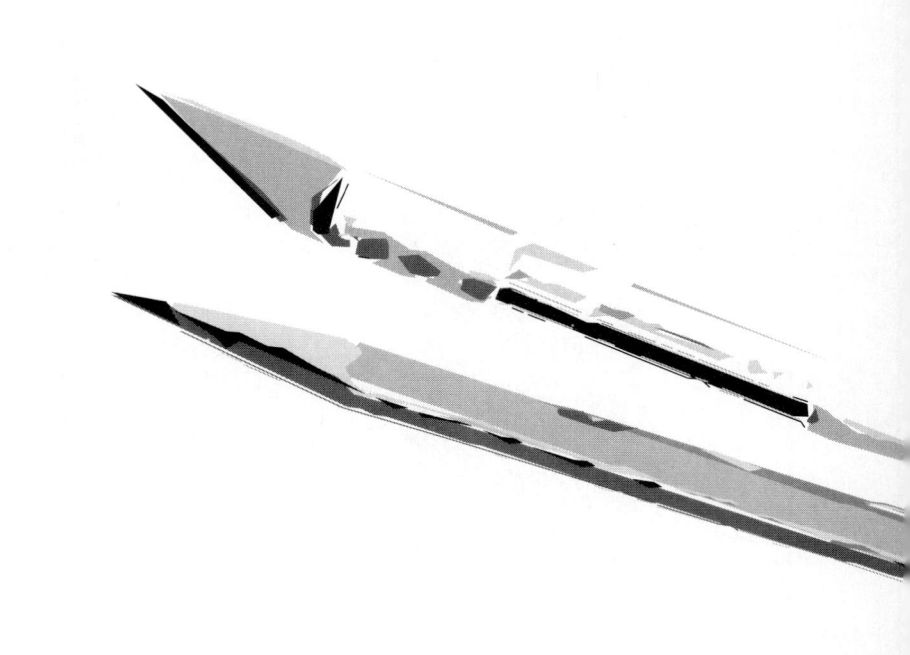

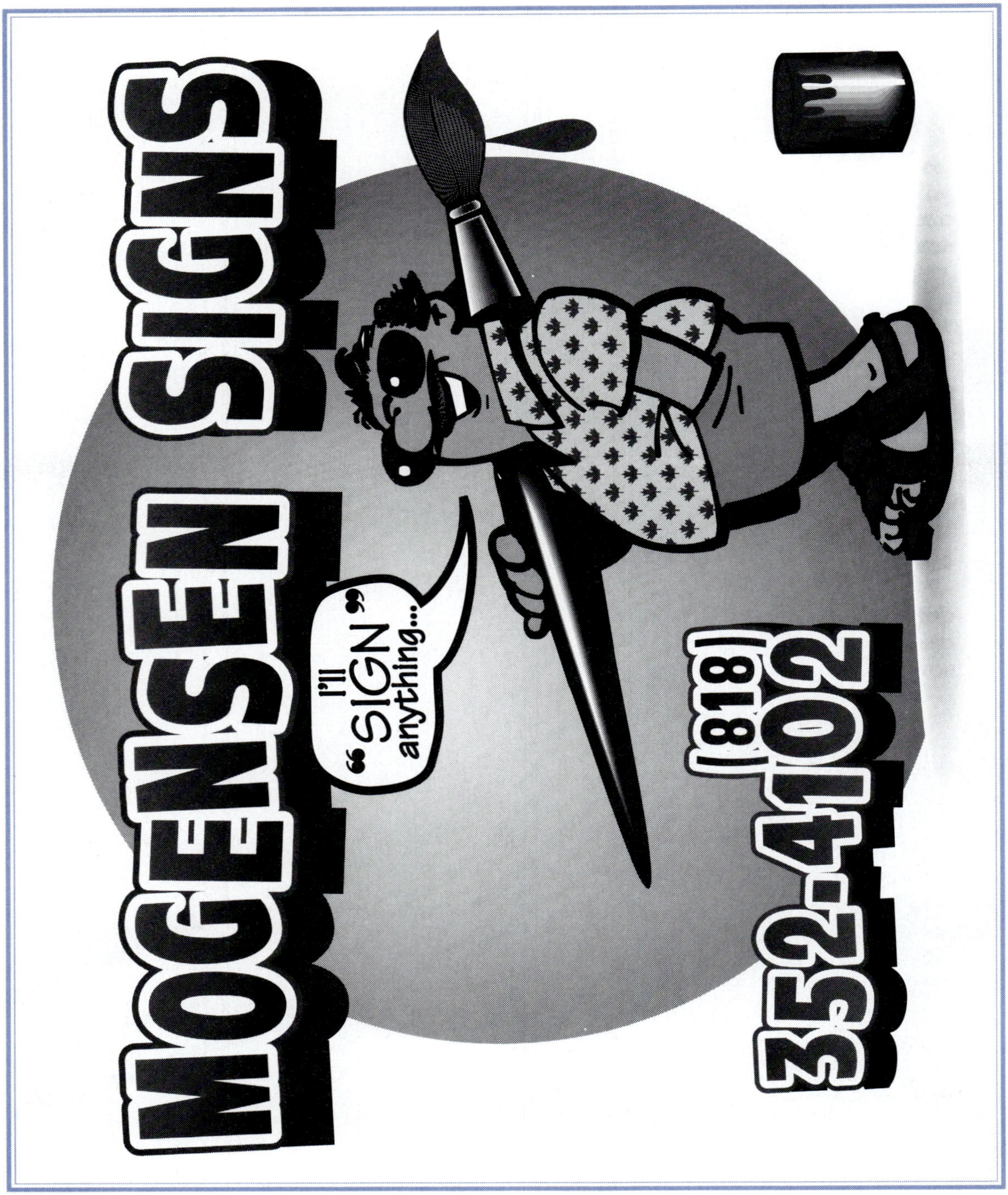
MOGENSEN SIGNS
I'll "SIGN" anything...
(818)
352-4102

CorelDRAW! in Action

WILLIAM MOGENSEN
Mogensen

William found the man for this self-promotional piece in the collection of clip-art included with an early version of CorelDRAW!. In the original clip-art piece the man was carrying a palm tree, so this had to be removed and replaced by the brush. The clip-art was imported, and the objects that made up the clip-art were ungrouped so that they could be individually manipulated. Then, using the Shape tool, the nodes associated with the various parts of the palm tree were selected and deleted.

William next created the brush handle shape with the Freehand tool, and fine-tuned the handle's curvature by moving the control points of individual nodes. To add the highlight to the black brush handle a narrow shape with a white fill and no outline was first created in the center of the handle. Then the highlight and handle objects were selected and blended, using the Blend roll-up. Similarly, the highlight on the ferrule of the brush was created by blending a narrow black shape with the white ferrule shape.

The large jumbled lettering consists of four layers: the black shadows, the dark (red) outlines, the white outlines, and the top letters which have no outline and a fountain fill. After typing the block letters for the first layer, the Shape tool was used to select the character node of every other letter. Then the letters were dragged up a bit. Next, William double-clicked on the selected nodes to get the Character Attributes dialog box and gave the letters a tilt by adjusting the Character Angle option. This first layer of lettering was then duplicated three times and the outline and fill of the various layers were varied. The bottom layer, which has a black outline and a black fill, was dragged down to create a 3-D effect. In addition, a rounded corner was selected for the outline pen of two of the layers.

The balloon that contains the man's speech is a symbol from the CorelDRAW! symbol library.

This piece was in CorelArtShow 4: Page 132, Number 29, File: PLD00097.CDR. You may contact William in care of:

> William Mogensen
> 10109 Janetta Way
> Shadow Hills, CA 91040
> Voice/Fax: (818) 352-4102

The art on the opposite page was created by and is the property of William Mogensen. It is used with permission.

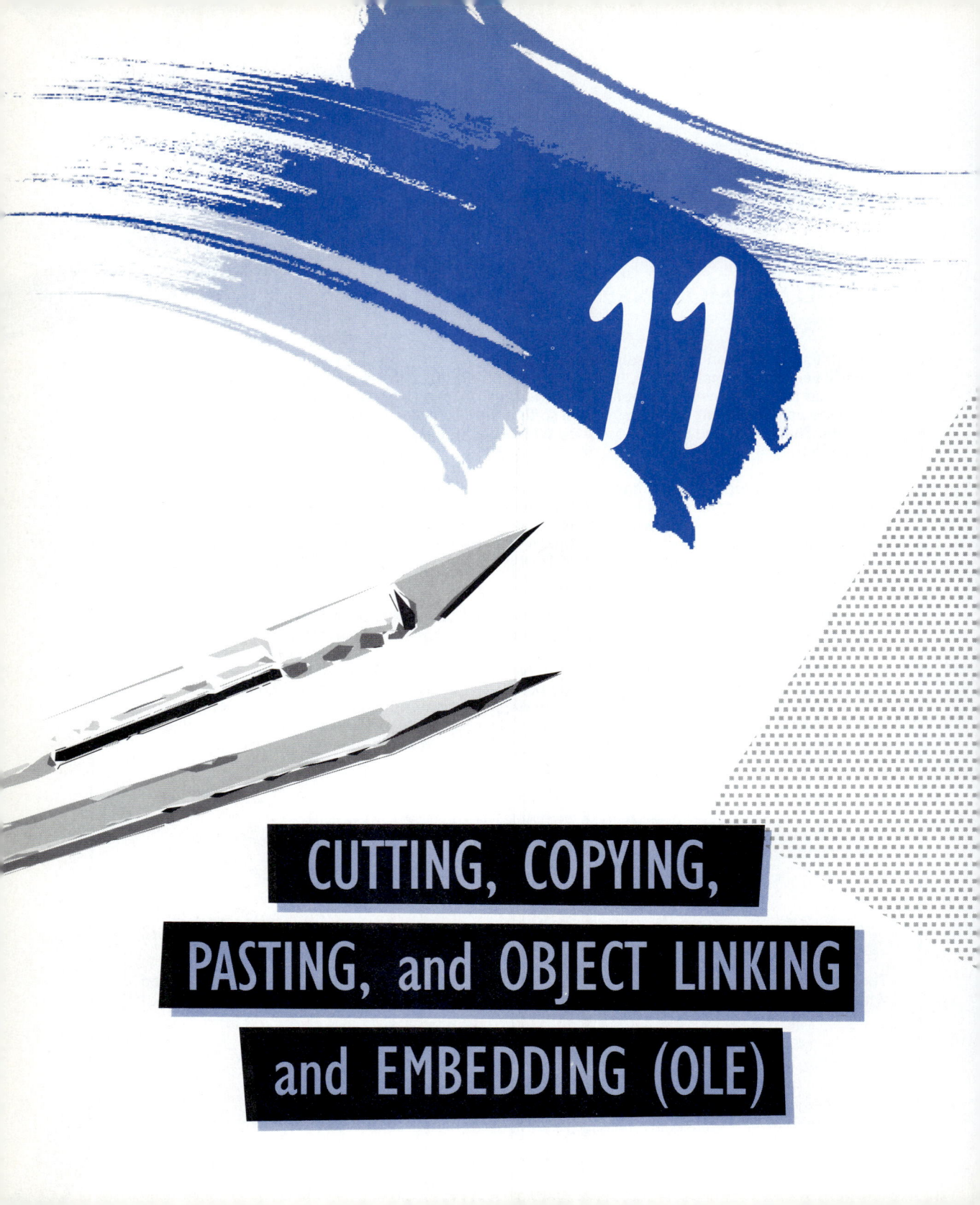

11

CUTTING, COPYING, PASTING, and OBJECT LINKING and EMBEDDING (OLE)

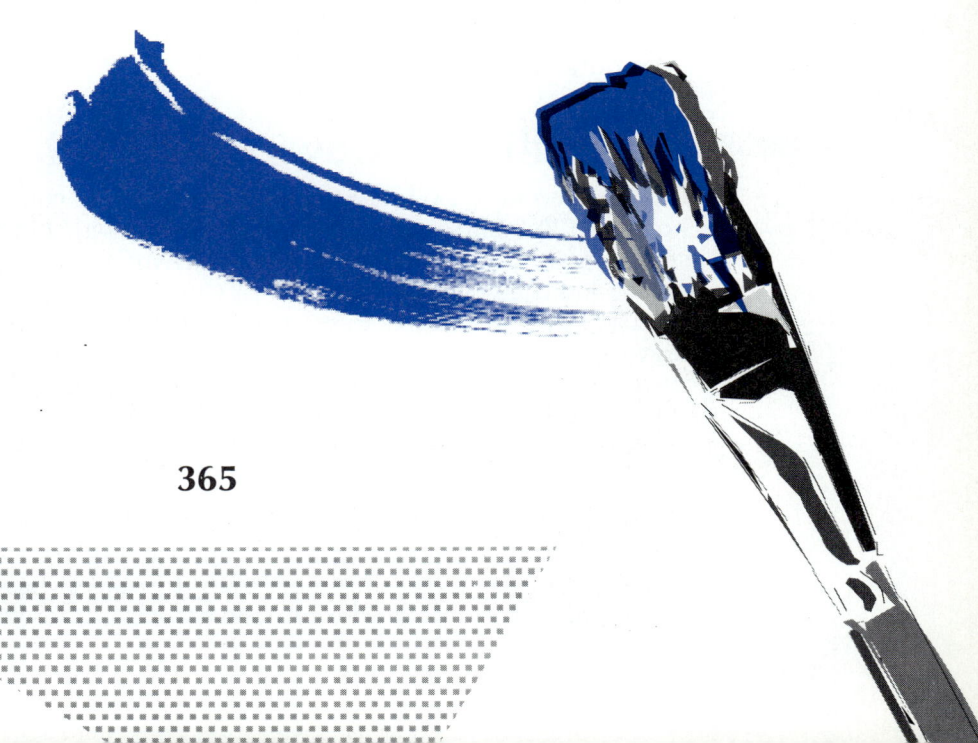

So far you have learned how to select, move, rearrange, transform, and reshape objects within a certain graphic. An equally important part of the editing process involves the *transfer of image information* within a graphic, between pictures, or between CorelDRAW! and other Windows applications. The editing functions that allow you to transfer image data include copying, cutting, and pasting objects and pictures; deleting or duplicating objects; and copying object attributes. You access these operations using the Cut, Copy, Paste, Delete, Duplicate, Clone, and Copy Attributes From options in the Edit menu.

These editing functions have many uses that will save you time and design effort. You don't have to start from scratch each time you need to duplicate an object or its style attribute. You can simply transfer image information, using the editing commands. You perform some of the transfer operations within a single picture; others allow you to transfer information between CorelDRAW! files and even between CorelDRAW! and other Windows applications.

CorelDRAW! allows you to transfer objects to and from the Windows Clipboard. This means that you can copy or cut and paste objects between different image files in CorelDRAW!, or from CorelDRAW! to a file in another Windows application. Conversely, you can copy or cut and paste objects from files in other Windows applications and paste them to the page of your choice in CorelDRAW!.

This chapter covers the use of the Windows Clipboard, both within CorelDRAW! and between CorelDRAW! and other Windows applications. It introduces you to some additional object and style copying functions in CorelDRAW! that complement the use of the Windows Clipboard. You'll find out how to duplicate objects within a drawing and how to copy attributes from one object to another. You'll review the difference between cutting objects from a file and deleting them permanently. Finally, you will work with Object Linking and Embedding, usually referred to by the acronym OLE (pronounced *O'lay*). OLE provides new ways to utilize objects from different applications.

About the Windows Clipboard

If you haven't used Windows applications before, you may be wondering how the Clipboard works. Think of the Windows Clipboard as a temporary storage place that can contain only one item at a time. When you select an object and then click on the Copy or Cut command in the Edit menu, you send a copy of the object to the Clipboard from its original place in your drawing. You can then choose Paste from the Edit menu to send a copy of the object from the Clipboard to the desired location. The copy you sent to the Clipboard remains there until you overwrite it by copying or cutting another object, or until you exit Windows and end a session.

Windows creates its own file format, called a *metafile*, out of the information that you send to the Clipboard. This standard metafile format allows you to share information between different applications that run under Windows. A metafile can be larger or smaller than the object you send to the Clipboard, depending on the complexity of the information you are trying to transfer. As a rule of thumb, the more complex an object is in terms of its attributes, the more memory it requires when you send it to the Clipboard.

Theoretically, all Windows applications should be able to trade information through the Clipboard. In practice, however, some types of information in objects or files transfer better than others. When you have completed the basic exercises on copying, cutting, and pasting objects within CorelDRAW!, turn to the section entitled "Working with Different Applications." There you will find tips for trouble-free transfer operations through the Clipboard.

Copy, Cut, Duplicate, Clone, or Delete

In order to duplicate or delete one or more objects, or copy or cut them to the Clipboard, you must first select the objects with the Pick tool. The Edit menu commands and their keyboard shortcuts are unavailable to you unless one or more objects are already selected.

You can select a single object, multiple objects, or all objects in a graphic for any of the Edit menu operations discussed in this chapter. To select a single object for one of the transfer operations, just click on its outline once. To select multiple objects for a transfer operation, use SHIFT or the marquee method you learned in Chapter 5. (You might also want to group the objects after you select them in order to avoid separating them from each other accidentally.) To select all of the objects in a graphic, click on the Select All command in the Edit menu.

Copying and Pasting Objects

The Copy and Paste commands in the Edit menu enable you to copy CorelDRAW! objects and paste them to the same file, to another file in CorelDRAW!, or to another Windows application. When you *copy* an object to the Clipboard, the original object remains in position on the page. When you *paste* the object, Windows makes another copy from the copy on the Clipboard. The copy on the Clipboard remains there until you overwrite it by copying or cutting another object or group of objects, or until you exit Windows.

To practice copying objects to the Clipboard and pasting them to the same or different pictures, you will use a file that you created in Chapter 5.

Tip: Cut, Copy, and Paste icons are available on the ribbon bar. Just click on them instead of using the Edit menu commands for a shortcut technique.

Copying and Pasting Objects Within a Picture

When you copy an object to the Clipboard and then paste it to the same picture, the copy overlays the original object exactly. The copy is selected as soon as it appears on the page, however, so you can move it safely without displacing the original object.

A more convenient way to copy an object within the same picture is to use the Duplicate command. When you invoke this command, CorelDRAW! automatically offsets the copy of the object from the original. See the "Duplicating and Cloning Objects" section of this chapter for more details.

For the exercises in this chapter, make sure that Rulers in the View menu and Show Status Line on the View tab of the Preferences menu on the Special menu are selected (turned on). Also check that Show Grid and Snap To Grid are selected in the Grid & Scale Setup option of the Layout menu. Then open the Chapter 5 file and practice copying a group of objects with these instructions:

1. Open the ARROW1.CDR file and group all of the text strings in the picture, using the Select All command in the Edit menu and then the Group command in the Arrange menu.
2. To copy the grouped objects to the Clipboard, either select the Copy command from the Edit menu, as shown in Figure 11-1, or press CTRL-C. The pointer turns into an hourglass until CorelDRAW! finishes copying the selected object to the Clipboard.
3. Select Paste from the Edit menu or press CTRL-V. The screen redraws, with the pasted object selected. You will not notice anything different because the pasted object appears exactly on top of the original.

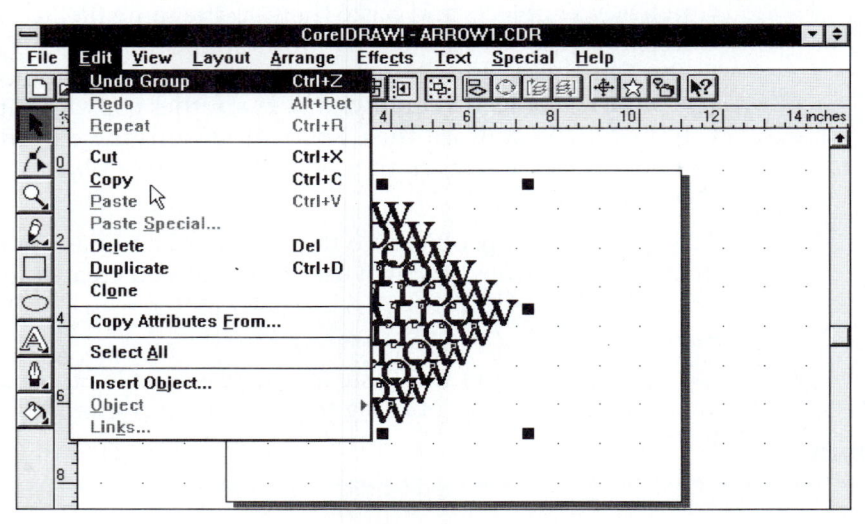

Selecting the Copy command
Figure 11-1.

4. To move the pasted object away from the original, press and hold the mouse button directly over any outline of the selected object and drag it as desired. You can now scale, rotate, stretch, skew, or otherwise edit the pasted object.
5. Select New from the File menu to clear the screen before continuing. Do not save any changes to the ARROW1.CDR document.

Next try copying an object to a different picture, and use it as a design enhancement there.

Copying and Pasting Between Pictures

In this exercise you will copy the text string from the DOINWHAT.CDR file created in Chapter 10 and paste it to the KITE.CDR file from Chapter 2.

1. Open the DOINWHAT.CDR file and select the text string.
2. Select Copy from the Edit menu or press CTRL-C to copy the text to the Clipboard. The pointer may temporarily turn into an hourglass, or you may get a message box telling you the status, until CorelDRAW! finishes copying the text string. This lets you know it's busy.
3. Open the KITE.CDR file and drag all of the guidelines off the screen. Make sure Wireframe is checked (turned on) in the View menu.
4. From the Edit menu, choose Select All; then from the Arrange menu, select Group. The status line will tell you that there is now a group of objects.
5. Position the pointer at any of the four corner boundary markers of the group. Then drag the marker diagonally inward to scale down the kite to 50 percent of its original size.
6. Drag the kite so it is approximately centered horizontally and leaves about one-third of the vertical white space at the top. See Figure 11-2 to see how it's positioned at this stage.
7. Select Paste from the Edit menu or press CTRL-V. The text string will come into the center of the page.
8. Drag the text to the top of the page to complete this exercise, as shown in Figure 11-3.
9. Select Save As from the File menu, type **kite2**, and select OK.

You don't have to start from scratch to design an attractive picture.

As you can see from the preceding exercise, you can copy and paste existing objects and images to an illustration in progress, saving yourself work without sacrificing quality or originality. In the next sections, you will experiment with the Cut and Paste menu commands and see how their operation differs from that of Copy and Paste.

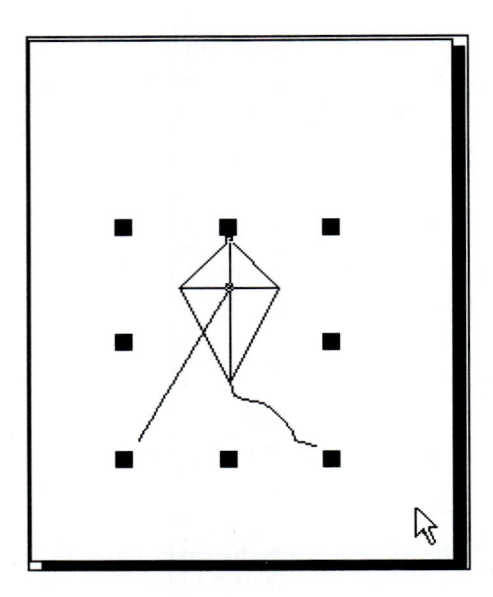

Kite positioned to receive pasted text
Figure 11-2.

Cutting and Pasting Objects

When you select an object and then invoke the Cut command in the Edit menu, the object disappears and goes to the Clipboard. When you then select the Paste command, Windows places a copy of the cut object on the page.

Copying and pasting an object to an existing image
Figure 11-3.

Cutting, Copying, Pasting, and Object Linking and Embedding (OLE)

The original object that you cut remains in the Clipboard until you overwrite it by cutting or copying another object, or until you end a Windows session.

To begin practicing cutting and pasting objects, you will use the LANDSCAP.CDR file you created in Chapter 3.

Cutting and Pasting Within a Picture

There are two ways to remove an unwanted object from a picture in CorelDRAW!. You can either cut it to the Clipboard using the Cut command, or delete it from the program memory entirely by using the Delete command. Use the Cut command unless you are absolutely certain that you will never need the object again. If you delete an object using the Delete command, CorelDRAW! doesn't store a copy anywhere; unless you immediately select the Undo command, you won't be able to recover the object.

CorelDRAW! always pastes a cut or copied object as the top layer of the picture. Therefore, when you cut and paste objects within an image that contains several layers of objects, remember to restore the original object arrangement using the commands in the Arrange menu.

1. Clear the screen by choosing New from the file menu and open the LANDSCAP.CDR file that you created in Chapter 3.
2. With the Pick tool, draw a marquee around the tree and its trunk to select it (make sure your marquee is large enough to completely enclose the boundary markers for the top of the tree).
3. From the Arrange menu, select Group.
4. Select Cut from the Edit menu or press CTRL-X. The tree disappears from the drawing.
5. Select Paste from the Edit menu or press CTRL-V, and the tree comes back onto the drawing in the same place it was originally. If the tree was not on the top layer of the drawing, it *will* be after pasting. In that case, it is not *exactly* where it was originally.
6. Select a bird and then choose Delete from the Edit menu or press DEL.

Tip: Once an object has been cleared or deleted from a drawing, you can use Undo to restore it. If you do so, select Undo prior to doing anything else; otherwise the object is gone. Undo only remembers the last action.

7. Press CTRL-V or select Paste again. Another tree comes onto the drawing, not the bird—the bird is not on the Clipboard; the tree still is. There

will be a second tree because the second tree came in on top of the original tree. Drag the second tree off to one side to see the other tree. Press DEL to get rid of the second tree.

Go immediately on to the next section of this chapter because you will need to use the contents of the Clipboard (the tree) in the next section, where you will cut and paste objects between different pictures in CorelDRAW!.

Cutting and Pasting Between Pictures

Earlier in this chapter, you created a poster by combining the kite you drew in Chapter 2 with some text you created in Chapter 10. In the following exercise, you will add two copies of the tree you cut from the LANDSCAP.CDR drawing and the word "CorelDRAW!," which you will cut from a drawing you create.

1. From the File menu, select Open. Answer No to saving changes to the LANDSCAP.CDR file and select KITE2.CDR as the file to open.

2. Press CTRL-V to paste the tree from the Clipboard onto the kite poster. When the tree comes onto the drawing, drag it down about a quarter of an inch.

3. Press CTRL-V to paste a second time, drag the second tree to the right side of the poster, and then approximately align it with the first tree, as shown in Figure 11-4.

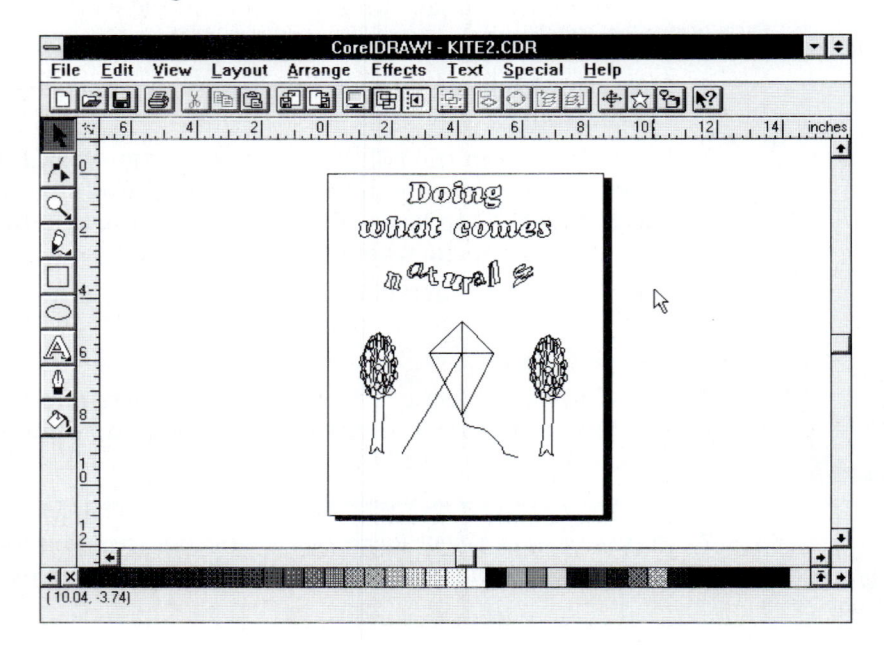

Trees pasted onto the kite poster
Figure 11-4.

Cutting, Copying, Pasting, and Object Linking and Embedding (OLE)

4. Save the file as KITE3.CDR and then select New from the File menu. From the View menu, click on Rulers to turn them off and click on Wireframe to change to full-color mode.
5. Select the Text tool and place the insertion point near the center of the page. Choose Text Roll-Up from the Text menu, then select the font, Times New Roman, 60-point, Normal-Italic. Select the center-justification button and click on Apply.
6. Using all capital letters, type **CORELDRAW!**, then press F4 to go to fit-in-window magnification (or select the third icon from the right in the flyout menu).
7. Select the Shape tool, then select all the characters in "DRAW!". From the Text roll-up, select the font FreeStyle Script 80 point, and then click on Apply. Close the Text roll-up. Select the Pick tool and from the Fill flyout select Black. Then click on any white space to deselect the text. Your screen should look like this.

CORELDRAW!

8. Select Save As from the File menu and name the drawing CDLOGO.CDR.
9. With the Pick tool, select the word "CorelDRAW!" and press CTRL-X , or select Cut from the Edit menu.
10. From the bottom of the File menu, select KITE3.CDR, and answer No if asked whether you want to save the current file.
11. Press CTRL-V or select Paste from the Edit menu. The word "CorelDRAW!" appears in the middle of the drawing.
12. Drag "CorelDRAW!" to the bottom of the poster. Then, by dragging on one of the corner boundary markers, scale it to fit in the space available, as shown in Figure 11-5.
13. Save the completed poster as KITE4.CDR and select New to clear your work space.

Working with Different Applications

The number of software packages running under Microsoft Windows is increasing almost daily. These programs include such diverse applications as word processors, desktop publishing and presentation software, database managers and forms generators, and, of course, paint and illustration

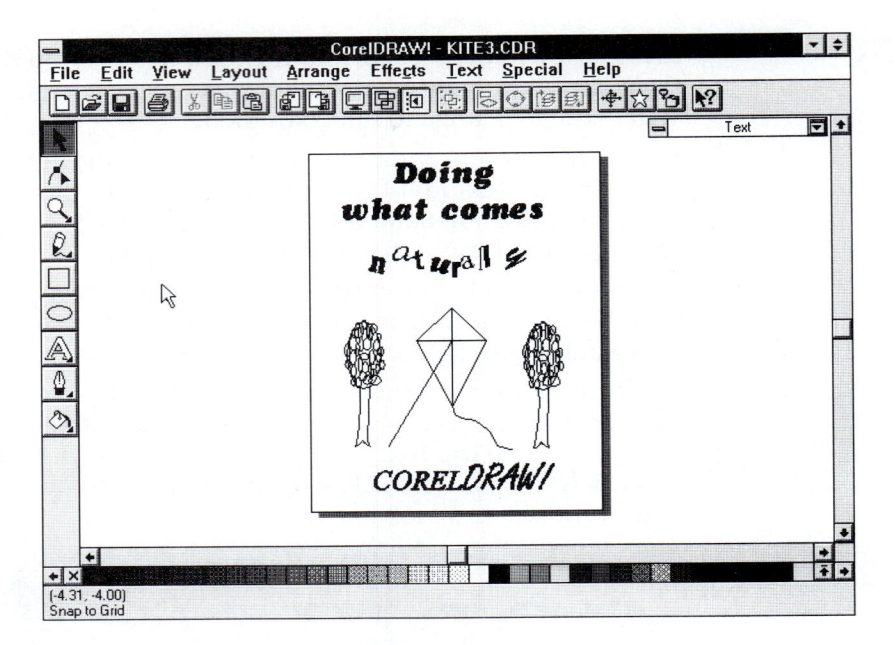

Completed poster with four pasted objects
Figure 11-5.

software. If your other favorite Windows applications also support the Windows Clipboard, you should be able to transfer data back and forth between them and CorelDRAW!.

Features and techniques differ with every application, however; as a result, not all visual information transfers equally well between programs. There are too many Windows applications to catalog what happens to each file type as it transfers to or from CorelDRAW! through the Clipboard. However, the following sections should give you an idea of how the Clipboard handles graphic information that you transfer between CorelDRAW! and some of the most popular software.

Clipboard Memory Limits

There is a slight chance that at some point you may get an error message that says "CorelDRAW! Clipboard format too large to put on Clipboard." Should this happen, you can break the object into smaller groups of objects and then transfer them in several passes. You can also save the object as a new drawing, then use the Import command to move it.

In most cases when you get the "CorelDRAW! Clipboard format..." message, CorelDRAW! will actually have copied the selected objects to the Clipboard in spite of the message. Check the Paste command in the Edit menu; if it is now available for selection, the objects have been successfully copied. If this command is not available, CorelDRAW! could not copy the selected object.

In general, you'll have the best chance of success when copying, cutting, and pasting CorelDRAW! objects that don't take advantage of too many advanced features at one time. An image that includes text, custom calligraphic outlines, PostScript fills, or Fountain fills, for example, will be more difficult to transfer to the Clipboard than an apparently complex geometrical image that contains none of these features.

Transferring Objects to Other Applications

When you copy or cut a CorelDRAW! object to the Clipboard, you are transferring not only the shape of an object, but also its attributes. Attributes include outline, outline fill, object fill, and text characteristics. Some attributes do not transfer well in their original form, owing in some cases to the diversity of Windows applications and in others to the complexity of CorelDRAW! features.

Most problems with transferring CorelDRAW! objects to the Clipboard have to do with objects taking too much memory. The following tips should help you avoid Clipboard memory or Windows metafile compatibility problems.

Fountain fills and PostScript fills (both discussed in Chapter 7) are extremely memory intensive from the standpoint of the Windows Clipboard, and they may go through unpredictable changes when transferred to another program. For example, when transferring an object containing PostScript fills, the object may be represented by blank or gray space when it is pasted into some applications. Even the outline disappears.

When an object with PostScript fill is transferred through the Clipboard, you often get the outline and then either no fill, or the little "PS"s that you see on the CorelDRAW! screen. The PostScript fill itself is not transferred in any instance.

Text sent from CorelDRAW! files to the Clipboard can be sensitive also. The greater the number of letters and/or attributes in a text string, the more likely that some information will not transfer properly. The specific program to which you want to send the text may further influence the transfer of information. As a general rule, text comes in as a graphic object rather than as editable text.

On the positive side, a number of applications such as PageMaker can import CorelDRAW!-produced lines, curves, fills, Fountain fills, and text, with all of their attributes, from the Clipboard without a problem.

Transferring Objects from Other Applications

When you transfer objects from your other favorite Windows applications to CorelDRAW!, you may not always receive exactly what you sent to the Clipboard. Sometimes this results from a limitation on what the Windows Clipboard can interpret; at other times, the apparent discrepancy is specific to the interaction between the other program and CorelDRAW!.

The Clipboard, for example, has difficulty transferring special text kerning or text rotation information, pattern or flood fills, pixel-by-pixel manipulations, and combined pen colors from other Windows applications to CorelDRAW!.

Text that you import into CorelDRAW! from another Windows application comes in with the default text attributes. If you know the font, style, alignment, and other attributes you want, set these before importing the text. You can import a maximum of 4,000 ASCII text characters at a time.

> You cannot use any of the Effects menu commands with OLE objects. Also, an OLE object cannot be rotated, skewed, cloned, combined, intersected, or welded with other objects.

Some features do not transfer well into CorelDRAW!. Bitmaps, for example, often don't transfer well. Text sent from other graphics applications (as opposed to word processors) often arrives in CorelDRAW! as curves. A fill or Fountain fill from another program may be transferred into CorelDRAW! as solid, or as an outline and separate fill object. Circles and ellipses may come in as connected line segments, while curves may become straight line segments. As CorelDRAW!, Microsoft Windows, and other Windows applications are constantly being upgraded, however, you can expect compatibility to improve. In the remaining sections of the chapter, you will learn about special commands in the CorelDRAW! Edit menu that make it easy for you to copy objects or their attributes within a CorelDRAW! file.

Object Linking and Embedding

Object Linking and Embedding (OLE) is similar to copying and pasting. With OLE, though, the source object is from an application other than the one you bring it into, and a connection is maintained to the source document, so that any editing in the source document will automatically appear in the destination document. Most importantly, with OLE you can double-click on an object in the destination application, and the source application will open and allow you to edit the object. With a normal copy and paste operation, you would not be able to edit the pasted object; you would have to delete the object, go to the source to change it, and then copy it back in. There are two forms of OLE: object *linking* and object *embedding*. They are the same, except that in embedding, a copy is made of the source document, and changes made to the copy do not affect the original.

Cutting, Copying, Pasting, and Object Linking and Embedding (OLE)   **377**

Linking

When an object is linked to its source, the object is not actually copied, but rather a dynamic link is formed. When you double-click on the destination object, the link causes the source application to open with the source object, and the changes are made there. When you return to the destination application, the changes will appear. To demonstrate linking, follow these steps:

1. Switch to the Program Manager and start CorelPHOTO-PAINT!.
2. Open the file, SAMPLE.CPT in the SAMPLES directory under the PHOTOPNT directory. Save this file to another name to prevent changes to the original; use the name LINKOBJ.CPT.
3. From the Select Tool flyout, choose the icon second from the left, the Box Selection tool. (The Select Tool is the top tool in the toolbox, similar to DRAW!'s Pick tool.) Select some part of the picture, as shown in Figure 11-6.
4. Select Copy from the Edit menu, and switch back to the CorelDRAW! window by pressing and holding ALT while pressing TAB once or twice.
5. Select Paste Special from the Edit menu to open the Paste Special dialog box shown here:

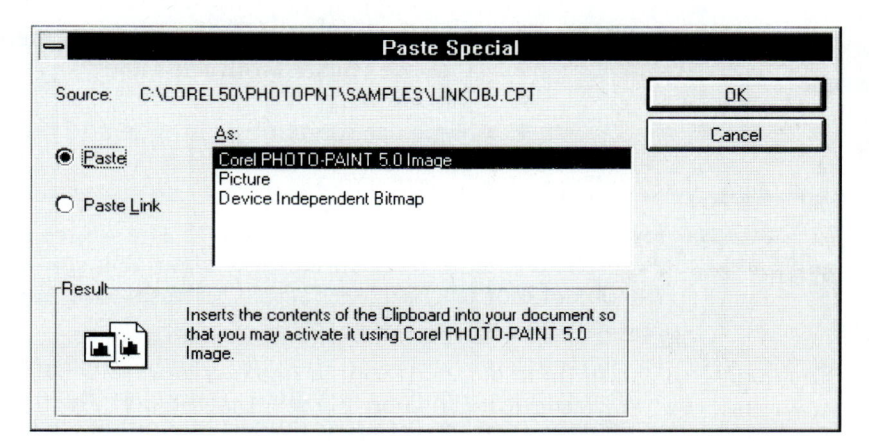

```
                      Paste Special
Source:   C:\COREL50\PHOTOPNT\SAMPLES\LINKOBJ.CPT        [  OK  ]
              As:
                                                         [ Cancel ]
 ● Paste      Corel PHOTO-PAINT 5.0 Image
              Picture
 ○ Paste Link Device Independent Bitmap

 ┌─Result────────────────────────────────────────────┐
 │        Inserts the contents of the Clipboard into your document so
 │        that you may activate it using Corel PHOTO-PAINT 5.0
 │        Image.
 └───────────────────────────────────────────────────┘
```

The Paste Special dialog box shows you the filename and path of the source object on the Clipboard and asks you how you want to bring it into CorelDRAW!. If you choose Paste, you will paste a *copy* of the object on the Clipboard, and you can modify it *without* affecting the original object. If you choose Paste Link, you will paste a *link* to the original object, and any modifications made will be made to the original.

Source application document
Figure 11-6.

> **Tip:** Another way to link an object is to
> - Select Insert Object from the Edit menu
> - Choose Create From File
> - Choose Link
> - Type the filename or Browse and then select it
> - Click OK

6. Select Paste Link and then click on OK. The source object is now on the page. Press F4 to go to fit-in-window view. You can now size and move the object, but to change its actual contents you must use the source application.

7. Double-click anywhere on the object and CorelPHOTO-PAINT! restarts, with the object ready to be edited. When you have finished making changes, close CorelPHOTO-PAINT! by double-clicking on its Control-menu box. The changes will appear on the CorelDRAW! screen.

> **Tip:** Another way to update a link is to
> - Select the linked object with the Pick tool
> - Select Links from the Edit menu
> - Choose Manual or Automatic
> - Click on the desired action

Cutting, Copying, Pasting, and Object Linking and Embedding (OLE) **379**

Embedding

Embedding is similar to linking, except that embedding makes a copy of the source object, and once the copy is pasted in the destination document, there is no connection between the copy and the source object. As in linking, you can double-click on the destination object and the source application will open. The difference is that you will be editing the destination copy and not the source object. To see object embedding in action, follow these steps:

1. Clear the screen by choosing New from the File menu and answering No to the question about saving the file. Then choose Insert Object from the Edit menu. The Insert Object dialog box appears, as you see here:

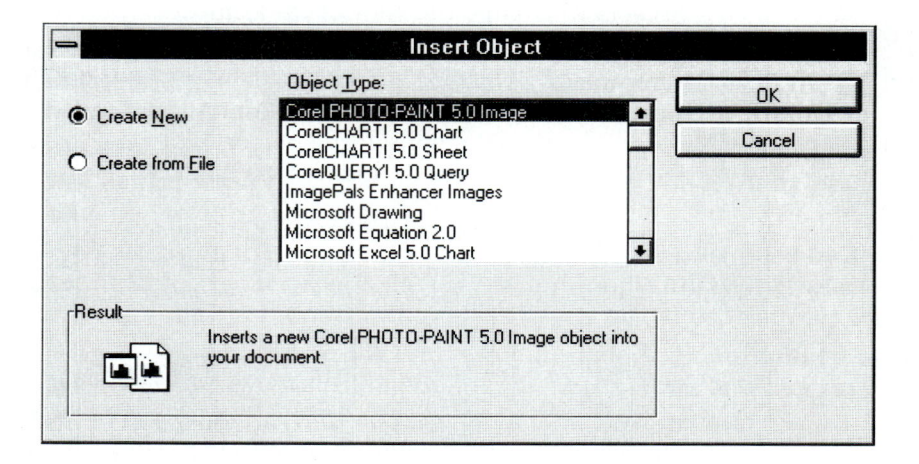

    The Insert Object dialog box is very similar to the Paste Special dialog box you just used. The major difference is that Insert Object brings in objects that are not on the Clipboard. You can either go out and create a new object in some application (the Create New option) or bring in an object that is a file on your hard disk (the Create from File option). In either case, you must first select the type of object you want to bring in.

2. Select CorelPHOTO-PAINT 5.0 Image as the type of object you want to bring in, make sure Create New is selected, and then click on OK.

    The Create a New Image dialog box will open, asking you the size and resolution of the new picture and showing you the memory required and available to hold the picture.

3. Click on OK to accept the default dimensions, and CorelPHOTO-PAINT! will open with a small onscreen window with a title bar. This new window is titled UNTITLED.CDR in CorelDRAW!.

4. Once again, open the LINKOBJ.CPT. Select an object in the picture and copy it to the Clipboard. Click on UNTITLED.CDR to select it.

5. Choose Paste from the Edit menu and then click on As New Object from the submenu that opens. The object you copied will appear in the UNTITLED.CDR window.

6. Choose Exit and Return to CorelDRAW! from the File menu and then click on Yes to update UNTITLED.CDR in CorelDRAW!, click No to save changes to LINKOBJ.CPT. Click No to remove the image from the Clipboard. CorelPHOTO-PAINT! will close and CorelDRAW! will open with the copied CorelPHOTO-PAINT! object in the middle of the page.

7. Press F4 to enlarge the view of the embedded object.

8. Double-click on this embedded object to open the source application. After making changes, go to the File menu, select Exit and Return to CorelDRAW! (this may take a while). This menu option would not be present in the File menu if the objects had been linked instead of embedded. Click Yes to update CorelDRAW!.

If you now go back to CorelPHOTO-PAINT! and open the original object, it will not have the changes you just made. Had you linked this object rather than embedded it, the changes would have been transferred.

Duplicating and Cloning Objects

As you saw earlier in the chapter, you can use the Copy and Paste commands in the Edit menu to make a copy of an object within a picture. This process can be somewhat time-consuming if you use it frequently, because you need two separate menu commands or keyboard combinations to perform one action. A more convenient way of achieving the same end is to use the Duplicate command in the Edit menu or its keyboard shortcut, CTRL-D.

The offset of a copy makes it easier to move the duplicate to a new location.

The Duplicate command causes a copy of the selected object or objects to appear at a specified *offset* from the original. In other words, the duplicate copy does not appear directly on top of the original, but at a horizontal and vertical distance from it, which you specify.

Cutting, Copying, Pasting, and Object Linking and Embedding (OLE)

You can also use the Duplicate command alone or with the Combine command in the Arrange menu to achieve unusual logo or graphic designs, or special effects. In the next exercise, you will create and duplicate three different series of rectangles, each with a different specified offset. Then you will combine them to create the design shown in Figure 11-7.

1. Starting with a blank page, change the page format to landscape using the Size tab on the Page Setup command from the Layout menu. Also, make sure that Rulers and Wireframe are turned on (as indicated by a check mark next to each option in the View menu).

2. Select the Preferences command from the Special menu. In the General tab, check that the Place Duplicates and Clones settings at the top of the Preferences dialog box are set to the default value setting of 0.250 inches, as shown in Figure 11-8.

   If the values are correct, select OK and exit the dialog box. If either of these settings is different, change it to 0.25 inches.

3. Select the Rectangle tool and draw a rectangle about three-fourths of the way down the left edge of the page. The rectangle should be wider than it is high.

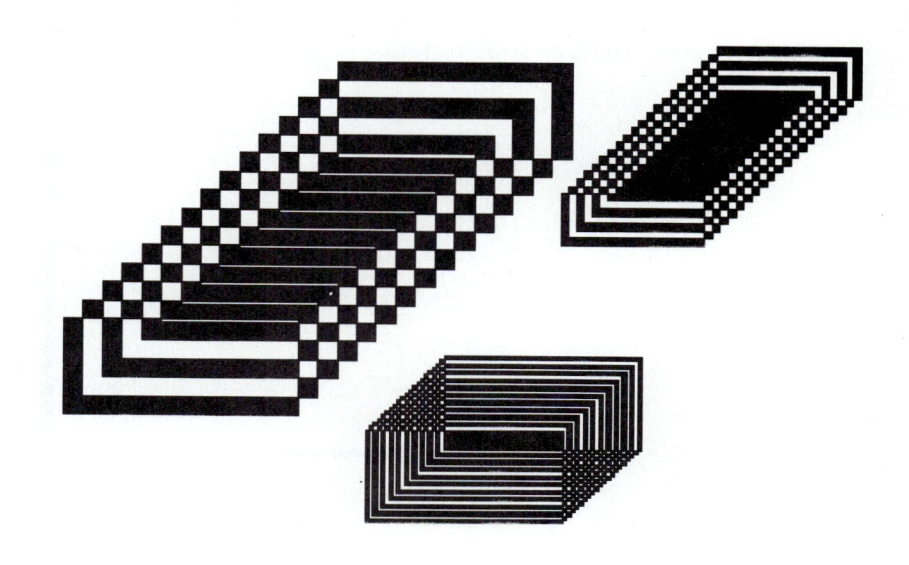

Special effects created with the Duplicate and Combine commands (with Full screen preview)
Figure 11-7.

Place Duplicates and Clones settings
Figure 11-8.

4. Press CTRL-D or select the Duplicate command from the Edit menu. An exact copy of the rectangle appears 1/4 inch to the right and above the original. Press CTRL-D repeatedly until you have created 14 copies of the rectangle, as shown here:

Cutting, Copying, Pasting, and Object Linking and Embedding (OLE)

5. Change the Place Duplicates and Clones setting in the General tab of the Preferences dialog box to 0.05 inches in both the Horizontal and Vertical numeric entry boxes. Click on OK.

6. With the Rectangle tool still selected, draw another rectangle to the right of the first series. Then, press CTRL-D 20 times in succession. This time, the duplicates appear at much shorter intervals, as shown here, giving a smoother appearance to the transitions between the series of duplicated objects.

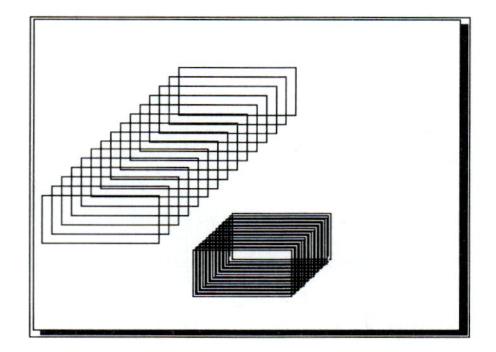

7. Refer to the Place Duplicates and Clones settings in the Preferences dialog box one more time, and change both values to −0.10 inches. The negative number indicates that the duplicates will appear below and to the left of the original object.

8. Draw a third rectangle near the upper-right corner of the page and press CTRL-D 20 times in succession. This time, the duplicates appear to the left of, and below, the original object, as shown here:

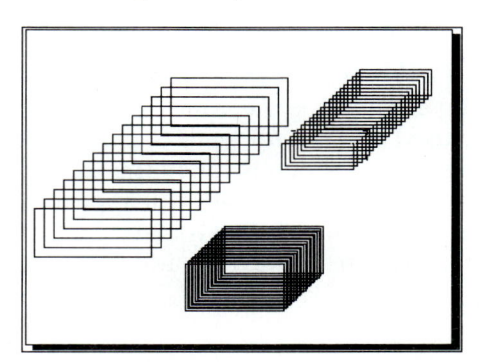

9. Now set the right mouse button so you can toggle between the Edit screen and Full screen preview. Do this in the General tab of the Preferences dialog box with the Right Mouse Button option by opening the drop-down box and clicking on Full screen preview. Click the OK button. With the Pick tool, select each of the series of objects in turn, and apply the Combine command from the Arrange menu to combine the series. While each object is selected, open the Fill tool at the bottom of the toolbox and click on the black solid fill in the bottom row of fills. You will recall from Chapter 5 that using the Combine command causes alternating objects in a group to become transparent. You won't see any change on the screen immediately.

> **Tip:** You can also fill all the objects at one time by using Select All from the Edit menu, applying the Combine command from the Arrange menu to all the objects, and then selecting the black solid fill for all.

10. After completing step 9, click the right mouse button to toggle to full screen preview. As you can see from Figure 11-7, the various offsets lead to different special effects when you combine each group of rectangles. Click the right mouse button to return to the normal view.
11. Save this file as DUPECOMB.CDR and then select New to clear the screen.

The preceding exercise shows you only one potential use for the Duplicate command. You can probably think of many others that will spark your creativity and enhance your design abilities, especially since you can apply this command to multiple or grouped objects as well as single objects.

Cloning an Object

Cloning an object is the same as duplicating; however, the resulting objects can be used in different ways. A cloned object will still have a link to the original object, which is called the *master*. When you make changes to the master, those same changes will appear in the clone. The connection will remain until some change is made to the clone itself, then the link is broken. Try this for yourself with the following steps:

Cutting, Copying, Pasting, and Object Linking and Embedding (OLE) **385**

1. Choose the Ellipse tool, make an ellipse near the top of the page, then press SPACEBAR to select it.
2. Choose Clone in the Edit menu. You see a duplicate appear on top of the original. Move this clone to the lower part of the page.
3. Click on the master (original) to select it, then drag one of the sizing handles to make the master about half the original size. The clone changes to match the master.
4. Now select the clone and change its size. Then go back and change the master. The clone will no longer follow the master.
5. Press CTRL-N to clear the screen and open a new drawing. Answer No to the question of saving any changes.

In the next section, you will see an example of another interesting CorelDRAW! copying technique—one that transfers attributes rather than the objects themselves.

Copying an Object's Attributes

Suppose that you have spent a lot of time designing an object, giving it a custom calligraphic outline, special fills, or a unique combination of text attributes. You would like to give the same set of attributes to another object, but you don't want to waste time setting up all those attributes from scratch. CorelDRAW! allows you to save time and enhance the design of your image by using the Copy Attributes From command in the Edit menu. You can practice using this command in the following exercise.

1. Select the Page Setup command in the Layout menu and change the page format on the Size tab to portrait. Then go to the View menu and turn off both Rulers and Wireframe.
2. Adjust magnification to actual size (1:1), activate the Text tool, select an insertion point near the top left of the screen, and type **Corel**. Activate the Pick tool, selecting the text object, and open the Text roll-up. Click on the Character Attributes command button to open the Character Attributes dialog box, change Spacing for Character to 40 percent, set text attributes to Aachen BT, style to Bold, size to 100 points, and alignment to None. Click on OK and then click on Apply. From the Fill flyout select the Black fill.

Preparing to copy text attributes from one text string to another
Figure 11-9.

3. Click on any white space to deselect the word "Corel." In the Text roll-up, set attributes to AvantGarde Bk BT Normal-Italic, 50 points, and left alignment. Click on Apply. When the Text Attributes dialog box opens, click on OK to apply this default to both Artistic and Paragraph text.

4. Select the Text tool again and place a second insertion point below the first one. This time type **DRAW!**. Select the text with the Text tool and from the Fill flyout select the Black fill. Your screen should look similar to Figure 11-9, after deselecting the text.

5. Close the Text roll-up and activate the Pick tool. Select the second text string. Click on the Copy Attributes From command in the Edit menu. The Copy Attributes dialog box appears, as shown here:

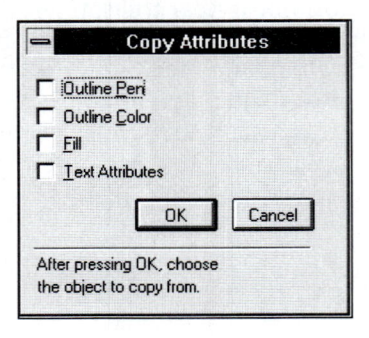

Cutting, Copying, Pasting, and Object Linking and Embedding (OLE)

The Copy Attributes dialog box contains four options: Outline Pen, Outline Color, Fill, and Text Attributes. You can choose to copy any or all of these attributes to the selected object. If you use the Shape tool instead of the Pick tool to select your text, the Text Attributes option will be dimmed and unavailable.

6. Click on the Text Attributes check box to place a check mark in it. Notice that a message at the bottom of the dialog box instructs you to select the object *from* which you want to copy the attributes.
7. Click on OK to exit to the page. The pointer changes to a thick arrow. This reminds you to click on the object from which you want to copy attributes.
8. Select the "Corel" text string by clicking anywhere on its outlines with the tip of the arrow. The "DRAW!" text string immediately changes to reflect the same attributes as the "Corel" text string, as shown in Figure 11-10. If you miss the outline when you click, a dialog box comes up giving you the chance to try again.
9. Select New from the File menu to clear the screen. Do not save these changes.

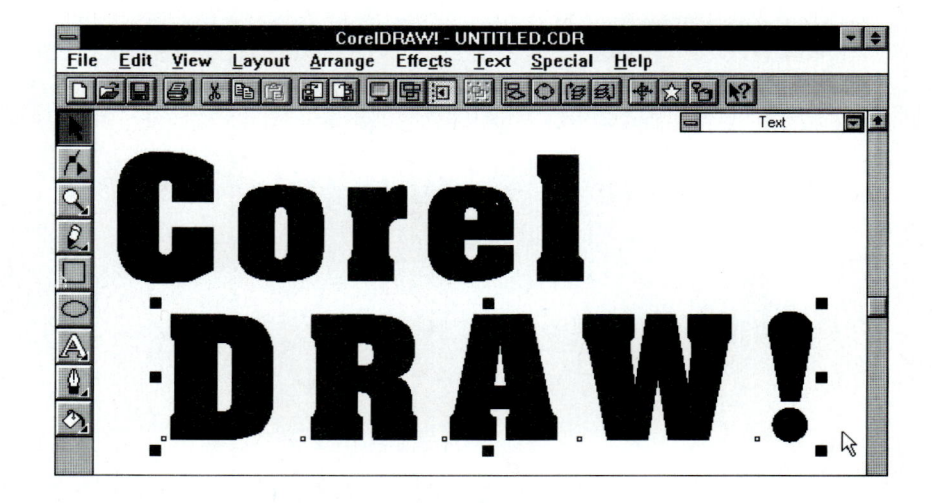

Selected object with attributes copied from adjoining object
Figure 11-10.

You have had and will have opportunities to use the Copy Attributes dialog box in other chapters.

At this time you may want to reset some of the default values, such as those in the General tab on the Preferences menu (Place Duplicates and Clones numeric values to .250 inches, and Right Mouse Button to whatever you want), Snap To Grid in Layout menu turned off, and Rulers in the View menu turned on.

You have experimented in this chapter with the available techniques for copying, cutting, and pasting objects and attributes within or between CorelDRAW! files, and between CorelDRAW! and other applications.

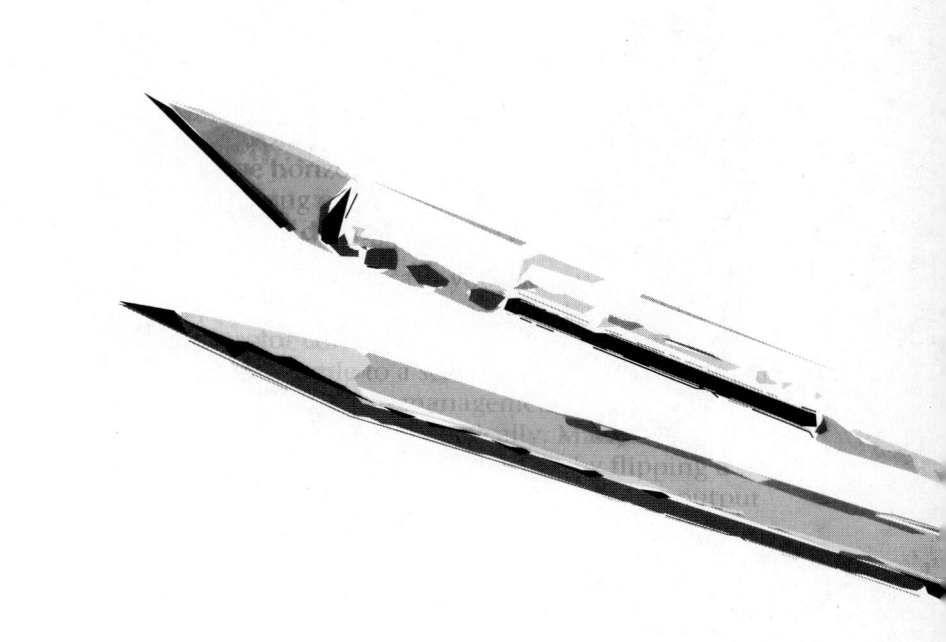

390 CorelDRAW! 5 Made Easy

CORELDRAW! in Action

REED FISHER
Cobra

Reed drew the outline and major shapes of the Cobra by referring to a color photograph of an actual automobile. He then used the Bèzier tool to adjust the nodes and control points of these objects until the main shapes in his drawing looked like those in the photograph. A large midtone shape was first created for the car's outline, the lightest areas of the shiny surface were added, then blends were created between the highlights and the midtones. He adjusted the nodes and control points until the blends looked just right, then he created blends for the darker areas.

To choose colors for his drawing, Reed matched colors from a Pantone Color Reference Manual with the actual colors in the photograph. For each color, he chose the Uniform Fill icon from the Fill tool flyout menu, then selected the corresponding Pantone Spot Color in the Uniform Fill dialog box. He then switched each color to the CMYK color model to get the percentages of Cyan, Magenta, Yellow, and Black for four-color printing of the drawing. All the objects viewed through the windshield were tinted lighter to help create the illusion of reflections on the glass, and highlights on the car contain a little blue to simulate reflections of the sky.

The cobblestones were scanned in from a hand drawing and traced, then placed on a separate layer behind the car's layer. The car was originally created on eight or ten layers which were later consolidated onto a single layer. Reed created a horizon line above the car on the guide layer. Near the ends of the horizon line he anchored perspective lines that met at right angles down on his drawing. He dragged the lower ends of these perspective lines around to aid in aligning objects like the headlights, windshield top, and grill.

This piece was in CorelArtShow 4: Page 76, File: PRD00149.CDR. You may contact Reed in care of:

>Reed Fisher
>2866 Via Bellota
>San Clemente, CA 92673
>Voice: (714) 498-0634

The art on the opposite page was created by and is the property of Reed Fisher. It is used with permission.

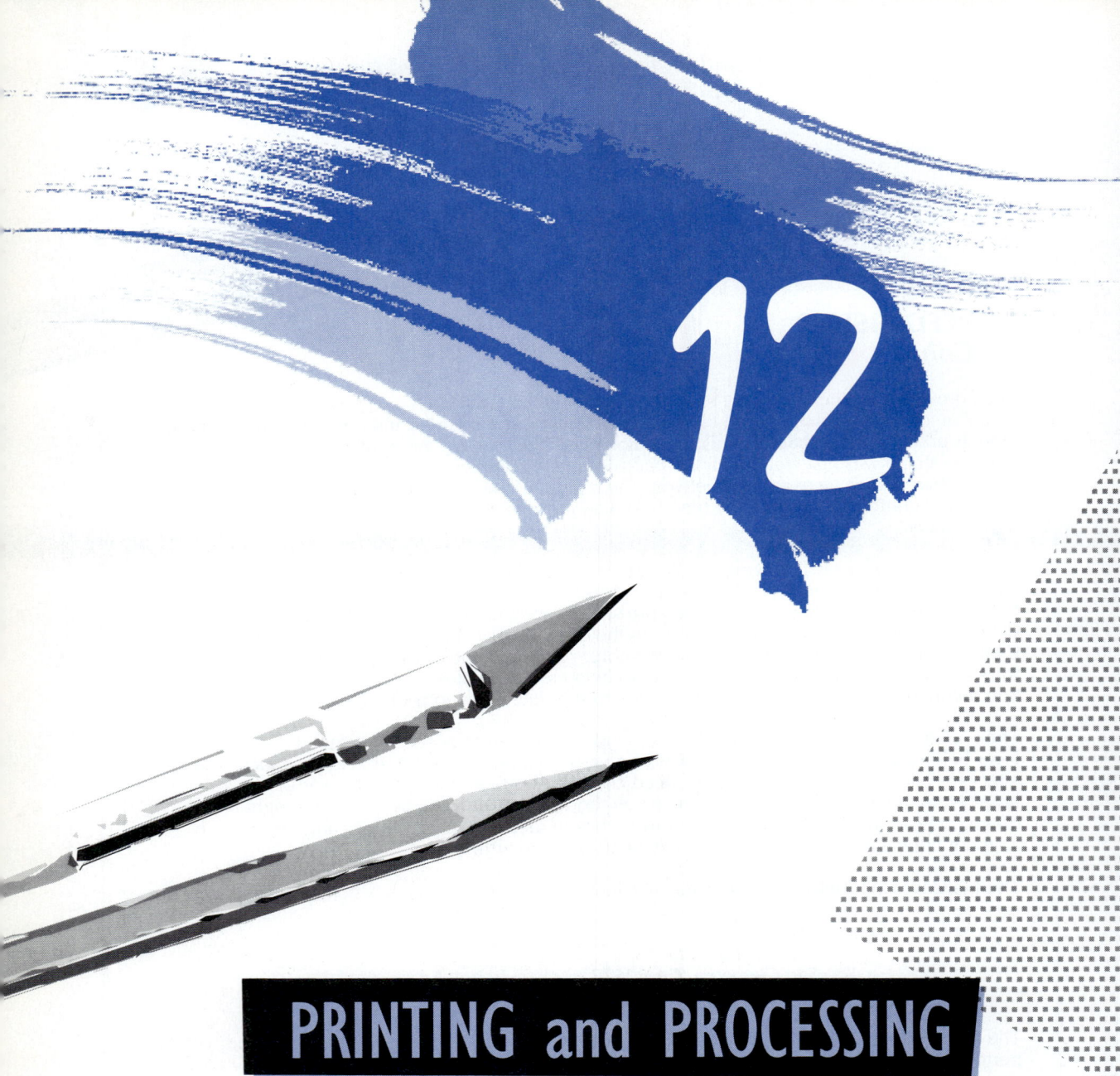

12

PRINTING and PROCESSING YOUR IMAGES

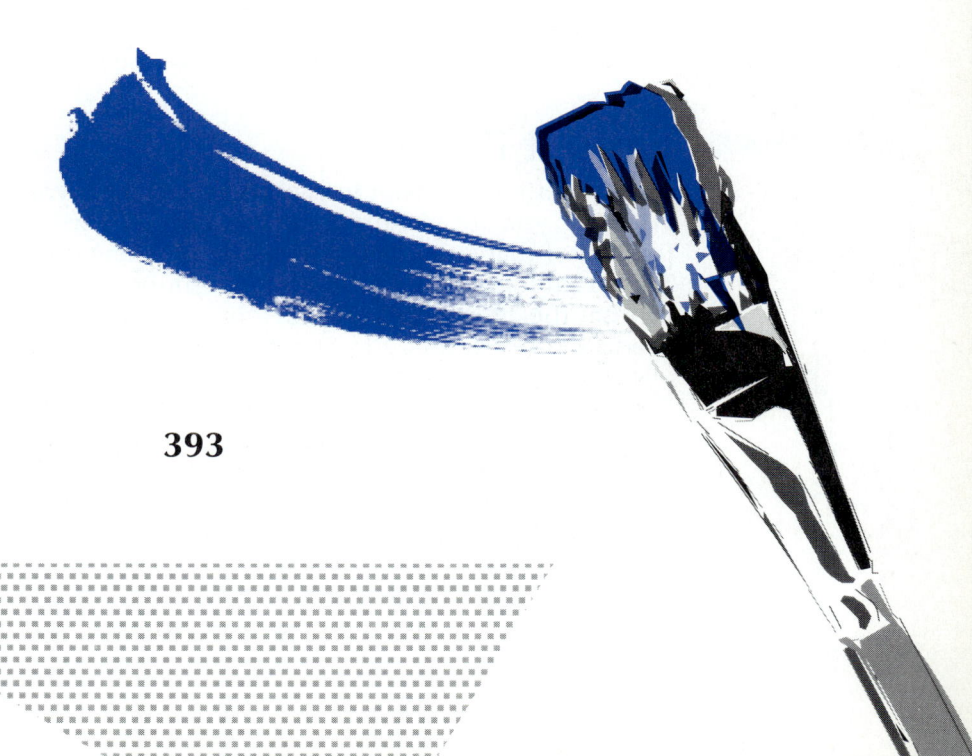

No matter how sophisticated an image may look on your computer monitor, you can judge its true quality only after it has traveled from your hard drive to the outside world. The means by which graphics travel from your computer to your intended audience is a question of output, and until recently output meant printer and paper. In today's world, however, paper is only one possible means by which your artwork can reach your audience. Appendix B explains how your CorelDRAW! files can be exported in various file formats that can be used in film, videotape, CD-ROM, and 35mm slide recorders. CorelDRAW! offers you a choice of all these media and their associated output devices.

If print media remain your preferred end products, you can produce your images using the Print command in the File menu. CorelDRAW! allows you to print selected objects within an image, scale your image to any desired size, print oversize images on multiple tiled pages, print from selected layers, or print to a file that you can send to a service bureau. You can prepare color separations for process color images, add crop marks and registration marks, print in film negative format, and add file information to your printouts. With a PostScript printing device, you can also reproduce the dotted and dashed outlines and fills, custom halftone screens, and PostScript textures you learned to use in Chapter 7.

If you want your images produced as slides or used in presentations, refer to Appendix B. You will use the Export command, not the Print command, to generate your output. CorelSHOW!, discussed in Chapter 22, allows you to assemble the slides, charts, and drawings you've created in CorelDRAW! into professional presentations. If you have the appropriate equipment, you can also output to a CD-ROM in Photo-CD format.

The first part of this chapter describes the output devices and media that CorelDRAW! supports. The middle portion of the chapter guides you step-by-step through the printing process using the Print and Print Setup dialog boxes. The concluding sections of the chapter contain tips to help you achieve satisfactory printing results, based on the type of printer you use.

Output Devices

In considering how your images will travel from your computer to your audience, you are actually concerning yourself with both equipment and the product of that equipment, or with both *output device* and *output medium*. The output device you work with determines what media you can produce, or what the end product of your work will be. For example, all printers produce paper output. PostScript printers and imagesetters, however, also allow you to prepare your images as color separations or in film negative format, so that you can eliminate costly steps in the commercial printing process. CorelDRAW! supports some printing devices better than others. As you may recall from Chapter 1, Windows provides drivers for many different printers and plotters, but not all of them work equally well with CorelDRAW!. The following list shows the printing devices that CorelDRAW! supports best, in the order in which you are likely to reproduce the fullest range of CorelDRAW! features.

Printing and Processing Your Images

- PostScript Level 2 black-and-white printers, color printers, and imagesetters
- HP LaserJet with Adobe-licensed PostScript Level 2 controller boards and plug-in cartridges
- PostScript Plus printers, such as the Apple LaserWriter II and HP LaserJet with Adobe-licensed PostScript Plus controller boards and plug-in cartridges
- Older PostScript printers compatible with the original Apple LaserWriter
- HP LaserJet printers and 100 percent compatibles
- HP DeskJet
- HP PaintJet

The PostScript printers and printers with genuine Adobe-licensed PostScript controller boards are the only ones in this list that let you generate output using PostScript printing options.

You can print your CorelDRAW! images with other printers, too, but the results may vary depending on the complexity of your images and the characteristics of a given manufacturer's device. With some of the following printers, your output may match your expectations exactly. With others, you may experience problems that are hard to predict because of the variety of standards in the industry.

- HP LaserJet clones that are not 100 percent compatible
- HP LaserJet printers, compatibles, and clones with PostScript-compatible controller boards and plug-in cartridges not licensed by Adobe
- Genuine HP Plotters
- HP Plotter clones and other plotters
- Dot-matrix printers

The "Hardware-Specific Tips" section of this chapter contains information about designing your images to obtain the best output results for the printer that you use. It also describes the kinds of limitations you are most likely to encounter with a specific type of printer and provides suggestions on how problems can be solved. The "Complex Artwork on PostScript Printers" section provides tips specific to working with PostScript printers.

In the next section, you will learn about general steps you can take before you print to ensure trouble-free output.

Preparing to Print

Before you select the Print command, you should make certain that your printer is correctly installed to run under Windows. You should also adjust several default settings in Windows in order to customize printing for the special needs of CorelDRAW!. Two of these settings, called "Printer Timeouts," determine how long Windows waits before sending you messages about potential printer problems. The settings you need to review are all in the Windows Control Panel.

Tip: If you work with a PostScript printer, you should be using Windows' own printer driver or a Windows-compatible PostScript driver that came with your printer (for example, the PostScript driver for the HP4M).

Another adjustment you should make is to disable the Windows Print Manager. You do this by deselecting the Use Print Manager check box in the Printers dialog box, reached from the Control Panel. The short sections that follow will guide you through the process of reviewing and editing your printer setup.

Printer Installation and Setup

If you did not specify the correct printer and port when you installed Microsoft Windows, you will not be able to print in CorelDRAW!. To check whether your printer is correctly installed to run under Microsoft Windows, follow these steps:

1. From CorelDRAW!, press CTRL-ESC to open the Task List and double-click on Program Manager.
2. From the Windows Main group, double-click on the Control Panel icon. The Control Panel window appears, like this (your Control Panel may have different icons in it):

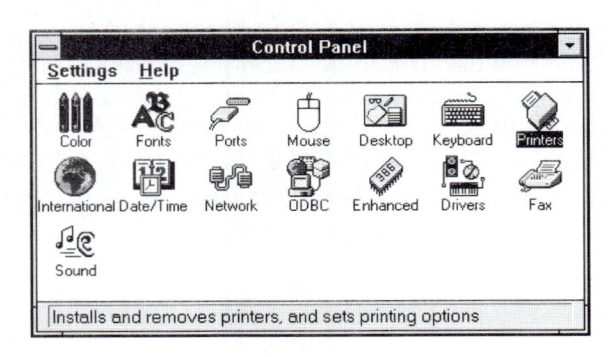

Printing and Processing Your Images

3. Double-click on the Printers icon in the Control Panel. The Printers dialog box will open and display a list of installed printers. An example of a Printers dialog box is shown next.

```
┌─────────────────────── Printers ───────────────────────┐
│ ┌─Default Printer──────────────────┐      ┌─────────┐  │
│ │ HP LaserJet 4/4M on LPT2:        │      │  Close  │  │
│ └──────────────────────────────────┘      └─────────┘  │
│ ┌─Installed Printers:──────────────┐      ┌─────────┐  │
│ │ HP LaserJet 4/4M on LPT2:      ↑ │      │Connect..│  │
│ │ HP LaserJet III on LPT1:         │      └─────────┘  │
│ │ HP LaserJet III PostScript on LPT1:│    ┌─────────┐  │
│ │ Linotronic 330 on FILE:          │      │ Setup...│  │
│ │ Microsoft At Work Fax on FAX:  ↓ │      └─────────┘  │
│ └──────────────────────────────────┘      ┌─────────┐  │
│         ┌───────────────────────┐         │ Remove  │  │
│         │ Set As Default Printer│         └─────────┘  │
│         └───────────────────────┘         ┌─────────┐  │
│                                           │ Add >>  │  │
│ ☐ Use Print Manager                       └─────────┘  │
│                                           ┌─────────┐  │
│                                           │  Help   │  │
│                                           └─────────┘  │
└────────────────────────────────────────────────────────┘
```

The Installed Printers list box should contain the name of the printer you are going to use, and this name should be highlighted. If the name of your printer is in the list box but is not highlighted, click on it with the mouse, click on Set As Default Printer, and click on OK to return to the Control Panel. Then skip to step 5.

4. If the name of your printer is missing from the Installed Printers list box, select Add. An extensive list of printers appears. Use the scroll bar to find the printer you want (they are in alphabetical order) and then double-click on it (or highlight it and select Install). You will be asked to insert one of the original Windows Install disks so that the printer's software driver can be copied to your hard disk. When your printer appears in the Installed Printers list box, select Connect, click on the port to which the printer is attached (LPT1, COM1, and so on), and then click on OK. Repeat these steps for all the printers you will use. When you are done, click on Close to return to the Control Panel.

5. If your printer is connected to a serial port, double-click on the Ports icon in the Control Panel. Select the port to which the printer is connected (COM1 through COM4), and click on Settings. The Settings for COM 1 (or whatever port you selected) dialog box will open, as shown next. Make sure that the Baud Rate, Data Bits, Parity, and Stop Bits are correct for your printer. More settings are available by clicking on the Advanced button, which opens an Advanced Settings dialog box. When you are finished, click on OK to return to the Control Panel.

Refer to your printer manual for help with special settings.

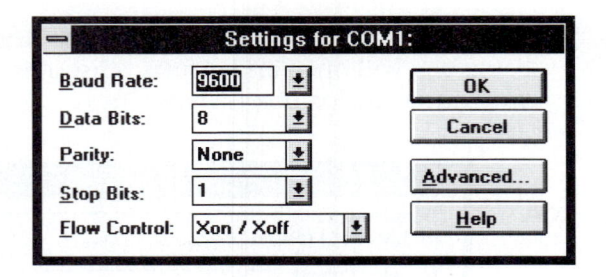

If you need to alter your printer installation after performing this check, refer to your Microsoft Windows 3.1x *User's Guide* and see the chapter that discusses the Control Panel and gives the necessary instructions.

Printer Timeouts

After checking for correct printer and port assignments, you should customize the Printer Timeouts settings, found under the Printers icon in the Control Panel. These settings define how long Windows waits before sending you messages about potential printer problems. The default Printer Timeouts settings installed with Microsoft Windows may be adequate for average Windows applications, but you should customize them to improve printing performance in CorelDRAW!. To edit Printer Timeouts:

1. From the Control Panel, double-click on the Printers icon again. With your printer selected, click on Connect. The Connect dialog box will open, as shown here:

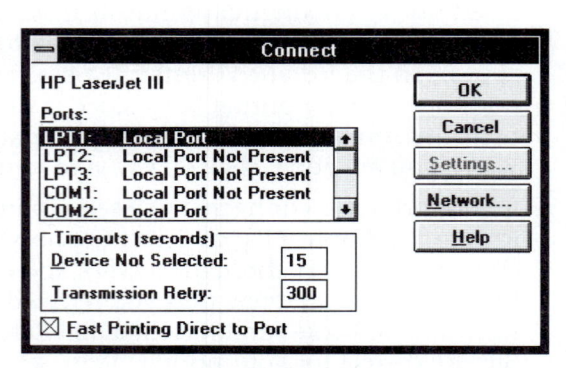

2. The Timeouts section of the dialog box shows two settings: Device Not Selected and Transmission Retry. The Device Not Selected setting determines how long Windows waits before informing you that the printer is not connected properly, not turned on, or otherwise not ready to print. Leave this setting at its default value of 15 seconds, because if

Printing and Processing Your Images

the printer is not ready to perform, you want to find out as soon as possible.

3. Adjust Transmission Retry from its default value of 45 seconds to 300 seconds (equal to 5 minutes), as shown in the illustration. The Transmission Retry value determines how long the printer waits to receive additional characters before a timeout error occurs. Although 90 seconds may be long enough for most software that runs under Windows, it is not always adequate for graphics applications such as CorelDRAW!. The output file that CorelDRAW! sends to your printer can contain complex information, requiring more time to transmit.

4. The Fast Printing Direct to Port check box should be left checked—its default mode. When it is checked, Windows bypasses MS-DOS interrupts and sends your output directly to the printer. The only time you would want to clear the check box is if you are using print spooler software that requires MS-DOS interrupts to control printing. Otherwise, clearing the check box will slow down your printing.

5. Click on OK to return to the Printers dialog box.

By verifying your printer setup and Timeouts settings each time you run CorelDRAW!, you can prevent potential printing and communications problems before you even attempt to print. You can eliminate one more potential printing pitfall by disabling the Windows Print Manager, about which you will learn in the next section.

Disabling the Print Manager

Windows, as it is normally installed, prints all files through the Print Manager. The Print Manager is a program that captures all the printing data and instructions, stores them on disk, and then sends them to the printer. The final step of sending the information to the printer is the slowest part of the process and is done in the background, so that you can continue working in your application without interruption. The Print Manager doesn't always work efficiently with graphics files, however. For this reason, you can avoid printing problems if you disable the Print Manager. When the Print Manager is disabled, the printing operation runs in the foreground; you must wait until printing is complete before you can continue with your work. Printing takes place faster this way than when the Print Manager is enabled, however.

To disable the Print Manager, follow these steps:

1. If necessary reopen the Control Panel and double-click the Printers icon. The Printers dialog box will again appear.

2. Look at the check box in the lower-left corner labeled Use Print Manager. If it is checked, click on it.
3. Click on Close to return to the Control Panel and then double-click on the Control-menu box to close the Control Panel.
4. Click once on the Program Manager Control-menu box to open it, choose Switch To, then double-click on CorelDRAW!.

Now that you have customized Windows' printer settings to improve printing performance in CorelDRAW!, you are ready to set up your printer in CorelDRAW!.

The Print Setup Dialog Box

To prepare for printing in CorelDRAW!, you first select a printer and options for your default CorelDRAW! printer setup. You do this by selecting the Print Setup command from the File menu. The following Print Setup dialog box is displayed:

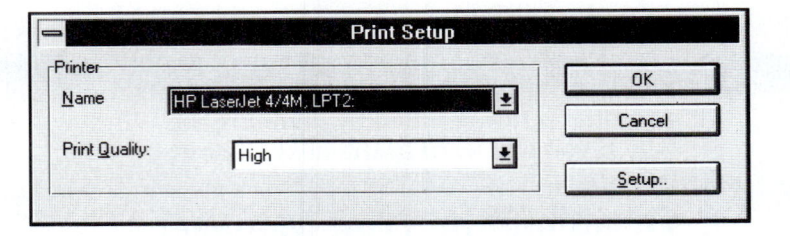

In the Print Setup dialog box you can select either the Windows default printer (selected in the Control Panel) or another printer, using the Specific Printer drop-down list box. The Print Quality drop-down list box may also offer several alternatives. If you click on Setup, the dialog box expands, as shown in Figure 12-1 and you can select paper size and source, the number of copies, and the page orientation. The other options will vary, depending on the printer selected. When you are done with the printer setup, click on OK twice to return to the drawing window.

Next, explore the options in the Print dialog box.

The Print Dialog Box

To begin the process of printing in CorelDRAW!, you must select the Print command in the File menu. An image must be on the screen before you can select this command. So that you can practice printing using the options in the Print dialog box, open a clip-art image and then use it in the exercises

Printing and Processing Your Images 401

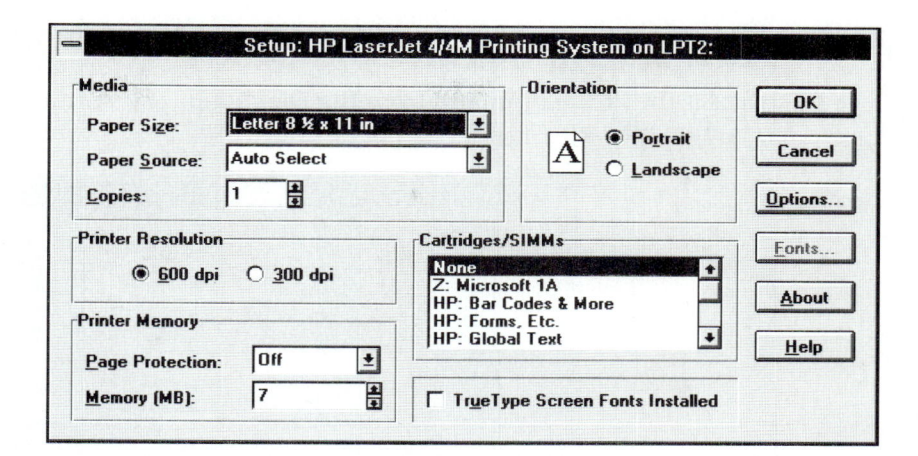

The Print Setup dialog box
Figure 12-1.

that follow. Each section explores one printing option or one aspect of the printing process. Start by getting the clip-art.

You can use any piece of clip-art that you want. The piece used here, shown in Figure 12-2, is BENZ.CMX from the \CLIPART\VEHICLE\CARS\ directory on the first CD-ROM. If you cannot see any color and you have a color monitor, turn off Wireframe in the View menu. Save this clip-art as BENZ.CDR in your \DRAWINGS\ directory.

\CLIPART \VEHICLE\ CARS\ BENZ.CMX used in printing exercises
Figure 12-2.

Selecting the Print Command

Select the Print command from the File menu. The Print dialog box appears, as shown here:

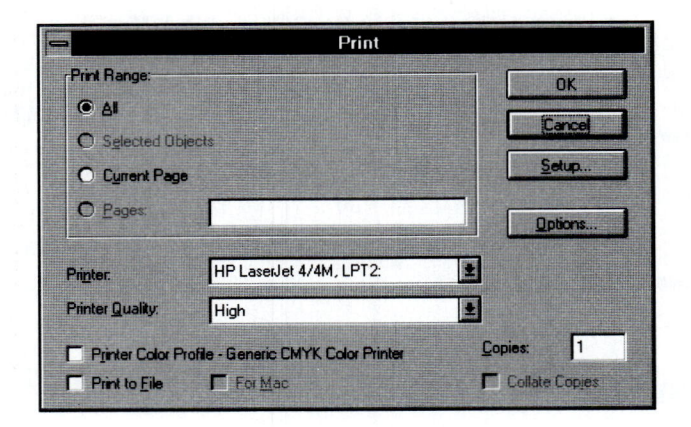

The Print dialog box allows you to determine what and how you want to print: All, Selected Objects, Current Page, or a range of pages; which printer you want to use and its resolution or quality; whether you want to print to a file or to a Macintosh; and the number of copies. If you click on the Setup button, you get a printer setup dialog box similar to the one you saw above. If you click on the Options button you get the greatly expanded Print Options dialog box shown in Figure 12-3.

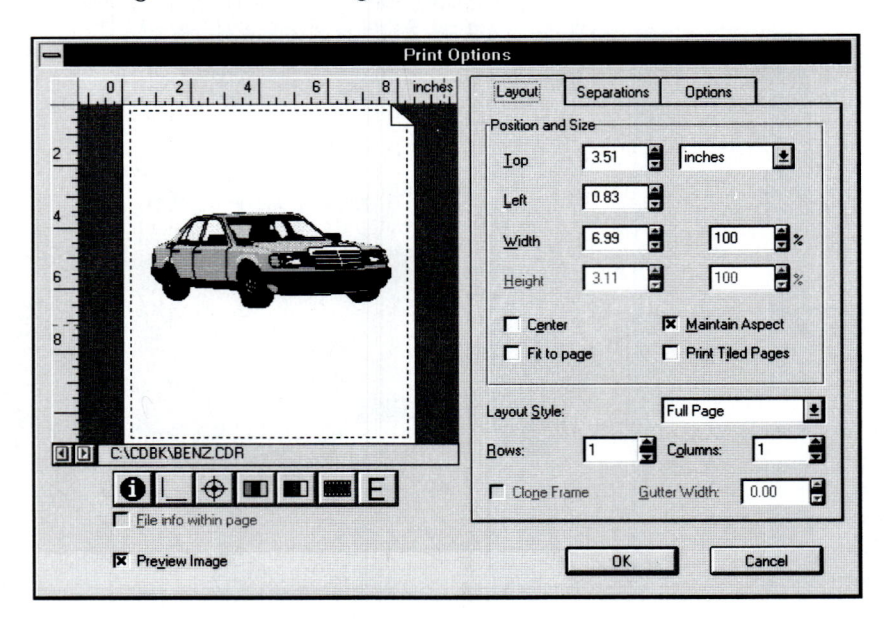

Print Options dialog box
Figure 12-3.

Printing and Processing Your Images

The Print Options dialog box allows you to preview how the printed image will look and fit on the page as well as to change the position of the image and the page layout style to be used. Also, you can specify that you want color separations, the features of those separations, and, if you are using a PostScript printer, several options for that. These features will be covered in detail later in this chapter.

The preview display box on the left, which displays the effects of the Position and Size settings when the Preview Image option is selected, can also be changed interactively by dragging any of the handles of the bounding box to the desired position. In addition, you can drag the graphic to any position on the page. These changes affect only the printed output, not the actual CorelDRAW! drawing.

Below the preview display box are a series of buttons that turn on or off various information or marks that are helpful if the image is to be commercially printed. Exactly how these items are used will be described later in this chapter, but the purpose of the buttons is shown in Table 12-1.

Before you experiment with the printing options, select Cancel to exit the Print Options Dialog Box, and return to the Print Dialog Box. Go on to the next section to learn how to check the printer setup.

Button	Purpose
	Prints the path and filename, the current date and time, the tile and plate number, and the screen frequency. If you are printing color separations, the color name and screen angle will be printed.
	Prints crop marks if the printed page is smaller than the physical paper size.
	Prints registration marks to align color separations.
	Prints a color calibration bar if you are printing color separations.
	Prints a densitometer scale if you are printing color separations.
	Prints a negative or reverse image for use with film.
	Flips the image from left to right for use with film, so that the emulsion side of the film can be placed down.

Print Information Buttons
Table 12-1.

Checking Printer Setup

Whenever you print, it is good to develop the habit of checking your printer setup *before* you select any print options. You do this with the same dialog box that you saw in Figure 12-1. It can be opened either from the File menu or from the Print dialog box. The Setup dialog box for your printer contains controls that allow you to define the desired number of copies; the paper size, source, and orientation; and other settings for your printer. The other items in the Setup dialog box will vary according to the printer you selected using the Printers icon in the Control Panel, Print Setup in the File menu, or the Print dialog box. For example, the Setup dialog box shown in Figure 12-1 shows the controls available for a non-PostScript printer.

Some of the variable controls are important because they help you avoid possible pitfalls when you attempt to print complex images. Later on, in the series of sections following "Hardware-Specific Tips," you will find hints on adjusting these settings to prevent or minimize printing problems. Take a moment to explore the contents of *your* printer Setup dialog box and of any nested sub-dialog boxes that are accessible by clicking on special command buttons. When you are ready, click on Cancel in the Setup dialog box.

Number of Copies

In either the Print dialog box or Printer Setup dialog box, you can enter the number of copies you want printed at one time in the Copies numeric entry box. This can be a number from 1 through 999. The entry you place in the Print dialog box overrides the number entered in the Printer Setup dialog box.

Pages

With multiple-page documents, you can specify the pages to be printed in the Print dialog box by choosing to print all the pages, just the currently selected page, a range of pages, or a list of pages. Both page ranges and page lists are entered in the text box opposite "Pages:" and can be intermixed. For example if you want to print pages 3, 5, and 7 and then pages 11 through 15, you would enter: **3,5,7, 11-15** in the text box.

Printing Only Selected Objects

The Print dialog box allows you to choose to print only Selected Objects. There are several reasons why you might want to do this, rather than print the entire graphic:

Printing and Processing Your Images

- You want to save printing time and need to check only a portion of the image.
- Your picture contains a great deal of fine detail, such as in a technical illustration, and you want to examine certain areas for accuracy.
- Some of your picture elements contain complex or PostScript-only features.
- You have experienced printing problems and want to locate the object or objects that are causing the trouble.

Whatever your reason, you can print just the selected objects within a picture by activating the Selected Objects check box in the Print dialog box. You must select the desired objects before you select the Print command, however, or you will receive an error message. Practice printing selected objects in the BENZ.CDR file now.

1. If the Print dialog box is still open on your screen, click on Cancel to exit and return to the BENZ.CDR file.
2. Click anywhere in the image to select it; the status line tells you that you have selected a group of 39 objects. Choose the Ungroup command in the Arrange menu to ungroup all of the objects.
3. Using the Pick tool, deselect the group, then select just the hood ornament by clicking on it; it's selected if the status line changes to "Group of 7 objects."
4. Leave the hood ornament selected and press CTRL-P. When the Print dialog box appears, review your print setup, and then click on the Selected Objects check box. If you open the Print Options dialog box by clicking on Options, the preview display box shows only the selected object—the hood ornament.
5. Select the OK command button (twice if you went in to look at the preview display box) to begin the printing process. After a short time, the image of the hood ornament should emerge from your printer. Leave the BENZ.CDR image on your screen for the next exercise.

As you learn about the other options in the Print and Print Options dialog boxes, you will think of effective ways to combine one or more of them with Selected Objects. Assume, for example, that you are working with a complex technical illustration and need to proof just a small area. If you activate both the Selected Objects and Fit To Page options, you can print the selected objects in magnified format in order to proof them more easily.

Tip: When you print complex, memory-intensive images, it is a good practice to use the Select All command in the Edit menu to select all objects before you click on the Print command, and then print with the Selected Objects option activated. Some objects in a complex image may be left out; by using the Select All command and the Selected Objects option, you minimize this problem.

In the next section, you will learn about a way to print proofs of a graphic that is larger than the page area.

Tiling a Graphic

You can choose from several different methods of sizing a graphic in CorelDRAW!. The most obvious method is to use rulers when creating objects. Another method involves defining a custom page size with the Page Setup command and the Page Setup dialog box. You can also use the Pick tool to scale an image to the desired size *after* you have created it.

Posters and other applications, however, require images that are larger than any paper size available for your printer. Even if you print final versions of these images on a Linotronic or other imagesetter that has fewer restrictions on paper size, how do you obtain accurate proofs? The answer is through tiling the image. Here, *tiling* refers to the process of printing an oversize image in sections that fit together precisely to form the complete picture. If, for example, you create a poster that is 11 inches wide by 17 inches high and select Tile on the Print Options dialog box as a printing option, the image will print on four 8 1/2-by-11-inch sheets (or on some multiple of whatever size paper you use for your printer).

In the following exercise, you will enlarge the page size for BENZ.CDR, scale the image to fit the page, and print the entire image with the Tile option enabled.

1. With the BENZ.CDR image still on your screen, click on the Select All command in the Edit menu to select all of the objects in the picture. Then select the Group command in the Arrange menu to keep all objects together.

Caution: Use the Group command sparingly for complex PostScript illustrations. Grouping objects slows PostScript printing by increasing print processing time and file size.

Printing and Processing Your Images

407

2. If necessary, activate the Rulers command in the View menu and then select the Page Setup command in the Layout menu. When the Page Setup dialog box appears, click on the Landscape option button and choose Tabloid in the paper size drop-down list box. Selecting Tabloid will result in a page that is 17 inches wide by 11 inches high in landscape format. Click on the OK command button to exit the dialog box. The rulers show you the change in page size.

3. With the Pick tool active, position the pointer at the upper-left corner boundary marker of the selected, grouped image. When the pointer turns to a crosshair, drag the mouse until you have scaled the image to fit the upper-left corner area of the page. Do the same for the lower-right corner boundary marker so your screen looks like Figure 12-4.

4. Move the scaled image so that it is centered on the enlarged page (use the Align to Center Page option in the Align dialog box to do this automatically and then select the Print command from the File menu.

5. When the Print dialog box appears, click on All in the Print Range, make sure the Printer and Printer Quality are correctly selected, and then click on Options. If you get a window advising you that the printer paper orientations do not match that of the document, click on Yes to have the printer adjusted automatically.

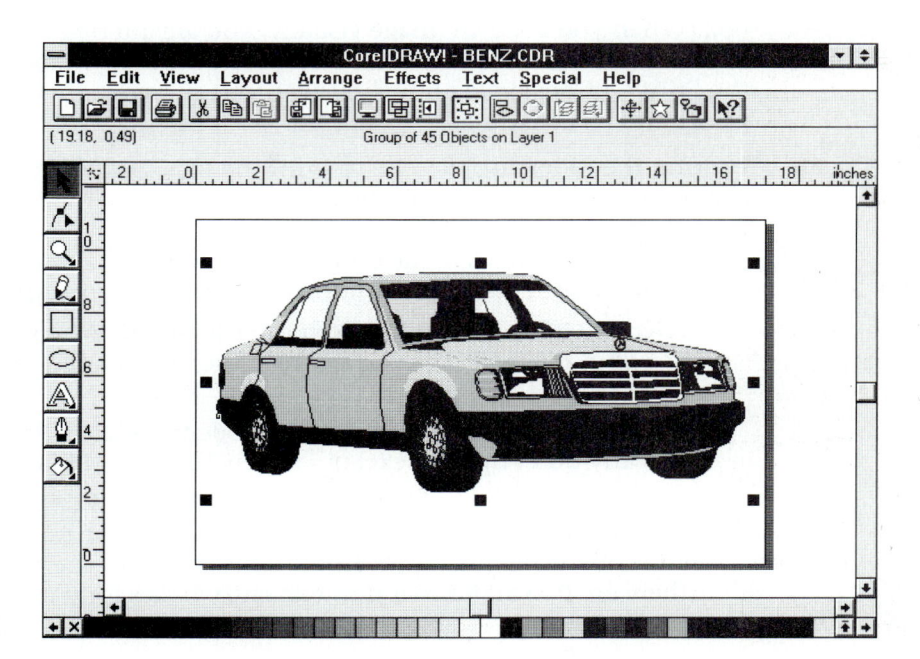

BENZ.CDR on tabloid page
Figure 12-4.

Depending on the algorithm your printer uses, the number of sheets used for tiling may vary.

6. When the Print Options dialog box opens, you can see in the Preview box that the image is larger than the paper size (assuming that the printer is set for 8 1/2-by-11-inch paper size). Deselect any options that are currently active, except Preview Image, and then click on the Print Tiled Pages option to activate it. Select OK twice. After a few moments, the image begins to print.

7. When the file has finished printing, deactivate the Rulers command, return to letter-size paper in the Page Setup dialog box, and then select Open from the File menu. Do not save the changes you have made to the picture. When the Open Drawing dialog box appears, double-click on BENZ.CDR to reopen this file in its original state. Leave BENZ.CDR on the screen for the next exercise.

Since most printers do not print to the edge of the page, you may need to use scissors or a matte knife to cut and paste the tiled pieces together exactly. Still, this method gives you a fairly exact representation of your image as it will print on the imagesetter. If your cutting and pasting skills are also exact, you may be able to use the tiled version of the image as the master copy for commercial printing.

Scaling an Image

There is a difference in CorelDRAW! between scaling an image on the screen with the Pick tool and defining a scaling value in the Print Options dialog box. When you scale an image visually, you are altering its actual dimensions. When you adjust the values in the scale numeric entry boxes in the Print Options dialog box, however, you change only the way the file prints, not its actual size.

Perform the following exercise to print the BENZ.CDR file at a reduced size using the scale numeric entry boxes:

1. With the BENZ.CDR file on the screen, click on any outline within the image. As the status line informs you, the entire image is grouped.

2. Select the Print command from the File menu. When the Print dialog box appears, make sure All is set for the Print Range, and then click on Options.

3. When the Print Options dialog box opens, deselect Print Tiled Pages and any other options except Preview Image and Maintain Aspect.

   Opposite Width and Height on the right of the Print Options dialog box are, first, two numeric entry boxes that are in the units you are currently using (inches in Figure 12-3); then, to the right of these boxes, there are two additional numeric entry boxes for entering percentages.

Printing and Processing Your Images

This second pair of boxes is used to scale the image for printing. The current values in the scale numeric entry boxes should be 100 percent (actual size). If Maintain Aspect is checked, the Height units and scale numeric entry boxes are dim, since they will automatically change as you change the width to keep the aspect ratio of width to height the same. Therefore, to scale the image for printing and maintain the aspect ratio, you only need to change the scale factor for Width.

4. Using the bottom scroll arrow in the Width scale numeric entry box, scroll to 10 percent, as shown here:

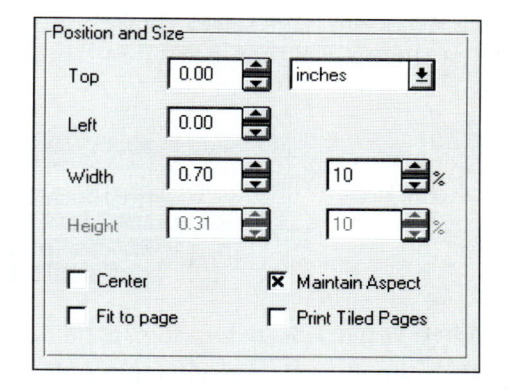

```
┌─Position and Size─────────────────────────────────┐
│                                                   │
│   Top     [ 0.00 ]   [ inches ]                   │
│                                                   │
│   Left    [ 0.00 ]                                │
│                                                   │
│   Width   [ 0.70 ]   [ 10 ] %                     │
│                                                   │
│   Height  [ 0.31 ]   [ 10 ] %                     │
│                                                   │
│   □ Center            ☒ Maintain Aspect           │
│   □ Fit to page       □ Print Tiled Pages         │
└───────────────────────────────────────────────────┘
```

Depending on your printer, you may not be able to print as small as 10 percent. If this is the case, increase the scale until your printer accepts the image.

5. Click on OK twice to begin the printing process. Again, depending on your printer, the image will probably print centered on your page, but it may be slightly offset.

6. Leave the current image on the screen for further work.

You have seen how you can reduce the scale of an image to 10 percent of original size. The lower limit is 1 percent of original size. You can also increase the scale of an image to an upper limit of 999 percent of original size. If you expand the scale of an image beyond the dimensions of the page, however, remember to activate the Tile option as well.

In the next section, you will experiment with another printing option that involves image size.

Fitting an Image to the Page

Like the Scale option, the Fit to Page option in the Print Option dialog box does not affect the actual size of the graphic. When you select this option,

CorelDRAW! automatically calculates how much it must increase the scale of the graphic or selected object(s) in order to make it fill the entire page. In the following exercise, you will combine the Fit to Page option with the Selected Objects option you learned about previously.

1. Click anywhere within the BENZ.CDR image; since the entire image is grouped, you select all objects automatically.

2. Click on the Ungroup command in the Arrange menu and then click on any white space to deselect all objects. Select several objects—like the grill, hood ornament, and head lights—by clicking on them. You can see what you have selected by choosing Preview Selected Only from the View menu and then pressing F9 (full screen preview). It should look like this:

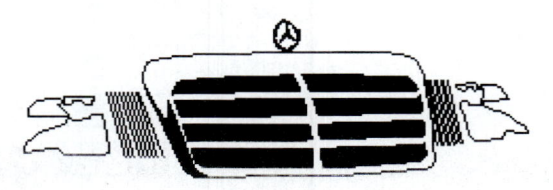

3. When you are done looking at the full screen preview, press F9 again.

4. With the objects selected, choose the Print command in the File menu. When the Print dialog box appears, click on the Selected Objects option and then on the Options button.

5. In the Print Options dialog box, deselect any options, except Preview Image, that are currently active, click on the Fit to Page option to activate it, and then click on OK twice to begin printing. After a few moments, the grill, headlights, and ornament appear on the paper, filling the entire sheet.

6. Leave the BENZ.CDR image on the screen for the next exercise.

When the Fit to Page option is selected, the centered option is also automatically enabled.

Next you will experiment with printing an image to a file.

Printing to a File

There are two common reasons why you might choose to print an image to a file:

♦ You are creating files to send to a service bureau for output on a Linotronic or other imagesetter.

♦ Your printer is busy and you prefer to copy the print information directly to the printer at a later time.

Printing and Processing Your Images

To print to a file, you select the Print to File option in the Print dialog box and name the output file in the Print to File dialog box that opens. Printer output files created in applications that run under Windows use the extension .PRN. The printing parameters included in the file are those that you set for the currently selected printer in the Print and Printer Setup dialog boxes.

The following exercise assumes that you are going to send an output file to a service bureau for use on a PostScript imagesetter. In order to do this, you do not need to have a PostScript printer, but you must have a PostScript printer driver installed in your Windows directory. If you do not have a PostScript driver installed, use the Add command in the Printers dialog box of the Control Panel. The service bureau should be able to provide you with the correct drivers for their equipment. Refer to the discussion under "Checking Printer Setup" earlier in this chapter for assistance. Once you have the PostScript driver set up, practice printing the BENZ.CDR image to a file in the following exercise:

1. With the BENZ.CDR file on the screen, deselect all objects in the image, choose Select All from the Edit menu, then Group from the Arrange menu.
2. Press CTRL-P, and when the Print dialog box displays, click on All for the Print Range, select the printer and printer quality you want to use, and then click on Print to File.
3. If you are going to print on a printer or imagesetter controlled by a Macintosh computer, select the For Mac option. Without this selection, the print files you produce will not work on a Macintosh.
4. Click on Options and, in the Print Options dialog box, turn off Fit to Page, return the two scale numeric entry boxes to 100%, and click on OK.
5. Select OK again; a second dialog box appears with the title "Print To File," as shown next. This dialog box looks like and operates similarly to the Save File As dialog box.

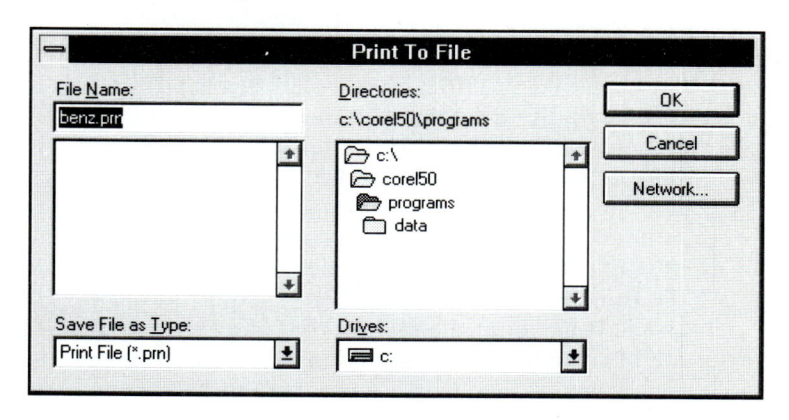

6. If the filename Benz is not already in the File Name text box, type it, and then select OK. CorelDRAW! adds the file extension .PRN automatically to designate this as a printer output file.
7. Make the changes you need in the dialog box and click on OK to begin the process of printing to a file.
8. When printing is complete, select New to clear the image from the screen without saving any changes.

When printing an image to a file, you can combine several options. For example, if you are creating color separations for commercial printing, you might choose to activate the Print as Separations and Print to File options at the same time.

Using Print Options

The Print Options dialog box, accessed through the Options command button in the Print dialog box, has not only the options that have been described above and that you saw in Figure 12-3, but two additional tabs with settings for creating color separations and for special PostScript features. The next sections introduce you to advanced print options, including those that are in the Separations and Options tabs as well as those that are in the Print Options dialog box itself and in the Layout tab. Since you may use some of these options in combination, the sections are ordered according to task, rather than according to their appearance in the Print Options dialog box.

Printing File Information with a Graphic

If you are like most illustrators and designers, you probably revise a graphic several times, renaming it with each revision so that you can choose the best version later. You are therefore familiar with the bewilderment of viewing multiple printouts of the same graphic and not knowing which sheet represents which version.

CorelDRAW! provides a convenient solution to this common frustration. By activating the file information option, you can print the path, filename, date and time of printing, and other information with your image. This information appears in 6-point Courier *outside* the top and bottom margins of your *page,* not on your graphic (unless you select the File info within page option). You select the file information option by clicking the leftmost button (with the "I" in it) under the preview display box. If you activate the file information option without the within page option, choose a page size in the Page Setup dialog box that is smaller than the actual paper size you are printing on. This step is necessary because the file information is visible *only* if you reduce page size below the size of the paper in your printer tray. If

Printing and Processing Your Images

you are using 8 1/2-by-11-inch paper, for example, you must use the Page Setup dialog box to define a custom page size of smaller dimensions, and then fit the graphic within that page. You can practice defining a custom 7-by-9-inch page size and printing file information in the following exercise. You'll start by loading another CorelDRAW! clip-art file, which you will use for the rest of the chapter.

1. Turn Rulers on and import the TOCAN.CMX file, which is in the \CLIPART\BIRD\ directory on the first CD-ROM. The toucan will appear, as shown in Figure 12-5. (Note the difference in spelling between TOCAN, the filename, and toucan, the actual birdname.)

2. Select the Page Setup command in the Layout menu. Select Custom in the paper size drop-down list box, and define a page 7 inches wide and 9 inches high. Then click on OK to exit the dialog box. The toucan is now larger than your page.

3. Click on the toucan to select it, open the Transform roll-up from the Effects menu, click on the Scale & Mirror button in the middle, enter 80% for both the horizontal and vertical scale factors, and click on Apply. The toucan is reduced so it fits on the page, as you can see in Figure 12-6. Save this image as TOCAN.CDR.

\CLIPART\BIRD\TOCAN.CMX image as it first appears

Figure 12-5.

TOCAN.CDR image reduced to fit a 7-by- 9-inch page
Figure 12-6.

4. Press CTRL-P to open the Print dialog box. Make sure that All is selected in the Print Range and that the Printer and Printer Quality are what you want. Then, if Print to File is still selected, click on it to deselect it and click on the Options command button. In the Print Options dialog box click on the file information button on the left under the preview display box and make sure that Fit to Page is not selected in the Layout tab. Click on OK twice to begin printing. After a few moments, the image emerges from your printer. The path and filename, date and time of printing, and other information appear just beyond the bottom boundary of the custom page, and the word Composite (meaning the print is a composite of all the colors) is printed at the top of the page, as shown in Figure 12-7.

5. Leave this image on the screen for subsequent exercises.

Since CorelDRAW! generates object-oriented art, you can scale your images without distortion. It is therefore convenient to change page size so that you can print file information for your own use. Another common use for the File Information option is in conjunction with the Print as Separations, Crop Marks, and Registration Marks options.

Printing and Processing Your Images

TOCAN.CDR printed with file information
Figure 12-7.

Color Separations, Crop Marks, and Registration Marks

When you specified outline fill and object fill colors in Chapter 7, you learned about the differences between spot color and process color in the commercial printing process. If you plan to send output files to a PostScript imagesetter, you can reduce your commercial printing expenses by generating color separations on paper or in a file. Doing this reduces the number of intermediary steps that commercial printers must perform to prepare your images for printing.

Put simply, *color separation* is the process of separating the colors that you specify for an entire image into the primary component colors. When you generate color separations using the process color system (CMYK), the output is four separate sheets, one each for the cyan, magenta, yellow, and black color components of the image. The commercial printer uses the four sheets to create separate overlays for each color, in preparation for making printing plates.

When you generate color separations using the spot color system, the output is one sheet for each color specified in the image, and the commercial printer creates overlays for each color. This process becomes very expensive as the number of spot colors in an image increases, so it is a good idea to use the process color system if you plan to have more than three colors in a given image.

Tip: Use the Focoltone color model to translate spot colors into CMYK colors.

When you generate color separations using the Print Separations option in the Separations tab of the Print Options dialog box, it is also important to include crop marks and registration marks. You can see examples of these marks in Figure 12-8. *Crop marks* are small horizontal and vertical lines printed at each corner of the image to show the exact boundaries of the image. A commercial printer uses crop marks to trim the piece to its finished size. *Registration marks,* two of which appear at each corner of an image, are crossed lines over a circle. Registration marks assist the commercial printer in aligning color separation overlays exactly; if misalignment were to occur, the final printed product would display a host of color distortions. When you activate the File Information option, CorelDRAW! prints the color for the page together with the halftone screen angle and density on the bottom and the filename, time, and date on the top.

If you have selected color separations, two other options are available in the buttons under the preview display box: color calibration bars and densitometer scales. Selecting color calibration bars prints a bar in each color in your drawing on the page. When your image is printed on a color printer, you can use these to adjust your monitor so that the printed colors are a close match to your monitor colors. Densitometer scales are used to check the accuracy of the printer used to print the separations. The densitometer strip on each separation page contains precise tints of the ink color for that page. These can be checked against standard reference values to determine the accuracy and consistency of the printer.

Caution: Just as with file information, you can see crop marks and registration marks from your printer only if you define a custom page size that is smaller than the size of the paper you are using, unless you select the Within page option. The exception to this rule is if you are printing to Linotronic or other imagesetting equipment.

Printing and Processing Your Images

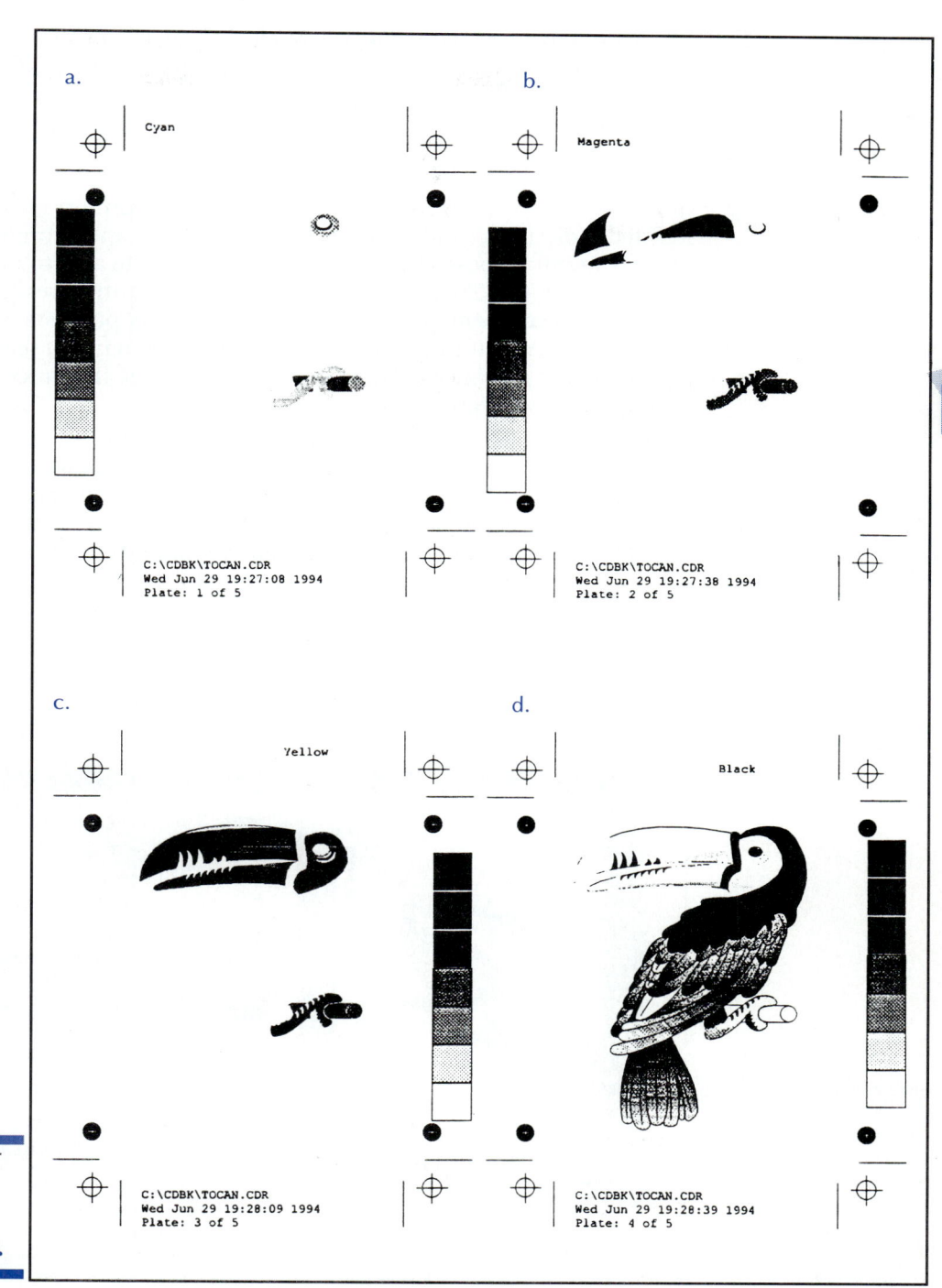

Figure 12-8. Process color separations for the tocan

In the following exercise, you will generate color separations for the tocan on your screen using the Print Separations, Crop Marks, Registration Marks, Calibration Bar, Densitometer Scale, and File Information options. If you send files to a PostScript imagesetter, you may perform this exercise as well with the Print to File option activated.

1. With the TOCAN.CDR image still on the screen, turn on Preview Selected Only in the View menu. Select the image and, from the Arrange menu, choose Ungroup. Click in any white area to deselect the ungrouped object. Then, select various objects in turn, pressing F9 to see just that object on the preview screen, magnifying portions of the image if necessary for more accurate selection. When you select a color object, open the Uniform Fill dialog box and check the process color values that have been specified.

2. After you have observed the fill colors of various objects, choose Select All from the Edit menu and then Group from the Arrange menu to regroup the bird. Then select the Print command in the File menu. When the Print dialog box appears, click on Options and the Separations tab. Finally, activate the Print Separations options.

3. Click on the first five buttons under the preview display box to print file information, crop marks, registrations marks, color calibration bars, and densitometer scales. Your dialog box should now look like Figure 12-9.

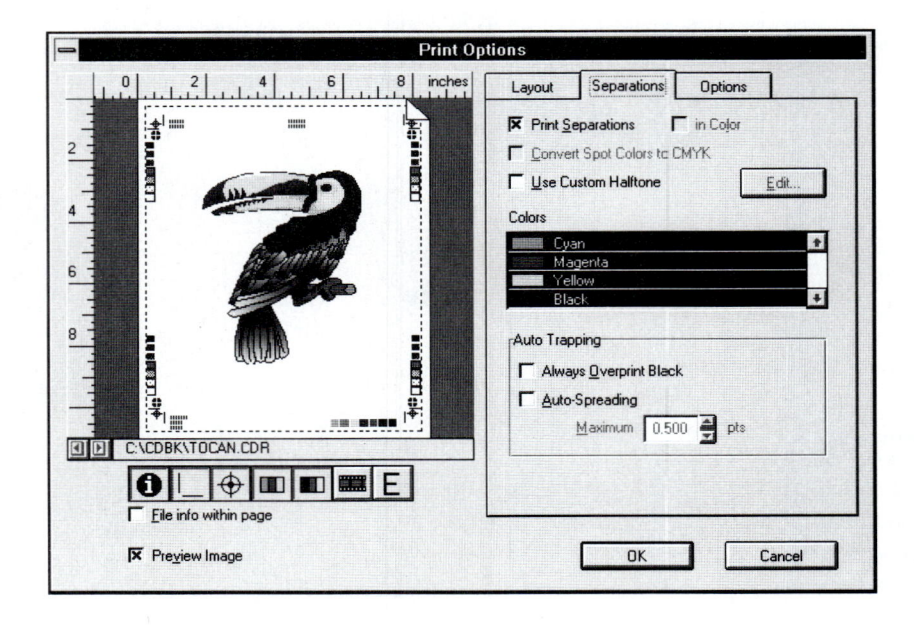

Print Options dialog box with the Separations tab active

Figure 12-9.

In the Separations tab is a list box containing the names of the four process colors. (If you were preparing to print an image using the spot color method, you would see specific color names here instead.) By default, all of the colors are selected and a separate sheet will print for each of them. You can deselect any or all of them by clicking on the color and then reselect them by clicking on the color again. For this exercise, leave all of the colors selected. For future reference, you can choose to print separations for either one color or a few colors at a time. To do so, just click on the color or colors in the list box that you do *not* want printed.

Above the Colors list box are four check boxes: Print Separations, Convert Spot Colors to CMYK, Use Custom Halftone, and In Color. If you have a color printer, you can select In Color to print your separations in color. Convert Spot Colors to CMYK converts Spot and RGB colors in your drawing to CMYK values; the conversion isn't exact, however, because the RGB and CMYK color models are based on different technologies. When the output for your drawing is to be process color, you should use only CMYK colors. Use Custom Halftone to specify custom halftone screen angles and line frequencies in the Advanced Screening dialog box, shown in Figure 12-10 and opened by clicking on the Edit button.

Below the Colors list box are two check boxes related to auto trapping. *Trapping* is the process of adjusting colors that print on top of each other. Normally, when objects with a uniform fill overlap, the bottom object is *knocked out*. This means that the part of the object being overlapped doesn't

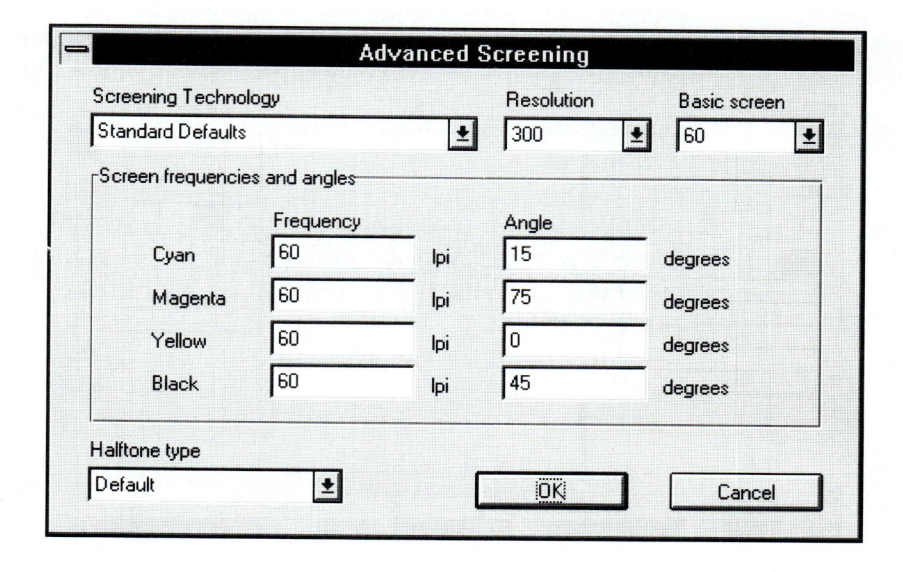

Advanced Screening dialog box for setting custom halftone screens and angles

Figure 12-10.

print, which prevents colors from interfering with each other when printed. When one of any two overlapping objects has a black value of 95% or higher, checking Always Overprint Black makes that object print without a knockout of the object beneath it. Auto-Spreading is used to minimize registration errors that can occur during printing. These errors show up as white spaces around colored objects. To minimize this problem, the lighter object is made larger or *spread*. The overlap created makes press registration less critical. When the lighter object is on top, it is made larger; this is called a *spread*. When the lighter object is on the bottom, the knockout is made smaller; this is a *choke*. Trapping can become very complicated in any but simple graphics.

In the Advanced Screening dialog box are four screen angle and frequency values, one for each of the Process colors. Do *not* alter these values unless you are very experienced in four-color printing and know exactly what you are doing. These angles and frequencies are preset to ensure the best possible color alignment and registration.

Tip: When sending output to a service bureau, enquire whether your screen settings should be adjusted for a specific imagesetter.

Printing color separation sheets takes longer than simply printing the file normally.

4. Click on OK to save the Separations settings and exit the dialog box; then click on OK once more. If you are printing directly to your own printer, CorelDRAW! now begins printing the separations. In several minutes, four sheets of paper appear. The first shows the color values for cyan, the second for magenta, the third for yellow, and the fourth for black. As shown in Figure 12-8, each sheet also contains crop marks, registration marks, filename and date information, and color and screen information.

5. If you chose to print to a file, the Print to File dialog box appears after you have exited the Options dialog box and clicked on OK in the Print dialog box. When you are prompted to name the output file, type **colorsep**, and select OK; CorelDRAW! adds the extension .PRN automatically.

6. Leave the TOCAN.CDR image on the screen for the next exercise.

Caution: If you fill objects with any PostScript halftone screen pattern other than the default pattern, your custom settings will have no effect when you print color separations for the objects, because CorelDRAW! uses the halftone screen function to calculate color separation angles. This limitation applies only to the objects for which you print color separations. If you require separations for only a few objects, you are free to assign PostScript halftone screen patterns to any remaining objects. If you assign non-default PostScript halftone screens to objects for which you must print color separations, your screen assignments have no effect.

Keep in mind that you can combine any number of options when you specify color separations. For example, you can tile separations for an oversize image, include file information, make selected objects fit a custom page size exactly, or scale the selected image for printing. If you are sure that the current image is in your final version, you can also print it in film negative format, as you will do in the next section.

Film Negative Format

In commercial black-and-white or color printing, the transfer of the image or of color separations to film negatives is one of the last steps to occur before the printing plates are made. Think of the difference between a snapshot and the negative from which it was produced: colors in the negative appear inverted and backward. You can do the same thing in CorelDRAW! when you activate the right two buttons under the preview display box in the Print Options dialog box. The button second from the right (see Table 12-1 earlier in this chapter) creates a negative image in which white portions of the original image fill with black and dark areas in the original image become light. The rightmost button flips the image horizontally, including the file Information and registration marks. This flipping of the image allows the printer to place the emulsion side of the film down during the plate making process.

Creating a negative and flipped image can save you money, but only if you are certain that the color separations in the image (if any) are in final form and will not need any further color correction or screen angle adjustments. If you intend to send a film negative file to a service bureau for output on a high-resolution imagesetter, ask the bureau management whether they can produce your file in film negative format automatically. Many imagesetters can print your color separation file as a film negative just by flipping a switch. This might be preferable if your aim is to achieve a higher output resolution than that provided by your own 300 or 600 dpi laser printer.

In the following exercise, you will print one color separation screen for the TOCAN.CDR file in film negative format. You can print this screen directly onto paper, or create a file to send to a service bureau. Steps are provided so that you can print the film negative format to your printer and to a file.

1. With the TOCAN.CDR file open, click on the Print command in the File menu. (If you printed to a file in the previous exercise and want to do that again, make sure that the Print to File option is still active.)
2. Open the Print Options dialog box, click on the Separations tab, and make sure that the print options that you used in the previous exercise—Print Separations, Convert Spot Colors to CMYK, and the file information, crop marks, registration marks, and densitometer scale buttons—are still active. Then, click on the print negative and emulsion side down buttons.
3. You do not need to print out all four color separation sheets to see how the Print Negative option works, so click on the Cyan, Magenta, and Yellow bars to turn them off, leaving only the Black to print. Click on OK to exit the Print Options dialog box and click on OK once more to begin printing.

   If you are printing directly to your printer, the color separation now begins to print. In a few moments, the color separation sheet for Process Black appears in film negative format, as shown in Figure 12-11. The image in the figure shows only the graphic and its file information, but your output sheet is covered with toner all the way to the edges of the printable page area. If you elected to print to a file, the Print to File dialog box appears, prompting you to enter a filename.
4. If you are printing to a file, type **neg-blk** in the File Name text box and then click on OK to generate your file. When you finish printing, leave the image on the screen.

You need not limit yourself to printing in film negative format when you are working with a spot or process color image. You can also use this printing option with black-and-white images.

Fountain Fill Steps

You can use the Options tab of the Print Options dialog box to control the number of steps used to create a fountain fill on both PostScript and non-PostScript printers. The steps are numbered from 2 through 250. You may want to change the number of fountain steps for either of two reasons: to increase the smoothness of the fill and get rid of banding or to increase the speed of printing. You increase the number of steps to increase the smoothness of the fill, and you decrease the number of steps to speed up

Printing and Processing Your Images

Figure 12-11.
Color separation sheet for Process Black printed in film negative format

Try out a series of values for fountain fill steps to see which are correct for your output device. Low-resolution (300 dpi) printers support only a limited number of steps.

printing. The "normal" number of fountain steps depends on the resolution of your printer. For a 300 dpi laser printer, the normal value is 64, while for a 1270 dpi imagesetter it is 128. A value below 25, while fast to print, produces obvious banding. On the other end, at around 100 for a 300 dpi laser printer, you can add fountain steps without any gain in the smoothness of the image but with a decided increase in print time.

Flatness Setting for PostScript

The Set Flatness to setting in the Options tab of the Print Options dialog box, which is active only for PostScript printers, allows you to reduce the complexity of the curves in a drawing and thereby improve the likelihood of being able to print the drawing and also reduce the printing time. As you increase the Set Flatness to setting, curves become less smooth with more straight ("flat") segments and, therefore, less attractive in some applications.

PostScript printers have upper limits on the number of curve segments they can handle, and they check for this limit. When a print image exceeds this limit, the image won't be printed. The normal Flatness setting is 1. If you are having problems printing a complex image, increase the Flatness setting in increments of 3 or 4 until you can print. By about 10, the curves are obviously less smooth. Selecting Auto Increase Flatness increases the flatness value by 2 until the object prints or the Auto Flatness value exceeds the

Flatness value by 10. You can choose values from 0.01 to 100. Settings below 1 increase the curvature (decrease the flatness).

Tip: Combine several objects in a drawing if it is too complex to print. Combining objects reduces the total number of nodes and eases the PostScript bottleneck.

Screen Frequency for PostScript

The Default Screen Frequency can be selected for a halftone screen in the PostScript Options dialog box. As you may recall from Chapter 7, you can access this dialog box whenever you assign a spot color to an outline or object fill. The frequency of the default screen pattern determines how fine the halftone resolution will appear on the printed page. Each type of PostScript printer has a default screen frequency, with the most common being 60 lines per inch for 300 dpi printers and 90 to 200 lines per inch for high-resolution imagesetters. The standard setting for Screen Frequency in the Options tab of the Print Options dialog box is "Default," because in most cases it is best to let the printer you are using determine the screen frequency.

You can override this standard value, however, by clicking on the down arrow on the right and either selecting the desired value from the drop-down list or entering the desired value in the associated numeric entry box. Thereafter, *all* of the objects in your image will have the custom screen frequency. The most common reasons for altering this value are as follows:

- You want to create special effects such as the fill patterns that result from altering the halftone screen settings, as discussed in Chapter 7.
- You experience visible banding effects while printing objects with fountain fills and want the color transitions to occur more smoothly.
- You are sending output files to a service bureau whose imagesetters are capable of variable resolutions and halftone frequencies.

In the first 2 cases, you would decrease the default screen frequency for the selected printer, while in the third case, you should ask the service bureau what screen frequency is best. If you have a 300 dpi PostScript printer, perform the following brief exercise to compare how reducing the default screen frequency alters the appearance of your output.

1. With the TOCAN.CDR image open, click on the Print command in the File menu. The Print dialog box appears.

2. Open the Print Options dialog box and make sure that the Print as Separations option is activated in the Separations tab. Click on Cyan, Magenta, and Yellow to turn them off and then click on Use Custom Halftone and on the Edit button to open the Advanced Screening dialog box you saw in Figure 12-10.

3. Change the value in the Black Frequency numeric entry box to 30 lpi (lines per inch). This setting will cause only the color separation for the color Black to print at a different screen frequency.

4. Click on OK to exit the Advanced Screening dialog box and click on OK again to exit the Print Options dialog box. Click on OK one more time to begin printing. After a few moments, the color separation sheet appears. If you compare this output sheet with the one produced in the "Color Separations, Crop Marks, and Registration Marks" section, you will not notice a big difference, but if you look closely you will see that the dot pattern of the 45-lines-per-inch screen printout appears coarser.

5. Select New from the File menu to clear the screen of the TOCAN.CDR file. Do not save any changes to the image.

If you alter the default screen frequency in order to proof an image, be sure to change the frequency back to Default before sending the final output file to a service bureau. Otherwise, your image will not appear to have a much higher resolution than what your printer could offer.

Note, however, that if you assign *custom* PostScript halftone screen patterns to an object while drawing, any changes you make to the *default* screen frequency at printing time will have no effect on the screen frequency of that object.

In the next section, you will become familiar with the use of Type 1 versus TrueType fonts.

Using Type 1 Fonts with PostScript

The Download Type 1 fonts and the Convert TrueType to Type 1 options in the Options tab of the Print Options dialog box are designed with the occasional user of PostScript Type 1 fonts and laser service bureaus in mind. As you are aware, CorelDRAW! comes supplied with both TrueType and Type 1 fonts. Although the TrueType fonts are of very high quality, they do not contain the "hints" (program instructions) that allow genuine PostScript Type 1 fonts to print at extremely small sizes with very little degradation. Therefore, if you use text with a small type size in a drawing, you might choose to substitute equivalent Type 1 fonts for the TrueType fonts at printing time. Activate the Download Type 1 fonts option if you have specified Type 1 fonts in your drawing and your printer does not already have the fonts stored in it. You use the Convert TrueType to Type 1 if you have specified TrueType fonts in your drawing but you prefer to print with Type 1.

These options are intended for temporary use. If you have purchased downloadable fonts from Adobe or other PostScript type vendors and *always* want your printer to automatically substitute Type 1 fonts for CorelDRAW! fonts, you can use the Download Type 1 fonts option. Also, if you use the Download Type 1 fonts option when you send output files to a laser service bureau, the fonts are stored with the data in the file, so the service bureau does not need to have the font.

In the final sections of this chapter, you will find tips for smooth printing based on the type of printer you are using and the features of your artwork.

Hardware-Specific Tips

Even if you closely follow all recommended printing procedures, such as checking the printer Setup options or setting Transmission Retry at 300 seconds, you may encounter printing difficulties on occasion. Some difficulties involve settings for your specific printer type, while others may involve features of the artwork you are trying to print. This section deals with printing problems that could be dependent on hardware and makes suggestions for solving them. The final section, "Complex Artwork on PostScript Printers," deals with printing problems that might be related to features of the artwork itself.

Tip: Regardless of the type of printer you use, you may sometimes encounter one of several error messages indicating that you should cancel the printing process. In most cases, click on the Retry command button. Repeated attempts to print often force the data through your printer.

PostScript Printers and Controllers

CorelDRAW! is designed for PostScript Level 2 printers, with their 11 resident font families and at least 3MB of RAM. CorelDRAW! also runs on older versions of PostScript printers that contain only four font families, but you may experience slower performance or other limitations if the memory in your printer is not sufficient. If this happens, check with your printer dealer to see whether a memory upgrade is possible.

A number of so-called PostScript-compatible controllers and plug-in cartridges are available for the HP LaserJet and compatible printers. You should be aware that there is a distinction between genuine PostScript controller boards and cartridges (licensed by Adobe) and

Printing and Processing Your Images

PostScript-*compatible* controller boards and cartridges, which are only as compatible as their interpreters. If your LaserJet printer is equipped with a genuine Adobe PostScript controller board or cartridge, you should be able to print everything that would be possible on a genuine Adobe PostScript printer. This is not necessarily true for a printer equipped with a PostScript-compatible controller board or cartridge, although some of these components work extremely well.

If you have a genuine PostScript printer, or if your printer has a genuine PostScript controller board or cartridge, the following tips should help you avoid printing problems when running CorelDRAW!. Potential problems are organized according to whether your printer is connected to a parallel or a serial port.

Parallel Printers

Printer or job timeout problems are common with PostScript printers that are parallel-connected. To avoid such problems, check for the following:

Additional tips for printing complex artwork with PostScript printers are in the "Complex Artwork on PostScript Printers" section.

- The Print Manager should be turned off (see "Preparing to Print," earlier in this chapter).
- Make sure that your printer is set up for batch processing mode, not interactive mode. Interactive mode does not permit the printing of imported bitmaps.
- See whether you can change Wait timeout directly from the printer as well as from the Windows Control Panel. Many PostScript printers provide utilities that let you specify these times independent of any software application.
- Set the Job timeout, Device Not Selected, and Transmission Retry settings as recommended in the "Preparing to Print" section of this chapter.

Serial Printers

Although most PostScript printers attach to IBM-compatible computers with a parallel cable (the faster and preferred printing method), some printers require the use of a serial cable. To ensure trouble-free printing with a serial-connected printer, compare your printer setup with the following checklist:

- Use the Ports icon in the Control Panel and make certain that the settings are correct. (Refer to your printer manual.) Make sure that hardware handshaking ("Flow Control") is active.
- Check the length and quality of your printer cable. Some long or unshielded serial cables do not always transmit all available data with graphics applications.

HP LaserJet Printers and Compatibles

Since the HP LaserJet and compatible printers connect to your computer by means of a parallel rather than a serial cable, you should refer to the earlier section "Parallel Printers." Printers that are guaranteed to be 100 percent LaserJet compatible perform equally well with the genuine HP LaserJet. Printers that are HP LaserJet clones and that do not guarantee 100 percent compatibility may present erratic problems, which vary with the printer driver and manufacturer.

If your LaserJet or compatible is an older model and you have only 512K of memory, you will find that you are unable to print full-page graphics with complex features such as outlines and fountain fills. Many LaserJet-type printers split a graphic that is too large for memory and tile it over several sheets. If you plan to print large graphics regularly, see whether you can expand your printer's memory. If this is not possible, try reducing the size of the graphic on the page. Since object-oriented graphics can be scaled up or down without distortion, this should be a satisfactory solution. As a last resort, reduce the printing resolution of the graphic to 150 dpi, or even 75 dpi, in the printer Setup dialog box.

HP DeskJet and PaintJet

While the HP DeskJet is a black-and-white inkjet printer and the Paint Jet is a color inkjet printer, both are almost completely compatible with the HP LaserJet. There are different versions of the software driver for these printers, however. Check to make sure that you have the latest model driver when printing graphics from CorelDRAW!. In addition, avoid designing large filled objects or layered objects; the ink for these printers is water-based and could run or smear if you layer it too thickly.

Genuine HP and Other Plotters

The Windows driver for plotters seems to be written specifically for the HP Plotter line. The HP Plotter supports only hairline outlines and no fills for objects that you create in CorelDRAW!. If you have a clone from another manufacturer, the Windows driver may not work well for you when you print images from CorelDRAW!. Contact your plotter manufacturer to see if a driver for CorelDRAW! is available.

Dot-Matrix Printers

The results of printing CorelDRAW! graphics on dot-matrix printers are very erratic, owing to the large number of printer types available and the many different drivers written for them. Some dot-matrix printers cannot print complex files at all, while others print part of a page and stop. Dot-matrix printers that have multicolored ribbons do not lay all colors down on the page in the same order as Corel expects them. This can result in muddy colors that do not match what you see on your screen. Depending on the problem, you may wish to contact your printer manufacturer to see if a driver for Windows is available.

Complex Artwork on PostScript Printers

The term "complex artwork," when applied to CorelDRAW!, can include a variety of features. Among them are curves with many nodes, multiple fountain fills in an image, PostScript halftone screens and textures, and text converted to curves. Many printing problems that are traceable to the complexity of features are encountered chiefly with PostScript printers. This happens because the PostScript language has certain internal limits. When these are exceeded, the affected object may not print at all or may print incorrectly. For example, objects that contain more than 200 to 400 nodes may cause your PostScript print job to crash. If you are having this problem, try increasing the Flatness setting in the Print Options dialog box by increments of 3. As discussed earlier, this reduces the number of nodes in curves, and after only a couple of increments, there is a noticeable improvement. You might also try combining some of the objects in your drawings to reduce the total number of nodes, or ungrouping grouped objects.

You might not experience a problem with the same object if you are printing to an HP LaserJet printer, because the HP LaserJet does not recognize nodes; it interprets all graphics images simply as collections of pixels. Some PostScript printer manufacturers, such as QMS, allow you to run PostScript printers in LaserJet mode. If you have such a printer, try switching to LaserJet mode and printing your "problem" image again. If the file prints correctly, it is safe to guess that an internal PostScript limitation is causing printing problems in PostScript mode.

Downloadable PostScript Error Handler

You may not be aware (since it is undocumented) that both CorelDRAW! 5 and Windows 3.1 include error handlers that help you diagnose PostScript printing problems. As of this writing, CorelDRAW!'s is better. To understand how an error handler works, you need to know that PostScript prints the "bottom" or first-drawn object in the image first, followed by each succeeding layer. When you download the error handler and try to print a problem file, the printer begins with the first object and prints as far as it can. When the printer encounters an object that is problematic, it stops and prints out the objects completed so far, together with an error message. Although the messages are in PostScript code language, they are, in many cases, intelligible enough for you to decipher what the basic problem might be. The purchase of a relatively inexpensive PostScript manual, of which several are available, can help you even further.

To download the PostScript error handler to your printer and keep it resident there until you turn the printer off, follow these steps:

1. From the Print dialog box, click on the Setup command button.
2. From the Setup dialog box, click on the Options command button to access the Options dialog box.
3. From the Options dialog box, click on Advanced. From the Advanced Options dialog box, make sure that Print PostScript Error Information is checked. This setting has no effect if you send a file to a service bureau, since most service bureaus use their own error handlers.

The PostScript error handler should be helpful in fixing problems that already exist within a graphic. However, there are other measures you can take to design a graphic that will cause no printing problems. The following sections explain a few of these measures briefly.

Printing PostScript Textures

The PostScript textures described in Chapter 7 are created with highly complex mathematical algorithms. Sometimes, you may not be able to make an object with a PostScript texture print correctly. If this happens, try adjusting the parameters to avoid extremely dense patterns. If the image does not print at all, try removing excess objects. PostScript textures can be so memory-intensive that they do not tolerate many other objects within the same graphic. In general, you should use these textures as fills in a limited number of objects within a given graphic. Short text strings used as headlines (but not converted to curves) are among the best applications for PostScript texture fills.

If you are a desktop publisher, you may sometimes find that a page containing a CorelDRAW! graphic with PostScript textures does not print. Try removing everything from the page except the PostScript texture graphic, and then attempt to print the page again. Sometimes a page becomes too complex for PostScript if it contains both PostScript textures and other elements.

Printing Complex Curve Objects

As previously mentioned, the current version of PostScript may give you difficulty when you try to print images that contain objects with a large number of nodes. The exact number of nodes that will create a problem depends on the type of fill the object has. If you suspect that an object has too many nodes and could be causing problems, click on it with the Shape tool. The number of nodes contained in the object appears on the status line. If the number of nodes seems too high or approaches the danger zone, reshape the object and eliminate any unnecessary nodes, then combine objects and reduce curve flatness.

When you drag one or more control points of a curve object outward by a great distance, the boundary markers of the object may extend much farther outward than you can see. If you print a file containing many curve objects and some objects just do not print, it may be that you have not selected them. One remedy is to click on the Select All command in the Edit menu before you begin to print, and then activate Selected Objects in the Print dialog box. This procedure ensures that all objects in the graphic are selected, no matter how extensively you may have reshaped them.

Printing Fountain Fills

A common complaint when printing fountain-filled objects on PostScript printers is that *banding* can occur. In other words, the edges of each fountain stripe are clearly visible and do not blend into the next stripe smoothly. This occurs more often with 300 dpi printers than with Linotronic or other imagesetters that have a higher resolution. With LaserJet and compatible printers, solving this problem is easy: you simply increase the Preview Fountain Steps value in the Preferences dialog box to create a smoother blend.

To reduce banding on Fountain Fills when you print to a 300 dpi PostScript printer, increase the value for Fountain Steps in the Print Options dialog box by 10 or 20. There is an upper limit, though. The maximum number of gradations that you can have is determined by the formula $(dpi / lpi)^2$. If a blend contains a greater number of steps than this, you will get banding no matter how much you increase the number of Fountain Steps.

Tip: If you alter the default screen frequency for a draft printout on a 300 dpi printer, remember to change the Default Screen Frequency setting back to Default before you create an output file to be sent to a high-resolution imagesetter. Also keep in mind that when you alter the default screen frequency, your image should contain no objects that have a nonstandard halftone screen pattern.

300 DPI Printers Versus High-Resolution Imagesetters

It may sometimes happen that your graphic prints on your own 300 dpi PostScript printer, but causes a high-resolution imagesetter to crash. This occurs because at higher resolutions, the amount of information in a file multiplies. It is possible that your graphic exceeds certain internal PostScript limits at these higher resolutions, but doesn't at the lower resolution. To avoid such problems, try reducing the resolution at which the imagesetter prints, by resetting the Default Screen Frequency in the printer Setup dialog box. Alternatively, you can define a custom default screen frequency for the imagesetter before you create the output file. If you do so, make certain that your custom frequency is lower than that of the imagesetter. These measures help reduce the amount of data in fills and outlines.

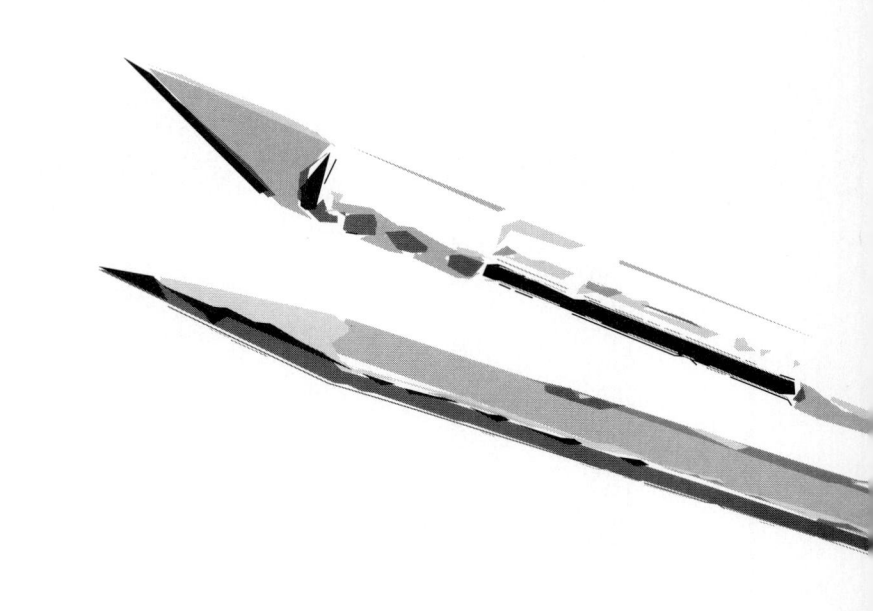

Imagination

CorelDRAW! in Action

WILLIAM SCHNEIDER
Imagination

Bill first scanned a photograph (of a man seated above Florence, Italy) in two different ways: as a gray-level bitmap, and as a monochrome bitmap. The monochrome bitmap (at the bottom, on the left) was given a navy blue color by selecting the Outline Color icon from the Outline Pen flyout menu, then specifying the color in the Outline Color dialog box. A transparent fill was chosen for the monochrome bitmap by choosing the X icon from the Fill Tool flyout menu. This allowed the fountain fill that lies behind the entire drawing to show through. The gray-level bitmap was cropped to a narrow vertical band centered on the man, then placed in front of and aligned with the monochrome bitmap.

The vertical riser above the man was created with two vertical rectangles exactly the same width as the gray-level bitmap of the man. The lower rectangle was given a fountain fill starting with a bottom color that matches the light gray at the top of the gray-level bitmap. This made the bitmap and the rectangle appear to be a continuous vertical band. Similarly, the upper rectangle contains a fountain fill that starts with a bottom color that matches the color at the top of the rectangle below it, so they also appear to be a continuous band. The curves that form the top end of the band were created by first making circles tangent to the left and right edges of the vertical band. Then, using the Shaping Tool, the circles were opened up into connecting arcs and given uniform fills. The three sets of clouds were hand drawn, scanned, then traced in CorelDRAW!. Using the Shaping tool, adjustments were made to the cloud objects to clean them up and smooth them, then they were each given a fountain fill. To ensure that the counters (the center curves in a, g, and o) printed correctly, each counter curve was combined with the outer curve of its letter.

Bill created the area behind the spheres by first creating a checkerboard, stretching it, removing and combining squares, and filling it with a fountain fill. To create the checkerboard pattern he first made a single square by dragging the Rectangle tool while holding down the CTRL key. Then, using the Pick Tool, he selected the square, held down CTRL, dragged one of its handles across the square until an adjacent outline appeared, then clicked the right mouse button before releasing the left button. This caused the square to leave a copy of itself as it was moved to the adjacent position. Then, using CTRL-R, he repeated the operation several times to create a chain of squares. He then selected every other one and offset them to create two rows or columns of the checkerboard. He duplicated this pattern to create the rest of the checkerboard pattern. All of the squares were combined into a single object for which a fountain fill was used.

This piece was in CorelArtShow 4: Page 14, File: ENV00039.CDR. You may contact Bill in care of:

> William Schneider
> 15 Morris Avenue
> Athens, OH 45701
> Voice: (614) 594-3205

The art on the opposite page was created by and is the property of William Schneider. It is used with permission.

13

CREATING
SPECIAL EFFECTS

The Effects menu, shown in Figure 13-1, is used to produce dramatic effects in your work. For example, as you have seen in earlier chapters, the Transform roll-up allows you to position, rotate, scale and mirror, size, or skew an object. With the Rotate or Skew feature, you can specify an angle at which the selected text is to be rotated or specify that the angle is to be skewed horizontally or vertically. The Size and Scale & Mirror features allow

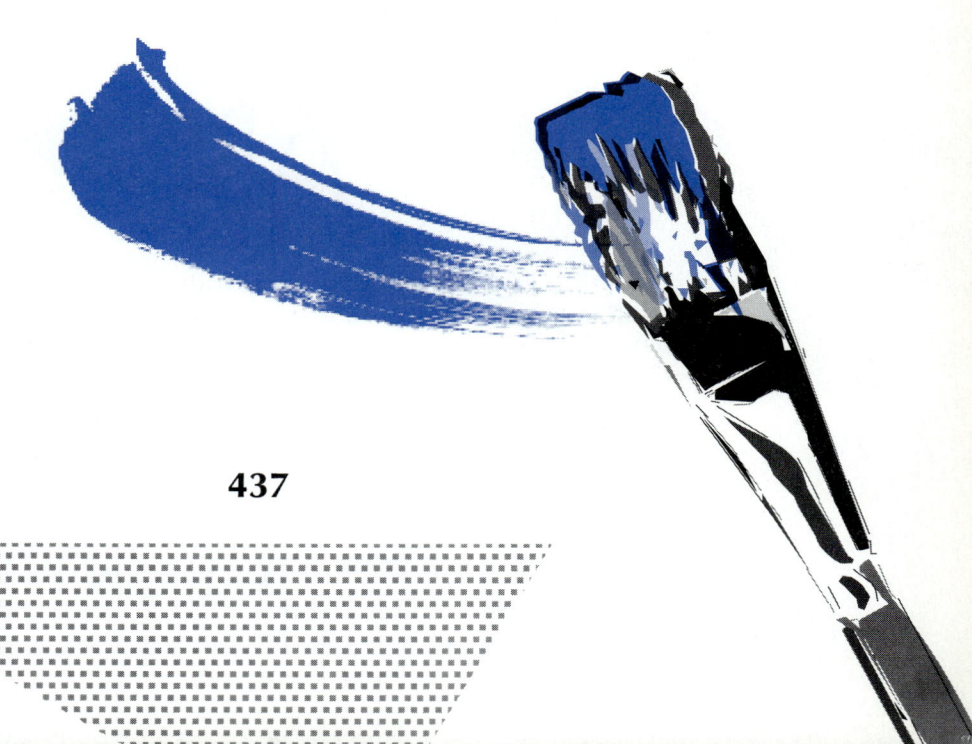

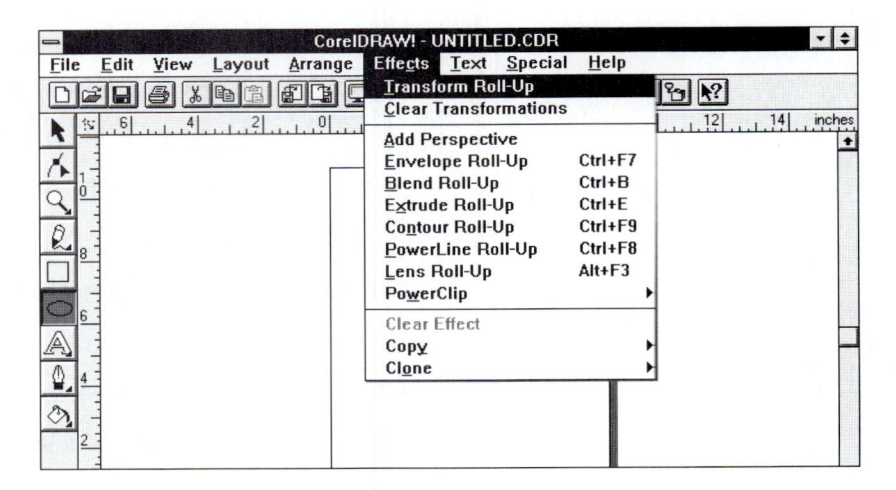

Effects menu
Figure 13-1.

you to elongate a text image, enlarge it on all sides, or cause it to mirror either horizontally or vertically. Figure 13-2 shows examples of these features; you can learn more about them in Chapter 8.

In this chapter, you will explore the rest of the features on the Effects menu. For instance, another special effect is the Add Perspective feature. It allows you to create depth in text or graphics by stretching the borders of an object. The object seems to fade away into the distance. You can create a simple 3-D effect or a more complex version, such as that seen here:

With the Envelope feature, you can cause text within the envelope to conform to any shape you make the envelope. In CorelDRAW! an *envelope* is a box that surrounds text or graphics. You can pull the envelope in different directions, distorting the shape as you might with putty. Any object within the envelope will follow the shape of the envelope, as seen here:

Creating Special Effects

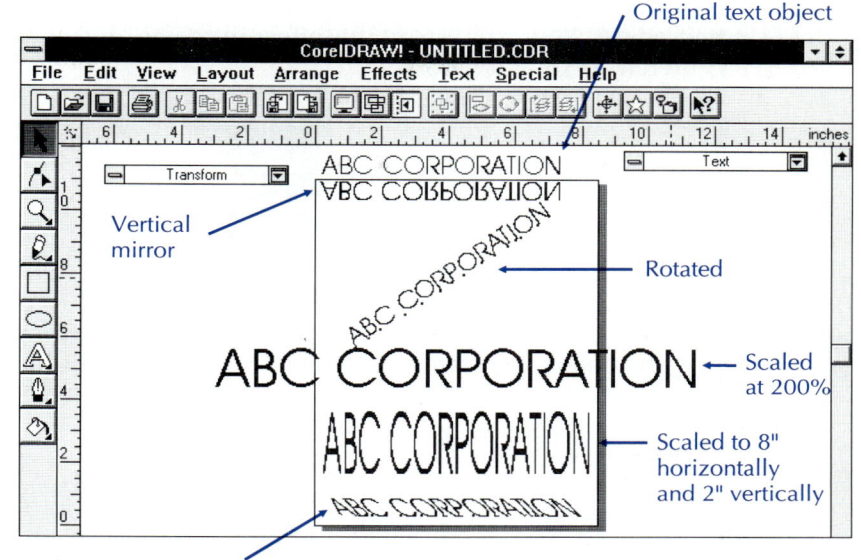

Examples of the Transform effects
Figure 13-2.

- Original text object
- Vertical mirror
- Rotated
- Scaled at 200%
- Scaled to 8" horizontally and 2" vertically
- Skewed to 45 degrees

Another special effect is the Blend feature, which allows you to blend one object into another, as shown here:

You define the beginning and ending points, and CorelDRAW! fills in the blend steps.

The Extrude feature gives depth to objects. An example of an open path extruded surface is shown here:

Contour allows you to create a blended type of effect with a single graphic or text object. You can display this effect inside or outside an object, or centered, as shown here:

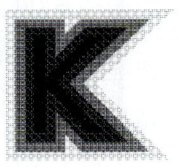

Another feature in the Effects menu is PowerLine. This feature allows you to draw a line of varying width and darkness. It differs from the Pencil tool in that the object is a graphic having its own fill, outline, and nib attributes. An example is shown here (this was created from the letter "H"):

A Lens feature is used to simulate placing a lens over an object, with the lens acting as a transparent window, a magnifier, a color filter (by filtering, adding or inverting colors), or a brightener. An example of a magnifier lens is shown here:

The final feature in the Effects menu is PowerClip, which allows you to place one object, or group or objects, into another. One object becomes a container and the other the contained item. In this example, an apple was placed into a box:

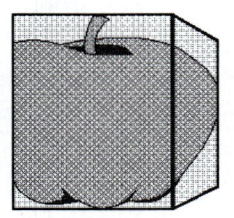

Creating Special Effects

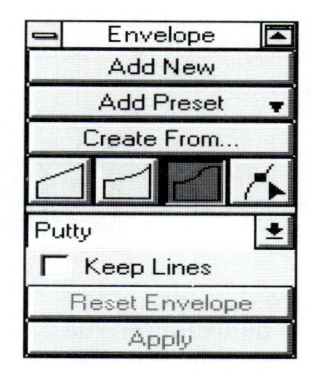

Envelope roll-up
Figure 13-3.

As you can see, the Effects menu contains many powerful and dramatic drawing effects. You will explore these special effects beginning with the Envelope feature. If your computer is not turned on, turn it on now and bring up CorelDRAW!.

Using an Envelope

An envelope is a bounding box with eight handles on it that surrounds the text or graphic. You pull the handles to reshape the object within the envelope.

The Envelope roll-up window contains the options for applying and editing envelopes. It contains eight basic operations, as shown in Figure 13-3.

You can add a new envelope to a selected object. You may either apply the first envelope to an object or apply a second object over an object shared by the first envelope.

With the Add Preset button, you can select from a predefined group of envelope shapes, as shown here:

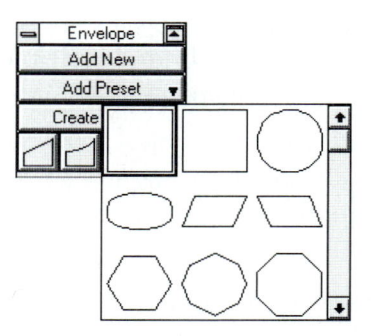

With the Create From button, you can also create an envelope shape from an existing object to place around a new object. You may select one of four editing modes that determine how the envelope can be reshaped, as shown here:

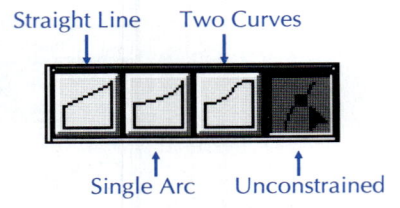

Straight Line   Two Curves

Single Arc   Unconstrained

The first three modes allow you to change the shape of a side of the envelope in a specific way. The first one allows you to pull the side in a straight line, the second in a curved line, the third in a line with two curves. The fourth envelope editing mode is unconstrained. It allows you to pull in any direction, and to change a line to a curve.

As you move the handles, the envelope changes shape. When you tell CorelDRAW! to apply the editing changes, the contents of the envelope are reshaped to conform to the new shape, as you will see shortly.

By clicking on the list box beneath the editing modes, you can see a list of mapping options, shown here:

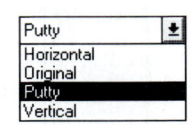

Putty
Horizontal
Original
Putty
Vertical

These options control how an object will be fitted to the envelope. There are five possibilities:

- *Horizontal* Maps the object to fit the horizontal dimensions of the envelope.
- *Original* Maps the object's boundary box (selected handles) to the envelope's shape. It produces an exaggerated effect.
- *Putty* Maps only the corners of the boundary box to the envelope's corners.
- *Vertical* Maps the object to fit the vertical dimensions on the envelope.
- *Text* Automatically applies when working with paragraph text. The other options are unavailable. The Text option can be used to flow text around graphics.

You will now create and duplicate some text to use for the first three editing modes.

Creating and Duplicating Text

To prepare for the first exercise, you need to create a piece of text and then duplicate it twice.

1. Set the screen to actual magnification (1:1). Click on the Text tool and then click on the page, at about the middle left.
2. Type **Happy Birthday** and select the text by dragging on it. Open the Text roll-up and change the type size to 36 points and the font to Cooper Md BT. Click on Apply to change the text. With the Pick tool, center the text on the screen. Now you will copy the text twice so that there are three copies, one for each of the first three editing modes.
3. From the Edit menu, select Duplicate for the first copy.
4. Press CTRL-D to duplicate another copy. The three copies will be stacked on top of each other with the edges of the bottom copies peeking out, as shown here:

Now you will move them apart.

5. Click on the Pick tool. Place the mouse pointer on an edge of the selected text. Press and hold the mouse button while moving the box outline to the bottom of the screen. Center the outline horizontally on the screen. When you release the mouse button, the selected copy of the text will be moved from the stack onto the screen.
6. Click on the top of the stack to select the next text object. Repeat step 5, but move the second copy from the stack to the top of the screen. The last copy will remain at the center of the screen.
7. Space the three text units so that you can easily work with each one. Figure 13-4 shows an example of the screen with the three copies rearranged.

Now you are ready to work with the first envelope editing mode.

Straight Line Envelope

The Straight Line editing mode allows you to pull envelope handles in a straight line. You can move one handle at a time.

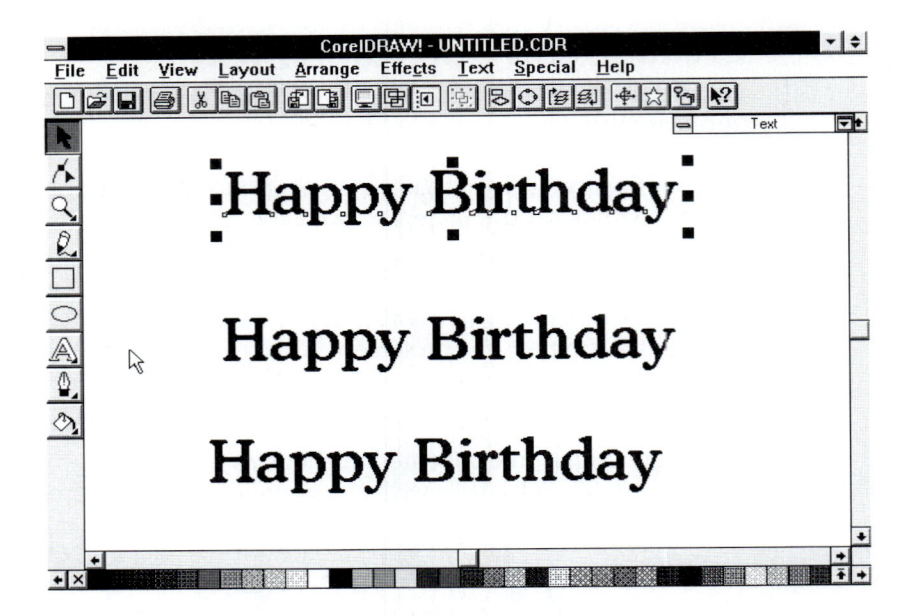

Text to be used for illustrating envelopes
Figure 13-4.

In Unconstrained mode, all handles move in any direction.

As in all of the first three editing modes, the handles can be moved only in a restricted way: handles located in the center of the sides move left or right; handles located in the top and bottom center move up or down; corner handles move up or down or left or right.

The easiest way to understand the feature is to try it out. Follow these steps:

1. If the top text object is not selected, select it by clicking on it so that the selection box surrounds it.
2. Display the Envelope roll-up from the Effects menu.
3. Choose the first editing mode, Straight Line.
4. Click on Add New.

   The envelope will appear on the screen surrounding the selected text. You can see the eight handles. Also, the Shape tool is selected, and the pointer turns into a shaping arrow.

5. Pull the top middle handle up, as shown here:

6. Pull the bottom center handle up as well.
7. Click on Apply to have the text conform to the envelope, as shown here:

Happy Birthday

You can see how the text conforms to the new straight line. Next you will see how the Single Arc editing mode differs.

Single Arc Envelope

The Single Arc editing mode allows you to create an arc by pulling the handles up, down, right, or left. Handles can be pulled only one at a time, and, as with the Straight Line mode, they can be moved only in a restricted way: handles located in the center of the sides move left or right; handles located in the top and bottom center move up and down; corner handles move up or down or left and right.

Follow these steps to try it out:

1. Click on the Pick tool, then select the second text copy by clicking on it so a selection box surrounds it. 
2. From the Envelope roll-up, choose the second option, the Single Arc.
3. Click on Add New.
4. Pull the top middle handle up.
5. Pull the bottom middle handle up.
6. Click on Apply.

The text will conform to the Single Arc envelope, as shown here:

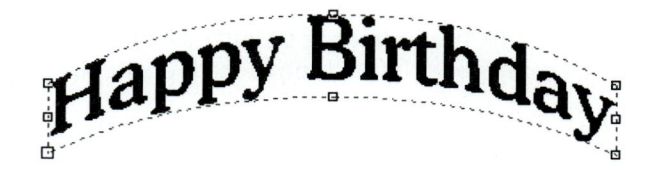

Happy Birthday

You can see how the Straight Line and Single Arc editing modes differ. Now try out the third editing mode.

Two Curves Envelope

The third choice allows you to create two curves by pulling one of the eight handles. You can move only one handle at a time, and the same restrictions apply as in the Straight Line and Single Arc modes.

Follow these steps to try the Two Curves editing mode:

1. Click on the Pick tool and click on the third text object so it is selected.
2. From the Envelope roll-up, choose the third item, Two Curves.
3. Click on Add New. The envelope will surround the third text object.
4. Pull the top middle handle up. Then pull the bottom middle handle up.
5. Click on Apply. The text will conform to the Two Curves envelope, as shown here:

You can see how two curves are created out of the line, shaping the text in an entirely different way. These three envelope editing modes have an additional feature that can be used to constrain the shapes.

Using CTRL and SHIFT with Envelopes

You can use CTRL or SHIFT with the three editing modes to produce surprising results. Three effects can take place:

- If you hold down CTRL while you drag on a handle, the opposite handle will move in the same direction.
- If you hold down SHIFT while you drag on a handle, the opposite handle will move in the opposite direction.
- Finally, if you hold both SHIFT and CTRL while dragging a handle, all four corners or sides will move in opposite directions.

You can use these keys with any of the first three Envelope options. Try the CTRL method now with the first text object on your screen.

1. Click on the top text image with the Shape tool so that the envelope and handles appear on the screen. Now experiment for a moment.

Creating Special Effects

2. From the Envelope roll-up, click on Add New to get an envelope around the text. Note that it is not the right one. The previous envelope correctly reflected its shape.
3. Click on Reset Envelope to restore the previous envelope.
4. Press CTRL while dragging the top middle handle down.
5. Click on Apply. The text should be changed, as shown here:

Happy Birthday

You can see two immediate effects: First, the top and bottom sides move in the same direction. You expected that. Second, and unexpectedly, the lines are *not* being shaped according to the Straight Line edit mode that was earlier applied to this particular text object. Instead, the lines are being shaped according to the Two Curves edit mode, the last mode applied. Whenever you apply a new editing mode to any envelope on the screen, all new edits will be assigned the new mode as well. If you need to change the shape of an object while retaining the original edit mode, simply reselect that mode before making your changes.

Now you will try the SHIFT method with the second text object.

1. Click on the middle text object so that the envelope and handles appear on the screen.
2. From the Envelope roll-up, select the Single Arc option.
3. Press SHIFT while dragging the top right handle out to the right. The left and right sides will move in opposite directions, as shown here:

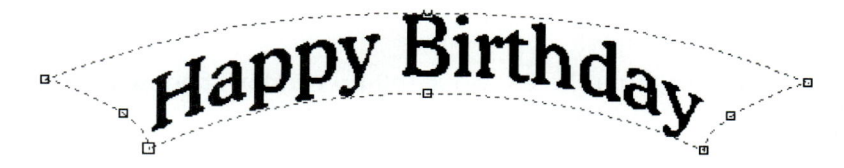

Happy Birthday

4. Click on Apply; you'll see an interesting effect.

The SHIFT-CTRL method is just as easy.

1. Click on the bottom text object to select it.

2. From the Envelope roll-up, select the Two Curves option.
3. Press SHIFT-CTRL while dragging the top right handle to the right. The top and bottom and both sides all move in opposite directions, as shown here:

Happy Birthday

4. Click on Apply.

These techniques are particularly useful when you are changing the shape of drawings located in circles or rectangles and you want one or all of the dimensions to be altered to the same degree.

Now you will explore the fourth envelope editing mode.

Unconstrained Envelope

The Unconstrained editing mode is the most dynamic of the four modes. The handles can be moved in any direction, and they contain control points that can be used to fine-tune and bend the objects even more dynamically. Unlike the first three Envelope options, the Unconstrained mode lets you select several handles and move them as a unit. To experiment with this, first clear the screen of its contents, then follow these steps:

1. Select New from the File menu. Click on No when asked about saving the current screen contents.
2. Select the Text tool and click on the middle left of the screen.
3. Type **Not Constrained**. Select the text and, from the Text roll-up, change the type size to 70 points and the font to Bookman. Click on Apply.
4. From the Envelope roll-up window, choose the fourth submenu option, Unconstrained.
5. Click on Add New.

   You will see the text object surrounded by the envelope and its handles. Also, the pointer turns into a Shape tool, and the handles of the bounding box become nodes.
6. Pull the top middle handle or node up and then the bottom middle node down, as shown in the following illustration.

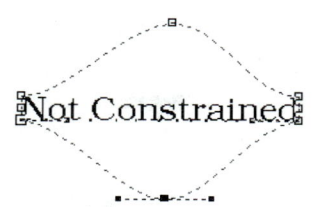

You can see that a pair of control points appeared first on the top middle, and then on the bottom middle, nodes. These control points, like Shape tool control points, allow you to alter the shape by exaggerating and bending the curve.

7. Place the pointer on the left control point of the bottom middle node and pull it down. (To experiment with it, move it down and then back up so that you will see what happens with the handle.)
8. Click on the top middle node to select it. Place the pointer on the right control point of the top middle node and pull it up, as shown here:

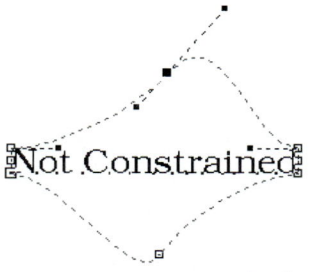

Click on Apply. Now, suppose you want the last letters to curve up at the end.

9. While holding SHIFT, click first on the bottom middle node and then on the bottom right node. Release SHIFT. Now you can move all selected nodes together.
10. Hold down the mouse button and pull the bottom middle node down, as shown here:

11. Click on Apply for another interesting effect.

One way that you can use the Unconstrained edit mode is to modify text to conform to a shape, for example, text within a circle or oval. First you create the circle, oval, or whatever shape you want as a border and then move the text with its envelope within the border. Next, you manually move the control points of the text so that they correspond with the border shape. Then, if you don't want the border to appear, you can delete it.

Continue to experiment until you are comfortable with the Unconstrained edit mode. Then you can move on to more Envelope features.

Adding a New Envelope

Sometimes you may want to use more than one of the editing modes on an object. Adding a new envelope allows you to do this. You apply an envelope and shape the object with it. Then you add a new envelope, which replaces the first envelope while retaining its shape. With the new envelope, you select a new editing mode and change the shape again. To try this out, follow these steps:

1. Clear the screen by selecting New from the File menu. Click on No when asked if you want to save the screen contents.
2. Select the Text tool and click on the middle left of the screen.
3. Type **New Envelope**, select the text and, from the Text roll-up, set the type size to 80 points and select the Futura Md BT font. Click on Apply.
4. From the Envelope roll-up window, attach an envelope by selecting the Straight Line editing mode and then Add New.
5. Click on the top left handle and drag it up.
6. Click on the bottom right handle and drag it down, as shown here:

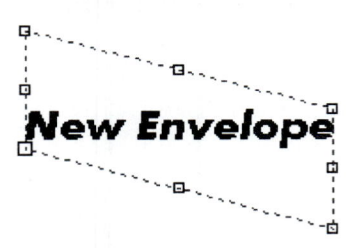

7. Click on Apply.

Now you will apply a new envelope and change the shape using another editing mode on top of the Straight Line editing mode.

1. From the Envelope roll-up, select the Two Curves editing mode. Click on Add New.

Creating Special Effects

2. Now drag the lower-right handle down, as shown in Figure 13-5
3. Click on Apply.

Notice that the text is limited by the original envelope's shape. The text adopts a new image within the constraints of both envelopes

Tip: One way that a new envelope can be used is with certain fonts that do not bend or reshape themselves exactly as you want. You can form the basic shape with one of the first three edit modes and then apply the Unconstrained edit mode to fine-tune the text. In this way you can manually form the letters with more precision than you might get with the font alone.

4. Remove the previous envelopes by clicking on Clear Transformations from the Effects menu.

Now you can copy an envelope to a new object.

Create From

The Create From command allows you to copy the envelope and its current shape to a new object. The new object does not need its own envelope.

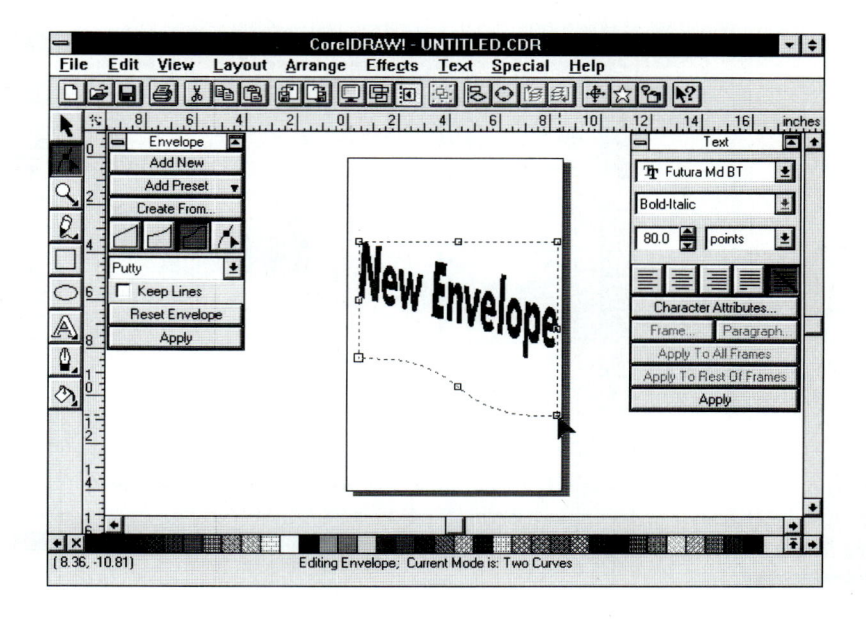

Using Add New Envelope to reshape a text object within the borders of a previous envelope
Figure 13-5.

However, the copied-from object must be a Single Curve object, having nodes and control points. To try out this feature, you will first create a new object.

1. Click on the Ellipse tool. Draw a circle below the text, using the CTRL key. (If necessary click on No fill in the color palette.)
2. Specify the Two Curves editing mode, select Add New, and click on Apply. Using the Shape tool, pull the top middle node down and the bottom middle node up. Click on Apply.
3. Select the text again with the Pick tool.
4. Select Create From in the Envelope roll-up.

   The pointer will turn into a thick arrow. You will move the arrow to the source of the envelope, which is the circle.

5. Move the arrow to the circle, and click on it.
6. Click on Apply.

The destination object, that is, the ellipse, will be reshaped with the new tool to match the text, as shown in Figure 13-6.

Sometimes you might want to start over again. Clearing an envelope allows you to do that.

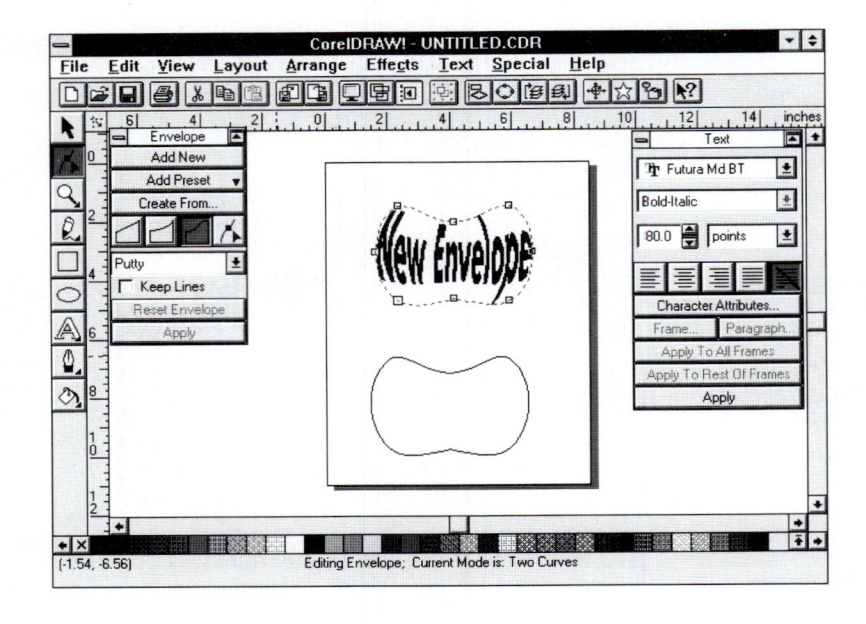

Using Create From to reshape a second object, in this case, text into a circle

Figure 13-6.

Clearing an Envelope

The Clear Envelope command on the Effects menu (not on the roll-up) removes the current envelope and all shape changes that occurred with it. The Clear Envelope appears on the Effects menu when you have chosen the Envelope roll-up. If you have applied more than one envelope, only the most recent one will be removed.

To clear the last envelope from the current text object, select Clear Envelope from the Effects menu. The drawing will be returned to the previous Straight Line edit mode. However, if you have applied a perspective (perspectives are discussed shortly) to the object after applying the most recent envelope, the perspective must be removed before you can clear the envelope.

Note: The Clear Transformations command, found on the Effects menu, removes all envelopes, restoring the drawing to its original shape. If you have applied perspectives, they will also be removed and the original shape restored.

Creating Perspective Effects

Perspective gives an object a sense of depth, as if the object were moving away from you. This effect can be applied from one- or two-point perspective views. Figure 13-7 shows the two kinds of perspective. The one-point perspective, on the top, gives the effect of moving away from you in a straight line. The two-point perspective, on the bottom, distorts the view so that the object is moving away and being twisted in the process.

Using One- or Two-Point Perspective

You apply perspective in much the same way that you change the shape of an envelope. A perspective bounding box with handles surrounds the object. You can drag the handles to shorten or lengthen the object, giving the perspective you want. Follow these steps to try it out:

1. Clear the screen by double-clicking on the Envelope roll-up's Control Menu, and then select New from the File menu. Click on No when asked if you want to save the screen contents.

2. If the rulers are not showing, click on Rulers in the View menu to display them. Pull the Zero Guides to the lower-left corner of the page. Place a horizontal guideline at 9 inches and a vertical guideline at 1 inch.

3. Select the Text tool and click at the intersection of the guidelines.

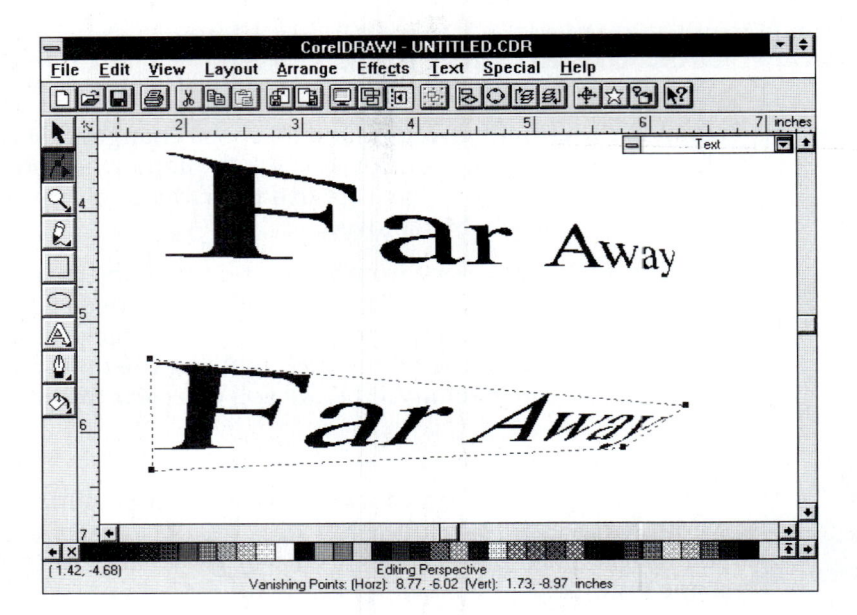

Examples of one-point and two-point perspectives
Figure 13-7.

4. Type **Moving Away**, select the text, and with the Text roll-up, set the type size to 60 points and the font to Times New Roman. Ensure that Normal is the selected style. Click Apply when you are done.

5. Select Add Perspective from the Effects menu.

    An envelope will surround the text, and the pointer will change to the Shape tool. When you place it on the handles, it will change to a crosshair. You move the handles according to the coordinates, which tell the location of the pointer. The coordinates are shown in the left corner of the status line.

    You will now change the shape of the text object. To change to one-point perspective, drag the handle either up, down, right, or left (that is, vertically or horizontally). In the following instructions and in the next several exercises, you will see sets of coordinates. These are meant as guidelines and are approximate. The coordinates are in inches and always have the horizontal displacement before the vertical.

6. Place the pointer on the bottom right handle and drag it vertically, straight down, until the coordinates are approximately 5.7 and 8.0.

7. Drag the bottom left handle vertically, straight down, until the coordinates are approximately 1.0 and 6.0, as in Figure 13-8. This is an example of a one-point perspective.

Creating Special Effects

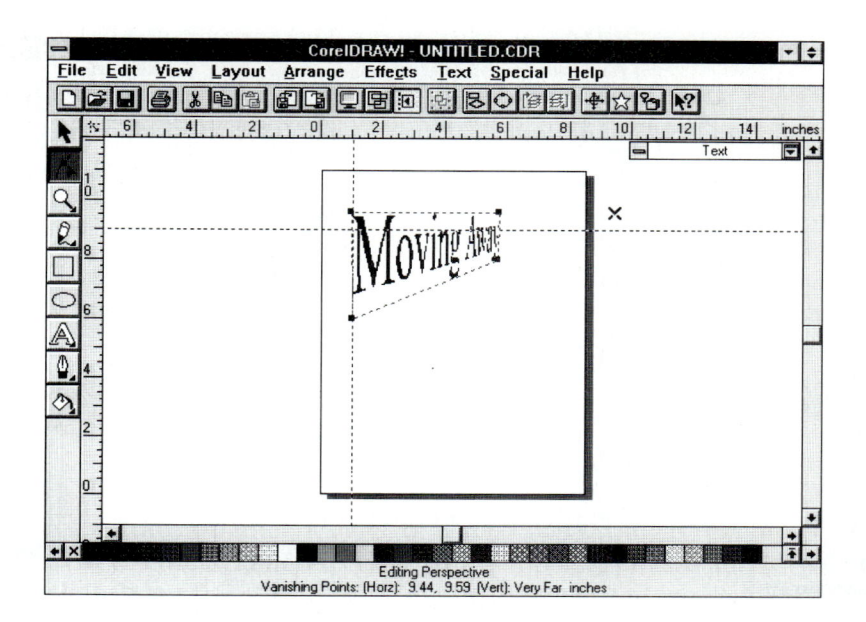

Example of one-point perspective created by dragging the handles straight down
Figure 13-8.

Now you will alter the shape to add the two-point perspective. You do this by dragging the handles either toward or away from the center of the object. If you drag toward the object, the shape is pushed under; if you drag away from the object, the shape is pulled out toward you.

8. Drag the handles as close as possible to the following coordinates, as shown in Figure 13-9.

    Upper-right corner: 6.9, 9.0
    Lower-right corner: 6.6, 8.0
    Lower-left corner: 2.0, 6.5

You should see two X symbols, known as *vanishing points,* which you will learn about next. One X may be hidden beneath the bottom of the screen. Scroll up to see it.

Using the Vanishing Point

In Figure 13-9, just off the page on the right, is the horizontal vanishing point. On the bottom of the page is the vertical vanishing point. Each of these points is marked with an X.

You can change the perspective by moving the vanishing point itself. By moving the vanishing point toward the object, the edge closest to the point becomes vertically shorter; the edge becomes vertically longer when the point is moved away from the edge.

Example of two-point perspective created by dragging the handles diagonally toward or away from the center of the object
Figure 13-9.

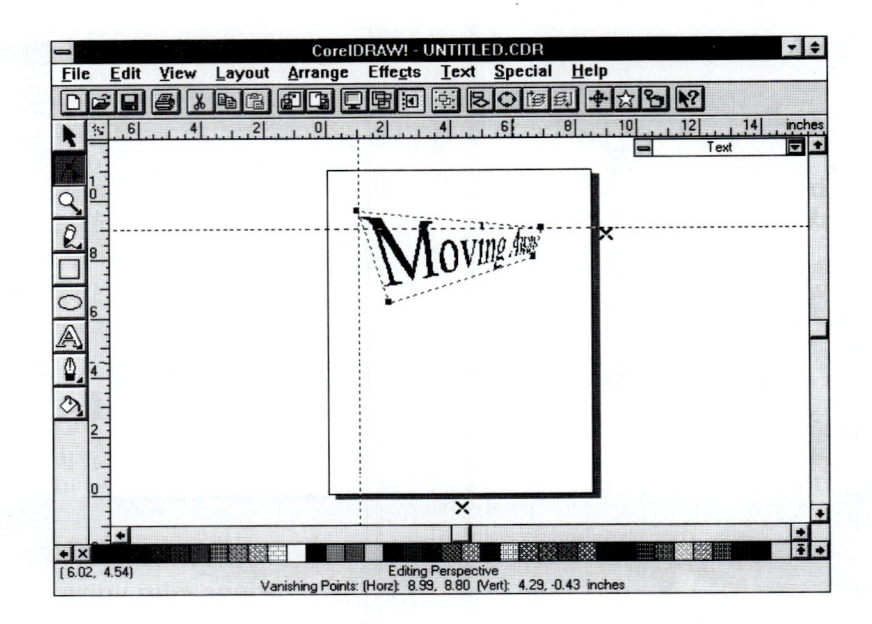

When you move the vanishing point parallel to the object, the far side will remain stationary, while the side nearest the point moves in the direction you drag the vanishing point.

Take a moment now to play with the vanishing point. When you are satisfied, you can explore some of the other perspective features.

Adding a New Perspective

You can add a new perspective to an object on top of one that already exists. This allows you to change the perspective, within the limits of the perspective already applied. To see how this is done, follow these steps:

1. Select Add Perspective from the Effects menu. A new, second bounding box will be applied to the object. Now you will change the perspective again.
2. Drag the handles to the following coordinates, or close to them, as shown in Figure 13-10.

   Upper-right handle: 5.6, 8.0
   Lower-left handle: 2.0, 6.3
   Lower-right handle: 8.2, 2.5

Now you will apply this perspective to a new object.

Creating Special Effects

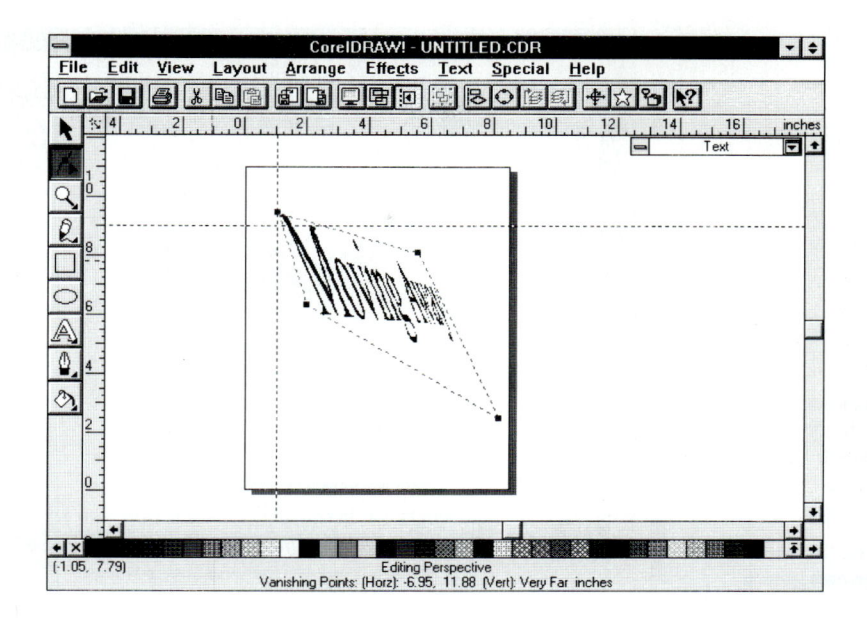

Changing shape with Add New perspective
Figure 13-10.

Copy Perspective From

When you select the Copy Perspective From option, you use the shape of one object to change the perspective of another one. First, you will create a form to which the perspective will be applied.

1. Select the Ellipse tool and draw a perfect circle under the text object.
2. From the Copy command on the Effects menu, select Perspective From in the submenu. The thick arrow will appear.
3. Move the tip of the arrow to the outline of the text object and click on it. The circle will be redrawn with the new perspective.
4. Use the Pick tool to drag the circle over the text object. (It doesn't matter if the reshaped circle isn't the same size as the text.)
5. Click on No fill (the X) in the lower-left corner of your screen.
6. The result should look like Figure 13-11. (It may differ because of the work you did with the vanishing point.)

Clearing a Perspective

Clear Perspective, similar to Clear Envelope, removes the most recent perspective applied to an object. The Clear Perspective option appears when

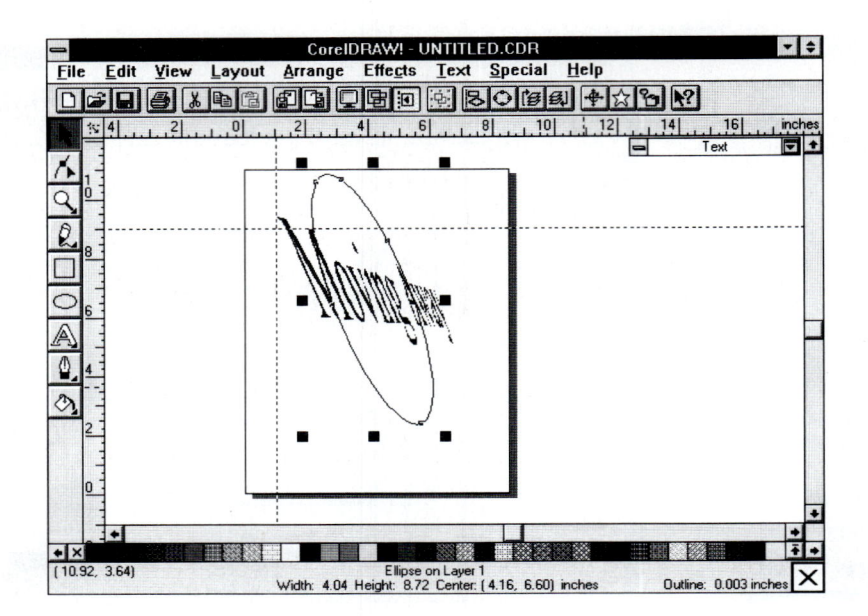

The circle reshaped with a copied perspective
Figure 13-11.

you have chosen Add Perspective. If you've applied more than one perspective, only the last one is removed.

If you've applied an envelope over a perspective, you must first remove the envelope before the perspective can be removed. Before you remove the envelope, be sure to duplicate the object in order to retain the shape you have created with the envelope. Then you can restore the shape by using the Copy Envelope From command after the perspective is removed.

Notice that Clear Transformations in the Effects menu will clear all perspectives and envelopes from an object at once. This is used when you want to restore an object to its original shape.

Now remove the perspective from the current object by following these steps:

1. Select the text and ellipse with the Pick tool.
2. Select Clear Perspective from the Effects menu. The shape will be changed.
3. Select Clear Transformations. See the change again.
4. Select New from the File menu. Do not save the changes.

Creating Special Effects

Blending Objects

The Blend command causes one object to be blended into another by a number of connecting images. For example, you can turn a square into a circle with 20 intermediate images. You can also use this feature to create highlights and airbrush effects. The images can be of different colors, line weights, fills, and so on.

Before the objects are blended, you must fill them and place them where you want them on the screen. And, of course, first you must create the objects to be blended.

1. Set the magnification to 1:1. Select the Text tool and click on the upper-left area of the screen.
2. Type **Happy**, select the text by dragging on it and, from the Text roll-up, set the type size to 60 points and the font to Revue BT, Normal. Click on Apply.
3. While the text object is still selected, click on the yellow in the palette at the bottom of your screen as the fill for the word "Happy."
4. With the text still selected, click on the lower-center area of the screen.
5. Type **Birthday**, select the text by dragging on it and, with the Text roll-up, set the type size to 80 points and the font to Revue BT. Click on Apply. Close the Text roll-up and move it to one side.
6. Click on a navy blue in the palette at the bottom of your screen for the word "Birthday."
7. Move both objects where you can see them on the screen.

Now you are ready to blend the two objects.

Blending Two Objects

Blending is done with the Blend roll-up window. To blend the objects, you must first select the two objects. Then you simply open the Blend roll-up window, tell CorelDRAW! how many steps are needed between the two objects, and click on Apply.

1. From the Edit menu, select Select All. You must be careful that both objects are selected. If they are not, you will not be able to use the Blend command.
2. When both objects are selected, select Blend Roll-Up from the Effects menu. The Blend roll-up window, shown on the following page, will appear.

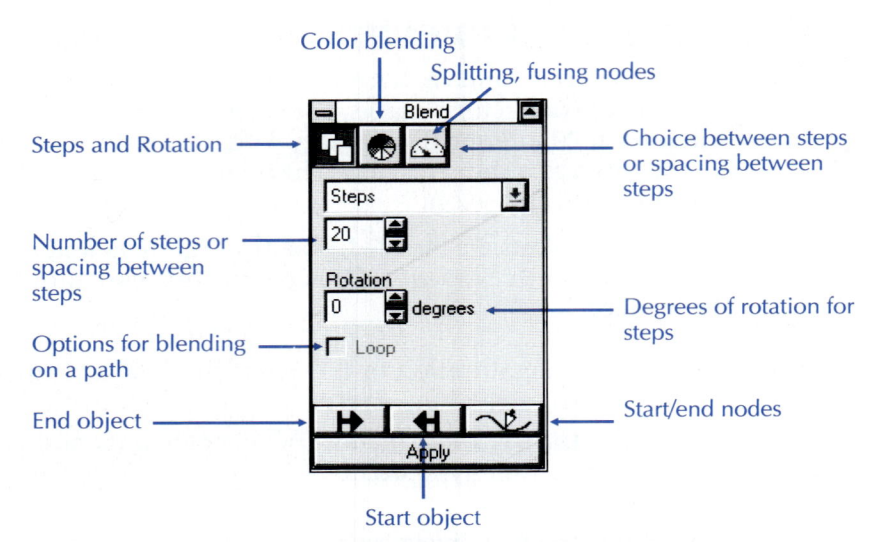

Blend roll-up callouts:
- Color blending
- Splitting, fusing nodes
- Steps and Rotation
- Choice between steps or spacing between steps
- Number of steps or spacing between steps
- Degrees of rotation for steps
- Options for blending on a path
- Start/end nodes
- End object
- Start object

The menu contains three main modes, represented by the icons on the upper left of the roll-up. The first displays the Steps and Rotation controls. The second displays color blending attributes, and the third provides controls for splitting and fusing blends.

The Steps and Rotation controls, on your screen now, are used to control how many steps you want in the blend and what degree of rotation will occur between the two objects. The Loop check box controls where the center of rotation is to be. You'll see its effects shortly. At the bottom of the menu are three controls. The two arrows allow you to select the start (the right-pointing arrow) and end (the left-pointing arrow) objects. The rightmost icon is used to manage the blend path.

You now tell CorelDRAW! the number of intervening steps between the two objects. It assumes 20 steps, which is acceptable for this example. You will indicate the degree of rotation and whether to map matching nodes in a minute.

3. Type in **10** steps and accept the 0 degrees of rotation. Click on Apply. You will see the two objects blended on the screen, as in Figure 13-12.

Next you will see what the rotation can do.

Rotating the Blended Objects

You can cause the blended objects to be rotated by putting a degree of rotation in the Blend roll-up window. You cause the intervening steps to be

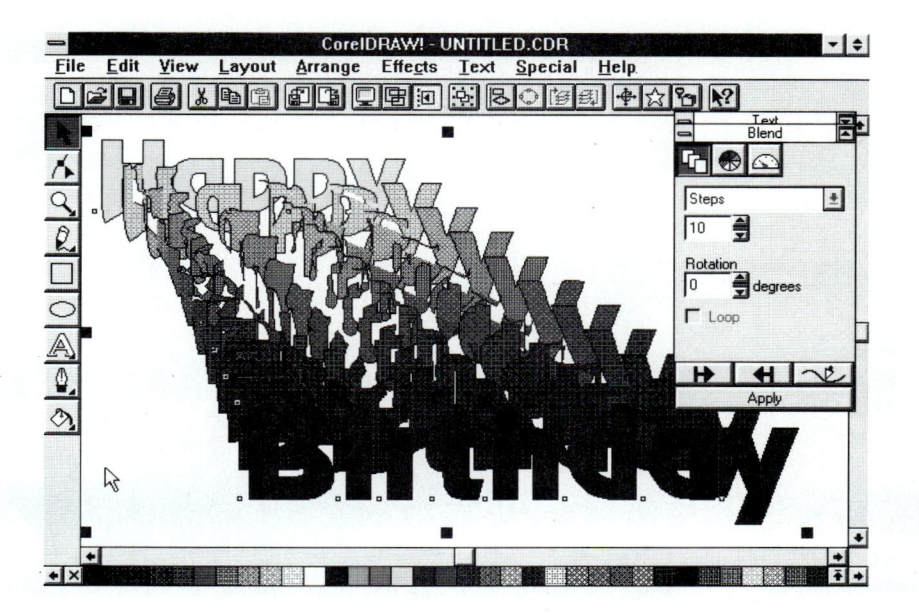

Creating Special Effects

Blending of "Happy" into "Birthday" with no rotation
Figure 13-12.

rotated counterclockwise if a positive number is entered; clockwise if a negative number is entered.

The Blend roll-up allows you to specify the degrees of rotation to be used in the intervening steps. Let's see how this is used.

1. Change the degree of rotation to 95.0 in the Blend roll-up window. Click on Loop and click on Apply.

Tip: Clicking on the Loop option makes the blend rotate around a center point midway between the beginning and the ending objects' centers of rotation. If Loop is not selected, the blend will rotate around the object's own center of rotation. Experiment to see the differences.

The effects of blending will appear on the screen, as shown in Figure 13-13.

Now try out clockwise rotation with these steps:

2. In the Blend roll-up, type **–90.0** for the degree of rotation and click on Loop to deselect it. Click on Apply. The results look something like Figure 13-14.

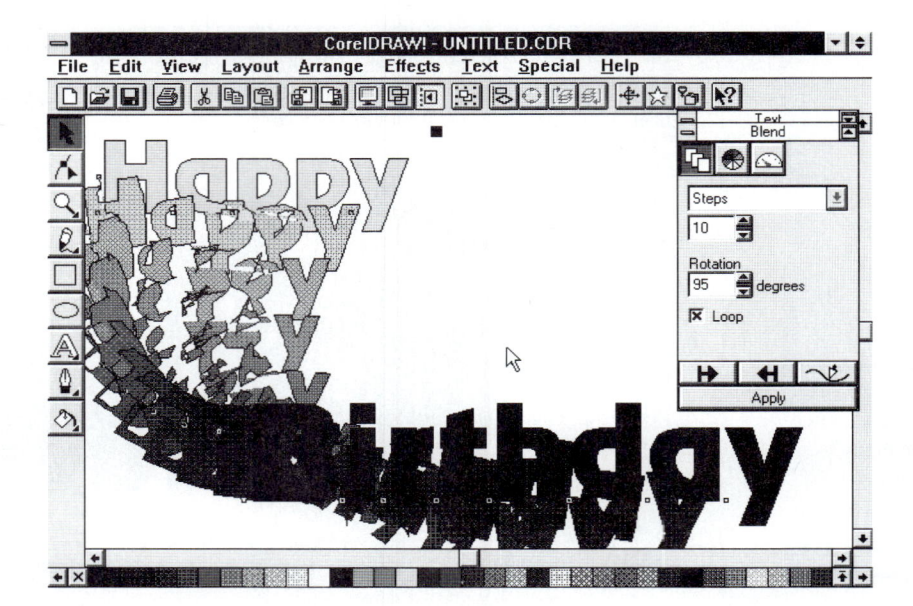

"Happy" blended into "Birthday" with 95 degrees of rotation
Figure 13-13.

3. To experiment, click on Loop and then Apply.

One other rotation feature, discussed next, can be used to create interesting effects.

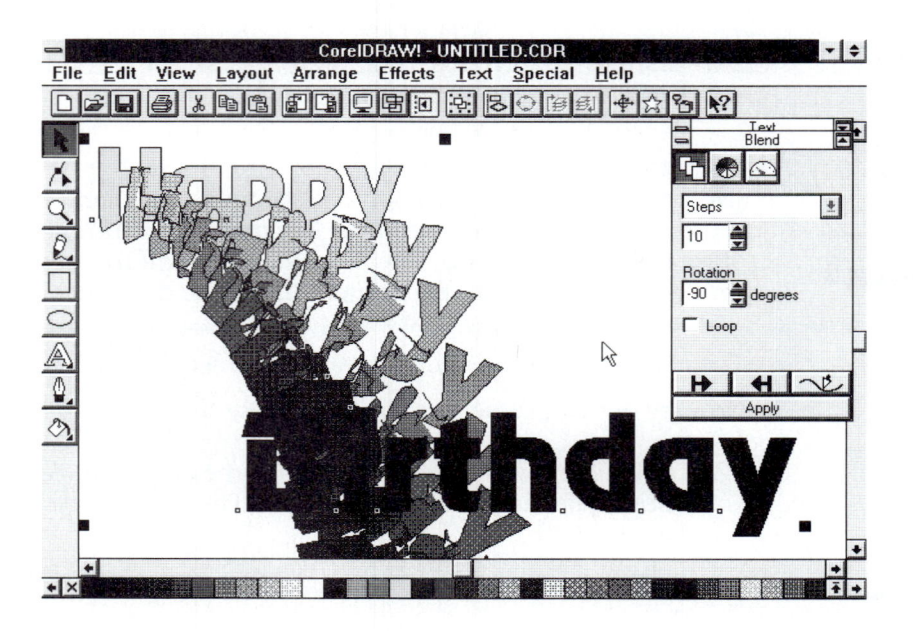

A blended arc created with −90 degrees of rotation
Figure 13-14.

Mapping Matching Nodes

By varying the beginning nodes of both of the objects, you can create some unexpected results. The nodes identify where the blend is to begin and end. You will try two different ways of identifying the nodes.

1. Begin with a new screen by selecting New from the File menu. Click on No.
2. Select the Rectangle tool and create four different-sized rectangles on your screen, as in Figure 13-15. Make sure that all four rectangles are unfilled. Click on the X in the lower-left corner of your screen for no fill.
3. Press SPACEBAR for the Pick tool and marquee-select the two rectangles on the left.
4. In the Blend roll-up, enter 20 Blend steps and 90 (positive) degrees of rotation, and click on Loop. Click on the Map Nodes option (third icon from the left) and then on the Map Nodes button. When you move the pointer off the menu out to the page, it will become a curved arrow, and one of the selected objects will have nodes displayed on each corner, as shown here:

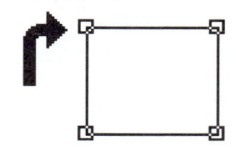

5. Select the upper-left corner node by moving the arrow to that node and clicking on it. The second object's nodes will be displayed.

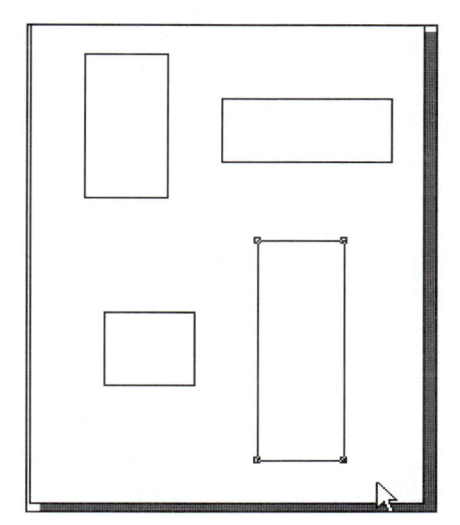

Figure 13-15. Placement of rectangles on the page

6. Select its upper-left corner node by moving the arrow to that node and clicking on it.
7. Click on Apply in the Blend roll-up.

    You will now see one result of mapping matching nodes.
8. Marquee-select the second two objects.
9. Click on Map Nodes in the Blend roll-up.
10. With the arrow, click on the lower-right node of the first object (the one with the corner nodes selected).
11. Click on the upper-left node of the second object and click on Apply in the Blend roll-up. The blend will occur, as in Figure 13-16.

    You can continue to experiment with Map Nodes, adding a different degree of rotation if you want to see its effects. When you are finished, you can look at another major feature found on the Effects menu, the Extrude feature.
12. Renew the screen by selecting New from the File menu. Click on No. Also, close the Blend roll-up.

Extruding Objects

Extruded objects appear to have a 3-D look. You can use the Extrude feature on text, closed shapes, or open paths. The results can be very dramatic.

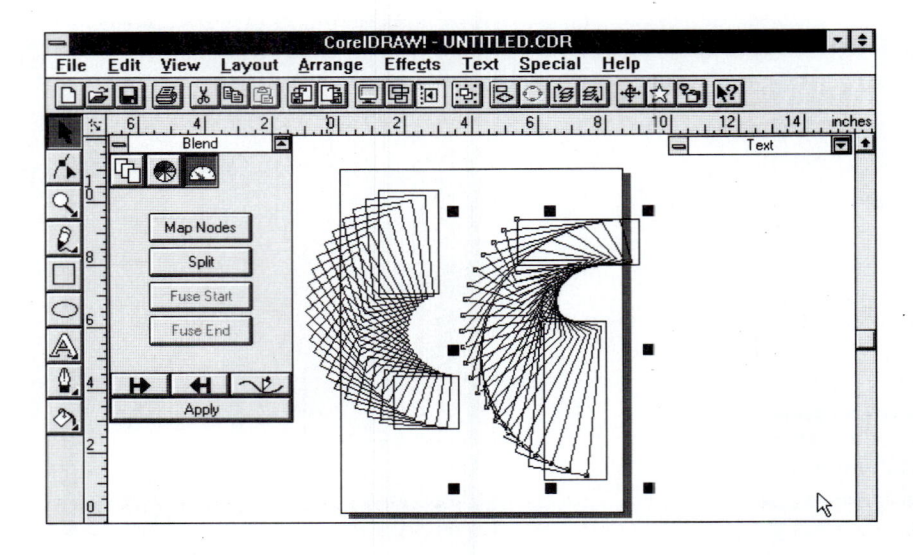

Examples of blends with two types of Map Nodes
Figure 13-16.

Creating Special Effects 465

There are three ingredients to the Extrude feature that affect the results: the depth and direction of the extrusion, the spatial alignment of the extruded object, and the shading and coloring of the extruded object. Each of these will be investigated separately. First create the objects to be extruded with the following steps:

1. Click on the Text tool and click in the upper-left quadrant of the page.
2. Type **T**, select the letter and, from the Text roll-up, select 120 points, NewCenturySchlbk font, and Normal. Click on Apply.
3. Click on purple from the color palette on the bottom of the screen. From the Outline Pen flyout click on the Hairline icon.
4. Click on Duplicate in the Edit menu to create a copy of the "T." Repeat it to make a second copy.
5. With the Pick tool, select each of the copies and drag one to the upper-right quadrant of the page, the other to the lower-left quadrant.
6. Click on the Pencil tool and draw a wavy line in the lower part of the page. Your screen should look something like Figure 13-17.

Pressing CTRL-D is a shortcut for the Duplicate command.

Now you are ready to experiment with extruding.

Placement of objects for experimenting with the Extrude feature
Figure 13-17.

Extrude Roll-Up Window

Extruding is controlled by the Extrude roll-up window, which you open from the Effects menu. The Extrude roll-up opens in its depth and direction mode (second icon from left), which you can see here:

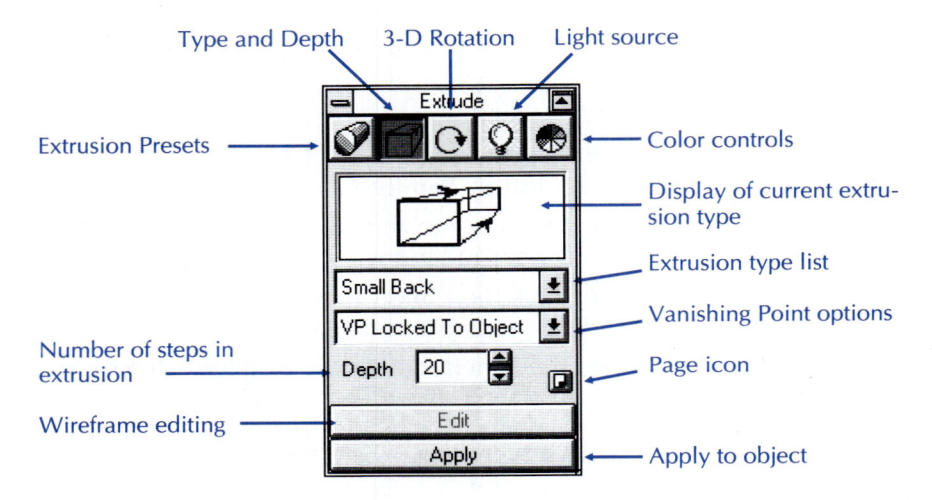

Callouts on the Extrude roll-up:
- Type and Depth
- 3-D Rotation
- Light source
- Extrusion Presets
- Color controls
- Display of current extrusion type
- Extrusion type list (Small Back)
- Vanishing Point options (VP Locked To Object)
- Number of steps in extrusion (Depth 20)
- Page icon
- Wireframe editing (Edit)
- Apply to object (Apply)

The type and depth mode is one of five modes that the Extrude roll-up can be in. These modes, which are activated by the five buttons on the upper part of the roll-up, perform the following functions:

- ◆ Extrusion Presets provide preestablished extrusion possibilities that you can choose to apply to an object.

- ◆ Type and Depth allow you to determine the depth of the extrusion, the location of the vanishing point, whether the vanishing point is in front of or behind the object, and whether the extrusion is in a perspective or orthogonal (parallel) view.

- ◆ 3-D Rotation allows you to rotate the extruded object in any of three dimensions.

- ◆ Light Source allows you to determine the location of the light source and its intensity to provide shading effects.

- ◆ Color Controls allows you to determine if the extruded object will use the same coloring as the original object, or whether the extruded portion and its shading should be different (and what those different colors should be).

Creating Special Effects

Selecting these modes significantly changes the options available in the Extrude roll-up, as you will see in the following sections.

Extrusion Presets

The Extrusion Preset mode presents you with a selection of preset extrusions that you can apply to an object. To explore this feature, follow these steps:

1. Select the topmost left "T" with the Pick tool.
2. From the Effects menu, choose Extrude Roll-up if it is not already on the screen.
3. Choose the first icon on the left.

    The roll-up shown here will be displayed (your display may show a different Preset option):

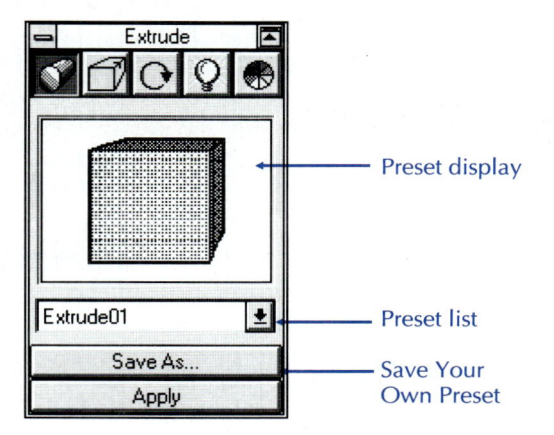

4. Click on the Preset Extrusion drop list and choose Extrude06.
5. Click on Apply. The "T" should look like this:

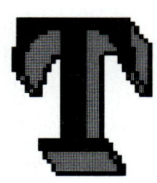

6. From the Effects menu, choose Clear Extrude.

You may want to experiment some more with the preset extrusions. If you do, clear the effects before continuing with the next extrusion mode.

Type and Depth

Type and Depth is the default mode for the Extrude roll-up—the window automatically opens in this mode. If you are in another mode and want to return to this mode, you can do so by clicking on the depth icon, the second from the left on the Extrude roll-up.

Examine the Extrude roll-up now by following these instructions:

1. With the Pick tool, click on the topmost left "T" to select it.
2. On the Extrude roll-up choose the Type and Depth mode, second from the left.

Perspective and Parallel Extrusions

You normally see an extrusion in a perspective view—it gets smaller as it extends away from you. Therefore, a perspective-type of extrusion is often what you'll want to use. The alternative extrusion is the Parallel view, or *orthogonal*, meaning that the lines forming the extrusion will be parallel to each other. The choices for extrusion types are shown here:

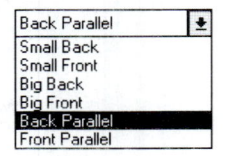

```
Back Parallel       ▼
Small Back
Small Front
Big Back
Big Front
Back Parallel
Front Parallel
```

The first four extrusions are perspective types, where you are looking from front to back or back to front. If you select the Back Parallel or Front Parallel type, the extrusion will be parallel. See this for yourself with this exercise:

1. Select Back Parallel type if it is not already selected. Click on Apply in the Extrude roll-up. The wireframe behind the "T" on the right is filled in to form a short extrusion, which does not grow narrower as it extends toward the center of the page—it is in a parallel view with a centered vanishing point, as you can see here:

2. Click on the right "T." (It takes two clicks to be selected.) From the Extrusion type drop-down list box, choose Small Back. Click on Apply.

Creating Special Effects

An extrusion is created behind the "T," narrowing as it extends toward the center of the page—it is very obviously in perspective.

3. Click on the black color fill on the Color Palette on the bottom of the screen to clearly distinguish the letter from its extrusion, as shown here:

Vanishing Point Options

The vanishing point is represented by a small X seen when an extrusion is being created. This marks the point to which the extrusion will extend given the current settings. You can use the vanishing point to modify the extrusion by dragging it from one location to another, or by moving the object and assigning the vanishing point a fixed location. The choices on the vanishing point options list give you several alternatives for working with vanishing points. The options have these meanings:

- *VP Locked to Object*   Locks the vanishing point in position relative to the object. As you move the object, the vanishing point moves with it.
- *VP Locked to Page*   Locks the vanishing point in one location on the page. As you move the object, the vanishing point remains locked in place.
- *Copy VP From*   Copies a vanishing point from one object for use with another. You will have two vanishing points in one location, each tied to a different object.
- *Shared VP*   Allows objects in a group to share one vanishing point.

Changing the Depth

The Depth counter is available only if you are working with an extrusion in perspective, and it determines how far toward the vanishing point the extrusion extends. You can think of this counter number as the percentage of the distance between the object and the vanishing point that is occupied by the extrusion. The Depth counter can go from 1 to 99. A value of 99 makes the extrusion extend all the way to the vanishing point, and a value of 1 creates no extrusion. A value of 0 or a negative number is not a valid entry.

Now you will reuse the "T" on the right, keeping the Small Back type.

1. Click on the up arrow of the Depth counter to increase the depth to 70. As you click on it the extrusion image reflects the new depth setting. (If 70 is not available, drag the counter and type in **70**.)
2. When the depth is at 70, click on Apply. A new, more elongated extrusion will appear, as shown here:

You can also affect the depth and direction of the extrusion by working directly with the vanishing point, as you'll see next.

Moving the Vanishing Point

You can move the vanishing point on the page in two ways: by adjusting the horizontal and vertical counters in the Extrude roll-up, or by clicking on Edit and dragging the X that indicates the vanishing point. Try both techniques:

1. Use the "T" on the right. Set the depth to 40, and keep the extrusion type Small Back.
2. Click on the Page icon beneath and to the right of the Depth numeric entry box. The following menu will appear:

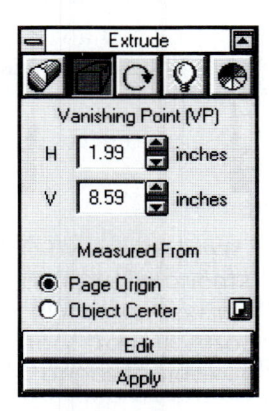

You can set the horizontal and vertical locations by typing an absolute number into the counters. You select how these numbers are to be measured by clicking either the Page Origin or Object Center option.

3. Change the horizontal and vertical counters for the vanishing point so they both have a value of 6.5. You can do this either by clicking on the

Creating Special Effects

up arrows or by dragging across the numbers and typing the new value. Keep the Page Origin default and click on Apply.

By moving the vanishing point, you've made the extrusion shift to follow it, as you can see here. If you rotate the vanishing point around the object, the extrusion will also rotate. If you move the vanishing point away from the object, the extrusion will extend out following the vanishing point (although the depth value doesn't change—it is a percentage, so it merely re-scales the extrusion).

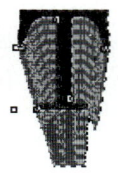

4. Drag the vanishing point to the upper-right corner of the page. Again, the extrusion will follow, as shown here:

5. Click on Apply to complete the extrusion.

Tip: You can also move the vanishing point by clicking on Edit and dragging the X representing the vanishing point wherever you want it. The extrusion will follow the X.

Clearing an Extrusion

If you have an extrusion that you want to remove without getting rid of the original object, you cannot just press DEL, which would get rid of everything, including the object. You must use the Clear Extrude option in the Effects menu.

1. With the extruded "T" on the right, select Clear Extrude from the Effects menu. The extrusion is removed, leaving the original selected object.
2. Press DEL to remove that letter, and to get ready for the next exercise.
3. Click on the extruded "T" on the left. Press DEL, and the entire object and extrusion are removed from the page.

    To prepare for the next exercise on 3-D Rotation, follow these steps:
4. Click on the remaining "T" to select it.
5. Click on the Page icon to return to the Type and Depth roll-up.
6. Select Small Back extrusion type and set the depth to 70. Click on Apply.
7. Click on a black color from the color palette to distinguish the letter from its extrusion..

Now you are ready to proceed with the next mode.

3-D Rotation

The second mode in which you can place the Extrude roll-up is 3-D Rotation. You change to this mode by clicking on the third button from the left on the Extrude roll-up. Try that now, and the Extrude roll-up will change to include the 3-D rotator that you see here:

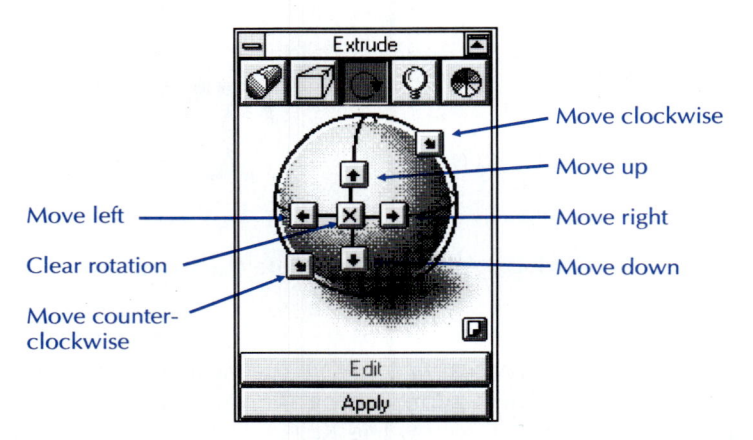

The 3-D rotator has six arrows that allow you to move the currently selected object in any of six directions—two in each of three planes. When you click on an arrow, the object is rotated five degrees in the direction of the arrow. In the center of the sphere is an X button that allows you to clear the current rotation. The 3-D rotator does not change the vanishing point, only the object and its extrusion. Try the 3-D rotator now with this exercise:

Creating Special Effects

1. Click several times on the upward-pointing arrow above the X on the sphere. The wireframe representing the extrusion will rotate upward—the face of the extrusion, the original letter, moves up, while the other end of the extrusion moves down, as you can see here:

2. Click on Apply to fill in the wireframe and complete the rotation.
3. Click on the X in the center of the sphere, and then click on Apply to remove the rotation and return the extrusion to its original position.
4. Click several times on each of the arrows on the rotator to observe their behavior. Click on the center X after each, to return the extrusion to its original position.
5. When you are through, click on X and then Apply.

With the 3-D rotator, you can look at the extruded object from literally any angle.

Shading and Coloring

You will remember that we originally set the color of the letter "T" to purple. Then, when the extrusion was produced, it was also purple, making the extrusion difficult to see. So you then placed a black fill in the letter so that the extrusion would more clearly be seen.

Altering the shading and coloring can also affect the clarity between the object and the extrusion. See now how you can change this, using the remaining "T" selected:

1. Click on the color wheel icon (the fifth from the left) to place the Extrude roll-up window in coloring mode. The roll-up's appearance will change, as you can see here:

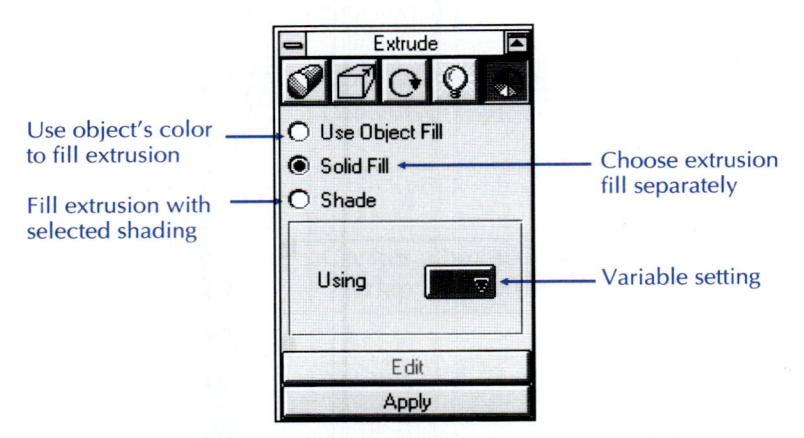

- Use object's color to fill extrusion
- Fill extrusion with selected shading
- Choose extrusion fill separately
- Variable setting

The coloring scheme is Solid Fill, where the object and the extrusion fills are determined separately. In other words, the object's fill color is not used as the color for the extrusion.

2. Click on Use Object Fill to make the extrusion's color the same as the objects.
3. Click on Apply.

The extruded object now has no clear differentiation, as shown in the following illustration. (Deselect the "T" to see it more clearly by clicking anywhere else on the screen, then select it again for the next step.)

4. Change it back by clicking on Solid Fill and then click on the Using color button. The current color palette will open. Click on the second gray from the right in the second row, then click on Apply.

This two-color scheme is nice, but you can improve on it with shading. When you select the Shade option, you can specify a range between two colors or shades for the extrusion. You will get a linear fountain fill

Creating Special Effects

along the extrusion, with the From color nearest to the original object, and the To color at the vanishing point.

5. Click on Shade to give the extrusion a shaded fill.
6. Click on the From color button and select the same gray you chose above. Then click on the To color button and choose the second from the right in the top row of the palette. Click on Apply. The extrusion changes to this:

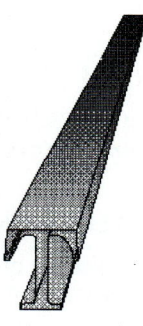

To give your extrusion even more life, you can put a spotlight on it and change the location of that light.

7. Click on the fourth button from the left of the Extrude roll-up. The Extrude roll-up changes once more, this time to include a device for setting up to three light sources, a slider to control intensity, and an On/Off switch for full color ranges:

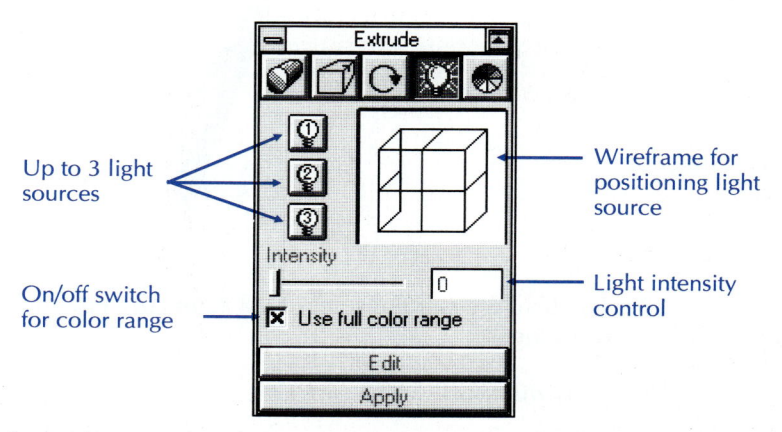

Up to 3 light sources

On/off switch for color range

Wireframe for positioning light source

Light intensity control

8. Click the first light bulb to turn the first light source on. Then drag the light source (represented by the circle-1) to the upper-left corner of the front surface of the wireframe. Next, drag the Intensity control to about 85.
9. Click on Apply. The extrusion will be redrawn like the following (your extrusion may differ depending on how you set it):

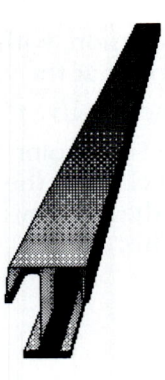

Now you will experiment briefly with how an open path can be used in a creative way with extrusions.

Applying Extrusions to Open Paths

Open paths can be used to create some dramatic effects with extrusions. In this case, you will create a ribbon from your wavy line.

1. Click on the wavy line to select it.
2. Click on the color wheel in the Extrude roll-up. Then click on Shade, if it isn't already selected. Make the From color a black, and the To color a gray. Click on Apply. Your wavy line will change to a shaded ribbon, like this:

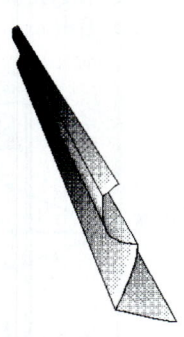

3. To clear the screen, select New from the File menu. Do not save the drawing.

Now you will work with contours.

Using Contours

Contours add concentric outlines either inward toward the center of an object, or outward away from the edge of it. Contours can be made to look

Creating Special Effects

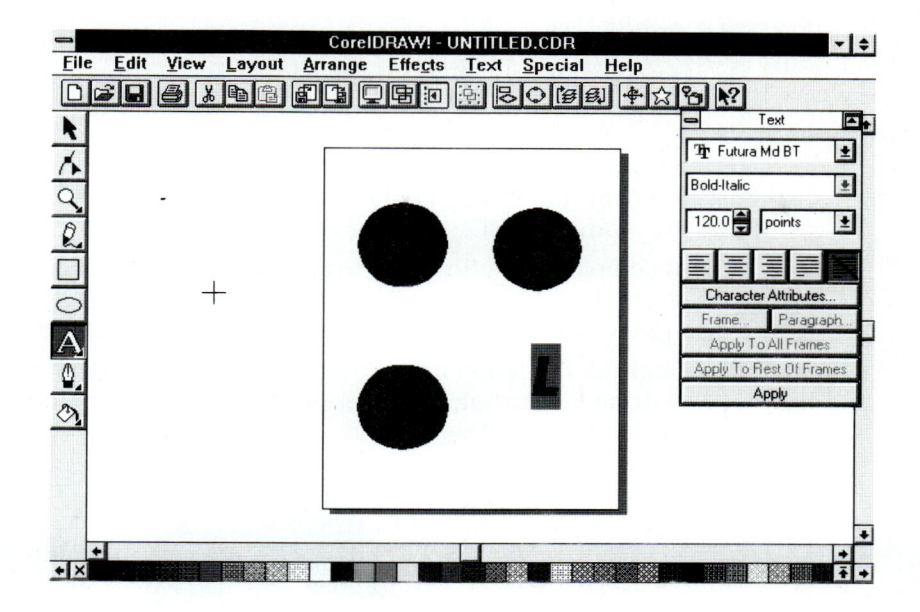

Screen set up to experiment with the Contour feature
Figure 13-18.

Fill must be on for contours to be seen.

like blending, but for a single object. They cannot be applied to groups of objects, bitmap objects, or OLE objects.

Follow these steps to get an understanding of what contours can do for you:

1. Using the Ellipse tool, create three circles, each filled with black, by selecting the Fill tool and clicking on black. With the Text tool, type **L**. Select the "L" by dragging on it. From the Text roll-up, set the "L" to 120 points and Furtura Md BT, bold-italic. Click on Apply. Select the Fill tool and click on black. Your screen will look like Figure 13-18.
2. With the Pick tool, select the first circle on the upper left.
3. From the Effects menu select Contour Roll-Up. The roll-up looks like this:

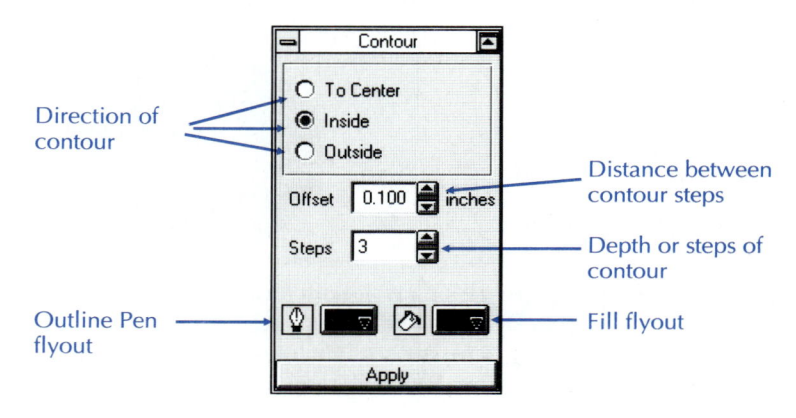

You have a choice of where the contour is to be applied: toward the center of the object, from the edges inward (not necessarily to the center, depending on the number of steps and the Offset), and from the edge of the object outward. Offset is used to define the thickness of each layer of the contour, and Step defines the number of layers you want in the contour. You can define the outline and fill colors or patterns from the menu as well.

In some of the following illustrations, the object being displayed is not selected (it does not have a bounding box around it) in order to show it more clearly. Your screen will have the object selected.

4. Click on To Center and set Offset to .2 inches. From the roll-up's Outline Pen flyout, select black. From the Fill flyout, select a light blue. Click on Apply. Your screen will look like this:

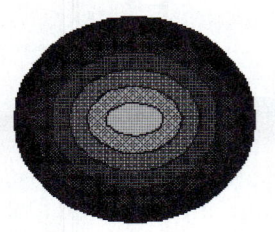

Note: Although the steps will not be used in the To Center option, you may have to have a value other than 0. If you get an error message warning you that the number of steps is between 1 and 99, set the Contour mode to Inside, type in **1** step, and click on To Center again. Then click on Apply.

5. Select the next circle to the right and click on Inside. Set Offset to .2 inches, set Step to 3, and click on Apply. Your circle looks like this:

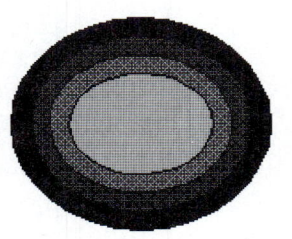

6. Select the third circle, click on Outside, keep Offset at .2 inches, keep Step at 3, and click on Apply. The results can be seen in Figure 13-19.

Creating Special Effects

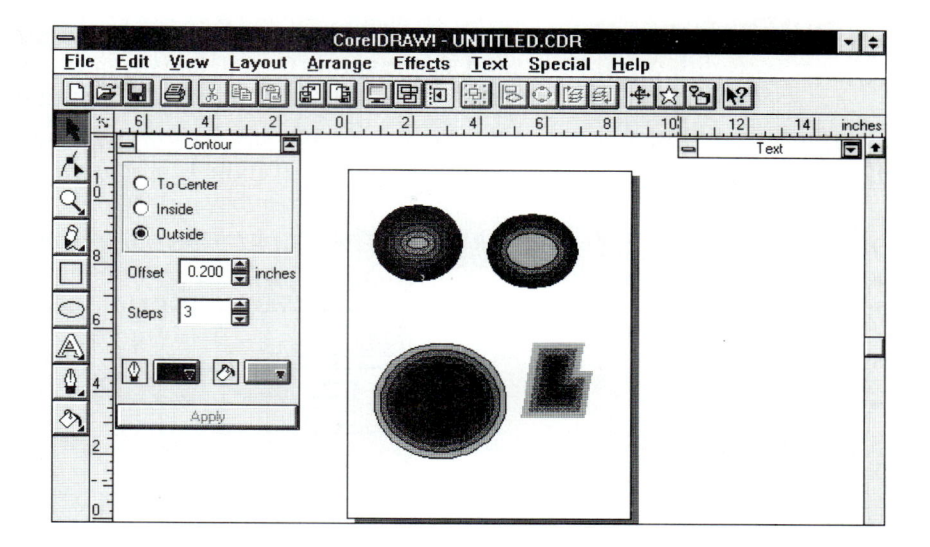

Results of contouring with and without outlines
Figure 13-19.

7. Click on the "L" to select it. Click on Apply to see how the contour setting affects text. Figure 13-19 shows the results.

   The fuzzy-edged blend effect is achieved by turning off the Outline Pen. The concentric outlines then blend into each other.

8. On the Outline Pen flyout, click on the X to turn off the outline. The black outlines are removed and the colors blend more readily.

Tip: To edit an individual contour, first select the contoured object and then select Separate from the Arrange menu. Hold down CTRL and click on a contour node. A bounding box surrounds a single contour, and the status line refers to it as "Child Curve." You can then edit the contour by resizing, rotating, or changing the fill or outline.

9. To prepare for the next section, select New from the File menu. Click on No to abandon the changes. Clear the Contour roll-up from the screen.

Another feature, PowerLine, is discussed next.

Using PowerLines

The PowerLine feature gives you a tool to create graphic lines. The lines resemble those drawn by hand, varying width and darkness, such as you get with calligraphic pens or paintbrushes. Since the line contains both outline and fill, it can be treated as a graphic. CorelDRAW! comes with 23 preset PowerLines, and you can create your own and then save them.

To get the PowerLines, you click on PowerLine Roll-Up on the Effects menu. It looks like this:

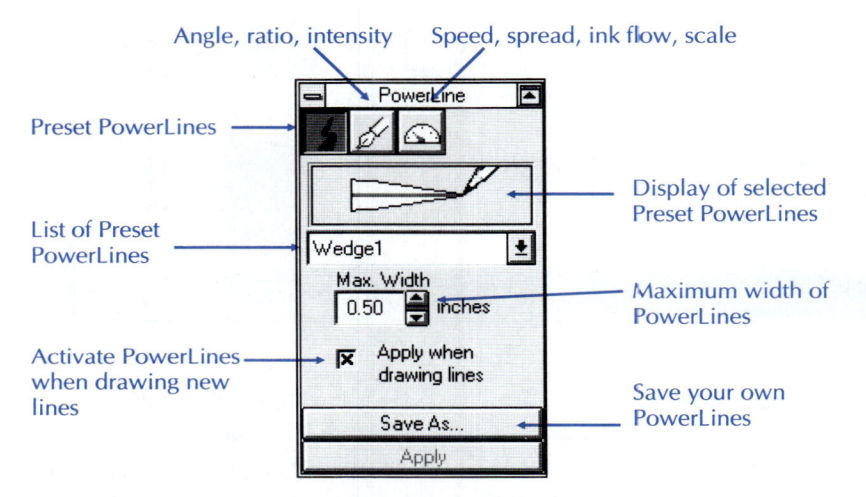

- Angle, ratio, intensity
- Speed, spread, ink flow, scale
- Preset PowerLines
- List of Preset PowerLines
- Display of selected Preset PowerLines
- Maximum width of PowerLines
- Activate PowerLines when drawing new lines
- Save your own PowerLines

The PowerLine feature has three modes or controls: The first, seen in the illustration, allows you to select preset PowerLines for your own use. The second, represented by the second icon from the left, allows you to set the angle, ratio, and intensity controls for the PowerLine in use. The third, represented by the third icon from the left, allows you to control the speed, spread, ink flow, and scale of the PowerLine.

The first mode displays the PowerLines available for your use. To see the whole list of PowerLines, you would click on the list box down arrow. Beneath the list box is a setting for maximum width, which defines the thickness the PowerLines may be. Clicking on the "Apply when drawing lines" check box allows you to apply the PowerLine settings to new lines you expect to create. You can save your own unique PowerLines to the preset list by clicking on the Save As command button.

To begin with, you will use a circle to experiment with the effects available with this new feature.

Applying PowerLines to an Object

You can apply PowerLines to existing objects. Follow these steps to see how you can create intriguing effects with an ordinary circle:

Creating Special Effects

1. With the Ellipse tool, draw a circle. Fill it with the second-from-the-right gray, in the second row on the Fill flyout. From the Outline Pen flyout, set the width to 2 points by clicking on the icon next to the hairline icon.

2. Click on PowerLine Roll-Up in the Effects menu, if it is not already on your screen.

3. Choose Wedge 1 as the type of PowerLine and leave the maximum width at .5 inch. Click on Apply. Your screen looks like this:

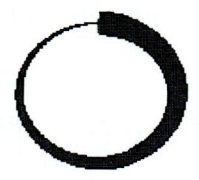

4. Click on the third icon from the left for applying speed, spread, and ink flow. The roll-up looks like this:

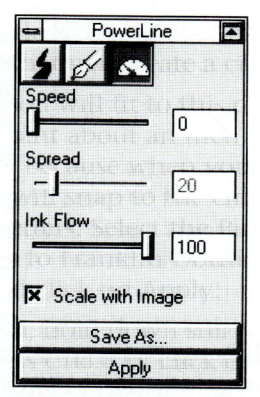

    You use the Speed setting to control the line sharpness on curves. The higher the number, the greater the "skid" around the curves. Use Spread to control smoothness and width. The higher the number, the smoother the line. A high number would be more like a paintbrush, while a lower number would be more like an ink pen. Use Ink Flow to control the darkness of the line and how much ink flows as you draw the line. A high number lets more ink flow, while a lower number restricts the ink flow. Finally, use Scale with Image to resize the PowerLine as the values change.

5. Set Speed to 20, Spread to 50, and Ink Flow to 50. Click on Apply. The circle looks like the following:

Varying the Nib

You can also vary the nib shape of the line by selecting the second icon from the left. The resulting roll-up looks like this:

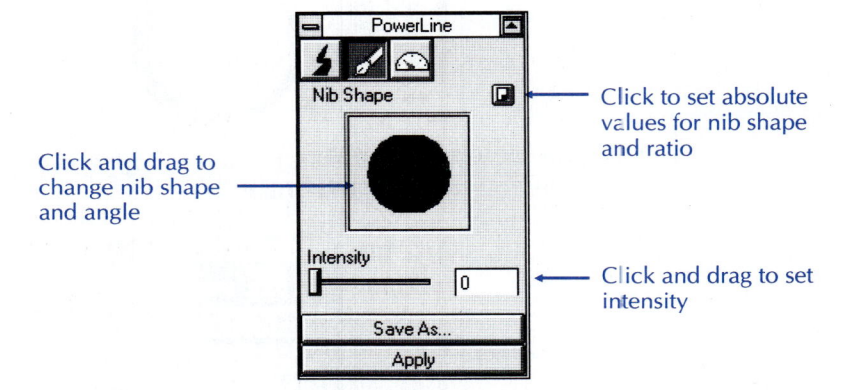

Click and drag to change nib shape and angle

Click to set absolute values for nib shape and ratio

Click and drag to set intensity

With this menu you can vary the nib shape, angle, and intensity. The display box contains a circle representing the nib shape. You can change it by placing the pointer on the display. As you drag the pointer, the nib shape and angle change. Beneath the display box is the slide control or numeric entry box for Intensity settings. This determines how strongly the nib is being pressed. Beneath the Intensity control icon at the top of the roll-up is a Page icon, which displays controls for entering absolute values for the nib shape angle, ratio, and intensity.

Follow these steps to experiment with the nib shapes:

1. Click on the second icon on the left.
2. Set Intensity to 75.
3. Click on the Page icon to the right of the PowerLine mode icons. Set the angle to 14 degrees and the nib ratio to 50. Click on Apply. The circle now looks like this:

Creating Special Effects

4. Select the circle with the Pick tool and press DEL to clear the screen.

Once you have a shape, you can pull it in different directions using pressure lines.

Using Pressure Lines

For more interesting effects, you can create your own pressure lines, and you can use the Shape tool to edit a pressure line.

1. Click on the first icon (top left) in the PowerLine roll-up to return to the first PowerLine mode. From the list box, select Pressure. Increase Max Width to 5.00 inches. Your pointer will turn into a hairline. Draw a squiggly line as shown here, and click the No fill button on the color palette.

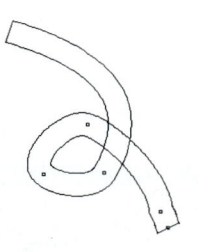

2. Select the Shape tool. Double-click on the pressure line. A Node Edit roll-up will appear. Click on Pressure Edit. The roll-up appears as shown here:

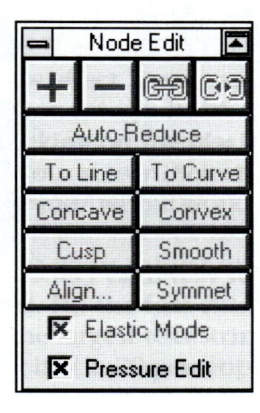

Two nodes on a straight line appear on each end of the line. You pull them along the line to broaden the line or make it more narrow.

3. With the Shape tool move the upper nodes right and left away from the line to broaden it; move the lower nodes to the center to narrow the line, as shown here:

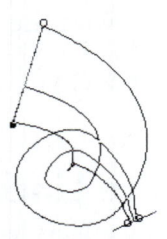

4. Select black fill from the Fill tool; the line will be filled in.
5. Turn off Pressure Edit in the Node Edit roll-up.
6. Using the Shape tool, shape the line however you wish by dragging the nodes.

One example is shown in Figure 13-20.

Now you will explore a new feature in CorelDRAW! 5, Lens.

Select New from the File menu and click on No to clear the screen. Remove the PowerLine and Node Edit roll-ups from the screen.

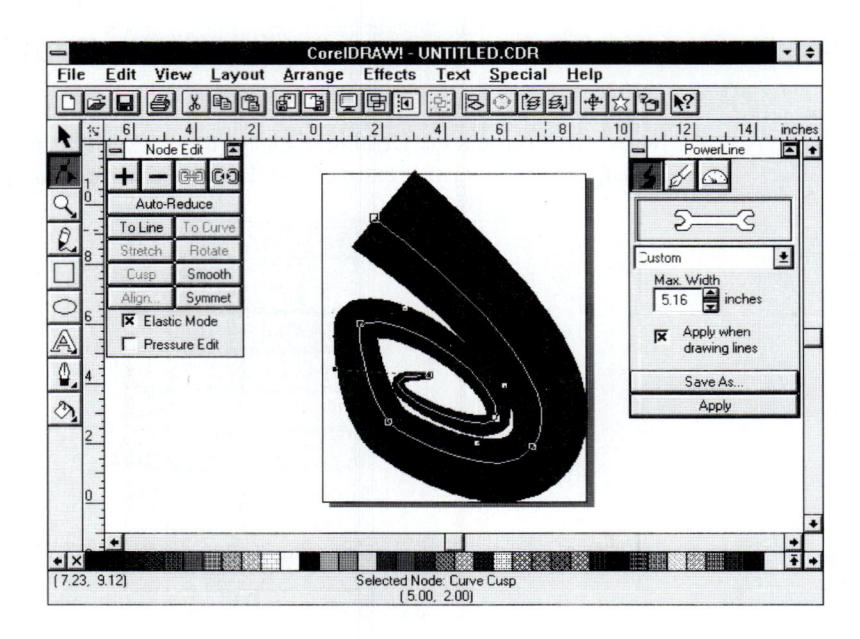

Results of shaping pressure PowerLines
Figure 13-20.

Creating Special Effects

Using Lens

The Lens feature can be used to achieve several interesting effects. You can place a "lens" over an object to make the object seem transparent where the lens is placed; to magnify a portion of the object; to filter out or add colors; to produce complementary, inverted, or negative colors; or to produce grayscale or infrared images.

A simple example is the easiest way to show the effects produced by the Lens feature. Follow these steps:

1. Pull the zero page guides to the upper-left area of the page. Then pull two horizontal ruler lines to 2 and 10 inches.
2. From the File menu, import COUGAR.CMX from the first CD-ROM disk in the \CLIPART\ANIMAL\ directory path. (If you do not have this available, use any clip-art you have.) Save the image as COUGAR.CDR. Drag the image off the page to the side. You are going to place a black rectangle beneath it.
3. With the Rectangle tool, draw a rectangle within the ruler lines and the page borders. Fill the rectangle with black, as shown in Figure 13-21.
4. Select the clip-art with the Pick tool and drag it into the center of the rectangle. From the Arrange menu, select Order and then To Front from the submenu to place the clip-art on top of the rectangle.

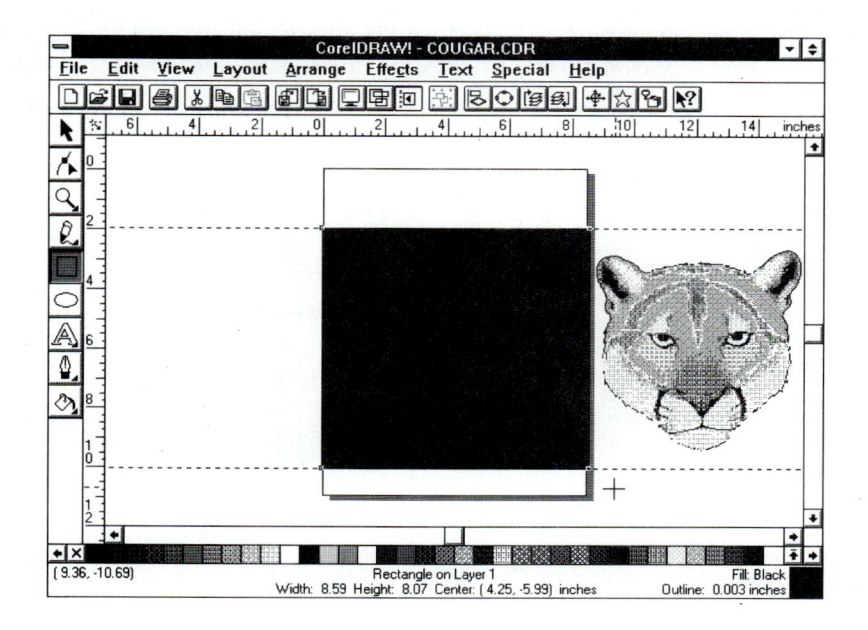

Black rectangle with clip-art on the side
Figure 13-21.

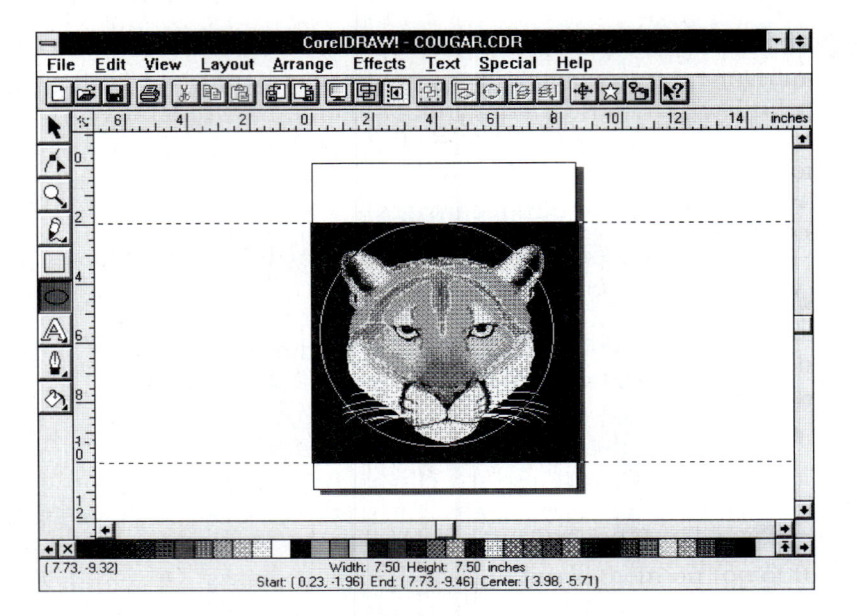

Circle drawn around clip-art image with Ellipse tool
Figure 13-22.

5. Using the Ellipse tool together with CTRL, draw a perfect circle around the clip-art image, as shown in Figure 13-22. When you release the Ellipse tool, the circle will disappear into the black background.

6. From the color palette on the bottom of the screen click on the bright red color. The clip-art will be hidden behind the red circle.

   Now you will experiment with some of the Lens effects. The circle will become the lens through which you can see the clip-art image beneath. Variations in images are created by selecting alternative lens types.

7. From the Effects menu select the Lens roll-up. It looks like this:

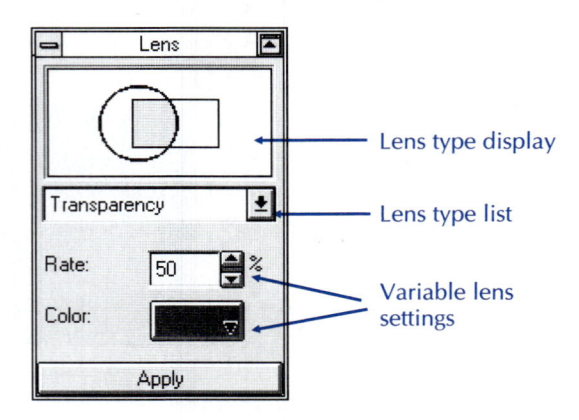

   — Lens type display
   — Lens type list
   — Variable lens settings

Creating Special Effects

Clip-art seen through a red-tinted transparent lens
Figure 13-23.

Transparency is the default lens type. At the top you can see a lens-type display that shows the effects produced by the selected type. Below the display is a drop-down list of eight lens types. You will use several of the lens types to illustrate their effects. Beneath the list is the Rate of transparency. The Rate percentage sets the clarity of the lens: 100% would appear as clear glass, and 0% would completely obscure the clip-art image. Each lens type has its own setting. Now you will see the effects of the Transparency type.

1. Set the Rate at 80% and click on Apply to see the image of the cougar through the red-tinted lens, as shown in Figure 13-23.
2. From the drop down list, select Magnify and set the Times to 3. Click on Apply. The results are shown here: 
3. From the type list, select Invert and click on Apply. The image now looks like this:

4. Finally, from the drop-down list, select Heat Map and click on Apply. You'll see another interesting result.
5. Set the Palette Rotation to 25% and click on Apply to see how that works.

   You now have seen an example of how the Lens feature works. Experiment with the other lens types to see how they can be used as well. Next you'll look at another feature that's new with CorelDRAW! 5, the PowerClip.
6. Select New from the File menu and do not save the image. Remove the Lens roll-up from the window.

Using PowerClip

PowerClip places one object within another. You use this to create one image out of two, where one object is the designated container, the other the contents of the container. You may have multiple layers of PowerClips where one completed image becomes the contents for another.

The following rules apply:

- Containers can be closed path objects, grouped objects, or artistic text.
- Contents can be closed path objects, grouped objects, artistic text, or bitmap images.
- Both containers and contents may contain uniform, fountain, or no fills; 2-color patterns; full color pattern; or textures.
- You may use PowerClips with other Effects menu features, such as Blend, Extrusion, or Transform options.
- You can copy a PowerClip with the Copy command in the Edit menu to create both a new container and its contents. If you create a new container object and use the Copy PowerClip in the Effects menu, the newly created container is filled with the contents of the copied PowerClip.
- You can clone a PowerClip using the Clone command on the Edit menu.
- You may group PowerClips and then ungroup them.

Follow these steps to experiment with this fun feature. You will create a rectangle within which a bull will be placed.

1. Open the clip-art BULLT.CDR from the CD-ROM, in the \CLIPART \ANIMAL\TOTEM directory path. Use any clip-art if this is not available to you.

Creating Special Effects

Figure 13-24.
BULLT-CDR clip-art opened and reduced in size

2. Select the bull with the Pick tool and reduce its size to about 1/4 of the page and place it in the lower-right quadrant of the page, as seen in Figure 13-24.
3. Select the Rectangle tool and draw a rectangle, about 1/4 the size of the page. With the Pick tool, place it in the upper-left quadrant of the page, as seen in Figure 13-24.
4. Select the Extrude Roll-up from the Effects menu and click on the Type and Depth icon, the second from the left. Choose Small Back from the Type list and change the Depth setting to 40. Click on Apply. Pull the vanishing point slightly to the right. This is the container for the bull, as seen in Figure 13-25.
5. Select the bull with the Pick tool and choose PowerClip from the Effects menu. A flyout menu will appear, as shown here:

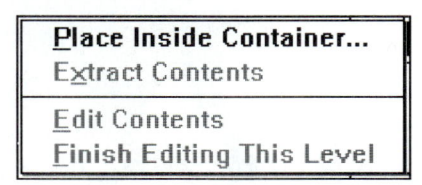

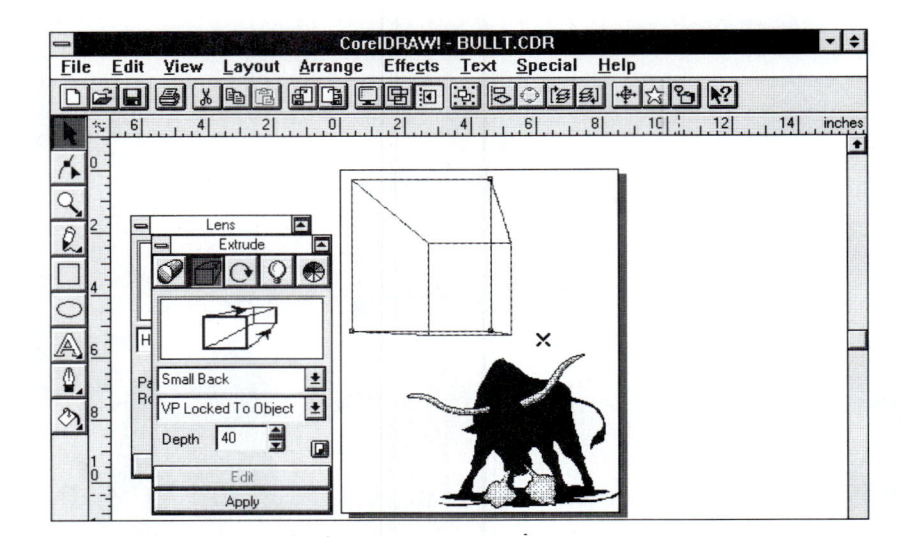

Container and bull for the PowerClip feature
Figure 13-25.

6. Choose the Place Within Container option. The pointer will turn into a thick arrow. Move the arrow to the box and click on it. The bull will be placed in the cylinder, as seen in Figure 13-26.

   You can see from the flyout that you can also extract the contents from a container, edit the PowerClip, or halt editing.

When you are finished, leave CorelDRAW without saving your test files. They can easily be created again.

Example of PowerClip placing one object (the bull) into another (the box)
Figure 13-26.

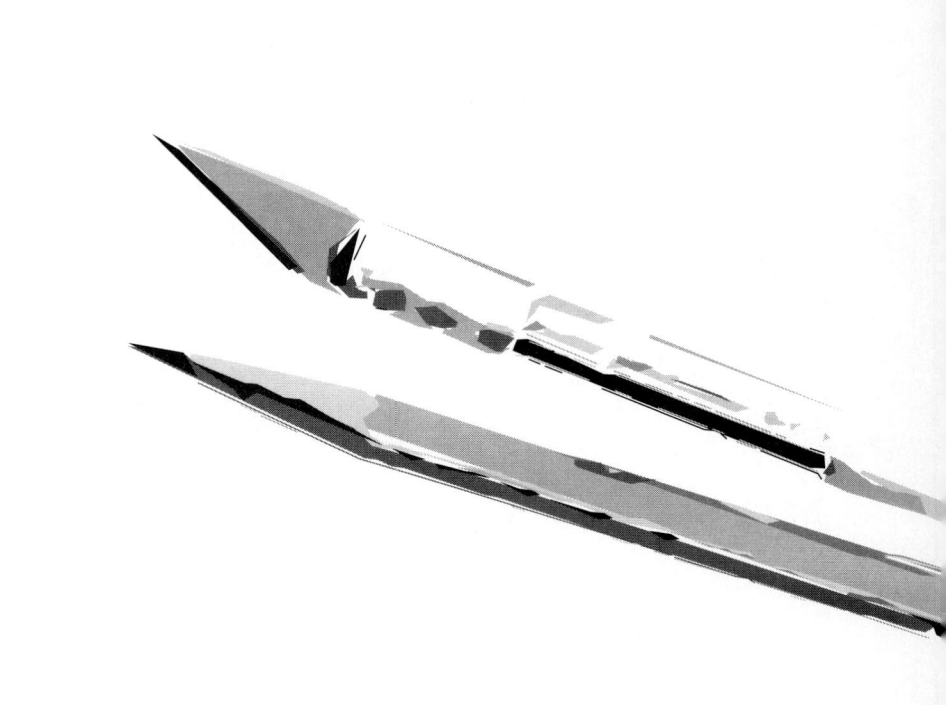

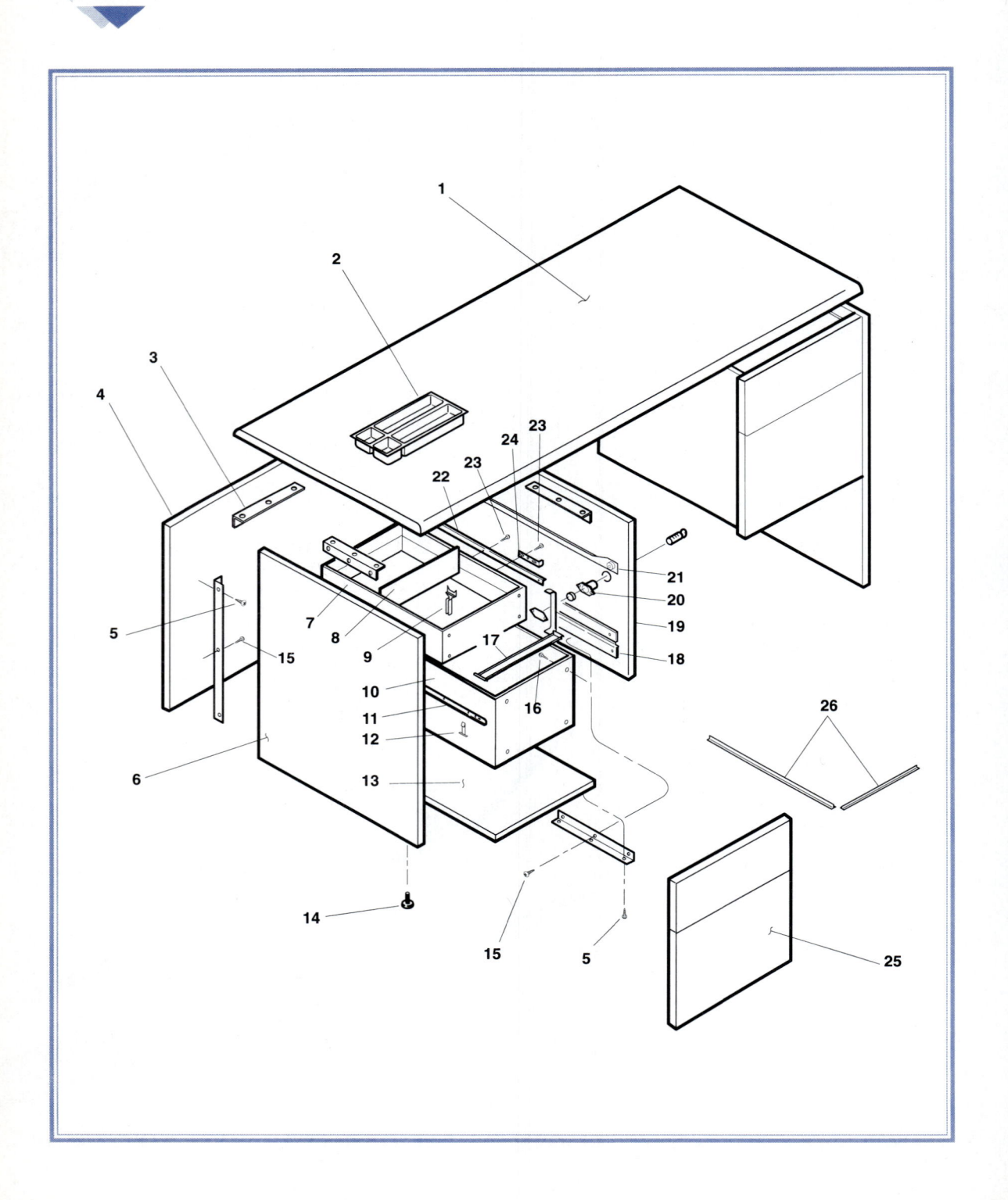

CorelDRAW! 5 Made Easy

Creating Special Effects

CorelDRAW! in Action

KEITH CALHOUN
Exploded Desk

Keith drew this exploded view of a double-pedestal desk entirely in CorelDRAW, using the Freehand tool. He used photographs, sketches, and actual parts for reference. This drawing uses an isometric view in which most edges make either a 30 degree or 90 degree angle with the horizontal. Using an isometric view rather than a two-point perspective (in which the angles depend upon the location in the drawing) allowed him to save and reuse various hardware parts of his drawings, such as hinges and drawer slides. To facilitate drawing lines at these angles, he set the Constrain Angle in the Preferences dialog box to 30 degrees. Also, in the Grid and Scale Setup dialog box, he specified millimeters as the unit for the Horizontal and Vertical Grid Frequency. This allowed him to use a scale of 1 millimeter = 1 inch. Then, after the drawing was finished (but before adding the numbers) he stretched the drawing to fit the page choosing Select All from the Edit menu and dragging the drawing's selection handles.

Keith used three general line widths for the desk parts in this drawing. Parts which are to be perceived as having space behind them use the heaviest lines (an Outline Pen Width of .028 inches); intermediate lines use a width of .014 inches; the finest lines have a width of 0.007 inches. In addition, the callout lines (which connect the numbers to their associated parts) use an outline width of .003 inches. All of these widths are specified in the Outline Pen dialog box. They also have the Scale With Image box checked so that they will retain their proportions after being stretched. Keith made corners and line ends slightly rounded by choosing the middle option in the Corners and Line Caps areas of the Outline Pen dialog box. This gave his drawing a slightly softer edge and makes it look very much like those hand-drawn with pen and ink.

To make the number 17 stand out, Keith removed the portion of the drawer edge behind it. Using the Shape tool, he double-clicked on the line at the location of the first break, then clicked on the Break button in the Node Edit roll-up. He repeated this at the location of the other break, then chose Break Apart from the Arrange menu. The small line segment was then a separate object which he selected and deleted.

This piece was in CorelArtShow 4: Page 34, File:TEC00067.CDR. You may contact Keith in care of:

> Keith Calhoun
> 17 Mountain Drive
> Candler, NC 28715
> Voice: (704) 667-2799

The art on the opposite page was created by and is the property of Keith Calhoun. It is used with permission.

14

COMBINING
CorelDRAW! FEATURES

The previous chapters in this book concentrated on teaching you a specific set of skills. The exercises throughout the book built on skills you had already learned, as you mastered new ones.

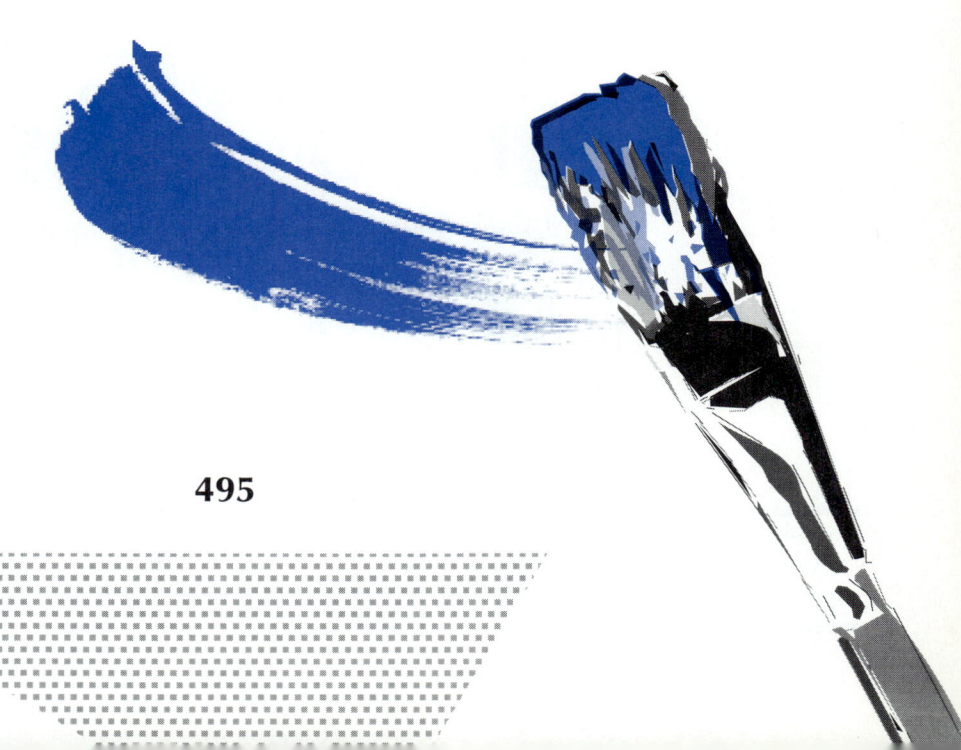

This chapter, however, takes a different approach. It assumes that you have mastered all of the basic skills in CorelDRAW! and are ready to explore applications that combine many different techniques. In this chapter you will find ideas, and perhaps some of these ideas will inspire you in your own work. However, you will not find a comprehensive catalog of every possible technique or special effect of which CorelDRAW! is capable. The three major exercises that make up this chapter feature text that is manipulated in various ways, amply demonstrating CorelDRAW!'s magnificent ability, unmatched by any other software for the PC, to turn text into word pictures.

Each of the three main sections in this chapter contains one exercise in designing a graphic. The title of the section describes the type of graphic; the introduction to each exercise briefly describes the main CorelDRAW! techniques that help you create the graphic. If you need to review certain techniques, you can refer back to the chapter or chapters that first introduced these skills. Bon voyage!

Integrating Clip-Art and Line Art

In the following exercise, you will design a poster that integrates clip-art images with line art—in this case, text. You can use this exercise to review text editing, size and scale, and outline and fill techniques (Chapters 4, 6, 7, 8, 10, and 13). Since the poster format is 20 inches by 15 inches, you also can brush up on the page setup, printing, and tiling skills you learned in Chapter 12. The end result of your exercise should look similar to Figure 14-1.

Completed auction poster
Figure 14-1.

Creating the Headline

To begin building the poster, create the 3-dimensional headline by following these steps:

1. Starting with a blank screen, turn on the Rulers and turn off the Wireframe commands in the View menu. Also, make sure the Snap To options (Grid, Guidelines, and Objects) in the Layout menu are turned off for this exercise.
2. Select Page Setup from the Layout menu, select Custom from the drop-down list box, assure that Landscape is selected, enter **20** for the Width and **15** for the height, and click on OK. In the Grid & Scale Setup dialog box reached from the Layout menu, type **15** in the Vertical Grid Origin numeric entry box to move the vertical zero point to the top of the page, and click on OK to return to the drawing window.
3. Save and name the planned image. Select Save As from the File menu and type **Auction** in the File Name text box. Then press ENTER or click on the OK command button to save the file and return to the CorelDRAW! screen.
4. Open the Text roll-up, select Bookman (BookmanITC Lt BT), Bold-Italic, 150 points, centered, and click on Apply. When the Text Attributes dialog box opens, click on OK to use this default for both Artistic and Paragraph text.
5. Activate the Text tool and select an insertion point at 2 inches vertically and 10 inches horizontally. Type **CLASSIC CAR**, press ENTER, and continue typing **AUTO AUCTION**.
6. Click on the Pick tool to select the text, click on Character Attributes in the Text roll-up, enter **35** in the Character Spacing and **80** in the Line Spacing, click on OK, and then on Apply. The text spreads out horizontally and moves together vertically, as shown in Figure 14-2. Click on the Save button in the ribbon bar.
7. If your status line does not say Fill: Black, Outline: none, open first the Fill flyout menu and click on Black, and then open the Outline Pen flyout and click on the X.

Headline after it has been correctly spaced
Figure 14-2.

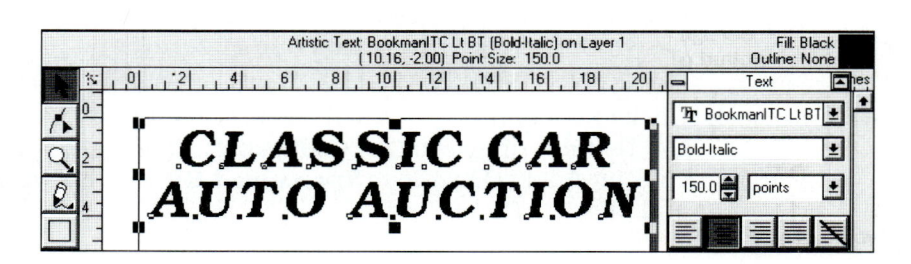

8. With the text selected, click on the Copy button in the ribbon bar (or press CTRL-C) and then click on the Paste button (or press CTRL-V) to make a copy of the text.

9. Click on the Fill tool and then on the white icon in the flyout menu (this is the second icon from the left in the bottom row). The text disappears from the screen and all you can see are the nodes.

10. Open the Transform roll-up from the Effects menu, select the Position option (leftmost button), click once on the down arrow opposite the horizontal position, click once on the up arrow opposite the vertical position, and click on Apply. This creates a white copy of the text offset by 1/10 inch from the original.

11. Again, copy and paste the selected white text, change its fill to black, and offset it by 1/10 inch to the upper left (down arrow horizontally, up arrow vertically). Your headline should now look like this (don't worry at the moment if your text is not perfectly centered).

12. Choose Select All from the Edit menu and then Group from the Arrange menu. If your text is not properly centered, center it now and then press CTRL-S to save the changes you have made to the file.

Entering Remaining Text

The remaining text can be entered quickly with these instructions:

1. If the headline is still selected, click on any white space to deselect it. Then, from the Text roll-up, click select Zapf Humanist, bold, 100 points, centered, and click on Apply. Click on OK when the Text Attributes dialog box appears.

2. With the Artistic text tool, click an insertion point at 14 inches horizontal and 6 inches vertical; next, type **April 19th, 11am** and press ENTER, then type **Paine Field, Everett** and press ENTER, and finally type **Admission: $10**.

3. Click the Text tool at 10 inches horizontal and 11 inches vertical. From the Text roll-up select Zapf Calligraphic, bold, 80 points, centered, and click on Apply. Then type **Sponsored By The Lynnwood Rotary** and press ENTER.

4. Reduce the point size in the Text roll-up to 60, and click on Apply; next, type **Cars may be previewed April 18th, 8am - 5pm** and press ENTER, then type **For Information** and press ENTER, and finally type **Call: 555-1234**. When you are done, select the Pick tool and click on any white space. Your screen should look like Figure 14-3. Click on the Save button to save your work.

Adding Clip-Art

The final step in building the poster is to add the clip-art. Three pieces will be added, one in the hole on center-left and the other two in the bottom-left and bottom-right corners. Add the clip-art now with these instructions:

1. If not done, click on the Pick tool and then click in any white space to deselect the text string.

2. Click on Import in the File menu and select All Files (*.*) in the List Files of Type drop-down list box. In the Import dialog box, select your CD-ROM drive and the \CLIPART\VEHICLE\CARS\ path, and then double-click on the file named ROLLZ.CMX. (If this piece of clip-art is not available to you, use any piece of clip-art you have.) The car will come into the center of your poster. Drag it to the left, resize it if necessary, and drag it into the hole that perfectly fits it, as shown in Figure 14-4.

Completed text entry
Figure 14-3.

First piece of clip-art in place
Figure 14-4.

3. Select Import from the File menu, make sure you are in the same directory as in step 2, and double-click on OLDCAR2.CMX. After resizing it, drag the second car to the lower-left corner, as shown here:

4. Select the Zoom-in tool from the Zoom-tool flyout menu and magnify the lower-left corner of the poster. Include enough of the text around the second car to give yourself a frame of reference.

5. Drag the upper-right sizing handle to the lower left in order to reduce the size of the car so that it fits in the space available for it, like this:

6. Press CTRL-S to save the poster, return the poster to fit-in-window view, and then click on any white space to deselect the second car.
7. Again, select Import from the File menu, make sure you are in the same directory as in step 2, and double-click on SAXON.CMX. After resizing, drag this third car to the lower-right corner.
8. Select the Zoom-in tool and magnify the lower-right corner of the poster. Include some of the text for a frame of reference.
9. Drag the upper-left sizing handle to the lower right in order to reduce the size of the car so that it fits in the space. Since the car is a little boxy for the space, drag the middle-left sizing handle to the left of the car, like this:

10. Return to fit-in-window view, deselect the third car, and save the poster. Select Full-Screen Preview from the View menu to look at the finished poster. What you see should look like Figure 14-1.
11. Press F9 to return to the normal drawing window and select New from the File menu to clear the screen.

The shortcut for Show Preview is F9.

You may choose to print this oversize poster on your own printer. If you do, be sure to activate the Print Tile Pages option in the Print Options dialog box. Your poster will print on four separate sheets, each containing one quarter of the graphic. If your printer does not have enough memory to print this graphic at 20 by 15 inches, try scaling the image down in the Print Options dialog box.

To add to your CorelDRAW! drawing gallery, continue with the next exercise. There, you will create a color design that takes advantage of CorelDRAW! features that fit text to a path and mirror images.

Fitting Text to a Path

If you have followed this book from the first chapter onward, you have learned nearly every available CorelDRAW! drawing technique. One important (and very creative) technique remains: fitting text to a path using the Fit Text To Path command in the Text menu. You can cause a text string to follow the outline of *any* object, be it a circle or ellipse, a rectangle or square, a line, a curve, a complex curved object, or even another letter that has been converted to curves.

Once you have fitted text to an object, you can delete that object without causing the text to lose its newly acquired shape. If you edit text attributes later, however, the text may change its alignment. You can remedy this simply by fitting text to the same path again. You can also make the curve object transparent by selecting the X (none) icon for both the object's outline and its fill.

Fit Text To Path Roll-Up

You open the Fit Text To Path roll-up by selecting Fit Text To Path from the Text menu. There are actually two Fit Text To Path roll-up windows: one for fitting text to an open line or curve, the other for fitting text to a closed rectangle or ellipse. The roll-up for fitting text to an open line or curve is shown on the left in the following illustration; the roll-up for fitting text to a closed rectangle or ellipse is shown on the right.

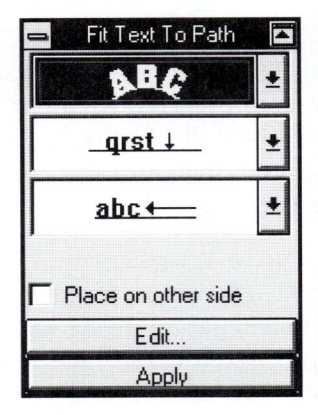

The shortcut for Fit Text To Path is CTRL-F.

The two roll-up windows share two drop-down list boxes: the list box at the top of the roll-up lets you determine the orientation of the text, while the second list box lets you select where the text will sit: above, below, or on the path of the object and its distance from it. Also, both roll-ups have a check box for moving the text to the opposite side of the path. The difference in the two roll-ups is in how to align the text on the object. For an open object, you have a drop-down list of alignment possibilities, whereas closed objects have a four-sided button to set their alignment. Each of these elements will be discussed in the next several sections. Figure 14-5 shows several examples of fitting text to a path that will be referred to in these sections.

Combining CorelDRAW! Features 503

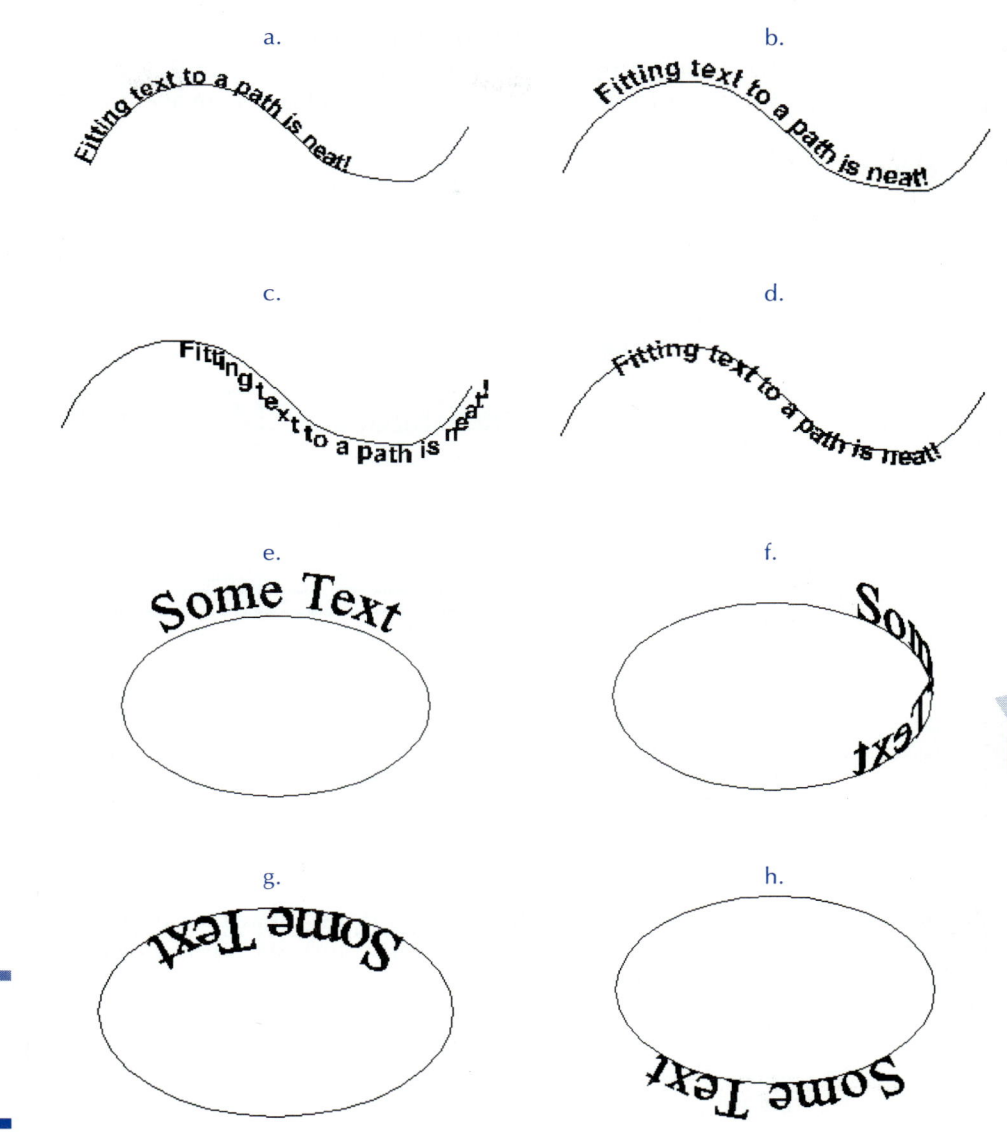

a.

Fitting text to a path is neat!

b.

Fitting text to a path is neat!

c.

Fitting text to a path is neat!

d.

Fitting text to a path is neat!

e.

Some Text

f.

Some Text

g.

Some Text

h.

Some Text

Examples of fitting text to a path
Figure 14-5.

Orientation of the Text

The orientation of the text is its degree of rotation, or skew, as it follows the path it is fitted to. There are four options for orientation in the drop-down list. Most of the examples in Figure 14-5 show the first (default) orientation; in this orientation, the letters rotate to follow the path. Figure 14-5f shows the second orientation, and Figures 14-5c and e show the fourth orientation.

Distance of the Text from the Path

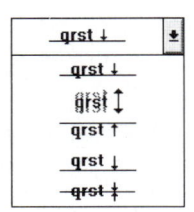

The second drop-down list box offers five alternative settings for the distance of the text from its path. (Not all five choices are always available.) Figure 14-5a and f show the first alternative, in which the text sits right on the path (the baseline of the text is on the path, and the descenders are beneath it). Figures 14-5b and e shows the second alternative: the text can be pulled away from the path either with the mouse or with the Fit Text To Path Offsets dialog box, opened with the Edit button in the roll-up, as shown next. Figure 14-5c shows the third alternative, in which the text sits underneath the path. Figure 14-5d shows the fifth alternative, in which the line runs through the text.

Aligning the Text on the Path

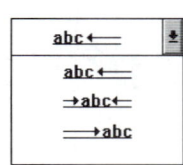

For open paths, the third drop-down list box on the roll-up provides three alternatives for aligning text on a path. Figure 14-5a shows the first alternative, in which the text is aligned with the left end of the path. Figure 14-5b and d show the second alternative, in which the text is centered on the path, while Figure 14-5c shows the third alternative, with the text aligned to the right end of the path.

For closed-path rectangles and ellipses, the text is aligned to the middle of one of four sides by clicking on the corresponding side of the four-sided button that is displayed. The text itself is rotated as it is moved to the right, as shown in Figures 14-5f and h. If you want to flip the text to the other side of the path, click on the Place on other side check box in the Fit Text To Path roll-up. Figure 14-5g shows the result of having this box checked, while Figure 14-5h shows the result of having the bottom side selected but not the Place on other side check box.

Using Fit Text To Path

In the following exercise, you will design a stylized "rainbow" image that consists of a series of scaled and aligned wedges. You will then fit the word "Rainbow" to a curve, combine the text string with a background object to create a mask, and overlay the transparent letters on the rainbow colors. The

Combining CorelDRAW! Features

result is shown later in Figure 14-10. If you have a color monitor, your results will appear much more vivid than the one shown in the figures. If you have a black-and-white display adapter and monitor, you can achieve a similar "rainbow" effect by filling the wedges with the gray shades indicated in parentheses in the following steps.

1. Starting with a blank screen, select Page Setup from the Layout menu. When the Page Setup dialog box appears, click on the Landscape and Letter option buttons and then select OK. This results in a page that is 11 inches wide and 8 1/2 inches high.

2. To prepare the CorelDRAW! screen for the exercise, activate the Rulers and Wireframe commands. Make sure that Snap To Grid from the Grid & Scale Setup on the Layout menu is activated, that the Vertical Grid Origin is set to 8.5 inches, and both Horizontal and Vertical Grid Frequency are set to 8 per inch.

3. Set new outline and fill defaults so that all of the objects you draw will be standardized. First, click on the Outline Pen tool and again on the X (for none) icon in the first row of the flyout menu. The Outline Pen dialog box appears, asking whether you want to define Outline Pen settings for objects you haven't drawn yet. Click on Artistic Text and accept the checked Graphic, so that both are selected. Select OK to set no outline as the new default for Graphic and Artistic Text objects.

4. Click on the Fill tool and then on the black icon. The Uniform Fill dialog box appears, asking whether you want to define fill colors for objects you haven't drawn yet. Click on Artistic Text and accept the checked Graphic, so that both are selected. Select OK to define a default fill color of black for all new Graphic and Artistic Text.

5. Activate the Ellipse tool, then position the pointer at the 6 1/2-inch mark on the vertical ruler and the 3 1/4-inch mark on the horizontal ruler. Press and hold CTRL-SHIFT and drag the mouse downward and to the right until the status line shows a width and height of 3 inches. As you may recall from Chapter 3, the use of CTRL and SHIFT together results in a circle drawn from the center outward. When you release the mouse button, the circle appears with the node at the top, as shown in Figure 14-6a.

6. Create a 90-degree wedge from this circle, as you learned to do in Chapter 9. Activate the Shape tool and position the Shaping pointer at the node of the circle. To turn the circle into a pie wedge, press and hold CTRL and drag the node in a clockwise direction until you reach the 9 o'clock position (90 degrees on the status line). (Hold the tip of the Shaping pointer *inside* the rim of the circle as you drag, or you will see an open arc instead of a wedge.) Release the mouse button when you reach the 9 o'clock position. The wedge appears, as in Figure 14-6b.

a.

b.

c.

d.

Creating a pie wedge from a circle and rotating it
Figure 14-6.

7. Activate the Pick tool to select the wedge automatically. Notice that the selection box is much larger than the wedge, just as in Figure 14-6c. CorelDRAW! continues to treat the wedge as though it were a full circle.

8. With the wedge still selected, open the Transform roll-up from the Effects menu. Click on the Scale & Mirror button in the middle, click on the horizontal mirror button, and then on Apply. The curve of the wedge now faces upward and to the right, as shown in Figure 14-6d.

9. To scale the wedge and leave a copy of the original, position the pointer at the boundary marker in the upper-right corner and scale the wedge upward and to the right, until the status line value reaches approximately 117 percent. When you reach the desired point, continue to hold the mouse button, but press the + key on the numeric keypad to leave a copy of the original. Then release the mouse button. The original wedge remains in position, and a scaled version overlays it, like this:

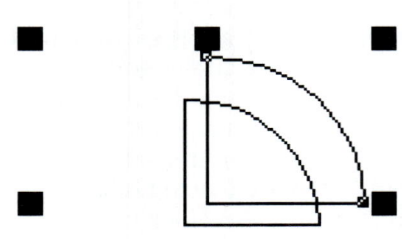

Combining CorelDRAW! Features

10. Press CTRL-R (the Repeat key combination) five times to create five additional wedges, each larger than the previous one. Your screen should show a total of seven wedges, resembling Figure 14-7.

11. Next, align the wedges so that they form one-half of a rainbow. Click on the Select All command in the Edit menu to select all seven wedges, and then select the Align command in the Arrange menu. When the Align dialog box appears, click on both the Horizontally Center and Vertically Center option buttons, click on the Align to Center of Page check box, and then select OK. The wedges realign with a common corner point in the center of the page, as you can see here:

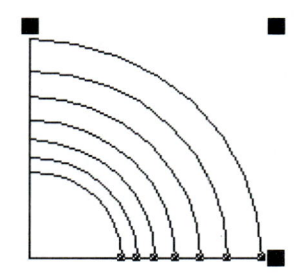

12. With the seven wedges still selected, click on the Order option in the Arrange menu and then on the Reverse Order command on the flyout. You will not see a visible change at this point, but you have positioned the larger wedges in the back and the smaller wedges in the front. When you turn on the preview window later in the exercise and begin to assign fill colors to the wedges, you will see each wedge as a ribbon-like band.

13. Select the Save As command from the File menu. When the Save Drawing dialog box appears, type **rainbow** and then press ENTER or click on OK.

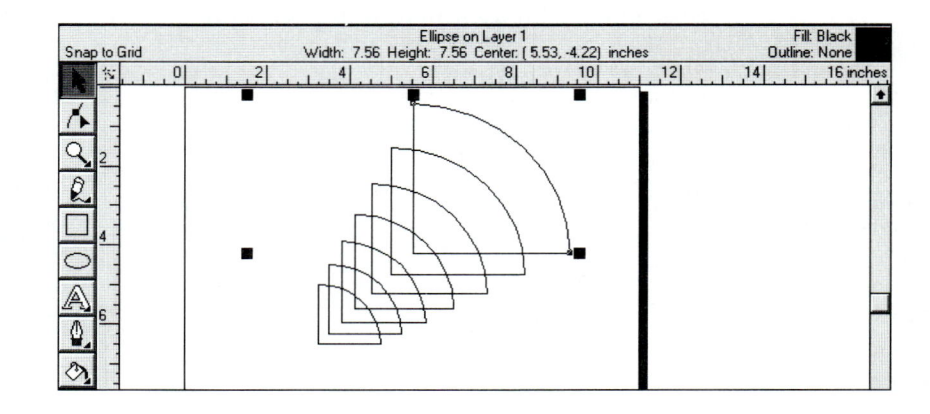

Series of scaled wedges created using the Repeat key combination
Figure 14-7.

14. To design the other half of the rainbow, you again create a horizontal mirror image of the currently selected image. In the Transform roll-up, which should be open, activate both the horizontal mirror button and Apply to Duplicate. The mirror image of the seven wedges appears and fits tightly against the original group of wedges, as shown in Figure 14-8.

15. You can now begin to assign fill colors to the wedges of the "rainbow." Activate the Preview Selected Only command in the View menu. Adjust magnification to fit-in-window by clicking on the Fit-In-Window icon in the Zoom tool flyout menu.

16. Deselect all of the wedges by clicking on any white space. Then select both the largest wedge on the left half of the "rainbow" and the smallest wedge on the right half. To select both of them, click on each of their curve outlines while holding down SHIFT. The editing window looks as though all of the wedges were selected, because the selection box of the largest wedge surrounds all of the objects. However the preview window, reached by pressing F9, shows you that only two wedges are selected, as you can see here:

17. With the two wedges selected, click on the bright red in the palette at the bottom of the screen. (If you have a black-and-white monitor, select 80 percent black, the third square from the left.) Turn off Preview Selected Only and press F9 again to see the color.

18. Deselect the previous wedges. Then select the second-largest wedge on the left half of the "rainbow" and the second-smallest wedge on the right half; then select orange fill from the palette at the bottom. (If you have a black-and-white monitor, select 60 percent black.)

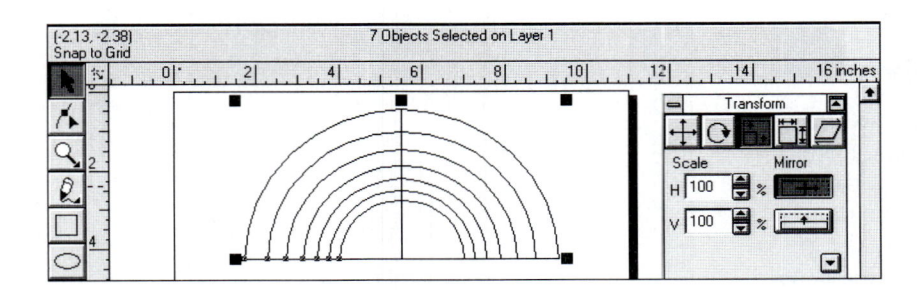

Original seven wedges with a horizontal mirror image
Figure 14-8.

Combining CorelDRAW! Features

You can also see the color by turning Wireframe off from the Display menu; then you do not have to use F9. With Wireframe off, though, you can't select the individual wedges.

19. Continue in the same way with the next five pairs of wedges. If you have a color monitor, assign colors as follows: third pair, yellow; fourth pair, green; fifth pair, light blue; sixth pair, dark blue; seventh pair, dark purple. Check your colors by pressing F9. (If you have a black-and-white monitor, assign 50 percent black to the third pair, 40 percent black to the fourth, 30 percent black to the fifth, 20 percent black to the sixth, and 10 percent black to the seventh.) When you are finished, make sure that all wedges are selected, and then press F9. The two halves of the rainbow show an opposite sequence of colors, as you can see by the black-and-white representation here:

20. Press F9 to return to your drawing, click on the Select All command in the Edit menu to select all 14 wedges, and then apply the Group command from the Arrange menu. This prevents you from accidentally moving or editing an individual wedge apart from the group.

21. Now you are ready to prepare the text that will eventually overlay the rainbow as a transparent mask. First, activate the Ellipse tool and position the pointer at the 1-inch mark on the vertical ruler and the 2 1/2-inch mark on the horizontal ruler. Press and hold CTRL and drag the mouse downward and to the right and draw a circle 6 inches in diameter. The circle overlays most of the "rainbow" for now, but you will delete it when it has served its purpose.

22. Activate the Text tool and select an insertion point in any white space on the page. Type **Rainbow**, click on the Pick tool, and open the Text roll-up. Set text attributes to Aachen bold, 105.0 points, alignment, None. Click on the Character Attributes command button, set Character spacing to 10 percent, and then select OK and on Apply to redisplay the text on the page.

23. Press and hold SHIFT and select the circle you just drew. Then press CTRL-F or click on the Fit Text To Path command in the Text menu.

24. When the Fit Text To Path roll-up opens, make sure that all of the defaults in the roll-up are set: rotated text orientation (the first alternative in the first drop-down list); text sitting on the path (the first alternative in the second drop-down list); the top quadrant in the four-sided button; and Place on other side not checked. After verifying these settings, click on Apply. In a few seconds, the text appears right side up, but on the circle, as shown in Figure 14-9.

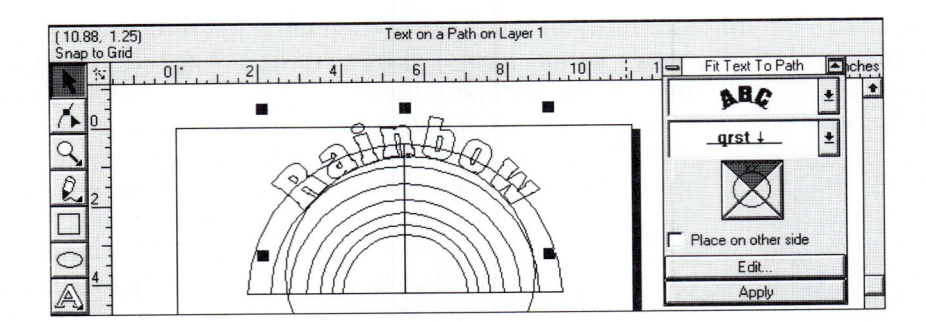

Fitting text to a circle
Figure 14-9.

25. Deselect the text to leave only the circle selected and then press DEL to delete the circle. The text retains its new shape.

26. Click again on the outline of the text string to select it, and then fill the text with white by clicking on the Fill tool and again on the white icon in the second row of the flyout menu.

27. Create a rectangle that will become the background of the mask. Activate the Rectangle tool and position the drawing pointer at the zero point on both the horizontal and vertical rulers. From this point, draw a rectangle 7.75 inches wide and 3.75 inches high, dragging downward and to the right.

28. Press the SPACEBAR to select the rectangle automatically. Give the rectangle a white fill by clicking on the Fill tool and then on the white icon in the flyout menu. If it isn't so already, make the edge (outline) of the rectangle transparent also by clicking on the Outline Pen tool and then on the No Fill icon in the first row of the flyout menu.

29. Select the text string and move it on top of the rectangle. Position it so that the bottom of the text string is 1/4 inch above the lower edge of the rectangle.

30. To center the text horizontally on the rectangle, select both objects, click on the Align command in the Arrange menu, and choose the Horizontally Center option button. Select OK to leave the Align dialog box and redisplay the newly aligned objects.

31. With both the text and rectangle still selected, move both objects into the empty space at the bottom of the page, out of the way of the rainbow wedges. Then select the Order command from the Arrange menu and choose Reverse Order to place the text behind the rectangle.

32. Press F9 to turn on full-screen preview. You cannot see the rectangle because it is white, and you cannot see the text because it has a white fill and is behind the rectangle. Press F9 again to return to the editing window and, with the text and rectangle both selected, click on the

Combining CorelDRAW! Features

Combine command in the Arrange menu. When the two objects combine, their common area, the text, becomes transparent "holes" in the white rectangle.

33. Move the newly combined object back over the grouped rainbow wedges and align the bottom edge of the curve object with the bottom edge of the wedges.

34. Choose Select All from the Edit menu and then press F9 for full-screen preview. With the white rectangle invisible against the page, all you can see are the rainbow colors behind the transparent text string, as shown in Figure 14-10.

Tip: The object that is in the background when you combine two objects determines the fill color of the combined object. If you see white letters over a transparent rectangle, you forgot to place the text behind the rectangle. Select Undo from the Edit menu, use the Reverse Order command in the Arrange menu to bring the rectangle to the foreground, and then combine the two objects again.

35. Return to the editing window and select both the combined object and the wedges and apply the Group command from the Arrange menu.

36. Press CTRL-S to save the changes to your work, then select New from the File menu to clear your screen.

The main emphases in this last exercise have been on fitting text to a path, working with color effects, creating a mask, aligning objects, repeating operations, and creating mirror images. In the next and final sample application, you can achieve 3-D effects using fountain and contrasting fills, outlines, and repeated scaling.

Rainbow colors appearing as fill through the mask object
Figure 14-10.

Achieving Special Effects with Text and Graphics

The "FAX" image in Figure 14-11 has a vibrant, 3-D look; the graphic represents the power of facsimile to quite literally "broadcast" to the world. Several special effects techniques contribute to the dynamic quality of the image:

- Text fitted to a curve
- Text objects with drop shadows (shadows placed behind and offset from the original)
- A "globe" with an off-center radial fountain fill
- Repeated duplication and expansion of a text string
- Judicious use of contrasting fills
- Inclusion of a backdrop that makes the image seem to burst beyond its boundaries

You already have practiced the basic skills that make all of these special effects possible. In the exercise that follows, you will recreate this image, using the Leave Original and Repeat keys, fountain fill and node editing techniques, and the Duplicate, Fit Text To Path, Group, and Page Setup commands. For a review of shadow and fountain fill techniques, see Chapter 7.

1. Starting with a blank screen, select Page Setup from the Layout menu. When the Page Setup dialog box appears, make sure that Landscape and Letter are still selected and then select OK.

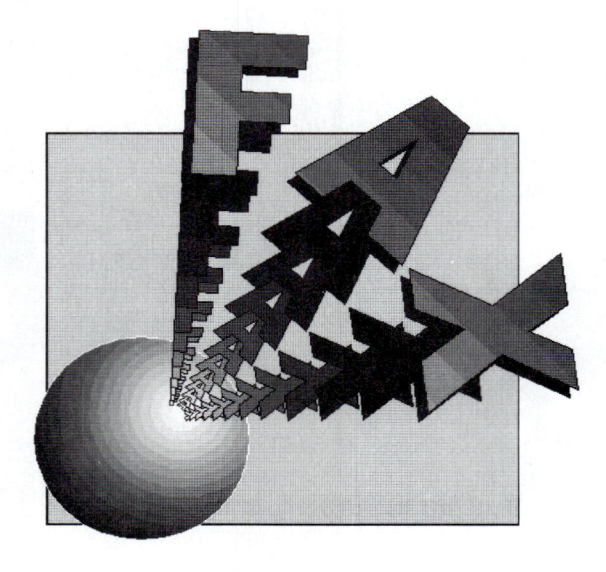

"Fax" illustration using fountain fill, drop shadows, and a background frame to enhance 3-D effects
Figure 14-11.

Combining CorelDRAW! Features

2. To prepare the CorelDRAW! screen for the exercise, activate the Snap To Grid command in the Layout menu, select the Grid & Scale Setup option, set both Horizontal and Vertical Grid Frequency to 8 per inch, and set the Vertical grid origin to 8.5 inches. From the View menu, activate the Rulers and Wireframe options as well.

3. Change the default outline type to a hairline by clicking on the Outline Pen tool and then on the hairline icon in the first row of the flyout menu (the icon with two arrows pointing at each other). When the Outline Pen dialog box appears, click on Artistic Text, accept the checked Graphic, and then click on OK.

4. Change the default outline color to black by clicking again on the Outline Pen tool and then on the black icon in the second row of the flyout menu. The Outline Pen dialog box appears; select Artistic Text, accept the checked Graphic, and click on OK, as you did in step 3.

5. Create a small circle to which you will fit text. To do this, activate the Ellipse tool and position the crosshair pointer in the center of the page at 4.25 inches vertically and 5.5 inches horizontally. Press and hold SHIFT and CTRL and draw a perfect circle 0.75 inches in diameter. When you complete the circle, remember to release the mouse button before you release SHIFT and CTRL to ensure that you create a circle rather than an ellipse.

6. Now enter the text that you will fit to this circle. Activate the Text tool and select an insertion point about an inch above the circle. The exact location does not matter, because when you invoke the Fit Text To Path command later, the text will snap to the circle no matter where it is. Type **FAX** in all-capital letters. Select the Pick tool and open the Text roll-up. Set text attributes to Franklin Gothic Heavy, Normal, 30.0 points, no alignment, and click on Apply.

7. With the text still selected, hold down SHIFT and select the circle. With both objects selected, press CTRL-F or click on the Fit Text To Path command in the Arrange menu. The Fit Text To Path roll-up will open, if it isn't already. Accept the defaults and click on Apply. The text wraps around the outside of the circle, centering itself at the top. Use the Zoom-in tool to magnify the image. The result is shown in Figure 14-12.

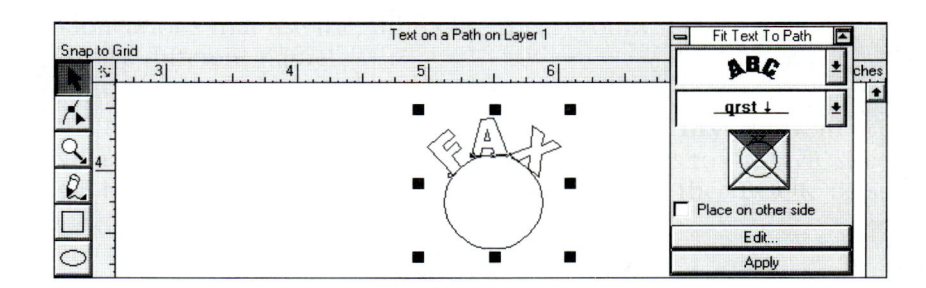

Magnified view of text fitted to a small circle
Figure 14-12.

8. Click on any white space to deselect the text string and circle and then select the circle and press DEL to delete the circle. The text remains curved, even though the circle is no longer there. Close both the Fit Text To Path and Text roll-ups.

9. Double-click on the text string to enter rotate/skew mode, and rotate the text by 45 degrees in a clockwise direction, so that it looks like this:

10. Move the text to the lower-left corner of the page, approximately 1/2 inch from the bottom-left page edge.

11. Now you are ready to begin creating a text pattern. Turn off Snap To Grid and, with the Pick tool still active, position the pointer at the upper-right corner boundary marker of the text object and begin to scale the object from this point. As soon as the dotted outline box appears, keep the left mouse button depressed and click the right mouse button or press and release + on the numeric keypad (to leave a copy of the original). Continue scaling the text until the status line indicates a value of approximately 129 percent. Then release the left mouse button. A larger-scaled version of the text string appears on top of, and offset from, the original.

12. Select the Show Page icon from the Zoom tool flyout menu to return to full-page view. Then press CTRL-R, the Repeat key, ten times, to repeat the scaling and duplication of the text. Ten scaled replicas of the text string overlay one another, each one larger than the previous one. The last text string exceeds the boundaries of the page, as shown in Figure 14-13.

13. Leaving the most recently created text string selected, click on Preferences in the Special menu. Make certain that the Place Duplicates and Clones values are both at 0.25 inches and then select OK. These values determine the placement of a duplicate object relative to the original.

14. Press CTRL-D to create an exact duplicate of the top text string, offset 1/4 inch above and to the right of the original. The duplicate is selected as soon as it appears.

15. Click on Select All in the Edit menu and then press F9 for the preview window. All of the text strings appear with black fills. Press F9 again to

Combining CorelDRAW! Features

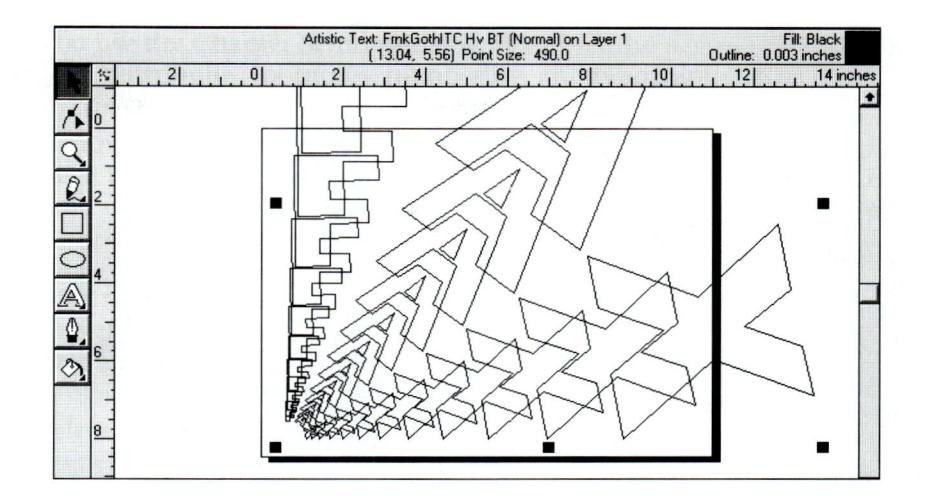

Scaled and repeated text strings exceeding the page boundaries
Figure 14-13.

return to the editing window and then click on the Group command in the Arrange menu to group all of the text strings. Then select the white icon in the Fill tool flyout menu and turn off Wireframe. The text strings redisplay with a fill of white, making it easier to distinguish them from one another.

16. With all text strings still selected, click on the Outline Pen tool and then on the Outline Pen Dialog tool to access the Outline Pen dialog box. Change the Width setting to 0.1 inch, turn on Scale With Image, and select OK. The text strings redisplay with a medium outline of uniform width.

17. Ungroup and deselect all text strings and then select only the last text string you created (the top). Click on the Fill tool and again on the Fountain Fill icon to access the Fountain Fill dialog box. Choose a linear fountain fill and an angle of 45 degrees. For the From color, click on white. Similarly, for the To color, click on black. Click on OK again to make this fill pattern take effect.

18. Now create a drop-shadow effect. Press TAB to select the text string in the layer just below the text string with the fountain fill. Assign a fill of black to this object by clicking on the black icon on the far left of the palette at the bottom of your screen. Select the Zoom-Out icon from the Zoom flyout menu to see your whole work. Figure 14-14 shows the result of your selection.

19. Continue pressing TAB to select each text string in the reverse order from which it was created. Fill the text strings in the following sequence, starting with the largest text string after the drop shadow: 90 percent black, 80 percent black, 70 percent black, 60 percent black, 50

Drop-shadow effect using duplicated text and black fill
Figure 14-14.

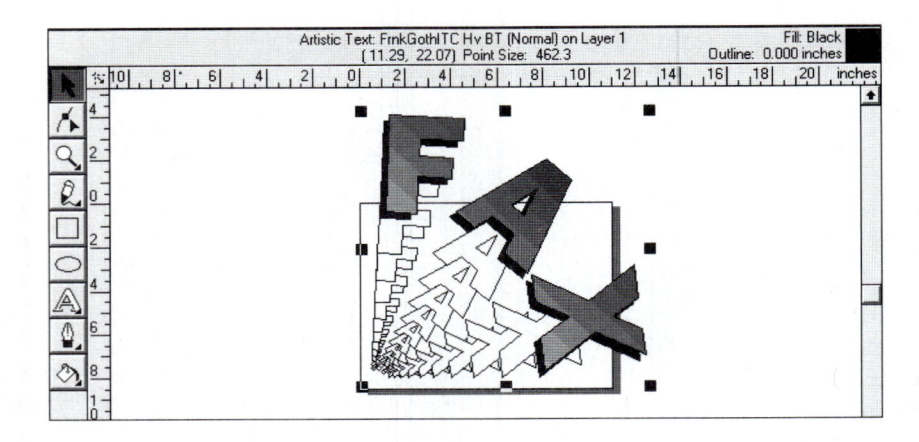

percent black, 40 percent black, 30 percent black, 20 percent black, and 10 percent black. Fill one more text string with 10 percent black and the remaining (smallest) text strings with white. You can quickly apply these shades by using the color palette at the bottom of the screen, beginning with the second black from the left. The resulting gradation of fills and the drop shadow make the repeated text strings seem to leap out of the screen, as shown in Figure 14-15.

20. To group all text strings so that you cannot separate them accidentally, click on Select All in the Edit menu and then on the Group command in the Arrange menu. Then move the group upward and away from the left side of the page. You will bring the group back later, but for now you need room to create more objects.

21. Activate the Ellipse tool and position the pointer 4 1/2 inches from the top of the page and 3/4 inch from the left margin. Press and hold CTRL

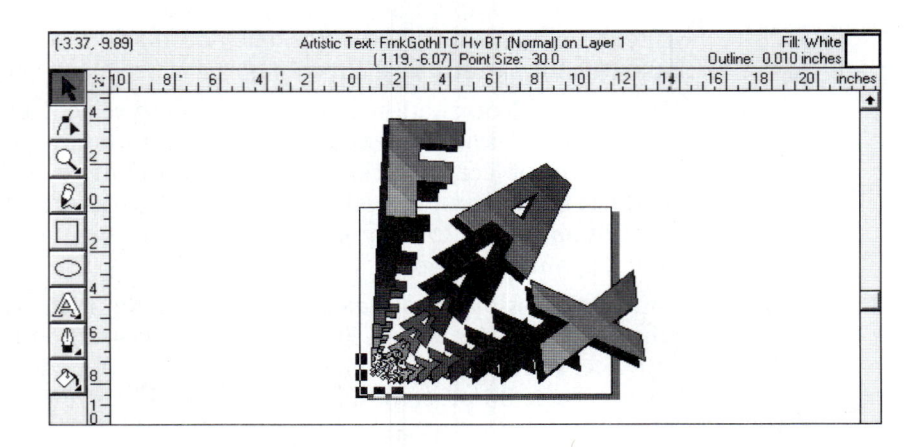

Gradation of fills, leading to a 3-D effect
Figure 14-15.

Combining CorelDRAW! Features

and draw a circle 3 inches in diameter, starting from the upper-left area of the rim. Use the status line as a guide.

22. Turn the circle into a 3-D globe by giving it a radial fountain fill. To do this, activate the Pick tool to select the circle automatically, and then click on the Fill tool and again on the Fountain Fill icon. When the Fountain Fill dialog box appears, select a radial fountain fill, but leave the other settings unaltered. Select OK to make the fountain fill take effect. The globe reappears with a white highlight in the center and the fill gradually darkening toward the rim.

23. Prepare to create an off-center highlight so that the light source seems to be coming from above and to the right of the globe. Activate the Freehand tool and draw a short line segment above and to the right of the globe. Select both the line segment and the globe, and click on the Combine command in the Arrange menu to combine these into one object. Whenever the window redraws from now on, CorelDRAW! extends the first stage of the fountain fill as far as the line segment, as shown in Figure 14-16. This means that you can control the placement of the highlight on the globe by moving the nodes of the line segment with the Shape tool.

24. If you wish to change the placement of the highlight on the globe, activate the Shape tool and move the uppermost node of the line segment in a clockwise or counterclockwise direction. You can move either or both nodes; experiment until you find the placement you want.

25. Now make the line segment invisible. Activate the Pick tool to select the combined object automatically, and then click on the Outline Pen tool and again on the white icon in the second row of the flyout menu. The line segment seems to disappear from the screen, but you can still use it to manipulate the highlight on the globe.

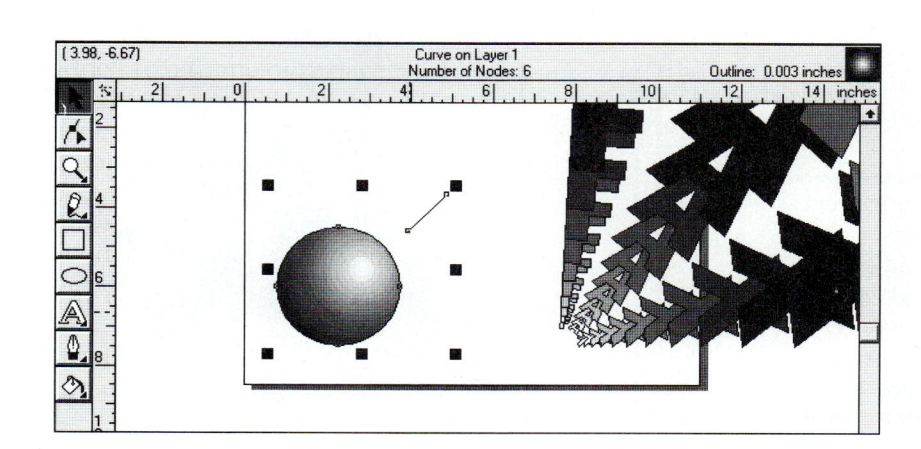

Changing the center of a radial fountain fill by combining a line segment with globe
Figure 14-16.

26. Create a rectangle that will form a backdrop for the rest of the image. Activate the Rectangle tool and begin a rectangle at the 1-inch mark on the horizontal ruler and the 1 1/2-inch mark on the vertical ruler. Extend the rectangle downward and to the right until you reach the 7 1/2-inch mark on the horizontal ruler and the 7 1/4-inch mark on the vertical ruler, then release the mouse button. The window shows that this object lies on top of all the other objects, obscuring them from your view.

27. Activate the Pick tool to select the rectangle automatically, click on the Order option in the Arrange menu and then on the To Back command. Now, the globe appears as the top layer (yes, the line reappears, but it will be obscured again in a moment).

28. With the Outline Pen and Fill tools, assign a black outline of 2.0 fractional points and a fill of 20 percent black to the rectangle.

29. To make the globe stand out in 3-D from the background, select it and assign an outline 0.1 inch wide, using the Outline Pen dialog box.

30. Select the "FAX" grouped text strings and move them on top of the globe, so that they seem to be emerging directly from the highlight. To make certain that the text strings are the top-layer object, click on the To Front command from the Order option on the Arrange menu. This also hides the line segment that you used as a "handle" to change the center of the globe's fountain fill, as shown in Figure 14-17.

31. Adjust viewing magnification to fit-in-window by clicking on the Fit-In-Window icon in the Zoom tool flyout menu. With the grouped

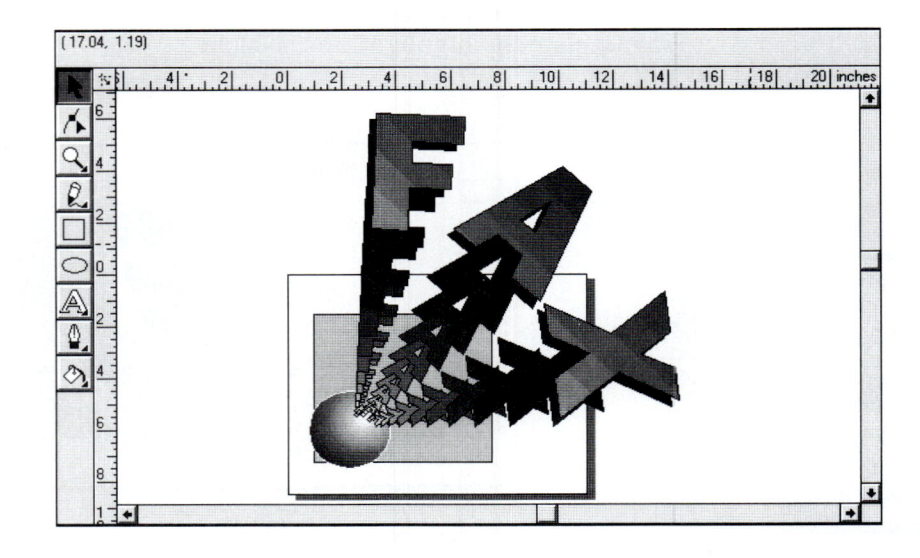

Grouped text strings overlaid on the globe highlight for 3-D effect
Figure 14-17.

text object still selected, scale the text strings down until the status line displays a value of approximately 47 percent. Return to fit-in-window magnification and select Full Screen Preview. Thanks to the insertion of the background rectangle, the text strings still seem to thrust outward in 3-D, as shown earlier in Figure 14-11.

32. Press F9 and click on the Select All command in the Edit menu and then on the Group command in the Arrange menu to group all of the objects in the image.
33. Select Save As from the File menu. When the Save Drawing dialog box appears, type **faxtrans**, and then press ENTER or click on OK.
34. Select New from the File menu to clear the screen.

If you have performed all three of the exercises in this chapter, you are well on the way to understanding how to combine many different CorelDRAW! features, tricks, and techniques. Perhaps these exercises have stimulated you to create your own original designs, or given you new ideas for embellishing existing ones. Whatever your field, your work in this tutorial has given you the tools to create more effective illustrations, documents, presentations, and designs. CorelDRAW! makes it all possible!

ARCHITECTURE

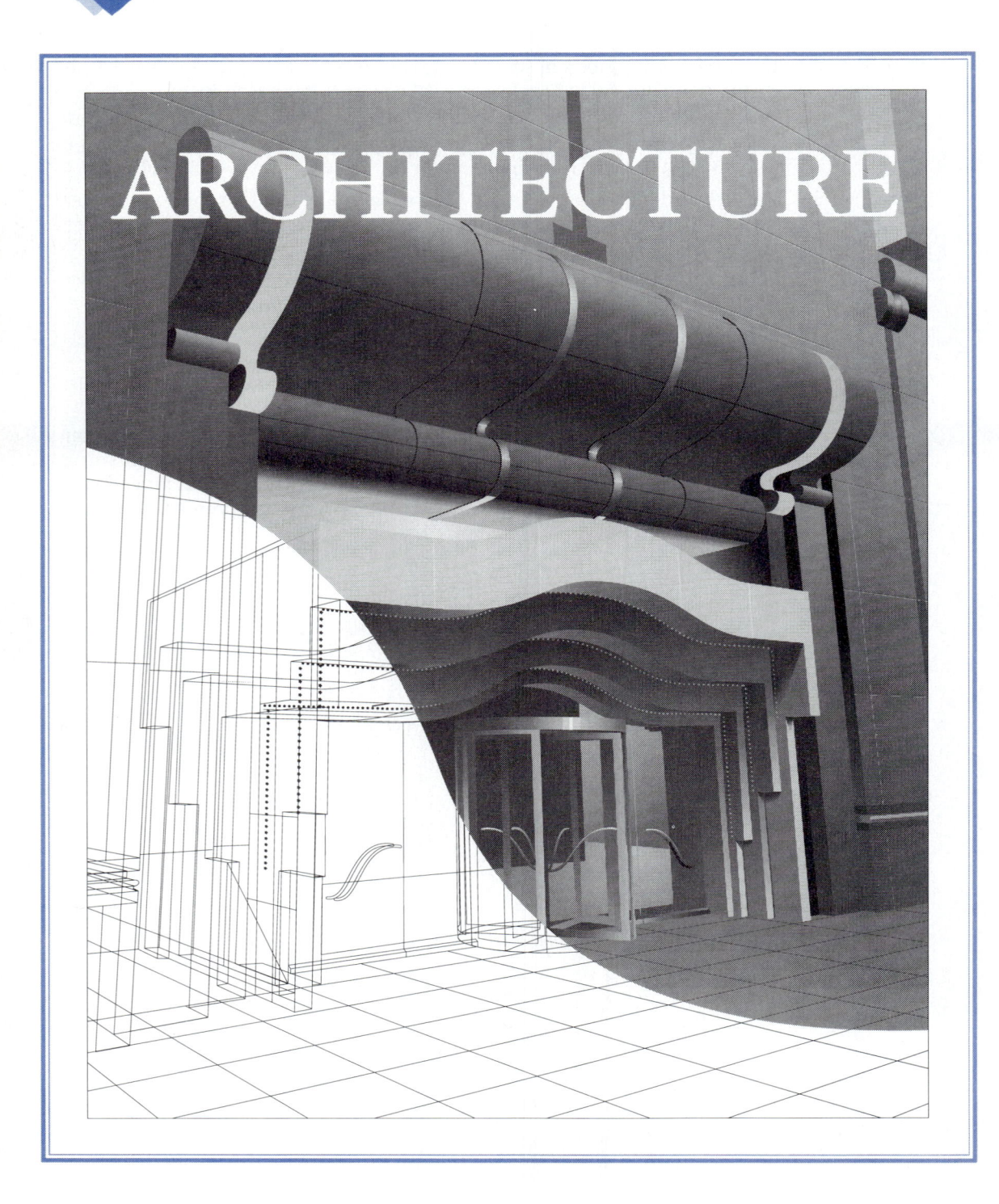

Combining CorelDRAW! Features

CORELDRAW! in Action

DAVID BRICKLEY
Entrance

David started with detailed photographs that he took of an interesting building entrance in San Francisco. He then scanned in one of the photographs, placed the bitmap on its own layer, and manually traced the major shapes with the Bézier tool. To duplicate the three-point perspective that the original photograph had, David zoomed out and up as far as possible, reduced the drawing a bit, then drew three perspective lines (originating at the extreme left and right on the horizon, and the extreme top center) that corresponded to perspective lines in the original photograph. He then used the Shape tool to move the lower end of the perspective lines about in his drawing, as guides.

The tiny twinkling lights on the underside of the arches above the revolving door are actually a string of asterisks (text) that are fitted to a path (the arches). First David typed a text string consisting entirely of asterisks (in a small point size). He selected both the text and the object that forms the edge of an arch, then chose Fit Text To Path from the Text menu. This caused the asterisks to follow the curve of the arch, and allowed them to be moved as a string for fine adjustments.

To create the large horizontal rolled shape near the top of the illustration, David first created three horizontal tubular shapes using the Blend feature. For each part of the rolled shape, he drew an ellipse at each end, then created a 40-step blend between them. Then he deleted most of the intermediate steps, leaving only the ends and the six intermediate bands that follow the curve from top to bottom. This enabled him to create the bands in the proper perspective. Then he made several skewed rectangles whose left and right ends were shaped to correspond to the blended ellipses. These rectangles (and most of the other shapes in the drawing) were given fountain fills to create the illusion of light falling on curved surfaces. The Edge Pad option in the Fountain Fill dialog box was adjusted up as far as 45% to create "compressed" color transitions in some shapes.

The skeletal area in the lower-left part of the illustration was created by layering a white curved object on top of the drawing. Any shape that continued into the white area was broken at the edge of the area using the Shape tool (as described for the exploded desk illustration by Keith Calhoun). The portion of the shape inside the white area was then moved on top of the white object and given a fine black outline and no fill. Additional lines were added to simulate shapes inside the building, giving the effect of x-ray vision.

This piece was in CorelArtShow 4: Page 36, File:CGR00038.CDR. You may contact David in care of:

> David Brickley
> 3318 Northeast Peerless Place
> Portland, OR 97232
> Voice: (503) 236-4883
> Fax: (503) 236-4952

The art on the opposite page was created by and is the property of David Brickley. It is used with permission.

Part 3

USING CorelVENTURA

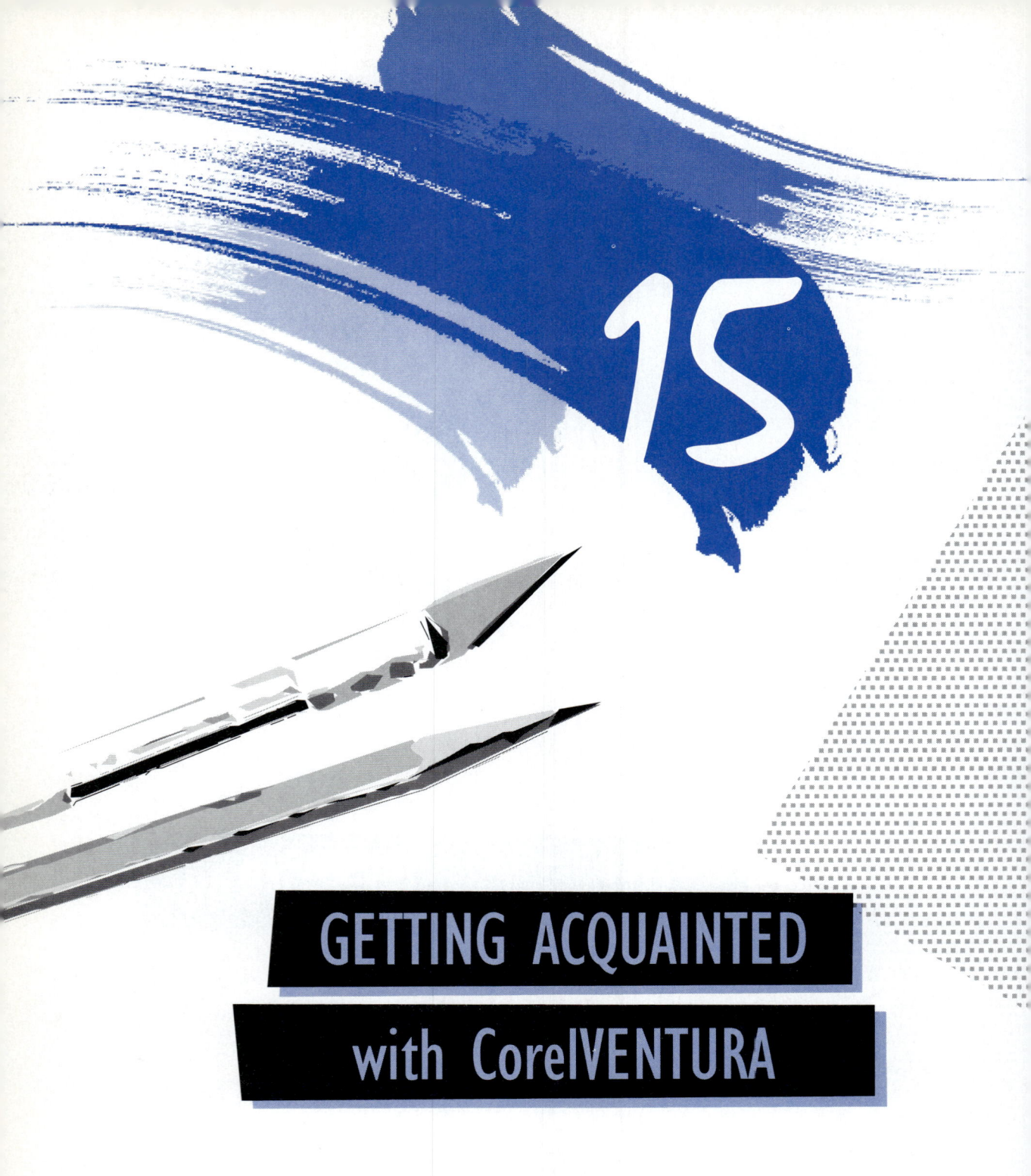

15

GETTING ACQUAINTED
with CorelVENTURA

CoreIVENTURA

is the desktop publishing component of CorelDRAW!. *Desktop publishing* covers the creation of a variety of publications, ranging from simple, single page flyers to complex books or catalogs with hundreds of pages and illustrations. The finished publication can be printed in full color and can include scanned photographs and line art. With the addition of CorelVENTURA, CorelDRAW! now provides all the creative and production tools you need to create both simple and complex publications. CorelDRAW!'s graphic capabilities are matched by CorelVENTURA's extensive text formatting and page layout options. Together they provide a complete desktop publishing solution.

Frames, Tags, Chapters, and Publications

With CorelVENTURA you build publications by combining text and graphic files created in other programs, such as CorelDRAW!, Word for Windows, WordPerfect, 1-2-3, or Excel. CorelVENTURA can import files from most popular word processors, spreadsheets, and databases. You import these text and graphic files into CorelVENTURA and then format, size, and arrange them to produce a complete publication. You can also create simple graphics and edit text using CorelVENTURA's own graphic and text tools, but CorelVENTURA's real strengths are in its powerful text formatting, page layout, and graphic handling controls.

Frames

The basic element of CorelVENTURA is a *frame*. A frame is simply a box that holds each text or graphic file you import into your CorelVENTURA document. Each file you import is placed in its own frame. The dimensions and other attributes of the frame will determine how the file will appear in your finished publication. For example, when you place a graphic in a frame, the size and location of the graphic will be determined by the size and location of the frame itself. If you want to change the size or appearance of the graphic, you will adjust the frame attributes.

CorelVENTURA offers an extensive array of options for formatting frames. Frame attributes include size, position, margins, number and width of columns, text formatting, text flow around the frame, ruling lines, borders, shading, and graphic attributes. These options will be covered in this and the following chapters.

Each page of a CorelVENTURA document has at least one frame for the page itself. This is called the *base page frame*, or just the *base page*. You set the size, margins, and other attributes of the base page when you create a new CorelVENTURA file. The base page will generally hold the main text file for your publication. If the text file is too long to be displayed on one page, additional pages will be automatically added to your document to display the complete text file. The base page for each automatically added page will have attributes identical to your first base page—the attributes *cannot* be changed for individual base pages. (Pages can also be manually inserted and deleted. The base page attributes for manually inserted pages *can* be changed. This is explained in Chapter 16.)

Getting Acquainted with CorelVENTURA

To add other text or graphic files to a page you need to create additional frames, called *free frames*. Unlike the base page, free frames can be individually formatted, sized, and even rotated in one degree increments. (Base pages can only be rotated in 90 degree increments.) You can also move, cut, copy, or delete free frames.

CorelVENTURA will also automatically generate frames that hold captions, headers and footers, and footnotes. Caption frames are used to hold the caption text for a graphic in a free frame. The caption frame is linked to the free frame so that they will always be placed together in your layout. You can adjust the size and other attributes of the caption frame independently of the free frame it is linked to.

Header and footer frames are created at the top and bottom of a page to hold header and footer text. Unlike free and caption frames, the size of header and footer frames will automatically adjust to display all the header and footer text. You can also set the attributes of header and footer frames independently of the other frames on a page, including the base page.

Footnote frames are generated at the bottom of a page or at the end of the document, depending on how you define them. These frames contain the footnote text you have defined in your text file. Footnote frames also automatically adjust to display all the footnote text, like header and footer frames.

Note: The term frame will be used in this book to describe free frames, while the other types of frames will be described by their full names.

Tags

Frame attributes are defined and saved as a *frame tag*. You use frame tags to quickly create frames with identical attributes. For example, in a catalog you might need to have a number of illustrations throughout the publication. By defining a frame tag containing the margins, borders, and other attributes that you want, you can very easily create any number of frames for your illustrations. You just draw a new frame and then tag it with the desired frame tag. If you decide to change the design of the frames containing your illustrations, you simply change the frame tag. All frames tagged with that frame tag will automatically reflect the new attribute settings.

You format the text placed in your document by using *style tags*. Like frame tags, style tags are a set of attributes that can be defined and saved. A style tag specifies the font, size, color, style, line spacing, alignment, and other attributes of the text for a *paragraph* (style tags are also referred to as *paragraph tags*). Paragraph and frame tags are stored in *style sheets*. Each CorelVENTURA document has a style sheet file attached to it. Each style sheet can be used by any number of documents. To use a style sheet other than the one currently attached to your document, you can either open another existing style sheet or create a new one. The paragraph and frame tags on the new style sheet can then be used in your document. Like frame tags, when a paragraph tag is modified, all paragraphs formatted with the tag are modified at the same time. Besides applying frame and paragraph tags, words and characters can be selected and formatted directly.

Tip: Frame and style tags enable you to establish a consistent overall design for a publication. Changes to the entire publication or to selected frames and paragraphs are easily made by editing the appropriate tags.

Chapters and Publications

CorelVENTURA documents are organized as *chapters*. Chapters are linked together to create a complete CorelVENTURA *publication*. You can generate an index, cross-references, and table of contents for a publication. Pages can be numbered consecutively for the publication and all or part of the publication can be printed at one time. CorelVENTURA's chapter and publication structure allows you to create large, complex documents with a minimum of effort.

When you place a text or graphic file in a CorelVENTURA chapter, only a *pointer* to the location of the source file is actually stored in the chapter, not a copy of the source file. The pointer tells CorelVENTURA where to find the source file. If a source file has been moved you will need to update the pointer to the file. A CorelVENTURA chapter file, then, contains the pointers to the text and graphic files placed in the chapter, and the formatting and special effects applied to each file. Like CorelVENTURA chapter files, publication files contain only the pointers to the chapters that have been added to the publication, not the chapters themselves.

Since the actual text and graphic files are not included in the CorelVENTURA publication, they can be opened and modified outside of CorelVENTURA. Also, any file can be used in a number of different publications. For example, an organization may need to produce a separate operations manual for each of several departments. Each manual could include a standard text file explaining the organization's goals. Only one copy of this file would have to exist in order for it to be included in all of the operations manuals. When the goals statement needed to be updated, only the one file would have to be modified, rather than every publication that used the file.

Getting Acquainted with CorelVENTURA

Caution: Always use the Publication Manager option in the File menu when copying or moving CorelVENTURA chapter and publication files. Using File Manager or similar utilities will not update the pointers to the source files referenced in the CorelVENTURA files.

The CorelVENTURA Screen

When you first start CorelVENTURA, after the copyright message is displayed, a screen similar to Figure 15-1 will appear. As you can see, the CorelVENTURA screen is similar to the CorelDRAW! screen. Common elements, such as the standard Windows control buttons, have been covered previously, so only the menus, toolbars, and screen elements unique to CorelVENTURA are discussed in the following sections.

Rulers

You can use the horizontal and vertical rulers to precisely position objects on a page and to determine the locations for margins, tabs, indents, and columns. Each ruler can be set independently to use inch, centimeter, or pica measurement systems. You can also move the zero point of the rulers in

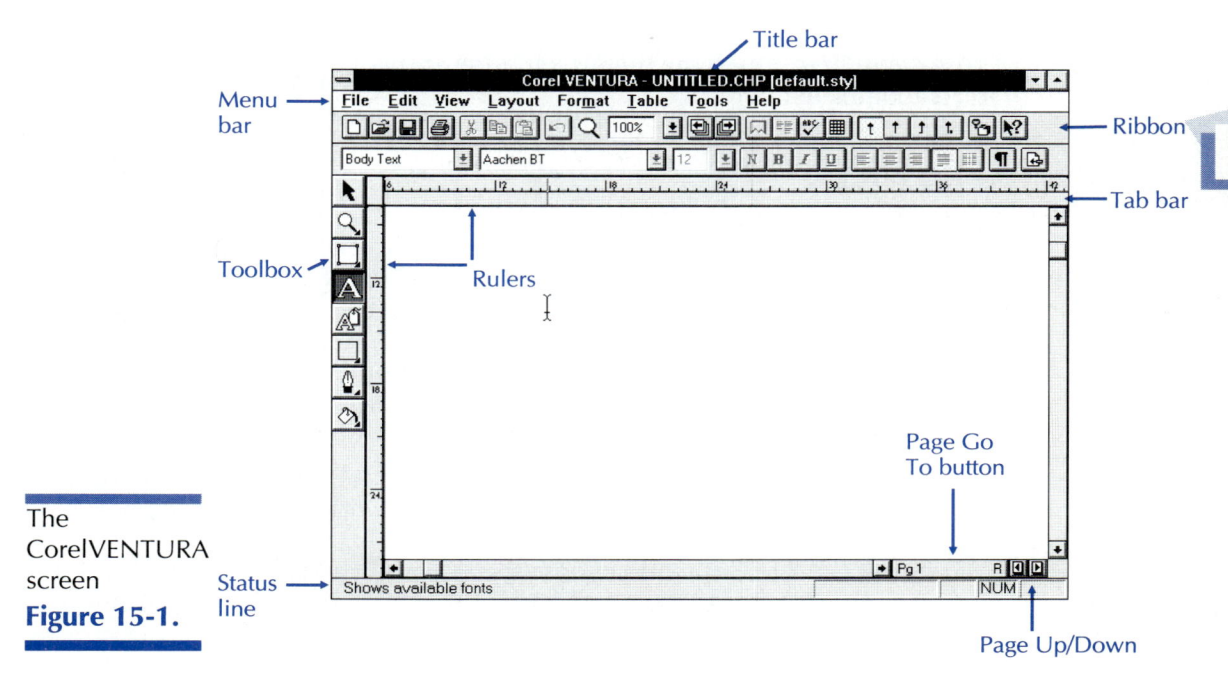

Figure 15-1. The CorelVENTURA screen

relation to the upper-left corner of the page by pointing on the box at the intersection of the rulers and dragging to the desired location on the page. To return the zero point to the upper-left corner, double-click on the same box.

When you select a frame, the zero point of the horizontal ruler aligns with the left edge of the frame, not the page. This simplifies setting indents and tabs for the frame. The zero point returns to the previous setting when the frame is no longer selected.

You can also move the rulers to make it easier to locate objects on your page. To move the rulers, point on the box at the intersection of the rulers, press the SHIFT key, and drag the rulers to the desired location. Double-clicking on the box at the intersection of the rulers will return them to the edges of the window.

Another function of the rulers is to place *guidelines*. Guidelines are non-printing lines you can use to align objects on a page. To place a guideline, simply point on either ruler, press and hold the mouse button, and then drag the guideline to the desired location. You can reposition guidelines by dragging them. Guidelines have a magnetic attribute that forces frames to align with them, making it easy to align frames across pages.

CorelVENTURA Menus

The CorelVENTURA menu bar contains seven menus in addition to the standard Windows Control and Help menus. Since the Control and Help menus are covered in Chapter 1, only the seven CorelVENTURA menus will be covered here. Open the menus and look at them on your computer as you read about them here.

File Menu

The File menu contains the options needed to create and manage publications. You can create, open, and save chapters and publications, and place, remove, or rename text and graphic files in a chapter either directly or with CorelMOSAIC. Publications are copied, moved, and deleted using the Publication Manager option. The Color Manager option allows you to calibrate your monitor, scanner, and printer for optimal results when working with color. You can also control printer setup and other printing options. Lastly, you also use the File menu to exit CorelVENTURA.

You can see how CorelVENTURA's chapter and publication structure works by opening the Publication Manager. Do so now with these instructions:

1. Select the File menu and choose the Publication Manager option. After CorelVENTURA scans your drives for publication files, the Publication Manager dialog box, shown in Figure 15-2, will be displayed.

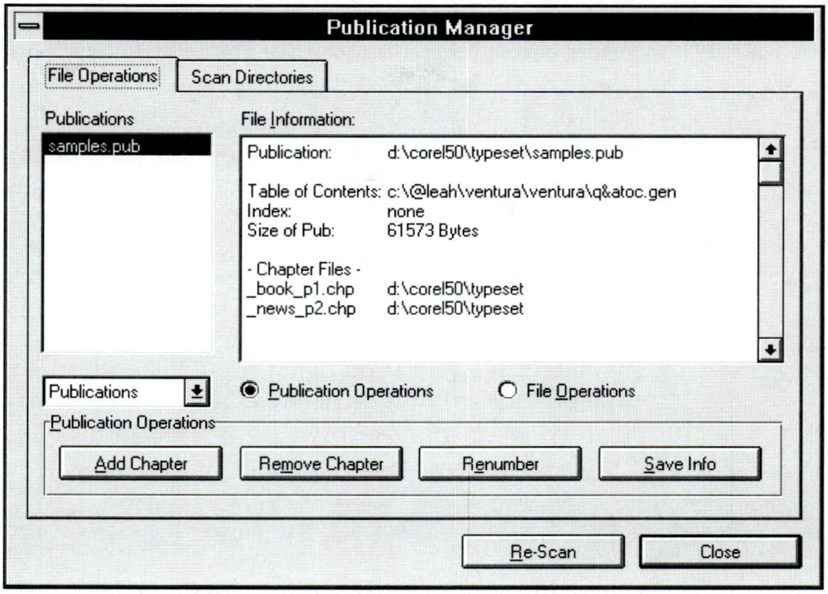

Getting Acquainted with CorelVENTURA

Publication Manager dialog box
Figure 15-2.

The Publication Manager dialog box contains two tabs: File Operations and Scan Directories. The File Operations tab should be selected. The Scan Directories tab is used to select the directories where CorelVENTURA will search for publication and chapter files. On the left side of the dialog box is the Publications list box. Your current CorelVENTURA publication files will be listed here. The File Information list box is to the right. It contains the names and locations of the chapter files that make up the selected publication. The location of the table of contents and index files, if any, are also listed here.

Below the Publications list box is a drop-down list box used to select either publications or chapters for viewing.

2. Click on the down arrow of the drop-down list box and choose Chapters. The Publications list box is now labeled Chapters. The Chapters list box displays all your chapter files. The File Information list box now displays the information for the selected chapter file, including the names of the text and graphic files included in the chapter. Use the scroll bars to see the entire list.

Below the File Information list box are two option buttons: Publication Operations and File Operations. Publication Operations should be selected. Below the option buttons are four command buttons—these control chapter operations. Chapters can be added or removed from a publication. This does not change the selected chapters, it simply adds or removes the link between the chapters and the publication. The order of chapters in a publication can be changed and then renumbered. You can also save the chapter information displayed in the File Information list box as a text file using the Save Info command button with Publications Operations selected.

3. Click on the File Operations option button. The four command buttons are now used to work with publications. Using these command buttons will ensure that all the component files in the publication are included in the selected operation. When you copy or move a publication CorelVENTURA checks all publications to determine which other publications share files with the publication being moved. The location of the shared files will be automatically updated in those other publications. When you delete a publication, files that are used in other publications will not be deleted. The Find File command button is used to search selected directories for specific files.

4. Click on Close to close the Publication Manager.

Edit Menu

With the Edit menu you can undo or redo the last operation you did to text, graphics, frames, and tags. You can also cut, copy, and paste text, graphics, frames and their contents, and tags. Text can be searched for specified text, text attributes, and style tags, which can then be replaced. You can insert and edit special text objects, such as footnotes, equations, and cross-references. You can also insert and edit special items such as footnotes, equations, and *frame anchors*. Frame anchors link a frame to a specific location in a text file. As you format your document, the anchored frame will automatically be located with the anchor in the text. You use a frame anchor to keep a frame containing an illustration with the relevant section of text. You can also establish OLE object links, and display and edit OLE properties.

View Menu

The View menu lets you control how your CorelVENTURA screen looks. You can select either the Story Editor view (to edit text files), Draft view (to speed up screen display by representing graphics as gray boxes), or Page Layout view (to place text and graphic files). Facing pages and specific pages can be displayed. You can control onscreen color correction and the toolbox can be fixed or floating. Rulers can be toggled on or off and you can hide graphics if you wish to speed up screen display. You can also redraw the screen at any time.

Layout Menu

You use the Layout menu to add and save chapters in your publication. You also control page formatting and attributes, such as page size and layout, for an entire chapter. Pages can be added or removed, and style sheets can be applied to the chapter, edited, and saved. By choosing the Chapter Settings option, you can also set character and line spacing, text placement within frames, column balance, numbering of paragraphs and tables, and control *widows* and *orphans*. A widow is the last line of a paragraph which is separated from the paragraph and placed at the top of the next column or page. An orphan is the first line of a paragraph which is separated from the paragraph and placed at the bottom of the previous column or page. The display of footnotes, headers, and footers for the chapter can be turned on or off and the sides of frames can be set to align with column guides and the top of frames can be set to align with the line spacing for the page.

Format Menu

The Format menu options control the attributes of the various CorelVENTURA elements such as paragraphs, selected text, frames, tables, and graphics. Frame margins, number of columns, frame size and location, and text flow around frames can all be controlled. Type attributes can be set for individual frames, replacing the chapter type attributes since frame attributes take precedence over default chapter attributes. Ruling lines can be placed above, below, and around text, and the frame can be shaded. Page and section numbers, and tables of contents and indexes can be generated, and their numbering updated. Frame and style tags are also created and organized using the Format menu. Frame anchors can be updated and frames, their contents, and attributes can be duplicated on every page in a chapter, although you can have only six repeating frames per chapter.

Table Menu

Tables display information in a row and column format. With the Table menu you can select and format information to be displayed as a table. You can insert a blank table, copy a table from an existing CorelVENTURA publication, or import data from a database or spreadsheet to create a new table. Rows and columns can be added and removed, and cells (the intersection of one row and column) can be merged or split. The width of columns, the border style, and the shading of cells can also be controlled.

Database and spreadsheet tables are imported using CorelQUERY, a stand-alone database viewer included with CorelDRAW!. With CorelQuery you can select fields and establish criteria to extract data from databases and spreadsheets. This selected information is then placed in your

CorelVENTURA publication. CorelQUERY cannot change the data in the database or spreadsheet, it can only read and format the information.

Tools Menu

The Tools menu accesses the spell check, thesaurus, and TypeAssist options. TypeAssist is a sophisticated on-line spell checker and glossary that automatically corrects misspelled words and capitalization errors as you type. TypeAssist also automatically substitutes text strings when you type pre-defined text. For example, you may use the phrase "consult your operator's manual" several times in a publication. Using TypeAssist, you could define "cyom" as the shorthand for "consult your operator's manual." Every time you typed "cyom," "consult your operator's manual" would be substituted in your document. TypeAssist uses a user-defined dictionary for text substitution.

The various CorelVENTURA roll-ups are also accessed from the Tools menu, and grid and ruler settings are defined. You can also set your CorelVENTURA preferences with the Tools menu. Preferences include automatic back-up of files, hiding or displaying generated tags in the Tags list, text display options, and punctuation style. The Extension option is used to access CorelMOSAIC; CorelPHOTO-PAINT; CorelKERN, a stand-alone program used to customize the kerning, or spacing, between pairs of letters; CDBEdit, a stand-alone program used to create database files or tables for use with CorelVENTURA; and Tagwrite Editor, a stand-alone manager for frame and paragraph tags.

The CorelVENTURA Ribbon

Below the menu bar is the ribbon, shown in Figure 15-3, consisting of two rows of buttons and drop-down list boxes. Most of the buttons duplicate menu options. Table 15-1 lists the functions of the tools and drop-down list boxes on the ribbon.

CorelVENTURA Toolbox

The CorelVENTURA toolbox is similar to the CorelDRAW! toolbox. Like the CorelDRAW! toolbox, the CorelVENTURA toolbox can be hidden or visible, and fixed or floating depending on the settings in the Toolbox option in the View menu. The Pick, Outline, and Fill tools and their flyout menus are identical to their CorelDRAW! counterparts. The tools unique to CorelVENTURA, and their flyout menus, are covered in the following sections.

CorelVENTURA ribbon

Figure 15-3.

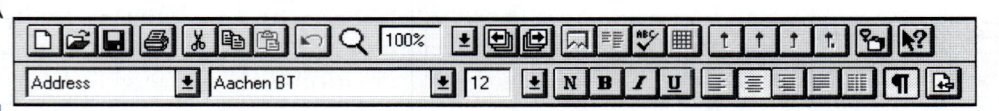

Getting Acquainted with CorelVENTURA

Tool	Nme	Function
	New	Displays the New Publication dialog box
	Open	Displays the File Open dialog box
	Save	Saves the current publication. If the current publication has not been saved previously the File Save As dialog box is displayed
	Print	Prints the current chapter or selected pages
	Cut	Removes the selected text or object and places it on the Clipboard
	Copy	Copies the selected text or object to the Clipboard
	Paste	Pastes the contents of the Clipboard at the current insertion point
	Undo	Reverses the last action
	Zoom	Selects the magnification factor for displaying the current page
	Chapter Down	Displays the first page of the previous chapter
	Chapter Up	Displays the first page of the next chapter
	Breaks	Displays the Breaks dialog box to set page, column, or line breaks
	Side-by-Side Paragraphs	Places selected paragraphs side-by-side on a page
	Spell Check	Checks the spelling of files
	Insert Table	Displays the Table Settings dialog box to create a table
	Tabs	Sets left, center, right, or decimal tabs
	Mosaic Roll-up	Opens the Corel Mosaic roll-up to import graphic files

Ribbon Tool Functions
Table 15-1.

Tool	Nme	Function
	Help	Activates the Help pointer which, when clicked on an item (such as a tool), displays the help file for that item
Body Text	Tags List	Displays tags available in the current style sheet so they can be selected
Aachen BT	Files List/Font Name	Displays the files available to be placed in the current publication or if the text tool is selected, displays the list of fonts that are available
12	Type Size	Selects the type size of the selected text or style tag
N B I U	Type Style	Selects normal, bold, italic, and underline styles for the selected text or style tag
	Justification	Selects left, center, right, or full justification or decimal alignment for the selected paragraph or style tag
¶	Tabs and Returns	Toggles the display of paragraph, tab, end of file, and other symbols in text
	Quick Format Roll-up	Opens the Quick Format Roll-up allowing application of pre-defined table formats

Ribbon Tool Functions (*continued*)
Table 15-1.

Zoom Tool

The Zoom tool is used to select the area of your document to be displayed on your screen. Displaying the entire page lets you check your overall layout, while zooming in allows you to precisely place objects. Table 15-2 lists the tools available on the Zoom flyout menu and their functions.

Frame Tool/Shape Tool

The Frame tool is used to create free frames on a page and the Shape tool is used to modify the shape of frames. The Shape tool is used when you want to flow text around irregularly shaped objects. Either the Frame or the Shape tool will be displayed depending on which tool was last selected from the Frame tool flyout.

Getting Acquainted with CorelVENTURA

Zoom Flyout Menu Tools
Table 15-2.

Tool	Name	Function
🔍	Zoom-in	Zooms in on the area of a page you select
🔍	Zoom-out	Either zooms out of your current view by a factor of two or, if your screen currently shows a zoom-in view, returns to the previous view
1:1	Actual Size	Displays your document at the actual size it will be printed
	Full Page	Displays the entire page
	Full Width	Displays the full width of a page
	Full Height	Displays the full height of a page

Once a frame has been created, the Pick tool is selected. Multiple frames can be created by pressing the SHIFT key while using the Frame tool. The Pick tool will be selected when the SHIFT key is released.

Text Tool

The Text tool is used to edit existing text or to add additional text to your publication.

Tag Base Text Tool

The Tag Base Text tool is used to select paragraphs and sections of text to apply or define style tags. Individual paragraphs are selected by clicking on them, consecutive paragraphs and sections of text are selected by dragging the Tag Base Text tool, and non-consecutive paragraphs are selected by pressing the SHIFT key while clicking on the desired paragraphs.

Drawing Tool

The Drawing tool is used to add and edit graphic elements in your publication. Selecting the Drawing tool displays a flyout menu. The flyout menus tools and their functions are shown in Table 15-3.

Tool	Name	Function
/	Line	Draws straight lines
▢	Rectangle	Draws rectangles
◯	Round Rectangle	Draws rectangles with rounded corners
⬭	Ellipse	Draws circles and ellipses
AB	Box Text	Creates a box to contain text which can overlap any text or graphics on a page

Drawing Flyout Menu Tools
Table 15-3.

Page Controls

CorelVENTURA offers you several methods for moving between pages in a chapter. The Go to Page option in the View menu (or CTRL-G), which allows you several options for selecting a page, and the Next and Previous Page buttons in the lower left of the window on the line with the horizontal scroll bar, shown here:

Pg 3   R ◀ ▶

Clicking on the Next Page button (the right pointing arrow) will make the next higher numbered page in the chapter the active page. Pressing the CTRL key while clicking on the Next Page button will make the last page in the chapter the active page. The Previous Page button (the left pointing arrow) works in the same manner—clicking once selects the previous or lower numbered page in the chapter and pressing the CTRL key while clicking moves to the first page in the chapter.

The current page and whether the current page is a left or right page is displayed next to the Next and Previous Page buttons. Clicking on the bar with the page number opens the Go To Page dialog box, and pressing PGUP and PGDN goes from page to page as you would expect.

Status Line

The status line at the bottom of the CorelVENTURA window, shown next, provides you with information about what you are currently doing. The left side of the status line displays a brief description of the last button or tool you pointed on. The right side of the status line displays the formatting codes in selected text as well as the status of the CAPS LOCK, NUM LOCK, and SCROLL LOCK keys.

```
Use the Text Tool to edit text on the current page        Paragraph End   CAP NUM SCRL
```

In the next chapter you will begin to work with CorelVENTURA's frame and page structure. You will learn how to apply frame attributes, import text files, and apply text formatting.

16

IMPORTING TEXT
and USING STYLE SHEETS

The design of books, newsletters, forms, and other publications combines page layout—the position of text and graphics on a page—and text formatting—the appearance of the text. With CorelVENTURA you can control virtually every aspect of page layout and text formatting. Whether your publication is a simple brochure or a complex book, CorelVENTURA gives you the tools you need to create effective publications that are visually pleasing. In CorelVENTURA you have two powerful aids for effective design: frames and style sheets.

Frames are the basic building blocks of CorelVENTURA publications. Frames are boxes or containers that hold the text and graphic files you place in your document. Each text or graphic file is placed in a frame or a series of frames. The attributes you select for a frame, such as size, margins, and number of columns, will determine the layout of the text or graphic in that frame. Frame attributes are stored in tags associated with the frame and are called *frame tags*. Text formatting features, such as font, style, and size, are also stored in tags associated with paragraphs and are called *style tags*. Style sheets, which are independent of publications, contain sets of frame and style tags that can be applied to a publication to determine the design information for both the pages and the text placed on pages. With style sheets, even a complex design can be created and changed quickly and easily.

In this chapter you will learn how to create a new CorelVENTURA chapter, how to open and modify style sheets, how to set frame attributes, how to import a text file, and how to *tag* paragraphs by applying styles from your style sheet. In Chapter 17 you will learn how to place graphics in frames.

Creating a CorelVENTURA Chapter

Your first step in creating a CorelVENTURA publication is to create a new chapter file. You can create a new chapter by opening a style sheet, or by opening a template. To create a chapter using a style sheet, you open a style sheet that contains the page size and the base page frame attributes (such as margins and columns) that you want. Opening the style sheet will create a chapter with a single blank page having the attributes contained in the style sheet. The style sheet also contains the style tags used to format your text.

When you want to create a new chapter with the same attributes as an existing chapter you can use the existing chapter as a *template*. A template is a chapter that has had some or all of the text and graphic files removed. Using a template allows you to keep selected elements the same for all publications based on that template. For example, a newsletter usually includes a list of the people who created it (editor, writers, and so on) and a title, which can include a graphic. This material generally remains the same from issue to issue. In a newsletter template, files for these elements would be included in the template.

Caution: If you modify a file included in a template, the changes will be reflected in all publications that include the file. Rename the file if you want to edit it for a single publication only.

When you start CorelVENTURA, a new chapter is automatically created using the default style sheet. The default style sheet is simply the style sheet named DEFAULT.STY in your style sheet directory (usually the COREL50\TYPESET directory). The new chapter will consist of one page with at least one frame, the base page. Other frames can be added to any page, and the attributes for each added frame can be individually set.

Note: The style sheet name DEFAULT.STY is reserved by CorelVENTURA. This means you can change the attributes of the style sheet, or copy them, but you cannot rename or delete this style sheet.

When you import a text file that is too long to fit on one page, CorelVENTURA will automatically create the additional pages needed to hold the complete text file. The inserted pages will have the same base page attributes as the default page. The base page attributes for individual pages that are automatically inserted *cannot* be changed. You can also manually insert and remove pages using the Insert and Delete Pages options in the Layout menu. The base page attributes for manually inserted pages *can* be changed.

Note: It is important to understand the difference between pages automatically created by CorelVENTURA and pages that you manually insert in your chapter. If your design requires you to modify the base page attributes on a page, you will have to manually insert the page. For example, you can have different margin or border settings in a chapter by manually inserting pages and then changing the base page attributes for the inserted pages. You can add design elements, such as ruling lines or frames, to either manually or automatically inserted pages. You cannot change from portrait to landscape format on any page, however.

Selecting a Style Sheet

When you select a style sheet for a chapter, you can use the default style sheet, open an existing style sheet, open a template, or create a new style sheet. New style sheets are created by copying and then modifying an existing style sheet. In this exercise you will open an existing style sheet and then modify it, creating a new style sheet. Do that now with the following instructions:

> **Tip:** When creating a new style sheet, start with the existing style sheet most like the style sheet you intend to create. This will minimize the number of changes you have to make.

1. Load CorelVENTURA if it isn't running already.
2. Select the File menu and choose New. The New Publication dialog box will be displayed, as shown here:

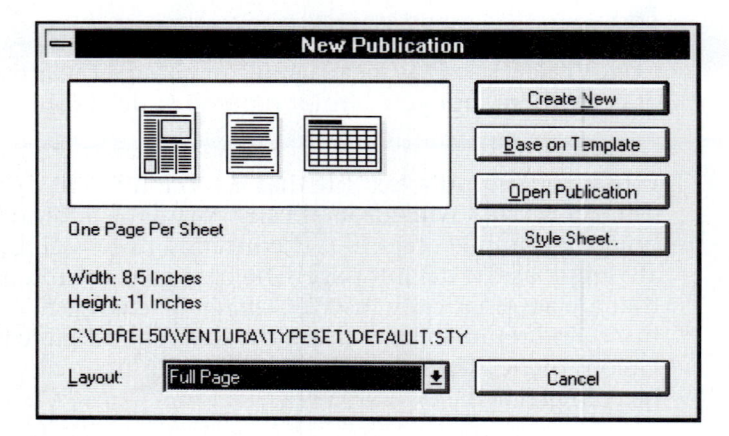

![New Publication dialog box showing One Page Per Sheet, Width: 8.5 Inches, Height: 11 Inches, C:\COREL50\VENTURA\TYPESET\DEFAULT.STY, Layout: Full Page, with buttons Create New, Base on Template, Open Publication, Style Sheet.., Cancel]

The Layout drop-down list box contains the standard page layouts available. The page layout determines how the selected page size will be arranged. These are the same page layouts as are available for CorelDRAW!. A preview of the selected page layout is shown above the Layout drop-down list box. The path and filename of the style sheet are displayed also. Create New will create a chapter with a single blank page using the selected style sheet. Selecting Base on Template will display the File Open dialog box. After selecting the file for your template, the Specify Template Destination dialog box will be displayed, as shown in Figure 16-1. This allows you to select the existing chapter (and its style sheet) and the other elements that will be used as the basis for the new chapter.

The chapter file to use for the template is selected in the File Name list box, and the text and graphic files to be included in the template are selected from the files list at the bottom of the dialog box. If you

Importing Text and Using Style Sheets

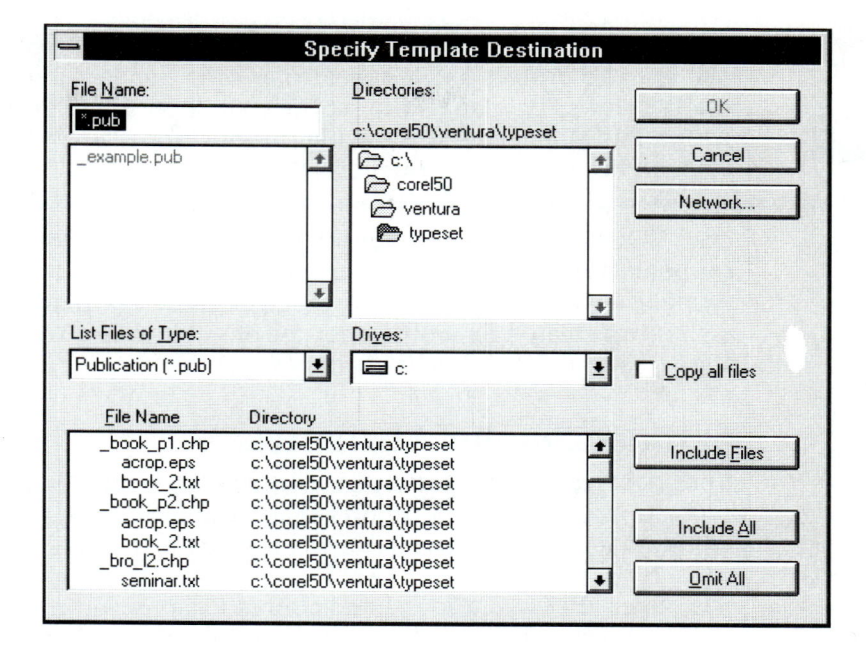

Specify Template Destination dialog box
Figure 16-1.

opened the Specify Template Destination dialog box, click on Cancel to close it.

You will use the _BOOK_P1.STY as the starting point for your new style sheet.

3. Click on the Style Sheet command button. When the File Open dialog box is displayed select _BOOK_P1.STY in the files list box. If _BOOK_P1.STY is not displayed in the current directory, use the Directories list box to select the directory containing your style sheets (\COREL50\VENTURA\TYPESET\ in this case).

4. Click on OK. A new chapter based on the _BOOK_P1.STY style sheet is created.

   You will be changing some of the attributes of the _BOOK_P1 style sheet. Since you do not want these changes to affect the existing publications that use the same style sheet, you will save _BOOK_P1.STY using a different name.

5. Select the Layout menu, then choose the Save Style Sheet As option. The File Save As dialog box will be displayed. Type **my_book** in the File Name text box and click on OK. Now your changes to the style sheet will be saved in the MY_BOOK style sheet, leaving the _BOOK_P1 style sheet unchanged.

> **Tip:** To protect a style sheet from being accidentally modified you can use Windows File Manager to set the style sheet file to Read Only. From within File Manager, select the file, choose Properties from the File menu, click on Read Only, and then on OK.

The _BOOK_P1 style sheet already contains a number of style tags suitable for book layout and design. By using a copy of this style sheet, you will have to make fewer changes to create a new book design than you would with a style sheet created for a different type of publication. You can now modify the MY_BOOK style sheet's attributes.

Setting Chapter Attributes

Your next step in creating a new chapter is to set the page size, chapter typography, and other attributes that are applied to the entire chapter. You will do that now with the following instructions:

1. Open the Layout menu and choose Chapter Settings. The Chapter Settings dialog box shown in Figure 16-2 is displayed.

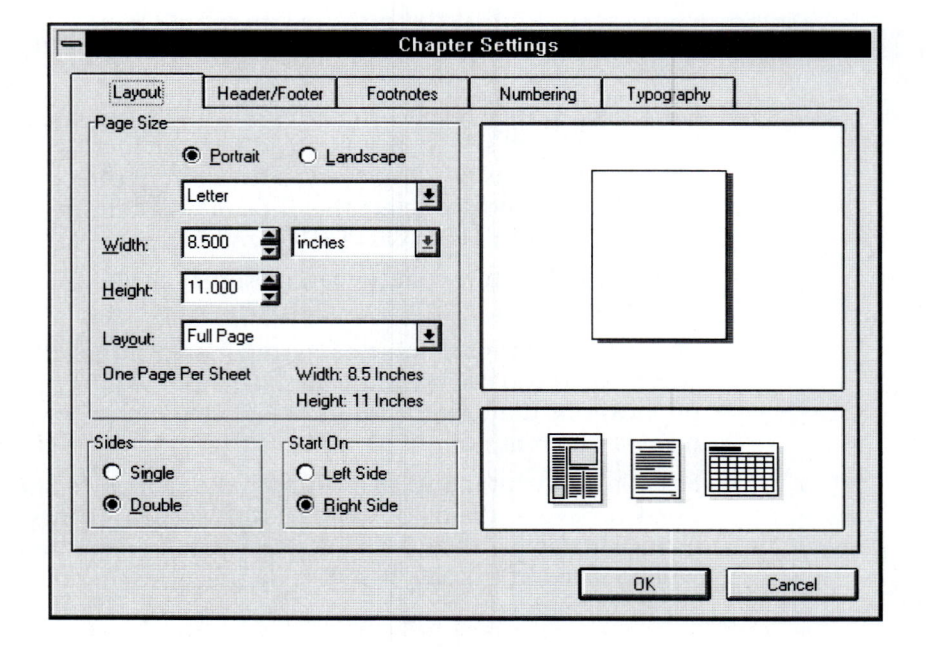

Chapter Settings dialog box
Figure 16-2.

You use the Chapter Settings dialog box to set the page size, header and footer attributes, footnotes, numbering, and typography for the chapter.

In the Layout tab, the Page Size drop-down list box contains a limited number of standard paper sizes that are commonly available. You may need to use a page size that does not match a standard paper size, or your design may require printing to the very edge of the page, known as a *bleed*. (Since printers cannot print to the very edge of the paper, you must use a paper size larger than the page size for bleeds. The paper is trimmed to the correct size after printing.) For example, the finished size of your publication in this exercise will be a book with a page size of 7 by 9 inches. Since this paper size is not available in the Page Size drop-down list box, you will need to set a custom page size.

2. Select **Custom** in the Page Size drop-down list box and confirm that inches is selected in the units drop-down list box to the right of the Width spinner. CorelVENTURA allows you to use more than one measurement system in a chapter. (You can choose from inches, picas and points, points, centimeters, or millimeters.) Many of the dialog boxes you will use allow you to select the measurement system for the settings in that dialog box without affecting any other settings. In this exercise, you will be using inches to specify most of the dimensions for your chapter layout.

3. Double-click on the Width spinner and type **7**.

4. Press TAB twice and type **9**.

5. Confirm that Portrait and Full Page Layout are selected for Page Size, and that Double Sides and Start On Right Side are also selected.

   You will use the current MY_BOOK style sheet settings for Headers/Footers, Footnotes, and Numbering. You can select these tabs to review the settings without changing them. The next group of attributes you will modify are the Chapter Typography defaults.

6. Click on the Typography tab. The tab shown in Figure 16-3 is displayed.

7. Confirm that Widows and Orphans are set to two lines. The Widows and Orphans settings determine the minimum number of lines of a paragraph that will be left at the top or bottom of a column or page. When Widows is set for two lines it means that no fewer than two lines of a paragraph will be placed at the top of a column or page. When Orphans is set to two lines it means that no fewer than two lines of a new paragraph will be placed at the bottom of a column or page. If there isn't enough room to place at least two lines at the bottom, the lines will be moved to the top of the next column or page.

8. Select the Column Balance check box. Column Balance is used to automatically adjust the text flow in multiple columns on a page. When

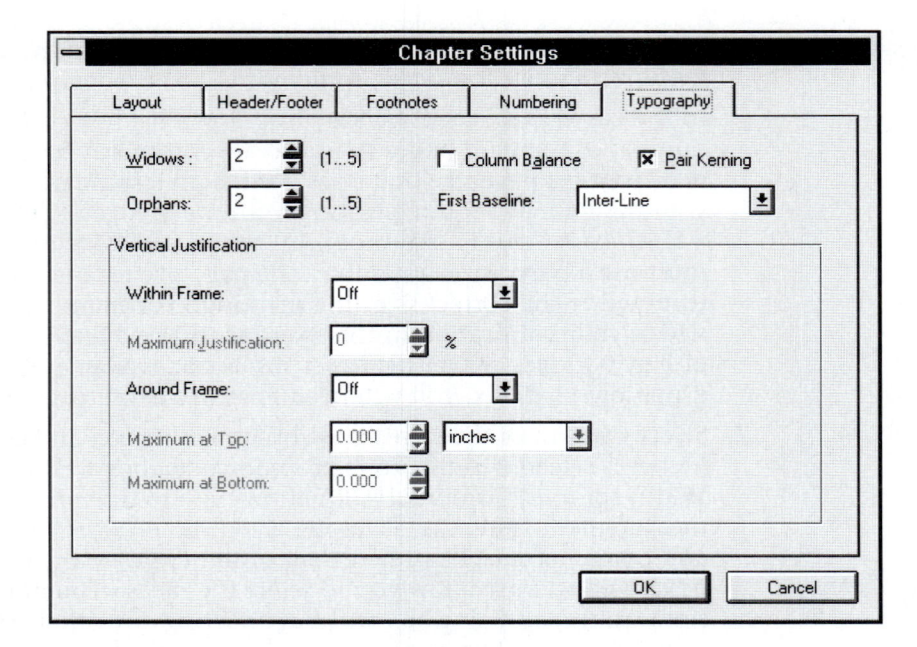

Chapter Settings Typography tab
Figure 16-3.

Column Balance is turned on, CorelVENTURA will adjust the text so that each column is equal in length.

9. Confirm that Pair Kerning is selected. Pair Kerning is used to control the spacing between pairs of letters. For example, the letter pairs "Yo" and "yo" require different spacing between the letters to create a balanced look. Even though the effects of kerning are often only apparent with larger type sizes, you will want to have Pair Kerning selected so that you can control the settings for individual style tags. If Pair Kerning is turned off, you cannot use it for any style tags; with it turned on in Chapter Typography, you can turn kerning on or off in individual style tags.

Leaving kerning on will slow down the redrawing of the screen and printing. Generally, with body text type sizes, you can turn off kerning with no ill effects. If you decide a particular letter pair needs to be kerned, the kerning can be applied manually. In style tags using larger type sizes, you can turn kerning on for that style tag when you define it.

Tip: The kerning between letter pairs can be adjusted manually by selecting the letter pair and then using the SHIFT-RIGHT ARROW keys to increase the spacing or the SHIFT-LEFT ARROW keys to decrease the spacing.

10. Confirm that Inter-Line is selected in the First Baseline drop-down list box. This setting determines how the baseline of the first line on a page or column will be aligned. You have two choices: *Cap Height* and *Inter-Line*. Cap Height aligns the top of the tallest capital letter with the top of the column (the top of the column includes the top margin). *Inter-Line* uses the spacing between lines to determine where to place the baseline of the first line of text. With Inter-Line you will generally have a small space between the top of the tallest capital letter and the top of the column.

    The remaining Chapter Typography options control Vertical Justification. Vertical Justification Within Frame is used to force text to always fill an entire column. Space is added (never subtracted) between paragraphs, added frames, tables, and lines of text until the text fills the entire column. You can apply vertical justification in one of two ways: by *feathering* or by *carding*. Feathering applies the exact amount of space needed to force the text to the bottom of the column. Carding adds space in increments equal to the space between lines of text. With carding, your lines of text will be aligned evenly across columns. With feathering, adjacent lines of text may be of differing heights. Feathering would be used in a brochure, for example, where the design requires the text and graphics to fill an entire column and there aren't adjacent columns or pages. For publications with facing pages or adjacent columns, such as books, carding is generally a better choice. Carding can sometimes add too much space between heads and paragraphs.

11. Select Carding from the Within Frame drop-down list box.

12. Confirm that 100 is displayed in the Maximum Justification spinner. This sets the maximum amount of space used to vertically justify a column to 100 percent of the amounts specified in the Maximum at Top and Maximum at Bottom spinners. Setting the Maximum Justification to zero turns Vertical Justification off.

13. Select Moveable in the Around Frame drop-down list box. Vertical Justification Around Frame is used to determine how space will be added to a frame on a page, such as a frame containing a graphic. When Fixed is selected, the frame will not be moved and space will only be added below the frame. Fixed is a better choice for small anchored graphics and large graphics that must remain aligned at the top or bottom of a page. When Movable is selected, the frame will be moved down as space is added both above and below the frame. Moveable is good for large anchored graphics such as figures that move with text.

    The remaining options are used to set the allowable amounts of space that will be used for vertical justification. Since type sizes and line spacing are measured in points, it is usually preferable to use points for these measurements.

14. Click on the down arrow on the units drop-down list box to the right of the Maximum at Top spinner, and select points from the drop-down list.
15. Double-click on the Maximum At Top spinner and type **12**.
16. Press TAB twice and type **12**, then click on OK to close the Chapter Settings dialog box.

Note: If the amount of space needed to vertically justify a column exceeds the allowable amount, the column will not be vertically justified.

The same options you have just set in the Chapter Settings Typography tab are available for individual frames using the Frame option in the Format menu. The Frame Settings Typography tab is similar to the Chapter Settings Typography tab with one exception: each drop-down list box contains one additional choice, which is Default. When the Default option is chosen, the settings in the Chapter Settings Typography tab will be used. When any of the other options are chosen, they will override the Chapter Typography settings.

Tip: Attributes are applied to text using CorelVENTURA's hierarchy: Chapter level, style tag and frame level, selected text or individual frame level. Settings changed for the lower levels always override the higher levels. In other words, applying attributes to selected text will override the chapter settings.

Now you will set the frame attributes for the base page.

Setting Frame Attributes

The Frame option on the Format menu is used to set the attributes for the base page, free frames, and the other types of frames. This option is only available when a frame is selected. The selected attributes will be applied to the selected frame. The attributes can also be defined as a frame tag. The frame tag can then be used to apply the same frame attributes to other frames you create. Set the base page attributes now using these steps:

1. Click on the Zoom tool in the toolbox (the second tool from the top). In the Zoom flyout menu, click on the Full Height tool (the rightmost tool).
2. Select the Pick tool (the topmost tool in the toolbox) if it's not already selected; click on the base page to select it. Figure 16-4 shows how your screen should appear.

Importing Text and Using Style Sheets

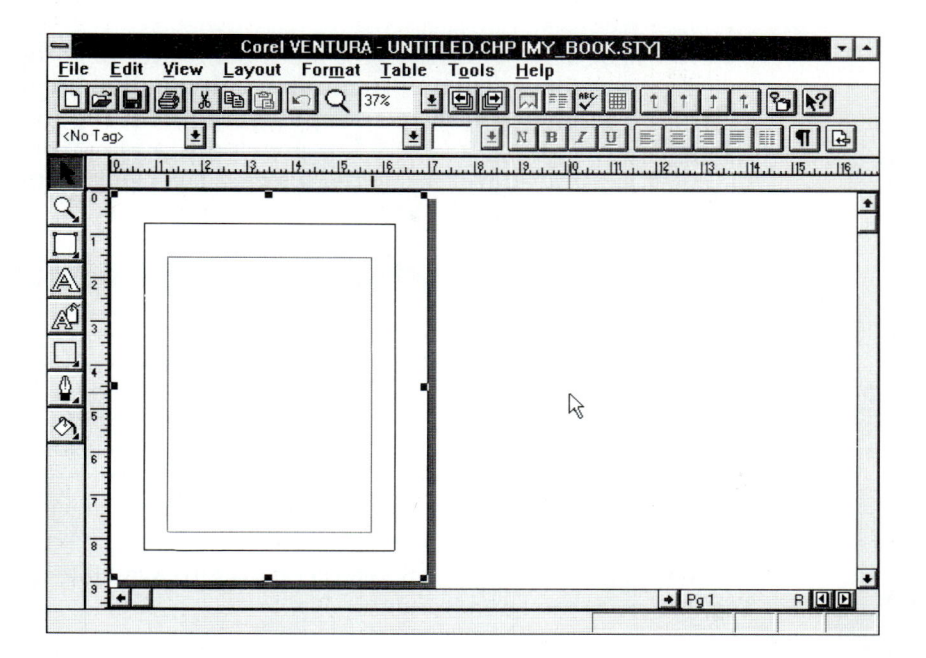

Base page selected
Figure 16-4.

3. Open the Format menu and choose Frame. When the Frame Settings dialog box is displayed, click on the Margins tab. Figure 16-5 shows the Frame Settings Margins tab.

Frame Settings Margins tab
Figure 16-5.

At the bottom of the Margins tab is the Frame Tag drop-down list box. This drop-down list box appears in each tab. You use it to select the frame tag the settings will be applied to. The + and – buttons to the right of the drop-down list box are used to add or delete tags. Clicking on the – button will delete the selected tag. Clicking on the + button will display the Add Tag dialog box, shown here:

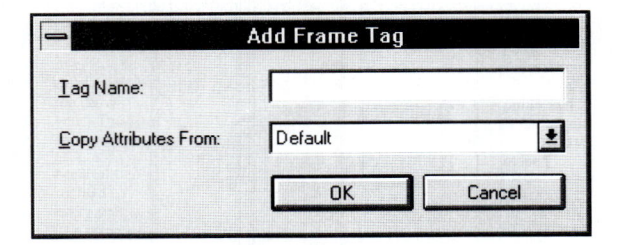

Tip: The Add Frame Tag dialog box is also available using the Add New Tag option in the Format menu.

You can select an existing frame tag to base the new tag on by selecting a frame tag in the drop-down list box. You then make the changes to the tag using the options in the Frame Settings dialog box.

The attributes you will define in these exercises will be applied to the default frame tag in the MY_BOOK style sheet. You will set the margins on your page to .5 inch. Since the _BOOK_P1 style sheet specified double-sided pages, you can specify different margins for right and left side pages. When your book is printed, the left margin on the right pages and the right margin on the left pages will be bound together, forming the spine of the book. You will need to allow extra space in these margins to compensate for this.

4. Select inches in the Units drop-down list box.
5. Confirm that the Left page option button is selected.
6. Double-click on the Top spinner and type **.5**.
7. Press TAB to select the Left spinner and type **.5**.
8. Press TAB to select the Bottom spinner and type **.5**.
9. Press TAB to select the Right Margin spinner and type **.75**. Setting the right margin of the left page to .75 inch allows an extra .25 inch for binding.

The final step in setting your base page inside margins is to mirror the settings from the left page to the right page. In other words, the right

Importing Text and Using Style Sheets 553

page left margin becomes the left page right margin. This means the binding margin will be on the correct side of the page.

10. Click on the Mirror to Facing Page command button.

    Since you are setting the attributes for the base page, the Outside Margins settings do not apply. You can also place up to two vertical rules on the base page, or within a frame. The Rule # spinner is used to select each rule, and the Position and Thickness spinners are used to set the attributes for the selected rule.

11. Confirm that the Position and Thickness values for both Vertical Rules are set to zero.

Next you will set the column attributes for the base page. Each frame can have up to eight columns. The columns can be equal in width or you can specify a different width for each column. The *gutters* (the space between columns) can also be set equally or individually. You will set your page to have two equal columns with a .25-inch gutter.

1. Select the Columns tab. Figure 16-6 shows the Columns tab that will be displayed.
2. Confirm that the Left page option button is selected, and set the # of Columns to 2 using the spinner.
3. Select the Equal Widths check box.

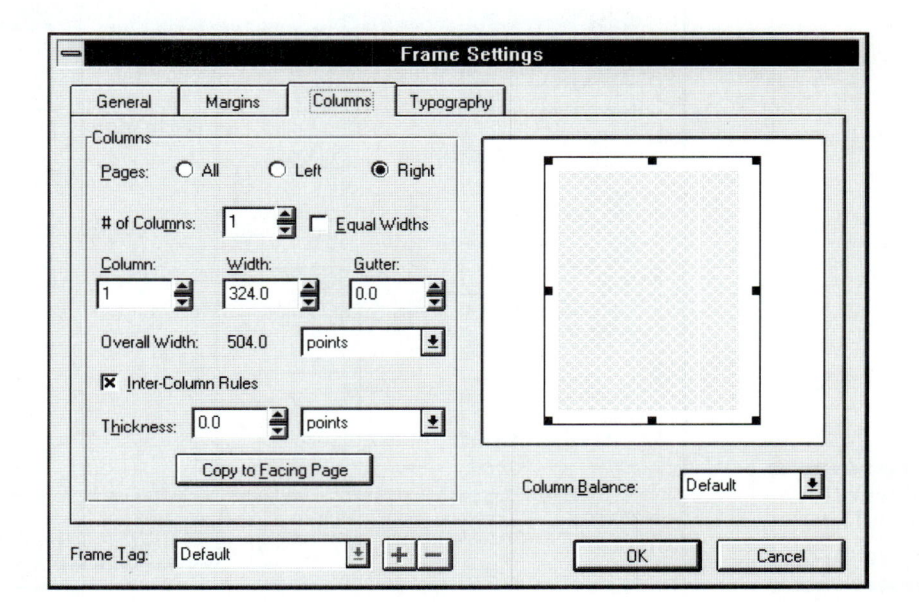

Frame Settings Columns tab
Figure 16-6.

4. Select inches in the Units drop-down list box.
5. Double-click on the Gutter spinner and type **.25**. CorelVENTURA will automatically calculate the proper column widths based on the frame width, margins, and gutter width.
6. Deselect the Inter-column Rules check box. Selecting this option allows you to automatically place vertical rules between columns on a page.
7. Click on the Copy to Facing Page command button, and then click on OK.

Tip: You can also set completely different column widths and margins for right and left side pages when a document has double-sided pages.

The _BOOK_P1 style sheet also includes a border around the base page. You will remove this border with the following steps:

1. Select the Format menu and choose the Ruling Lines option. The Ruling Lines dialog box is displayed.
2. Click on the Around tab. The Ruling Lines Around tab, shown in Figure 16-7, is displayed.

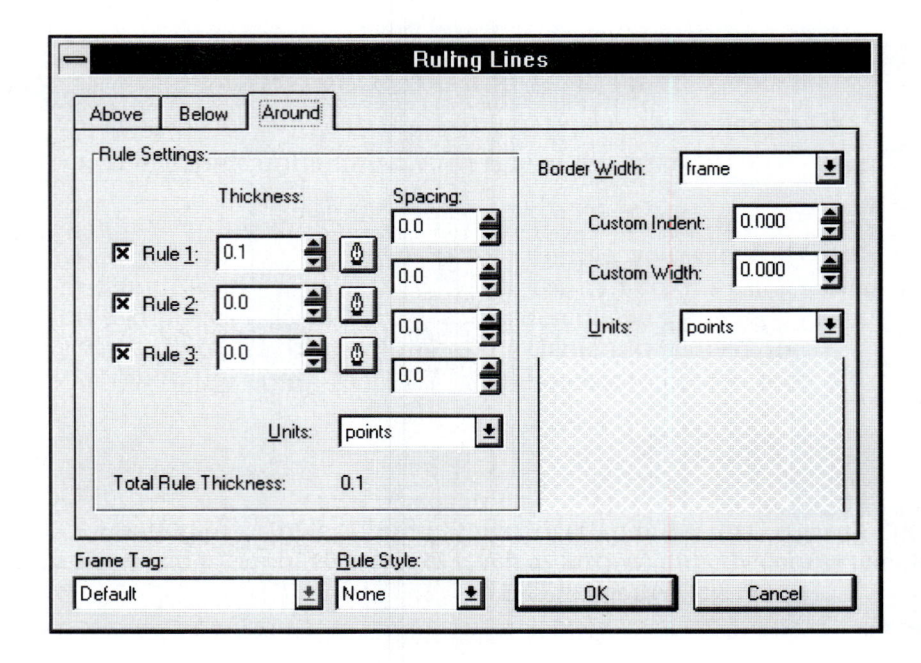

Ruling Lines Around tab
Figure 16-7.

Importing Text and Using Style Sheets

3. Click on the Rule 1 check box to deselect it. This will remove the border rule.
4. Click on OK to close the Ruling Lines dialog box.

You have now completed setting the basic page layout for your chapter. Before importing a text file, you should save your work as a new chapter file. Saving the chapter will also save your changes to the style sheet. Save the chapter now with these steps:

1. Select the File menu, then choose the Save As option. The Save File As dialog box will be displayed.
2. Type **my_book** in the File Name text box and click on OK.

Your chapter file is now ready for importing a text file. When you need to create another chapter with the same page layout, you will simply open the same style sheet.

Importing Text Files

A CorelVENTURA chapter may contain a single text file or it may contain a number of text files. Publications such as books generally contain one text file per chapter, while newsletters will generally contain several text files. In either case, the steps you follow to import text into your chapter are similar. Text files can either be imported directly into the active frame or they can be added to the Files list on the ribbon, and then placed in a frame. All files imported are added to the Files list even if they are not placed in a frame.

Caution: When a text file is imported into CorelVENTURA, any changes are made to the source text file, not a copy of the file. If other publications use the file, the changes will be reflected in those publications. Create a copy of the file before importing it if you don't want the changes to appear in all publications.

When an imported text file is first saved in CorelVENTURA, all paragraph formatting is removed. This includes line spacing, tab settings, justification, and margins. Character attributes, such as bold and italic, are retained in the file. You can also have CorelVENTURA automatically convert two hyphens (--) to an em dash (—) and convert standard quotes (") to open and closing quotes, also called typographer's quotes (" "). You use the Preferences option in the Tools menu to change these settings.

When you import a text file you have several options for how it can be placed. If the base page or another frame is selected using the Pick tool or the Text tool, the file will be placed in the frame and added to the Files list on the ribbon. If you want the text file to be placed at a specific point in an existing file, use the Text tool to place the insertion point at that spot. If no frames are selected, the text file will be added to the Files list. You can then place it in a frame by selecting the frame and then selecting the file from the Files list. Once the file has been placed in a frame you can use the style tags in the style sheet to format the text.

The first step in the next exercise will be to create a copy of the text file you will place in your chapter. This will leave the original file unchanged. You will then import the copy of the text file and place it in the base page of your chapter. Create a copy of the text file using these steps:

1. Press ALT-TAB to switch to the Program Manager.
2. Open the Windows File Manager.
3. Select the drive and path where you have installed the CorelVENTURA files—probably the \COREL50\VENTURA\TYPESET\ directory.
4. Select the file BOOK_2.TXT. In the File menu, choose the Copy option.
5. In the To text box, type **my_book.txt** and click on OK.
6. Close the File Manager and press ALT-TAB again to return to CorelVENTURA.
7. Click inside the base page with the Pick tool to select the base page, if it's not already selected.
8. Select the File menu, then choose the Load Text option. The Load Text dialog box is displayed, as shown in Figure 16-8. You can click on the Options command button to expand the dialog box.
9. Select Text Files (*.txt) in the List Files of Type drop-down list box.
10. Click on MY_BOOK.TXT in the Files list box.
11. Click on OK.

The text file will be imported and placed in the base page, and the filename will be added to the Files list on the ribbon. It is too long to fit in one page, so CorelVENTURA will automatically add the pages needed to display the entire file. Your screen should look similar to Figure 16-9. The name of the text file, MY_BOOK.TXT, now appears in the Files drop-down list box on the ribbon.

The Full Page view shows the general layout of the page, but the text is too small to read. In order to be able to read the text you will need to switch to a

Importing Text and Using Style Sheets

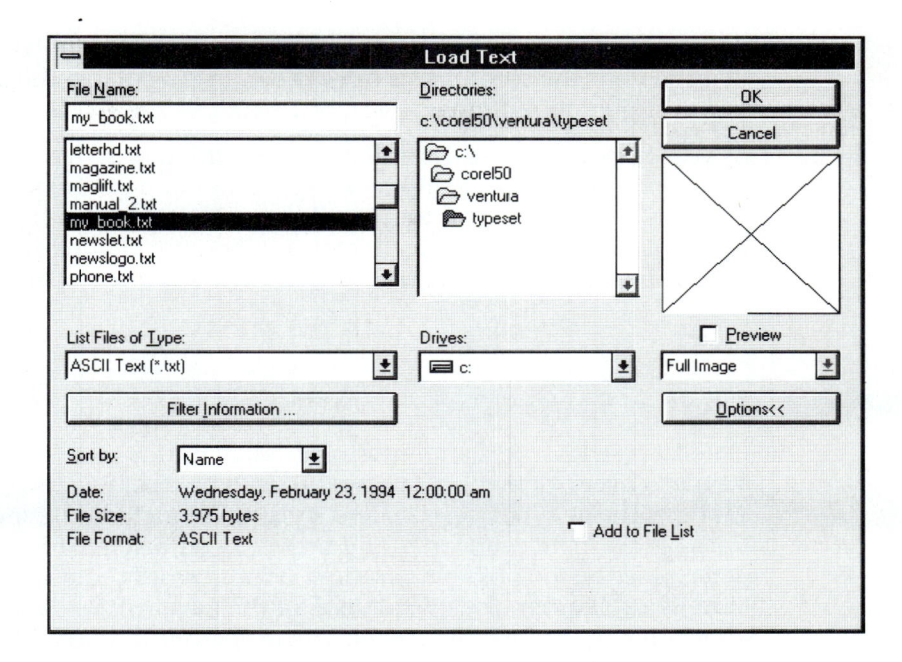

**Load Text dialog box
Figure 16-8.**

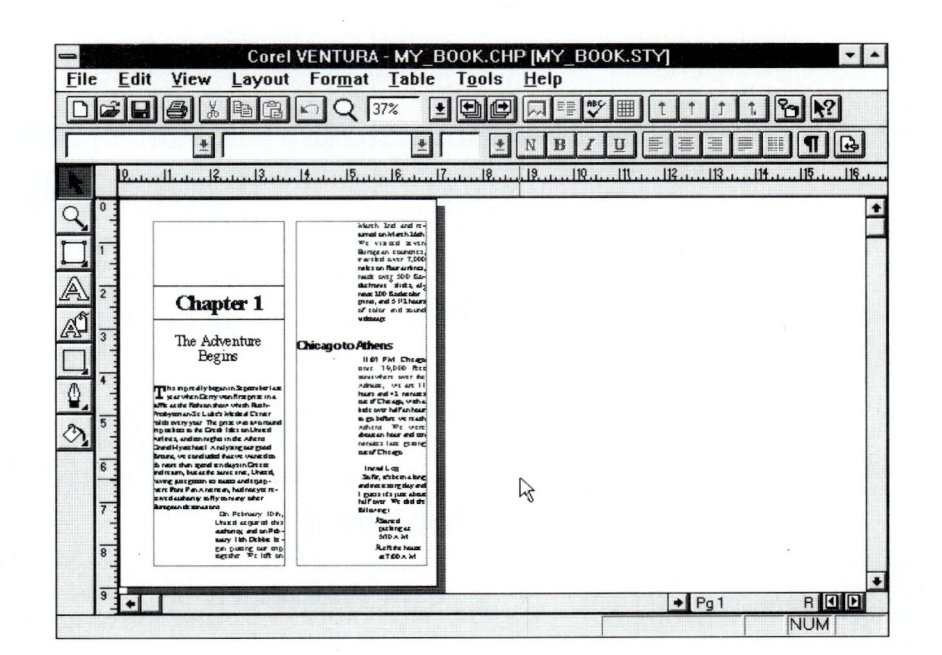

**CorelVENTURA screen with text file imported
Figure 16-9.**

different view. Click on the Zoom tool and select the Full Width tool on the flyout menu (the second tool from the right) to enlarge the page image. Your screen should look similar to Figure 16-10.

As you can see, the text is formatted with different styles. However, these styles were created for a different page layout and no longer represent an effective design. You will want to change the style tag definitions to apply different formatting for the chapter number, the chapter title, and the body text. You will use the style tags in your style sheet to do this.

Using Style Tags

CorelVENTURA offers an imposing array of options for formatting text. Virtually every element of typography can be modified using these options. Along with the typeface, size, and style, these include the spacing between lines of text, between words, and between characters. These settings determine the look of a publication. If lines, words, and characters are placed close to each other, the overall look of the page will be darker than if you allow more space between them. The proper settings for these attributes will depend upon the font chosen for the chapter and your personal taste. A

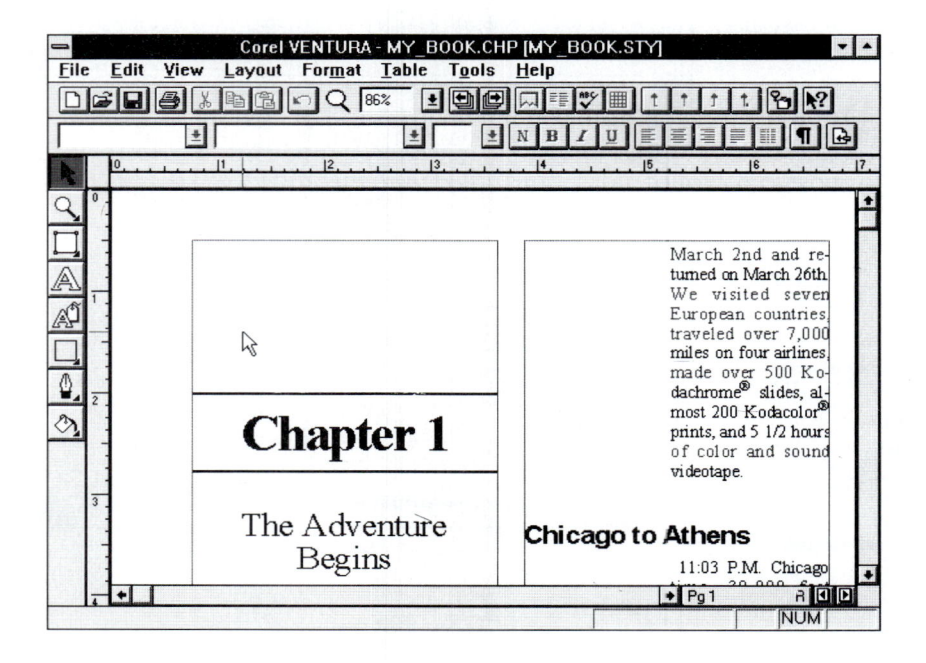

CorelVENTURA screen in Full Width view
Figure 16-10.

Importing Text and Using Style Sheets

"heavy" font (such as Bookman) will need more space than a "lighter" one (such as Times New Roman) to create a pleasing design.

Tip: Selecting a suitable font for a design requires familiarity with the overall appearance of the fonts you have available. One way to achieve this is to create and print a sample page, using a different font each time. It will help to look at these pages from a distance so you can see the overall tone of the page. You will soon learn which fonts require more white space than others.

The original style sheet you opened for your chapter, _BOOK_P1.STY, contains a number of style tags useful for formatting text in a book. It contains style tags for body text, chapter numbers and titles, as well as footnotes and other special types of paragraphs. When you saved _BOOK_P1.STY as MY_BOOK.STY, all these tags were retained. You will modify these tags and use them to format the text in your chapter.

Note: The tag name Body Text is reserved by CorelVENTURA. This means you can change the attributes of the tag, or copy them, but you cannot rename or delete the tag.

Formatting the Body Text Tag

Most of the text in a chapter is formatted with the Body Text tag, so you will begin formatting your chapter by modifying the Body Text tag. You will first select the typeface and size, then the alignment, spacing, and other text attributes.

Character Attributes

You select the Body Text font, size, and other attributes using the Paragraph option in the Format menu. When you do this, the Paragraph Settings dialog box is displayed, as shown in Figure 16-11.

The options in the Character tab allow you to select the font, style, size, color, and special effects for the style tag displayed in the Style Tag drop-down list box at the bottom of the dialog box. This is the Body Text tag in this case. The Font list box contains a list of the available fonts, the Style list box shows the available styles for the selected font, and the Size spinner allows you set the size of the selected font. You can use any of the measurement systems available (inches, centimeters, millimeters, picas and points, or points). Type is traditionally measured in points, and this is the

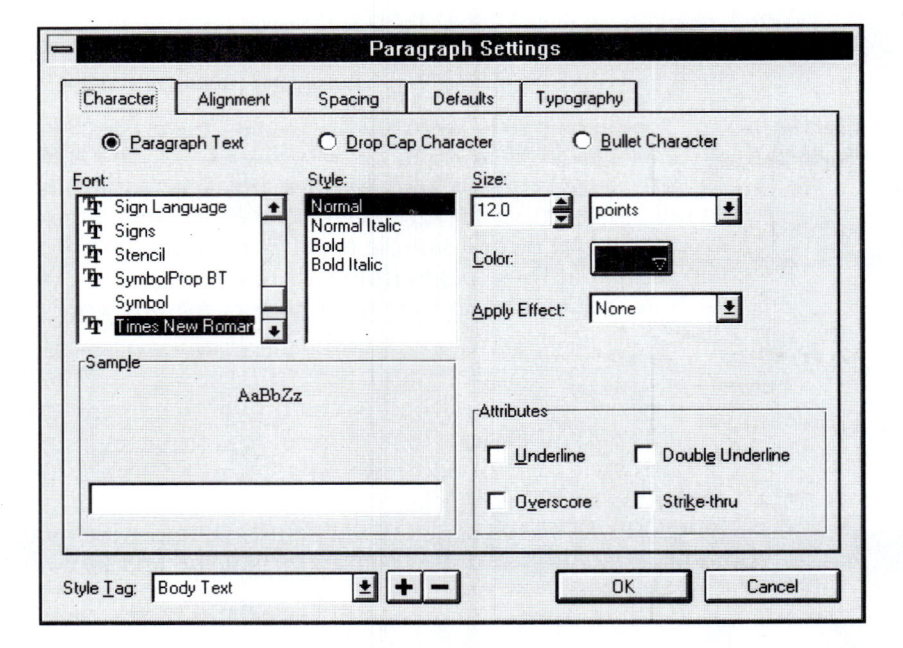

Paragraph Settings dialog box with Character tab selected

Figure 16-11.

measurement unit used in this book for indicating the font size. The information in these three list boxes is determined by the printer you have selected and the fonts you have installed on your computer.

The Paragraph Text, Drop Cap, and Bullet option buttons allow you to specify whether the attributes being defined apply to the paragraph text, a drop cap, or a bullet. A *drop cap* is the first letter of a paragraph that is formatted larger than the rest of the text. Normally this is done with the first paragraph in a chapter or section. This helps draw the reader's eyes to the beginning of the paragraph. Usually the drop cap will occupy the same amount of space as two or three lines of text. You can have the top of the Drop Cap even with the top of the first line of text, or position it above the first line. A *bullet* is a symbol placed in front of the first character of the paragraph. Bullets are generally used as a means of setting apart items in a list. After the drop cap or bullet attributes are defined, they can be applied to the style tag by selecting the effect in the Apply Effect drop-down list box.

The Color selector allows you to set the color of the typeface, and the Apply Effect drop-down list box allows you to display additional options for setting the Drop Cap and Bullet attributes. The Attributes check boxes allow you to select underlining and other text effects. A sample of the font selected in the Font list box is displayed in the Sample field. You can enter text in the Sample text box to check the appearance of specific characters.

You can also set ruling lines as part of the style tag using the Ruling Lines dialog box. This is the same dialog box you used earlier to remove the border around the page frame.

The current Body Text default font is Times New Roman, Normal style, 12 points, Black, and no Attributes. You will keep these defaults for your Body Text tag.

Alignment Attributes

The Alignment attributes (horizontal and vertical alignment, tabs, and breaks) are set using the Alignment tab. Use the following steps to set your Body Text alignment:

1. Select the Alignment tab. Figure 16-12 shows the Paragraph Settings Alignment tab.

   The Alignment tab controls how text is aligned in a frame or column. The Horizontal Alignment buttons present five choices: Left (text is aligned along the left edge and the right edge is ragged), Center (text is centered across the width of the frame or column), Right (text is aligned along the right edge and the left edge is ragged), Justified (text is aligned along both the left and right edges), and Decimal (text is aligned to a specified character, such as a period or comma, used to align columns of numbers in a table). If you choose Decimal alignment, the In From Right spinner is used to set the space from the right margin to the alignment character position. The alignment character is set using the Alignment Character spinner.

   The Vertical Alignment buttons offer three choices: Top (text is aligned with the top of the frame), Center (text is centered vertically in the frame), and Bottom (text is aligned with the bottom of the frame).

Caution: Center or Bottom aligned text should not be preceded or followed by Top aligned text in the same frame. In other words, Text with Center or Bottom alignment should be placed by itself in a frame.

   Frame Wide Text is selected to align text across the width of a frame, regardless of the number of columns. This allows you to have a headline spanning a frame while having the rest of the text in several columns.

2. Click on the Left Horizontal Alignment button (the leftmost button).

Tabs are also set with the Alignment tab. You can specify default tabs using the Default Tab spinner, or you can set tabs at specified locations using the

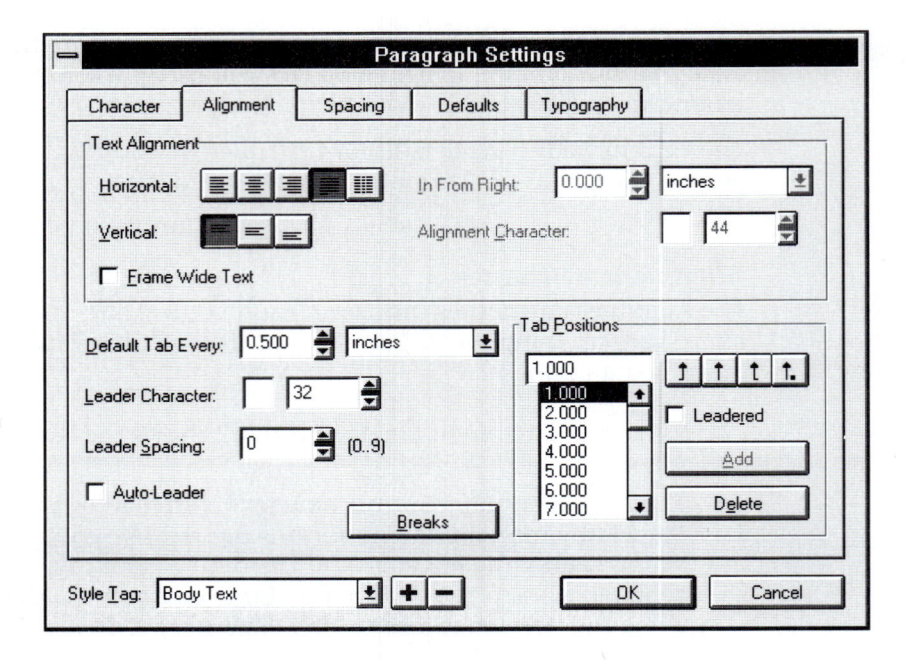

Paragraph Settings Alignment tab
Figure 16-12.

Tab Positions options. Tabs can be Left, Center, Right, or Decimal. You can set up to 16 tabs for each style tag. Tabs are measured from the edge of the column, not the edge of the frame. Tabs can also be set using the Tab bar.

The Leadered check box allows you to automatically insert a line of characters (such as a line of periods), selected with the Leader Character option, before the tab. You can define a character using the Leader Character spinner, or by entering a single character in the Leader Character text box.

Leader Spacing sets the number of spaces between each character when Leadered is selected. Up to nine spaces can be inserted between each character. When Auto-Leader is selected, the leader character will be inserted between the end of the last line of a paragraph and the right margin, even if you have not placed a tab there.

Set your default tabs now with these steps:

1. If the units drop-down list box to the right of the Default Tab spinner is set to a unit other than inches, select inches.
2. Double-click on the Default Tab Every spinner and type **.25**. This will set tabs every .25 inch, measured from the edge of the column.
3. Click on the Left Tab alignment button (the leftmost tab button), if necessary.

You also use the Alignment tab to set *breaks*. Breaks are used to control the flow of text by forcing paragraphs, columns, and lines to move to the next column or page. Open the Breaks dialog box and set your break attributes now with these steps:

1. Click on the Breaks command button. The Breaks dialog box is displayed, as shown here:

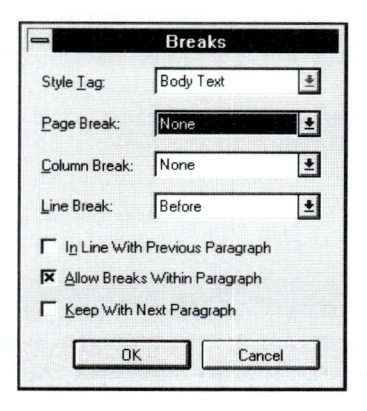

Note: Each break setting is overridden by the setting below it. In other words, the Line break setting takes precedence over the Column break setting, and the Column break setting overrides the Page break setting.

Page breaks are used to force a paragraph to begin at the top of the next page or frame. The options available are None, Before, After, Before & After, Before/Until Left, and Before/Until Right. Selecting None in the Page Breaks drop-down list box turns off page breaks. This is the setting you will usually use. When Before is selected, paragraphs with the selected tag will be placed at the top of the next page. When After is selected, the following paragraph will be placed at the top of the next page. Before & After forces both paragraphs to separate pages; this setting allows you to tag a paragraph to appear on a page by itself. Before/Until Left forces the paragraph to the next left page and will insert a blank right page if necessary. Before/Until Right forces the paragraph to the next right page, inserting a blank left page if needed.

Column breaks force a paragraph to begin at the top of a column. The options are None, Before, After, and Before & After. Again, you will usually set Column breaks to None. The Before option forces the paragraph to the next column, After forces the following paragraph to the next column, and Before & After puts the paragraph in a column by itself.

Line breaks are used to determine how space is added between paragraphs. The amount of space between paragraphs can be affected by several different settings. When Before, After, or Before & After are selected for consecutive paragraphs, the spacing between them is determined by the settings in the Paragraph Settings Spacing tab. (The settings in the Spacing tab are explained in the next section.)

When None is selected for Line breaks (and None is also selected for the Page and Column break options), the spacing applied is determined by the setting of the In Line With Previous Paragraph check box. When this option is not selected, one paragraph will print on top of the other. The value of this is that you can set the Left and Right Paragraph Indents (in the Spacing tab) so that the paragraphs will print side-by-side in the same column. This can be used for section heads, for example.

Tip: You can use the Side-by-Side Paragraphs button on the ribbon to quickly format two paragraphs to be placed side-by-side in a column. You can use this option to quickly create the look of a table without actually creating a table. This will not change the style tags of the selected paragraphs.

Selecting the In Line With Previous Paragraph option button allows you place separate paragraphs on the same line. For example, if you wanted the first three words of a paragraph to be 16 points and bold and the body text to be 12 points normal, you would make the first three words a separate paragraph. This paragraph would have Line Break set to Before and the typeface set to 16 point bold. The next paragraph would have Line Break set to After, the Add Width of Previous Line option in the Spacing tab selected, and the In Line With Previous Paragraph check box selected. The two paragraphs would appear to be one line. You could produce the same result by selecting the first three words of each paragraph and formatting them using the Text menu, but then any changes in formatting would require you to manually change every affected paragraph in your publication, rather than make one global change.

2. Confirm that Page and Column breaks are set to None, and Line Break is set to Before.

3. Confirm that the In Line With Previous Paragraph and Keep With Next Paragraph are not selected. The Keep With Next Paragraph option allows you to keep consecutive paragraphs together. For example, heads followed by body text would be set to Keep With Next so the head

Importing Text and Using Style Sheets

would not be placed in a different column or page than the body text. When selected, the consecutive paragraphs will not be split across columns or frames. You will usually not select this option.

4. Confirm that Allow Breaks Within Paragraph is selected. The Allow Within Paragraph option allows you to prevent a paragraph from being split across columns or frames. When the option is not selected, the paragraph will not be split (headings, for example, are a type of paragraph that should not be split). You will usually select the option to allow the paragraph to be split.

5. Click on OK to close the Breaks dialog box.

Spacing

The Spacing tab controls the spacing between lines and paragraphs, indents and outdents for lines and paragraphs, and text rotation. Set the spacing for the Body Text tag with these steps:

1. Select the Spacing tab, shown in Figure 16-13.

    The Paragraph Indents options set the spacing between the edge of the column or frame and the left and right edges of the paragraph.

2. Click on the All Pages option button and set the Left and Right spinners to zero.

Tip: Indented margins can also be set for paragraphs by selecting the paragraph and then using the left and right margin markers on the Tab bar.

The Line Indents options set the number of lines to be indented and the amount of the indent. Indent Amount can be set to a positive or negative value to create an indent or an outdent, also called a *hanging* indent, where the first line hangs out from the body of the paragraph. The Add Width of Preceding Line check box determines if the Indent Amount will be added to the width of the last line in the preceding paragraph. This is normally used with the Line Break option to create lead-in paragraphs, as explained in the previous section.

3. Confirm that the Lines to Indent is set to 1, Add Width of Previous Line is not selected, and Units is set to inches.

4. Select the Indent Amount spinner and type **.25**.

    The Spacing Above and Below spinners set the space that is added before and after a paragraph. The Inter-Line space (usually called *leading*) is the space between the lines of text (the actual measurement is

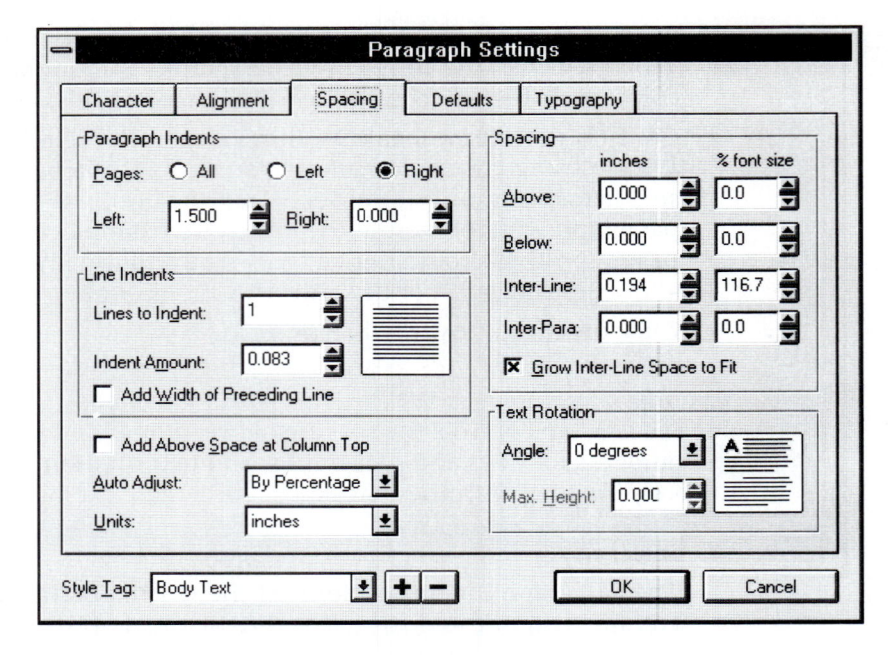

Paragaph Settings Spacing tab
Figure 16-13.

from the baseline of one line to the baseline of the line above). Since your type size is measured in points, it is easier to also measure these spaces in points. These distances can be expressed either as a value or as a percentage of font size.

A rule of thumb to use for determining inter-line space is to use a value that is 120 percent of the type size. You have already set your Body Text type size to 12, so the inter-line spacing is set to 14.4 points, or 120 percent of the type size. In order to keep adjacent lines of text even, you will use the same value for the space Above setting. The Below space will be set to zero.

T ip: Setting the Above or Below spacing to the same amount as the Inter-Line spacing produces the same effect as inserting an extra line between paragraphs. By using Above or Below spacing to change line spacing on a global basis, you simply change the values in the Above or Below spinners instead of having to repeat the change throughout the entire document to produce the same result.

5. Select points in the Units drop-down list box.
6. Double-click on the Above % of font size spinner and type **120**. The Above points spinner will display 14.4.

7. Confirm that the Below points spinner is set to zero.
8. Select the Inter-Line % of point size spinner and type **120**.

    Inter-Paragraph spacing is used to create paragraph spacing different from the Above and Below values. Inter-Paragraph spacing is applied *only* to consecutive paragraphs that have the same inter-paragraph spacing values. This allows you to create layouts where similar paragraphs will have inter-paragraph spacing that differs from the preceding or following paragraphs. For example, if your document contains a number of quotes, you could use inter-paragraph spacing to set the spacing between paragraphs of quotes to be different than the rest of the document. When only one paragraph of quotes was between regular paragraphs, the inter-paragraph spacing would be determined by the settings in the Above and Below text boxes. When consecutive paragraphs of quotes were included, the inter-paragraph spacing between them would be determined by the value in the Inter-Paragraph text box.

9. Press TAB to select the Inter-Para spinner and type **0**.

    When Grow Inter-Line to Fit is selected, the space between lines is increased when you format part of the line in a larger type size. Otherwise the larger type will run into the line above it.

> **Tip:** The Grow Inter-Line to Fit setting is useful when a paragraph contains in-line graphics that are of a different height than the surrounding text.

10. Confirm that the Grow Inter-Line to Fit check box is selected.
11. Confirm that By Percentage is selected in the Auto Adjust drop-down list box. This is used to automatically change the spacing values when the type size changes.
12. Confirm the Add Above Space at Column Top check box is not selected. This setting is used to determine when the space in the Above text box is applied. When the check box is not selected any space above a paragraph will be suppressed when it is at the top of a column.

    The Text Rotation Angle drop-down list box allows you to rotate text in 90 degree increments. Except for special effects, such as printing text vertically on the edge of a page, you will usually not rotate text. The Max Height spinner is used to set the height that rotated text will occupy. It is only available when the Text Rotation Angle drop-down list box contains a value other than zero.

13. Confirm that 0 degrees is selected in the Text Rotation Angle drop-down list box.

Defaults

The Defaults tab controls defaults for overscore, strike-through, and underline rules, as well as the size of superscript, subscript, and small-cap characters. These settings can be auto-adjusted as the font size is changed. You will use the default settings. You can select the Defaults tab, shown in Figure 16-14, to review these settings; next, select the Typography tab.

Typography

The Paragraph Settings Typography tab allows you to fine-tune the text spacing of your style tag. You can adjust the space between characters, words, and lines and set the minimum and maximum space widths. When CorelVENTURA adjusts any of these spaces as you are placing your text, it will use the range of values you set in the Paragraph Settings Typography tab. Use these steps to set your paragraph typography:

1. Select the Typography tab, if it's not already selected. The Typography tag is shown in Figure 16-15.

Tip: Space between characters is usually represented as a percentage of an *em* space. An em space is simply the amount of space a capital "M" occupies in the selected font and size.

The Justified Text settings control the minimum and maximum amount of space that will be placed between words when text is justified, measured as a proportion of the normal word spacing or an em space. When selected, the Automatic Letter Spacing option adds spacing between letters (up to the Maximum Limit value) when the spacing between words exceeds the Max. Word Spacing.

Normal Word Spacing sets the space that will normally be placed between words when an alignment other than justified is used. Character Tracking controls that amount of space that will be placed between characters. Loose tracking places more space between characters than tight tracking. Tracking can be used to shorten a line (such as a headline) that is slightly too long to fit the space available. Tight tracking in fonts with narrow character widths is fashionable in design circles. Looser tracking is used to expand text to make it fill the space available. Using looser tracking can make your publication more

Importing Text and Using Style Sheets

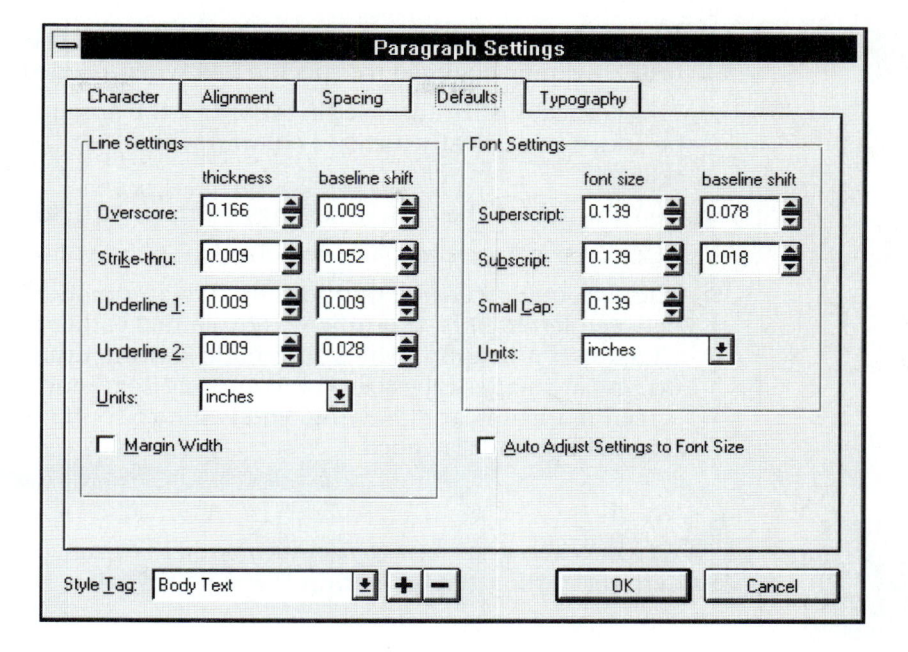

Paragraph Settings Defaults tab
Figure 16-14.

Paragraph Settings Typography tab
Figure 16-15.

readable. The correct tracking setting depends on the font and personal taste. It can be changed for specific text when needed.

The Vertical Justification settings control the amount of space that will be added to vertically justify a column when Vertical Justification is selected.

You will accept the current settings for these attributes.

2. Click on the Automatic Kerning check box to deselect it.

The Automatic Kerning option is used to automatically adjust the space between letter pairs. (Kerning was explained earlier in the section on Chapter Typography.) Since automatic kerning usually has little effect on text at smaller type sizes (such as Body Text) and slows down the screen redrawing and printing, you will turn it off here. You can still use manual kerning if needed.

Note: When you want to use Automatic Kerning you must first select Pair Kerning in the Chapter Settings Typography tab.

3. Click on the Automatic Hyphenation check box to select it. Automatic Hyphenation, when selected, will hyphenate words based on the dictionary selected in the Dictionary drop-down list box.

If you work in a specialized field, such as medicine, you may have a hyphenation dictionary containing specialized words and terms, otherwise, you will generally use the American English hyphenation dictionary when hyphenation is applied. Successive Hyphenation sets the number of consecutive lines that can be hyphenated.

Tip: When hyphenation is turned off and text is justified, excessive spacing between words and characters can occur. On the other hand, more than two successive hyphens is usually considered bad typography.

4. Select American English in the Dictionary drop-down list box, if necessary.
5. Confirm that 2 is selected in the Successive Hyphens spinner.
6. Click on OK.

You have now completed setting the attributes of the Body Text style tag. The depth of the controls CorelVENTURA offers for type settings can make this an involved process. The process is simplified by using an existing tag as

Importing Text and Using Style Sheets

the basis for the new tag. You will then only have to change the settings that are different between the two tags.

Your screen should now look like Figure 16-16. The second paragraph in the right column, which is formatted with the Body Text style tag, is now wider than the paragraph above it. This is because it is formatted with the Firstpar style tag, which you have not changed yet. With the exception of a drop cap, the Firstpar style tag should be identical to the Body Text style tag. Rather than go through all the steps you just went through to modify the Body Text tag, you will simply copy the Body Text tag as Firstpar and add a drop cap.

Create a new Firstpar style tag with these instructions:

1. Select the Format menu and choose Paragraph. When the Paragraph Settings Character dialog box is displayed, confirm that Body Text is selected in the Style Tag drop-down list box.
2. Click on the + button to the right of the Style Tag drop-down list box. The Add Paragraph Tag dialog box will be displayed.
3. Type **Firstpar** in the Tag Name text box.
4. Confirm that Body Text is selected in the Copy Attributes From and Next Tag drop-down list boxes.

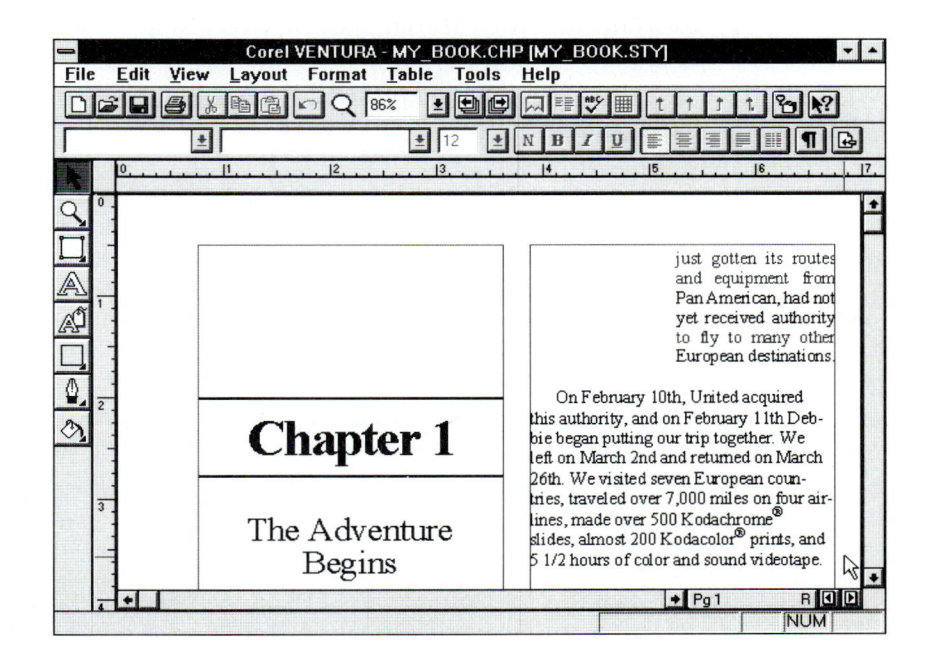

Body Text style tag applied
Figure 16-16.

5. Select Body Text in the Tag Type drop-down list box. The Add Paragraph Tag dialog box will now look like this:

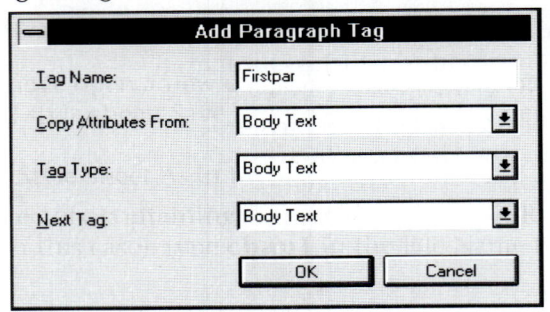

```
┌─────────────────────────────────────┐
│          Add Paragraph Tag          │
├─────────────────────────────────────┤
│  Tag Name:          │ Firstpar    │ │
│                                     │
│  Copy Attributes From: │ Body Text │▼│
│                                     │
│  Tag Type:          │ Body Text  │▼│
│                                     │
│  Next Tag:          │ Body Text  │▼│
│                                     │
│              [  OK  ]   [ Cancel ]  │
└─────────────────────────────────────┘
```

6. Click on OK.
7. Click on the Drop Cap Character option button in the Paragraph Settings Character tab.
8. In the Font list box, select Times New Roman, if it's not already selected.
9. Select Bold in the Style list box.
10. Confirm that points are selected in the Units drop-down list box, then double-click on the Size spinner and type **36**.
11. Confirm that the Color selector is set to Black and the Apply Effect drop-down list box is set to Drop Cap.
12. Confirm that the Custom Spacing check box is selected and the lines spinner is set to 2.
13. Select the Spacing tab and set the Lines to Indent spinner to 0.
14. Click on OK.

The Firstpar style tag is now identical to the Body Text style tag you created previously, with the exception of the drop cap and line indent. You need to make some changes in the other style tags also, to adapt them to your chapter layout. The following steps will take you through the process of modifying the other style tags used in the chapter:

1. Select the Format menu and choose Paragraph.
2. Select Chapter # in the Style Tag drop-down list box in the Paragraph Settings dialog box. The following dialog box will be displayed:

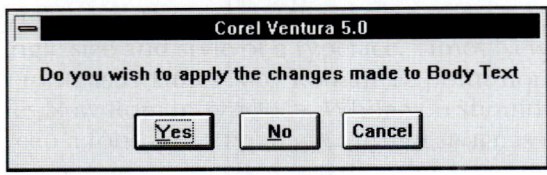

```
┌─────────────────────────────────────┐
│           Corel Ventura 5.0         │
├─────────────────────────────────────┤
│ Do you wish to apply the changes made to Body Text │
│                                     │
│       [ Yes ]   [ No ]   [ Cancel ] │
└─────────────────────────────────────┘
```

This dialog box will be displayed whenever you change the Selected Paragraph Tag.

3. Click on OK and select the Alignment tab, then click on Frame Wide Text to select it.
4. Confirm that Center Horizontal Alignment is selected.
5. Click on the Spacing tab, then click on the Add Above Space at Column Top to deselect it.
6. Click on OK.

Now you will modify the Chapter Title style tag.

1. Select the Format menu and choose Paragraph.
2. Select Chapter Title in the Style Tag drop-down list box in the Paragraph Settings dialog box.
3. Select the Alignment tab, then click on Frame Wide Text to select it.
4. Select Left Horizontal Alignment.
5. Click on OK.

There are two other style tags requiring small adjustments: Minor Heading and Bullets. Both style tags have left Paragraph Indents that are too large. Both will be changed using the Paragraph Settings Spacing tab.

1. Select the Paragraph option in the Format menu, then select the Spacing Tab.
2. Select Minor Heading in the Style Tag drop-down list box.
3. Double-click on the Left Paragraph Indents spinner and type **0**.
4. Select Bullet in the Style Tag drop-down list box.
5. Double-click on the Left Paragraph Indents spinner and type **0**.
6. Click on OK.

The remaining style tag used in the chapter (Major Heading) will remain unchanged.

You've now completed the formatting of your chapter. You should save your work and then print it.

1. Press CTRL-S to save your work.
2. Press CTRL-P to display the Print dialog box.
3. Confirm that the Current Chapter option button is selected and that the other settings match your printer setup.

4. Click on the Options command button. The Print Options dialog box will be displayed.
5. Click on the Crop Marks button (the second button from the left) if it is not already selected. When using a page size smaller than the paper size crop marks indicate the dimensions of the page.
6. Click on OK, and then click on OK in the Print dialog box.

In the next chapter you will learn more about using frames and how to use them with graphics.

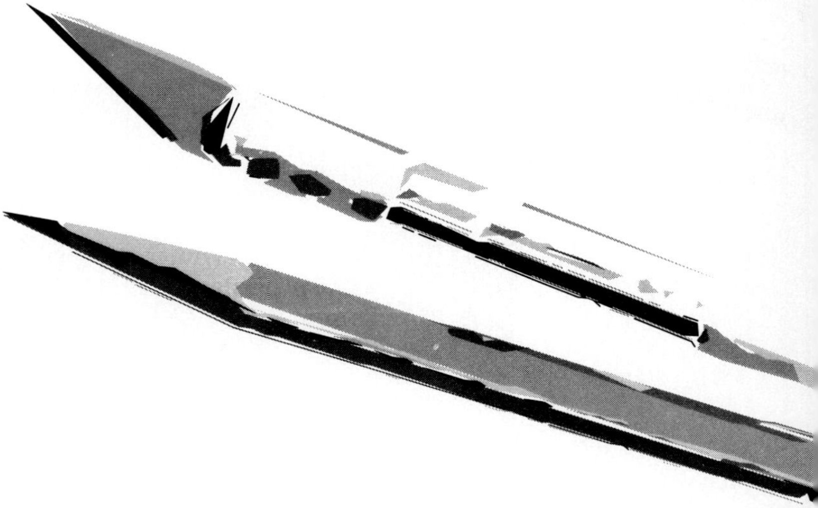

17

USING FRAMES and IMPORTING GRAPHICS

The base page you used to set your basic page layout in Chapter 16 is only one type of CorelVENTURA frame. You can create other frames to hold additional text or graphic files. The attributes for these frames can be set in the same way you set the base page attributes. CorelVENTURA will also generate frames to hold certain types of text, such as captions, headers and footers (text placed at the top and bottom of each page in a chapter), and footnotes.

In this chapter you will create additional frames for your chapter, set frame attributes and create frame tags, and add graphics to your publication.

Using Frames

The base page holds most of the text used to create a chapter and determines its attributes. Your design may require you to add graphics to the text in the base page, or you may need to add additional text that is not part of the main text file. The additional text may require frame attributes, such as borders or columns, that are different from those set for the main text. In these situations, you can add frames to your basic layout to hold the additional text and graphics. These frames can also have their own set of attributes.

Using the Frame Tool

You create new frames with the Frame tool in the toolbox. After selecting the Frame tool, you draw the frame by placing the pointer at the upper-left corner of the area where you want the new frame to be placed and then dragging to the lower-right corner. You do not have to precisely place or size the new frame when you create it. You can use the Frame option in the Format menu or the Pick tool to precisely place and size the frame at any time. You can also define a frame tag that includes the size of the frame and other attributes. Tagging a frame will then force it to the defined size.

Create a new frame now using the following steps:

1. Load CorelVENTURA if it's not already running.
2. Click on the Open button on the ribbon. The File Open dialog box is displayed.
3. Select the correct path to your publication files, if necessary, then select the MY_BOOK chapter file you created in Chapter 16, and then click on OK.
4. Click on the Full Page tool in the Zoom flyout menu (fourth from the left) if it's not already selected. Your screen will display the first page of your MY_BOOK chapter.
5. Click on the Frame tool in the toolbox. The pointer will change to the Frame pointer.
6. Place the Frame pointer at about 3 inches on the vertical ruler and 2.25 inches on the horizontal ruler, then drag the pointer to 5 inches on the vertical ruler and 5.25 inches on the horizontal ruler. The exact placement and size will be adjusted using the Frame option in the Format menu.

Using Frames and Importing Graphics

> **Note:** When a frame is created or selected, the rulers' zero points reset to the upper-left corner of the frame.

7. While the frame is still selected, open the Format menu and choose Frame. The Frame Settings General tab should be displayed, as shown in Figure 17-1.

8. Select the Flow Text Around Frame check box if it isn't selected already.

   When a frame is placed on a page, the text covered by the new frame will either flow around the frame, or it will remain underneath the new frame. Generally you will want your text to flow around the new frame. The Flow Text Around Frame check box controls text flow. The amount of space that will be left around the frame is determined by the values in the Outside Margins text boxes in the Frame Settings Margins tab. You can also flow text around an irregular object, and not just rectangles. This technique will be covered in Chapter 18.

> **Tip:** Turn Flow Text Around Frame off for a frame that contains a light screened-back graphic. Text will overprint the graphic, which then appears in the background of the page. Make sure that the colors or gray shades of the graphic are considerably lighter than the text that overprints it.

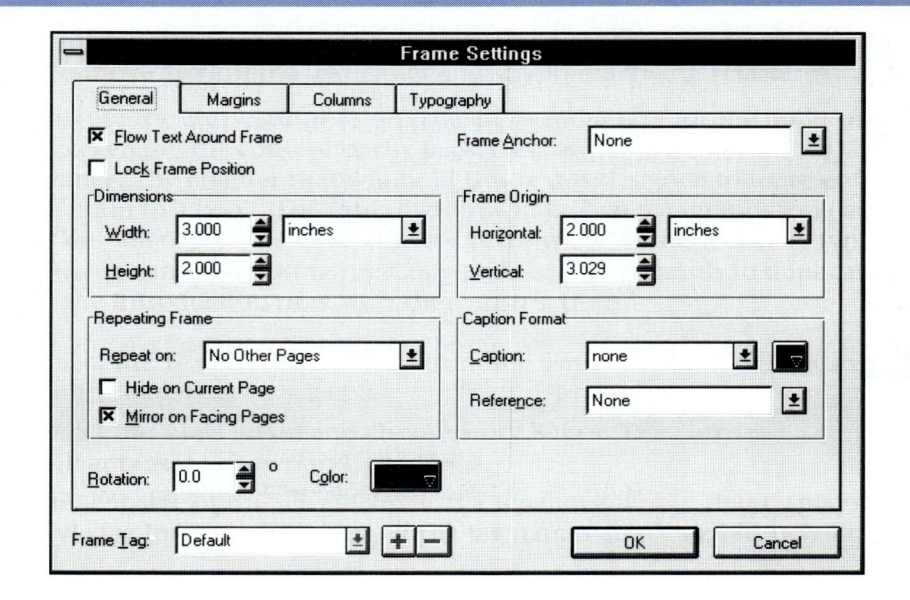

Frame Settings dialog box
Figure 17-1.

9. Select inches in the units drop-down list boxes for both Dimensions and Frame Origin, if necessary.
10. Double-click on the Dimensions Width spinner and type **3**.
11. Press TAB twice and type **2**.
12. Double-click on the Horizontal Frame Origin spinner and type **2**, then press TAB twice and type **3**. The new frame is 3 inches wide by 2 inches tall, and is located 2 inches from the left edge and 3 inches from the top edge of the base page.
13. Select the Margins tab. Confirm that the units drop-down list box is set to inches.
14. Double-click on the Horizontal Outside Margins text box and type **.25**.
15. Press TAB and type **.25**. Text will flow around the frame you have created and will leave a border of .25 inches around the top, bottom, and sides of the frame.

Next you will set the inside margins for the frame.

16. Click on the All Pages option button, if it's not already selected.
17. Double-click on the Top Inside Margins text box and type **.1**.
18. Press TAB and type **.1**.
19. Press TAB, type **.1**, press TAB again, and type **.1**. All four margins should now be set to 0.1 inch.
20. Click on OK.

You will now use the Ruling Lines dialog box to create a border for the frame.

1. Select the Format menu and choose Ruling Lines. The Ruling Lines dialog box will be displayed.
2. Select the Around tab to display the Ruling Lines Around tab.
3. Confirm that Frame is selected in the Border Width drop-down list box.
4. Confirm that Points is selected in both units drop-down list boxes.
5. Click on the Outline Pen tool to the right of the Rule 1 Thickness spinner. The Outline Pen dialog box is displayed, as shown in Figure 17-2.
6. Select Points in the units drop-down list box to the right of the Width spinner.
7. Double-click on the Width spinner and type **1**.
8. Click on OK to close the Outline Pen dialog box. Click on OK again to close the Ruling Lines dialog box.

Using Frames and Importing Graphics

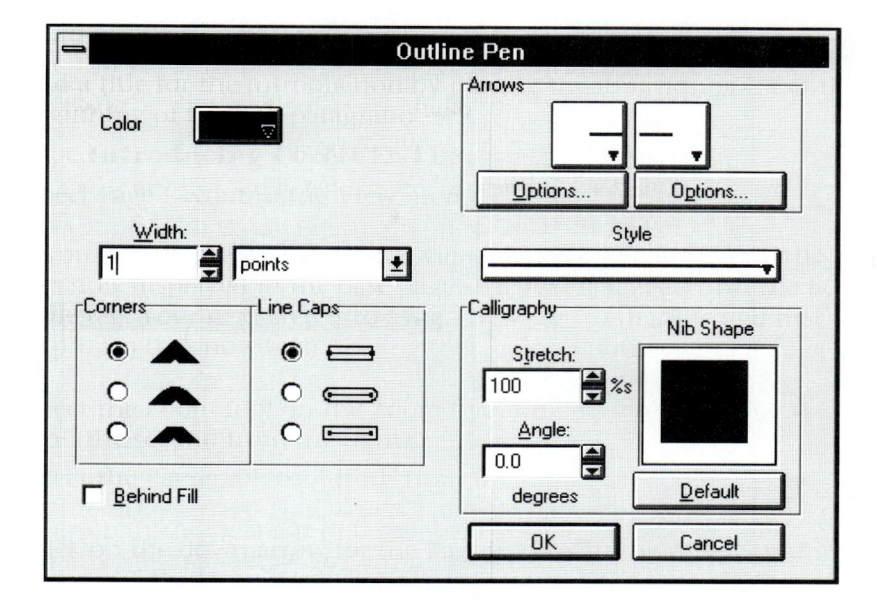

Outline Pen dialog box
Figure 17-2.

> **Tip:** To change just the width of a ruling line, you can use the Thickness spinner in the Ruling Lines dialog box, instead of the Outline Pen dialog box.

The size, location, and border for the selected frame have now been defined. Frame attributes can also be set using frame tags, which are used in much the same manner as style tags. When you create a new frame, it will have the default attributes that are saved with the chapter file, but it will not have a frame tag.

Frame Tags

Frame tags allow you to maintain a library of standard frame attributes that can be easily applied to frames at any time. When a frame tag is modified, all frames with the tag will change to the new attributes.

> **Note:** Frame tags cannot be applied to the base page, header and footer frames, footnote frames, caption frames, or repeating frames.

Frame tags are created by drawing a frame, applying the desired attributes, and then defining the tag using the Add New Tag option in the Format menu. You will create a new frame tag for the frame you have just created using the following steps:

1. Select the frame you just created, if it is not still selected, using the Pick tool.
2. Select the Format menu, then choose the Add New Tag option. The Add Frame Tag dialog box will be displayed:

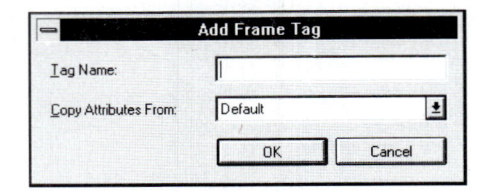

3. Default should be selected in the Copy Attributes From drop-down list box. Type **Picture** in the Tag Name text box and press ENTER. The Tags list on the ribbon will display the new tag name for the selected frame.

Tip: Frame tags from other chapters can be merged into the current chapter using the Update Tag List option on the Format menu.

Working With Graphics

CorelVENTURA can import graphics in a variety of formats. Graphics placed in a CorelVENTURA publication can be sized and scaled, cropped, and rotated. You can also add additional graphic elements and backgrounds using CorelVENTURA's drawing tools.

Importing Graphics

Graphic files are placed in your CorelVENTURA publication the same way you import text files. You select the graphic, add it to the files list, and place it in a frame. When a frame is selected, the graphic file will be placed directly into the frame. The graphic can then be sized and scaled. Use the following steps to import a graphic file:

1. Click on the frame you created to hold the imported graphic with the Pick tool, if it isn't already selected.

Using Frames and Importing Graphics

2. Click on the Zoom tool, then select the Full Width tool in the Zoom flyout menu (second from the right).
3. Use the Vertical scroll bar (on the right side of the screen) to scroll down the page until the selected frame is completely visible on the screen.
4. Select the File menu and choose Load Graphic. The Load Graphic dialog box will be displayed.
5. Select ACROP.EPS in the Files list box and click on OK. The graphic file will be placed in the selected frame, as shown in Figure 17-3, and the filename will be added to the Files list on the ribbon.

You can also import graphics using CorelMOSAIC, the CorelDRAW! graphics file manager. To use CorelMOSAIC, you create and select a frame as described above. You then click on the Mosaic roll-up button (the second button from the right in the top ribbon bar). The Mosaic roll-up, shown here, is displayed. When the graphic you want to place in your frame is displayed, you simply drag it from the Mosaic roll-up and drop it into the selected frame.

Sizing, Scaling, and Cropping Graphics

When a graphics file is placed in a frame it will be scaled to the maximum size the frame will hold. When the selected frame includes a ruling line around, above, or below you can use the inside margin settings to leave a space between the graphic and the border. When the frame does not have a border, the outside margins settings in the Frame Settings Margins tab are used to provide space between the graphic and text.

You can also size and scale graphics using the Frame option in the Format menu. Use the following steps to size and scale the graphic you just imported (the frame containing the graphic should still be selected):

1. Select the Format menu and choose Frame. The Frame Settings dialog box is displayed. Select the Graphic tab, shown in Figure 17-4.

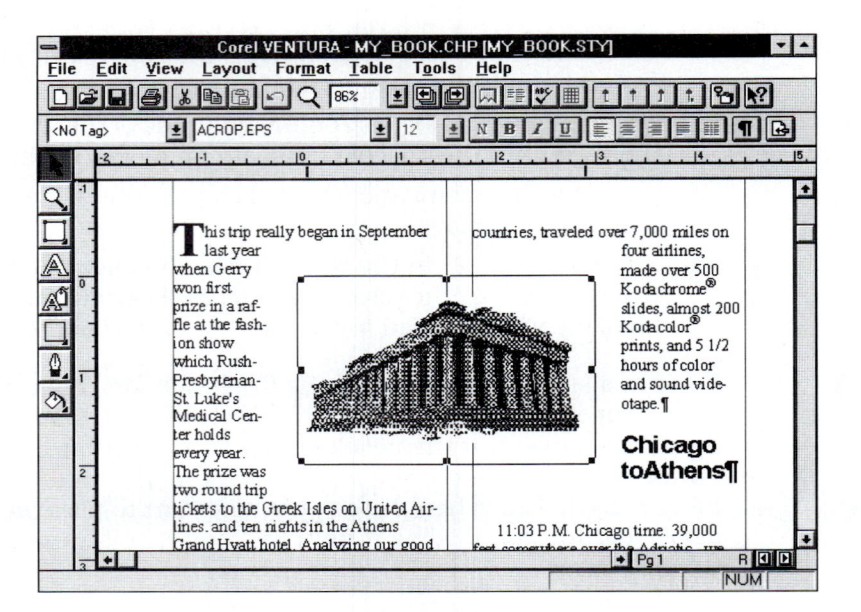

Page with graphics file imported
Figure 17-3.

2. Click on the Fit in Frame check box to deselect it.

   The size and scaling of a graphic are controlled using the Dimensions options. The Fit in Frame check box, when selected, will size the graphic

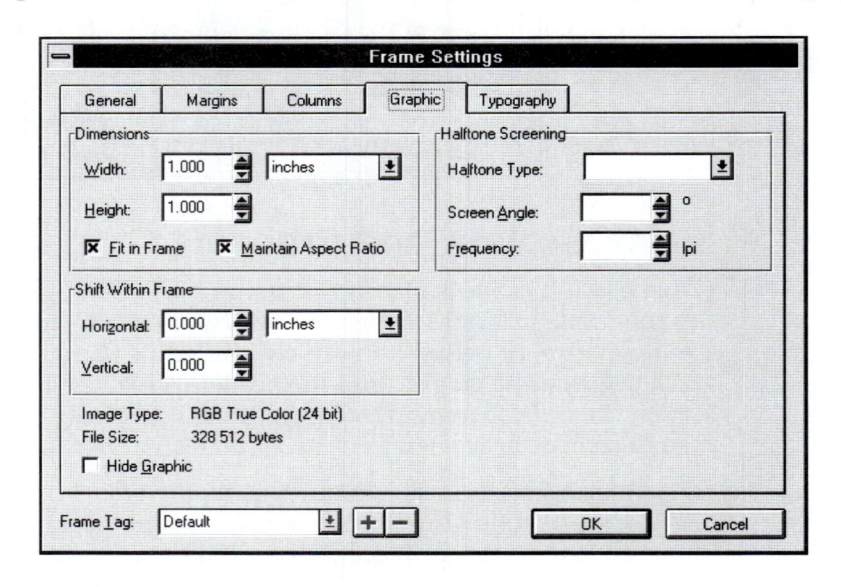

Frame Settings Graphic tab
Figure 17-4.

Using Frames and Importing Graphics

to fill the frame. You can then scale the graphic by changing the size of the frame. When the Maintain Aspect Ratio check box is selected, the ratio of height to width of the graphic will remain unchanged as the graphic is sized. When one dimension is changed the other will also change to keep the aspect ratio constant. If the Maintain Aspect Ratio check box is not selected, and Fit in Frame is selected, the aspect ratio will be adjusted until the graphic completely fills the frame, resulting in a distorted graphic.

You can change the size of the graphic independent of the frame dimensions by changing the values in the Width and Height spinners.

3. Confirm that the Maintain Aspect Ratio check box is selected, and the units drop-down list box is set to inches.
4. Double-click on the Width spinner and type **1.5**.
5. Click on OK to close the Frame Settings dialog box.

The graphic has been reduced in size and the aspect ratio has stayed the same. However, the graphic is no longer centered in the frame. Center the graphic with these steps:

1. Press and hold down the ALT key.
2. Point on the graphic and drag it to the center of the graphics frame.
3. Release the mouse button and then the ALT key when the graphic is positioned.

The graphic could be precisely positioned within the frame using the Shift Within Frame options in the Graphic tab. You can see how the graphic can be distorted with the following steps:

1. Select the Format menu and choose Graphic. The Frame Settings dialog box is displayed.
2. Select the Graphic tab.
3. Click on the Maintain Aspect Ratio check box to deselect it.
4. Double-click on the Width spinner and type **3**.
5. Press TAB twice and type **1** in the Height spinner.
6. Click on OK. Your graphic should look similar to the illustration shown next.

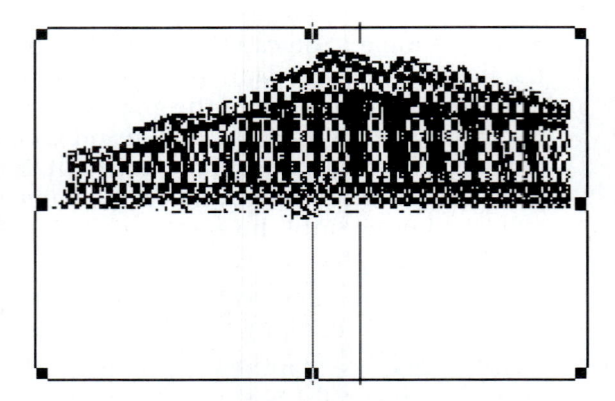

Restore the aspect ratio with these steps:

1. Open the Frame Settings Graphic tab.
2. Select the Maintain Aspect Ratio and Fit in Frame check boxes.
3. Click on OK.

When you want to use only part of a graphic you *crop* it to remove the part you do not want displayed. The graphic itself will remain unchanged. If you want to use the entire graphic, simply select the Fit in Frame check box in the Frame Settings Graphic tab. Use the following steps to crop the graphic so that only the left side of the Acropolis is displayed:

1. Open the Frame Settings dialog box and select the Graphic tab.
2. Click on the Fit in Frame check box to deselect it.
3. Double-click on the Width text box and type **6**, then click on OK.
4. Drag the graphic until only the left side of the Acropolis is displayed.

When working with graphics, you will sometimes need to draw attention to a particular part of a graphic, as when, for example, you want to identify the name or significance of part of the graphic. You can do this using a *callout*. A callout is text placed next to a graphic that describes a graphic element, usually with a line or arrow pointing to the element described. In CorelVENTURA, the easiest way to create callouts is to use *box text*.

Box Text

Box text differs from other text placed in your chapter in several ways: it is always formatted in a single column, it may overlap other text or graphics on the page, and it can have graphics (such as arrows) directly connected to it. Box text is formatted with the Z_BOXTEXT generated tag.

Using Frames and Importing Graphics

Tip: Box text should be used only for short, non-repetitive text, such as callouts.

You will add a callout to the graphic using box text with the following steps:

1. Click on the Drawing tool in the toolbox (the third tool from the bottom). In the Drawing flyout menu, click on the Box Text tool.

   You create a box text frame the same way you create any other frame: place the pointer on the upper-left corner and drag to the lower-right corner.

Note: When a paragraph is selected, the zero point of the vertical and horizontal rulers will reset to the top and left edges of the column that the text is in. This allows you to change the indent/outdent and tab settings relative to the column edge, not the base page edge. To reset the zero point to the upper-left corner of the base page, double-click on the box at the intersection of the rulers.

2. Place the pointer in the upper-left corner of the graphics frame, at about one-eighth of an inch on the vertical and horizontal rulers.
3. Drag the pointer to about .5 inches on the vertical ruler and 1.25 inches on the horizontal rulers.
4. Click on the Text tool and then click inside the box text frame.
5. Type **Our room**. Your frame should look like this:

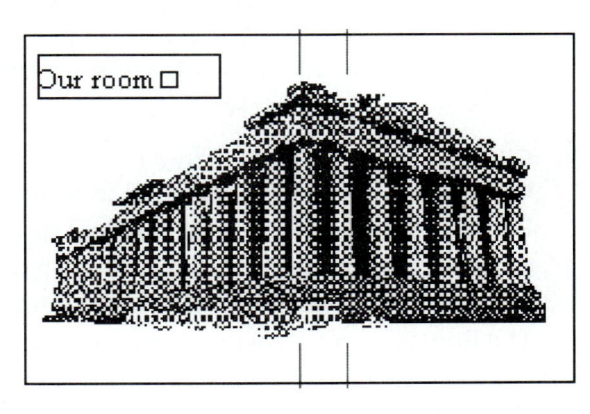

The exact location of the box text is not important. It should be within the frame containing the graphic and it should not be touching the graphic. Otherwise its location is a matter of personal taste. To place the box text where you want it, follow these steps:

1. Click on the Pick tool.
2. Point on the box text frame and press the mouse button. The pointer will turn into a four-headed arrow.
3. Drag the box text to the desired location and release the mouse button.

Tip: You can move and position any frame (except the base page) by dragging it with the Pick tool.

The box text frame has been created with a border and fill. Unlike the previous frame you created, the box text frame border is a graphic element, not a frame attribute. To remove the border you will use the Outline Pen tool in the toolbox. You will remove the border with these steps:

1. Select the box text frame, if necessary
2. Click on the Outline Pen tool.
3. Click on the Remove Outline tool in the Outline Pen flyout menu.

Next remove the fill:

1. Click on the Fill tool.
2. Click on the No Fill tool in the Fill flyout menu.

Now you will add an arrow to point to the part of the graphic referenced by the box text.

1. Click on the Drawing tool (the third tool from the bottom of the toolbox), and select the Line tool from the flyout menu.
2. Point on the right side of the box text, just after the last character.
3. Drag the pointer until it is close to the left side of the Acropolis, then release the button. A line now runs from the box text to the graphic.

    The line needs an arrowhead at one end to actually make it an arrow.

4. Click on the Outline Pen tool in the toolbox to open its flyout menu and select the Outline Pen roll-up.

Using Frames and Importing Graphics

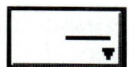

5. When the Outline Pen roll-up is displayed, click on the left arrowhead selector for the left end of the line.

6. The Arrowhead drop-down list box will be displayed, as shown here. Click on the open arrow located second from the left in the top row.

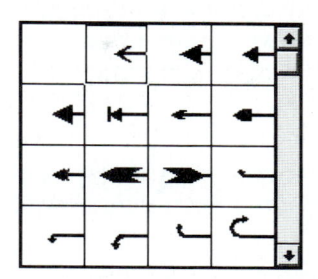

7. Click on Apply and then close the Outline Pen roll-up. Your box text arrow should look similar to this:

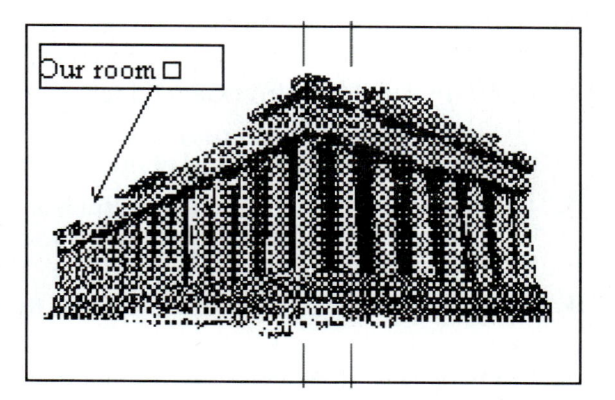

Other Text Frames

In addition to the frames you have used so far, there are several types of frames that CorelVENTURA creates automatically to hold text or graphic files. These include caption frames, repeating frames, header and footer frames, and footnote frames.

Captions

Graphics included in a publication will often include a caption that describes the graphics. When captions are included as part of the frame tag, CorelVENTURA will automatically generate the caption frame for the graphics frame when it is tagged. The caption can include a chapter number and a figure or table number. For example, the first figure in chapter three could be written as Figure 3-1. You would include "Figure" as part of the frame tag and CorelVENTURA will automatically generate the chapter and figure numbers when the appropriate options are selected.

Just as a caption frame is *anchored* to a graphics frame, other frames can be anchored to text. A frame that is anchored to a specific piece of text will always be placed on the same page as that text.

Note: Anchors cannot be set as part of a frame tag since each frame must be anchored to its own unique text.

Define a caption for the Picture frame tag with these steps:

1. With the Pick tool, select the frame containing the graphic file (not the box text frame).
2. Open the Frame Settings General tab.

    The Caption Format options, in the lower-right corner of the General tab, control the location and contents of the caption frame.
3. The frame tag Picture should be displayed in the Frame Tag drop-down list box. If it isn't, use the down arrow to display the list of tags and then select it.
4. Select Below in the Caption drop-down list box.
5. Click on the down arrow for the Reference drop-down list box. The drop-down list that appears contains several preformatted options for the caption text. These include Figure and Table followed by the codes [F#], [C#], and/or [T#] for figure number, chapter number, and table number. When the caption frame is generated, these codes will be replaced by the figure, chapter, and table number, respectively.
6. Select Figure [C#]-[F#].
7. Select the word Figure in the Reference drop-down list box and type **Illustration**. Include a space after the text. This text will be placed in each caption frame generated by CorelVENTURA. The trailing space will separate "Illustration" from the following text.
8. Click on OK.

When you tag a frame with the Picture frame tag, a caption frame will be generated by CorelVENTURA and attached to the tagged frame. The text in the caption frame will consist of two paragraphs, the generated text "Illustration," followed by the chapter and figure number separated by a hyphen. This is the text defined by the contents of the Reference drop-down list box in the Frame Settings General tab. You will enter the second paragraph directly in the caption frame since this text will describe the image in the graphics frame.

Generated Tags

When you create a caption, header, footer, or other type of frame containing generated text, CorelVENTURA will also generate tags for the text. The attributes of the generated tags will be based upon the attributes of the Body Text style tag. You can modify these tags in the same way you would other tags you create. These tags will be added to the Tags list box on the toolbar. Table 17-1 shows the names of the generated tags and the type of text they are applied to.

Tag Name	Text Applied To
Z_BOXTEXT	Box Text
Z_CAPTION	Text typed in the caption frame
Z_FNOT#	Footnote numbers
Z_FNOT ENTRY	Footnote text
Z_FOOTER	Footer text
Z_HEADER	Header text
Z_INDEX LTR	The letter head for each index section
Z_INDEX MAIN	Index body text
Z_INDEX TITLE	Index title text
Z_LABEL CAP	Text generated in the caption frame
Z_LABEL FIG	Figure number
Z_LABEL TBL	Table number
Z_SECx	Section numbers (x is replaced by the actual section number)
Z_TOC LVLx	Table of contents text (x is replaced by the actual table of contents level number)
Z_TOC TITLE	Table of contents title

Generated Tags Table 17-1.

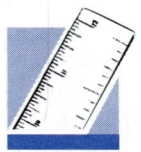

Tip: The names of generated tags can be hidden (not displayed in the Tags list) by setting the Generated Tags option to Hidden, using the Preferences option in the Tools menu. The tags will still be applied to the appropriate text but they will not be displayed, even when the tagged text is selected.

You will add a description of the graphic in the caption frame with these steps:

1. The text "Illustration 1-1" should be visible in the caption frame. Click on the Text tool (the fourth tool from the top) in the toolbox.
2. Click on the figure label text. The tag Z_LABEL FIG is displayed in the Tags list box.

    At the end of the text "Illustration 1-1" is a paragraph symbol, the ¶ character. This symbol indicates the end of the figure label paragraph. Following the paragraph symbol is a hollow square. This character indicates the end of the caption paragraph, the text that will describe the graphic that will be placed in between symbols in the captions frame.

3. Place the text cursor just to the left of the hollow box. The tag listed in the Tags list box will change to Z_CAPTION.
4. Type **Our hotel**. Your frame will look similar to the frame shown here:

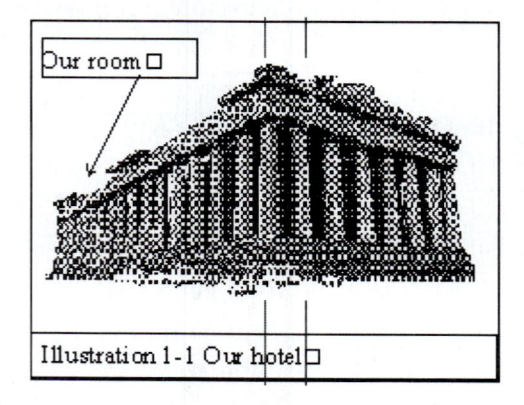

As you can see, both paragraphs (the generated text and the caption) are on the same line. This feature is useful when you need to have a lead-in to a paragraph that is formatted differently from the body of the paragraph. You can see how this is accomplished by looking at the settings for the Z_LABEL FIG and Z_CAPTION tags. The following steps point out the settings that

Using Frames and Importing Graphics

you use to place both paragraphs on the same line (the other options do not affect the placement in this case):

1. Click on Illustration with the Text tool. Z_LABEL FIG will be displayed in the Tags drop-down list box.
2. Select the Format menu and choose Style Tag. Confirm that Z_LABEL FIG is displayed in the Paragraph Settings Style Tag drop-down list box.
3. Select the Alignment tab. The Horizontal Text Alignment is set to Left.
4. Click on the Breaks command button. In the Breaks dialog box, the Line option will be set to Before. Click on Cancel.
5. Select the Spacing tab. The Spacing Below option is set to 0.

Now look at the settings for the Z_CAPTION tag:

1. Select Z_CAPTION in the Style Tag drop-down list box.
2. In the Spacing tab the Add Width of Preceding Line option is selected. This means the width of the preceding line will be added to the value in the Indent Amount spinner to determine the total indent amount. The Spacing Above option is set to 0.
3. Select the Alignment tab and click on the Breaks command button. In the Breaks dialog box, Line Break is set to After, and the In Line With Previous Paragraph check box is selected. Click on Cancel.
4. Click on Cancel to close the Paragraph Settings dialog box.

These settings place the first paragraph (Illustration 1-1) at the left edge of the caption frame. The Line Break settings cause the two paragraphs to be placed on the same line. The Relative Indent option causes the second paragraph (Our plane) to be indented from the left margin by the length of the last line of the previous paragraph plus the amount set in the Indent Amount spinner.

Repeating Frames

Repeating frames are used to place the same text or graphic on each page of a chapter. You would use repeating frames to place a logo, custom crop marks, or thumb tabs on each page. Repeating frames are created using the Frame Settings General Tab.

After creating the frame you want to repeat (including its contents, borders, and so forth), you use the Repeating Frames options in the Frame Settings General Tab to set the pages on which the frame will appear (All, Left, Right,

None). You can also hide a repeating frame on the current page. When double-sided pages are selected, repeating frames can be either mirrored or copied to facing pages. Copying to a facing page will place the frame in the same place on each page. In other words, if the frame is located two inches from the right edge of the right page, it would also be located two inches from the right edge of the left page. If the frame was mirrored, it would be two inches from the left edge of the left page.

Note: You can have a maximum of six repeating frames in each chapter. Repeating frames cannot be tagged or include captions. If you require repeating captions for a repeating graphic, draw the caption frame as a separate frame and make it repeating.

Headers and Footers

Headers and footers are used to place text at the top and bottom of each page in a chapter. For example, the chapter title could be placed as a header (causing it to appear at the top of each page), and the page number could be placed as a footer (causing it to appear at the bottom of each page).

Headers and footers are created using the Chapter Settings option in the Layout menu. When the option is selected, the Chapter Settings dialog box is displayed. Selecting the Header/Footer tab displays the tab shown in Figure 17-5. The Enable check boxes are used to turn headers and footers on or off. Separate headers or footers can be set for facing pages, or copied, or mirrored from one side to the other. The Define drop-down list box determines which header or footer the text in the Header/Footer Left, Center, and Right text boxes will be applied to.

The buttons at the bottom of the tab allow you to place variables in headers and footers. The buttons and their uses are described in Table 17-2.

When selected, the First Match and Last Match option buttons locate the first or last text tagged with the tag specified in the appropriate text boxes, and places it in the selected header or footer. The text formatting is copied with the text. This allows you to automatically place chapter and section heads in headers and footers.

Headers and footers can be locally formatted (as distinguished from formatting with a tag) using the Text Attributes button. In other words, you can use the Text Attributes button to change the attributes of *selected* text within the header or footer. Selecting the button displays the Selected Text Attributes dialog box shown in Figure 17-6. You can use these options to format the selected header and footer text. Headers are normally formatted

Using Frames and Importing Graphics

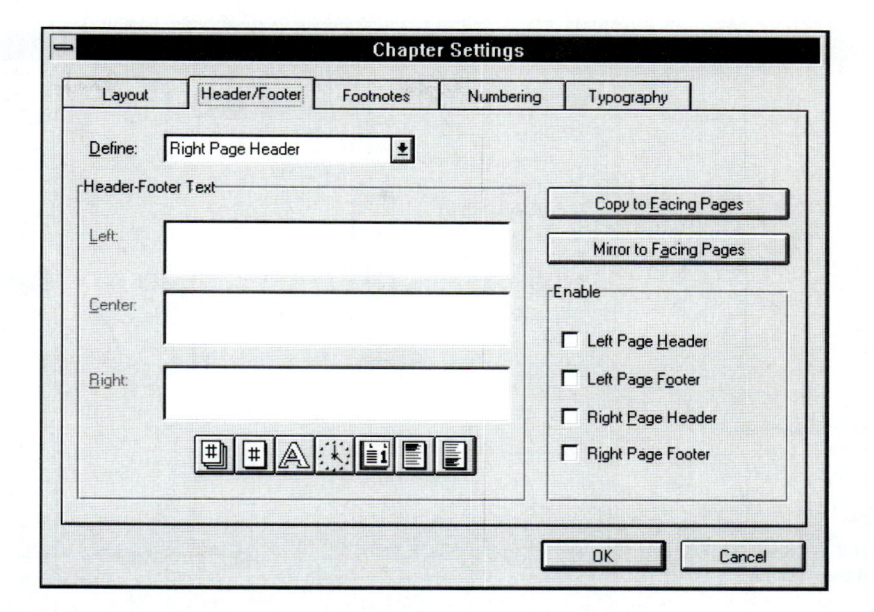

Header/Footer tab
Figure 17-5.

Button	Function
	Chapter number
	Page number
	Text attributes for selected text
	Current time
	Current date
	First match of formatted text
	Last match of formatted text

Header/Footer Insert Buttons
Table 17-2.

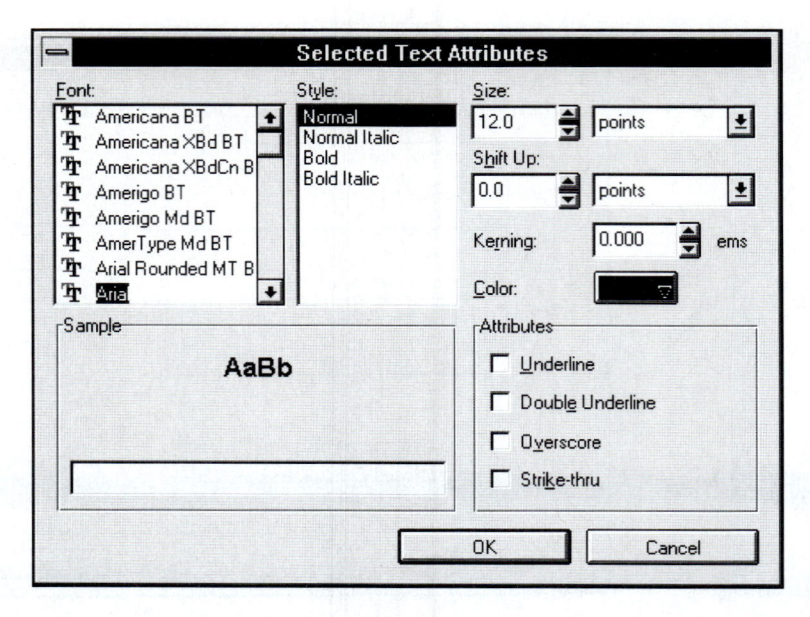

Selected Text Attributes dialog box
Figure 17-6.

with the Z_HEADER generated style tag, and footers with the Z_FOOTER generated style tag.

Add headers and a footer to your publication with these steps:

1. Select the Layout menu and choose Chapter Settings.
2. Select the Header/Footer tab in the Chapter Settings dialog box.
3. Select all four Enable check boxes.
4. Select Left Page Header in the Define drop-down list box.
5. Click on the Left Header-Footer Text text box and type **CorelVENTURA for Fun and Profit** (do not end with a period).
6. Select Right Page Header in the Define drop-down list box.
7. Click on the Right Header-Footer Text text box, then click on the First Match Insert button. The Tags list box shown in Figure 17-7 is displayed.
8. Double-click on the Chapter Title tag. The text [<Chapter Title] is inserted in the Right Header-Footer Text text box.
9. Select Left Page Footer in the Define drop-down list box.
10. Click on the Center Header-Footer Text text box, then click on the Chapter Number button. Type - (a hyphen) and click on the Page Number Insert button. The text [C#]-[P#] is placed in the text box.
11. Click on the Mirror to Facing Pages command button.
12. Click on OK.

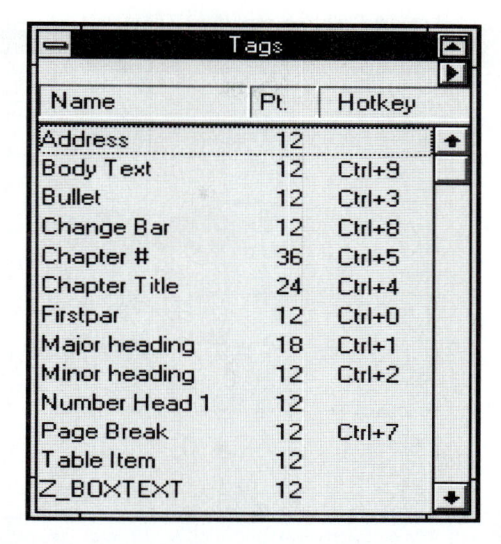

Tags list box
Figure 17-7.

You should save your work again by clicking on the Save tool on the ribbon or by choosing Save in the File menu. You can use the Vertical scroll bar on the right side of the CorelVENTURA screen to view the headers and footers that have been included with your chapter.

Footnotes

Footnotes are used to provide additional information about statements in the main text file. For example, the text may quote another publication; a footnote would then be used to provide the source and author of the quoted work. Footnotes consist of a footnote number inserted into the text and a footnote frame that contains the footnote text and the footnote number. To insert a footnote, the text tool is selected and the cursor is placed at the appropriate point in the text. You then choose the Footnote option in the Insert Special Item submenu in the Edit menu. Footnote attributes are then set using the Footnotes tab in the Chapter Settings dialog box. The Footnotes tab is shown in Figure 17-8.

The Numerical, Custom, and Off option buttons determine if standard Arabic numbers will be used, if a custom numbering system will be used, or if footnotes will be turned off. When Numerical is selected, Arabic numerals will be used. You can enter other characters before and/or after the footnote number by entering the characters directly in the Reference text box. Type the preceding character(s), then a # (pound sign), followed by the succeeding character(s). The Position drop-down list box allows you to select Normal, Superscript, or Subscript positioning for the footnote.

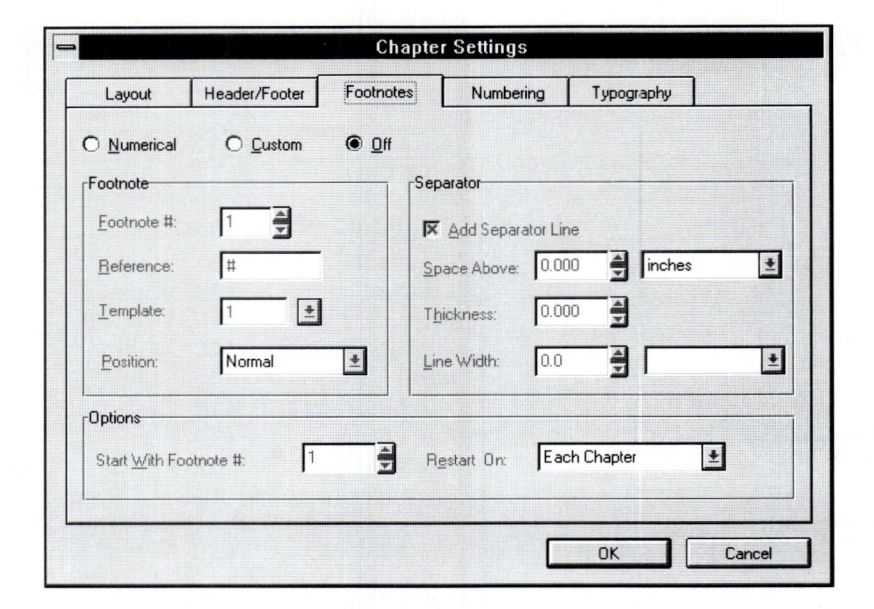

Chapter Settings Footnotes tab
Figure 17-8.

When the Custom option button is selected, the footnote you want to define is selected in the Footnote # spinner, and the custom characters are entered in the Reference text box. Templates for footnotes are selected with the Template drop-down list box.

The Start With Footnote # option allows you to specify a number other than 1 (the default) for the footnote starting number. The Restart On drop-down list box sets whether the footnotes will be placed on each page or at the end of the chapter. A ruling line can be placed above the footnote text with the Separator Line Width, Space Above, and Thickness spinners.

Footnote frames can be modified in the same manner as other frames, except that you cannot change the number of columns. Footnote text is tagged with the Z_FNOT# and Z_FNOT ENTRY generated tags.

In the next chapter you will bring together CorelVENTURA's and CorelDRAW!'s features to create a complete publication.

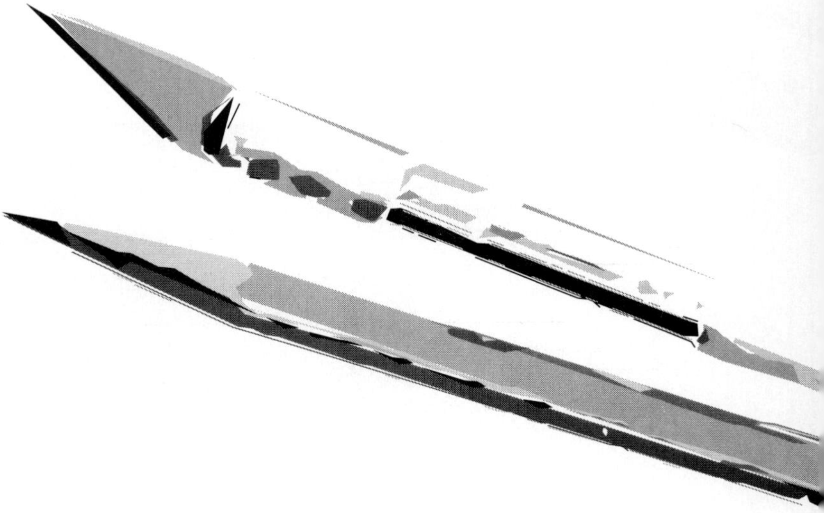

18

INTEGRATING CorelDRAW! and CorelVENTURA

A CorelVENTURA publication is a combination of text, graphics, and data produced by word processors, graphics programs, databases, spreadsheets, and other applications. In fact, if an application can produce an output file in any of a number of common file formats, CorelVENTURA can integrate its information into a publication.

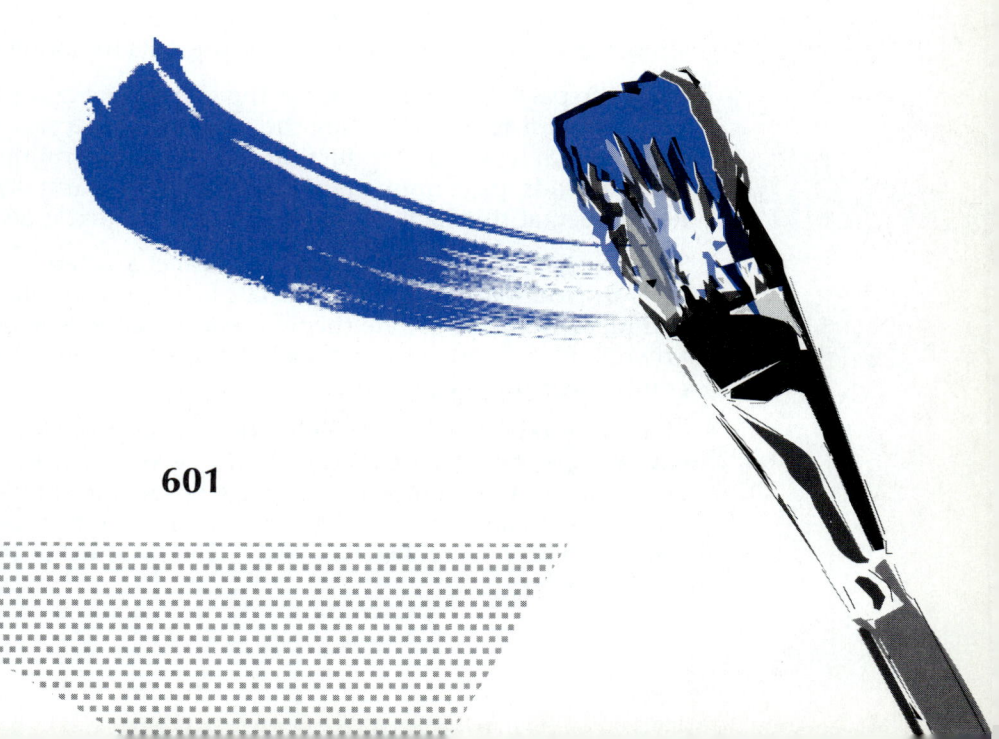

CorelVENTURA is the director, organizing the cast of characters into a coherent production. As you've seen in previous chapters, CorelVENTURA's frames, tags, and style sheets give you extensive flexibility to organize and format text and graphics into publications. In this chapter, you will expand your knowledge of CorelVENTURA and learn how to combine its page layout capabilities with the graphics power of CorelDRAW!.

Designing a Publication

Before importing and placing information in a CorelVENTURA document, you need to design the overall appearance of your publication. During this design "stage," CorelVENTURA presents the available options for the components that make up a complete publication. At this stage in the process, text should also be considered a graphic element—integrated into the overall design based on its appearance, rather than its content.

The page size is the most basic element of publication design. Some common book page sizes are 5.5 by 8.5 inches, 7 by 9 inches, and 8 by 10 inches. Books designed to primarily present text (such as this book) will use page sizes around 7 by 9 inches. This size allows the designer to place text in a single column that is not too wide to read comfortably (when a column of text becomes too wide, the reader's eyes will tire from moving side to side). A magazine or newsletter, on the other hand, will often have pages around 8.5 by 11 inches, and text will be placed in multiple columns. Specialty books, such as books of artwork that consist mostly of images, will have page sizes that allow the designer to present the images most favorably. Page sizes for specialty books may range from 8.5 by 8.5 inches to 11 by 14 inches, but almost any size is usable as long as it presents its contents favorably.

Once the page size is determined, the graphic elements that will appear on each page are added. These are the supporting players—often overlooked, but essential to a good production. These include ruling lines, chapter and section heads, page numbers, and especially the font chosen for the text. Remember, at this stage of the design process, text is also a graphic element.

The stage is now set to bring on the main characters—the text file that will form the foundation of the publication, and the graphics that will be used to complement and illustrate the text. For some types of books (collections of artwork, for example) the roles will be reversed, with the text supporting and complementing the graphics.

Like any good director, CorelVENTURA knows how to bring out the best in its cast. You not only have CorelVENTURA's text formatting and layout tools, but also CorelDRAW!'s integrated package of graphic abilities. CorelDRAW! itself allows you to add structured graphics and text effects (such as text that follows a path), Corel PHOTO-PAINT gives you extensive control and effects

Integrating CorelDRAW! and CorelVENTURA

for bitmapped images (such as scanned artwork), and CorelCHART makes creating and placing charts in a publication quick and easy.

CorelVENTURA and CorelDRAW! have been designed to work together to make it easier and faster for you to design and produce many types of publications. In the rest of this chapter, you will work with CorelVENTURA and CorelDRAW! to create a complete publication, integrating both text and graphics. You will see that you can directly import CorelDRAW! CDR files into CorelVENTURA, something you can do with no other application.

Chapter Layout

The publication you are creating in this chapter is composed of two chapters of a book illustrating some of the features of CorelVENTURA. The first chapter will consist of a single page that is an introduction to the book. It will include imported graphics. The second chapter will demonstrate how tables are added to a publication.

The emphasis is on combining the elements that make up a publication, rather than creating a specific type of chapter. The content of the text you will use is of less importance than its appearance. After you learn how the elements work together, you are encouraged to experiment with the placement of elements to create your own design.

The page size will be 8.5 by 11 inches. This page size is large enough to use multiple columns, and provides enough space for graphics in a wide range of sizes. The pages will be double-sided, with the left page having the book title as the header and the right page having the chapter title as a header. The page number will be placed at the bottom of each page—in the left corner on left pages and in the right corner on right pages.

To create this publication, you will begin with the default style sheet (DEFAULT.STY) included with CorelVENTURA. As originally installed, the default style sheet includes only one style tag—Body Text. When you open CorelVENTURA, a chapter consisting of a single page formatted with the default style sheet is created. If CorelVENTURA is not open, open it now. Use the steps on the following page to create a new chapter:

Note: If you have modified your DEFAULT.STY style sheet, it may contain style tags other than Body Text. These tags will be included when you save the new style sheet. Since you are saving them to a new style sheet, any changes you make to them will not affect existing publications.

1. Choose New in the File menu.
2. Click on the Style Sheet command button, select DEFAULT.STY, and click on OK.

You should now have open a new chapter with a single page formatted with the DEFAULT.STY style sheet. Save the style sheet with a new name now:

1. Choose Save Style Sheet As in the Layout menu.
2. Select the directory containing your style sheets (\COREL50\VENTURA\TYPESET\ in this case), type **chap1** in the File Name text box, and press ENTER.

The changes you will make in the style sheet will be made to CHAP1.STY, not the DEFAULT.STY style sheet. Any publications formatted with the DEFAULT.STY style sheet will not be affected by the changes you make in the new style sheet.

Tip: You should create new style sheets for your publications rather than making changes to the DEFAULT.STY style sheet. Since changes to a style sheet will be reflected in every publication formatted with that style sheet, you should be careful when changing a style sheet to avoid surprises when you use it later on.

Choosing a Font

Modifying the Body Text style tag and adding tags to your style sheet are the next steps in the process. The Body Text style tag is applied to all untagged text when it is first placed in a publication. It is also the style that CorelVENTURA copies when it generates automatic style tags, such as header and footer style tags. Since most of the text in your publication will have this style tag, your choices will have a large impact on the overall appearance of your publication.

The first step is to choose a font or typeface for the style tag. The terms *font* and *typeface* are commonly used interchangeably, even though they actually have different meanings. A typeface is a *family* of characters. A typeface family includes the normal (or *roman*) version of the characters, as well as italic, bold, bold italic, and other styles of the characters. A font is technically a single size and style of a typeface. Times New Roman 12 point italic is a single font, as is Times New Roman 12 point normal, but both are part of the Times New Roman typeface. While you should understand the difference between a font and a typeface, current usage is to use either term interchangeably.

Figure 18-1. Examples of type styles

Roman	Dutch 801 (Times New Roman)
Italic	*Dutch 801 (Times New Roman)*
Bold	**Dutch 801 (Times New Roman)**
Bold Italic	***Dutch 801 (Times New Roman)***
Semibold	Dutch 801 (Times New Roman)
Extrabold	**Dutch 801 (Times New Roman)**
Headline	Dutch 801 (Times New Roman)

When you select a font to use for the body of your text, you should use a typeface family that includes, at a minimum, normal, italic, bold, and bold italic type styles. These style changes allow you to place different amounts of emphasis on words in your text. Some families will include even more variations, such as expanded, condensed, light, medium, black (an extra heavy bold effect), and combinations of these styles. Figure 18-1 shows examples of different type styles. Among the typefaces included with CorelDRAW!, good choices for body text fonts are Dutch 801 (Bitstream's version of Times), ITC Garamond, and Swiss 721 (Bitstream's version of Helvetica).

Body Text - Dutch 801

Body Text - Times New Roman

Body Text - Garamond

Body Text - Arial

Body Text - Swiss 721

On the other hand, typefaces such as ITC American Typewriter (with only medium and bold styles) and Calligraphic 421 (one style only) are poor choices for body text. However, these typefaces could work well in shorter publications, such as advertising or posters, or as headlines.

ITC American Typewriter

Calligraphic 421

An assortment of typefaces allows you to select the typeface that best suits the mood of the publication you are creating. In this chapter, you will use Times New Roman and Arial. These typefaces are supplied with Windows and are equivalents of Times and Helvetica.

Note: You will often see typefaces with different names that appear to be identical. The names of typefaces (such as Times or Helvetica) can be copyrighted, but the actual shape of the characters cannot. Most type manufacturers, or type foundries, will have a version of a standard typeface with their own name. For example, Times New Roman (The Monotype Corp.) and Dutch 801 (Bitstream) are basically the same typeface. While the differences between these typefaces may be small, they can have a significant impact in a publication because of character spacing and other attributes.

Caution: If a typeface doesn't include a style, such as italic, it sometimes can be simulated onscreen by the application. However, even if the typeface appears as italic on your screen, it may not print properly on a PostScript printer or typesetter, such as a Linotronic. It is best to use only fonts that are installed on your computer; if you submit your document for publication, be sure that the fonts are included in your output files or are available on your publisher's computers.

A body text font should be easy to read at body text type sizes (generally 10 to 12 points). Generally *serif* typefaces (a serif is the short stroke at the ends of the bars of a character) are easier to read than *sans serif* typefaces (those without strokes at the ends of the bars). Times New Roman is a serif typeface, Arial is a sans serif typeface. Typefaces that are too ornate are also poor choices for body text. For these exercises, Times New Roman will be used for the body text. This is a very common font, and is almost always a safe choice for the body text. It can also be a very boring choice because it is so common.

Tip: Try different fonts as you work through these exercises to get a feel for how they look and fit on a page. Different fonts will require more or less space for a specific amount of text. Changing the style tag definition will apply the new font to the tagged text. Remember that, with fonts, more is not always better. Too many (more than three) different fonts on one page makes for unpleasant reading.

Define the Body Text style tag in your style sheet now with these steps:

1. Choose Paragraph in the Format menu. In the Paragraph Settings dialog box, Body Text should be displayed in the Style Tag drop-down list box at the bottom of the tab.

2. In the Character tab, the following options should be selected: Times New Roman Font, Normal Style, 12 points, Black—no special effects or attributes should be selected. Change to these settings, if necessary, and then select the Alignment tab.

   In the Alignment tab, the following options should be selected: Justified Horizontal Alignment and Top Vertical Alignment. Change to these settings, if necessary, and then click on the Breaks command button.

   Body text will generally have either Left or Justified horizontal alignment. As you read from left to right, if each line starts in a different horizontal position the reader's eyes have to search for it. This soon becomes tiring. Justified text give a smoother appearance to columns of text, but can produce excessive space between words and letters if the columns are too narrow. Center alignment is more appropriate for headlines, captions, or other short pieces of text. Right alignment is best used for special effects, such a caption located on the left side of an illustration. Decimal alignment is used for aligning columns of numbers.

3. In the Breaks dialog box, the following options should be selected: no Page or Column breaks, Line Break Before, and Allow Breaks in Paragraphs. Change to these settings if necessary, then click on OK.

4. Select the Spacing tab. In the Spacing tab, the following options should be selected: All Pages, Left and Right Paragraph Indents should be set to zero, Line Indents should be one Line to Indent at .25 inch, and the Above, Below, and Inter-Line spacing should be 120 percent. Change to these settings if necessary.

   The Spacing attributes you select will have a large impact on the overall look of your publication. One way to look at the design of a publication is to look at the empty space created by the text and other elements. This white space balances the text and other elements. Good design recognizes the importance of this balance. The spacing between lines of text (Inter-Line spacing or *leading*) determines, in large part, how light or dark a page will be. Darker typefaces will need more, while lighter typefaces can get by with less. Words become harder to read as the space between letters (*tracking*) gets too narrow or too wide.

   Paragraphs break up the text on a page, preventing the page from becoming a dark mass. Spacing before and after paragraphs uses white space to define each paragraph. Indents also establish for the eye the beginning of each paragraph. Indenting a paragraph places more emphasis on it, because it breaks up the flow of the text

5. The attributes of the Defaults tab will be accepted as is. The Defaults tab attributes determine the thickness and location of the rules used to underline, overscore, and strike-thru text, and the values for superscripts, subscripts, and small caps. These settings reveal the extensive control CorelVENTURA gives you in defining the appearance of text.

6. Select the Typography tab. Automatic Hyphenation should be selected, American English should be the Dictionary, and Successive Hyphenations should be set to 2.

The Paragraph Typography tab also defines the maximum and minimum limits CorelVENTURA will use to justify text, both horizontally and vertically. If the letter or word spacing in your publication appears too loose or too tight, use these settings to adjust it.

The next style tag to set is the Firstpar tag. This tag is identical to the Body Text tag, except that it specifies a drop cap for the first letter of the paragraph. Drop caps help bring the reader's eyes to the beginning of the text. Drop caps can use the Body Text font, or a different font can be chosen. This style will be used for the first paragraph of a chapter or section. Set the Firstpar style tag now with these steps:

1. Click on the + button to the right of the Style Tag drop-down list box in the Paragraph Settings dialog box. The Add Style dialog box is displayed.

2. In the Add Style Tag dialog box, type **Firstpar** in the Tag Name text box.

3. Confirm that Body Text is selected in the Copy Attributes From and Next Tag drop-down list boxes.

4. Select Body Text in the Tag Type drop-down list box, and then click on OK.

5. Select Firstpar in the Style Tag drop-down list box at the bottom of the dialog box. A dialog box is presented asking if you wish to apply the changes made to Body Text. Click on Yes.

6. Select the Character tab, and click on the Drop Cap option button. The Character tab will display the font, size, and other attributes for a drop cap, as shown in Figure 18-2.

7. Select Arial in the Font list box, Bold in the Style list box, and set the size to 24 points.

8. Select Drop Cap in the Apply Effect drop-down list box.

9. Select the Spacing tab and set the Indent Amount to 0.

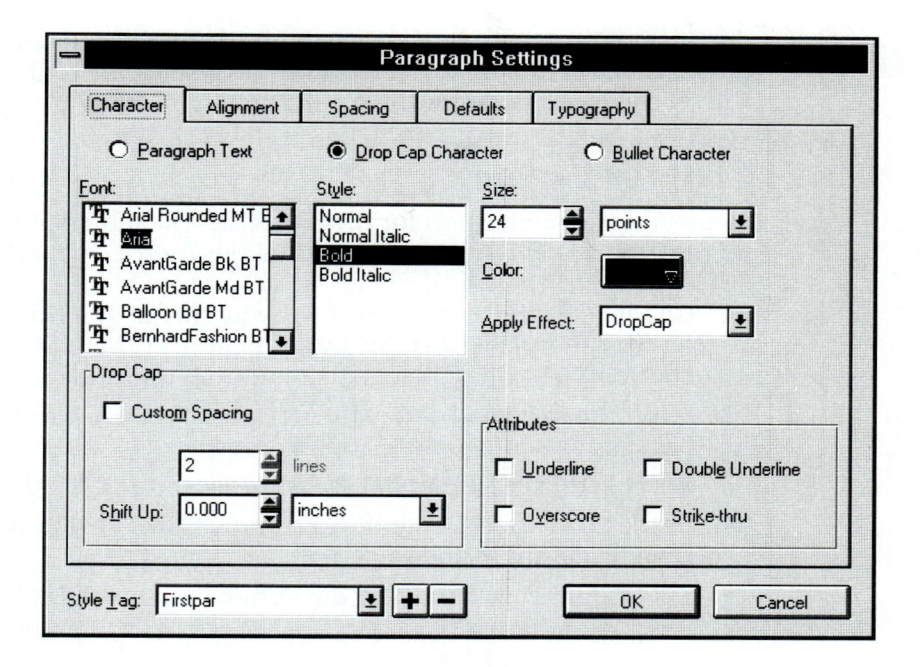

Drop Cap settings in the Character tab
Figure 18-2.

You will add one more style tag before setting the chapter layout. This is the Chapter Title style tag. This tag will be used once per chapter to set the style for the title of the chapter. Set the Chapter Title attributes now with these steps:

1. Click on the + button to the right of the Style Tag drop-down list box in the Paragraph Settings dialog box.
2. In the Add Style Tag dialog box, type **Chapter Title** in the Tag Name text box.
3. Confirm Body Text is selected in the Copy Attributes From and Next Tag drop-down list boxes.
4. Select Body Text in the Tag Type drop-down list box, and then click on OK.
5. Select Chapter Title in the Style Tag drop-down list box in the Paragraph Settings dialog box. A dialog box is presented asking if you wish to apply the changes made to Firstpar. Click on Yes.
6. In the Character tab, Times New Roman should be selected for the font. Select Bold for the style and 24 points for the size.
7. Click on OK.

This gives you a basic set of style tags for your publication. New style tags can be added at any time you feel they are needed for your design. Next you will set the page layout for the publication.

Chapter Layout

To prepare the publication for the imported text and graphics, you need to set the page size and the headers and footers for the publication.

1. Choose Chapter Settings in the Layout menu. The Layout tab should be set for Letter size paper (8.5 by 11 inches), Portrait, Double-sided, and Start on Right side. Change these settings if necessary.
2. Select the Headers/Footer tab. Activate all the Enable check boxes—right page headers and footers, and left page headers and footers.
3. Select Left Page Header in the Define drop-down list box.
4. In the Left Header-Footer text box type **CorelVENTURA for Fun and Profit** (do not include a period).
5. Select Right Page Header in the Define drop-down list box.
6. Click on the Right Header-Footer text box, then click on the First Match button (the second from the right in the button bar at the bottom of the tab). The Tags roll-up will be displayed.
7. In the Tags roll-up, double-click on Chapter Title.
8. Select Left Page Footer in the Define drop-down list box.
9. Click on the Left Header-Footer text box, then click on the Page Number button (second from the left) at the bottom of the tab.
10. Click on the Mirror to Facing Pages command button to generate a page number in the bottom-right corner of right pages.
11. Click on OK.

The attributes for your chapter have been set. The final step in preparing the publication is to set the base page attributes.

Frame Attributes

The frame attributes determine the margins and columns of each page. This is the space your design will use. The space outside the margins also plays a part in the overall design. This white space balances the space within the margins. Graphics and text effects can also spill over onto this space for special effects. Set the margins and other frame attributes with the following instructions:

1. Using the Pick tool, click on the page displayed on your screen. This is the base page.
2. Choose Frame in the Format menu.
3. Select the Margins tab in the Frame Settings dialog box.
4. Confirm that the Left Pages Inside Margins option button is selected.
5. Confirm that Units are set to inches, then double-click on the Top spinner and type **1**. Press TAB and type **1**.
6. Press TAB, type **1**, press TAB again, and type **1.5**.
7. Click on the Mirror to Facing Page command button.
8. Click on OK to accept the Frame Settings.
9. Save your file now by clicking on the Save File button in the ribbon. Type **MY_BOOK2** in the File Save As dialog box and press ENTER.

The stage has been set to import your text and graphic files.

Using the Story Editor

You have previously imported a text file into CorelVENTURA, which is how you will normally add text to a publication. You can also enter or edit text directly in a frame, or use the Story Editor to enter or edit longer sections of text. The Story Editor is easier to use than editing in the frame when working with longer sections of text. The Story Editor displays all the text in the same font and size. The style tags for the text are displayed on the left side of the screen. Because the Story Editor is working only with the characters, and not the formatting, more text can be displayed on the screen at one time. You can also move around the text easier and screen redrawing is faster.

You will use the Story Editor to prepare an introduction for the publication. For this exercise, the content of the text is less important than the appearance. The chapter that will hold this text is designed to represent the introduction to a book. The introduction will be two paragraphs long and will fit on one page. You will create the text for the introduction by typing one sentence and then using the Copy and Paste commands to duplicate it. Create the introduction now with these instructions:

1. Select the Text tool (the fourth from the top in the toolbox) and click on the base page to select it.
2. Select the View menu and choose Story Editor. The Story Editor screen will appear, as shown in Figure 18-3.

    The left side of the screen contains a separate column that displays the style tag for each paragraph. If the tag names aren't visible, point on the

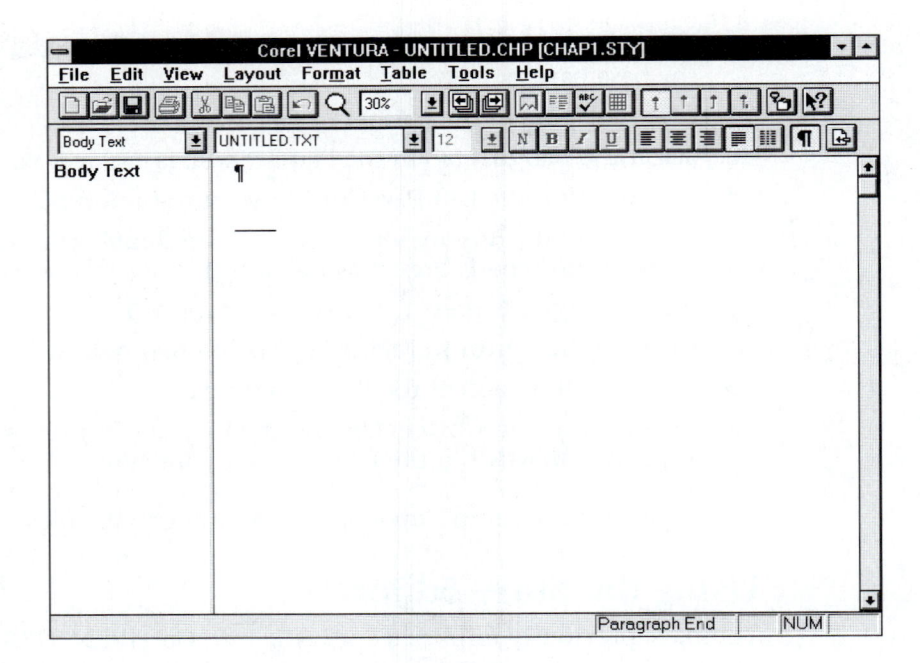

Story Editor screen
Figure 18-3.

left edge of the screen. The pointer will change to a two-headed arrow. Drag the pointer to the right. The tag names should now be displayed. The main portion of the screen will display the text you are editing.

3. The text cursor will be located at the top of the screen. Type the following sentence:

   This paragraph will allow you to see the effects of applying different style tags to text in CorelVENTURA.

   Leave a space after the period.

4. The cursor should be at the end of the text, just to the left of the paragraph symbol. Select the text by pressing and holding the SHIFT key while clicking on the beginning of the sentence.

5. Press CTRL-C to copy the selected text.

6. Place the insertion point just to the left of the paragraph symbol and press CTRL-V to paste the text.

7. Repeat steps 4 through 6 two more times. Your paragraph should now have eight sentences.

8. Copy the paragraph using steps 4 and 5, then place the insertion point just before the paragraph symbol and press ENTER.

9. Press CTRL-V to insert the second paragraph of the introduction.
10. Add a title for the introduction by placing the insertion point at the beginning of the first paragraph.
11. Type **Introducing CorelVENTURA** and press ENTER.
12. Select Page Layout in the View menu.

When you return to the Page Layout view, the text you entered in the Story Editor is now displayed in the base page. The text is tagged with the Body Text style tag. Your next step is to assign new tags to the title and first paragraph. Do that now by following these instructions:

1. Select the Zoom tool, in the Zoom flyout menu select the Full Width tool (the second from the right).
2. Select the Paragraph tool (fifth from the top in the toolbox), and click on the title "Introducing CorelVENTURA," to select it.
3. Click on the down arrow for the Tags list box in the ribbon and select Chapter Title. Once the text is tagged with the Chapter Title tag, it will also appear as the header for the page.
4. With the Paragraph tool still selected, click on the next paragraph.
5. Click on the down arrow for the Tags list box and select Firstpar.

Your screen should look similar to Figure 18-4.

Your chapter is now ready for adding graphics.

Importing Graphics with Corel MOSAIC

In the previous chapter, you imported graphics and placed them in rectangular frames. With CorelVENTURA you can also have text flow around the outline of an irregular graphic. You will use this technique to add a graphic to the introduction. Import the graphic now with these instructions:

1. Select the Frame tool (third from the top of the toolbox).
2. Place the pointer at about 2.5 inches on the vertical ruler and 6 inches on the horizontal ruler. Drag to about 5 inches on the vertical ruler and 8 inches on the horizontal ruler. When you release the button, the rulers' zero points will reset to the upper-left corner of the new frame.

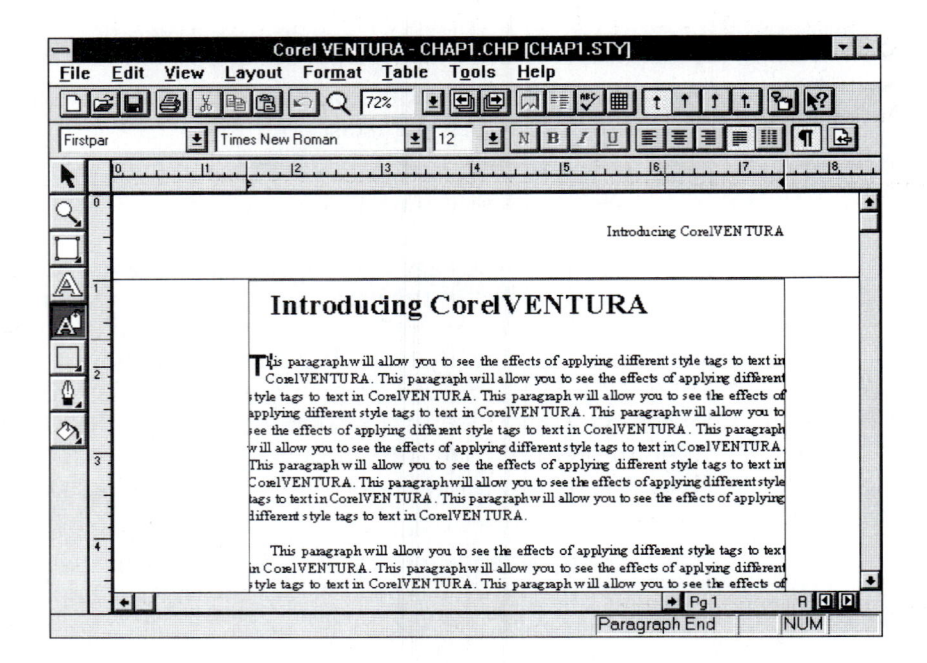

CorelVENTURA screen with tagged text
Figure 18-4.

3. Click on the MOSAIC roll-up button (second from the right) on the ribbon. The MOSAIC roll-up will be displayed, as shown here:

4. At the top of the MOSAIC roll-up, below the title bar, the current directory is displayed. The image you are going to place in your chapter is a CorelDRAW! file located in the \CLIPART\BIRDS\ directory on the CorelDRAW! CD-ROM. You can use another clip-art example if you want. If the correct directory is not displayed, use the drop-down list box in the upper-left corner of the roll-up to select the correct path.

5. Using the vertical scroll bar, scroll until TOCAN.CDR is displayed.

6. Point on the thumbnail of TOCAN.CDR, then drag it to the frame you just created and release the mouse button. The graphic will be placed in the frame.

Integrating CorelDRAW! and CorelVENTURA

7. Close the MOSAIC roll-up by double-clicking on the control button in the upper-left corner.

   Now you will flow the text around the graphic.

8. With the frame still selected, choose Frame in the Format menu and click on the Flow Text Runaround check box. Click on OK.

A path following the outline of the graphic has been created. You can use the Shape tool (in the Frame tool flyout menu) to edit the outline. You can also use the Curve Editing roll-up in the Tool menu to edit the path. You edit the path in exactly the same manner as you would in CorelDRAW!. Your screen should now appear similar to Figure 18-5.

Editing Graphics in CorelDRAW!

The ability to place graphics created in CorelDRAW! without having to change the file format is just one of the many ways in which these two programs cooperate. Editing a CorelDRAW! graphic while in CorelVENTURA is as simple as double-clicking on the graphic. The graphic must first be placed as a *linked object,* using CorelDRAW!'s Object Linking and Embedding (OLE) features. OLE is explained in detail in Chapter 11; in the following

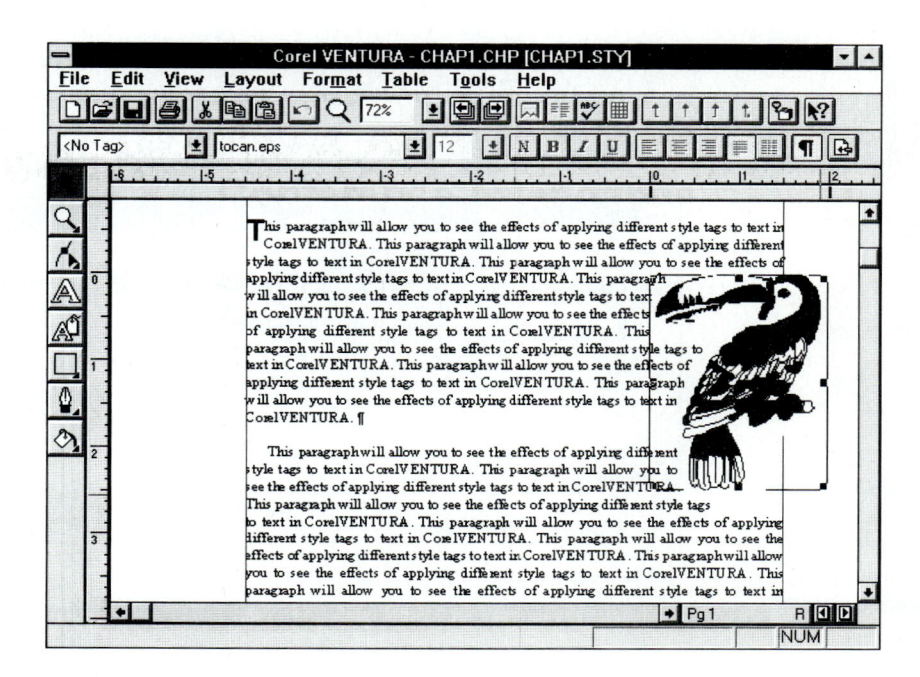

CorelVENTURA screen with TOCAN.CDR placed

Figure 18-5.

exercise you will learn how to use it to edit an imported graphic. Place a linked graphic now with the following steps:

1. Select the Zoom tool, and click on the Full Page view tool in the Zoom flyout menu.
2. Click on the base page to reset the rulers' zero points to the upper-left corner.
3. Select the Frame tool and place the pointer at 5 inches on the vertical ruler and 1.5 inches on the horizontal ruler.
4. Drag to 8 inches on the vertical ruler and 3.5 inches on the horizontal ruler.
5. While the frame is still selected, select the Edit menu and choose the Insert Object option. The Insert Object dialog box, shown in Figure 18-6, is displayed.
6. Click on the Create from File option button. The Object Type list box is replaced by the File text box.
7. Click on the Browse command button. In the Browse dialog box that is displayed, select the \CLIPART\BIRDS\ directory on the CorelDRAW! CD-ROM, then select TOCAN.CDR and click on OK.
8. Confirm that the Link check box is selected, then click on OK. A copy of the selected file is placed in the selected frame.

The graphic displayed is linked to the original file. This means that when the original file is modified, the changes will be reflected in the copy of the file

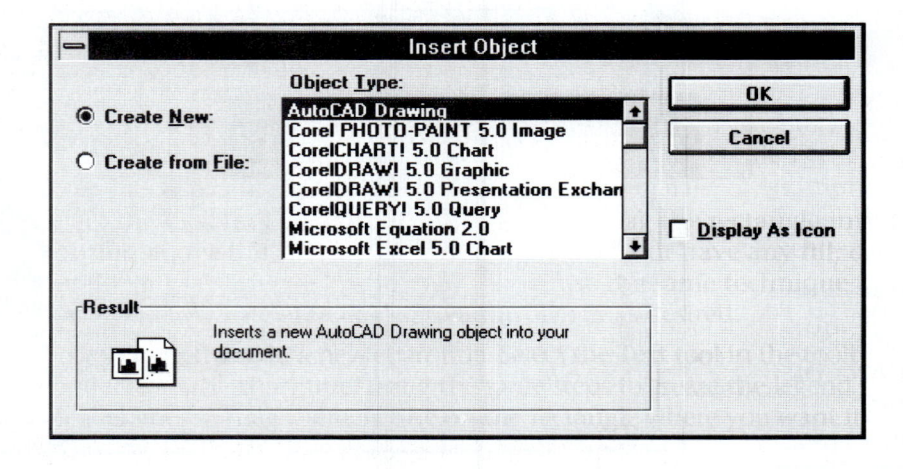

Insert Object dialog box
Figure 18-6.

Integrating CorelDRAW! and CorelVENTURA

in your CorelVENTURA publication. The next set of instructions will demonstrate the process of editing a linked object.

1. Double-click on the graphic you just placed.
2. CorelDRAW! will open with the graphic file displayed, as shown in Figure 18-7.

   Since you are going to modify the file, you should save it using a different name and make your changes to the copy.
3. Select the File menu and choose Save Copy As.
4. In the Save Drawing As dialog box, type **tocan2.cdr** in the file text box. Choose the desired target directory and click on OK.
5. Select the drawing by clicking on it.
6. Select the Effects menu and choose Transform roll-up.
7. In the Transform roll-up, click on the Mirror button (the center button in the top row), then click on the Horizontal Mirror button (the top Mirror button).
8. Click on Apply. The drawing will be mirrored horizontally so that the toucan is facing to the right.
9. Save your copy by choosing Save in the File menu.
10. Select the File menu and choose Exit & Return To. CorelDRAW! closes, and the modified graphic appears in CorelVENTURA.

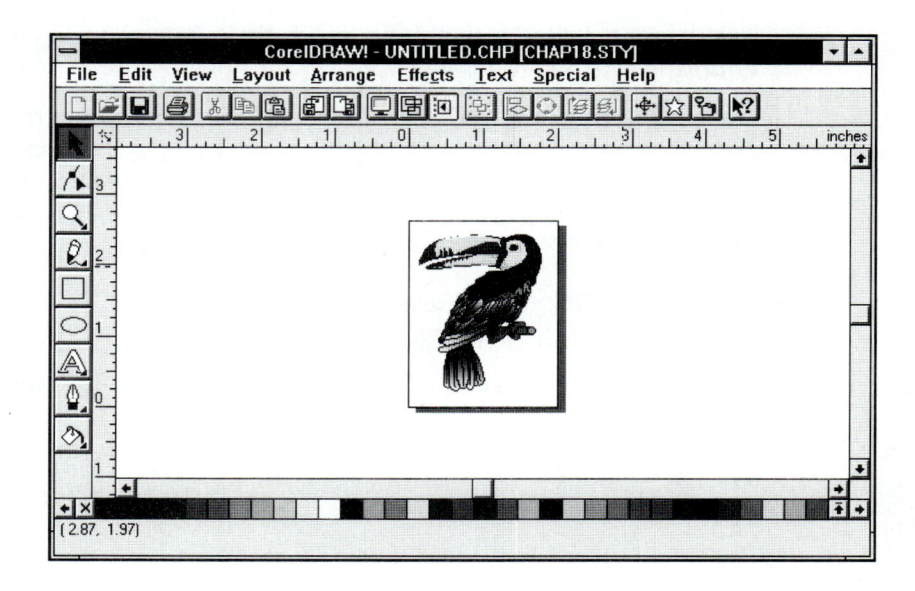

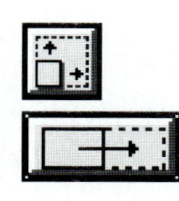

CorelDRAW! with TOCAN.CDR displayed
Figure 18-7.

11. Flow the text around the new graphic by choosing Frame in the Format menu and click on the Flow Text Runaround check box. Adjust the runaround path if necessary, using the Shape tool. Click on OK.

    You do not have to have CorelVENTURA running to have changes to this graphic appear in CorelVENTURA. If you change the graphic, CorelVENTURA will reflect those changes the next time the publication file is opened.

    This completes the first chapter of your publication. Before continuing with the second chapter you should save your work.

12. Choose Save in the File menu.

The same technique you used to add a CorelDRAW! graphic can be used to place a CorelPHOTO-PAINT graphic, or a CorelCHART chart in a CorelVENTURA publication. The same technique can also be used for any file from an OLE2 aware application.

In the next section you will add another chapter to your publication.

Adding Chapters to a Publication

CorelVENTURA publications can consist of as many chapters as you need. You can add additional chapters by inserting a chapter break in the existing chapter, or by creating a new chapter. You cannot change the sequence of, or use a different style sheet with, chapters that are added using a chapter break. Therefore, it is better to create a new chapter using the Add New Chapter option, as you will do in the following exercise. Chapters added with the Add New Chapter option can be reordered and different style sheets can be used. Add a new chapter now by selecting the Layout menu and choosing Add New Chapter.

A new chapter consisting of a single page formatted with the CHAP1.STY style sheet is created. You will be placing a table in this chapter, but first you need to place a text file. The content of the text file is unimportant, it is simply being placed to provide a background for the table. Place a text file now with these steps:

1. Use the Pick tool to select the base page.
2. Choose Load Text in the File menu.
3. In the Import dialog box select the CHAP1.TXT file you created previously. Click on OK.

In the next section you will learn how to place tables in your CorelVENTURA publication.

Working with Tables

Tables present information in a row and column format. In CorelVENTURA, tables can be created by defining a set of rows and columns and typing the information in directly or by extracting information from databases or spreadsheets.

Information extracted from databases and spreadsheets can be updated in CorelVENTURA as the source file is updated. This capability can be very useful in such publications such as catalogs or financial reports that use the same basic entries in each issue. Updating these publications can be as simple as updating the source file.

Tables can be inserted directly into the text, or a separate frame can be created for a table. As with other items, tables placed in separate frames can have captions added to them. When a table is relatively short (that is, only a few rows and columns), inserting it directly in the text may work best. Larger tables that would generally be placed in a separate frame include those that, for example, show the stock numbers, weight, price, and other information relating to auto parts.

Tip: If a table is short and you are sure that it will remain on the same page as its reference after your document has been edited, place it directly in the text. For a table that is long, runs the risk of breaking across pages, requires editing separate from the surrounding text, or requires callouts or captions, you retain better control over location and cell flow by placing the table in its own frame. Tables in their own frames can be saved as separate text files, while tables placed directly in text cannot.

Creating a Table

Tables are created using either the Table tool in the ribbon, or the Create option in the Table menu. In each case, the Table Settings dialog box, shown in Figure 18-8, is displayed.

In the Table Settings General tab, the number of rows and columns is set using the Rows and Columns spinners. The number of rows and columns

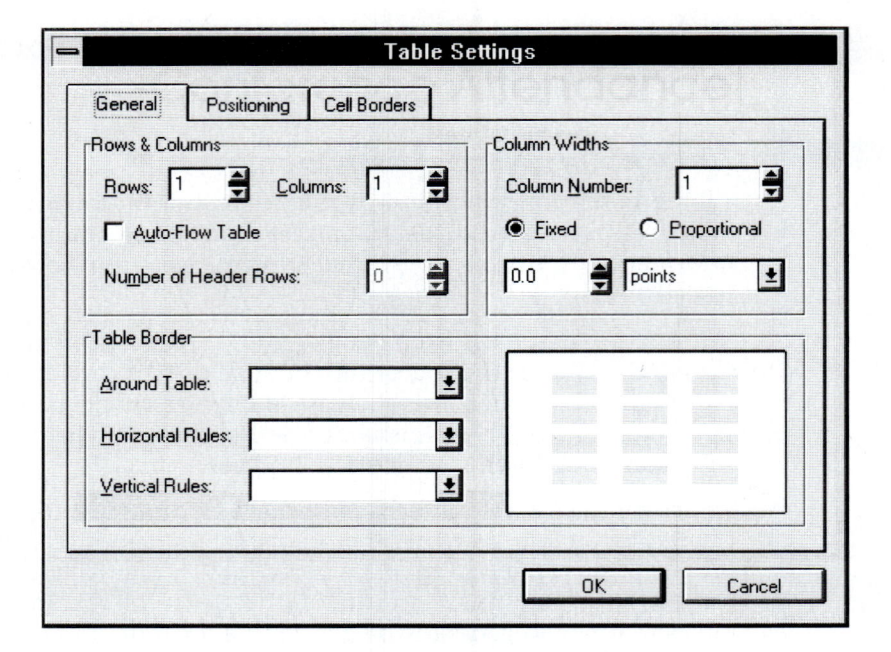

Table Settings dialog box
Figure 18-8.

needed for a table includes the number required for the data, as well as row and column headers. When Auto-Flow Table is selected, the table can be split across page and column boundaries. If you want your table in one column, frame, or page, Auto-Flow should not be selected. When a table is split across a column or page, the value in the Number of Header Rows spinner determines the number of header rows (rows containing the description of the contents in the columns) that will be placed at the top of the table on the next page or column.

Tip: If you place a large table requiring more than one page in a separate frame, you can create another frame on the page on which you want it to continue. To cause the table to flow from the first frame to the second, click on the first frame and then go to the page that contains the continuation frame and click on it. Remember to have selected Auto-Flow Table in order to preserve the table headings in the continuation frame.

The width of each column can be fixed or proportional. When a table is first created, all columns will have the same width. You can then change the

Integrating CorelDRAW! and CorelVENTURA

widths by using the Table Settings General tab or by using the mouse and ALT key to drag the column border to the desired location. In the Table Settings General tab, the width of fixed width columns is determined by the value in the Column Width spinner. Each column can have its own fixed width. The width of a proportional column is the proportional share of the space remaining after all the fixed width columns are set. The proportional value is set by the value in the Column Width spinner. A column with a value of 2 will be twice as wide as a column with a value of 1. If all the proportional width columns have the same number, regardless of the number, all will be the same width. You can set the narrowest column to a value of 1, and then have the remaining columns be a multiple of 1, or you could set all the proportional columns as a percentage. For example, you could set three proportional columns to 30, 30, and 40. The columns would be 30 percent, 30 percent, and 40 percent of the space available after the fixed width columns were set. If you set proportional columns as a percentage, the total of all proportional columns must equal 100.

The Table Border options set the thickness of the rules between columns, rows, and the border around the table. You can create single thick or thin rules, double rules, or no rules at all.

The Table Settings Positioning tab, shown in Figure 18-9, allows you to set the amount of space that will be placed above and below the table in the column or frame. Cell Spacing determines the amount of space that will be placed between rows and columns. These are, in effect, the inside margins for each cell. The Vertical Justification settings control the amount of space that can be added above and below the table when vertical justification of text is turned on for the chapter. The Alignment & Indent options control the positioning of the table within a column or frame. When a table is created it will be the same width as the column or frame it is placed in. You can then adjust the width of the columns as described previously. With the Alignment & Indents options you can set a custom width for the table, set an indent from the left edge of the column or frame, and align the table within the column or frame.

The Cell Borders tab is shown in Figure 18-10. The Cell Borders options allow you to establish a custom border style for your table, in much the same way as you define borders for frames. Border styles can be tagged using the Border Tag drop-down list box.

You can also shade cells using the Fill roll-up, shown on page 623. The Fill roll-up is displayed using the Cell Color option in the Table menu, or by

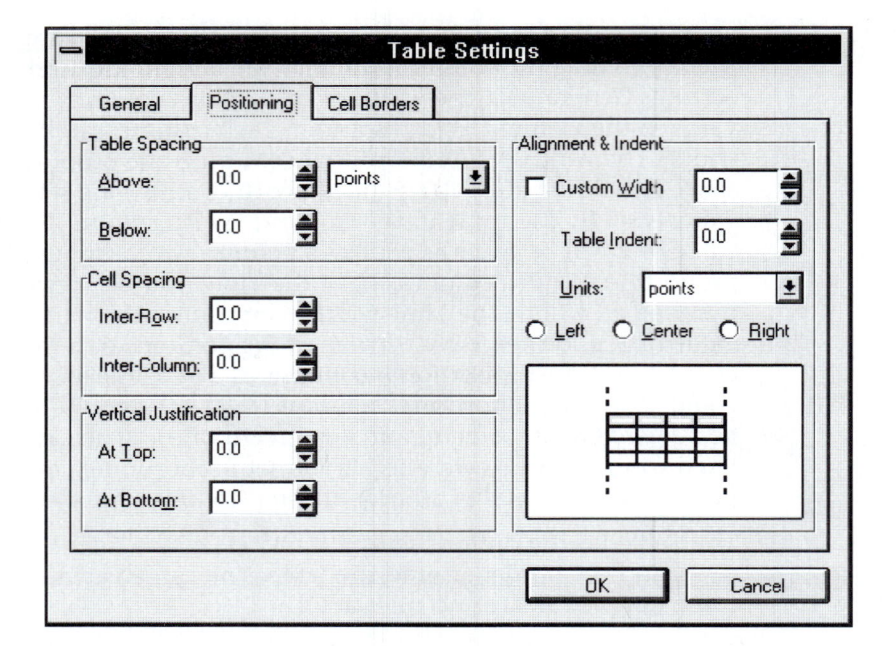

Table Settings
Positioning tab
Figure 18-9.

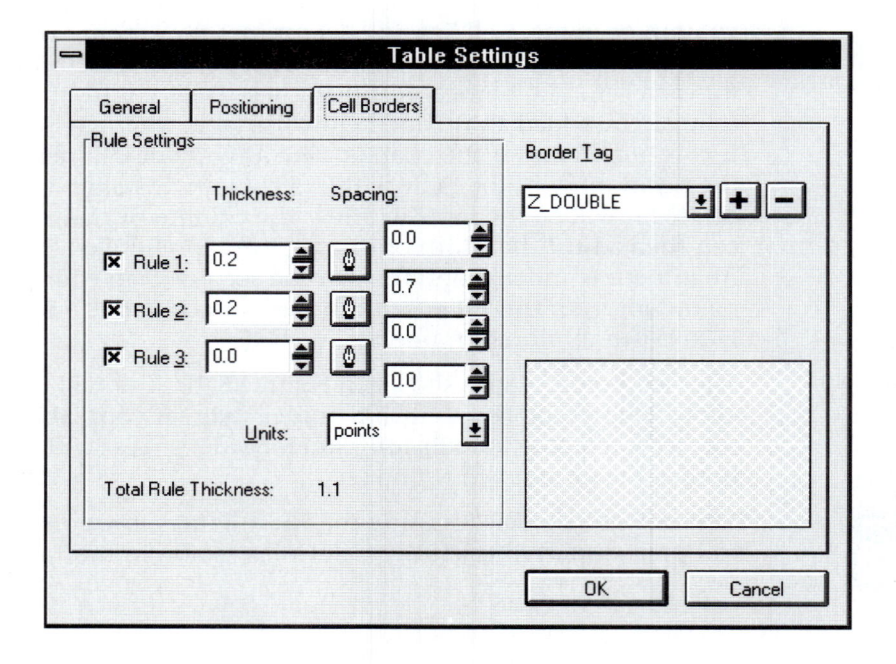

Table Settings
Cell Borders
tab
Figure 18-10.

selecting the Fill roll-up tool in the Fill flyout menu. You define and apply cell fills in the same manner as you apply fills in CorelDRAW!.

Importing Tables with CorelQUERY

You can also create tables in CorelVENTURA using information contained in databases and spreadsheets. To import data from these programs you use CorelQUERY, a stand-alone program included with CorelDRAW!. CorelQUERY allows you to select information included in database and spreadsheet data files, even if the applications that created the files are not on your computer, and place that information in a CorelVENTURA table. You use CorelQUERY to define a *query*, a set of criteria that will be applied to the selected database or spreadsheet file. The information that meets the criteria in the query will then be copied into CorelVENTURA.

Note: You cannot add, delete, or modify data in any database or spreadsheet file using CorelQUERY. You can only copy selected information into a CorelVENTURA table.

CorelQUERY can be opened from within CorelVENTURA by choosing Create from Database in the Table menu, or by double-clicking on the CorelQUERY icon in your Corel program group. When CorelQUERY is opened, the screen shown in Figure 18-11 is displayed.

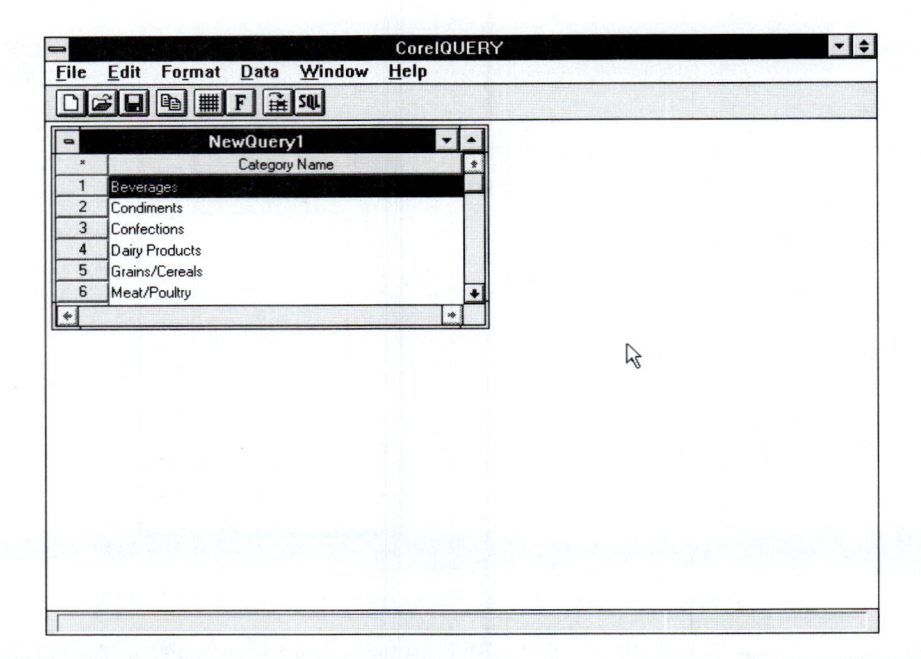

Figure 18-11.
CorelQUERY screen

Note: Until a query is created or opened, only the File and Help menus will be displayed.

The File menu is used to open, create, and save queries. The Edit menu allows you to copy a selection to the Clipboard, select records or fields in the query, and adjust the width of columns. With the Format menu you can turn grid lines on or off, select a font, and set the CorelQUERY preferences. You use the Data menu to move to a specified cell in the query and to change the current query. The standard Windows and Help menus contain the same options as with other Corel applications.

The ribbon below the menu duplicates some of the options contained in the menus. The buttons and their functions are described in Table 18-1.

CorelQUERY accesses databases and spreadsheets using Windows' Open Database Connectivity (ODBC) interface. ODBC is a method of transferring data between applications. Many applications such as databases now include ODBC interfaces. Any application that includes an ODBC interface can be accessed by CorelQUERY. You simply use CorelQUERY's dialog boxes to select the data source—the nuts and bolts of ODBC are transparent to you.

Integrating CorelDRAW! and CorelVENTURA

Tool	Name	Function
📄	New	Connects to a data source to create a new query
📂	Open	Displays the Open Query dialog box
💾	Save	Saves the current query
📋	Copy	Copies the selected information to the Clipboard
▦	Grid	Turns grid lines on or off
F	Font	Displays the Select Font dialog box to set font attributes
⇥	Goto	Displays the Goto dialog box
SQL	SQL	Creates a new query or modifies an existing query

CorelQUERY Tools
Table 18-1.

Queries are created using the Query Builder dialog box. The actual queries are built in the Structured Query Language (SQL). SQL is a sophisticated language used to extract information from databases and spreadsheets. Again, you do not need to know anything about SQL to build a query. You simply use the CorelQUERY dialog boxes to select the information you want, then CorelQUERY builds a SQL query and extracts the desired information from the data source using the ODBC interface.

Note: Information in databases and spreadsheets is classified as tables, records, and fields. A table is a collection of records containing similar information, such as customer data. Each record would be all the information for one customer. A field would be one piece of information, such as the customer's name or address. Database and spreadsheet tables, like CorelVENTURA tables, are organized in rows and columns, where each row is one record and each column is one field.

When you choose New in the File menu, or click on the New button in the ribbon, the Data Source dialog box, shown here, is displayed:

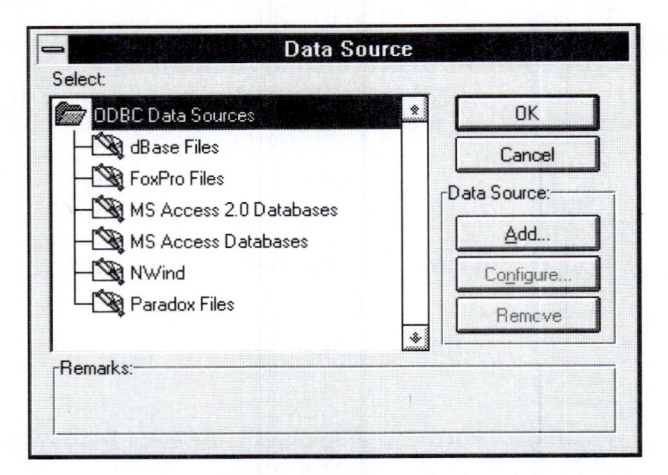

This is where you select a data source for your query. When you double-click on the ODBC data source icon, the Select list box will display the applications for which ODBC interface drivers have been installed. You do not have to have the application installed on your computer in order to be able to access a data file created by that application. You do have to have the ODBC driver for that application installed, however. Many database and spreadsheet applications include ODBC drivers for the file types they can read.

After you have selected the type of file you want to access and click on OK, the Select the Default Database dialog box is displayed, as shown here:

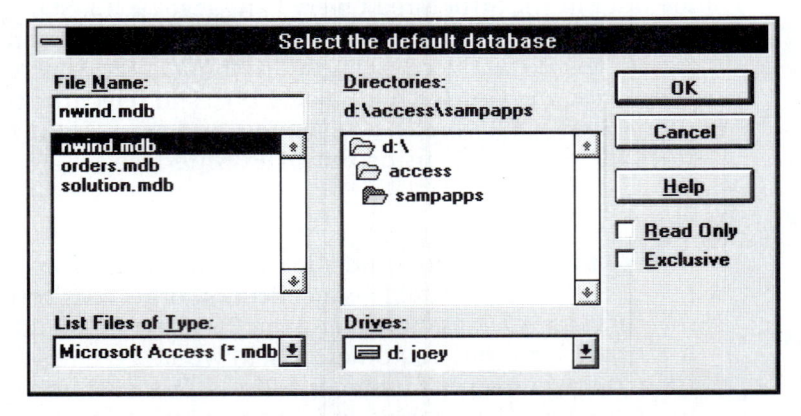

The available data files for the application you selected are displayed in the files list box. Selecting a file will make that file the default for the SQL query you will create.

Integrating CorelDRAW! and CorelVENTURA

Once a default data file has been selected, the Query Builder dialog box is displayed, as shown in Figure 18-12. The Select tab allows you to select the data tables and fields to be included in your query. The Relations list box displays the available tables in the data file. Tables that will be included in the query are selected by double-clicking on them. After being selected, they will be marked with a check mark. The Fields list box displays the fields for the selected tables. The fields to be included are also selected by double-clicking on them. After being selected, they will also be marked with check marks.

Once the tables and fields are selected, the data selection criteria are defined using the Criteria tab, shown in Figure 18-13. The Field Name drop-down list box is used to select the field for which the criteria will be defined. The Operator drop-down list box selects the relationship and the value specified in the Value drop-down list box. Table 18-2 lists the Operator criteria available.

Clicking on the List Values command button will import from the data file the existing values for the field selected in the Field Name drop-down list box. You can then select any of the values in the Criteria drop-down list box. Clicking on Add adds the defined criterion to the list box. Multiple criteria can be defined for each field, and multiple fields can be used. The And/Or option buttons determine if the relationship between criteria will be And (both criteria must be met) or Or (either criterion must be met). For example, if you want to select the records for all the customers in Argentina who ordered Dungeness Crabs, the selection criteria would be Country = Argentina AND Product = Dungeness Crabs. If you want to find the Argentine customers who ordered Dungeness Crabs or Quilcene Oysters, the

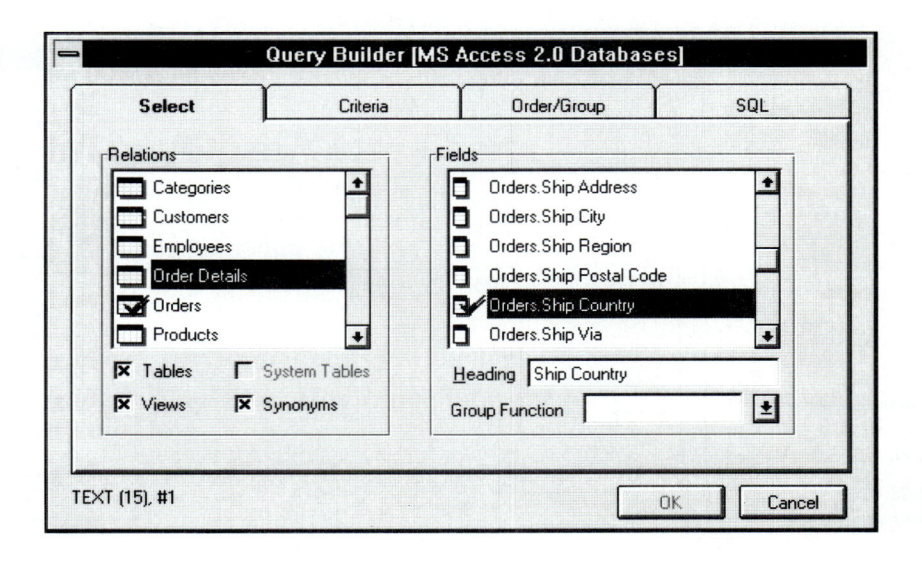

Query Builder dialog box
Figure 18-12.

Operator	Name	Effect
<	Less than	Selects all records in which the field value is less than the criteria value
<=	Less than or equal to	Selects all records in which the field value is less than or equal to the criteria value
<>	Not equal	Selects all records in which the field value is not equal to the criteria value
=	Equal to	Selects all records in which the field value is equal to the criteria value
>	Greater than	Selects all records in which the field value is greater than the criteria value
>=	Greater than or equal to	Selects all records in which the field value is greater than or equal to the criteria value
like	Like	Selects all records in which the field value is similar to the criteria value (used with fields containing text values)

Query Builder Operators
Table 18-2.

criteria would be Country = Argentina AND Product = Dungeness Crabs OR Product = Quilcene Oysters.

The Order/Group tab, shown in Figure 18-14, defines the order in which the data in the selected fields will be sorted. The data can be sorted in ascending (A to Z) or descending (Z to A) order.

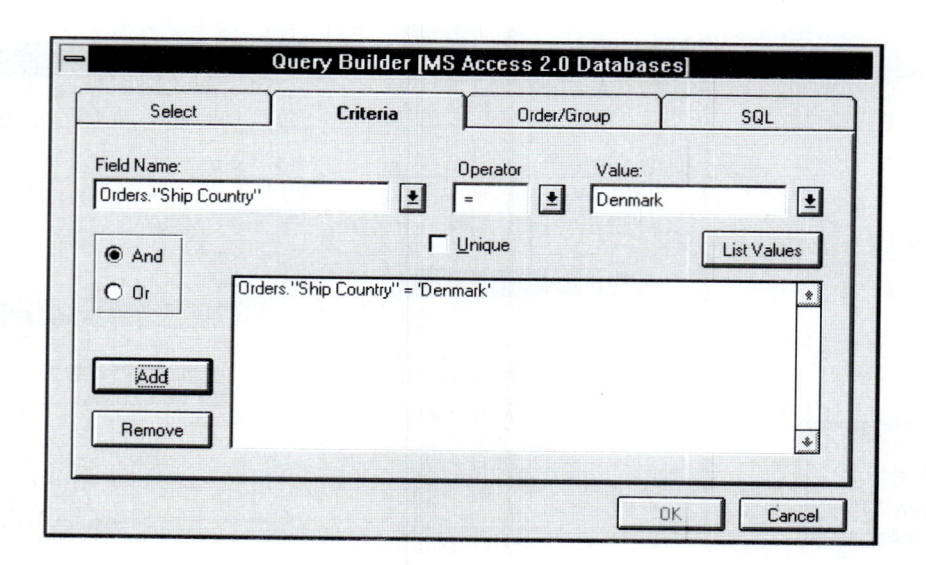

Query Builder Criteria tab
Figure 18-13.

Integrating CorelDRAW! and CorelVENTURA

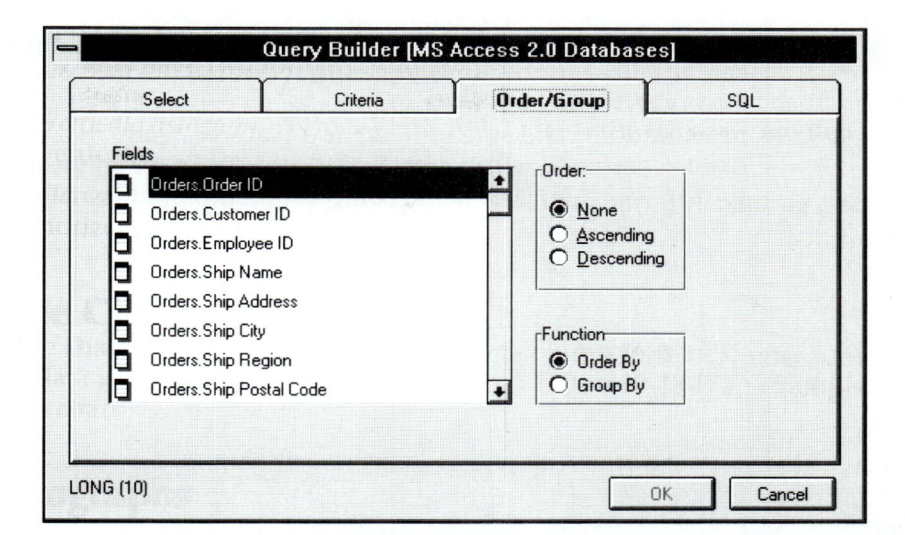

Query Builder Order/Group tab
Figure 18-14.

The SQL tab, shown in Figure 18-15, builds a SQL query from the selections you made in the other query Builder tabs. Queries can also be saved and loaded using the SQL tab. Clicking on OK applies the query to the selected data source. The information in the data source that matches the criteria is then copied to CorelQUERY and used to create a CorelVENTURA table.

CorelVENTURA is a powerful tool for creating a wide variety of publications. As you've seen, it is more than simply a program that combines information.

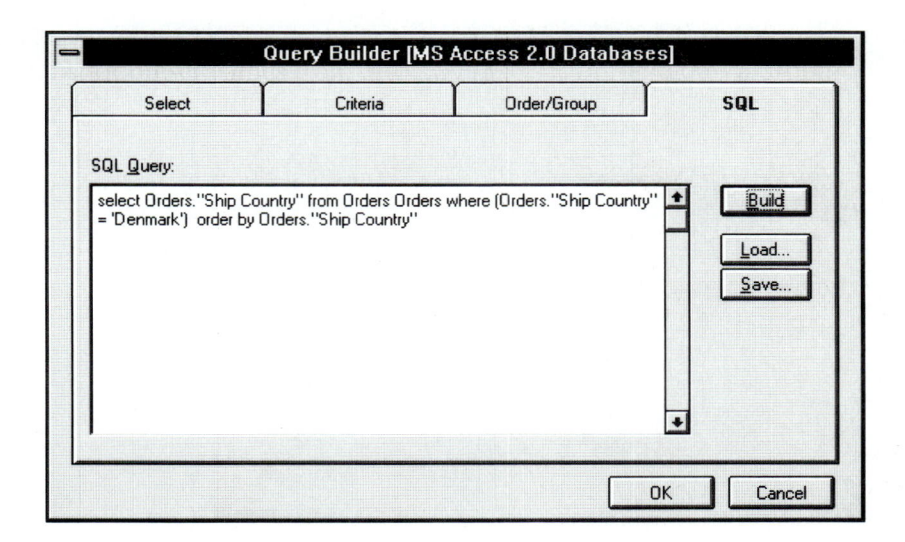

Query Builder SQL tab
Figure 18-15.

Virtually every aspect of typography can be controlled, imported files can be edited in the applications that created them without leaving CorelVENTURA, and information can be extracted from databases, presentations, and spreadsheets and placed directly in a CorelVENTURA table. Combined with CorelDRAW! and the other applications in the Corel 5 suite, CorelVENTURA is the complete desktop publishing solution.

Part 4

USING OTHER
COREL 5 COMPONENTS

19

USING CorelCHART

CorelCHART

is a stand-alone program for creating several different kinds of charts. Charts let you view information in graphical form and are commonly used in publications and presentations. Many people find it easier to understand information presented in visually concrete form, rather than by abstract numerical values.

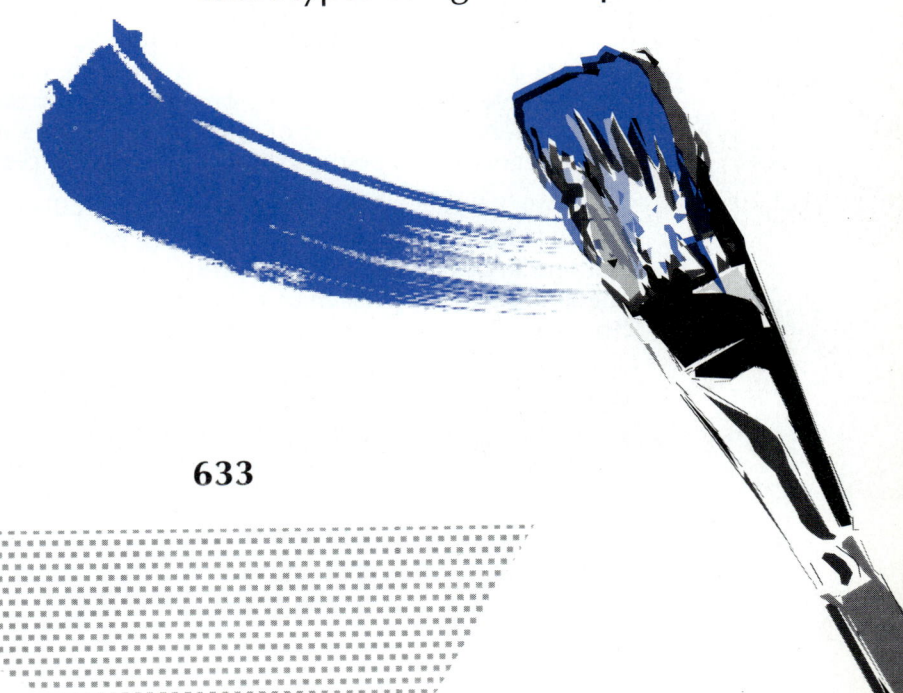

CorelCHART can create 16 different chart types using data imported from spreadsheet and database programs or entered directly into CorelCHART. Each basic chart type is available in up to nine formats.

Charts can be customized with titles and other text labels. Graphics can be imported, or created with CorelDRAW! or with CorelCHART, and added to the charts. Customized charts can be saved and repeatedly used as *chart templates*—that is, preformatted starting points for new charts. The chart templates for each basic chart type include the chart format, the color palette, and graphics. CorelCHART comes with an assortment of templates for each basic chart type. You can also create and save your own templates.

The exercises in this chapter will demonstrate how to create a new chart; how to import data for the chart; how to add titles, labels, and graphics to charts; how to modify chart objects; and how to use chart templates. The different types and formats of charts will also be covered.

Charting Basics

The objective of using a chart is to present information in a graphic form that makes it easier to understand and highlights the message the information is carrying. Not all charts accomplish this objective. It is important to learn not just how to create charts, but how to create effective charts.

Each value that is plotted on the chart is called a *data point*. Data points are grouped in data series and data categories. *Data series* are groups of related data points. In a chart of sales figures from several sales offices, for example, the data points (sales figures) for one office are one data series. *Data categories* are groups containing one data point from each data series, taken at one interval. If the chart of sales figures reflects monthly sales, then one data category could be the sales from all the offices for one month.

Figure 19-1 shows a Vertical Bar chart, which displays the attendance at a series of conferences in four cities over a period of four years. The four years of attendance for each city constitute one data series. Each year constitutes one data category. This chart makes it easy to see the differences among the cities (the data series) in any year (the data category).

Figure 19-2 shows the same data as Figure 19-1, except that the data series and data categories have been reversed. Each year is now a data series, and each city a data category. This chart highlights the differences among the years (the data series) in any one city (the data category). When creating your charts, the relationship you want to emphasize will determine how you define your data series and data categories.

CorelCHART can create both two- and three-dimensional charts. Two-dimensional (2-D) charts have two axes. The horizontal or *x* axis is

Using CorelCHART

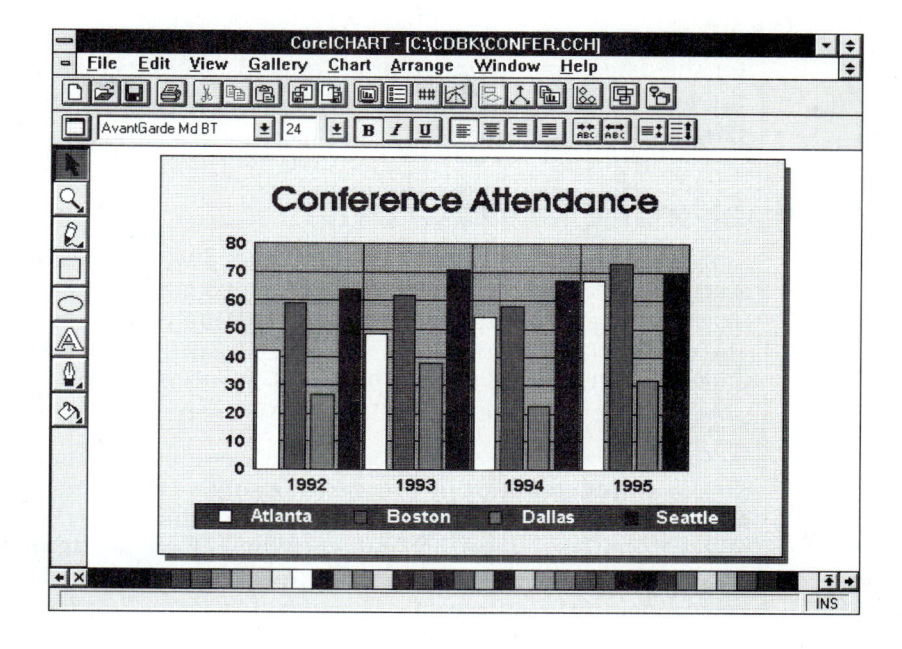

Figure 19-1.
Conference attendance with each city as a data series

usually the category axis. Each data category is plotted along the category axis. The vertical or y axis is the data axis. Each data point is plotted against

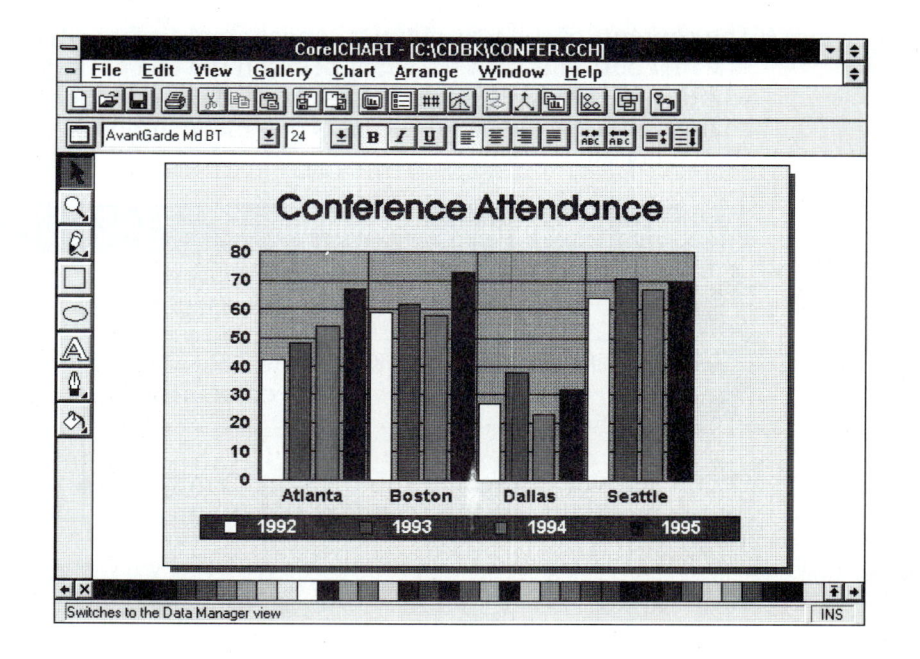

Figure 19-2.
Conference attendance with each year as a data series

the data axis. The data axis usually has a scale indicating the range of values for the data points. Three-dimensional (3-D) charts have an additional axis, the *z* axis, which is at a right angle to the *x* and *y* axes, and adds depth to the chart.

Starting CorelCHART

CorelCHART is a separate program included with CorelDRAW!. It is installed in the Windows Program Manager's Corel 5 group along with CorelDRAW!. To start CorelCHART, open the Corel 5 group window and double-click on the CorelCHART icon. The initial CorelCHART screen appears after the title screen and looks like Figure 19-1 or 19-2 without a chart. As you can see, it is similar in appearance to the CorelDRAW! window.

Across the top of the screen, below the menu bar, you see the *ribbon bar*, a row of command buttons that provide single-click access to many common menu commands. The left seven buttons of the ribbon bar offer the familiar file maintenance, printing, and editing you have seen in CorelDRAW!. The next two buttons are for importing and exporting spreadsheets, while the remainder of the buttons are specifically designed for working with charts and change according to what you are doing.

Below the ribbon bar, the *text ribbon* contains a set of drop-down list boxes and command buttons that you use to select the text attributes—the font, size, and other characteristics—for the text used in your charts. The text ribbon is similar to CorelDRAW!'s Text roll-up and is used in the same way. The contents of the text ribbon changes according to what you are doing. The first button is used to switch between the chart window and the data window, both of which you will learn about in a moment. The button changes its appearance on the basis of which window is currently active, as shown below:

Button	Description	Function
	Chart View	Makes the chart window the active window when in the Data Manager
	Data Manager	Makes the Data Manager the active window when in chart view

On the left side of the screen is the CorelCHART toolbox. The tools operate for the most part like their CorelDRAW! counterparts and are explained in Table 19-1.

Using CorelCHART

Tool	Description	Function
▶	Pick	Selects elements in a chart
🔍	Zoom	Presents a flyout menu to change the magnification of the chart
✏️	Curve (Pencil)	Presents a flyout menu with three drawing modes: straight lines, polygons, and freehand lines
▭	Rectangle	Draws rectangles in the same manner as its CorelDRAW! counterpart
⬭	Ellipse	Draws ellipses and circles in the same manner as its CorelDRAW! counterpart
A	Text	Adds text to a chart
✍	Outline	Opens the Outline Pen flyout menu, which has the same options as in CorelDRAW!
🪣	Fill	Opens the Fill flyout menu, which has most of the same options as in CorelDRAW!

CorelCHART Toolbox Table 19-1.

Below the chart area is the color palette. To use the palette, simply select the chart element whose color you want to change and then click on the desired color in the palette. The color of the selected element will change to the chosen color. Clicking with the left mouse button changes the element's fill color, clicking with the right mouse button changes its outline color. To undo any color change, choose Undo in the Edit menu. The View menu (not visible until a graph is open or ready to be created) Color Palette option allows you to display six different color palettes, or none at all. By clicking on the upward-pointing arrow on the right end of the palette, you will open an expanded palette with a scroll bar for viewing more colors at one time.

Undo reverses only the last action taken, so use it before you continue working with the chart.

On the bottom of the screen is the *status line*. The left end of the status line provides information on currently selected tools, buttons, and commands. You can simply move the mouse to a button (don't click on it), and the status line will tell you what that button does. The small box on the far right gives an onscreen indication of whether you are in insert or overwrite mode.

Creating a New Chart

When CorelCHART is started, only the File and Help menus are available. The File menu is used either to load an existing chart or to create a new chart. This exercise will create a new blank chart. Then, in the exercise that follows, data will be added to the chart with the Data Manager.

1. From the File menu, choose New. The New dialog box, shown in Figure 19-3, is presented.

    On the left in the New dialog box is the Gallery list box, which is a listing of the 16 basic chart types. To the right of the Gallery list box is the Chart Types list box. This is a pictorial display box containing specific templates for the basic chart type chosen in the Gallery list box. Both a basic chart type and a template must be chosen for a new chart. The various chart types will be covered later in this chapter.

2. For this exercise, click on Bar in the Gallery list box, then click on the chart template for a Vertical Side-by-Side Bar (middle icon in the second row). Make certain the Use Sample Data box is *not* checked and click on OK.

This chart template will create a Vertical Bar chart. A window for the chart is created and overlaid by a window for the Data Manager, as shown in Figure 19-4. The Data Manager is the element of CorelCHART that is used to enter or import data for the chart. It also is used to format and prepare data for charting.

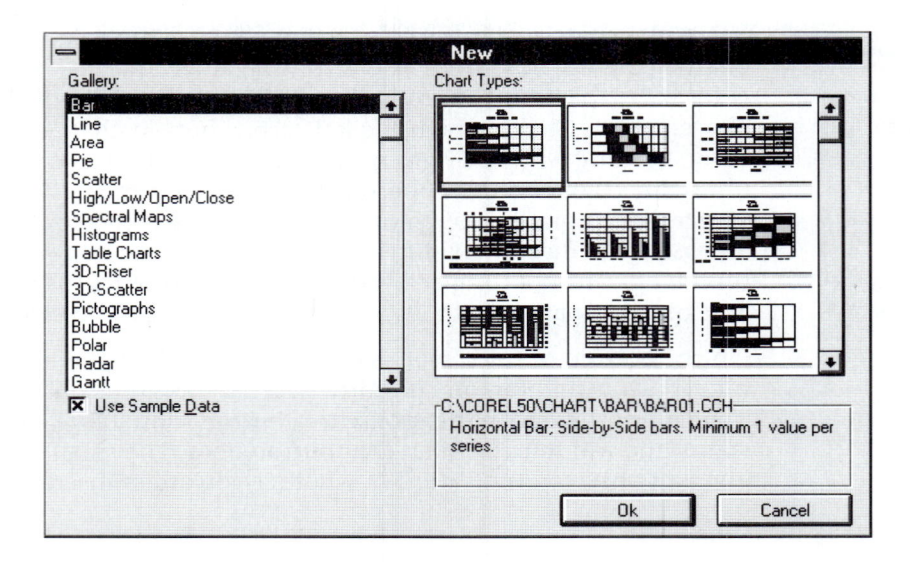

New dialog box

Figure 19-3.

Using CorelCHART

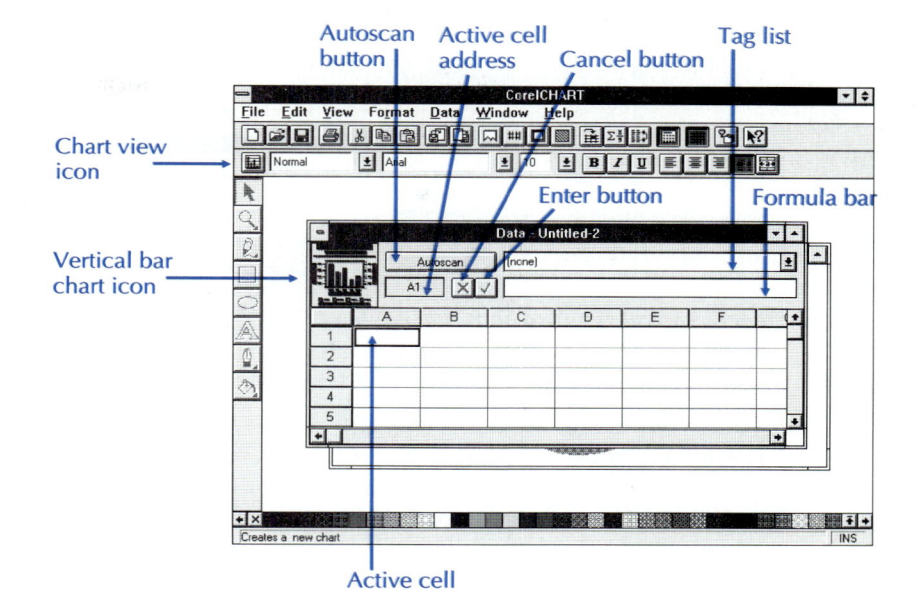

The Data Manager window
Figure 19-4.

Labels in figure: Autoscan button, Active cell address, Cancel button, Tag list, Chart view icon, Enter button, Formula bar, Vertical bar chart icon, Active cell

Using the Data Manager

The Data Manager presents a grid of rows and columns, like a spreadsheet, to hold the data that will be used to create the chart. The intersection of a row and a column is called a *cell*. Cells are referenced by the cell *address*, which is the column letter and row number that describes the cell. The first cell in the upper-left corner of the Data Manager is A1, meaning column A, row 1. Each cell can contain one value. The *value* may be a numeric data point to be charted in the form of a number or a formula, or the value may be text for a label.

Cells are selected by clicking on the cell—the selected cell then becomes the *active cell*. The active cell has a heavier border around it and is referenced above the chart. A rectangular group of contiguous cells is called a *range*. Ranges of cells are selected by clicking on the cell that is one of the corners of the range and dragging the mouse until the desired range is highlighted. Ranges are referenced by the addresses of the cells in the upper-left corner and the lower-right corner, separated by a colon. A range of cells from A1 (in the upper-left corner) to B2 (in the lower-right corner) is referred to as A1:B2 in this book.

In the upper-left corner of the Data Manager window is an icon showing the type of chart the Data Manager will create. At the upper right of the Data Manager window is a drop-down list box, the tag list, which is used to tag the contents of each cell. The information in each cell is *tagged* to tell CorelCHART which values are to be plotted and which values are to be used as labels for row and column headers, titles, and other chart elements. The opened tag list, shown next, presents some of the available tags.

Use the scroll bar to see all the tags in the drop-down list box.

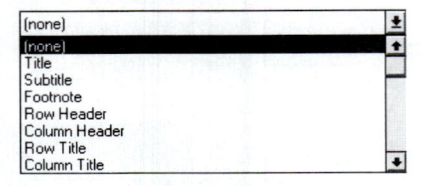

```
(none)
(none)
Title
Subtitle
Footnote
Row Header
Column Header
Row Title
Column Title
```

Most of the tags are self-explanatory. The Data Range tag is used to define the range of cells containing the data points to be plotted on the chart. The other tags define cells containing text for the chart's titles.

To the left of the tag list is the Autoscan command button. When Autoscan is selected, the Data Manager is scanned for a range of cells containing data. Separated rows of text at the top of the spreadsheet are considered titles. If a range of cells containing data is found, the row and column immediately above and to the left are tagged as the row and column headers. The rest of the range is tagged as the data range. Any text below the data range is tagged as subtitles and footnotes.

Below the tag list is the *formula bar*. The formula bar is used to enter and edit the contents of cells. When you select a cell and start to type information into it, the information will be entered in the formula bar. When ENTER, TAB, or one of the arrow keys is pressed, the information is entered in the selected cell. When you select a cell, the contents of that cell will be placed in the Formula, where it can be edited.

To the left of the formula bar are two command buttons, one with an X, which is used to cancel the contents of the formula bar, and one with a check mark, which enters the contents. These two buttons, Cancel and Enter, are available when the formula bar is activated, which occurs by clicking in the formula bar or by pressing F2.

The box to the left of the formula bar displays the address of the currently selected cell. If a range of cells is selected, only the address of the first cell is shown.

Entering Data with the Data Manager

Data for charting can be entered directly into the Data Manager, as the next exercise shows. The data will represent attendance at a series of conferences.

1. Click on the maximize button in the data window if it is not already maximized, then in cell A1, which should be selected, and type **Conference Attendance**. Press ENTER.

Using CorelCHART

2. Use the arrow keys or mouse to move to cell B2.
3. In cell B2 type **1992**. Press TAB to move to the next cell in the row, C2. In cell C2 type **1993**. Repeat this process until cells D2 and E2 contain the dates 1994 and 1995.
4. Use the arrow keys or mouse to move to cell A3.
5. In cell A3 type **Atlanta**. Press TAB to move to cell B3.
6. In cell B3 type **42**. Press TAB to move to the next cell in the row, C3. In cell C3 type **48**. Repeat this process to place 54 and 67 in cells D3 and E3 respectively.
7. Select cell A1. In the tag list, select Title to tag the selected cell as the title for the chart.
8. Select the range of cells B2:E2 by dragging the mouse across them. In the tag list, select Column Header to tag the selected range as the column headers for the chart.
9. Select cell A3. In the tag list, select Row Header to tag the selected cell as the row header for the chart.
10. Select the range of cells B3:E3. Again in the tag list, select Data Range to tag the selected range as the data to be charted.
11. Click on the Chart View button above the toolbox to view the chart. Figure 19-5 shows the chart created from the information in the Data Manager. (Note that there is no reference to Atlanta on the chart; you'll add that in a moment.)

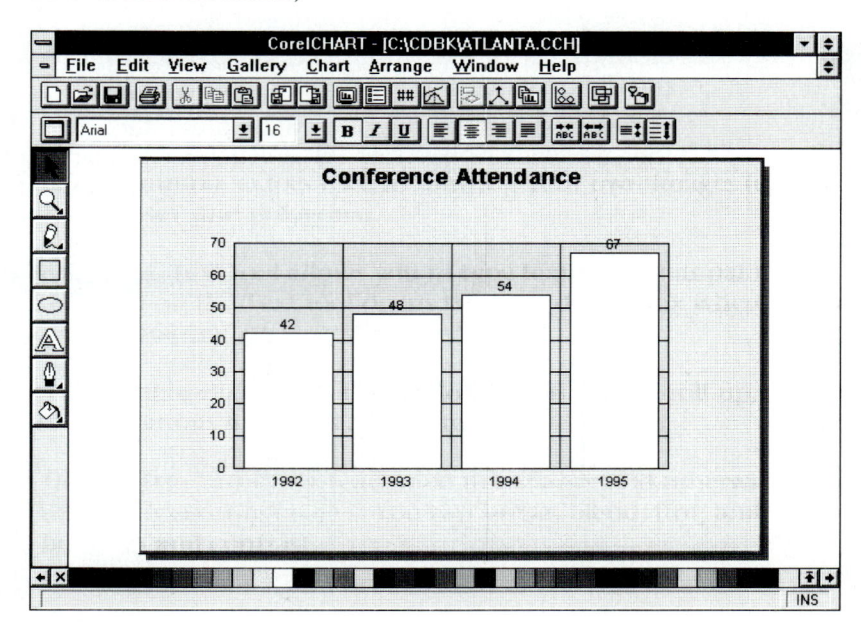

Conference attendance in Atlanta
Figure 19-5.

12. Use the File menu to save the chart and your data.

In this chart there is one data series, the attendance in Atlanta. Each year is one data category.

Importing Data with the Data Manager

The Data Manager also allows you to import information from spreadsheets and databases to use in charts. CorelCHART can import data in the file formats shown in the following table:

File Format	Extension
ASCII (Tab and Space Separated)	.TXT
ASCII (Comma-Separated Value)	.CSV
Corel Sheet	.CDS
Corel Sheet (version 4.0)	.TBL
Excel (versions 3 and 4)	.XLS
Rich Text Format	.RTF

The steps to import an Excel worksheet are as follows:

1. To import data, select File New, choose the chart type and format you want to create, and then click on the Data Manager tool to make it the active window.

2. From the File menu, choose Import or click on the Import button from the ribbon bar.

    The Import Data dialog box will be presented. In the lower-left corner is the List Files of Type drop-down list box for selecting the file type to import. For example, if you wanted to import an Excel worksheet, you would select "Excel 3 & 4 (*.xls)" in this drop-down list box, like this:

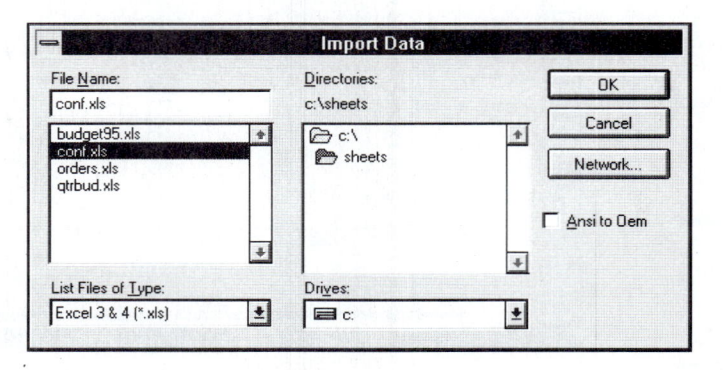

Using CorelCHART

3. Select a file to import and click on OK. The imported data will replace any data already in the Data Manager.
4. The imported data needs to be tagged before it will be charted properly. This is done by clicking on Autoscan if the data is in a normal order. You can also tag the data in the same manner as in the previous exercise: select the cell with the title and tag it as the Title. Select the range containing the row headings and tag it as the Row Heading; and so on.
5. To see the new chart, switch to chart view by clicking the Chart View tool.

Using OLE

In addition to importing text manually from other applications, you can also use the convenience of object linking and embedding (OLE) in CorelCHART. OLE, as you know from Chapters 11 and 17, can link text and objects created in one application, the server, with a file in another program, the client. When you change the text or object in the original linked file, the client file will be similarly modified. Embedded objects are not linked but when double-clicked will open their parent application, ready to be edited. Within CorelCHART, Chart View acts as an OLE server but not a client, while Data Manager is fully compliant with OLE.

Customizing Charts

CorelCHART provides a number of ways to customize your charts. Text can be formatted by selecting a different font, color, size, placement, and style. Labels can be added to emphasize elements of your chart. Graphics, including arrows, can also be placed on the chart.

Formatting Text

Text is formatted with the text ribbon at the top of the CorelCHART screen, below the ribbon bar. This exercise will use the text ribbon to format the chart title and the axes label or scale. The Atlanta conference attendance chart that you created before should still be on your screen. (You may have to close other charts overlaying it.)

1. Click on the Chart View button on the left of the text ribbon, if necessary to see the chart. You can format text in either the Data Manager view or in chart view, but in chart view you can immediately see the result.
2. Select the chart title, "Conference Attendance," by clicking on it.
3. Open the font drop-down list box and scroll to the top, as shown here:

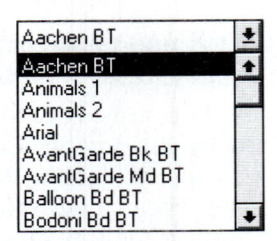

4. Select a font, say Avant Garde Md Bt, by clicking on it.
5. The size of the text is set with the size drop-down list box, which is to the right of the font drop-down list box. Select 24 in the size list box by clicking on it.
6. Click on the number 70 at the top of *y*-axis scale on the left of the chart. Any formatting you now do will effect all of the *y*-axis scale.
7. Select 12 points to increase the size and click on the "B" in the text ribbon to make the *y*-axis scale bold.
8. Similarly, click on 1992 and make it 12 points and bold.

Changing the Bars

You can change the size, spacing, and color of the bars by simply clicking on the bars and choosing the formatting you want to apply to them. Try that now with these steps:

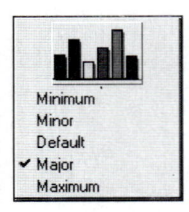

1. Click on one of the bars, and then click on Bar Thickness in the Chart menu. The submenu shown on the left opens.
2. Click on "default" and you will see a thinner, more attractive bar.
3. With the bar still selected, click on a color that you think will be attractive in the color palette at the bottom of the screen.

Adding a Legend

With a single bar, a legend is not necessary, but to see how it is done, add a legend to the chart on your screen.

1. Click on the white space outside the chart to deselect the bar and not select anything else for the moment.
2. In the Chart menu, click on Legend. The dialog box shown in Figure 19-6 opens.
3. Click on Display Legend and then on OK. Your chart will redisplay and look like Figure 19-7.

Using CorelCHART

Legend dialog box
Figure 19-6.

Adding Labels

You have already seen how to add text for chart titles and headings using the Data Manager. Other text, such as labels to draw attention to a specific element of the chart, can be added using the Chart toolbox. This exercise will add a label and an arrow to identify the largest attendance on the chart.

1. To add labels to the chart, the chart window must be the active window. Once again, click on the Chart View tool in the toolbox, if necessary to display the chart.

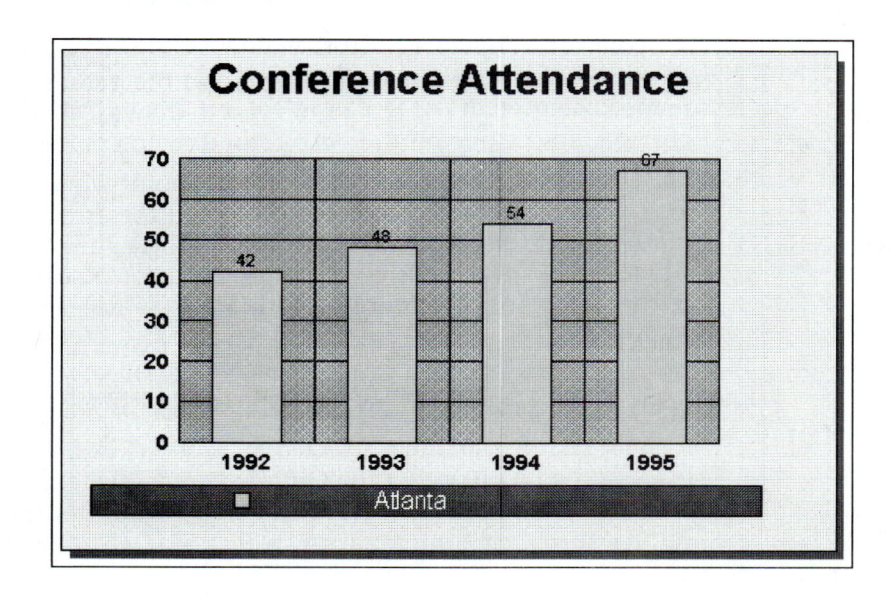

Conference data after changing the titles and columns and adding a legend
Figure 19-7.

2. Select the Text tool in the Chart toolbox by clicking on it. The mouse pointer will turn into a crosshair.

3. Click on the chart in the approximate location where you want the text to be placed. (The text can be moved after it has been added to the chart.)

   This label will identify the largest attendance on the chart—which is 67, the attendance in Atlanta in 1995—so click on the area above the chart on the right side. The I-beam insertion point will appear where you clicked. Type **Best Attendance** and then click on the Pick tool. The text you just typed will reflect the current text attributes (font, size, and so forth) that you selected in the text ribbon for the title. The attributes can be changed with the text ribbon while the new text is selected.

4. If the text needs to be larger or smaller, it can be adjusted in two ways. The first way is to select the text and then use the type size drop-down list box to change the size of the text. The other method is to select the text and use the scaling or sizing handles to increase or decrease the size of the text box.

5. When you are satisfied with the appearance of the text, drag it into its final location with the mouse.

6. Next, add an arrow to the chart to point out the bar representing the best attendance. Click on the Pencil tool in the toolbox, shown here:

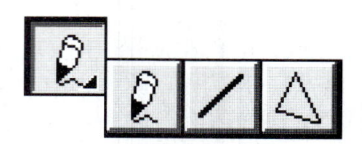

7. A flyout menu opens, allowing you to select the type of line you want to draw. Click on the straight-line tool in the middle of the flyout menu. The tool on the left allows you to draw freehand lines and curves, and the one on the right is for drawing polygons.

7. Press and hold the mouse button on the point where you want the arrow to start (this will be the end without the arrowhead). Drag the mouse to set the length and direction of the arrow. When the line is where you want it, release the mouse button. You can add the arrowhead by using either the Outline Pen or the Pen roll-up.

8. Click on the Outline Pen tool to open the flyout menu. Click on either the first tool to open the Outline Pen dialog box or the second tool to open the Pen roll-up.

9. First make sure the line is selected and then click on the rightmost line-ending box in either the Outline Pen dialog box or the Pen roll-up. Choose an ending-arrow shape and click on OK (for the dialog box) or Apply (for the roll-up). An arrow will appear with the arrowhead where

Using CorelCHART

you ended the line. The arrow can be moved by choosing the Pick tool in the Chart toolbox, selecting the arrow, and dragging it with the mouse.

Figure 19-8 shows the conference chart with the label and arrow described in this exercise.

Graphics

Graphics can be added to your charts by creating them with CorelCHART's drawing tools or by importing them from other programs. Graphics created with CorelDRAW! can be placed directly onto a CorelCHART chart. Also, graphics you create in CorelCHART can be exported for use in other applications.

Adding Graphics

Graphics and text are placed on the chart in layers, in a manner similar to CorelDRAW! drawings. The chart layer, which contains all the information on the Data Manager, is the bottom layer. All other layers are placed above the chart layer. The label "Best Attendance" and the arrow you added in the previous exercise are both above the chart layer. The next exercise will add a simple graphic to the chart, using CorelCHART's drawing tools. The graphic will appear behind the chart title. To do this, you will first create the background graphic and then create a new chart title to be placed above it.

1. To modify the chart, the chart window must be the active window. Click on the Chart View tool in the text ribbon, if necessary.

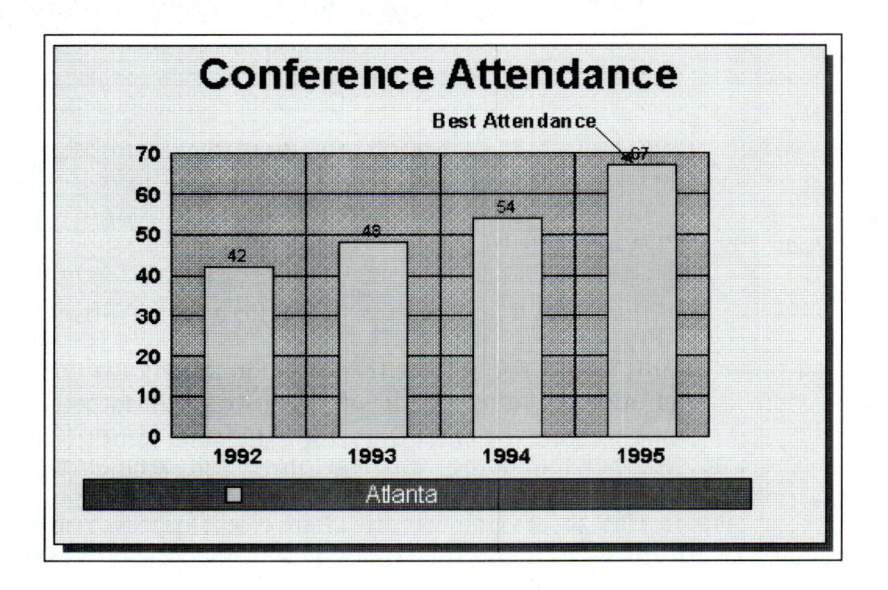

Chart with annotation
Figure 19-8.

2. Since the existing chart title will be covered by the graphic, you can turn the title off. In the Chart menu, choose Display Status. The Display Status dialog box shown here will open:

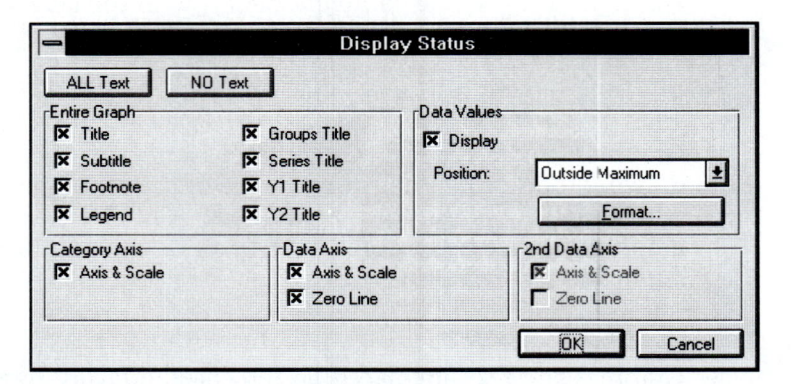

3. To turn off the chart title, click on the Title check box, so there is no longer a check mark in the box, and then click on OK.
4. If you feel you might not have enough room for the rectangle, drag the "Best Attendance" label and possibly its arrow down a bit.
5. Now you will create a rectangle. Select the Rectangle tool from the toolbox. The mouse pointer will turn into a crosshair.
6. Place the mouse pointer in the area that will be the left side of where you want the rectangle and drag the mouse to the opposite corner, as shown next. The rectangle can be moved with the Pick tool after it is created, so the exact placement isn't critical.

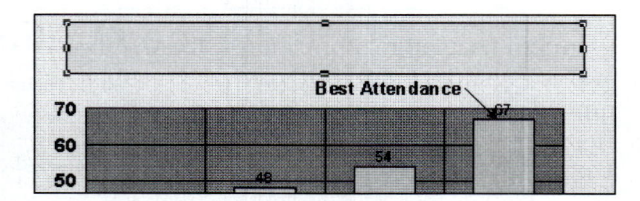

7. Select the Pick tool in the Chart toolbox and drag the rectangle into position above the chart. If your rectangle does not have any fill, or if the fill and outline are not to your liking, use the same technique that you would use in CorelDRAW! to adjust them as desired.
8. Now you need to add a new chart title. Select the Text tool in the toolbox and recreate the chart title, using the same steps to create the legend. Use the Pick tool to drag the new title on the rectangle where you want it.

Figure 19-9 shows one way the chart could appear. You should experiment with the Fill tool and the color palette to see the effects they can create.

Using CorelCHART

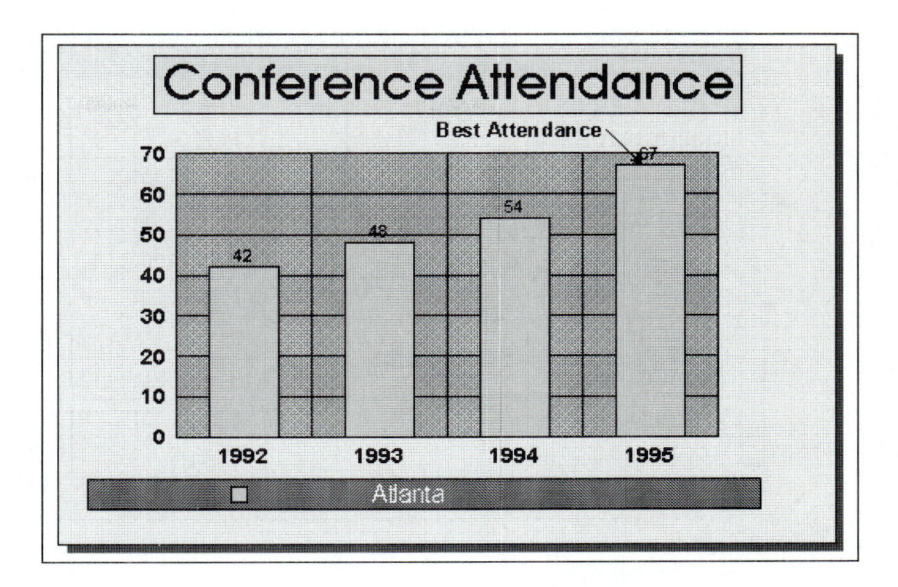

Rectangle added to chart
Figure 19-9.

Importing Graphics

Graphics can also be imported into CorelCHART by using the File Import command or the Import tool located on the ribbon bar. Imported graphics can be in a number of different formats, as shown in the following table.

File Format	Extension
Adobe Illustrator 1.1, 88, 3.0	.AI, .EPS
AutoCAD	.DXF
CompuServe Bitmap	.GIF
Computer Graphics Metafile	.CGM
CorelDRAW! Presentation	.CDR, .PAT
Corel Presentation Exchange	.CMX
CorelTRACE	.EPS
GEM File	.GEM
HPGL Plotter File	.PLT
IBM Pif	.PIF
JPEG Bitmap	.JPG, .JFF, .JTF, .CMP
Kodak Photo CD Image	.PCD

File Format	Extension
Lotus Graphics	.PIC
Macintosh PICT	.PCT
Micrografx 2.x, 3.x	.DRW, DRX
Paintbrush (CorelPHOTO-PAINT)	.PCX
PostScript (Interpreted)	.EPS, .PS
Scitex CT Bitmap	.CT, .SCT
Targa Bitmap	.TGA, .VDA, .ICB, .VST
TIFF Bitmap	.TIF, .SEP, .CPT
Windows Bitmap	.BMP, .DIB, .RLE
Windows Metafile	.WMF
WordPerfect Graphic	.WPG

Exporting Graphics

You can easily export graphics created in CorelCHART to other applications by choosing Export from the File menu or clicking on the Export tool from the ribbon bar. The file formats CorelCHART can export to are listed in the following table:

File Format	Extension
Adobe Illustrator	.AI, .EPS
AutoCAD	.DXF
CompuServe Bitmap	.GIF
Computer Graphics Metafile	.CGM
GEM File	.GEM
JPEG Bitmap	.JPG, .JFF, .JTF, .CMP
HPGL Plotter	.PCT
IBM PIC	.PIC
Macintosh PICT	.PCT
Matrix/Imapro SCODL	.SCD
OS/2 Bitmap	.BMP
Paintbrush (CorelPHOTO-PAINT)	.PCX

Using CorelCHART

File Format	Extension
Scitex CTI Bitmap	.CT, .SCT
TARGA Bitmap	.TGA, ,VDA, .ICB, .VST
TIFF Bitmap	.TIF
Windows Bitmap	.BMP, .DIB, .RLE
Windows Metafile	.WMF
WordPerfect Graphics	.WPG

Modifying Chart Elements

In the previous exercises you modified charts by adding text and graphics to them. Charts can also be modified by changing the objects on the charts, such as the width of the bars (as you have also done). You can also change the distance between bars, the shape of the bars, and many other features. The options for modifying chart elements are in the Chart menu; the exact options displayed vary, depending on the type of chart being modified. For example, when a Bar chart is the selected chart, the Chart menu contains options that modify the bars on the chart. When a Pie chart is selected, the Chart menu contains options for modifying segments of the pie.

The commands in the Chart menu can be accessed in three different ways. For each method, you first select the chart object to be modified. You can then choose the desired option from the Chart menu, using the mouse or keyboard; or you can also select a pop-up menu associated with the object. By clicking on the selected object with the right mouse button, a pop-up menu containing similar options as the Chart menu is presented next to the selected object. The pop-up menu will contain only the options that can be used with the selected object. For example, if you want to remove or change the data values at the top of each bar, you would click with the right mouse button on one of the data values. This dialog box would open:

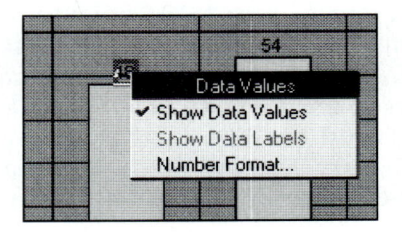

If you wanted to turn off the data values, simply click on the Show Data Values option. If you want to change the shape of a bar (or the width, as we did above), click on a bar with the right mouse button. From the dialog box

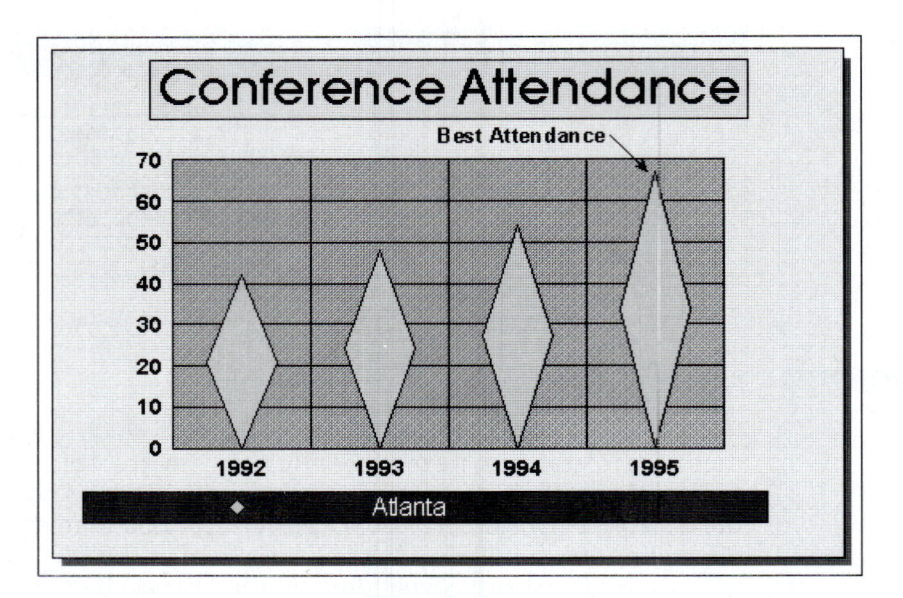

Figure 19-10.
Bars shaped as diamonds

[Chart: Conference Attendance, Atlanta, 1992–1995, with Best Attendance arrow pointing to 1995 bar]

that opens, click on Marker Shape and another dialog box opens, giving you a choice of a number of shapes. Figure 19-10 shows the example chart with the Marker Shape set to Diamond. Experiment with the different combinations CorelCHART provides to discover what effects you prefer for your own charts.

Creating Chart Templates

Any chart you design can be used as a chart template. You can insert your template in the Chart Types pictorial display box in the New dialog box, so it will be available when you are creating a new chart. You can also use a chart as a template after you have created it as a regular chart.

To include your chart template in the New dialog box, you must save it to the directory where CorelCHART stores the other chart templates. In the directory containing your Corel applications, there will be a subdirectory named CHART. The CHART subdirectory will itself contain a series of subdirectories, one for each type of chart. The chart templates are stored in these directories. If you installed CorelDRAW! using the default parameters, the path is C:\COREL50\CHART\BAR (or other chart type) *.CCH. Any chart saved to these directories will be available in the Chart Types pictorial display box.

A chart template is simply a regular CorelCHART chart. When it is loaded as a template, if Use Sample Data is not checked, the existing data (including text) is ignored. Only the chart type, graphics, color palette, and other modifications are presented.

Placing a template chart in the CorelCHART directories makes it readily available when you are creating a new chart. However, any chart can be used as a chart template, no matter where it is located. If you want to use a chart as a template after you have saved it as a regular chart, follow these steps:

1. Open the chart you wish to start with and then, in the File menu, select Apply Template.
2. Select the drive and directory containing the chart file you want to use and then select the file in the File Name list box.
3. Click on the filename and then click on OK, or just double-click on the filename.

The selected chart file will apply its format characteristics to the current chart.

Chart Types

CorelCHART can create 16 chart types, with most of these chart types available in several formats. Each chart type and format presents your data in a different pictorial form. The chart type that best presents your data will depend upon the kinds of relationships you are illustrating. You can preview the various chart types in the File New dialog box or from the Gallery menu. In the remaining sections of this chapter, you can have the File New dialog box open on your screen to see the different pictorial representations of each chart type. Or, you can look at the Gallery menu, which has a more orderly list of the chart types.

Bar Charts

Bar charts are used to show how values compare with one another and how they change over time. Each bar represents one data point—the value in one cell of the Data Manager. Bar charts can be configured as Vertical Bar charts or as Horizontal Bar charts.

Vertical and Horizontal Bar charts have seven formats, as shown in the Gallery menu. The Bar, Line, and Area charts have the same set of formats. These formats will be covered in detail in this section and mentioned only briefly in the sections on Line and Area charts.

The available formats are as follows:

- *Side-by-Side Bar* The bars representing each data point are placed next to each other.
- *Stacked Bar* Each bar in the data category is placed on top of the previous bar, rather than next to it. Each overall bar represents the sum of values for one data category. The Stacked Bar chart is used to compare

sums of data points between categories and to see the relative contribution of each data point.

- *Dual-Axis Side-by-Side* The charts shown so far have had one category axis (the x axis) and one data axis (the y axis). The Dual-Axis Side-by-Side format has two data axes. In a Horizontal Bar chart, one data axis is at the bottom of the chart and the other data axis is at the top of the chart. Some of the data series are plotted against the bottom data axis, and the other series are plotted against the top data axis. In a Vertical Bar chart, one data axis is on the left side and the other data axis is on the right side.

- *Dual-Axis Stacked* This is identical to the Dual-Axis Side-by-Side chart, except that each bar in the data category is placed on top of the previous bar, rather than next to it. Each bar represents a sum of data points.

- *Bipolar Side-by-Side* The Bipolar Side-by-Side chart divides the chart into halves, horizontally for a Vertical Bar chart and vertically for a Horizontal Bar chart. There are two data axes; each starts at the center of the chart and increases in value toward the edge of the chart. Figure 19-11 shows a Vertical Bar Bipolar Side-by-Side chart of the conference data. As you can see, the baseline for the data axes is the center of the chart, and values increase as they approach the top and bottom of the chart. The Horizontal Bar Bipolar Side-by-Side chart is similar, except that the data values increase as they get closer to the left and right sides of the chart.

- *Bipolar Stacked* This is identical to the Bipolar Side-by-Side chart, except that each bar in the data category is placed on top of the previous bar, rather than next to it.

Vertical Bipolar Side-by-Side chart
Figure 19-11.

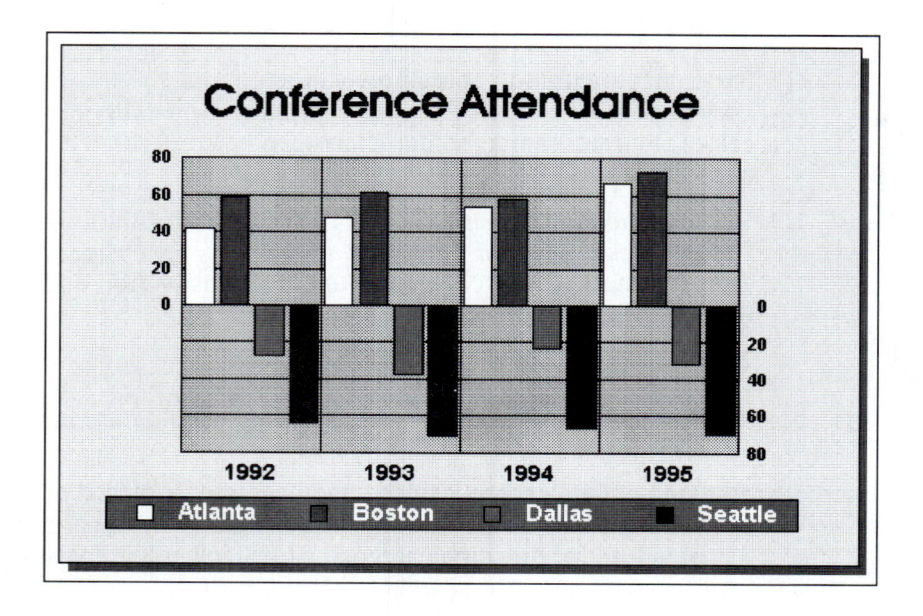

Using CorelCHART

- *Percent* A Percent chart is a type of Stacked Bar chart. In the Percent chart, the sum of all the numbers in each data category is represented as 100 percent. Each number in the data category is shown as a percentage of the total, rather than its actual value.

Line Charts

Line charts are primarily used to show the change over time in a series of values. Each data series is plotted side by side, allowing you to readily observe trends between the data series. A marker is placed at each data point, and the markers in each data series are connected. Line charts can be either vertical or horizontal.

Vertical and Horizontal Line charts offer seven formats that are similar to the ones available for Bar charts. The Line chart formats are as follows:

- *Absolute* Each data value is plotted at its actual value on the data axis. The values in each category are plotted in line with each other on the category axis.
- *Stacked* The Stacked Line chart is similar to the Stacked Bar chart—each value is plotted above the previous value in the data category, and the largest marker represents the sum of the values.
- *Bipolar Absolute* This is an Absolute Line chart in a Bipolar format, similar to the Bipolar Bar chart described in the previous section. The data is presented in the same manner as the Bipolar Side-by-Side Bar chart.
- *Bipolar Stacked* This is a Stacked Line chart in the Bipolar format. Data is presented in the same manner as the Bipolar Stacked Bar chart.
- *Dual-Axis Absolute* This is an Absolute Line chart in the Dual-Axis format. Data is presented in the same manner as the Dual-Axis Side-by-Side Bar chart.
- *Dual-Axis Stacked* This is a Stacked Line chart in the Dual-Axis format. Data is presented in the same manner as the Dual-Axis Stacked Bar chart.
- *Percent* The Percent format shows each value as a percentage of the total, in the same manner as the Bar Percent chart.

Area Charts

Area charts are similar to Line charts. The difference is that Area charts fill the areas between the lines with a color or pattern. Area charts can also be vertical or horizontal and offer formats similar to Bar and Line charts.

The Area chart formats are as follows:

- *Absolute* Each data value is plotted at its actual value on the data axis. The values in each category are plotted in line with each other on the category axis.
- *Stacked* The Stacked Area chart is similar to the Stacked Bar or Line chart—each value is plotted above the previous value, and the largest value marker represents the total of all the values in the data category.
- *Bipolar Absolute* This is an Absolute Area chart in a Bipolar format, similar to the Bipolar Bar charts described previously. The data is presented in the same manner as the Bipolar Side-by-Side Bar chart.
- *Bipolar Stacked* This is a Stacked Area Chart in the Bipolar format. Data is presented in the same manner as the Bipolar Stacked Bar chart.
- *Dual-Axis Absolute* This is an Absolute Area chart in the Dual-Axis Format. Data is presented in the same manner as the Dual-Axis Side-by-Side Bar chart.
- *Dual-Axis Stacked* This is a Stacked Area chart in the Dual-Axis format. Data is presented in the same manner as the Dual-Axis Stacked Bar chart.
- *Percent* The Percent format shows each value as a percentage of the total, in the same manner as the Bar Percent chart.

Pie Charts

Pie charts show the percentage distribution of your data. The entire pie represents 100 percent of one data series. Each data point is plotted as a wedge, representing a percentage of the total.

Pie charts have six formats as follows:

- *Pie* This is the single Pie chart.
- *Ring Pie* This is identical to the single Pie chart, except that the pie is shaped like a ring with a hole in the center.
- *Multiple Pie* This format uses several Pie charts together, to represent several data series.
- *Multiple Ring Pie* This is like the Multiple Pie chart, but with ring-shaped pies.
- *Multiple Proportional Pie* Each pie is sized in relation to the other pies. The pie that represents the largest total value will be the largest pie. The pie that represents the smallest total value will be the smallest pie.
- *Multiple Proportional Ring Pie* This is like the Multiple Proportional Pie format, but uses ring-shaped pies.

3-D Riser Charts

The 3-D Riser chart is the general name for a 3-D Bar chart. Each bar represents one data point. The 3-D Riser has four formats:

- *3-D Bars*   Each bar is rectangular.
- *Pyramids*   Each bar is a pyramid.
- *Octagons*   Each bar is an octagon.
- *Cut-Corner Bars*   Each bar is rectangular with a cut corner, as shown in Figure 19-12.

CorelCHART also provides three variations of the 3-D Riser chart:

- *3-D Floating*   This chart displays three dimensional data with 3-D cubes or spheres.
- *3-D Connect Series*   This chart connects data points in a series to form three-dimensional floating lines or areas. Ribbon and step lines let you see below them, while areas rise from the floor.
- *3-D Connect Group*   The same as 3-D Connect Series, except groups are connected instead of series.

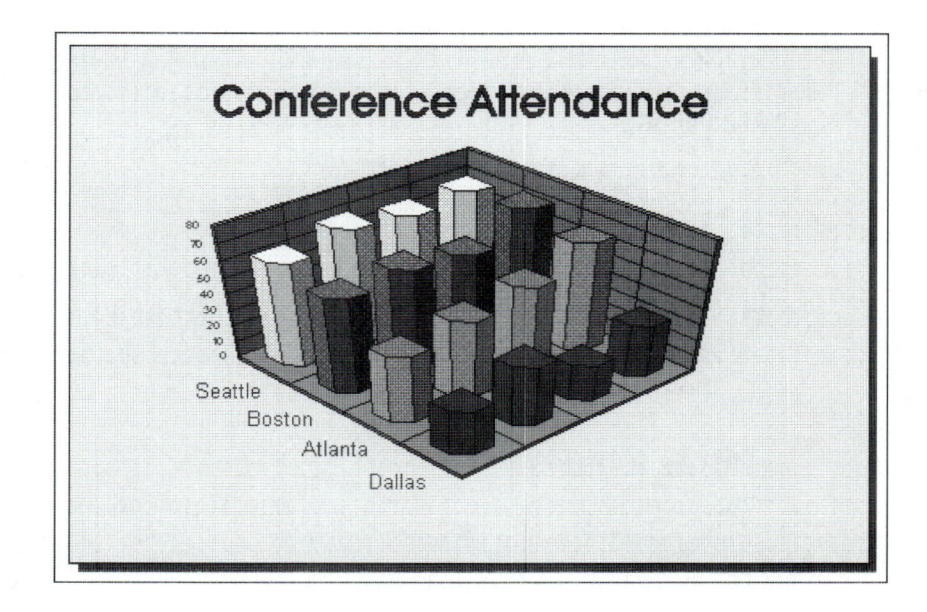

Conference data displayed as a Cut-Corner 3-D Bar chart
Figure 19-12.

3-D Surface Charts

The 3-D Surface chart shows what appears to be a rubber sheet stretched over a 3-D Riser chart. This chart is especially useful in spotting high and low points within large amounts of data. There are three 3-D Surface formats:

- *Surface*   This is the basic chart with a floating, flexible surface.
- *Surface with Sides*   This chart provides sides to the floating surface portrayed in the basic chart.
- *Honeycomb Surface*   This is similar to the Surface with Sides chart with colors added to create depth to the top surface.

3-D Scatter Charts

The 3-D Scatter chart is similar to the normal Scatter or X-Y chart (see the description of Scatter charts in the following section) with the addition of a third axis. The 3-D Scatter chart has two formats:

- *XYZ Scatter*   This is like a normal Scatter chart, but with a third data series.
- *XYZ Scatter with Labels*   This is an XYZ Scatter chart with data labels.

Scatter Charts

Scatter, or X-Y charts, show the relationship between pairs of numbers and the trends they represent. In each pair of numbers, one is plotted on the category axis, the other on the data axis. A marker is placed on the chart at the point where the value on the category axis intersects the value on the data axis.

Scatter charts have four formats:

- *Scatter*   This is the basic Scatter chart.
- *X-Y Dual-Axis*   This is a basic Scatter chart with two data axes.
- *X-Y with Labels*   This is a basic Scatter chart with the data points labeled.
- *X-Y Dual-Axis with Labels*   This is a Dual-Axis Scatter chart with the data points labeled.

Polar Charts

This chart type represents each data point as the distance (or radius) and angle from the origin on an X-Y plane.

The two Polar chart formats are

Using CorelCHART

- *Polar*   This is the basic Polar chart.
- *Dual-Axis Polar*   This is the basic Polar chart with two data axes.

Radar Charts

This chart can display several series of data on one chart. The data points in each series are connected by lines to represent the occurrence of data or the variation of data in relation to each other.

The three Radar chart formats are

- *Regular*   This is the basic Radar chart.
- *Stacked Radar*   This chart provides a summation of the data.
- *Dual-Axis Radar*   This chart stacks the data on two data axes.

Bubble Charts

This chart is similar to a Scatter chart with the added feature of displaying a third variable. In addition to the standard x and y axes, the Z variable is represented by the size of the data point, or bubble.

Bubble chart formats include

- *Bubble*   This the basic Bubble chart.
- *Dual-Axis Bubble*   This is the basic Bubble chart with two data axes.
- *Bubble with Labels*   This is the basic Bubble chart with the data points labeled.
- *Dual-Axis Bubble with Labels*   This is a Dual-Axis Bubble chart with the data points labeled.

High/Low/Open/Close Charts

The High/Low/Open/Close chart is a type of Line chart. It is also known as a Stock Market chart because a common use for High/Low/Open/Close charts is to show opening, low, high, and closing prices for shares of stock.

High/Low/Open/Close charts have six formats:

- *High/Low*   This format plots just the highest and lowest values.
- *High/Low Dual-Axis*   This format plots the highest and lowest values with dual axes.
- *High/Low/Open*   This format plots the highest, lowest, and starting values.

- *High/Low/Open Dual-Axis*   This format plots the highest, lowest, and starting values with dual axes.
- *High/Low/Open/Close*   This format plots the highest, lowest, starting, and ending values.
- *High/Low/Open/Close Dual-Axis*   This format plots the highest, lowest, starting, and ending values with dual axes.

Spectral Mapped Charts

Spectral Mapped charts are used to show relationships between sets of data. In Spectral Maps a range of values, not a data series, is marked with colors or patterns. Spectral Mapped charts are like topographical maps, where elevation ranges are marked with different colors. Spectral Maps have only one format.

Gantt Charts

Gantt charts are used in project scheduling to show the start, end, and duration of individual events. There is only one Gantt chart format.

Histograms

Histograms are use to show how often values occur in a set of data. For example, if temperature was recorded over a period of time, a Histogram

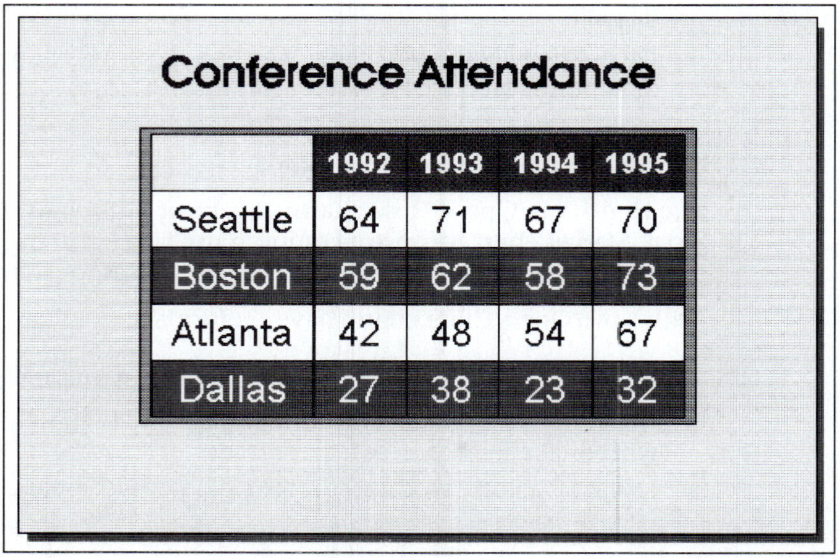

Conference Attendance

	1992	1993	1994	1995
Seattle	64	71	67	70
Boston	59	62	58	73
Atlanta	42	48	54	67
Dallas	27	38	23	32

Table Chart displaying the conference data

Figure 19-13.

Using CorelCHART

could be used to show how often each temperature was recorded. Histograms have two formats as follows:

- *Vertical Histogram*   As in a Vertical Bar chart, the bars are oriented vertically.
- *Horizontal Histogram*   As in a Horizontal Bar chart, the bars are oriented horizontally.

Table Charts

Table charts present the data in a row and column format, similar to the way the data is contained on the Data Manager. Figure 19-13 is an example of a table chart.

Pictographs

A Pictograph uses a graphic element to replace the plain bars in Bar charts and Histograms. For example, you could display the conference data from Atlanta, using the image of stacks of computers in place of a solid bar.

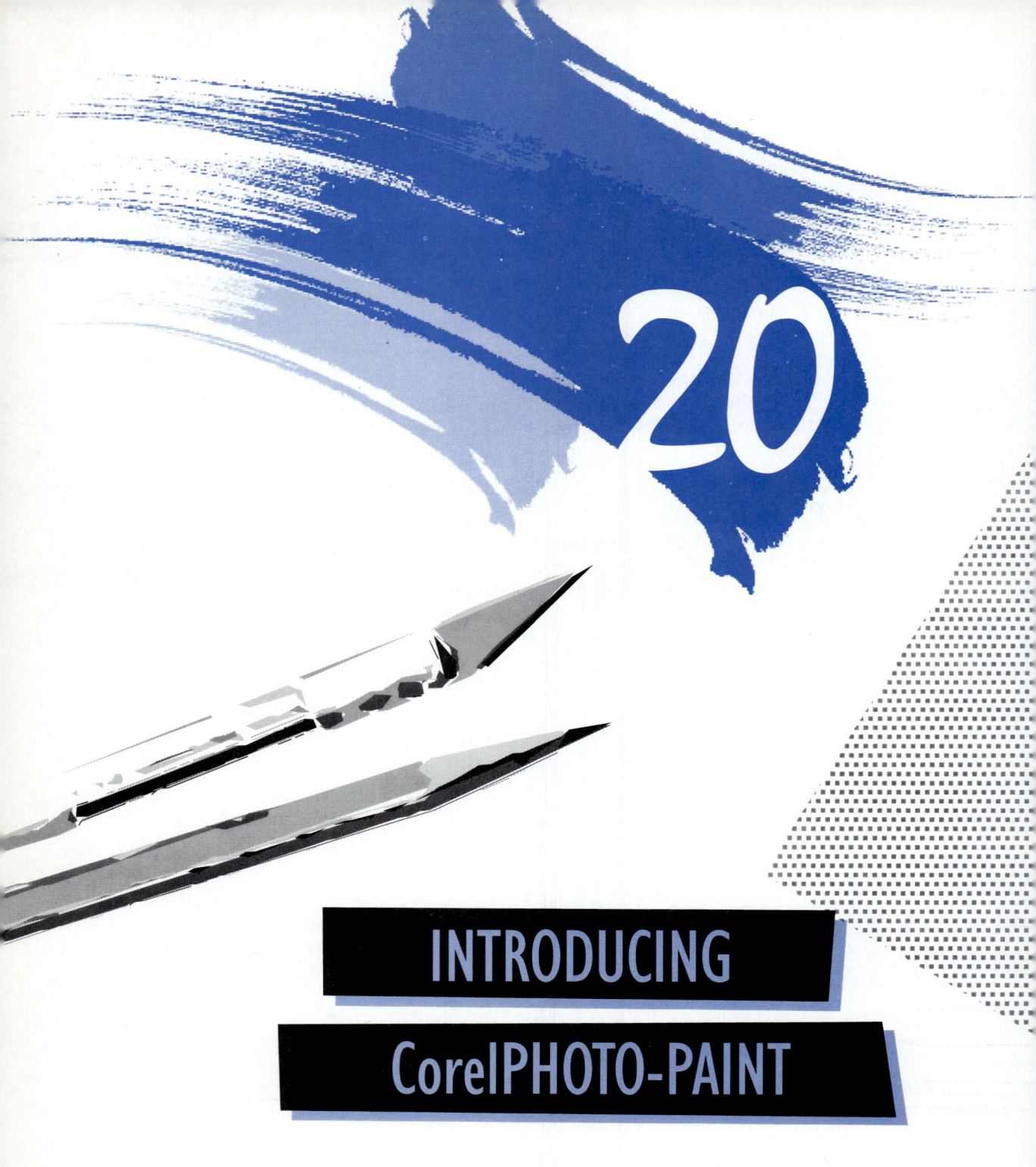

20

INTRODUCING
CorelPHOTO-PAINT

Basic

paint capabilities are combined with photographic enhancement features in CorelPHOTO-PAINT. Working with CorelPHOTO-PAINT, you can produce bitmapped "paintings" as well as retouch and enhance scanned photographs. This chapter introduces CorelPHOTO-PAINT by discussing its features and tools, and how to get started using it.

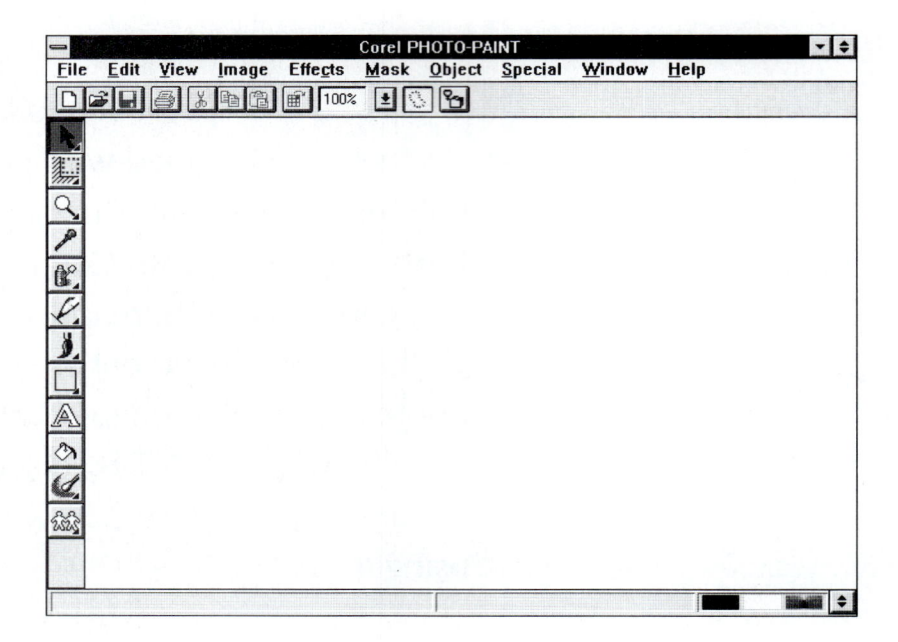

Initial CorelPHOTO-PAINT screen
Figure 20-1.

CorelPHOTO-PAINT Overview

CorelPHOTO-PAINT is a multifaceted paint program. It allows you to create bitmap images with an extensive toolkit of drawing tools, and it also enables you to enhance and retouch scanned photos. You can include the resulting images in CorelSHOW presentations, CorelDRAW! graphics, CorelVENTURA documents, CorelMOVE animations, or in other applications.

Getting Started with CorelPHOTO-PAINT

To start CorelPHOTO-PAINT, first bring up Windows, open the Corel5 Group, and then double-click on the CorelPHOTO-PAINT icon.

After a short time you will see the screen displayed in Figure 20-1 (maximized).

At this point you can either open an existing picture on disk or create a new one. If you want to create a new image, select the File menu and choose New; confirm or change the defaults in the Create a New Image dialog box, (shown on the following page) and a blank window will open, where you can create the picture.

Introducing CorelPHOTO-PAINT

If you want to open an existing picture, select File Open and identify the file you want. Once you've loaded a picture into CorelPHOTO-PAINT, your screen will look something like Figure 20-2. In this case, a sample file called APPLE.PCX, from the \COREL50\PHOTOPNT\SAMPLES\ directory, has been opened.

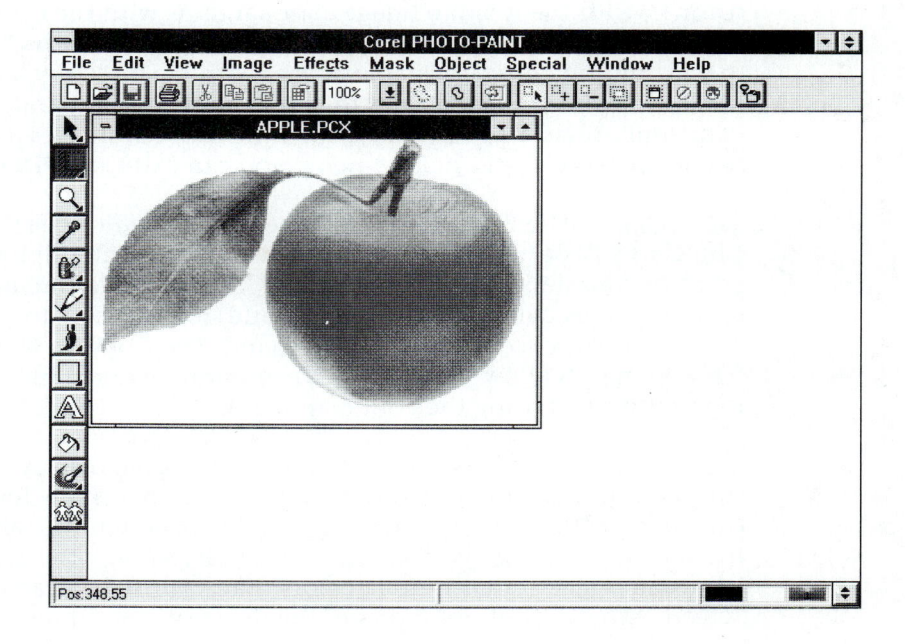

Opening an existing picture
Figure 20-2.

CorelPHOTO-PAINT Screen Elements

The CorelPHOTO-PAINT window contains many features to help you create pictures or retouch photos.

At the top of the screen is the title bar. On the right are the maximize and minimize buttons, which allow you to resize or restore the CorelPHOTO-PAINT window.

The menu bar, which is discussed shortly, is beneath the title bar. Beneath the menu bar is the ribbon bar. Below the ribbon bar is the CorelPHOTO-PAINT picture window, where you can create or open a picture. The status bar, beneath the picture area, displays messages, pointer coordinates, and paint, paper, and fill colors as you work with a picture. The button on the rightmost end of the status bar allows you to maximize the work area by hiding the title and menu bars.

The Menu Bar

The menu bar contains 10 menus. Open each of them in turn as they are discussed in the following paragraphs.

File Menu   The File menu contains the normal file-handling and printing features. You can also acquire images by selecting a source device, such as a scanner, with the Acquire Image command. As with the other Corel applications, there is the MOSAIC Roll-Up command, which allows you to view thumbnails of available images within a directory, and the Color Manager, which offers settings to best capture, display, and print color on your equipment. You can also reopen the last four images previously opened. Finally, from the File menu, you can exit CorelPHOTO-PAINT.

Edit Menu   The Edit menu offers the standard editing features like Undo, Cut, Copy, Paste, and Clear. You can also save an interim image at a certain point in your design process using the Checkpoint command; you can then try out various enhancement features and return safely to your saved image with the Restore to Checkpoint command. The Copy To File and Paste From File commands allow you to copy to and from external files. Text formatting is accomplished using the Font command.

View Menu   The View menu manages the screen display of images. You can zoom in and out of pictures; selectively hide or show four roll-up menus, the ruler, or the toolbox; and maximize the screen in the same way as with the status bar button. Full-Screen Preview shows only the active picture. When an image contains more colors than your screen can display, the Screen Dithering option improves the onscreen appearance of the image by optimizing color transitions. Color Correction improves the linearity of the monitor.

Image Menu   The Image menu allows you to add special effects to a picture or scanned photo with options to flip, rotate, or distort a picture. The Resample command allows you to change the size and/or resolution of an image, while Paper Size lets you increase or decrease the total number of pixels while changing the placement of the subject relative to the background. The Convert To command converts to another color. You can use the Split Channels To command to separate an image into color component channels that you can edit; then, you can recombine the image with the Combine Channels command. Finally, the Info option displays measurements and technical details about an image.

Effects Menu   The Effects menu allows you to select and apply special effects filters to pictures or cutouts. Later in this chapter you will see how these filters can enhance an image.

Mask Menu   The Mask menu, along with the Color Mask roll-up, provide options to apply a protective shield against filters or enhancements, or to limit filter or enhancement effects to a selected area.

Object Menu   The Object menu allows you to manipulate selections, or *objects*, that are extracted from an existing image. The Object features will provide unlimited opportunities for you to create composite images from multiple sources or to transfer portions of your images to other applications.

Special Menu   The Special menu allows you to adjust color tolerances, select your preferences (such as units of measurement), use third-party special effects filters, and create brushes of various sizes for paint operations. The selection commands are used to modify existing selection areas, masks, and objects.

Window Menu   The Window menu has the standard arrangement and activation commands. Also from the Window menu, you can duplicate pictures so you can see them at different magnifications and you can refresh the screen.

The Roll-Up Menus

The six roll-up menus, shown in Figure 20-3, can be displayed by selecting them from the View menu (Color, Canvas, Fill, and Tool Settings roll-ups), Mask menu (Color Mask roll-up), or the Object menu (Layers/Objects roll-up). They stay on the screen and can be rolled up or down like the roll-ups in CorelDRAW!.

a. b. c.

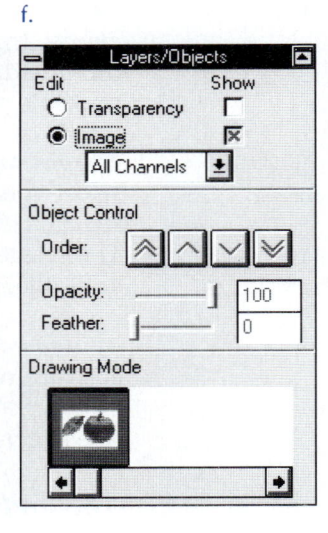

d. e. f.

Roll-up menus
Figure 20-3.

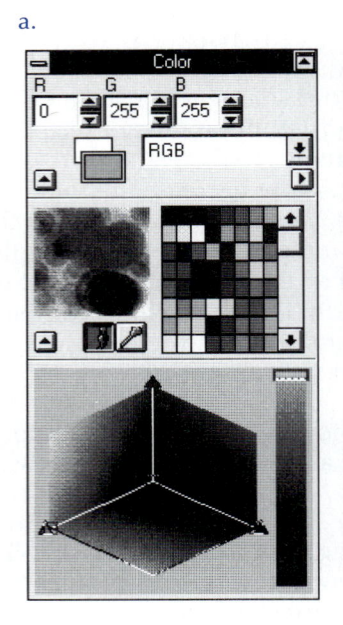

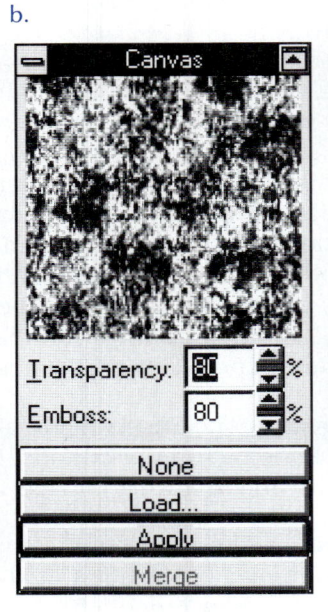

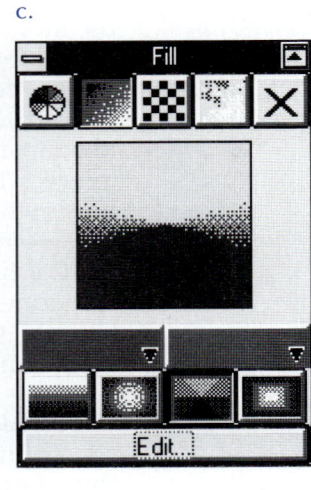

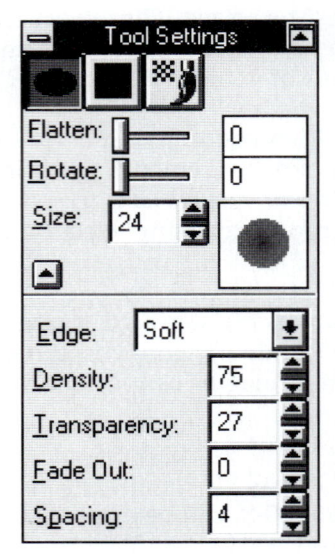

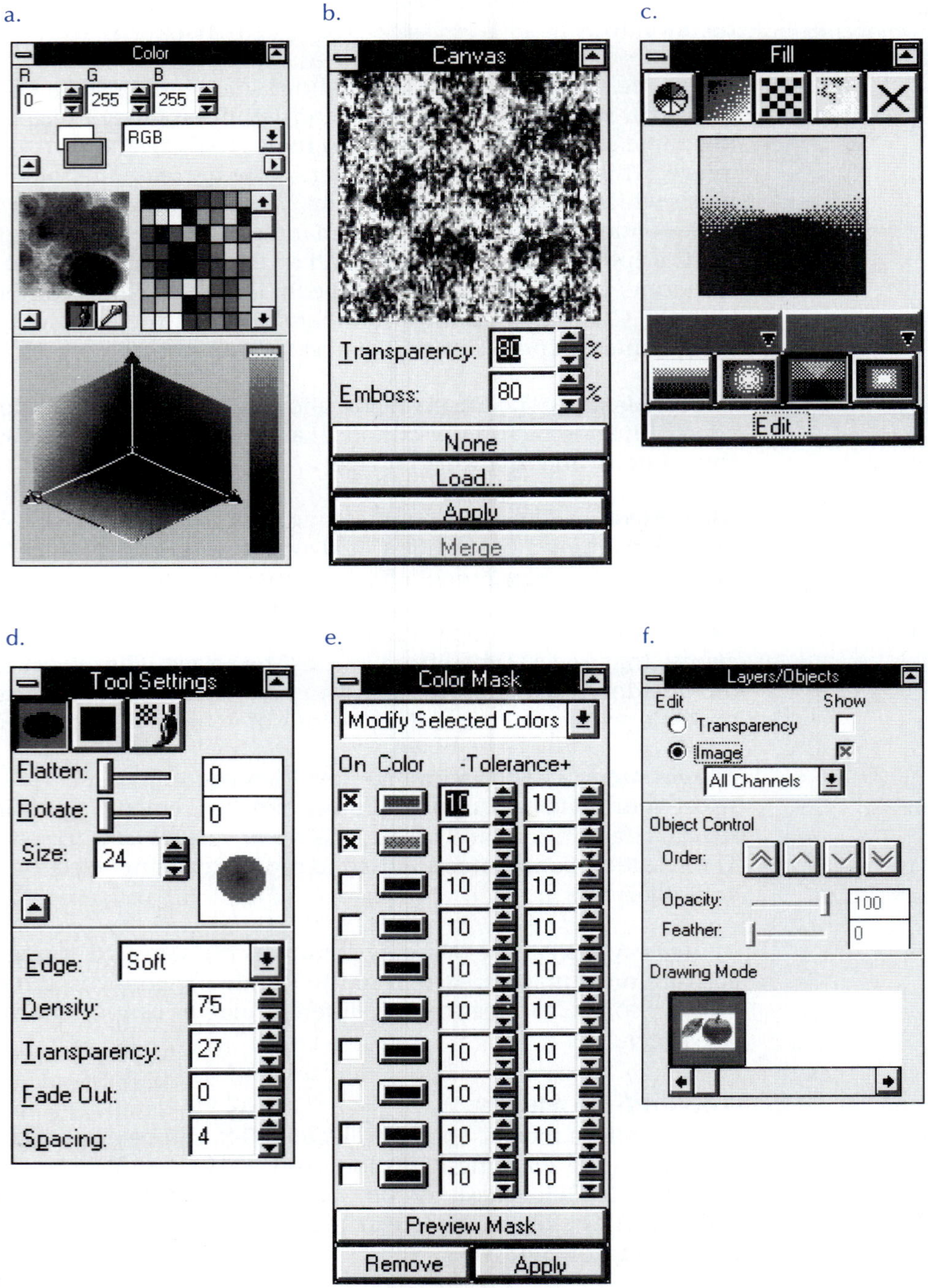

Introducing CorelPHOTO-PAINT

The shortcut for displaying the Color roll-up is F2.

Color Roll-Up The Color roll-up, shown in Figure 20-3a, allows you to select foreground and background colors for paint and masking operations in an image. It can be used to adjust or select a color palette, and you can paint with the selected colors in a preview window. You can create a fountain fill by controlling the To/From values that are displayed when the Gradient Fill tool is selected.

The shortcut for displaying the Canvas roll-up is F3.

Canvas Roll-Up The Canvas roll-up, shown in Figure 20-3b, allows you to load a textured pattern from disk or the Clipboard. When the pattern is loaded, it is displayed in the display box of the roll-up. This can be applied as a background to a painting, or it can overlay a picture for a transparency effect.

The shortcut for displaying the Fill Settings roll-up is F6.

Fill Roll-Up The Fill roll-up, shown in Figure 20-3c, is very similar to the Fill Roll-up in CorelDRAW!. The buttons across the top of the roll-up allow you to use existing patterns or to create your own. Each button provides access to its representative fill. From the left, the buttons access uniform fill, fountain fill, tiles, textures, and no fill. For example, clicking on the Texture button (third from the left) and then clicking on the Edit command button opens the Texture Fill dialog box, as shown in Figure 20-4.

The shortcut for displaying the Tool Settings roll-up is F8.

Tool Settings Roll-Up The Tool Settings roll-up is used to control the width, shape, or thickness of a brush tool, depending on the tool selected. The spinners below "Width" (Edge, Density, Variances, and so on) are used with the Impressionist, Impressionist Clone, Pointillist, and Pointillist Clone tools, which you will learn about later in the chapter. The Tool Settings roll-up is shown in Figure 20-3d.

The shortcut for displaying the Color Mask roll-up is F4.

Color Mask Roll-Up The Color Mask roll-up, shown in Figure 20-3e, allows you to either modify or protect masking colors using the drop-down list box at the top of the roll-up. The colors are set by clicking on the button in the Color column. The pointer turns into an eyedropper that allows you to pull color from an image. You can expand or contract the amount of color that is used by increasing or decreasing the tolerance settings. The command buttons at the bottom of the roll-up are used to preview, remove, and apply your settings.

The shortcut for displaying the Layers/Objects roll-up is F7.

Layers/Objects Roll-Up The Layers/Objects roll-up is used to edit available transparency masks and images, control the order of the object layers, and specify the degree of opacity and feathering of the object. You can isolate individual objects for applying different effects by using the Drawing Mode preview box, which displays thumbnails of the entire image and its associated objects. The Layers/Object roll-up is shown in Figure 20-3f.

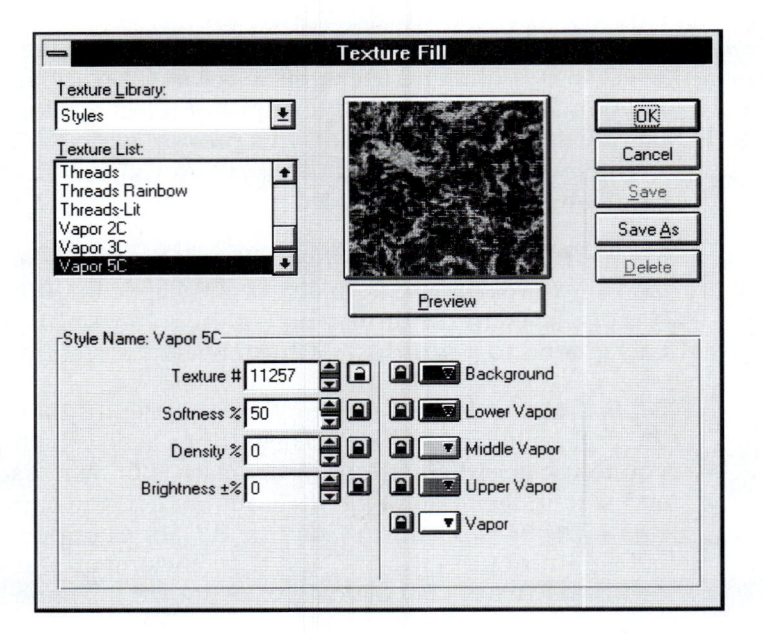

Texture Fill dialog box
Figure 20-4.

Ribbon Bar

Below the menu bar, CorelPHOTO-PAINT provides a collection of commonly used features on the *ribbon bar*. As with the ribbon bars you've already used in other Corel applications, the buttons that appear on the ribbon bar change depending on the current task. To see what each button does, simply point on a button and its function appears in the status bar. The buttons that appear when CorelPHOTO-PAINT opens are shown here:

The first four buttons in the default ribbon bar perform the same functions as selecting the New, Open, Save, and Print commands in the File menu. The next three buttons perform the same functions as the Cut, Copy, and Paste commands in the Edit menu. The next button, which looks like a grid, is used to select a partial area of an image so that you can save that area in a file.

Tip: If your system has a limited amount of RAM, editing partial files can speed your work and avoid draining system resources.

Introducing CorelPHOTO-PAINT

The Zoom drop-down list box, the next item on the ribbon bar, allows you to magnify or shrink your view of an image.. The second button from the right turns the marquee on objects on or off, while the rightmost button opens the Mosaic roll-up. Other buttons, which are optionally added to the ribbon bar according to what you are doing, deal with adding and removing items from a selection and with text formatting.

CorelPHOTO-PAINT Tools

> Pressing CTRL-T is a shortcut toggle that hides or displays the toolbox.

The CorelPHOTO-PAINT toolbox is either in its default location on the left edge of the screen or as a floating window that you can move around on the screen. You can choose to display or hide the toolbox, or make it a floating toolbox, by using the View Toolbox submenu.

Tools within the toolbox are arranged according to function. There are 12 tools shown on the toolbox, as you can see here:

- Object Picker
- Mask
- Zoom
- Eyedropper
- Local Undo
- Line, Curve, Pen
- Paint Brush
- Rectangle, Ellipse, Polygon
- Text
- Fill
- Smear
- Clone

Most buttons represent groups of tools; these can be identified by a small black triangle in the lower-right corner of the tool button. When you click on a button with a triangle and momentarily hesitate, a flyout menu displays the tools in the group. If you choose to float the toolbox, you can ungroup the tools by using the toolbox Control menu to view the entire tool ensemble, as shown in the following illustration.

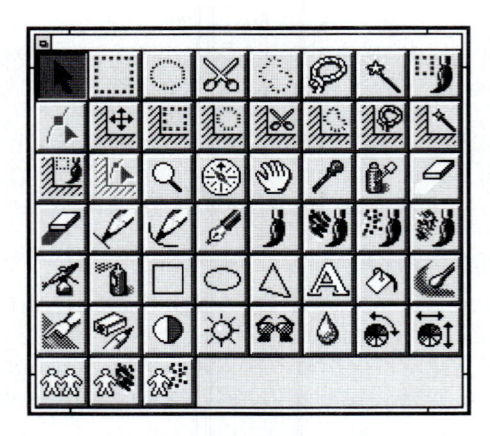

The tools within the toolbox can be selected by clicking on a tool button or, in the case of group tools, by dragging the cursor on a flyout menu until the tool you want is highlighted. To see what a particular tool does, point on the tool and view its function on the status bar. Most tools have a Tool Settings roll-up associated with them. By double-clicking on a tool you can open its roll-up and adjust settings for that particular tool (with some tools, a dialog box or other roll-up opens and performs a similar function). Settings are saved until you next change them.

A brief summary of each of the tool groups is provided in the following sections.

Object Picker Tools   Object Picker tools are used to select, or cut out, an area of a picture. Once selected, an area, or *object*, can be cut, copied, pasted, stretched, rotated, or otherwise manipulated. The Object Picker tools define the area that will be selected using various methods:

- Object Picker defines and selects an object by clicking on it;
- Rectangle Object defines and selects a rectangular area by dragging a rectangle around the objects to be selected;
- Circle Object defines and selects a circular area by dragging a circle;
- Polygon Object defines and selects a polygon area by clicking and defining the polygon;
- Freehand Object defines and selects an irregular shaped area by drawing the selection with a Freehand pencil;
- Lasso Object defines and selects irregular shapes with similar colors by "drawing" the area with a lasso;
- Magic Wand Object defines and selects objects with similar colors by touching them with the wand;

Introducing CorelPHOTO-PAINT

- Object Brush defines and selects objects to paint with the Paint Brush by brushing the area within the objects;
- Object Node Edit defines and selects nodes to be edited with the Node Edit roll-up by dragging a rectangle around the nodes.

Mask Tools   The Mask tools allow you to create masks in various shapes and different color configurations. You use masks to protect or change the colors of a selected area.

Zoom Tools   Zoom tools are used to manipulate the display of the picture in some way, including by magnifying, locating, and moving it.

Eyedropper Tool   Eyedropper picks up a color from a picture so the same shade can be applied elsewhere. As with the Smear tools, the Eyedropper is used to refine or apply hand-retouching (painting with a brush after choosing a color with the Eyedropper) to parts of a picture. Filters are usually used to manipulate entire selected areas of a picture.

Local Undo Tools   The Local Undo tools are used to reverse your last action, erase portions of an image, or apply the paper color to the image color.

Line, Curve, Pen Tools   The Line tools create lines, curves, and irregular shapes and lines which may be filled or hollow.

Paint Brush Tools   Painting tools are the bread and butter of the PHOTO-PAINT program. They allow you to add to a picture (or delete from it) color, texture, or text.

Rectangle, Ellipse, Polygon Tools   These hollow box tools let you quickly create many common shapes used in drawing your own images (unfilled): rectangles, ellipses, and polygons.

Text Tool   The Text tool allows you to type text onto your painting. Double-clicking on the Text tool opens the Font dialog box where you can set the text formatting attributes.

Fill Tool   Double-clicking on the Fill tool opens the Fill roll-up, which allows setting various fill colors and patterns.

Smear Tools   The Smear tools are used to enhance and otherwise correct any blemishes in existing images. You can smear, blend, tint, and smudge as well as brighten and contrast.

Clone Tools   The last icon on the toolbox is for the Clone tools. Clone duplicates painting or drawing strokes elsewhere within a picture, or applies them to a duplicate of a picture. As you draw, a clone is produced.

This section has provided a brief introduction to CorelPHOTO-PAINT's many tools and their capabilities. To really appreciate the power and versatility of CorelPHOTO-PAINT you have to apply the magic these tools offer to onscreen images. The remainder of this chapter is dedicated to showing how some of the more exciting features of this program work.

Using CorelPHOTO-PAINT Features

The two major tacks that you can take with CorelPHOTO-PAINT are to modify existing images and to create new ones. The next section will start out with one of the existing sample files provided by CorelPHOTO-PAINT. Using this file we will explore various ways you can manipulate the image by selecting segments to create masks and objects. The next logical step—enhancing your images through one or more filters or the retouching tools—makes it possible to transform existing pictures with amazing effects. Finally, you will see how to create your own images.

Making Selections

Before you can create masks or objects, which are described in the following sections, you have to define, or select, a portion of an existing image. CorelPHOTO-PAINT provides a collection of tools to solve the different problems you might face in selecting just the right detail. The selection tools are contained with the flyout associated with the first tool in the toolbox, as shown here:

In order to put the selection tools to use, an image has to be present in the painting area. We will use a sample file of the apple shown in Figure 20-2.

1. Select the File Open command. In the Open an Image dialog box, use the Drives and Directories browser boxes to locate your CorelPHOTO-PAINT files. These are in the \COREL50\PHOTOPNT\SAMPLES\ directory.

2. When you locate the correct directory, select the APPLE.PCX file. You can also use any bitmap file (PCX, TIF, BMP) you have available.

3. The image appears on your screen in a window. Maximize the window as shown in Figure 20-5.

Introducing CorelPHOTO-PAINT

The APPLE.PCX sample file maximized on your screen
Figure 20-5.

The .PCX file extension identifies this file as one of the more popular graphics formats supported by CorelPHOTO-PAINT. Originally developed for use in the PC Paintbrush painting program, PCX has become a widely supported format among graphics and painting programs.

4. Click on the Object Picker tool, the first tool in the toolbox, to open its flyout menu.

   Point on each tool in the flyout and read its function displayed on the status bar. As you can see, CorelPHOTO-PAINT offers a number of ways for you to select a portion of the image. In this example, you want to isolate the apple.

Tip: As you select tools, notice how the ribbon bar sometimes changes to a smaller or larger selection of tools to accommodate tasks associated with the selection.

5. Click on the Freehand Object tool—the middle tool, fifth from either end. Since the apple is an irregular shape, this tool allows the highest degree of flexibility in defining the object.

Notice how the Freehand Object tool now becomes the tool that appears in the toolbox and that the mouse pointer turns into a crosshair when you move it into the image area.

6. Click and drag the crosshair around the apple, being careful not to catch any more of the leaf than a section of the stem. Don't be too concerned about how much white space is between the apple and the marquee. Complete the selection by dragging the crosshair back to the starting point.

The area around your selection is now surrounded by eight handles. Your screen should now look similar to Figure 20-6.

You have created your first simple object—a copy of the apple without the leaf. Now you can manipulate the object by performing actions (probably familiar to you) such as moving, sizing, rotating, and skewing, and a few others described in the following section.

Working with Objects

You can create multiple objects from one image; cut, copy, or drag and drop objects into other images and applications; and order them as layers. In the following example, we will extract our selection, manipulate it, and save it for use later in the chapter.

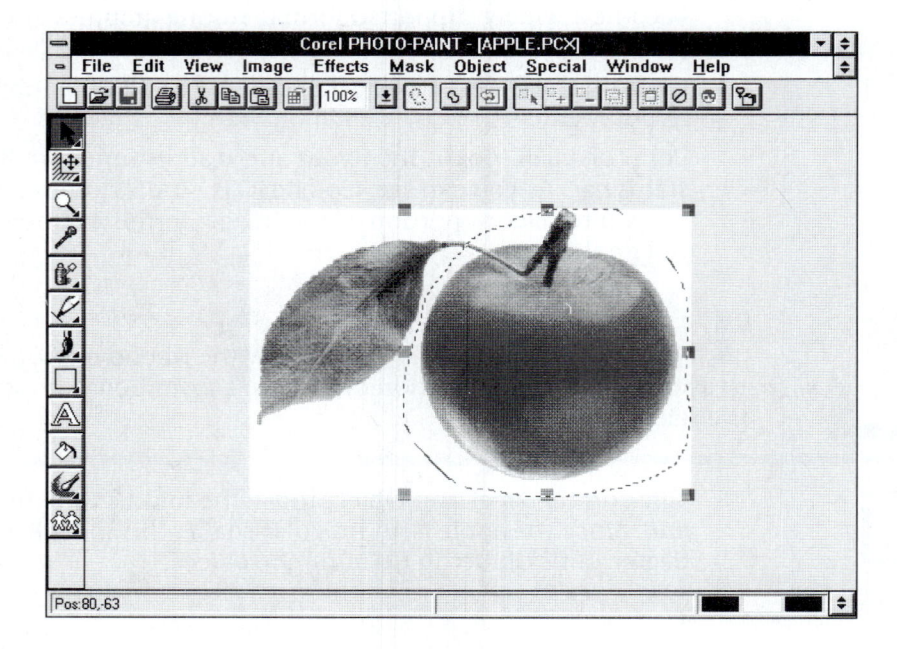

Selected area defined by a visible marquee
Figure 20-6.

Introducing CorelPHOTO-PAINT

To gain more working room, the paper size should first be increased.

1. Select the Image menu and choose the Paper Size command. In the Paper Size dialog box, change the Width dimension to approximately 800 pixels. Make sure the Maintain Aspect check box is selected so the height is increased proportionately and that the Placement option is Central. Click on OK.

   After a few moments, the new paper size fills the painting area and the image redisplays in the lower-right corner.

2. Use the vertical scroll bar to center the image vertically, open the selection tools flyout, and click on the Object Picker tool. Click in the area within the eight handles and drag that object to the left of the original image. Position the object in an area where it doesn't overlap the original image. If you deactivate the marquee (the marquee button acts as toggle to activate/deactivate the visible marquee), your screen should look similar to Figure 20-7.

   When you first used the Freehand Object tool to surround the object, you used the left mouse button as you drew a line around the apple. This caused a copy to form when the selection was moved. If you use the right mouse button to select part of an object and then move it, it will be cut from the original image.

Isolating an object from its image
Figure 20-7.

3. Experiment moving, sizing, rotating, skewing the apple. See Chapters 5 and 8 if you need to review these features. When you are through, return the object to something close to Figure 20-7, even if you have to reload the image from the disk and reselect the object.

4. Select the cropped object if it isn't already selected, and open the Layers/Objects roll-up by choosing it from the Object menu or by pressing F7. Adjust the Opacity and Feather sliders to see what effect they have on the object.

5. Open the Object menu to see what other options are available to you. Again, choose some of the commands and observe their effects. If you change the object so drastically you cannot get it back to the appearance of a normal apple, close the window and start fresh with a new copy of the APPLE.PCX file.

6. With the cropped object still selected, click on the Copy button and choose Copy from the Edit menu or press CTRL-C. Doing this copies the object to the Clipboard, from where you can paste it into a new window. You can now close all open files. Choose No when prompted to save.

7. Click on the New button at the left end of the ribbon bar or choose New from the File menu. Accept the default settings in the Create a New Image dialog box by clicking on OK.

8. Click on the Paste button (or choose one of the other methods) and choose As New Object. Maximize the drawing window so your object looks like Figure 20-8.

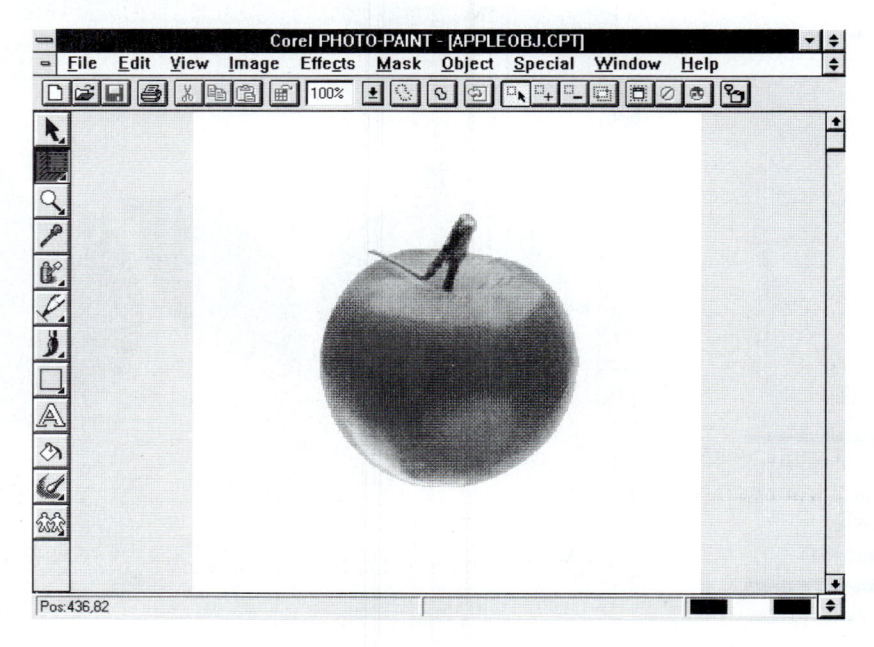

Object pasted into a new file
Figure 20-8.

9. Click on the Save button and save the file as APPLEOBJ in your DRAWINGS directory. Notice that the default file extension is .CPT, identifying it as CorelPHOTO-PAINT file. Click on OK. The object you saved is now an independent bitmap taken from the APPLE.PCX file.
10. Click on Close in the File menu to remove the image from your screen. In the next exercise you'll go back to the original apple.

Masks and Filters

Masks have two functions in general. They can act like a protective film over an area of your image or can define an area where color is to be modified. You can protect or modify colors either inside or outside of the defined area. Masks can protect or modify specific colors or they can protect according to the degree of transparency you assign them. The second tool group in the toolbox contains the Mask tools as shown here:

The Mask tools look and are used very much like the Object Picker tools. The first tool in the flyout selects a mask once it is defined, and the other Mask tools define portions of an image to be masked. Also as with objects, mask options are available from their own menu and roll-up. Try the Mask tool with these instructions:

1. Again open the APPLE.PCX sample file. Maximize its window. In this example, it will be all right to use the default paper size.
2. Click on the Mask tool and open its flyout. Choose the Lasso Mask tool (looks like a rope—fourth from the right) and, as before, encircle the apple to isolate it from its leaf.
3. Select the Effects menu and choose the Mapping option. In the submenu that appears choose the Tile option. Accept the default settings in the Tile dialog box and click on OK. The apple mask changes into multiple smaller images of itself within the confines of the mask, as shown in Figure 20-9.
4. Save the image (using a new filename), if you want, and close the file.

By default the mask applies the effects of the tiling within its boundaries and protects or modifies colors to the area outside the boundaries. By choosing Inverse from the Mask menu, you can cause the tiling to affect the area outside the mask. By opening the Color Mask roll-up, you can protect individual colors. The transparent mask options on the Mask menu allow

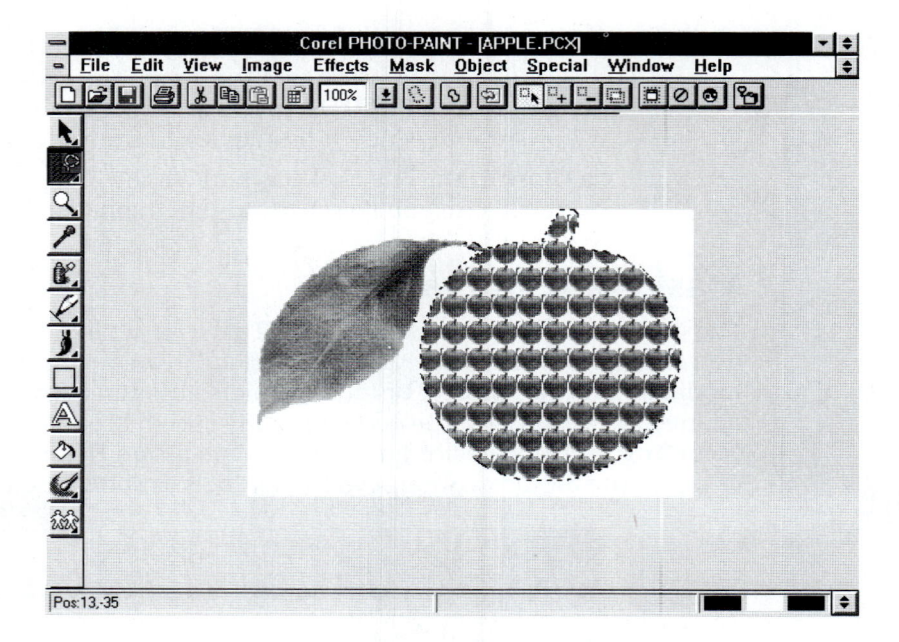

One type of masking protects the area outside of the mask
Figure 20-9.

you to load existing images to mask an image. You can adjust the degree of transparency to vary the opacity of effects applied to the masked area.

The tiling effect that was applied to the mask was one of the filters provided by CorelPHOTO-PAINT. The following section describes the filters in more detail.

Filters

Filters can create professional results and can be used in creative, complex ways. They also provide an easy way to enhance images and to try out various special effects. As demonstrated in the previous example, filters are easy to apply; they are just as easy to remove: simply choose the Edit menu Undo command. Their ease of use and no-fuss removal make filters the predominant way to professionally strengthen your images. In addition to the ample number of filters provided by CorelPHOTO-PAINT, you can use third-party filters such as Adobe and Kai's Power Tools plug-in filters.

CorelPHOTO-PAINT filters are grouped in the Effects menu. Most filters have associated dialog boxes that allow you to adjust their respective settings. A handy feature CorelPHOTO-PAINT offers is the ability to select any filter within a group from any one of the group's associated dialog boxes, as shown in the following illustration.

Introducing CorelPHOTO-PAINT

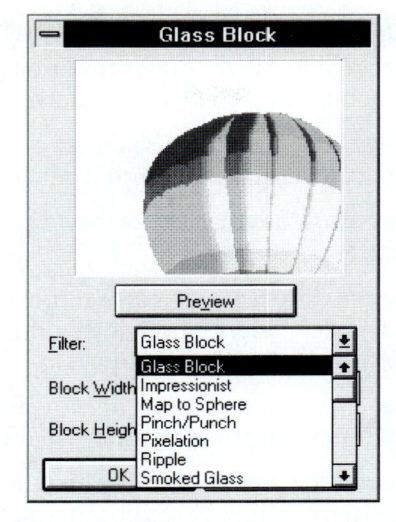

The best way to see a filter's effect is to open an image and use the preview box in the filter's dialog box to display the results of different settings. The following section briefly describes each filter within the ten Effect menu groups.

Artistic Filters

Pointillism adds a random array of multicolored dots. You can change dot size and spacing, as well as vary the colors.

Impressionism adds impressionistic brush strokes to an image. You can customize the brushes by setting such attributes as length, number, weight, and direction.

Color Filters

Brightness and Contrast allows you to modify the relative lightness or darkness of an image.

Gamma provides a means to adjust the midtones of an image without affecting the darker (shadow) and highlighted areas.

Hue/Saturation provides control over the degree of color ("colorness") of a selection without affecting its brightness. When changing the hue, you are shifting the color around an imaginary color wheel, with red at 0 and 360 degrees and the other colors in a rainbow sequence in between. Saturation is a measure of how intense you want a particular color.

Tone Map provides an interactive means of creating and saving color corrections. All colors (using the RGB color model) can be modified, or each color channel can be individually changed.

Fancy Filters

Edge detect creates an outline or textured effect. You can adjust the edge sensitivity, color, and lightness or darkness.

Emboss gives you the ability to create a 3-dimensional appearance to an image. You can set the color and direction of the light source.

Invert flips colors; a white background becomes black, yellows become blues, and so forth.

Jaggy despeckle diffuses colors and removes jagged edges from bitmaps by changing the dot height and width values. You can introduce new colors or use the identical colors in the image.

Motion blur creates the illusion of movement. You can set the speed (or amount of blur) and the direction the motion.

Outline creates a grayscale outline around the image or selected area. It may create multiple outlines throughout an image, or the appearance of holes.

Mapping

Glass Block gives a distorted appearance of viewing an image through several thicknesses of blocks of glass. You can adjust the glass block width and height.

Impressionist provides an oil or watercolor painting-like impressionist style to an image.

Map to Sphere adjustably wraps the image around a sphere, or around a horizontal or vertical cylinder.

Pinch/punch compresses and expands an image in a three-dimensional way.

Pixelation creates block-like segments of an image in a rectangular or circular pattern. You can adjust width, height, and opacity of the blocks.

Ripple gives a wave-like appearance to an image. You can set the period, amplitude, and orientation of the wave effect.

Smoked Glass darkens an image by adjusting the amount of tint and its percentage.

Swirl rotates an image around its center. You can set the angle of rotation.

Tile creates multiple images of the original image within its boundaries. You can adjust the width and height of the multiple image (see Figure 20-9).

Vignette creates an oval spotlight on a image that shades off gradually into the surrounding area. Adjustments can be made to the offset, fade, and color of the vignette.

Introducing CorelPHOTO-PAINT

Wet Paint gives the appearance of running paint. You can control the effect by changing the degree of wetness and the percentage of the depth of the object that is effected.

Wind produces a wind-blown effect by creating thin lines in the image. The effect is adjusted by the opacity and strength of the pseudo-wind.

Noise

Add noise provides a granular effect to an image. Choose from a heavy and larger grain size (Gaussian), a thinner and lighter colored grain (Spike), or moderate grainy appearance (Uniform).

Maximum lightens an image by decreasing the number of colors present. Adjustments are made by increasing or decreasing the percentage of pixel values affected.

Median removes noise from images that have a grainy appearance.

Minimum darkens an image by decreasing the number of colors present. Adjustments are made by increasing or decreasing the percentage of pixel values affected.

Remove noise softens edges in scanned images by comparing pixels to those surrounding it. The maximum variance from the average value can be adjusted.

Sharpen

Adaptive unsharp highlights details along edges without affecting other areas of the image or selection.

Directional sharpen determines from which direction to apply the greatest amount of sharpening.

Edge enhance accentuates edges along boundaries of areas of different colors and shades.

Enhance sharpens or clarifies the entire image.

Sharpen brings out detail and sharpens edges.

Unsharp mask is most pronounced in higher-resolution images. It blurs contrast boundaries, enhancing and "adaptively unsharpening" the edges in the image.

Soften

Diffuse scatters colors.

Directional smooth loses a minimal amount of detail among differences in adjacent pixels.

Smooth tones harshness with minimal loss of detail.

Soften smoothes and softens color. It also softens transitions between shadows and lighter areas.

Special

Contour uses lines to outline the edges of an image while reducing the number of colors drastically.

Posterize reduces the overall number of colors and creates areas of solid colors and grays from gradations.

Psychedelic randomly applies colors to an image to produce a chaotic explosion of colors.

Solarize allows you to select areas of an image to reverse its appearance, as in a photo negative.

Threshold enables everything below a certain color threshold value to be darkened and values above it to be lightened.

Tone

Equalize redistributes shades of colors, making the darker colors black, the lighter colors white, and stretching those in between. This is useful for color images that will be color separated and printed using a high-resolution imagesetter.

Transformations

3D Rotate provides a representative 3-dimensional box that displays the vertical and horizontal rotation effects you apply.

Mesh warp covers an image with an adjustable mesh whose intersections can be dragged to alter the appearance of the image.

Perspective allows you to distort an image by dragging on corner control points.

Retouching Images

The last of the features designed for use on existing images allows you to correct any imperfections and enhance their overall appearance. The majority of the tools that are used to retouch images combine colors by tinting, blending, smearing, and smudging. These tools are all located in the Smear tool group (second tool from the bottom of the toolbox). Additional tools that are commonly used are those in the Local Undo group and the Eyedropper. In the following example, you will retouch the apple that you isolated earlier.

Introducing CorelPHOTO-PAINT

1. Close the APPLE.PCX image and open APPLEOBJ.CPT to display the apple you earlier separated from its attached leaf. Your image should look something like this:

   As you probably already noticed when you removed the leaf, the leaf's stem was abruptly cut off. Let's see what you can do to enhance the image.

2. Double-click on the Paint Brush tool to open its Tool Settings roll-up. Set the brush size to 4 to allow for more detailed use.

3. Select Zoom from the View menu and choose 200% from the submenu. You can experiment with other magnifications to see which one you are most comfortable working with.

4. From the Local Undo group click on the Erase tool in the middle of the flyout. Carefully drag the pointer, in the shape of a small rectangle, over the portion of the leaf's stem that extends beyond the apple. Do not be too concerned if you erase a piece of the apple. You can undo the action now or retouch it later.

   You might want to select Checkpoint from the Edit menu to save your work to this point. This will allow you to try a few different retouch techniques and safely return to the image with the stem removed.

5. Click on the Eyedropper tool and click the eyedropper-shaped mouse pointer in the red color next to the leaf's stem. This picks up the local color so you can use it to disguise the dark color of the stem. Check the paint color in the status bar (the leftmost color) to make sure you picked up the color you want to use.

6. Click on the Paint Brush tool and drag the mouse pointer across the leaf stem in the area where you picked up the red color. Continue covering the leaf's stem with red, moving toward the apple's stem. Depending on how well you want to exactly match the adjacent coloring, you might

want to pick up the lighter shades near the apple's stem and use them to disguise the leaf stem.

7. At this point you have a much better looking apple. You can accomplish similar results by using the Smear, Blending, Smudging, and Tinting tools. Choose Restore to Checkpoint from the Edit menu to try some of these other techniques. You can also work on the base of the apple's stem to provide a more uniform shading. When you are through, your image could look something like Figure 20-10.

8. If you are connected to a printer, choose Print from the File menu and click on the Options command button. In the Layout tab, size and position the image to your liking, and then click on OK to return to the Print dialog box. Click on OK.

9. Present the printed apple to your favorite teacher!

Drawing Tools

Up to this point you have been using CorelPHOTO-PAINT to work on existing images. The second facet of CorelPHOTO-PAINT provides the ability to create your own images with an assortment of drawing tools. The Painting, Line, Fill, and Cloning tool groups include the majority of tools you will need to draw your own pictures. You are probably familiar with the basics of using these tools from CorelDRAW! and other painting

Retouched apple
Figure 20-10.

applications, like Windows' Paintbrush. There is an infinite variety of drawing possibilities that exists—too extensive to cover here—and you are encouraged to fine-tune your artistic talents by trying out the available tools as you desire and as time allows.

This introduction only touches on the numerous capabilities found in CorelPHOTO-PAINT. The program contains many more surprises. Continue to experiment with it, and you will be impressed with its capabilities.

21

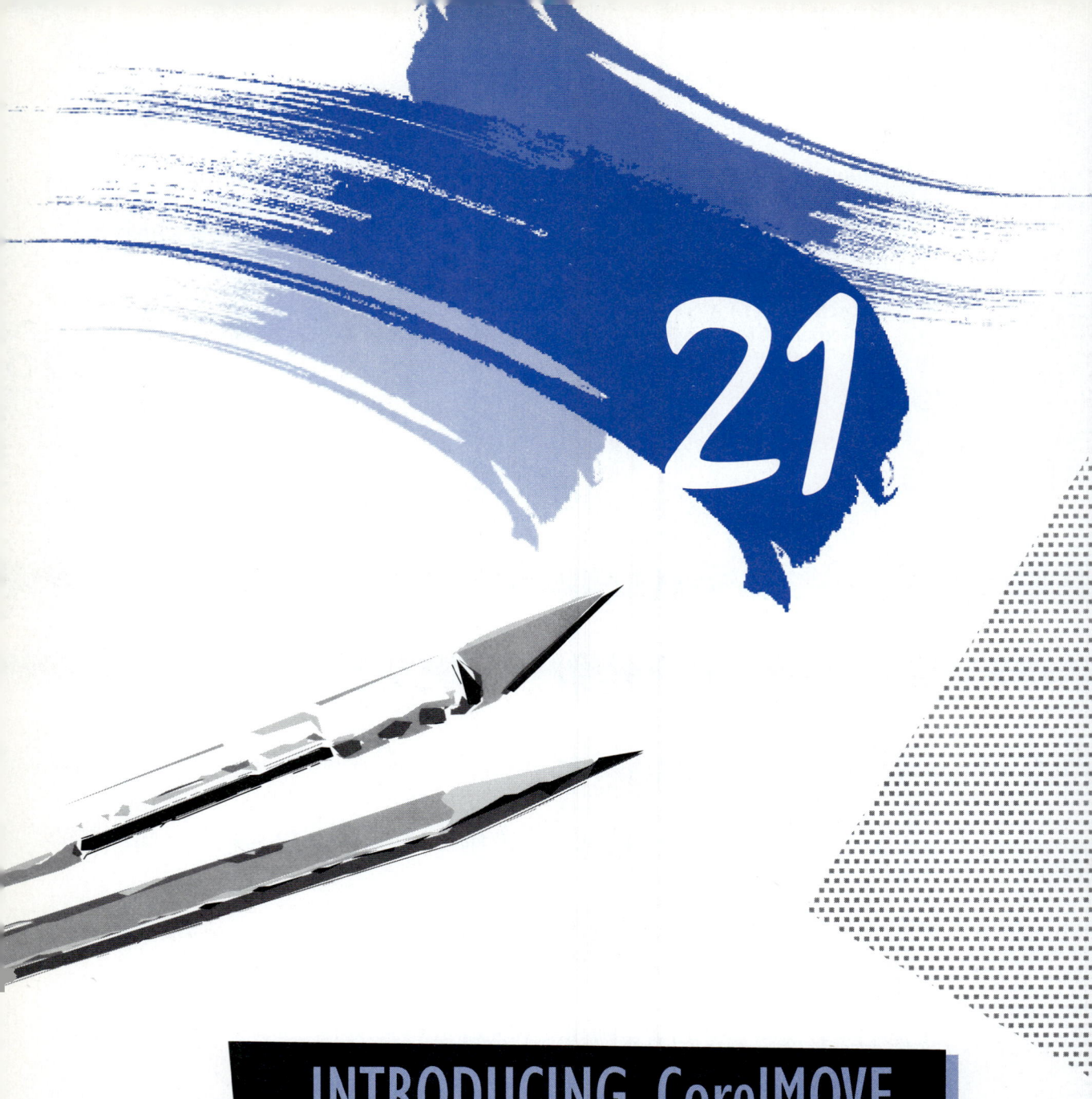

INTRODUCING CorelMOVE

CorelMOVE

is a complete multimedia animation program. With CorelMOVE, you can create simple or complex animations using graphics created in CorelDRAW!, you can record and edit sounds, and you can import graphics and sounds from other programs to use in your animations.

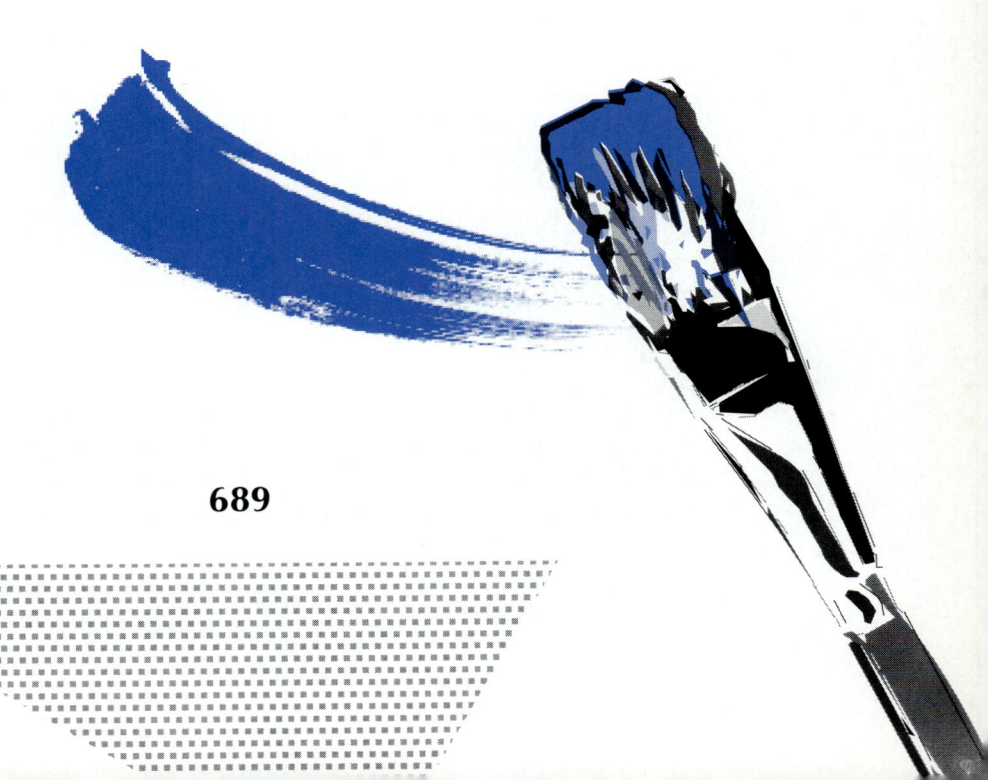

This chapter introduces CorelMOVE by briefly discussing the basics of animation, how to get started using CorelMOVE, and how to use its principal tools.

Animation Basics

Traditionally, animations are created by drawing a series of individual images, called *frames,* that are viewed in sequence. Each frame contains a number of cels of different objects. *Cels* are the individual images that make up an animated object. For example, to animate a walking figure, each frame would contain a cel of the figure with its legs and body in a slightly different position. First one leg would move to the front, then the other. The arms would be drawn in a similar manner. A series of ten cels might be needed to show a complete cycle of movement. To create a longer animated sequence, these same ten cels would be shown over and over again. For example, an animation 100 frames long would have the same ten cels of the figure repeated ten times. Each object in the animation has its own set of cels.

Objects in an animation are either *actors* or *props*. The difference between actors and props is that props are single objects, with only one cel, not a series of cels. This means that props cannot be animated. A chair and a tree could be examples of props. If you wanted to have a tree moving in the wind, however, the tree would have to be an actor, because it would be animated. Props can be moved around in an animation, but in each frame the prop will be identical in appearance. In other words, it would not be animated.

Actors can be either *single-cel* or *multiple-cel*. The walking figure mentioned previously is an example of a multiple-cel actor. Multiple-cel actors are used when an object changes its shape or appearance in an animation. A single-cel actor is similar to a prop; both have only one cel. Single-cel actors can be combined with multiple-cel actors to conserve resources in an animation. For example, to show a ball bouncing, a single-cel actor could be used to show the ball while it's in the air. When the ball strikes the ground, a multiple-cel actor is used to show the ball compressing and then expanding as it bounces.

Both actors and props can change position in an animation. This movement is independent of the animation of the object. If the walking figure actor is placed in the same place in each successive frame of an animation, for example, the figure will appear to be walking without moving. The feeling of movement is created either by having the actor move across the screen, or by having other objects (actors or props) move in relation to the walking figure.

You control how actors and props move in an animation by defining *paths* for the objects to follow. A path has one point in each frame of the animation, and each actor or prop has its own path. When the points of a

Introducing CorelMOVE

path are close together, movement is relatively slow; when the points are farther apart, movement becomes more rapid. For example, the path for the bouncing ball would have the points of its path close together at the top and bottom of its bouncing motion, where the ball would naturally be traveling slower. In the middle of its path, where the ball is either rising or falling, the points would be farther apart, because the ball would be traveling faster.

With CorelMOVE you can control all of these animation attributes. In the following sections you will learn more about CorelMOVE's animation tools.

Getting Started with CorelMOVE

To start CorelMOVE from Windows, double-click on the CorelMOVE icon. After a few moments, the initial CorelMOVE screen will be displayed.

Only the File and Help menus are available when CorelMOVE is started. In the File menu you can either open an existing animation file or create a new file. To become familiar with the CorelMOVE menus and screen elements, open a new file.

1. Select the File menu and choose New. The Select Name For New File dialog box will be displayed.
2. Click on OK to accept the default filename, UNTITLED.CMV. The main CorelMOVE screen, shown in Figure 21-1, is displayed.

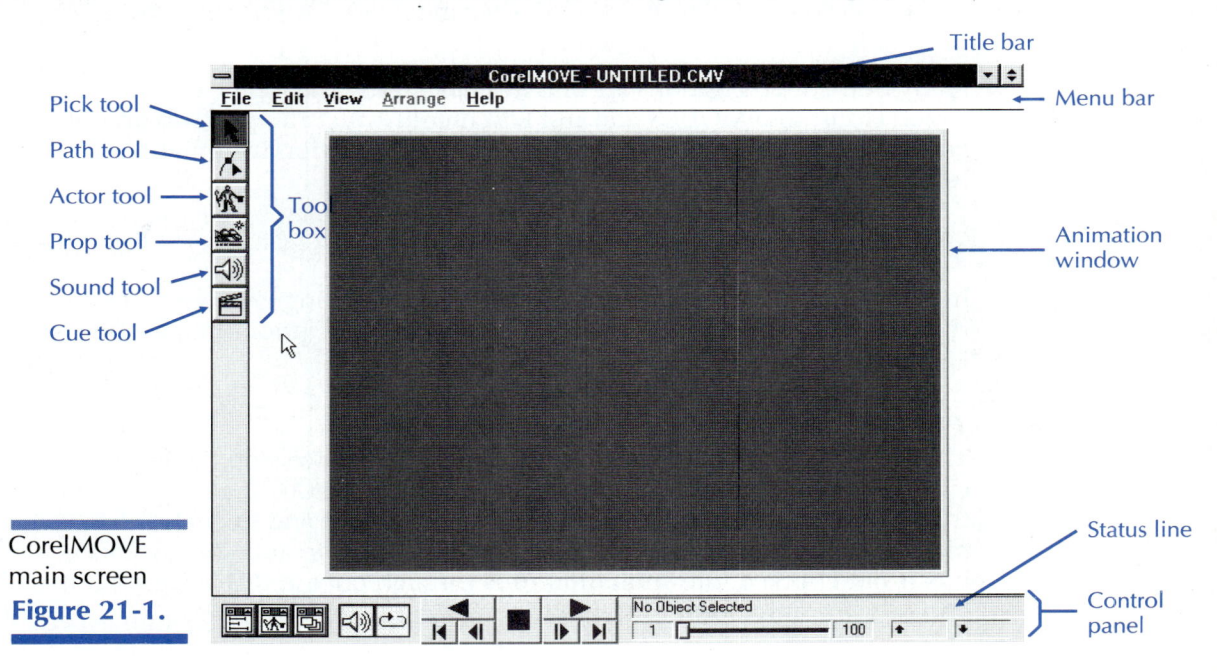

CorelMOVE main screen
Figure 21-1.

CorelMOVE Screen

In the center of the CorelMOVE screen is the Animation window. This is the work area for building and displaying your animations. Both the height and width of the window can be adjusted. The Animation window displays one frame of your animation while you are working on it. It is also where your animation is displayed when it is played. At the top of the screen is the title bar, and below that, the menu bar. To the left is the toolbox. At the bottom of the screen is the Control Panel. Each of these elements is described in the following sections.

CorelMOVE Menus

At the top of the screen, below the title bar, is the menu bar, which contains five menus. The File menu contains the options for: creating, opening, and saving files; importing and exporting files to use in your animations; displaying the Mosaic roll-up; creating a profile that matches your monitor, printer, and scanner for improved color display and printing; and setting user preferences. The Edit menu offers basic editing features, such as copy and paste, different methods for editing CorelMOVE objects, settings to change animation features, and the ability to insert actors, props, and sound files. The View menu opens the CorelMOVE roll-up menus, hides or displays screen elements, provides color correction, and allows you to play animations and also view them in single-frame mode. Like CorelDRAW! drawings, CorelMOVE animations consist of layers; the Arrange menu is used to control the layers in an animation. The Help menu contains standard help options.

Many of the menu options are also available using the toolbox and Control Panel. From CorelMOVE's File and Edit menus, you can open two unique and important dialog boxes: Preferences and Animation Information, respectively.

Preferences Dialog Box

In the File menu is the Preferences command. Selecting Preferences presents the Preferences dialog box, displaying the Playback Options tab, as shown in Figure 21-2.

Playback Options Tab

The Playback Options tab allows you to control how to stop the animation, either by a mouse button click or by pressing CTRL-BREAK. It also allows you to display or hide the toolbox, menu bar, and cursor and to enable the playing of sounds included with the animation. If the Auto Replay check box is not checked, the animation runs through once and then stops; if it is checked, the animation runs continuously.

Introducing CorelMOVE

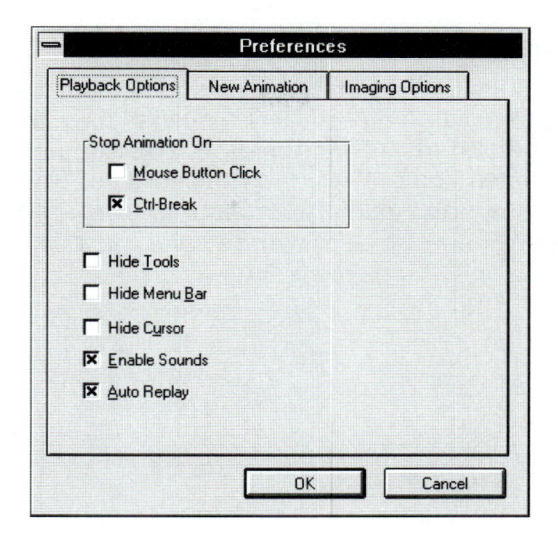

Figure 21-2.
Preferences dialog box

New Animation Tab

The New Animation tab allows you to establish the initial settings for a new animation. The width and height of the animation window can be adjusted using the Width and Height numeric entry boxes. These setting allows you to adjust the size of the animation to the intended output device, such as video tape or computer monitor. The number of frames in an animation can be set in a range of from 1 to 9999 frames. The Thumbnail Frame numeric entry box allows you to choose which frame you want to display as a thumbnail of your animation in Preview boxes. The speed of the animation can be set in a range of from 1 to 18 frames per second (fps). Grid Spacing functions much like grid spacing and Snap To Grid in CorelDRAW!, except that a list of preset values from 5 to 200 pixels is presented in a drop-down list box. The New Animation tab looks like this:

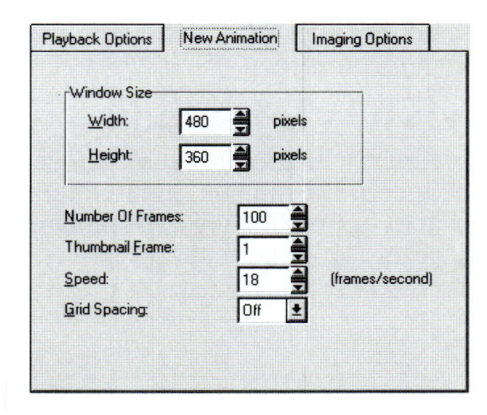

Imaging Options Tab

Defaults for imported images and animations are changed from the Imaging Options tab. You can elect to always have this tab screen appear when you import an image or animation. You can perform high quality dithering on imports. You can select White, Black, or None as the transparent color for the imported image or animation. By specifying a color tolerance, you can control how black or white a color must be before it is transparent. The Imaging Options tab is shown here:

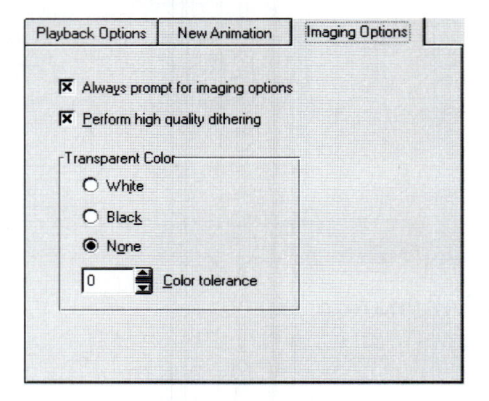

Animation Information Dialog Box

Selecting Animation Info in the Edit menu opens the Animation Information dialog box, shown in Figure 21-3. This dialog box presents information about your current animation, such as the number of actors, props, sounds, and cues used. It also allows you to adjust the same attributes that you may have set using the previously described New Animation tab. The difference between these two sets of identical attributes is that the New Animation tab sets them for all new animations, whereas the Animation Information set affects the attributes of the current animation.

CorelMOVE Toolbox

The CorelMOVE toolbox has some similarities to the CorelDRAW! toolbox. The first tool in the toolbox, the Pick tool, is used for selecting objects, like the Pick tool in CorelDRAW!. The remaining five tools are for working with specific parts of your animation.

Introducing CorelMOVE

**Animation Information dialog box
Figure 21-3.**

Path Tool

The second tool in the toolbox, the Path tool, is used to create and modify the paths that actors and props follow. This tool looks similar to the Shape tool in CorelDRAW!, but here it controls the movement of objects in your animation. When the Path tool is selected, the Path Edit roll-up is displayed, as shown here:

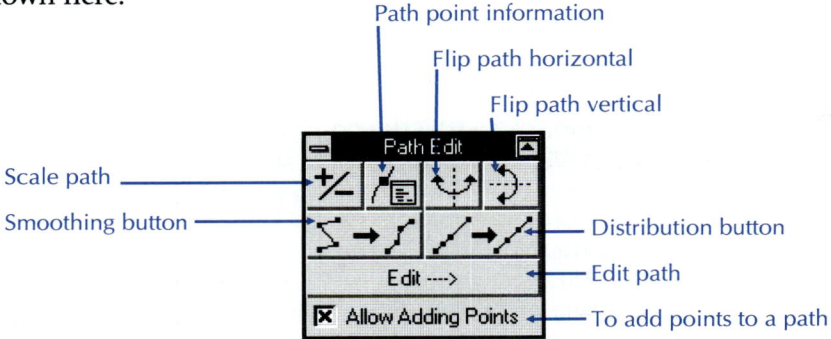

- Path point information
- Flip path horizontal
- Flip path vertical
- Scale path
- Smoothing button
- Distribution button
- Edit path
- To add points to a path

The Allow Adding Points check box is selected when you want to add points to a path using the mouse. To add a point, make sure this check box is selected, then click on the location in the path for the new point.

The Scale Path button (+/–), in the upper-left corner of the Path Edit roll-up, is also used to change the number of points in a path. The path will have the same starting and ending points, but the object's movement will be distributed over the new number of points. The more points along the path, the shorter the distance between the points and the slower the actors movement. Fewer points in the path speeds up movement. Selecting the Scale Path button opens the Scale Path dialog box, as shown here:

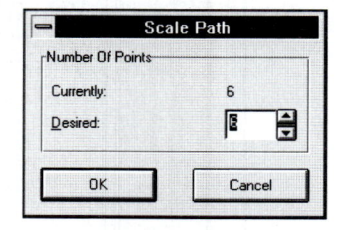

Selecting the Path Point Information button, located to the right of the Scale Path button, opens the Point Information dialog box shown here:

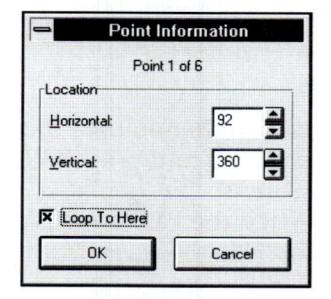

The location of a point on a path can be set by using the Horizontal and Vertical numeric entry boxes in this dialog box, or it can be set directly, using the mouse to drag the point to the desired location. When the Loop To Here check box is selected, the selected point becomes the *loop point,* and the object will move from the end point of the path to the loop point. The loop point does not have to be the start point of the path. If a point in the middle of the path is set as the loop point, the object will follow the path from the start point to the end point. It will then jump to the loop point and continue to the end point, where it will jump to the loop point again. When there is no loop point in a path, the object will move along the path once and then disappear from the animation.

The next two buttons on the Path Edit roll-up (Flip Path Horizontal and Flip Path Vertical) are used to mirror the selected path vertically and horizontally.

Introducing CorelMOVE

The Smoothing button, the left button in the second row, is used to make an angular path smoother. Repeated application to a path will make the path flatter.

Next to the Smoothing button is the Path Points Distribution button, which is used to distribute the points in a path more evenly. This has the effect of making the speed of an object's movement along the path more consistent.

The Edit command button opens the Edit Path menu shown here:

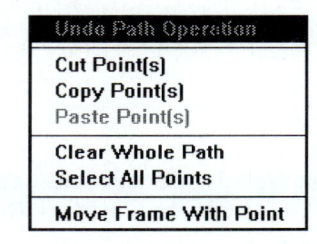

```
Undo Path Operation
Cut Point(s)
Copy Point(s)
Paste Point(s)
Clear Whole Path
Select All Points
Move Frame With Point
```

This menu contains the familiar editing commands of Undo, Cut, Copy, and Paste, which can be applied to individual points, a selected group of points, or the entire path. Copy and Paste can be used to duplicate a range of points. For example, to have a ball bounce across the screen, the path for one complete bounce would be created, then copied and pasted so that the start point of the second bounce was also the end point of the first bounce.

The Move Frame With Point command attaches the path's object to the current point. As you move the point, the object moves with it. This allows you to position your object along its path more precisely.

Actor Tool

Selecting the Actor tool, located below the Path tool, opens the New Actor dialog box, shown in Figure 21-4. When the Create New option button is selected, the Object Type list box displays the available programs you can use to create a new actor. If you select an application other than CorelMOVE, that application is opened. The object that you create in the application will then be embedded in the CorelMOVE animation file.

An existing object can be placed in your animation file by clicking on the Create from File option button in the New Actor dialog box, as shown in Figure 21-5. In this case, you would enter the path and filename in the File text box, or use the Browse command button to locate the appropriate file.

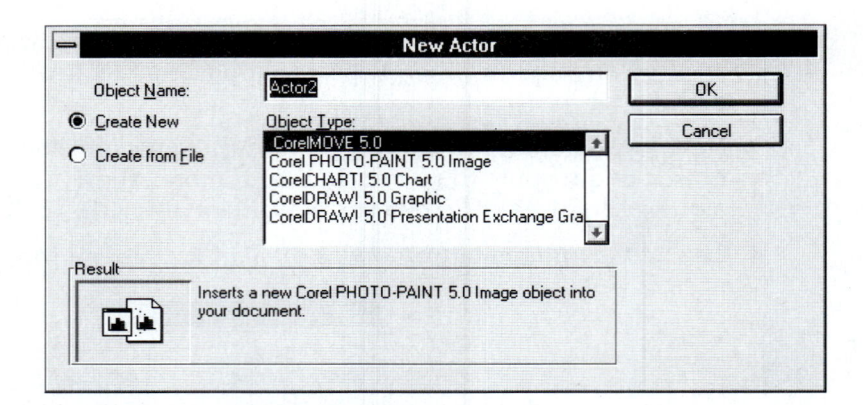

New Actor dialog box
Figure 21-4.

When Create New is selected and CorelMOVE is the selected application, clicking on OK opens the Paint toolbox and Painting window shown here:

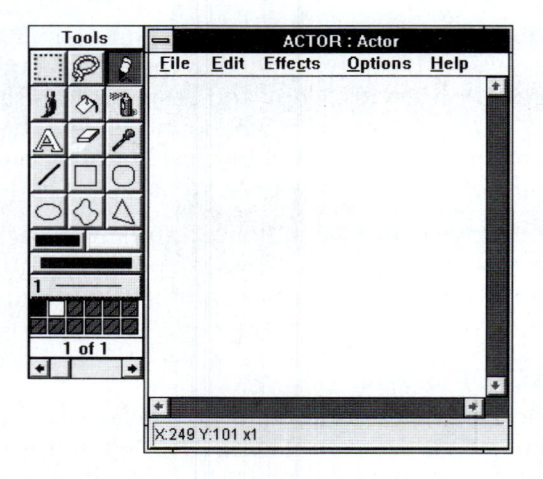

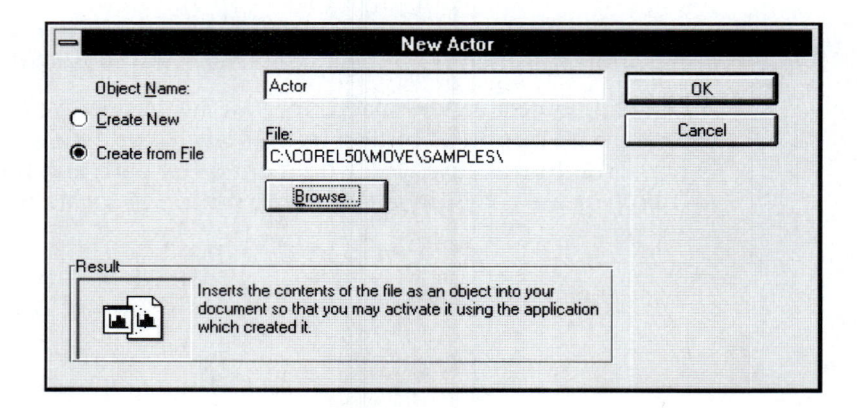

New Actor dialog box with Create from File selected
Figure 21-5.

Introducing CorelMOVE

The tools in the Paint palette are similar to the tools available in CorelPHOTO-PAINT. A brief summary of each tool follows.

Tool	Name	Function
	Marquee	Selects a rectangular section of the image
	Lasso	Selects an irregular section of the image
	Pencil	Draws freehand lines
	Brush	Draws with the current pattern and brush shape
	Paint Bucket	Fills the selected object with the current color and pattern
	Spray Can	Sprays the current color and pattern into an area, similar to an airbrush
	Text	Adds text to an object. All the fonts available with CorelDRAW! can be used with CorelMOVE
	Eraser	Removes the parts of images it is dragged over
	Color Pick-up	Changes an existing color in an image to the current color
	Line	Draws straight lines
	Rectangle	Draws rectangles with square corners
	Rounded Rectangle	Draws rectangles with rounded corners
	Oval	Draws circles and ovals
	Curve	Draws free-form shapes
	Polygon	Draws polygons with irregular sides
	Foreground Color Selector	Opens a pop-up palette for selecting the foreground color

Tool	Name	Function
	Background Color Selector	Opens a pop-up palette for selecting the background color
	Pattern Selector	Opens a pop-up palette with the available patterns
	Line Width Selector	Selects the current line width
	Recent Color Pick-up	Displays the 12 most recently selected colors
	Cel Cycle Arrows	Cycle through the cels of a multiple-cel actor. The box above the Cel Cycle Arrows displays the number of the current cel and the total number of cels

Four menus are available for working with your animations in the Painting window: File, Edit, Effects, and Options. The File menu is where you apply changes to the Actor or Prop, and where you can set horizontal and vertical cel dimensions. The Edit menu contains the familiar commands for image editing. The Edit menu also contains the Registration command, which is used to define a *registration point* for each actor. The actor will always be the set distance and direction from its registration point. It is the registration point that moves along a path. For example, if you want your animation to have two figures walking side by side, you could either create a separate path for each actor, or you could use one path and offset the registration points for each actor. The Edit menu also allows you to insert, delete, and reverse cels.

The Effects menu offers special effects that can be applied to the actor being created or edited. The commands apply special effects to all of the object's cels, or to a selected area of one cel. Morph Cel allows you to create the appearance of a metamorphosis between two cels in a multiple cel actor. This is the feature that is used, for example, to transform the picture of a person into a monkey or other animal. The Tint all cels feature blends the selected color with the current foreground or background color. Anti-Alias all cels is used to smooth the edges of objects by blending the colors along the edge of an object. Rotate all cels rotates the object either clockwise or counterclockwise in one-degree steps. Mirror all cels flips an object either horizontally or vertically. Scale all cels is used to change the size of an object.

The Options menu provides an assortment of display and special features. Zoom allows you to zoom in for detail work. Font opens a dialog box to access all the fonts available with CorelDRAW!.

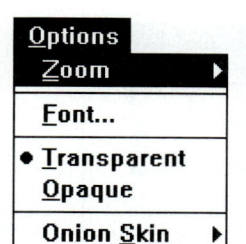

Ink effects are adjusted with the Transparent and Opaque commands. When an object is *opaque*, any object underneath it is invisible; when it is *transparent*, any object underneath it is visible.

The Onion Skin command duplicates the traditional method of creating cels for animated objects. *Onion skin* refers to a type of translucent paper animators use to draw on. Each successive cel would be placed on top of the previous cel. The animator could then make sure each cel was properly aligned with the preceding cel. Selecting the Onion Skin command shows the preceding or following cel of the actor behind the current cel. The onion skin cel will be lighter than the current cel.

Prop Tool

Selecting the Prop tool, located beneath the Actor tool, opens a dialog box identical to the New Actor dialog box, with the same options for creating objects. The title bar will contain "New Prop," however. When Create New and CorelMOVE are selected, a Paint toolbox and Painting window identical to the New Actor Paint toolbox and Painting window are displayed. The only difference between the Actor and Prop Paint toolbox is that the Prop Paint tools do not include the Cel Cycle Arrows and display, since a prop cannot have multiple cels. Also, multiple cel features are omitted from the Prop Painting window menu commands.

Sound Tool

If you have a sound board, such as a Creative Labs Sound Blaster card or Microsoft Windows Sound System, you can record, edit, and play sounds with your animations. Selecting the Sound tool opens the New Wave dialog box. You can either select an existing sound or record a new one. Sounds can be edited using the Wave Editor, which is accessed from the Edit menu and the Insert Object, Sound option.

Cue Tool

The Cue tool, located at the bottom of the toolbox, controls one of CorelMOVE's more advanced features—the ability to control the playback of an animation with external events (such as a mouse click). You could use this in a situation where the presenter wants to stop the show to make comments. The Cue Information dialog box, shown in Figure 21-6, is displayed when the Cue tool is selected. At the top of the Cue Information dialog box is the Name text box. This allows you to name a cue and then reference the cue by that name. Below the Name text box are two numeric entry boxes: Enters At Frame and Exits At Frame. The values in these boxes

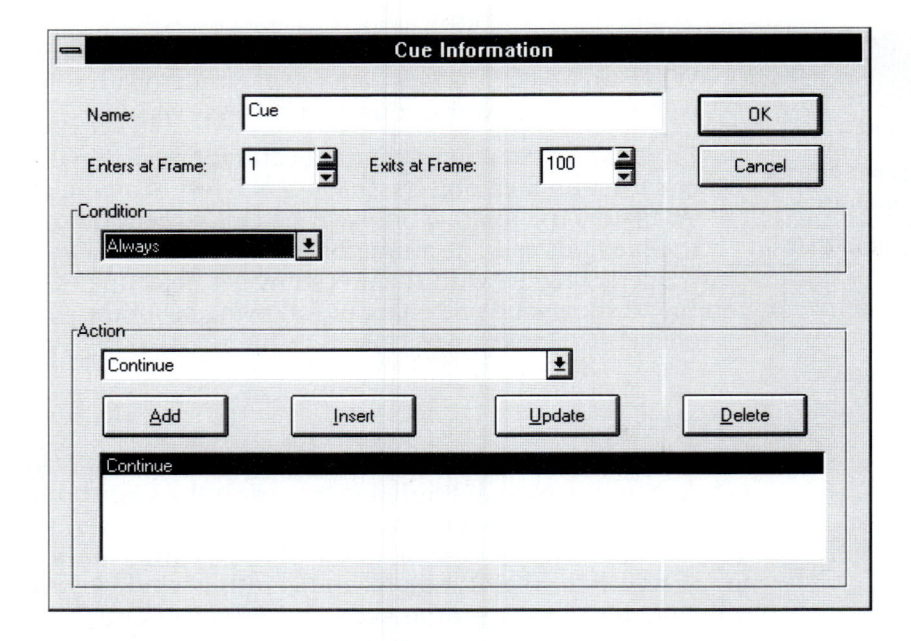

Figure 21-6.
Cue Information dialog box

determine the portion of the animation for which the cue will be in effect. This may be the entire animation, or just a part of it.

The section labeled "Condition" is used to define the event or events that trigger the action defined by the cue. The appearance of the Condition section will vary depending on the conditions selected. When you open the Condition drop-down list box, you'll see this submenu:

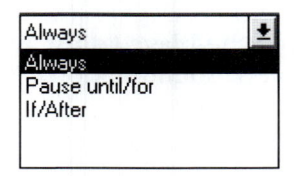

The three conditions are

- *Always*   The action is always executed without any other condition being met.
- *Pause until/for*   The animation stops and waits for a condition to occur.
- *If/After*   When the If condition is met, the After action will occur. When the If condition is not met, the After action occurs.

Introducing CorelMOVE

A second drop-drop list box is displayed if you select the Pause until/for and If/After conditions. It shows three additional options: time delay of, mouse click on, and key down.

- *time delay of*   The animation continues after a preset delay. A numeric entry box allows you to enter a time value.
- *mouse click on*   The animation waits for a mouse click. A third drop-down list box displays the options for Mouse Click:
    - *anything*   Any mouse click will meet the condition.
    - *actor*   The mouse pointer must be on the named actor when clicked.
    - *prop*   The mouse pointer must be on the named prop when clicked.
- *Key down*   The animation waits for a specific key to be pressed. A key can be selected when the Choose A Key dialog box is displayed, which takes place when key down is chosen and the button to the right is pressed

The Action section at the bottom of the Cue Information dialog box is used to establish the action that will occur when the defined condition is met. The options displayed vary depending on the conditions selected. Choices are made by clicking on an action in the Action drop-down list box, as shown here:

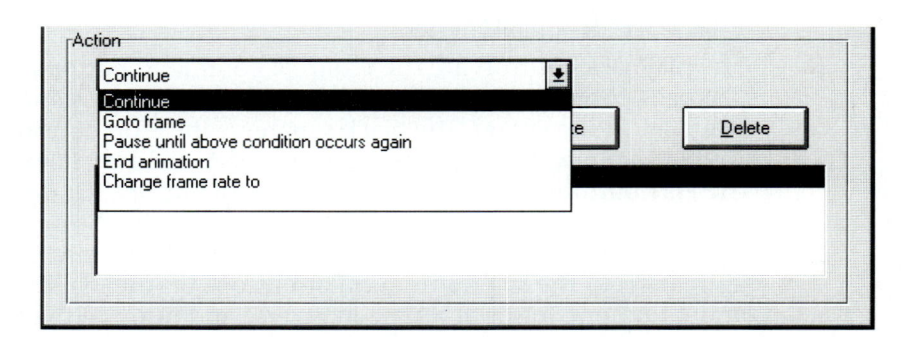

```
Action
Continue                                    ±
Continue
Goto frame
Pause until above condition occurs again          Delete
End animation
Change frame rate to
```

The drop-down menu choices are

- *Continue*   The animation continues.
- *Goto frame*   The animation continues from the selected frame.
- *Pause until above condition occurs again*   The animation stops until a condition is met.
- *End animation*   The animation ends.
- *Change frame rate to*   The playback rate of the animation is changed.

You highlight the option you want and click on the four command buttons, Add, Insert, Update, or Delete, to add or remove an action.

CorelMOVE Control Panel

Located at the bottom of the CorelMOVE screen is the Control Panel, shown in the following illustration. It provides controls for the playback of your animations and displays information about them.

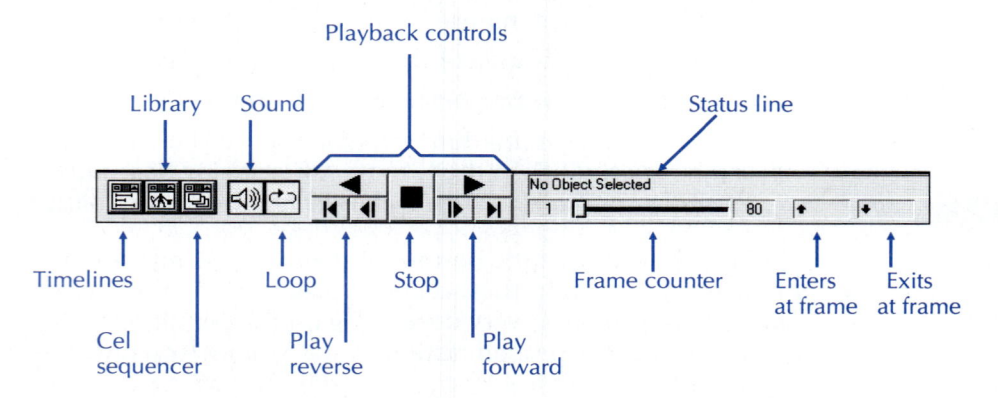

Playback controls

Library   Sound   Status line

Timelines   Loop   Stop   Frame counter   Enters at frame   Exits at frame

Cel sequencer   Play reverse   Play forward

Playback Controls

The playback controls are the group of command buttons that look like the playback controls on a VCR, and they are used in the same manner as VCR controls. In the center (the black square) is the Stop button, on the right side is the Play Forward button, and on the left is the Play Reverse button. Below the Play buttons are two additional control buttons. Under the Play Forward button are the Step Frame Forward button, which advances the animation in single-frame increments, and the Fast Forward button, which advances the animation to the last frame. Similar buttons on the left side step through the animation one frame at a time in reverse and jump to the first frame.

To the left of the playback controls are the Sound and Loop icons. The Sound icon turns the sound on or off, and the Loop icon, when selected, plays your animation continuously.

To the right of the playback controls is the status line, which displays information about the animation or selected objects. Below the status line is the frame counter. A slider is used to move through the animation. The left side of the slider displays the current frame number; the right side displays the total number of frames. Two additional display boxes are visible to the right of the frame counter. When an object is selected, the left box (with the

Introducing CorelMOVE

upward-pointing arrow) displays the number of the frame in which the selected object first appears in the animation; the other box displays the number of the last frame in which the object appears.

Icons for the Timelines, Library, and Cel Sequencer roll-ups are located on the left side of the Control Panel. You will learn about their functions after you open a sample CorelMOVE animation.

Opening a CorelMOVE Animation

If you have installed your CorelMOVE sample files, you will find a file called SAMPLE.CMV in your MOVE\SAMPLES directory. Open the SAMPLE.CMV file now with these instructions:

1. Select the File menu and choose Open. The Open dialog box will be displayed. Navigate to the MOVE\SAMPLES directory.
2. Double-click on SAMPLE.CMV to open the sample animation file. In a few moments your screen should look like Figure 21-7.

Before continuing, play the animation by clicking once on the Play button (to the right of Stop). Remember, if the Loop button is selected, the animation will play continuously. Either deselect the Loop button to stop

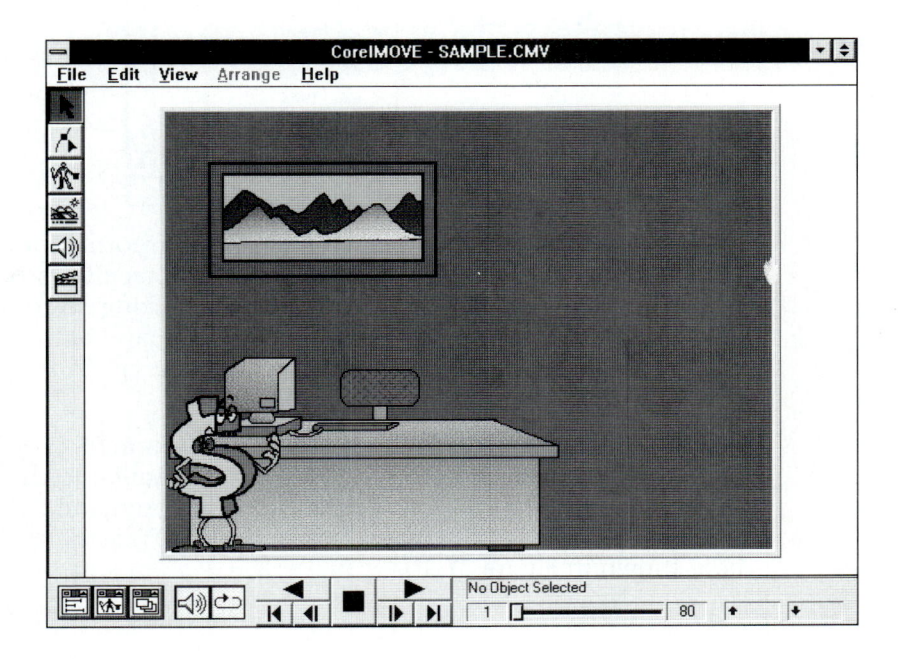

First frame of SAMPLE.CMV animation
Figure 21-7.

the animation, or click on the Stop button, and then click on the Rewind button to jump to the first frame of the animation. In the next section you will learn more about how the different elements of an animation are combined to create a finished movie.

Timelines Roll-Up

The Timelines roll-up in the View menu and shown in the following illustration, is used to edit actors and props and their actions or placement at specific times in your animations. The features of the Timelines roll-up should look familiar to you. At the top of the roll-up are the Actor, Prop, Sound, and Cue icons. These control which elements will be displayed in the list box below them. Objects with a check mark are displayed in the animation window; if you deselect an object by clicking on its check mark, it will be removed from the animation window.

When you double-click on an actor, the Actor Information dialog box, shown in Figure 21-8, is displayed. The dialog box allows you to edit when the actor enters and exits the animation, its starting position, and the path starting point. Clicking on the Edit Actor command button opens the Actor Paint toolbox and Painting window (which you saw in the "Actor Tool" section), with the selected actor displayed.

When you double-click on a prop, the Prop Information dialog box, shown in Figure 21-9, is displayed. This dialog box is similar to the Actor Information dialog box. Clicking on the Edit command button in the Transition section of the dialog box opens the Transitions for Prop dialog box, shown in Figure 21-10.

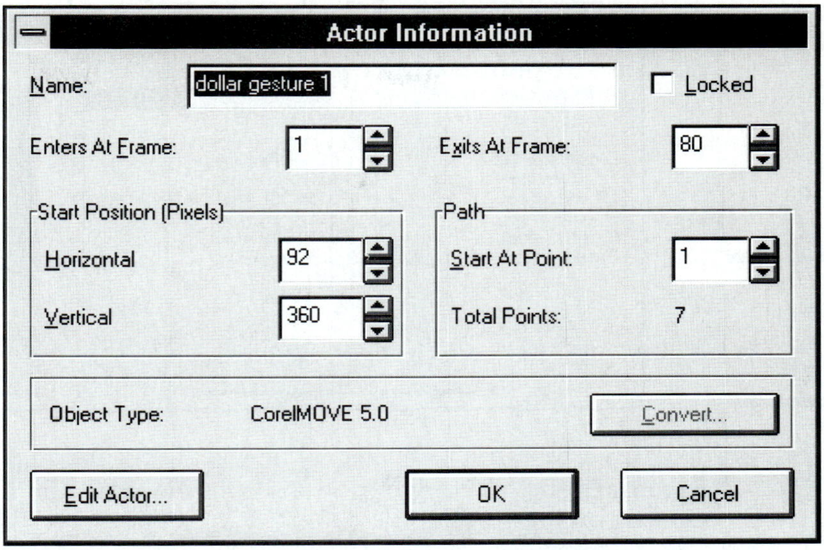

Introducing CorelMOVE

Figure 21-8.
Actor Information dialog box

The Transitions for Prop dialog box controls how props enter and exit an animation. Separate transitions are established for the prop's entry and exit.

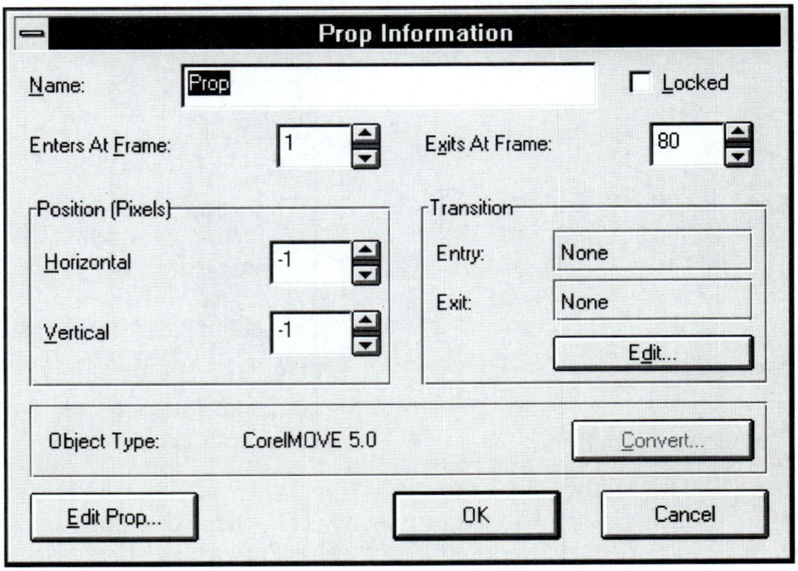

Figure 21-9.
Prop Information dialog box

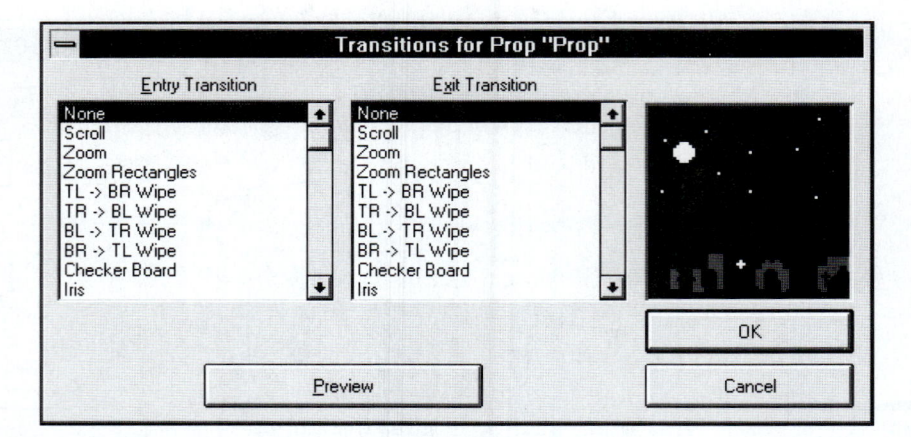

Transitions for Prop dialog box
Figure 21-10.

Experiment by selecting transitions from the Entry and Exit list boxes, and clicking on Preview.

Library Roll-Up

You can create libraries (or files) of actors, props, and sounds to use in your animations through the Library roll-up in the View menu. If no library is selected you will first see the Open Library dialog box. If you click on SAMPLE.MLB in the COREL50\MOVE\SAMPLES directory you will see the Library roll-up similar to this.

The Library flyout menu is opened by clicking on the right-pointing arrow underneath the roll-up arrow. The menu commands allow you to create a new library, open a library, or modify an existing one. Objects can be added, deleted, or renamed. The preview box displays objects in the library according to which of the three buttons at the top of the roll-up (actors, props, or sound) are selected. The slider below the preview box allows you to display the objects whose button(s) you selected. Actors and wave files are run by choosing the Play button. The Place button copies an object from the preview box to the Animation window, where you can include it in your animation.

Cel Sequencer Roll-Up

You use the Cel Sequencer roll-up in the View menu and shown in the following illustration, to control how the cels of an actor are used in your animation. You can control the order in which cels are shown, and apply effects to groups of cels.

Frame	1	2	3	4	5	6	7	8
Cel	1	2	3	4	5	6	7	8
Size%	100	100	100	100	100	100	100	100

Actor: dollar gesture 1

In the Frame row at the top of the Cel Sequencer roll-up, you select eight contiguous frames to view by using the slider at the bottom of the roll-up. The Cel row displays the cel number that corresponds to a particular frame. The right-pointing arrow at the end of the Cel row opens the Sequence Effect flyout, as shown here:

Select All
Normal Cycle
Reverse Cycle
Ping Pong
Slow Forward
Slow Reverse
Random

Before you can apply an effect, you have to select a cel sequence. Choose Select All to select all the cels in the animation, or select a sequence by clicking on the sequence's first cel and then press SHIFT and click on the last cel in the sequence. You can then choose one of the effects listed in the

Effects Sequence flyout. The Size% row and its associated flyout, shown next, work in a similar manner in scaling the size of the cel (useful for creating the impression of an actor coming toward or moving away from the viewer) and setting the cel display sequence.

```
Select All
Normal Size
Small to Large
Large to Small
Normal to Large
Large to Normal
Small to Normal
Normal to Small
Constant
First to Last
Random
```

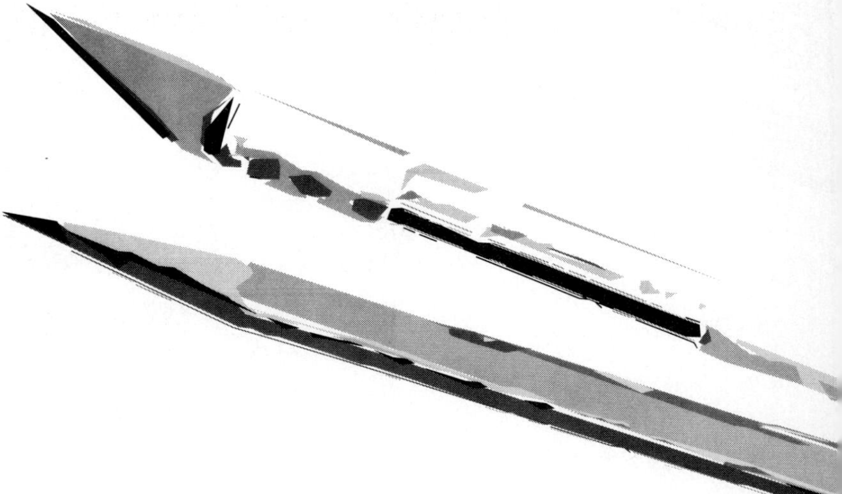

22

INTRODUCING
CorelSHOW

With CorelSHOW you can assemble drawings and graphics from other products to produce slide presentations, computer screen shows, documents (such as online brochures), or overhead transparency presentations.

This chapter introduces CorelSHOW by briefly discussing the features it offers, how you get started using it, and the principal tools.

CorelSHOW Overview

CorelSHOW lets you integrate drawings, charts, and other art for the purpose of creating a presentation. CorelSHOW has no editing or artistic tools of its own. Rather, it lets you gather art from other OLE (Object Linking and Embedding) applications, such as CorelDRAW! and CorelCHART, and then move around or resize the art until it is arranged for the presentation.

A presentation can be a computer screen show, where the slides are displayed on the computer screen one at a time, in a timed display. You can set the time that each screen will be displayed. If you want the presentation to ultimately be recorded on slides, overhead transparencies, or paper, you can first preview the show on your computer screen.

The OLE connection is a basic component of CorelSHOW. (Chapter 11 explains this feature in more detail.) If you want to import a chart created with CorelCHART, for example, you have two options for bringing it into CorelSHOW. You can paste a *linked* copy into CorelSHOW, which causes the contents of the original chart to be mirrored in CorelSHOW. To make changes to the linked copy, you open CorelCHART either directly, from within CorelSHOW, or from Windows, and then modify the original chart. Any changes are reflected in the linked copy. Alternatively, you can *embed* a copy of the chart in CorelSHOW. In this case, if changes are made to the embedded copy, the changes are again made with CorelCHART, but they are not reflected on the original chart.

CorelSHOW has some limitations: it cannot import *files* from applications that are not OLE applications. As described in the preceding paragraph, if a linked or embedded copy must be modified, this has to be done in the OLE application from which it came. CorelSHOW has no tools to modify its art. Further, if you want to assemble a document, such as a brochure, CorelSHOW has no word processing capabilities for flowing text around graphics or changing fonts. You must do this in other OLE applications and link or embed the results into CorelSHOW. If you must bring in something from a non-OLE application, cut or copy it to the Windows Clipboard from the originating application, then load or switch to CorelSHOW, and paste the item. If you need to edit this item, you must leave CorelSHOW, open the originating application, and, after editing, repeat the copy and paste procedure.

Getting Started with CorelSHOW

You load CorelSHOW from the Corel5 group in the Windows Program Manager. Follow these steps to get started:

1. Start Windows, open the Corel5 group if necessary, and then load CorelSHOW by double-clicking on the CorelSHOW icon.

When CorelSHOW has been loaded, after the initial title screen, you'll see a blank screen as displayed in Figure 22-1. You must either open an existing presentation or create a new one in order to have any tools available to you. To start a new presentation you would either select New from the File menu or click on the New presentation icon in the ribbon bar under the menu bar. At this point you will open an existing presentation, which may be found in: COREL50\SHOW\SAMPLES\SAMPLE.SHW.

2. Open an existing presentation either by using the File Open command or by clicking on the Open presentation icon.
3. Click on SAMPLE.SHW in the COREL50\SHOW\SAMPLE\ directory.

When you open the sample file, the screen shown in Figure 22-2 will be displayed.

CorelSHOW Screen Elements

At the top of the screen, beneath the title bar, is the menu bar. It contains seven menus: *File* offers various options to manage your files, presentations, and printing; You can display the CorelMOSAIC application as a roll-up or run a screen show from the File menu. *Edit* provides limited editing options, such as Cut, Copy, and Paste, plus Edit Cue, which sets the conditions for pausing and restarting a presentation. This is also where fonts, bullet styles

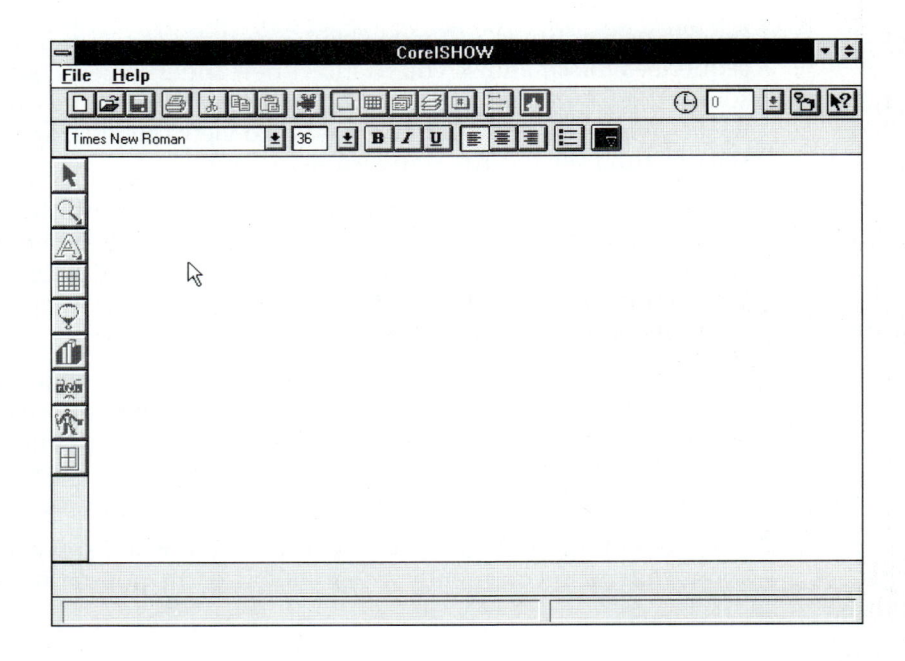

Initial CorelSHOW screen
Figure 22-1.

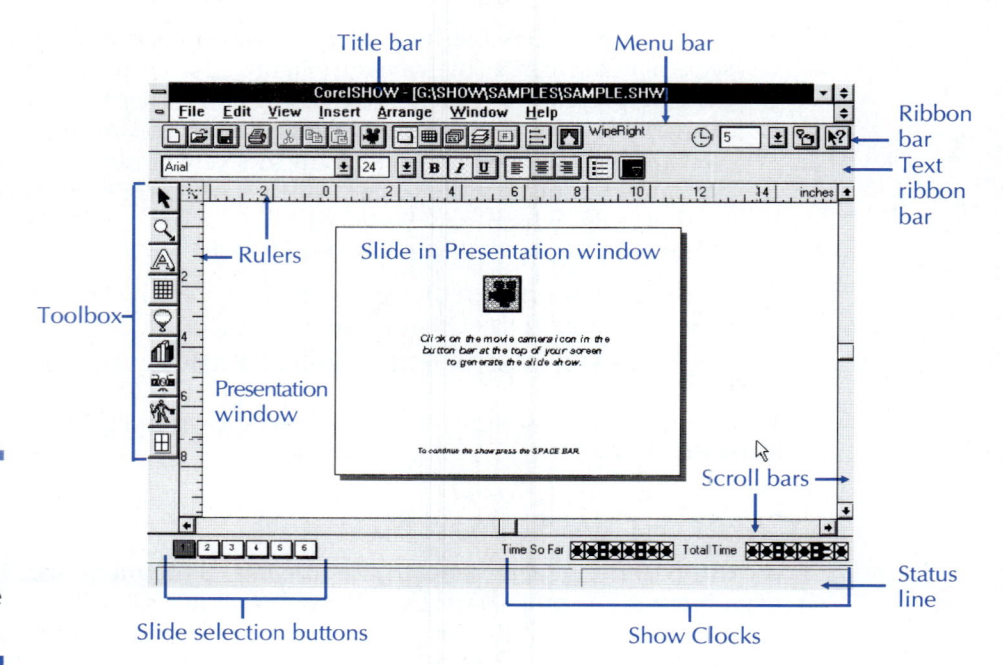

Figure 22-2. Sample from CD-ROM of Slide view, for working on an individual slide

and OLE connections can be found. *View* provides rulers, guidelines, and other display aids. You also can switch between viewing the background mode, speaker notes, individual slides or slides as a group so they can be sequenced. *Insert* allows you to insert new slides, objects, animation, and sound files. *Arrange* offers several options for rearranging objects on different levels; *Window* offers a variety of ways to view the presentations on the screen; and *Help* has the standard help options.

The toolboxes, discussed shortly, are displayed beneath the menu bar (the ribbon bar and Text ribbon bar) and along the left side of the screen (the toolbox). The presentation window is below and to the right of the toolbox. It contains the ruler guides (if specified with the View menu) and the contents of the current slide in the slide area.

The top line at the bottom of the screen contains the slide number icons on the left, which allow you to switch from one slide to another by simply clicking on the slide number you want. To the right are the Show Clock icons, which assist you in timing your presentation by displaying the Time So Far and the Total Time for previewing the presentation.

The status line, the bottom line on the screen, will display information about the menu commands when you bring the pointer to rest on them. Try

Introducing CorelSHOW

moving the pointer from one icon on the ribbon bar to another to see how this works.

CorelSHOW Modes

You can view a presentation in three modes: *background view*, which displays art elements common to all slides; *slide view*, to view an individual slide (shown in Figure 22-2); and *slide sorter view*, to display all slides. The tools in the toolbox may perform different tasks depending on the current mode. (There is a fourth mode, speaker notes, that allows you to enter and edit notes about the slide presentation.)

Now you will take a look at the toolbox and the ribbon bars.

CorelSHOW Toolbox

The toolbox, found on the left of the screen, contains various tools to help you view and create presentations:

The Pick Tool

The Pick tool, in background or slide views, is used to position, select, scale, and stretch objects. In these modes, it is also used to cut and copy to the Clipboard or to connect to the OLE application to which the object is linked. When you are in slide sorter view, the Pick tool is used to resequence slides.

Zoom Tool

The Zoom tool is exactly like the Zoom tool in CorelDRAW! and has the same subsidiary tools. You can use the Zoom tool to magnify a part of a slide to better align objects you are placing on it.

Artistic Text/Paragraph Text Tool

The Artistic/Paragraph Text tool can be switched between the two features by pressing the mouse button on the icon until the following flyout menu appears.

Click on the first icon for Artistic Text. The Artistic Text tool creates text characters without a frame that can be stretched and scaled like other objects. When this is done, the point size is changed. The Paragraph Text tool, the second icon on the flyout, creates text within a frame in which the point size is retained when the frame is stretched or scaled.

Background Library Tool

The Background Library tool displays the library of backgrounds that you can assign to a slide presentation. To insert a background from the CorelSHOW library of backgrounds, click on the Background Library icon. (Samples are found in the COREL50\SHOW\BACKGRDS directory.) If no background files are in use, a dialog box displays the background files that are available, as shown below. You then click on the file you want, and the backgrounds it contains will be displayed, as shown in Figure 22-3. If you have background files in use, a screen similar to Figure 22-3 will be displayed.

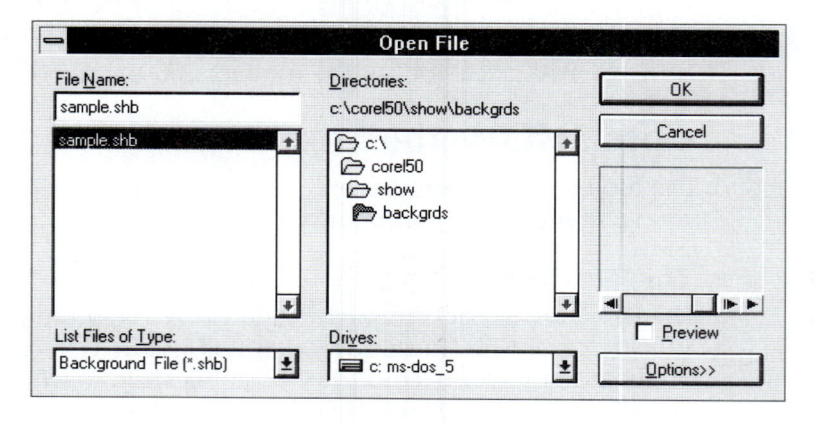

OLE Application Tools

From the slide view, you can easily integrate a drawing, chart, or other object from another application. This can be done either by clicking on the

A sample Background Library file containing a variety of backgrounds
Figure 22-3.

Introducing CorelSHOW

appropriate icon, shown in the following table, or by pulling down the Insert menu, selecting Object, and choosing the file to be inserted. Click on:

Icon	Description
	For CorelDRAW!
	For CorelCHART
	For CorelPHOTO-PAINT
	For Animation Insert Tool
	For other OLE applications

If you click on the icon for CorelDRAW! or one of the other applications, you will be placed within the selected application, but with a link that allows you to easily return to CorelSHOW. For example, clicking on the CorelDRAW! icon takes you to CorelDRAW!. There, you can import a drawing or, using Paste to copy the work being used in CorelSHOW from the Clipboard, you can modify the drawing and then copy it to the Clipboard. When you return to CorelSHOW (by choosing Exit and Return to CorelSHOW from the File menu), you can then paste the modified drawing onto the slide. The appropriate links with CorelDRAW! are automatically established to ensure that changes to the original will be reflected in the copy. Refer to Chapter 11 for more information about how to move from one OLE application to another, and back.

If you insert a file with the Object, Animation, or Sound commands from the Insert menu, you can select the file to be linked or embedded into CorelSHOW *without* switching to another application.

The Ribbon Bar

The ribbon bar contains both common and unique icons. The first seven icons (New presentation, Open presentation, Save presentation, Print presentation, Cut, Copy, and Paste) are familiar to you already. If you need to review them, you can refer to discussions of them in earlier chapters on CorelDRAW!.

The icons unique to CorelSHOW are discussed next.

Run Screen Show
The Run Screen Show icon activates a presentation and runs it on the screen. You can also choose this command from the File menu or by pressing F5. The Presentation tab in the Preferences command of the File menu contains several run-time options for a presentation.

Tip: To stop the slide show while it is in process, press ESC.

Slide View
Slide view is selected by clicking on the Slide View icon, or the Slide command in the View menu. This view displays all the attributes of a single slide, both in background and foreground. Use slide view to create or edit the foreground of an individual slide. Figure 22-2 shows this view.

Background View
You can select background view by clicking on the Background View icon or by selecting Slide Background from the View menu. Background view is used to create or modify the background of the slides. CorelSHOW has a series of backgrounds you can select from, or you can create your own in another application and then assemble it in CorelSHOW. Once you identify and insert a background, it will appear in all slides (unless the contents of a slide cover it up). In Figure 22-4 you see only a background common to all slides.

Speaker Notes View
Speaker notes view is used to display pages of notes for a slide that have been prepared as aids to the presentation. They may be used as notes for the speaker giving the presentation, or as handouts for the audience. In this view you can modify these notes.

Slide Sorter View
Slide sorter view, shown with the sample application in Figure 22-5, displays the slides in a reduced size. (You can revert quickly to slide view by double-clicking on any slide that you want to examine in detail.) With this screen, you can manipulate the collection of slides. You can drag the slides from one position to another, thereby reordering the slides within the presentation.

Introducing CorelSHOW

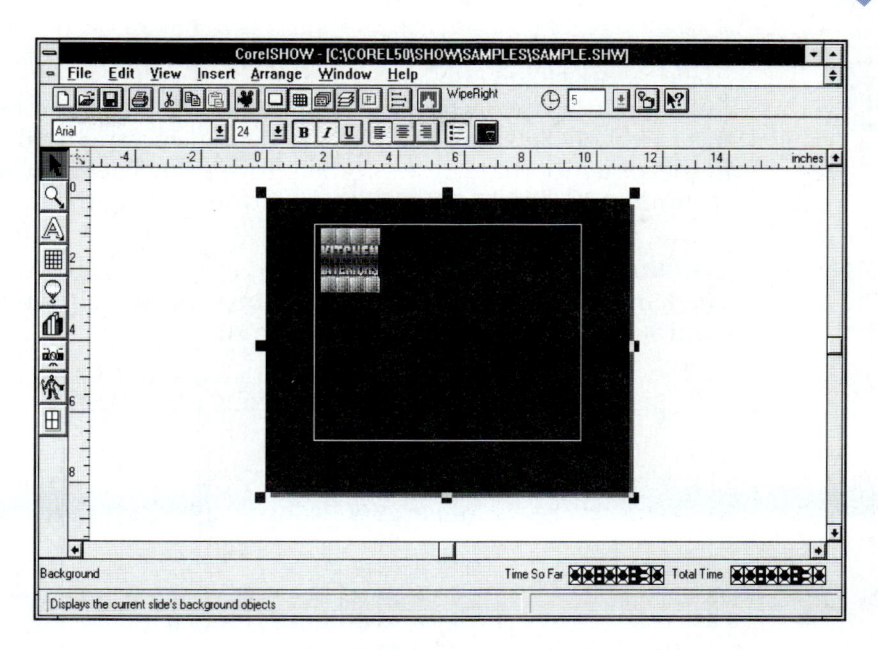

Background view of a slide
Figure 22-4.

If you have more than one presentation open at one time, you can copy, cut, and paste slides from one presentation to another using the slide sorter view. The Tile command in the Window menu displays two windows side by side, so that you can use the Copy, Cut, and Paste commands on the Edit menu to move slides between the two presentations.

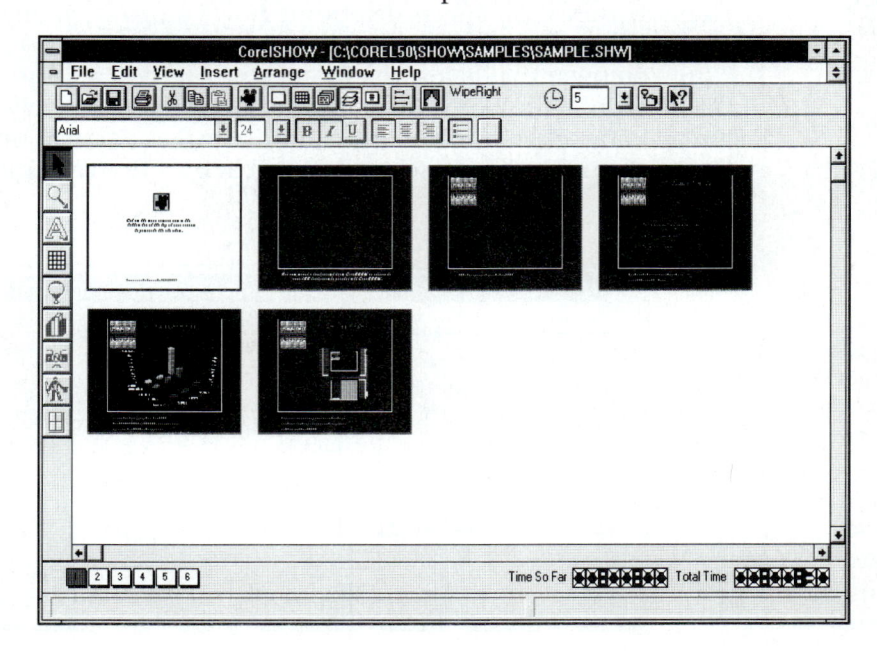

Use slide sorter view for working on slides as a group
Figure 22-5.

Slide Numbering

An alternative way to reorder the slides is to use the Numbering feature. In this case, you click on the Slide Numbering icon and then click on the slides in the sequence that you want them to appear. The slides will be renumbered in the sequence in which you click on them.

Timelines

The Timelines icon displays the Timelines window shown below. It lets you control the elements and cues for each slide.

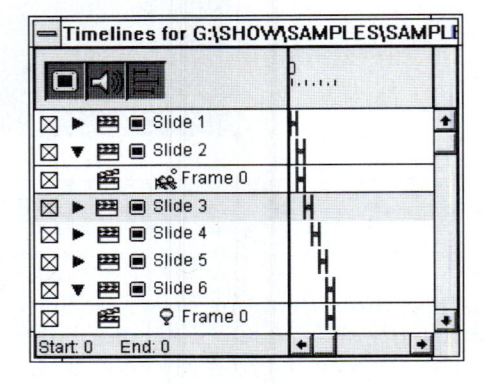

Transition Effects

The slide transition effects determine how you go from one slide to another. This is accomplished with the Transition Effects dialog box, shown in Figure 22-6. You open the dialog box by clicking on the Transition Effects icon in the horizontal toolbox. The dialog box allows you to apply special effects to the opening and closing of any slides. To assign a transition effect to a slide, first click on the slide to select it, then click on the Transition Effects icon.

Transition Effects dialog box for choosing how to go from one slide to another
Figure 22-6.

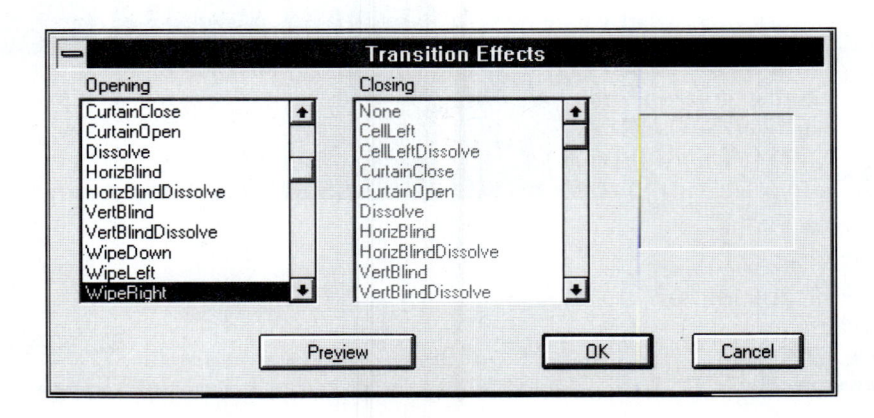

Introducing CorelSHOW

You can get a quick look at the transition by pressing the Preview button and observing the small display window on the right of the dialog box.

With these options, you can create effects such as a curtain opening to reveal a slide, or a curtain closing to mask a slide. You can zoom in to a slide, or out from a slide, quickly or slowly. Or, you can open a slide with a shutter effect, in which the shutters of a blind gradually open to reveal the slide. These are just a few tricks to make a slide presentation more interesting and animated, without having actual movement in the slides.

Time On-Screen List

The Time On-Screen List (also called the Slide/Frame Duration list box), allows you to assign the length of time each slide should be displayed. You click on the down arrow to display a drop-down list of various standard times from 1 to 240 seconds. Click on each slide, then either select a time value from the drop-down list, or enter a specific time in the entry box.

Mosaic Roll-Up

Clicking on this icon will activate the CorelMOSAIC application. This application allows you to open and peruse thumbnail views of graphic files, an example of which is displayed below.

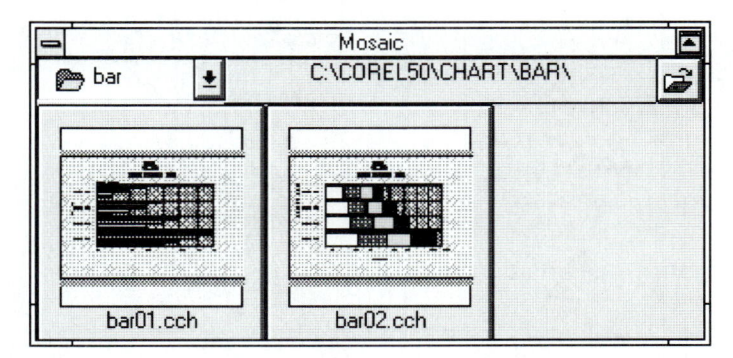

From viewing the thumbnails, you can then select or import selected graphics to insert in a presentation. To import a graphics file, you drag it from the mosaic dialog box onto the CorelSHOW screen. If you want to change the graphic before you import it, double-click on the mosaic thumbnail image and you will be transferred to the application that created the graphic.

Screen/Menu Help

Clicking on the Screen/Menu Help icon allows you to see a context-sensitive message about a specific item. You can click on anything on the screen or menu and a message will be displayed.

Text Ribbon Bar

The Text ribbon bar contains text editing tools. These are familiar to you and will just be listed here: Font, Point Size, Bold, Italics, Underline, Align left, Center, Align right, Bullets (to place a default bullet style next to text), and the Color Selection Box.

Previewing a Presentation

To preview a presentation, you can click on the Run Screen Show icon on the ribbon bar. If you want to change defaults affecting how the presentation will run, first choose the Preferences command from the File menu and make any desired changes in the Presentation tab, an example of which is shown below. You have the options of advancing to the next slide either automatically or manually, of repeatedly running the presentation until ESC is pressed, of displaying a mouse pointer on the screen, or of generating the slide show in advance, so that the presentation moves from slide to slide more smoothly. Finally, the Software Video Decompression option offers a technique of enhancing a bitmap object if necessary.

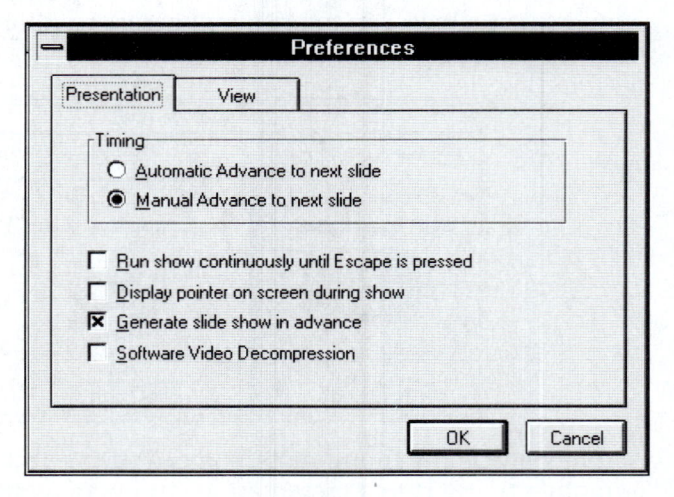

After completing the dialog box, you can click on the Run Screen Show icon or select Run Screen Show from the File menu.

Pop-up Menu

There is another tool that has not been discussed: the Pop-up Menu tool. The Pop-up Menu tool, displayed by clicking the right mouse button, allows you to click on an object in a slide and get a set of menus that relate to that object. For example, clicking on the border of a slide produces this menu:

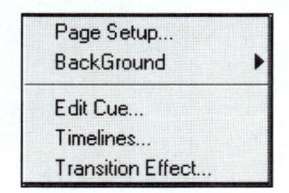

```
Page Setup...
BackGround          ▶
Edit Cue...
Timelines...
Transition Effect...
```

With these menus, you can edit or change a characteristic of the selected object. For example, click on BackGround to change the background of the current slide.

CorelSHOW Runtime Player

A limited version of CorelSHOW is available as CorelSHOW Runtime Player. CorelSHOW Player can be used for only displaying screen shows, such as for a conference or sales presentation. It allows you to display the screen show without all the CorelSHOW programs.

To transfer the CorelSHOW Player programs to a diskette so it can be transported, you will need to save your presentation as a screen show (*.SHR) and then copy it and the CORELPLR.EXE program to a diskette.

To run the CorelSHOW Player screen show, simply run the CORELPLR.EXE program, or load CorelSHOW Player by clicking on the CorelSHOW Runtime Player icon. A dialog box will be displayed for you to enter the filename or the screen show and some operating preferences.

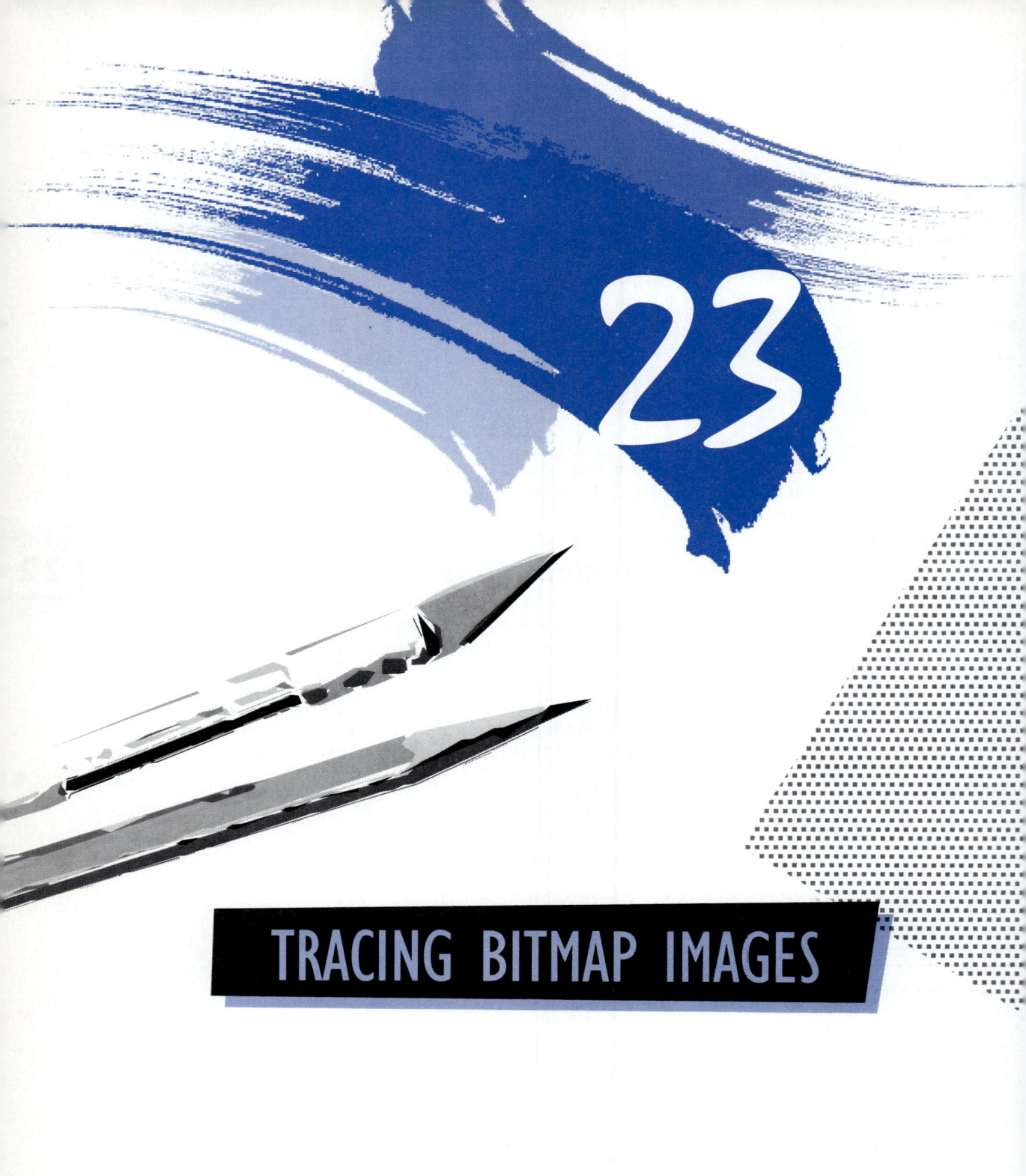

23

TRACING BITMAP IMAGES

Bitmap

images contain no objects for you to select; they consist entirely of a fixed number of tiny dots or *pixels*. If you enlarge or reduce the size of the bitmap without converting it to a CorelDRAW! object, distortion or unsightly compression of the pixels results. The solution is to trace the bitmap in CorelDRAW! or CorelTRACE and turn it into an object-oriented drawing.

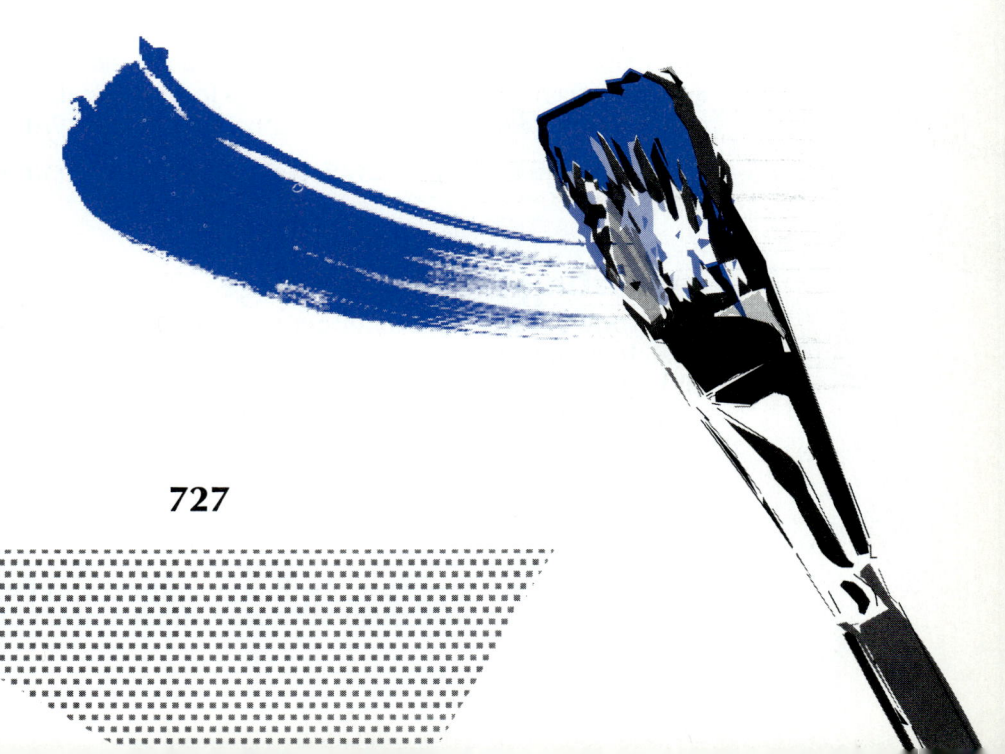

You can then change the shape of the object's outline and the color of its fill, edit it normally, and print it, all without distortion. The CorelDRAW! package offers you three different methods for tracing an imported bitmap. The most sophisticated of these is CorelTRACE, a separate program included with CorelDRAW!. You will be amazed at the speed and accuracy with which this product can turn even the most complex bitmap into a finished curve object ready for editing. CorelTRACE will be discussed later in this chapter in the section, "Tracing with CorelTRACE."

In CorelDRAW! itself you can choose between manual tracing and the semiautomatic AutoTrace feature. These methods are slower than CorelTRACE and require more work on the part of the user, but they offer you a high degree of control over the curves that result from your tracing. They are discussed in the early sections of this chapter.

Creating a Bitmap Image

CorelDRAW! treats a bitmap image as a unique object type, separate from other object types such as rectangles, ellipses, curves, and text. Unlike all of the other object types, bitmaps must be created outside of CorelDRAW!.

There are several ways to secure a bitmap image for importing into CorelDRAW!. The easiest method is to import a Photo CD image from a CD-ROM or to import a finished clip-art image or a sample file having one of the many extensions related to bitmap files (see Appendix B). The next easiest method is to scan an existing image from a print source, such as a newspaper or magazine. Alternatively, you can sketch a drawing by hand and then scan the image in PCX or TIF format. Finally, you can create your own original pixel-based images with CorelPHOTO-PAINT.

Once the bitmap image is available, you are ready to import it into CorelDRAW!.

Importing a Bitmap Image

CorelDRAW! accepts many bitmap file formats for import: TIF, BMP and PCX, to name a few. The PCX format is native to the ZSoft PC Paintbrush and Publisher's Paintbrush family of paint software and is also used in CorelPHOTO-PAINT. The TIF format is the one that most scanners support, and BMP is the Windows Paint file format. If the bitmap you want to import is in another format, you can convert it to PCX or TIF using an image conversion program, such as Inset Graphics' Hijaak or U-Lead Systems' ImagePals.

To import a bitmap, you use the Import command in the File menu and select the appropriate bitmap file format in the Import dialog box.

Tracing Bitmap Images

The standard CorelDRAW! package includes a number of bitmap files in the \CLIPART_BITMAPS\ directory on the first CD-ROM. In the following exercise, you will see how to import one of the sample bitmap files.

1. Starting with a blank CorelDRAW! screen, open the View menu and make sure that Rulers and Wireframe are turned off (not checked).
2. Select the Page Setup command from the Layout menu and make certain that the page is set for Portrait and that the page size is Letter. Click on the OK command button to save these settings. Also in the Layout menu, none of the Snap To options should be checked.
3. Select the Import command from the File menu. The Import dialog box appears.
4. Open the List Files of Type drop-down list box and select TIFF Bitmap.
5. In the Drives and Directories boxes, specify the drive and directory that contains the CorelDRAW! sample TIFF files. This is the \CLIPART_BITMAPS\ directory on the first CD-ROM.
6. To open a TIF file, double-click on the filename in the File Name list box, or highlight the filename and click on OK. After a few seconds, the image appears, centered on the page and surrounded by a selection box, as shown in Figure 23-1. The status line displays the message "Color Bitmap on Layer 1" (or "Monochrome Bitmap on Layer 1" for a black and white TIFF file) in the center.

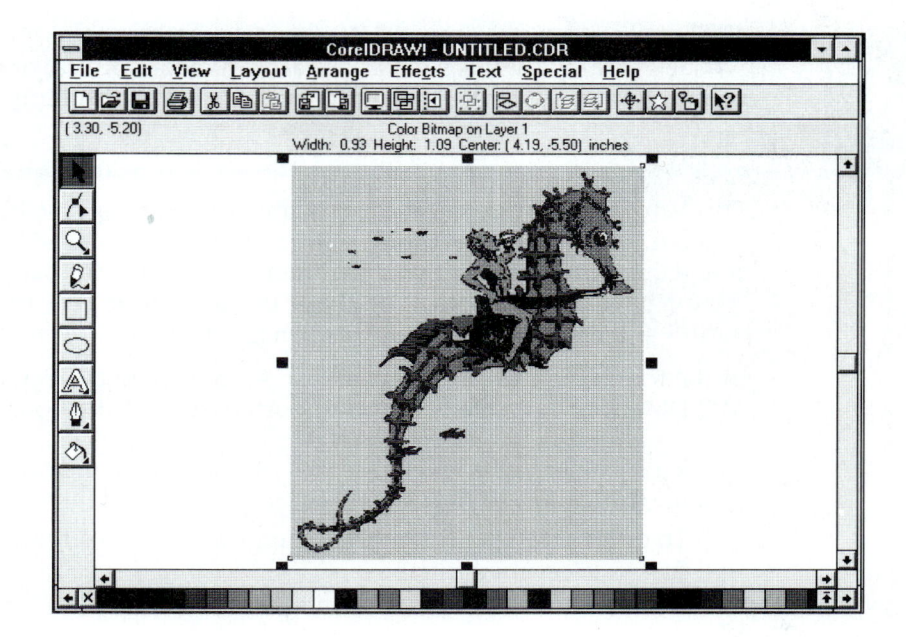

Bitmap image, imported for tracing
Figure 23-1.

> **Note:** The file used here is named SEARIDE1.TIF in the \CLIPART_BITMAPS\FANTASY\ directory on the first CD-ROM. If you do not have it available, select any other TIF file you do have, so that you can follow these steps.

7. Select the Save As command from the File menu. When the Save Drawing dialog box appears, change the directory to the one in which you save your CorelDRAW! drawings. Type a name, for example, **auttrace**, in the File Name text box, and then choose OK. You do this to prevent overwriting the original file.

AutoTracing an Imported Bitmap

As mentioned earlier, CorelDRAW! lets you turn an imported bitmap image into a resolution-independent curve object by tracing the image. You can trace a single bitmap image either semiautomatically, using the AutoTrace feature, or manually. You can also use the fully automatic CorelTRACE program described later in this chapter. Manual tracing is a good choice if you desire total control over the appearance and placement of the outline curves. If you find it cumbersome to use the mouse for tracing long paths manually, however, use the AutoTrace feature instead. You have less control over the results, but you will spend less time manipulating the mouse.

> **Tip:** Using a stylus such as one from Wacom, Kurta, or CalComp gives you more natural control over curves and hand movements.

The AutoTrace feature becomes available to you when the bitmap object is selected. AutoTrace is semiautomatic in the sense that the software draws the actual curves for you, but you must define a number of parameters before tracing begins. You control the shape of the Outline Pen, the color of the outline fill, the interior fill of the object, and the smoothness of the curves.

In the following exercise, you will use AutoTrace to trace portions of the AUTTRACE.CDR image that you imported earlier from your TIF file.

1. With the image you will use still on the screen and selected, adjust magnification to fit-in-window view.

   To establish the Outline Pen settings for the traced object, you must first deselect the bitmap.

Tracing Bitmap Images

2. Deselect the object and click on the Outline Pen tool and then on the hairline icon in the first row of the flyout menu. This will result in hairline curves of a very fine width. Click on OK in the Outline Pen dialog box to apply this default to all graphic objects.

3. With the object still deselected, click on the Fill tool and on the X (the no fill icon). Again, accept this as the default for all graphic objects.

4. Reselect the bitmap and crop it so that only the portion you are tracing is visible. You do this by activating the Shape tool and positioning it over the middle boundary marker of each edge in turn. When the pointer changes to a crosshair, drag the edges inward until the object is the size you want. The status line shows the percentage that has been cropped from each side, as shown in Figure 23-2.

5. Choose the Preferences command from the Special menu and then click on the Curves tab. In the Preferences-Curves dialog box, adjust the settings as follows: AutoTrace Tracking, 5 pixels; Corner Threshold, 8 pixels; Straight Line Threshold, 3 pixels; AutoJoin, 10 pixels; and leave Freehand Tracking and Auto-Reduce at their current settings. These settings will result in smoother curves, smooth (rather than cusp) nodes, curves rather than straight line segments, and curve segments that snap together when they are as far as 10 pixels apart, as shown in Table 23-1. Click on OK to make these settings take effect.

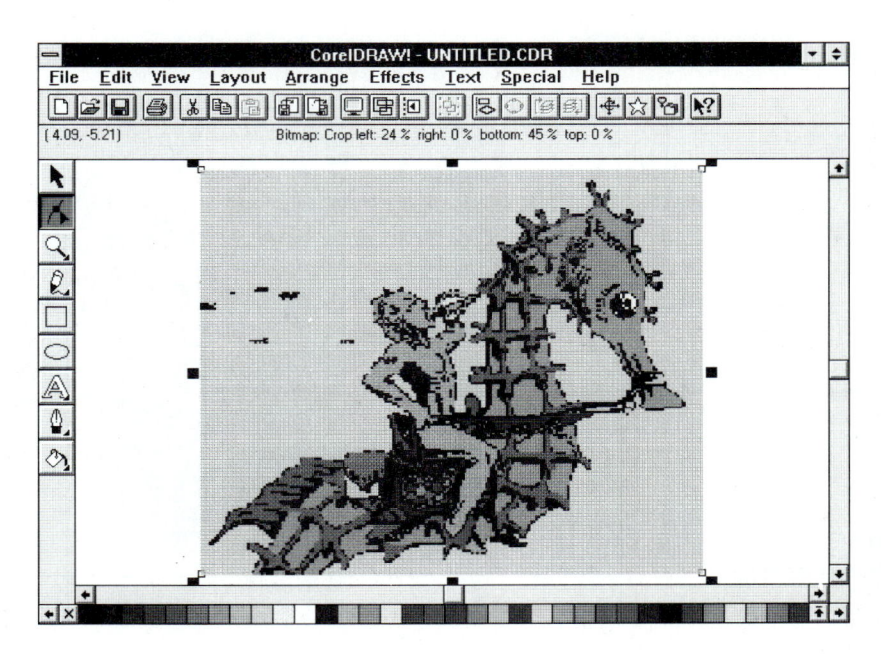

AutoTrace does not give you the same degree of control available with manual tracing.

Cropped bitmap
Figure 23-2.

6. Turn on Preview Selected Only in the View menu. Select the Zoom-In tool and magnify only the portion of your bitmap object that you want to start tracing. The editing window should show your figure, similar to Figure 23-2.

7. Now you are ready to begin AutoTracing. Make sure that the bitmap is still selected and then select the Freehand tool. Notice that the pointer looks different (as shown on the left): instead of being a perfectly symmetrical crosshair, it has a wand-like extension on the right. This is the AutoTrace pointer. It appears only when you activate the Pencil tool with a bitmap object selected. The phrase "AutoTrace on Layer 1" appears on the status line, indicating that you are now in AutoTrace mode.

8. Position the wand of the AutoTrace pointer to the left of an area that you want to trace and then click once. After a moment, a closed curve object appears, completely enclosing the contours of the area that you clicked on, as shown in Figure 23-3. Press F9 while the curve is still selected, and you see the traced line similar to Figure 23-4.

9. Position the AutoTrace pointer along the remaining closed portions of your bitmap object and click on each of them. Another closed curve appears each time you click.

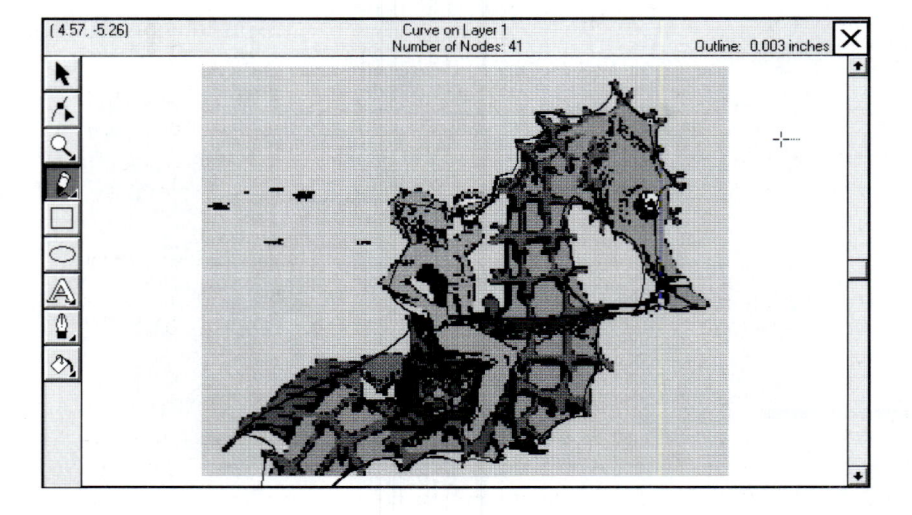

AutoTracing a closed curve—editing screen
Figure 23-3.

Tracing Bitmap Images

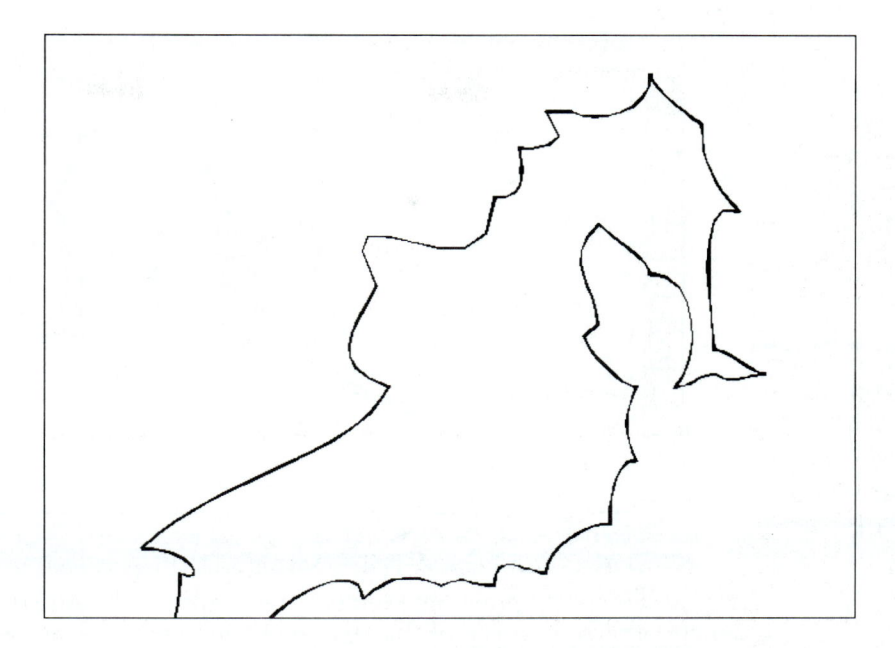

AutoTraced closed curve—preview screen
Figure 23-4.

10. Select the Zoom-In tool and zoom in on a part of your bitmap that has many small details. Position the intersection point of the AutoTrace pointer inside one of the closed regions and click. A closed curve object quickly appears.
11. Create more detailing curves in the same way and then move around the bitmap, tracing the objects you see.
12. Press SHIFT-F4 to show the full page. Select the Pick tool and click on the bitmap somewhere other than where you were tracing. Press DEL to remove the bitmap and see your handiwork. AutoTrace produces a rough approximation of your bitmap object, as you can see in Figure 23-5.
13. Save your changes to the image by pressing CTRL-S.
14. Select New from the File menu to clear the screen.

Tip: If you have trouble selecting a region that results in the curve you need, try pointing at the desired region using the tip of the wand on the AutoTrace pointer instead of its center point. You will find that you can aim the wand more accurately when you are working in a magnified view.

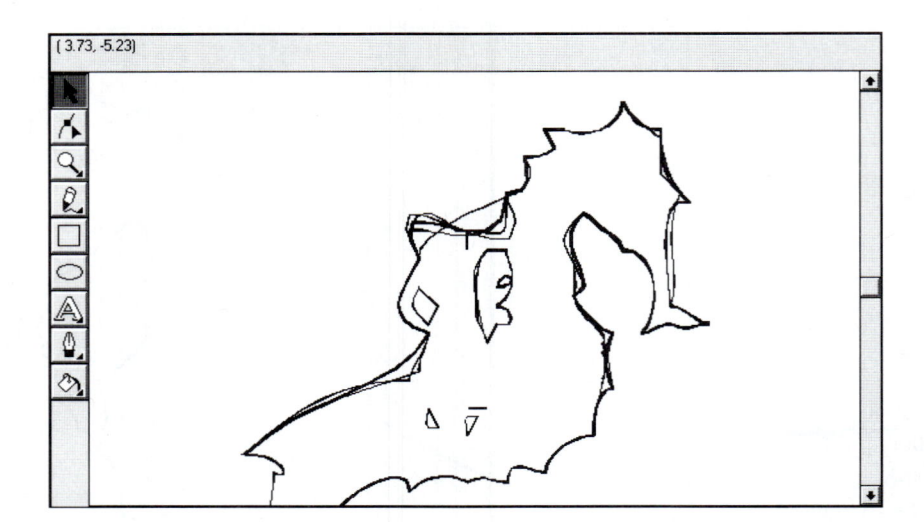

Result of AutoTracing part of a bitmap
Figure 23-5.

As you saw in the previous exercise, the results of the AutoTrace feature depend on your choice of the area to outline and on exactly how you position the AutoTrace pointer. Even if you use AutoTrace to trace the same area twice, CorelDRAW! may change the number and positions of the nodes each time. The path that an AutoTrace curve takes can sometimes seem to be quite unpredictable, especially if there are not clear separations between light and dark areas or between areas of different color. With practice, you will gain skill in positioning the AutoTrace pointer for the best possible results.

Tracing Manually

You don't have to be a superb drafter to trace a bitmap with precision in CorelDRAW!. By magnifying the areas you trace and adjusting the Lines and Curves settings in the Preferences dialog box, you can trace swiftly and still achieve accurate results. To trace a bitmap manually, you deselect the bitmap just before you activate the Pencil tool. This action prevents the Pencil tool from becoming the AutoTrace pointer.

Manual tracing is faster and easier than AutoTracing if the imported bitmap contains multiple subjects with no abrupt changes in brightness levels or colors from one pixel to the next. Most commercial clip-art fits this description. Using the manual method avoids the problem of AutoTrace curves that extend beyond the subject with which you are working. As a result, you usually need to do less editing after your initial manual tracing than after using AutoTrace.

Tracing Bitmap Images

Table 23-1. Guidelines for Setting Options in the Preferences-Curves Dialog Box

Option	Determines	Settings Low no. (1-3)	Settings High no. (7-10)
Freehand Tracking	How closely Corel follows your freehand drawing	Many nodes	Few nodes
AutoTrace Tracking	How closely the AutoTrace pointer follows bitmap edges	Rough curve	Smooth curve
Corner Threshold	Whether a node is cusped or smooth	Cusp nodes	Smooth nodes
Straight Line Threshold	Whether a segment should be a curve or a straight line	More curves	More lines
AutoJoin	How close together two line or curve segments must be in order to join	Less joining	More joining
Auto-Reduce	How many nodes are removed by Auto-Reduce in the Node Edit roll-up	Fewer nodes	More nodes

Just as when you use the AutoTrace feature, you can define the default shape of the Outline Pen, Outline Color, the interior fill of the object, and the smoothness of the curves before you begin tracing. In the following exercise, you can manually trace portions of your TIF file.

1. Once again, import a TIF file as you did earlier. You can use the SEARIDE.TIF used earlier in this chapter, or you may use a different image.
2. When the bitmap object appears, adjust magnification to fit-in-window. Also, make sure Snap To Grid, Rulers, and Wireframe are turned off, and Preview Selected Only is turned on.
3. Deselect the object and click on the Outline Pen tool and then on the hairline icon in the first row of the flyout menu. This will produce hairline curves of a very fine width. Accept this setting as the default for all graphic objects.
4. Click on the Fill tool and again on the X icon to change the object fill color to none. This prevents any closed paths that you trace from filling with an opaque color and obscuring other traced areas that lie beneath. (You can edit the fill colors of individual objects later.) Again, accept this as the default and then reselect the object.
5. Reselect the bitmap with the Shape tool and then crop the bitmap so that only the part of the picture you want to trace is visible. Start this by

positioning the pointer directly over a corner boundary marker of a corner you want to remove. When the pointer changes to a crosshair, depress and hold the mouse button and drag this corner diagonally. Release the mouse button when the area you want is in the box, as in Figure 23-6. You might also want to drag the center boundary markers inward to get the final shape that you need.

6. Select the Preferences command from the Special menu and click on the Curves tab. Adjust the settings as follows: Freehand Tracking, 1 pixel; Corner Threshold, 10 pixels; Straight Line Threshold, 1 pixel; AutoJoin, 10 pixels; and leave AutoTrace and Auto-Reduce as they are. These settings will result in curves that closely follow the movements of your mouse. You will generate smooth (rather than cusp) nodes, curves rather than straight line segments, and curve segments that snap together when they are as far as 10 pixels apart. These settings promote ease of editing should you need to smooth out the traced curves later. Click on OK to save these settings.

7. Click on Fit-in-Window view so that the cropped bitmap fills the drawing area.

8. Deselect the bitmap object and activate the Pencil tool. (If you see the AutoTrace pointer instead of the regular Pencil pointer, you haven't deselected the bitmap.) Position the Pencil tool anywhere along the outline of a closed area, then depress and hold the mouse button, trace all the way around, and end the curve at the starting point. Should you make any errors, you can erase portions of the curve by pressing the SHIFT key as you drag the mouse backward.

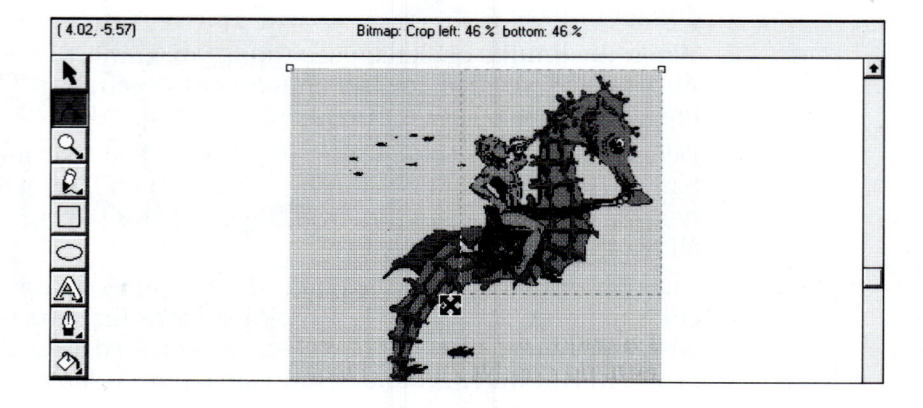

Cropping a bitmap in preparation for manual tracing
Figure 23-6.

Tracing Bitmap Images

Tip: For even smoother curves, trace in a series of small joined segments, placing a node every time the angle of the curve changes. This "connect-the-dots" approach avoids the jaggedness that can occur when you try to trace large areas with a single sweep of the mouse.

9. Zoom in and trace more of the picture with the Pencil tool. You can trace the outline of small details in the bitmap as open curves and use AutoTrace as well as manual, all in the same picture.

10. In order to do some AutoTracing in your bitmap, activate the Pick tool and select the entire bitmap object. Remember that unless the bitmap is selected, you cannot enter AutoTrace mode.

11. Activate the Pencil tool again with the bitmap selected. Position the AutoTrace pointer inside one of the small detail areas of your bitmap and click to trace a curve around this tiny area automatically.

12. Using AutoTrace, trace a few more small details of your picture. When you have finished, your screen should look roughly similar to the way it looked in the previous section, "AutoTracing an Imported Bitmap." Save the image at this point under the filename, MANTRACE.

13. Select the Pick tool and click on the bitmap somewhere other than where you were tracing. Press DEL to remove the bitmap and see your handiwork. Your screen should show the curve objects, as you see in Figure 23-7.

14. Save your changes by pressing CTRL-S, and then select New from the File menu to clear the screen.

As you have just seen, it is possible and sometimes even preferable to combine both the manual and AutoTrace methods when tracing complex bitmap images. Manual tracing is best for obtaining exact control over the placement of curves in bitmaps that contain several subjects close together, as is the case with most clip-art. The AutoTrace method is useful for tracing small closed regions, like the details of the bitmap in the previous exercises. The AutoTrace method is also more convenient to use when the bitmap image has a single, clearly defined subject with sharp contours and/or clear delineation between light and dark areas and between colors.

Whether you use the AutoTrace feature, manual tracing, or a combination of both methods, you can always edit the curve objects you create.

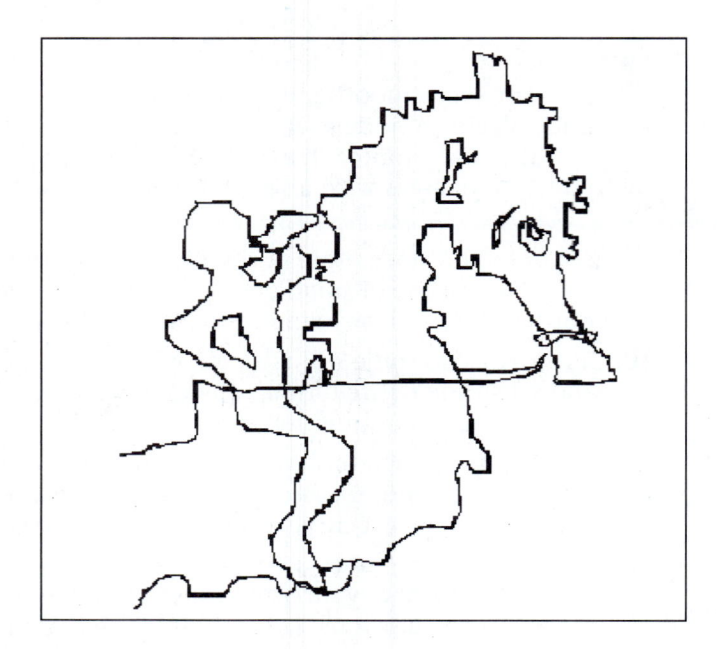

Combining
AutoTracing
with manual
tracing
Figure 23-7.

Tracing with CorelTRACE

A third method of tracing bitmap images is available to you—one that is more rapid, sophisticated, and efficient than either the manual or the AutoTrace method. The CorelTRACE batch tracing utility allows you to trace one or more bitmaps automatically at high speeds and save them in the Adobe EPS format. You can choose from two default methods of tracing, or you can customize tracing parameters to suit your needs. When you are finished tracing files, you can edit the resulting object-oriented images in any drawing program that can read the Adobe EPS file format, including CorelDRAW!.

CorelDRAW! comes with sample files with which you can practice changing the tracing parameters.

The following sections provide instructions for preparing to use CorelTRACE, for selecting and tracing bitmaps, and for customizing and editing tracing parameters.

Preparing to Use CorelTRACE

CorelTRACE is installed in the same directory and Windows group where you installed CorelDRAW!. Before you begin using CorelTRACE for the first time, check the amount of free space available on your hard drive. When you trace bitmaps using CorelTRACE, temporary files are generated on your hard drive. If you trace large bitmaps, or more than one bitmap during a session, you are almost certain to require several megabytes of hard drive space for these temporary files. You should have at least 5MB of space free, and 10MB is recommended.

If your selected hard drive does not have enough space available, you can either remove unnecessary files or specify a different hard drive, if you have one, as the drive where CorelTRACE can place the large temporary files it generates. For example, if CorelDRAW! and CorelTRACE are installed in drive C and you wish to locate temporary files in the TRASH directory of drive D, you would first open your AUTOEXEC.BAT file in a text editor. Then either add the following line, or edit any existing "set temp=" line to match the following:

```
"set temp=d:\trash"
```

This statement tells Windows always to place temporary files in the specified drive and directory. Be sure to reboot after you edit the AUTOEXEC.BAT file in order to make your changes take effect. Also be sure that the directory you named exists on the specified hard drive.

Caution: Never select the Windows directory as the directory in which to store the temporary files that Windows applications generate. Errors could result that might cause your system to crash unexpectedly.

Loading CorelTRACE

Unless you have over 4MB of memory, do not run any other Windows applications in the background while you are running CorelTRACE. This means that you should exit CorelDRAW! while running CorelTRACE; not just switch out of it. CorelTRACE requires a large amount of memory to work efficiently. If you run other applications concurrently, CorelTRACE may not run or may function very slowly.

To load CorelTRACE, double-click on the CorelTRACE icon in the Corel5 group window. The opening screen appears and is then replaced by the main window, shown in Figure 27-8.

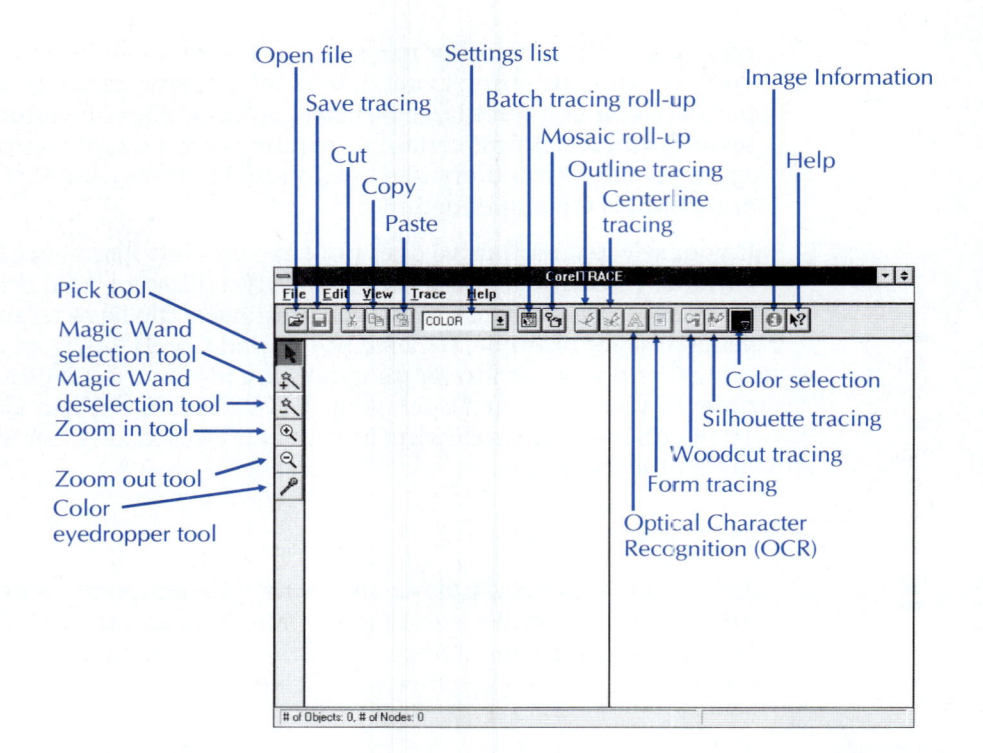

Figure 23-8.
CorelTRACE window upon opening

Labels in figure:
- Pick tool
- Magic Wand selection tool
- Magic Wand deselection tool
- Zoom in tool
- Zoom out tool
- Color eyedropper tool
- Open file
- Save tracing
- Cut
- Copy
- Paste
- Settings list
- Batch tracing roll-up
- Mosaic roll-up
- Outline tracing
- Centerline tracing
- Image Information
- Help
- Color selection
- Silhouette tracing
- Woodcut tracing
- Form tracing
- Optical Character Recognition (OCR)

The CorelTRACE window is split into two halves, with the original image to be traced on the left and the traced image on the right. (When you open CorelTRACE, both windows are blank. Upon loading an image to be traced, it is placed in the left window and when you complete the tracing you will see it on the right, as shown in Figure 23-9.) Like most other CorelDRAW! applications, CorelTRACE has a ribbon bar across the top of the window, a toolbar down the left side, and a status line across the bottom.

CorelTRACE contains five menus: File, Edit, View, Trace, and Help. The File menu provides the normal Open, Save, and Exit options as well as access to the Batch File and Mosaic roll-ups and to Scanner output. The Edit menu provides the normal Undo, Cut, Copy, Paste, and Clear options, plus the ability to open a bitmap image editor, such as CorelPHOTO-PAINT. The View menu lets you look at information about the image you are tracing and lets you refresh the window and clear the window. The Trace menu provides access to the six different tracing methods (outline, centerline, woodcut, silhouette, OCR, and form), all of which are buttons in the ribbon bar. The Trace menu also opens a very extensive tabbed dialog box of options for editing the traced image. The Help menu, which you can also get to by pressing F1, provides assistance in using CorelTRACE.

Tracing Bitmap Images

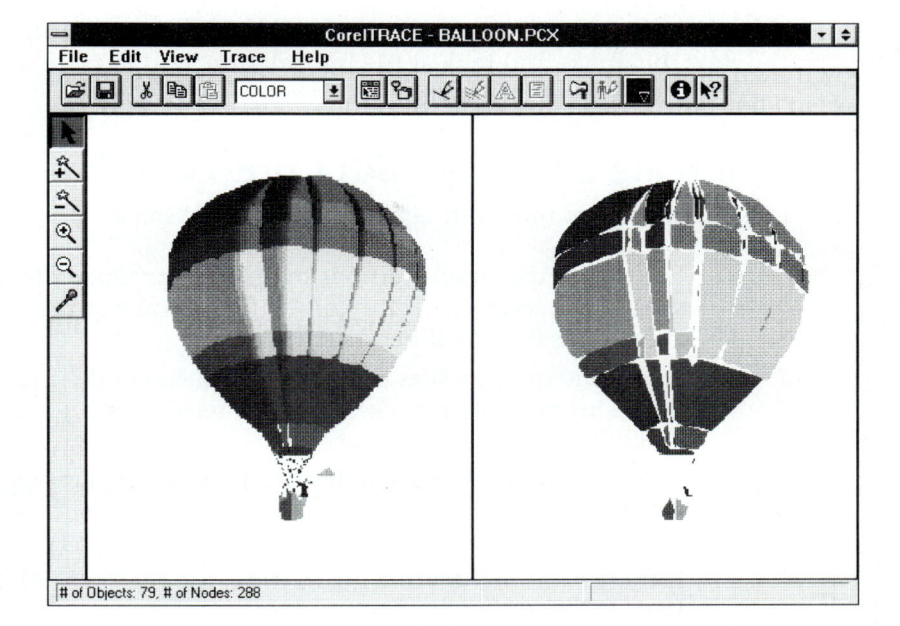

**CorelTRACE window with the original image on the left and the traced image on the right
Figure 23-9.**

Opening Files to Trace

In order to trace one or more bitmaps, you must open the files in CorelTRACE in one of three ways: by clicking on Open in the File menu, by clicking on the File Open button in the ribbon bar, or by clicking on the Batch Files roll-up button (just to the right of the drop-down list box in the ribbon bar) and then on the Add button in the Batch Files roll-up. In all cases, the Open Files dialog box appears. If you have only one file to trace, the first two methods are faster than the Batch Files roll-up. If you have several files to trace, though, the Batch Files roll-up, shown next, provides a good way to handle them all at one time.

The Batch Files roll-up allows you to add and delete files from the list, to view the image and look at file information, and to trace selected files only or all those in the list.

Tracing a Bitmap with CorelTRACE

Tracing one or more bitmaps involves several steps:

1. Use one of the three methods to display the Open dialog box and then specify the source directory of the file(s) you want to trace, using the Directories list box if necessary.
2. Select one or more files to trace by clicking on their names in the File Name list box. Then click OK. If you selected more than one file, the Batch Files roll-up appears.
3. Edit the tracing options, if desired, by selecting Edit Options in the Trace menu.
4. Click on one of the trace buttons to begin tracing the selected file(s). If there is more than one file to trace, use the Trace All button in the Batch Files roll-up.

In the following exercise, you will tell CorelTRACE to *batch trace* (trace one after the other) two bitmap files. You can use any two bitmap graphics files that are available to you.

1. Click on Open and change to the drive and directory where your bitmap files are located.
2. Click on two bitmap (PCX, BMP, or TIF) filenames in the File Name list box at the left side of the dialog box. Click on OK, and the Batch Files roll-up will appear with the selected filenames listed and the first of the two images in the roll-up, as shown in Figure 23-10.
3. Choose Save Options in the File menu. The Save Options dialog box appears, as you see next. Here you tell CorelTRACE where to send the traced files and whether to replace an older version of the same filename. You are also given the opportunity to make the files "Read Only" and to decide how text is to be handled.

Tracing Bitmap Images 743

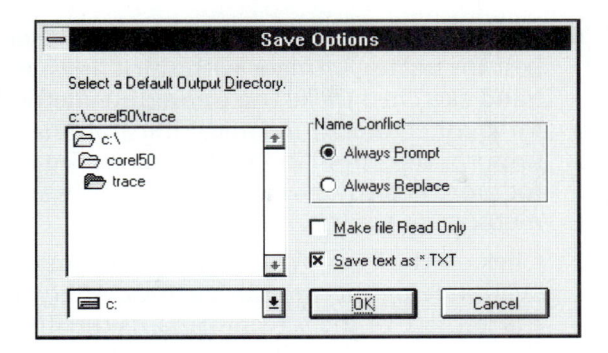

4. Click on OK to close the Save options.
5. Other settings can be changed with the Edit Options in the Trace menu, but for now they should all have their default settings.

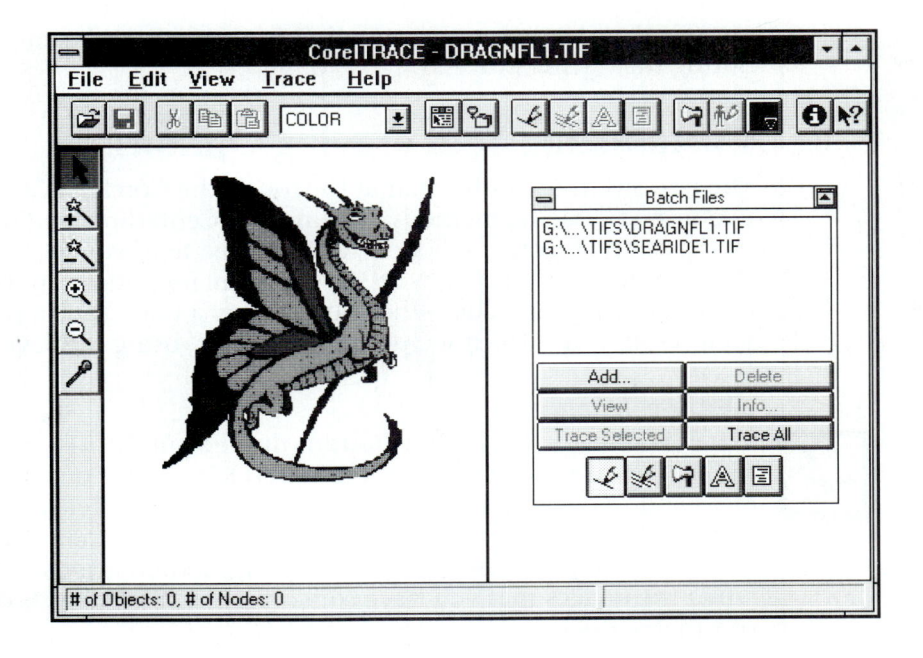

Batch Files roll-up opened with two images to be traced
Figure 23-10.

6. Make sure the Outline Tracing button is selected. The Outline method is best for tracing bitmaps with thick lines, many fills, and a hand-sketched look. The Centerline method, on the other hand, is best for architectural or technical illustrations that have thin lines of fairly uniform thickness and no fill colors. See the next section of this chapter for more details on the differences between the Outline and Centerline methods of tracing.

7. Click on the Trace All command button in the Batch Files roll-up to begin tracing the two sample files. After a few seconds, the window on the left side of the screen contains the first of the two bitmaps. When the tracing is complete, the first bitmap disappears automatically and is replaced by the second bitmap. When both tracings are done, both images will disappear—they will be saved as EPS files, which you can edit from another program, such as CorelDRAW!.

The preceding exercise gave you a glimpse of what CorelTRACE can do. In the next section, you will learn more about how you can customize the options that determine the smoothness, fineness, and clarity of the curves during the tracing process.

Customizing Your Tracing Options

The buttons in the ribbon bar at the top of the CorelTRACE window contain two primary tracing methods, Outline and Centerline, and four secondary methods: OCR, Form, Woodcut, and Silhouette. If you wish, you can modify the parameters associated with the two primary options to define your own custom tracing methods. When you modify a tracing option, you can save your result in the Tracing Options dialog box, using the Save buttons.

Outline Tracing

When you select the Outline button (ninth from the left or right in the ribbon bar) as the tracing method, CorelTRACE seeks out the *outlines* of areas and traces around them. Every curve becomes a closed object that is then filled with black or white, a color, or a gray shade to match the original bitmap as closely as possible. This method is most appropriate when the images that you trace contain many filled objects or have lines of variable thickness.

Centerline Tracing

When you select the Centerline button (eighth from the right) as the tracing method, CorelTRACE seeks out the *center* point of lines in a bitmap and traces down the middle of those lines. No attempt is made to close paths or fill them. The resulting accuracy and attention to fine detail makes this tracing method the best choice for scanned images of technical or architectural drawings. Centerline is also appropriate for tracing drawings in which line thickness is fairly uniform.

Note: Centerline tracing, as well as OCR and Form tracing, are available only when you select Mono or Form settings in the Settings list.

Other Types of Tracing and Tools

Besides Outline and Centerline tracing, there are four other types of tracing you can perform with CorelTRACE: OCR, Form, Woodcut, and Silhouette. These tools are selected with the fourth through the seventh buttons from the right in the ribbon bar at the top of the screen and are described in Table 23-2.

When you use Woodcut or Silhouette tracing, you can choose a color for the area you are tracing (*before you do the tracing*) either by selecting it from the Color selection tool or by using the Eyedropper tool to pick it up from the original image (just click on the color with the eyedropper). This procedure works well with the Magic wands, which select (the wand with a plus sign) and deselect (the wand with a minus sign) areas of the object to be traced that are a constant color. Therefore, to do custom tracing, you select the area

Tracing Tools
Table 23-2.

Button	Description
A	Optical character recognition (OCR) converts text brought in as graphics to text that CorelDRAW! can edit as text.
≣	Form tracing allows you to trace the lines and text of a form and then edit them with CorelDRAW!.
🪓	Woodcut tracing produces a special effect similar to old-fashioned hand woodcuts.
👤	Silhouette tracing produces an outline of the traced area filled with a single color that can be selected with either the color selector or the eyedropper (described a little later).

to be traced with the Magic wand selector, pick the color, either by choosing it from the palette that appears when you click on the Color selection tool or by using the Eyedropper tool to pick up the original color, and then click on the Silhouette tool to do the tracing.

Defining Custom Tracing Settings

What if the image you want to trace contains both filled areas and line art? In CorelTRACE, you can adjust a variety of tracing options in the Tracing Options dialog box reached from the Trace menu. You can then save the settings under a name you choose or replace one of the standard settings names (Color, Dithered, Form, and Mono) and select these settings from the Settings list in the ribbon bar. Follow these steps to define custom tracing settings:

1. Click on Edit Options in the Trace menu to open the Tracing Options dialog box shown in Figure 23-11.
2. Select the area you want to change by clicking on its tab, and make the necessary changes.
3. When you are finished making the changes you want, enter a description and a filename in the Settings area at the bottom of the dialog box. Remember that the filename must be eight or fewer characters. Finally, click on Save. The new setting will now appear in the Settings List drop-down list box, as shown here:

CorelTRACE Help has a section on each of the tabs in the Tracing Options dialog box.

```
NEW
COLOR
DITHERED
FORM
MONO
NEW
```

Tracing Bitmap Images

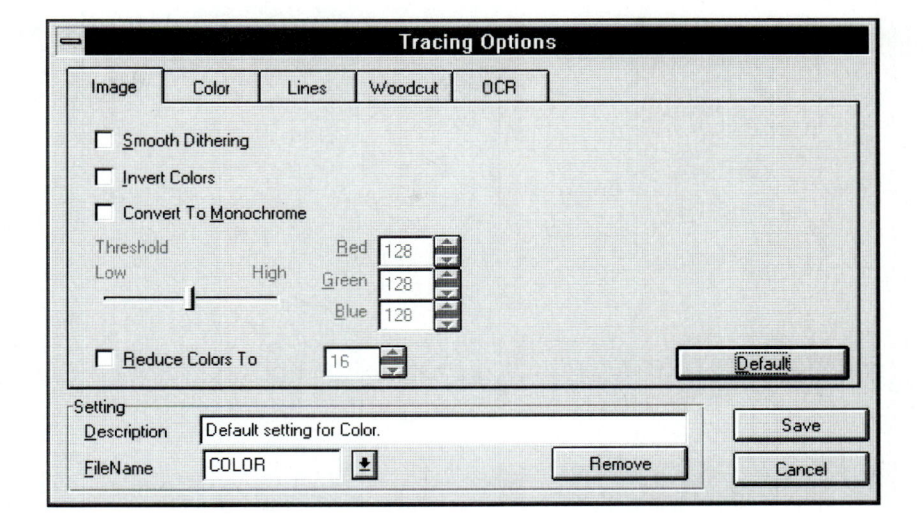

Tracing Options dialog box
Figure 23-11.

Editing the parameters for tracing options will save time if you repeatedly import similarly traced graphics into CorelDRAW!. For example, if you know in advance that you need to invert colors of a particular bitmap or that you require a larger or smaller number of nodes in the traced graphic, you can change tracing parameters to give you the desired results automatically.

Part 5

APPENDIXES

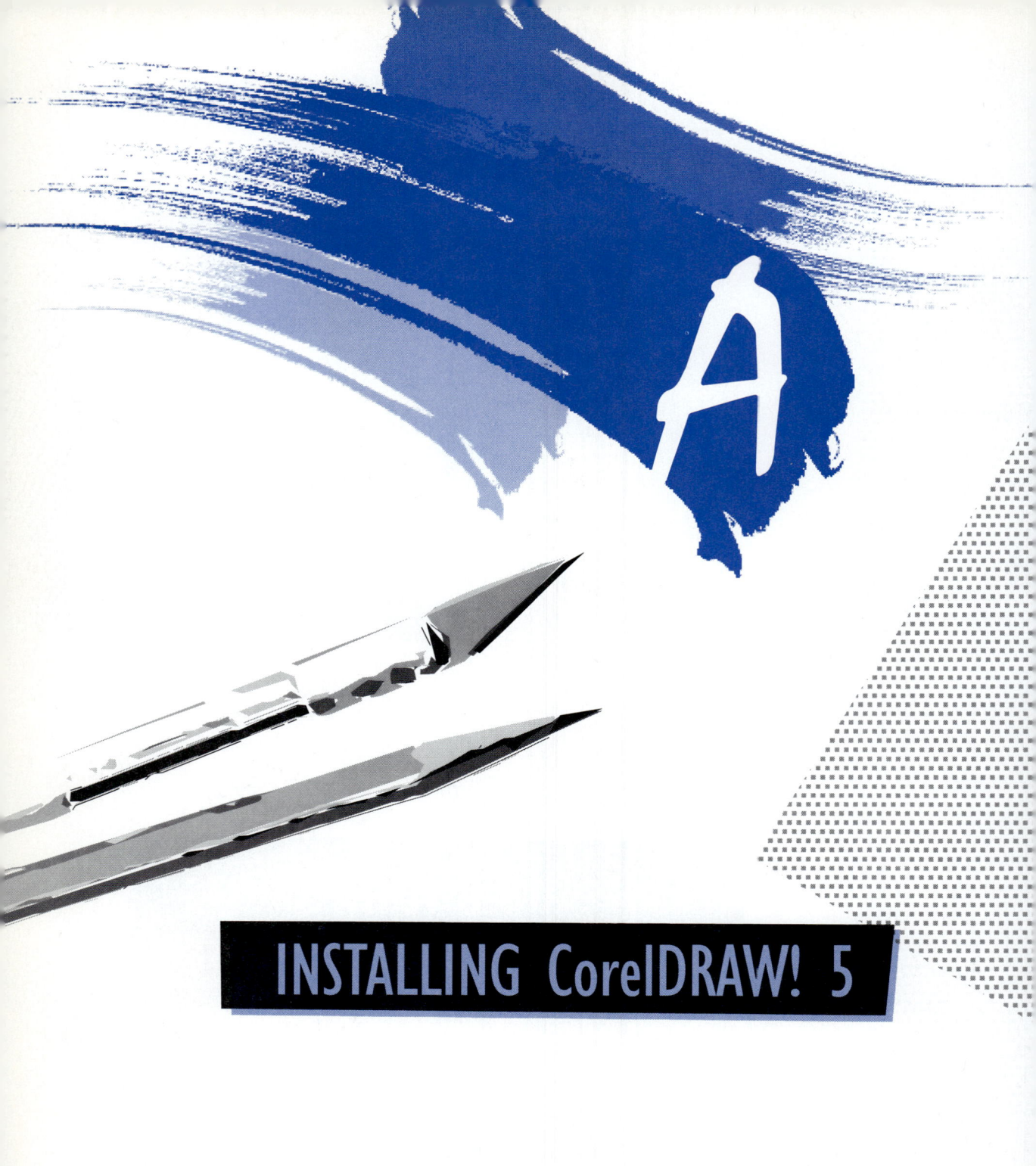

INSTALLING CorelDRAW! 5

This appendix guides you through the process of installing CorelDRAW! 5. If you or someone else has installed your software already, you do not need to use this appendix. If you have an earlier version of CorelDRAW!, many of the steps are the same, but you should be aware that this discussion describes the installation of CorelDRAW! 5.

You must install Windows 3.1 or later and ensure that it is working properly before you install CorelDRAW! 5. Refer to the documentation that came with your Windows software for full instructions on installing Windows correctly.

System Requirements

Before you begin the installation procedure, review the hardware and software requirements explained in this section. You can help ensure trouble-free operation of CorelDRAW! 5 by checking to see that your system meets all of the requirements.

Computer

Your computer must be based on an 80386, 80486, or compatible microprocessor with a hard disk drive and at least one floppy disk drive. (An 80286-based computer will not work. A 486 is recommended for response time considerations.)

Memory

You must have a minimum of 8MB (megabytes) of memory, and 16MB is strongly recommended. All memory above 1MB should be configured as *extended* memory. You should be running HIMEM.SYS, which comes with Windows 3.1 or DOS 5 or DOS 6. You can find out how much memory you have by exiting Windows, changing to your Windows directory, and typing **msd**. By clicking on Memory, you can see your memory usage and availability. Your Windows and DOS manuals, as well as your dealer or internal company support people, can help you change or add to your memory. Increasing the memory size beyond 4MB will speed up the running of both Windows and CorelDRAW! and give you more flexibility in what you can do.

Hard Disk Space

Your hard disk must have approximately 50MB of space available for a full installation of CorelDRAW! and its associated applications, including CorelVENTURA, plus an additional 10MB for the Windows swap file, and another 10MB for the storage of temporary files. The amount of disk space for the Windows swap file may be permanently assigned and not showing as available space. You can determine this from within Windows by opening the Control Panel from the Program Manager, clicking on the 386 Enhanced icon, and then clicking on the Virtual Memory button.

If you do not have this much space available on your hard drive, you can perform a Custom installation and selectively install the programs, features, fonts, and graphic sample files you think you will use. The amount of disk

Installing CorelDRAW! 5

space that you will use for storage of CorelDRAW! files will be displayed. Be cautious about installing too many fonts, which could drag on the system (unless you also install the bundled copy of Ares Fontminder to manage the amount of disk space taken up by fonts).

Monitor and Display Adapter

You should have a color or paper-white VGA graphics monitor and VGA adapter that is supported by Windows 3.1, with at least a 640-by-480 resolution. A color SVGA monitor and higher-resolution video display adapter (32,000, 64,000, or 16 million colors) are highly recommended to take full advantage of CorelDRAW!'s full-color mode.

Drawing Device

You must have a mouse or another drawing device, such as a graphics tablet, in order to run CorelDRAW!. If you use a graphics tablet instead of a mouse, choose one that has the activation button on the side rather than on the top. This type of design gives you the best results because it minimizes unwanted movement on the screen.

This book assumes that most users work with a mouse instead of some other type of drawing device. References to a mouse therefore apply to any drawing device.

Output Device

Using the Print and Export commands in the File menu, you can produce your CorelDRAW! images on paper (standard printers) or in formats used by film recorders, Photo CD service centers, and slide generation equipment. Appendix B discusses the file formats needed to output to 35mm slide generation or presentation equipment in greater detail. If you normally print your images to paper, however, you will achieve the best results with the following types of printers:

- PostScript printers, imagesetters, PostScript controller boards, and PostScript plug-in cartridges licensed by Adobe Systems
- HP LaserJet series or 100 percent compatible printers
- HP PaintJet and DeskJet printers

For more information on printers, see Chapter 12.

Although Windows supports other printers as well, many of these cannot reproduce complex CorelDRAW! images exactly as expected. In addition, a few of the most complex CorelDRAW! features can only be produced on PostScript printers.

CD-ROM Disk Drive

A CD-ROM disk drive is not mandatory to run CorelDRAW! but it is highly recommended. CorelDRAW! 5 is cheaper if you buy the CD-ROM only version and you will have access to the full 825 fonts, 22,000 pieces of clip art, and 100 high resolution photos. This book makes use of both fonts and clip art that are only on the CorelDRAW! CD-ROM. You can substitute other fonts and clip art, but it will be easier to follow the book if you are using the items discussed. Finally, it is significantly easier to install all of the Corel applications from the CD-ROMs than it is to install them from approximately 20 floppy disks.

Operating System and Windows Requirements

CorelDRAW! 5 requires Windows 3.1 or later, and the combination of DOS 6.X and Windows 3.1 is recommended to make full use of CorelDRAW!'s extended memory and OLE capabilities. CorelDRAW! 5 will work with earlier releases of DOS (3.3 and above), but you won't have the high memory optimization and other features of DOS 5 or 6.

Installing the Software

The SETUP program for CorelDRAW! 5 installs CorelDRAW! program files, fonts, sample files, and clip art onto your hard disk. Depending on your choice of installation method (Full or Custom), you can install some or all of the programs and utilities that make up the total CorelDRAW! 5 ensemble.

The directions that the SETUP program gives you vary according to which installation method you choose. The Full installation method requires the least interaction on your part and is recommended for new users of CorelDRAW!. If disk space is a concern, you might do a minimum Custom installation and then later selectively add other CorelDRAW! programs, again using the Custom installation method, as your needs and disk space allow.

If you have very little hard disk space and you do have a CD-ROM, you can install CorelDRAW! to *run off* (not just *install* off) of the CD-ROM and therefore take very little hard disk space. If there is any possible way around this, it is strongly recommended that you *do not* run CorelDRAW! this way—it is excruciatingly slow! If you do want to run off the CD-ROM, use the Setup2 command in place of the Setup command in the instructions below.

Before you begin, decide on the name of the hard disk directory in which you want to install CorelDRAW! 5 (the default name is \COREL50), and have the Windows Program Manager on your screen. The following example assumes you will perform a Full installation.

Installing CorelDRAW! 5

1. Insert CorelDRAW! Disk 1 into the floppy drive or the first CD-ROM into the CD-ROM drive from which you want to install CorelDRAW!. This book assumes that you are installing the software from drive A, but you can use any drive.
2. Click on the Program Manager's File menu, choose Run, and type **a:\setup** (or **a:\setup2** if you want the installed version to run off the CD-ROM) in the Command Line text entry box. (If you are installing CorelDRAW! from a different drive, type that drive name instead of **a:**.) Press ENTER or click on OK.
3. After a short period, an initial welcome message appears on your screen. Press ENTER or click on Continue to proceed with the installation.
4. Type your name, press TAB, enter your serial number which appears just after the registration card inside the front cover of your CorelDRAW! 5 User Manual Volume 1, and press ENTER or click on Continue.
5. The next window provides buttons for the two installation methods, Full Install (the default) and Custom Install. If you are unsure of your installation method, you can choose either button and explore some of its features before committing to the corresponding method. For example, choosing the Custom installation method accesses its menu of choices. If you decide not to continue with the Custom installation, click on the Back button to return to the window with the two installation buttons.
6. After choosing the installation method you want to use, you are asked if you want to install CorelDRAW! in the C:\COREL50 directory on your hard drive. If this is satisfactory, press ENTER or click on Continue. If you want the CorelDRAW! files in another directory, type your path name in the text entry box and press ENTER or click on Continue to continue with the installation.
7. If you chose Full Install you are next asked which of the filter, font, and driver files you want installed. If you chose Custom Install you are asked which applications you want installed before being asked about filters, fonts, and drivers. Beside many of the options, especially Filters and TrueType Fonts, there are Customize buttons. By clicking on these buttons you are given detail options about what items you want installed. It is often difficult to know what you will need in the future. The predominate criteria is usually whether or not you have adequate disk space. If you do, then the best starting position is to select the defaults throughout the installation. If you do not have a lot of disk space, then you need to make a lot of tough choices about what you will really be using. The one salvation is that, if you find that you need something you did not install, you can always run Setup again.

8. Choose which files you want to install from the options that are presented. When you are done press ENTER or click on Continue.

   Finally, you are next told that CorelDRAW! is ready to be installed. If you wish to precede, click on Install or press ENTER.

9. Next you are asked to choose the path for the temporary drive and directory that CorelDRAW! will use. Choose the one with the most space available and press ENTER or click on Continue.

10. CorelDRAW! now begins copying files to the destination you established in step 6. If you are installing from floppy disks, when prompted, insert CorelDRAW! Disk 2 in the drive you are using. Press ENTER or click on OK. Continue to insert the remainder of the installation disks when prompted. Depending on the speed of your computer, the installation process will take approximately 30 minutes (less time if you are installing from a CD-ROM, more if from floppy disks).

11. SETUP finishes by creating a Program Manager application group called Corel5 and placing icons there to start all of applications and utilities that come with CorelDRAW! 5. Chapter 1 shows what this application group looks like.

This completes the automatic installation procedure.

Creating a Directory

You need a directory in which to store the drawings created with CorelDRAW!. When you installed Windows and CorelDRAW!, directories were automatically created in which the program, font, and other files that came with Windows and CorelDRAW! are stored. While you could use these directories to store your CorelDRAW! drawings, it is unwise to do so for two reasons. First, when you get an update to Windows or CorelDRAW! you will want to remove the old program files and replace them with the new ones. The easiest way to do that is to erase the entire directory with a single command. If your drawing files were in the directory at the time, you would lose them. Second, if you want to do some file maintenance with either DOS or the Windows File Manager, the large number of product-related files will make looking for drawing files difficult.

Therefore, create a new directory now to hold your drawing files. You can name your directory anything you want as long as the name is from one to eight characters long and does not include the following characters:

   " + ; , * ? "

This book will use DRAWINGS as the example directory in which drawings will be stored. Your directory should be a full directory branching off the

Installing CorelDRAW! 5

root directory. Its path then is \DRAWINGS. Use these instructions to create this directory either from the DOS prompt or from the Windows File Manager.

At the DOS prompt:

1. Type **cd** and press ENTER to make sure you are in the root directory.
2. Type **md\drawings** and press ENTER to create the new DRAWINGS directory.

From Windows:

1. Double-click on the File Manager icon located in the Program Manager's Main application group.
2. Select the File menu and choose the Create Directory option.
3. Type **c:\drawings** in the Name text entry box. Press ENTER or click on OK to create the new DRAWINGS directory.

If you use the other applications in the Corel5 suite frequently (for example, CorelPHOTO-PAINT and CorelCHART), consider creating specially named directories for the files you will create with those applications, too.

The only remaining step is to start CorelDRAW! and begin using it. Do that now by following the directions in Chapter 1.

B

IMPORTING and EXPORTING FILES

As more graphics applications for IBM-compatible computers become available, the need to transfer files among different applications becomes more acute. *Connectivity*, or the ability of a software program to import and export data in various file formats, is rapidly becoming a requirement for graphics applications. Whether your work involves desktop publishing, technical illustration, original art, or graphic design, it is essential to be able to export your CorelDRAW! graphics to other programs, to import clip art, and to polish your work from other programs.

Tip: All of the clip-art that is on the CD-ROM in the CorelDRAW! package must be imported into CorelDRAW!.

CorelDRAW! offers you two different methods of connectivity. In Chapter 11, you learned how to use the Windows Clipboard to transfer files between CorelDRAW! and other applications that run under Microsoft Windows. The Windows Clipboard is not your only option for transferring files, however. CorelDRAW! has its own independent import and export utilities specifically designed for transferring data between different graphics formats. These utilities allow you to import graphics from and export them to a variety of drawing, painting, desktop publishing, and word processing applications, even though some of these programs may not run under Windows. The use of the Import and Export commands in CorelDRAW! is the subject of this appendix.

Bitmap Versus Object-Oriented Graphics

CorelDRAW! imports from and exports to both bitmap and object-oriented applications, as well as text files. It is important to have a clear understanding of the differences between bitmap and object-oriented graphics. You will then have a firm basis for choosing how and when to import and export graphics files.

There are many different graphics file formats, but only two kinds of graphics: bitmap, also known as *pixel-based,* and vector, also known as *object-oriented*. The differences between these two kinds of graphics involve the kinds of software applications that produce them, the way the computer stores them in memory, and the ease with which you can edit them.

Paint programs and scanners produce bitmap images by establishing a grid of pixels, the smallest visual unit that the computer can address, on the screen. These applications create images by altering the colors or attributes of each individual pixel. This way of storing images makes inefficient use of memory, however. The size of an image (the number of pixels it occupies) is fixed once it is created, and is dependent on the resolution of the display adapter on the computer where the image first took shape. As a result, finished bitmap images are difficult to edit when you transfer them from one application to another. If you increase the size of a finished bitmap image, you can see unsightly white spaces and jagged edges. If you greatly decrease the size of a finished bitmap image, parts of the image may smudge because of the compression involved. Apparent distortion can also occur if you transfer bitmap graphics to another computer that has a different display resolution.

Tip: To store images more efficiently, you can crop a bitmap image as you import it. The storage will be reduced according to the extent of the crop. If you want to crop the image after importing it in CorelDRAW!, you will still need storage space for the full-sized image

Object-oriented graphics, on the other hand, have fewer limitations. They are produced by drawing applications such as CorelDRAW! and are stored in the computer's memory as a series of numbers (not pixels) that describe how to redraw the image on the screen. Since this method of storing information has nothing to do with the resolution of a given display adapter, line art is considered to be *device-independent*; no matter what computer you use to create an object-oriented graphic, you can stretch, scale, and resize it flexibly without distortion. Object-oriented graphics also tend to create smaller files than bitmap graphics because the computer does not have to "memorize" the attributes of individual pixels.

How can you use each type of graphic in CorelDRAW!? As demonstrated in Chapter 23, you can import bitmap images in order to trace them and turn them into object-oriented graphics. Alternatively, you can simply import them and incorporate them into an existing drawing. Your options for editing an imported bitmap image do not end with the editing capabilities available in CorelDRAW!, however. When you need your finished work to issue from a paint or photo editing application, or if you prefer to polish your artwork in pixel format, you can export CorelDRAW! graphics back into a paint program, such as CorelPHOTO-PAINT.

If you work with other object-oriented drawing and design programs, you can import line art in order to enhance it with advanced features that only CorelDRAW! offers. You can introduce clip art and edit it flexibly. When you are finished editing, you can export CorelDRAW! artwork back into your favorite object-oriented application or to the desktop publishing application of your choice. You can even export your CorelDRAW! graphics to a format that film recorders and imagesetters will be able to use to create professional-looking presentation materials.

Tip: To import an unsupported file format, open it in another application and try to copy and paste it into CorelDRAW! via the Clipboard.

CorelDRAW! supports an ever-growing number of file formats that include both pixel-based and object-oriented graphics. Table B-1 lists all of the file formats you can import into CorelDRAW!, while Table B-2 lists the file formats to which you can export CorelDRAW! graphics. Both tables list for each file format, the file type (bitmap or "Pixel," object-oriented or "Line," or "Text"), and the file extension.

File Format	File Type	Extension
Adobe Illustrator 1.1, 88, 3.0	Line	.AI, .EPS
Ami Pro 2.0, 3.0	Text	.SAM
ASCII Text	Text	.TXT
AutoCAD	Line	.DXF
CompuServe Bitmap	Pixel	.GIF
Computer Graphics Metafile	Line	.CGM
CorelDRAW!	Line	.CDR
CorelPHOTO-PAINT	Pixel	.PCX, .PCC, .CPT
CorelCHART	Line	.CDR, .CCH
Corel Presentation Exchange	Line	.CMX
CorelTRACE	Line	.EPS
EPS Placeable	Line	.AI, .EPS, . PS
Excel For Windows 3.0, 4.0	Text	.XLS
GEM File	Line	.GEM
HPGL Plotter File	Line	.PLT
IBM PIF	Line	.PIF
JPEG Bitmap	Pixel	.JPG, .JFF, .JTF, .CMP
Kodak Photo CD	Pixel	.PCD
Lotus Pic	Line	.PIC
Lotus 1-2-3 1A, 2.0	Text	.WKS, .WK2
Lotus 1-2-3 3.0 and for Windows	Text	.WK3
Macintosh PICT	Line	.PCT
Micrografx Designer 2.x, 3.x	Line	.DRW
Rich Text Format	Text	.RFT
Microsoft Word 5.0, 5.5	Text	Any
Microsoft Word for Mac 4.0, 5.0	Text	Any
Micorsoft Word for Windows 1.x, 2.x	Text	Any, .DOC
Microsoft Word for Windows 6.0	Text	Any, .DOC

CorelDRAW! 5 Import File Formats
Table B-1.

Importing and Exporting Files

CorelDRAW! 5 Import File Formats (*continued*)
Table B-1.

File Format	File Type	Extension
OS/2 Bitmap	Pixel	.BMP
Paintbrush	Pixel	.PCX
PostScript (Interpreted)	Line	.EPS, .PS
SciTex CT Bitmap	Pixel	.SCT, .CT
Targa Bitmap	Pixel	.TGA, .VDA, .ICB, .VST
TIFF Bitmap	Pixel	.TIF, .SEP, .CPT
Windows Bitmap	Pixel	.BMP, .DIB, .RLE
Windows Metafile	Line	.WMF
WordPerfect Graphic	Line	.WPG
WordPerfect 5.0, 5.1, and for Windows	Text	Any
WordPerfect 6.0 for Windows	Text	Any

CorelDRAW! 5 Export File Formats
Table B-2.

File Format	File Type	Extension
Adobe Illustrator 88, 3.0	Line	.AI, .EPS
Adobe Type 1 Font	Line	.PFB
AutoCAD	Line	.DXF
CompuServe Bitmap	Pixel	.GIF
Computer Graphics Metafile	Line	.CGM
GEM File	Line	.GEM
HPGL Plotter File	Line	.PLT
IBM PIF	Line	.PIF
JPEG Bitmap	Pixel	.JPG, .JFF, .JTF, .CMP
Macintosh PICT	Line	.PCT
Matrix/Imapro SCODL	Line	.SCD
OS/2 Bitmap	Pixel	.BMP
PaintBrush (CorelPHOTO-PAINT)	Pixel	.PCX
EPS Placeable (Encapsulated PostScript)	Line	.EPS
SciTex CT Bitmap	Pixel	.SCT, .CT
Targa Bitmap	Pixel	.TGA, .VDA, .ICB, .VST
TIFF Bitmap	Pixel	.TIF
TrueType Font	Line	.TTF

CorelDRAW! 5 Export File Formats (*continued*)
Table B-2.

File Format	File Type	Extension
Windows Bitmap	Pixel	.BMP, .DIB, .RLE
Windows Metafile	Line	.WMF
WordPerfect Graphics	Line	.WPG

Using Help for Importing and Exporting

You can use CorelDRAW! Help to get detailed technical information on the different formats available for importing and exporting. To get help, press CTRL-F1 or click on the Help menu and then on Search For Help On. The Search dialog box appears. In the Search dialog box, type a search argument, such as **bmp**, and the requested subject appears in the window, as shown in Figure B-1.

You can then choose either the import or export notes and click on Show Topic to put them into the lower window. Click on OK and the help subject is displayed. If you need a hard copy of the subject, click on Print in the File menu.

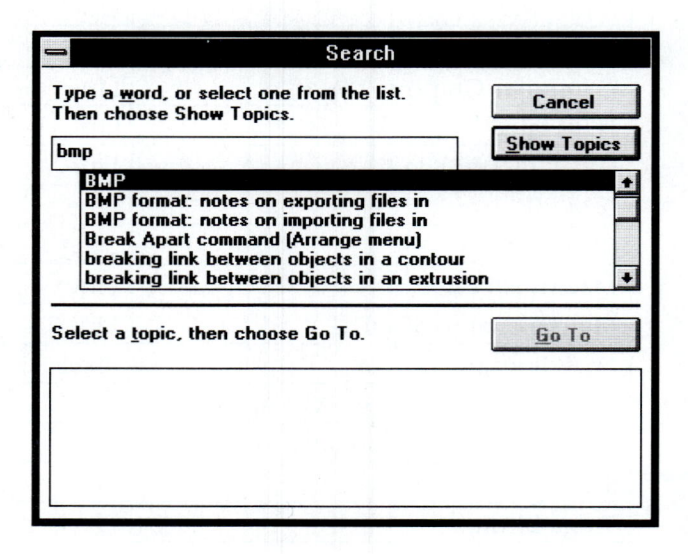

Searching for help on exporting to a .BMP format
Figure B-1.

Importing and Exporting Files

Importing: An Overview

The process of importing into CorelDRAW! from other file formats always involves these three steps:

1. Select the Import command from the File menu.
2. Select one of the file types listed in the Import dialog box's List Files of Type drop-down list box.
3. Specify the directory and filename of the file you want to import and click on OK.

You will find more information on the CorelDRAW! bitmap tracing features in Chapter 23.

Once you import the file, you have several editing options, depending on the kind of application it comes from. If the imported object originated in a paint program, you can trace it automatically or manually and turn it into a distortion-free, object-oriented image, or incorporate it into an existing line art drawing.

When you select the Import command from the File menu, the Import dialog box appears, as shown in Figure B-2. Clicking on the drop-down list box in the bottom left of the dialog box displays the list of file formats available for import.

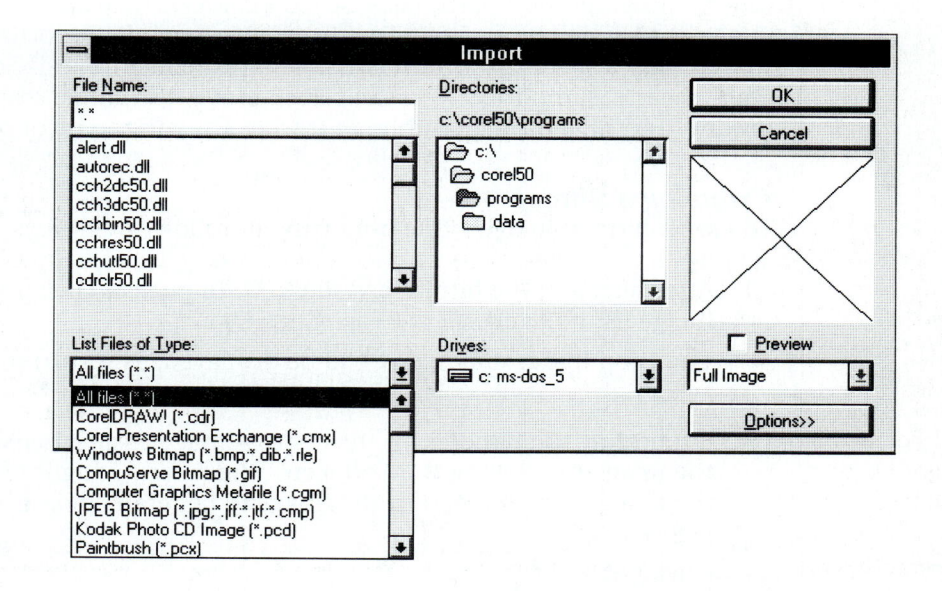

Import dialog box
Figure B-2.

Bringing in a File

To select the format for the file you wish to import, and actually bring the file into CorelDRAW!, follow these steps.

1. Select the Import command from the File menu. The Import dialog box appears.
2. In the Directories list box, select the path to the directory that contains the file you want to import.
3. Click on the down arrow in the List Files of Type drop-down list box. If the file type you want does not immediately appear in the window, use the scroll arrows to move through the list.
4. Select the filename you want and click on OK, or double-click on the filename. The image will begin importing to the CorelDRAW! page.

What happens to the image during the import process depends on the specific file format you have chosen.

Importing Bitmap Graphics

CorelDRAW! can import bitmap graphics in many different formats, as you saw in Table B-1. Once imported, you cannot break bitmap images down into their component parts, because CorelDRAW! treats the entire bitmap image as a single object. You can crop a bitmap while importing it, however, so that only a specified section is visible. This reduces the size of the file. Once the file is imported, you can select, move, rearrange, stretch, scale, outline, and fill a bitmap as though it were any other type of object.

Cropping a Bitmap

To crop a bitmap image while importing it, follow these steps:

1. After selecting the bitmapped file to be imported, click on the Full Image list box and select Crop. Click OK.

   The Crop Image dialog box will be displayed, as shown in Figure B-3.
2. Click OK.
3. Either drag the handles on the display image to another size, or crop the image by clicking the Top, Left, Width, and Height arrows to move the marquee to the part of the image to be retained, as is shown in Figure B-3.
4. Click OK.

Importing and Exporting Files

Crop Image dialog box with crop marquee moved to identify area to be cropped
Figure B-3.

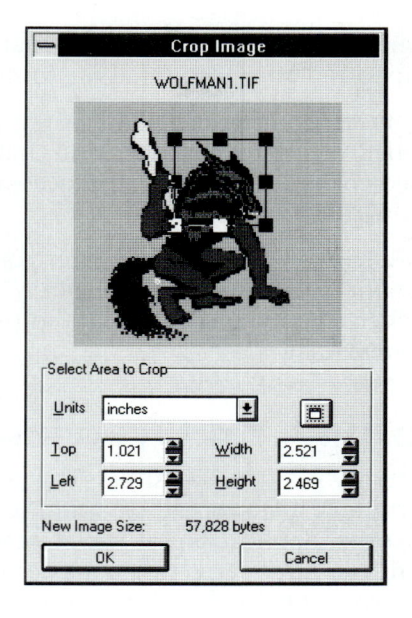

Resampling an Image

During the import operation, you can also resample a bitmap image. Resampling an image changes the size or resolution. Follow these steps to resample an image:

1. After choosing an image to import, change the Full Image to Resample.
2. Click OK. The Resample dialog box will be displayed.
3. Change the Height, Width or Resolution values.
4. Click OK.

A rotated or skewed bitmap will only print on a PostScript printer.

In some respects, imported bitmaps behave differently from other objects when you edit them. If you rotate or skew a bitmap, the original image in the preview window changes to a series of bars, unless you are in Edit Wireframe, in which case it will appear as a gray box.

Importing Object-Oriented Graphics

The original release of CorelDRAW! allowed you to import three object-oriented graphics file formats: .CDR (the native CorelDRAW! format), Lotus .PIC graphs, and .AI and .EPS files created by Adobe Illustrator or clip-art manufacturers. Since then, the ranks of supported object-oriented file formats have swelled to include many more file formats. Table B-1 lists each supported object-oriented file format.

Specific notes on importing and working with each file format are provided in CorelDRAW! Help. Keep in mind that software applications are being upgraded continually, and that process may alter the way certain file formats interact with CorelDRAW!.

The CorelDRAW! import filters offer you a rich world of possibilities. But the uses to which you can put CorelDRAW!'s advanced graphics features are even richer when you consider the software applications to which you can export your images.

Exporting: An Overview

Connectivity is a two-way street. The ability to import any number of different file formats would be of limited use if you could not export your work to other applications as well. CorelDRAW! also has a large number of export filters. After perfecting a masterpiece in CorelDRAW!, you can send it to your favorite paint program, object-oriented drawing software, desktop publishing application, or film-recording device.

The process of exporting a CorelDRAW! file to another application always involves these five steps:

1. Open the CorelDRAW! image file you want to transfer and save it before beginning the export procedure. If you want to export only certain objects rather than the entire file, select those objects.
2. Select the Export command from the File menu.
3. Select a file type from the choices in the Export dialog box's List Files of Type drop-down list box.
4. Choose whether to export the entire file or selected objects only.
5. Specify the directory and filename for the object you want to export.

Depending on the export file format you choose, other choices in various secondary Export dialog boxes may also become available to you.

Preparing for Exporting

If you are planning to export an existing file, open it before you select the Export command. If the page is empty when you attempt the export procedure, you'll find you can't select the Export command.

If you are preparing to export a new file or one you have imported and edited, always save the file as a .CDR image before exporting it. This is

Importing and Exporting Files

extremely important if there is any chance that you might need to edit the image again later. Although most files are both importable and exportable, in some cases you may not be able to import a file that was exported earlier from CorelDRAW!

If you want to export only a part of the CorelDRAW! file rather than the entire image, select the desired objects before beginning the export procedure. An option in the Export dialog box will allow you to specify the export of selected objects only.

The Export Dialog Box

When you select the Export command from the File menu, the Export dialog box appears, as shown in Figure B-4.

At the lower-left corner of the dialog box, the List Files of Type drop-down list box contains the names and extensions of the file formats to which you can export the current file. Depending on the format selected, there are several secondary Export dialog boxes for entering further options; these include Bitmap Export, Export EPS, HPGL Options, and Export AI, to name a few. One of these boxes will appear if you select the corresponding file type in the drop-down list and click OK.

To select and highlight the file format to which you will export the CorelDRAW! image, scroll through the list box until it appears and then click on it.

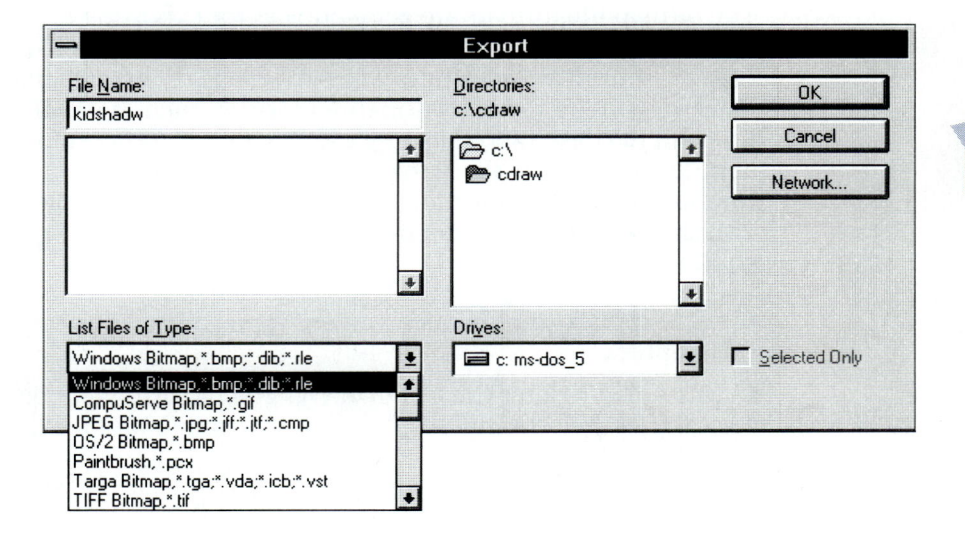

Export dialog box
Figure B-4.

Selected Only Option

The Selected Only option is available for any export file format that you choose. It lets you choose to export only certain objects from your on-screen graphic. However, you must have one or more objects selected before the Selected Only option is available.

The Export dialog box in Figure B-4 indicates that no object has been selected, since the Selected Only option is unavailable.

Specifying the Filename and Destination Directory

To specify the destination drive and directory for the exported image, click on the appropriate drive in the Drives drop-down list box and double-click on the appropriate directory in the Directories list box. Use the scroll bars if the desired directory is not visible. The path of the highlighted drive and directory appear above the box.

To name the export image file, double-click in the File Name box to select the default extension. Then type the desired filename; CorelDRAW! will restore the correct extension. Click on OK. Select the needed options in the secondary Export dialog box, and click OK to begin transfer of the image.

Exporting to Bitmap Graphics Formats

When you have a choice of several different export file formats, your primary concern should be the end use to which you will put the exported graphic. Add to that, the CorelDRAW! features that can or cannot be retained, and the convenience of working with the image in the export file format.

The bitmap file formats are good choices for exporting to paint programs and can also be used with desktop publishing programs if you do not use a PostScript printer and cannot take advantage of the .EPS file format. However, one of the object-oriented formats such as .WMF or .EPS (for professional desktop publishing use) is a better choice for desktop publishing applications. Unlike the bitmap formats, the object-oriented formats are easy to resize without distortion, and they preserve more attribute information. You should select a bitmap file format only when one of the following conditions applies:

- ♦ The application to which you are exporting accepts only bitmap graphics.
- ♦ You plan to alter the CorelDRAW! graphic using techniques available only in the pixel-by-pixel editing environment of a paint program.

As shown in Table B-2, CorelDRAW! can export drawings in many bitmap formats. When you choose a bitmap format from the File Export dialog box, the secondary Bitmap Export dialog box opens, as shown in Figure B-5.

You can export full-color and gray-scale images with these bitmap formats. The files they create, if uncompressed, would be quite large—as high as tens of megabytes for a full-color, rasterized magazine cover, for example—as shown in the bottom of the dialog box. When you have the option of compressing a file, the Compressed check box will be available for selection.

Specifying a Bitmap Graphics Resolution

Assuming you have chosen a pixel-based export file format and then selected OK, you can choose the bitmap resolution from the Bitmap Export secondary dialog box. The available resolution is from 75 dpi (dots per inch), up to 300 dpi. You can also specify FAX Fine, FAX Normal, or Custom resolutions. A higher resolution is the option to choose if you want to give the exported image the best possible appearance—but it will also take up more disk space.

Because of the way a computer stores pixel-based graphics, an image that is large in CorelDRAW! can occupy an enormous amount of memory (for example, 5MB for a medium-sized image) when you export it at a high resolution. Rather than export the graphic at a lower resolution, consider

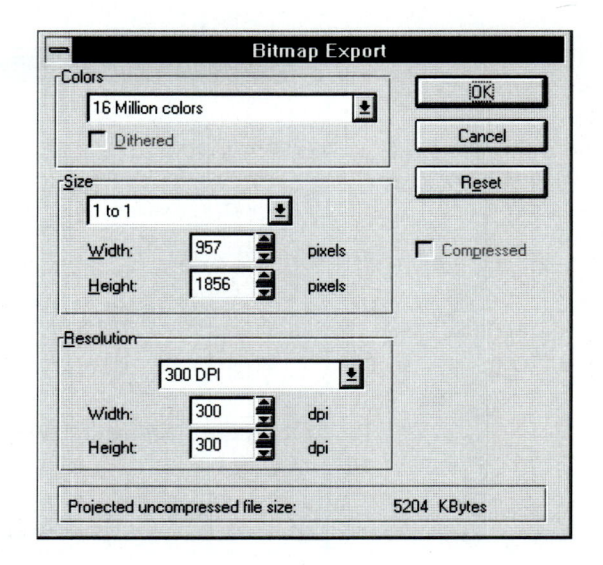

Bitmap Export
dialog box
Figure B-5.

using the Pick tool to scale the CorelDRAW! image down to the size it should be in the final application. For example, if you plan to export the graphic to a desktop publishing program and know the desired image size on the page, scale it down to that size before exporting it from CorelDRAW!. This precautionary action will also prevent you from having to resize the bitmap later, thereby causing its appearance to deteriorate.

Exporting to Object-Oriented Graphics Formats

As mentioned earlier, object-oriented formats transfer color, outline, fill, and attribute information more accurately than is the case with bitmap formats. In addition, object-oriented formats are device-independent, which means that their images look the same despite resizing or changes in the display resolution.

Your main concerns when choosing an object-oriented export format are the final use to which you plan to put the image and the kinds of information you cannot afford to lose during the export process.

Use CorelDRAW! Help any time there is doubt about the way the import or export filters handle a particular format.

Exporting to an EPS Format

EPS is a good example of an object-oriented format that is widely used. As with most of the objected-oriented formats, a secondary dialog box will appear when OK is selected in the Export EPS dialog box, as shown here:

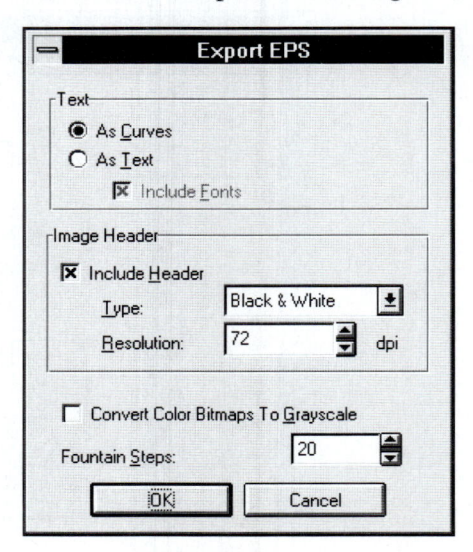

Importing and Exporting Files

Translating Text
You can choose to translate text into curves or to export it as text. If you export As Text, the Include Fonts checkbox will be available and checked as the default. This insures that those Type1 fonts (or TrueType Fonts after being converted to Type1 fonts) which are used in the image will be exported along with the image. If you disable the Include Fonts checkbox, the PostScript names of the fonts only will be identified and fonts may have to be downloaded in the new application.

Including an .EPS Image Header (Thumbnail)
An image header is a thumbnail visual representation of a PostScript graphic for display on your screen. The Header Resolution option is available only when you select the .EPS Placeable export file format for PostScript images and the Export EPS secondary dialog box appears. While not truly WYSIWYG, the image header helps you position or crop the .EPS image in desktop publishing applications such as Aldus PageMaker and CorelVENTURA where thumbnails are supported. If you choose not to include an image header, select the 0 dpi option in the Header Resolution drop-down list box. In this case, you will not have a visual representation of an .EPS image in your desktop publishing application.

Choose the 0 dpi option only if you plan to use the exported .EPS image in an application that cannot display an .EPS image header.

The image header resolution you select does *not* affect the actual PostScript graphic. If conserving memory and disk space is a concern, you should select the Low Resolution option for the smallest image header. If accurate representation is more important to you than memory conservation, select the 300 dpi option to obtain an image header that is true to the proportions of the actual graphic. The 300 dpi Header Resolution option can result in an image header that adds more than 64K to the .EPS file.

Converting Color to Grayscale
You can convert color bitmaps to grayscale by clicking on this option. This allows color bitmaps to print as black and white on some PostScript Level 1 printers.

Setting Fountain Steps
Setting Fountain Steps is used to control the gradations in fountain fills.

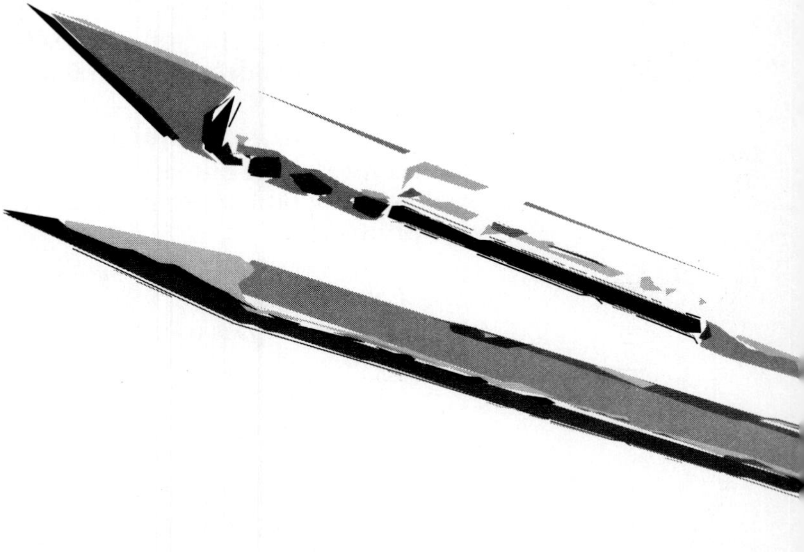

INDEX

+ key, 152
    for retaining original objects, 264
+ (on the numeric keyboard), with the Shape tool, 310
> (Greater than) operator, in Query Builder, 628
>= (Greater than or equal to) operator, in Query Builder, 628
< (Less than) operator, in Query Builder, 628
<= (Less than or equal to) operator, in Query Builder, 628
<> (Not equal) operator, in Query Builder, 628
= (Equal to) operator, in Query Builder, 628
1:1 tool, 28-29
2-D charts, 634-636
3-D Bar charts, 657
3-D Bars format, for 3-D Riser charts, 657
3-D Connect Group chart, 657
3-D Connect Series chart, 657
3-D effects, with radial fountain fills, 242
3-D Floating chart, 657
3-D globe, drawing a, 517
3-D Riser charts, 657
3-D Rotate filter, 684
3-D Rotation mode, in the Extrusion roll-up, 466, 472-473
3-D rotator, 472-473
3-D Scatter charts, 658
3-D Surface charts, 658
300 dpi printers, versus high-resolution imagesetters, 432

A

Absolute Area chart, 656
Absolute Line chart, 655
Action section, in the Cue Information dialog box, 703-704
Active cell, 639
Actor Information dialog box, 706, 707
Actor tool, in CorelMOVE, 697
Actors, 690
    controlling cels of, 709-710
    creating libraries of, 708-709
    defining registration points for, 700
    editing, 706
    multiple-cel, 690
    single-cel, 690
    special effects for, 700
Actual Size tool, 23, 28-29
    in CorelVENTURA, 537
Adaptive Unsharp filter, 683
Add (+) command, from the Node Edit roll-up, 308, 309, 310
Add Above Space at Column Top check box, 567
Add Frame dialog box, 582
Add Frame Tag dialog box, 552
Add New Chapter option, in the Layout menu, 618
Add Noise filter, 683
Add Paragraph Tag dialog box, 571-572
Add Perspective option, on the Effects menu, 438, 456
Adobe Illustrator file format, 762, 763
    exporting from CorelCHART, 650
    importing into CorelCHART, 649
Adobe PostScript controllers, genuine versus compatible, 427
Adobe TYPE 1 Font file format, exporting from CorelCHART, 650
Adobe Type file format, 763
Advanced Screening dialog box, 419
.AI extension, 649, 650, 762, 763
Aleatory characteristics, 253
Align command
    in the Arrange menu, 160, 162
    in the Node Edit roll-up, 323-324

Align dialog box, 160-163
Align To Baseline command, in the Text menu, 352
Align to Center of Page option, 162, 163
Align to Grid option, 162, 163
Alignment, for body text, 607
Alignment attributes, setting, 561-565
Alignment tab, in the Paragraph Settings dialog box, 561-565
Allow Adding Points check box, 695
ALT-BACKSPACE, 47
ALT-F, 33
ALT-F4, 33, 72
ALT-SPACEBAR, 8
Always condition, for cues, 702
Always Overprint Black option, 420
Ami Pro file format, 762
Anchors, 590
And relationship, between criteria, 627-628
Angle attribute, 181
Angle settings, 200-201, 203
Angles, constraining lines to, 41-42
Angular dimension line tool, 55
Animation Information dialog box, 694, 695
Animation Insert tool, inserting files into CorelSHOW, 719
Animation window, 692
Animations
    basics of, 690-691
    controlling the playback of, 701-703
    opening, 705-706
    settings for new, 693
Anti-Alias all cels option, 700
Apparent fill, 233-234
Applications
    selecting from CorelSHOW, 719
    working with different, 373-380
Arcs, creating open, 330-331
Area charts, 655-656
Area Percent chart, 656
Ares Fontminder, 753
Around tab, in the Ruling Lines dialog box, 554
Arrange menu, 11
    in CorelMOVE, 692
    in CorelSHOW, 716
Arrow keys, for moving objects, 149
Arrowhead drop-down list box, 589
Arrowhead Editor, 180, 196-198
Arrowhead pointer, with the Shape tool, 296, 297
Arrowheads
    adding, 195-196
    editing, 196-198
Arrows
    with box text, 588-589
    two-way, 276
Arrows attribute, for the Outline Pen, 179-180
Arrows line-ending display box, 195
Artistic filters, 681

Artistic text, 21, 97
Artistic Text tool
    in CorelSHOW, 717
    selecting, 21
Artwork, complex, 429
ASCII file format, importing into CorelCHART, 642
ASCII Text file format, 762
Aspect ratio, 259
    maintaining for graphics, 585
    restoring, 586
Attributes
    copying an object's, 385-388
    copying from Outline Pen, 204
    editing for text strings, 340-342
    setting for frames, 550-555, 581-582
    transferring to the Clipboard, 375
Auto Flatness value, 423-424
Auto trapping, 419-420
Auto-Flow Table setting, 620
Auto-Leader spacing, 562
Auto-Panning, 262
Auto-Reduce option, 735
Auto-Spreading option, 420
AutoCAD file format, 762, 763
    exporting from CorelCHART, 650
    importing into CorelCHART, 649
AutoJoin, 62-65, 735
AutoJoin threshold, adjusting, 63-65
Automatic Hyphenation, selecting, 570
Automatic Kerning option, 570
Automatic Letter Spacing option, 568
Autoscan command button, 640
AutoTrace pointer, 732-733
AutoTrace Tracking option, 735
AutoTracing, 730-734
    combining with manual tracing, 737-738

B

Back One command, 154, 155
Back Parallel type, of extrusion, 468
Background Color Selector tool, 700
Background illustrations, settings for, 203
Background Library tool, in CorelSHOW, 718
Background View icon, 720
Background view mode, 717
Backgrounds, displaying the library of, 718
Banding, 431
Bar charts, creating, 653-655
Bar Percent chart, 655
Bars, changing in charts, 644
Base page, 526
Base page frame, 526
Baseline, 345
    constraining text to, 352
Batch Files roll-up, 741-742

Index

Batch processing mode, setting PostScript printers for, 427
Batch trace, 742
Beginning node, of a line, 179
Behind Fill check box, 182
Behind Fill setting, in the Outline Pen dialog box, 187-188, 202
Bevel corner, 181
Beveled corners, 190
Bézier drawing, of straight lines, 46-47
Bézier mode, 38
    of drawing curves, 51-54
    selecting, 44
Bézier tool, 45
Bipolar Absolute Area chart, 656
Bipolar Absolute Line chart, 655
Bipolar Side-by-Side Bar chart, 654
Bipolar Stacked Area chart, 656
Bipolar Stacked Bar chart, 654
Bipolar Stacked Line chart, 655
Bitmap Export dialog box, 771
Bitmap fill patterns, 246-252
Bitmap graphics, 760
    cropping, 766
    importing into CorelDRAW!, 766-767
    resampling, 767
    specifying resolution for, 771-772
    versus object-oriented graphics, 760-764
Bitmap graphics formats, exporting to, 770-772
Bitmap images, 246, 727-728
    AutoTracing, 730-734
    creating, 728-730
    importing, 728-730
    tracing with CorelTRACE, 742-744
    tracing manually, 734-738
Bitmap Pattern Editor, 249
Bitmap texture fills, 250
Black, outlining with, 225-226
Blemishes, correcting in existing images, 673
Blend command, 459
Blend roll-up, 11, 438, 439
Blend roll-up window, 459-460
Blended objects, rotating, 460-464
Blends, splitting and fusing, 460
.BMP extension, 650, 651, 763
Body text, alignment for, 607
Body text fonts, selecting, 604-607
Body Text style tag
    defining, 607-608
    modifying, 604-608
Body Text tag, 559-574
Border styles, customizing for tables, 621
Borders, creating for frames, 580
Bottom alignment, of text, 561
Boundary markers, 259
Bounding box, in Paragraph mode, 119
Box text, 586-589

Box text arrows, creating, 589
Box text frames, removing the borders of, 588
Box Text tool, 538
Break Apart command, from the Arrange menu, 320
Break command button, in the Node Edit roll-up, 319
Breaks, setting, 563-565
Breaks tool, in CorelVENTURA, 535
Brickley, David, 520-521
Brightness filter, 681
Brush tool, in CorelMOVE, 699
Bubble charts, 659
Bullet style tag, 573
Bullets, 560
Butt end, 191, 192
Butt line end style, 181
Buttons, ribbon bar, 17-18

C

[C#] code, 590
Calhoun, Keith, 492-493
Calligraphic nibs, creating variable, 198
Calligraphic style, varying, 203
Calligraphy option, in the Outline Pen dialog box, 198-202
Calligraphy settings, 181-182
Callout lines, 492, 493
Callouts, 58-60, 587
Canvas roll-up, 669
Cap Height setting, 549
CAPS LOCK key, displaying the status of, 539
Caption frames, 527
    generating, 590-591
Captions, 589-591
Carding, 549
.CCH extension, 649, 762
CD-ROM disk drive, for CorelDRAW! 5, 754
CDBEdit, accessing, 534
.CDR extension, 7, 649, 762
.CDS extension, 642
Cel Cycle Arrows tool, 700
Cel Sequencer roll-up, 709-710
Cell address, 639
Cell Borders tab, in the Table Settings dialog box, 621, 622
Cell Spacing, in tables, 621
Cells, 639
    shading in tables, 621, 623
Cels, 690
    metamorphosis between two, 700
Center alignment
    of text, 106
    of text in CorelVENTURA, 561
Center of rotation, of objects, 279-281
Centerline tracing, 744-745
.CGM extension, 649, 650, 762, 763
Chapter Down tool, in CorelVENTURA, 535

Chapter layout, in CorelVENTURA, 603-604, 610
Chapter numbers, generating in captions, 590
Chapter operations, controlling, 531-532
Chapter Settings dialog box, 546-550, 594, 598
Chapter Settings Typography tab, 550
Chapter Up tool, in CorelVENTURA, 535
Chapters, 528
    adding to publications, 618-619
    creating, 542-555, 603-604
    setting attributes for, 546-550
Chapters list box, 531
Character Angle setting, in the Character Attributes dialog box, 345, 349-350
Character attributes, setting, 559-561
Character Attributes dialog box, 98-101, 115-117, 177, 344-350
    accessing, 344
    options in, 345-346
    values displayed in, 346
Character option, for adjusting spacing, 116
Character Reference Chart, 132
Character tab, in the Paragraph Settings dialog box, 560-561
Character Title style tag, modifying, 573
Character Tracking, 568
Characters
    adjusting the space between, 350-354
    entering special, 131-132
    kerning multiple, 353-354
    kerning single, 351-353
    representing space between, 568
    reshaping, 358-360
    shifting horizontally and vertically, 348
    stylizing, 358
    tilting to different angles, 349-350
CHART subdirectory, 652
Chart templates, 634
    creating, 652-653
Chart types, creating, 653-661
Chart Types list box, 638
Chart View, activating from Data Manager, 636
Charting, basics of, 634-636
Charts
    creating new, 638
    customizing, 643-651
    modifying elements of, 651-652
    using as chart templates, 653
Check boxes, 13-14
"Child Curve" status message, 479
Choke, 420
Circle Object tool, 672
Circles
    converting to curve objects, 332-334
    drawing, 87-88, 230
    shaping, 330-334
    starting from the rim, 87
Classes, of objects, 19

Clear Envelope command, 453
Clear Extrude option, in the Effects menu, 471-472
Clear Perspective option, 457-458
Clear Transformations command, in the Effects menu, 266, 453, 458
Clicking, 6
Clip-art
    adding, 499-501
    integrating images with line art, 496-501
Clipboard, 366-367
    copying objects to, 368-369
    copying text to, 123
    importing via, 761
    memory limits of, 374-375
    transferring attributes to, 375
Clone tools, 674
Cloning objects, 384-385
Closed curve objects, drawing, 49-50
.CMP extension, 649, 650, 762, 763
.CMX extension, 649, 762
CMYK color model, 208, 220-221
Cobra (drawing), 390-391
Color attribute, for the Outline Pen, 179
Color blending attributes, in the Blend roll-up window, 460
Color calibration bars
    printing, 418
    selecting, 416
Color Controls mode, in the Extrusion roll-up, 466, 473-475
Color drop-down palette, 215
Color filters, 681
Color Manager option, 530
Color Mask roll-up, 669
Color model, selecting, 209
Color Override, 165
Color palette, 9, 176
Color palettes, in CorelCHART, 637
Color Pick-up tool, 699
Color roll-up, 669
Color separations, 415-416
    generating, 418-421
    and halftone screen patterns, 421
Color units, 220
Color wheel icon, 474
Color-matching systems, 208
Colors
    adding to Custom Palettes, 223-225
    defining new, 223-225
    mixing area for, 221
Column attributes, setting, 553-554
Column breaks, setting in CorelVENTURA, 563-564
Column tab, in the Frame Settings dialog box, 553-554
Columns
    putting text in, 124, 125
    setting attributes for, 553-554
    in tables, 625

Index

Combine command, 158, 159
    in the Arrange menu, 322, 384
Command buttons, 14
Complex artwork, 429
Complex curve objects, printing, 431
CompuServe Bitmap file format, 762, 763
    exporting from CorelCHART, 650
    importing into CorelCHART, 649
Computer, required for CorelDRAW! 5, 752
Computer Graphics Metafile file format, 762, 763
    exporting from CorelCHART, 650
    importing into CorelCHART, 649
Condition section, in the Cue Information dialog box, 702
Conical fountain fills, 237
    defining, 245-246
Connect dialog box, 398
Connectivity, for graphics applications, 759-760
Constraining
    ellipses to circles, 87
    lines to angles, 41-42
    rectangles to squares, 78
Context-sensitive help, 13
    in CorelSHOW, 723
Contour filter, 684
Contour roll-up, on the Effects menu, 11, 440, 477-478
Contours, 476-479
Contrast filter, 681
Control Panel, in CorelMOVE, 704-710
Control Panel window, 396
Control points, 51-52, 294, 299-300
    for curve segments, 313
    dragging, 298
    moving, 304-307
Control-menu box, 8
Convert To Curves command, from the Arrange menu, 329
Convert TrueType to Type 1 option, 426
Copies, specifying the number for printing, 404
Copy Attributes dialog box, 204, 386-387
Copy Attributes From command, 204
Copy command, selecting, 368
Copy Perspective From option, 457
Copy tool
    in CorelQUERY, 625
    in CorelVENTURA, 535
Corel5 icon, 6
Corel5 window, 6
Corel MOSAIC, importing graphics with, 613-618
Corel Presentation Exchange file format, 762
    importing into CorelCHART, 649
Corel Sheet file format, importing into CorelCHART, 642
\COREL50 directory, 754
CorelCAPTURE, 4
CorelCHART, 4, 633-661
    initial screen, 636

    inserting files into CorelSHOW, 719
    starting, 636-637
    toolbox in, 636-637
CorelCHART file format, 762
    importing into CorelCHART, 649
CorelDRAW!, 4-5
    exiting from, 72
    file format, 762
    graphics, editing in CorelVENTURA, 615-618
    inserting files into CorelSHOW, 719
    installing, 754-757
    Presentation file format, importing into CorelCHART, 649
    quitting, 33-34
    running as an icon, 8
    screen components of, 7-10
    starting, 5-7
CORELDRAW.DOT, 194
CORELDRW.END, 197
CorelKERN, accessing, 534
CorelMOSAIC, 4
    accessing, 534
    activating from CorelSHOW, 723
    importing graphics into, 583
CorelMOVE, 4, 689-710
    Control Panel in, 704-710
    main screen for, 691-692
    menus in, 692-694
    starting, 691
    toolbox in, 694-704
CorelPHOTO-PAINT, 4
    accessing, 534
    features of, 674-686
    icon, 664
    initial screen for, 664
    inserting files into CorelSHOW, 719
    making selections in, 674-676
    overview of, 664-674
    screen elements of, 666-674
    starting, 664-665
    toolbox, 671-674
CorelPHOTO-PAINT file format, 762, 763
    exporting from CorelCHART, 650
    importing into CorelCHART, 649
CORELPLR.EXE program, 725
CorelQUERY, 4, 533-534
    importing tables with, 623-630
    screen for, 624
    tools in, 625
CorelSHOW, 4, 713-725
    limitations of, 714
    modes in, 717
    overview of, 714
    screen elements of, 715-717
    starting, 714-715
    toolbox in, 717-719
CorelSHOW Runtime Player, 725

CorelTRACE, 4, 728
   customizing tracing options in, 744-747
   loading, 739-741
   main window for, 740
   memory requirements for, 739
   preparing to use, 738-739
   tracing bitmaps with, 742-744
   tracing with, 738-747
CorelTRACE file format, 762
   importing into CorelCHART, 649
CorelVENTURA, 4, 525-526
   editing CorelDRAW! graphics in, 615-618
   importing graphics into, 582-583
   menus in, 530-534
   ribbon, 534, 535-536
   screen for, 529-530
   toolbox, 534, 536-538
Corner attributes, setting for Outline Pen, 189-190
Corner radius indicator, distorted, 328
Corner Threshold option, 735
Corners options, for the Outline Pen, 181
.CPT extension, 650, 651, 679, 763
Create Arrow command, in the Special menu, 198
Create From command, 451-452
Create from File option button, in the New Actor dialog box, 697, 698
Create a New Image dialog box, 664-665
Crescent moon, creating, 337
Criteria tab, in the Query Builder dialog box, 627-628
Crop Image dialog box, 766, 767
Crop marks, 416, 574
   printing, 418
Cropped bitmap, 731
Cropped graphics, 586
Crosshair mouse pointer, 20
.CSV extension, 642
.CT extension, 650, 651, 763
CTRL
   for constraining ellipses to circles, 87
   for constraining lines, 41
   for constraining text to the nearest baseline, 352
   with envelopes, 446-448
   with mirror images, 274
   for moving objects at a 90-degree angle, 147-149
   with page buttons, 538
   for rotating objects, 277-278
   for scaling objects, 268
   for sizing objects, 263
   with skewing, 284
CTRL-D, 380, 382, 443
CTRL-F, 509, 502
CTRL-F1, 764
CTRL-F2, 104, 260
CTRL-F3, 164
CTRL-G, 538
CTRL-J, 231
CTRL-P, 405, 411, 414

CTRL-R, 287
CTRL-S, 71
CTRL-SHIFT-HOME, 120, 124
CTRL-SHIFT-T, 98
CTRL-T, 104, 115
   in CorelPHOTO-PAINT, 671
CTRL-V, 123, 368
CTRL-X, 371
CTRL-Y, 60
CTRL-Z, 146, 266
Cue Information dialog box, 701-704
Cue tool, in CorelMOVE, 701-704
Curtain opening/closing, for slides, 723
"Curve" message, 50
Curve objects
   drawing closed, 49-50
   printing complex, 431
Curve (Pencil) tool, in CorelCHART, 637
Curve segments
   converting straight line segments to, 314-315
   converting to straight line segments, 314
   converting to straight lines, 313
Curve tool, in CorelMOVE, 699
Curves, 38
   breaking at single or multiple nodes, 319-320
   converting ellipses and circles to, 332-334
   converting rectangles to, 329
   drawing in Bézier mode, 51-54
   drawing in Freehand mode, 47-51
   drawing multisegment, 49
   erasing portions of, 48-49
   joining with lines, 62-65
   reshaping, 295
   selecting with the Shape tool, 295-297
   strategy for reshaping, 302
Cusp command button, in the Node Edit roll-up, 316
Cusp nodes, 298
   converting into smooth nodes, 317
   moving the control points of, 305, 306
Cusped nodes, creating, 315-316
Custom halftone screen angles, specifying, 419
Custom installation, 754, 755
Custom Palettes, adding colors to, 223-225
Custom tracing settings, defining, 746-747
Customize buttons, 755-756
Cut command, 370-373
Cut tool, 535
Cut-Corner Bars format, for 3-D Riser charts, 657

D

Dashed and dotted line styles list box, 193
Dashed line, selecting, 193-194
Data
   entering with the Data Manager, 640-642
   importing with the Data Manager, 642-643
Data categories, 634

Index

Data Manager, 639-643
    activating from Chart View, 636
    entering data with, 640-642
    importing data with, 642-643
Data Manager window, 639
Data menu, 624
Data point, 634
Data Range tag, 640
Data series, 634
Data Source dialog box, 626
Decimal alignment, of text, 561
Default style sheet, 543
Default tab attributes, 608
Default tabs, setting, 561-562
Defaults tab, of the Paragraph Settings dialog box, 568, 569
DEFAULT.STY, 543, 603, 604
Degree of rotation, of text, 503
DEL, for deleting objects, 146
Delete (-) command, from the Node Edit roll-up, 312
Delete command, 371
Densitometer scales, 416
    printing, 418
Depth, changing, 469-470
Depth counter, 469
Desk, exploded view of a, 492, 493
Desktop publishing, 525
Device-independent graphics, 761
Diagonal mirror images, creating, 273-274
Dialog boxes, 13-16
.DIB extension, 650, 651, 763
Diffuse filter, 683
Dimension labels, changing settings for, 57, 58
Dimension line tools, 55
Dimension lines, 55-58
Directional sharpen, 683
Directional Smooth filter, 683
Directory, creating a, 756-757
Display adapter, required for CorelDRAW! 5, 753
Display boxes, 15, 16
Display Status dialog box, 648
"distorted" message
    for ellipses, 331
    for rectangles, 328
Dot-matrix printers, printing CorelDRAW! graphics on, 428-429
Dotted line, selecting, 193
Double-clicking, 6
Download Type 1 fonts option, activating, 425-426
Draft view, 532
Drawing device, required for CorelDRAW! 5, 753
Drawing files, creating a directory for, 756-757
Drawing scale, setting, 55-56
Drawing tools, 19-21
    in CorelPHOTO-PAINT, 686-687
    in CorelVENTURA, 537
Drawings
    creating, 65-69

creating with ellipses and circles, 88-92
creating in layers, 164-168
creating with rectangles and squares, 82-85
increasing precision in, 60-62
saving, 69-71
Drop Cap Character tab, 608-609
Drop caps, 359, 560, 608
Drop-down list boxes, 15
Drop-shadow effect, creating, 515-516
.DRW extension, 650, 762
.DRX extension, 650
Dual-Axis Absolute Area chart, 656
Dual-Axis Absolute Line chart, 655
Dual-Axis Bubble format, for Bubble charts, 659
Dual-Axis Bubble with Labels format, for Bubble charts, 659
Dual-Axis Polar chart format, 659
Dual-Axis Radar format, for Radar charts, 659
Dual-Axis Side-by-Side Bar chart, 654
Dual-Axis Stacked Area chart, 656
Dual-Axis Stacked Bar chart, 654
Dual-Axis Stacked Line chart, 655
Duplicate command, 368, 380-381, 382
dx code, in the status line, 40
.DXF extension, 649, 650, 762, 763
dy code, in the status line, 40
Dynamic link, forming, 377

E

Edge Detect filter, 682
Edge Enhance filter, 683
Edge padding, 243-244
Edit command button, 697
Edit Layers dialog box, 165-166
Edit menu, 10
    in CorelMOVE, 692
    in CorelPHOTO-PAINT, 666
    in CorelQUERY, 624
    in CorelSHOW, 715
    in CorelTRACE, 740
    in CorelVENTURA, 532
    in the Painting window, 700
Edit Path menu, 697
Edit Text dialog box, 98-101
    entering text in, 102
Editing tools, 21-22
Editing window, toggling with full-screen preview, 285
Effects menu, 11, 437-441
    in CorelPHOTO-PAINT, 667
    in the Painting window, 700
Effects Sequence flyout, 710
Ellipse tool, 20, 85
    in CorelCHART, 637
    in CorelPHOTO-PAINT, 673
    in CorelVENTURA, 538

Ellipses
    aligning text in, 504
    converting to curve objects, 332-334
    drawing, 85-87
    drawing from the center outward, 86-87
    shaping, 330-334
    starting from any point on the rim, 85-86
em dash, converting hyphens to, 555
em space, 568
Embedding, 376, 379-380
Emboss filter, 682
Encapsulated PostScript file format (EPS), 763
End caps, selecting, 190-192
End nodes, 306
End point, for a line, 40
Ending node, of a line, 179
Enhance filter, 683
Entrance (drawing), 520-521
Envelope editing modes, 442
    using more than one, 450-451
Envelope roll-up, 11, 438, 441
Envelope shapes
    creating, 442
    selecting from predefined, 441
Envelopes, 438, 441-453
    adding new, 450-451
    clearing, 453
    copying to new objects, 451-452
    CTRL with, 446-448
    options for fitting objects to, 442
    SHIFT with, 446-448
.EPS extension, 649, 650, 763
EPS format, exporting to, 772-773
EPS image header (Thumbnail), including, 773
EPS Placeable file format, 762, 763
Equal to (=) operator, in Query Builder, 628
Equalize filter, 684
Eraser tool, in CorelMOVE, 699
Error handlers, for diagnosing PostScript printing problems, 429-430
Excel file format, importing into CorelCHART, 642
Excel for Windows file format, 762
    importing into CorelCHART, 649
Excel worksheets, importing, 642
Existing objects, 210
Exit command, 33
Exploded Desk (drawing), 492-493
Export dialog box, 769-770
Export EPS dialog box, 772-773
Export file formats, in CorelDRAW! 5, 763
Exporting
    from CorelDRAW!, 650-651, 768-770
    help for, 764
Extended memory, 752
Extract dialog box, 121
Extrude roll-up, on the Effects menu, 438, 439
Extrude roll-up window, 466-467
Extruded objects, 464-476

Extrusion Presets mode, in the Extrusion roll-up, 466, 467
Extrusions
    applying to open paths, 476
    clearing, 471-472
    depth of, 469-470
Eyedropper tool, 673

F

[F#] code, 590
F1, 13
F2, 24, 640
    in CorelPHOTO-PAINT, 669
F3, 24
    in CorelPHOTO-PAINT, 669
F4, 24, 30, 378
    in CorelPHOTO-PAINT, 669
F5, 20, 43
F6, 20
    in CorelPHOTO-PAINT, 669
F7, 20
    in CorelPHOTO-PAINT, 669
F8, 21
    in CorelPHOTO-PAINT, 669
F9, 233, 285, 410
F10, 297
F11, 238
Family, of characters, 604
Fancy filters, 682
Fast Forward button, 704
Fast Printing Direct to Port check box, 399
Feathering, 549
Fields, in tables, 625
Figure numbers, generating in captions, 590
File formats
    for imported graphics, 649-650
    in Windows, 366
File information
    printing, 418
    printing with graphics, 412-415
File Information list box, in the Publication Manager dialog box, 531
File menu, 10
    in CorelPHOTO-PAINT, 666
    in CorelQUERY, 624
    in CorelSHOW, 715
    in CorelTRACE, 740
    in CorelVENTURA, 530-532
    in the Painting window, 700
File Open dialog box, displaying, 535
File Operations option button, 532
File Operations tab, in the Publication Manager dialog box, 531
Files
    editing partial, 670
    exporting from CorelDRAW!, 768-770
    listing the most recent, 10

Index

opening to trace, 741-742
placing temporary, 739
printing to, 410-412
retrieving, 71-72
Files List/Font Name tool, 536
Fill attributes, setting default, 228
Fill color attributes, defining, 228-229
Fill Color icon, 228
Fill roll-up, 621, 623
    in CorelPHOTO-PAINT, 669
Fill Roll-up icon, 228
Fill roll-up window, 253
Fill styles, copying, 253-254
Fill tool, 22, 228, 208
    in CorelCHART, 637
    in CorelPHOTO-PAINT, 673
    hints about, 253-254
Fills
    increasing the smoothness of, 422
    placing outlines behind, 182, 187-188
Filters, in CorelPHOTO-PAINT, 680-684
Find dialog box, 129
Firstpar style tag, 571-572
Firstpar tag, setting, 608-609
Fisher, Reed, 390-391
Fit in Frame check box, 584-585
Fit Text To Path command, in the Text menu, 501-502
Fit Text To Path Offsets dialog box, 504
Fit Text To Path roll-up, 509-510
    opening, 502
Fit to Page option, in the Print Option dialog box, 409-410
Fit-in-Window tool, 23, 30-31
Fixed columns, width of, 620-621
Flatness, setting for PostScript printers, 423-424
Flip Path Horizontal button, 696
Flip Path Vertical button, 696
Flow Text Around Frame check box, 579
Flyout submenus, 18
FOCOLTONE Colors, 208
Font tool, in CorelQUERY, 625
Fonts, 100, 604
    accessing, 341
    assigning to characters, 346-347
    selecting, 109-114, 559
    selecting in CorelVENTURA, 604-610
Fonts list box, 99
Footer frames, 527
Footers, 594-597
Footnote frames, 527
Footnote tab, in the Chapter Settings dialog box, 598
Footnotes, 597-598
For Mac option, 411
Foreground Color Selector tool, 699
Form tracing, 745
Format menu
    in CorelQUERY, 624

in CorelVENTURA, 533
Formula bar, 640
Forward One command, 154
Fountain Fill dialog box, 237-240
    opening, 238
Fountain Fill icon, 228
Fountain fills
    custom, 237-246
    printing, 431
    steps for, 422-423
    transferring to other applications, 375
Fountain steps
    for enhancing previews and printing, 254
    increasing the value for, 431
Frame anchors, 532
Frame attributes, setting in CorelVENTURA, 610-611
Frame Attributes dialog box, 124
Frame counter, in CorelMOVE, 704
Frame option, on the Format menu, 550
Frame pointer, 578
Frame Settings dialog box, 551, 579
Frame Tab drop-down list boxes, 552
Frame tags, 527, 528, 542, 581-582
    selecting existing, 552
Frame tool, 578
    in CorelVENTURA, 536
Frames, 97
    in animations, 690
    in CorelVENTURA, 526-528, 542
    creating borders for, 580
    for graphics in CorelVENTURA, 578-582
    justification around, 549
    in Paragraph mode, 119
    repeating, 593-594
    setting attributes for, 550-555
    setting inside margins for, 580
Free frames, 527
Freehand drawing, of straight lines, 46-47
Freehand mode, 38
Freehand Object Picker tool, 675-676
Freehand Object tool, in CorelPHOTO-PAINT, 672
Freehand tool, selecting, 43
Freehand tool icon, 38
Freehand Tracking, 82, 735
Frequencies, of halftone screen patterns, 236
Frequency, of the default screen pattern, 424
Front Parallel type, of extrusion, 468
Full color fill patterns, 249-250
Full color mode, 50-51, 210
Full Color Pattern dialog box, 249-250
Full Color Pattern icon, 228
Full Height tool, in CorelVENTURA, 537
Full installation method, 754, 755
Full Page tool, 537
Full page view, 22
Full screen preview, toggling with the editing window, 285

Full Width tool, 537

G

Gallery list box, 638
Gamma filter, 681
Gantt charts, 660
Gaussian effect, 683
.GEM extension, 649, 650, 762, 763
GEM file format, 763, 762
    exporting from CorelCHART, 650
    importing into CorelCHART, 649
General tab
    in the Frame Settings dialog box, 579
    in the Table Settings dialog box, 619-621
Generated tags, 591-593
.GIF extension, 649, 650, 762, 763
Glass Block filter, 682
Globe, drawing a 3-D, 517
Glossary, 534
Go to Page option, in the View menu, 538
Goto tool, 625
Granular effect, adding to images, 683
Graphic lines, creating, 479
Graphic tab, in the Frame Settings dialog box, 583-585
Graphics
    adding to charts, 647-649
    centering, 585
    cropping, 586
    editing in CorelDRAW!, 615-618
    exporting, 768-770
    exporting from CorelCHART, 650-651
    fitting in windows, 30-31
    importing with Corel MOSAIC, 613-618
    importing into CorelCHART, 649-650
    importing into CorelVENTURA, 582-583
    positioning precisely, 585-587
    scaling in CorelVENTURA, 583-585
    sizing in CorelVENTURA, 583-585
    tiling, 406-408
    See also Clip-art; Images
Graphics files, importing from CorelMOSAIC into CorelSHOW, 723
Graphics tablet, 753
Gray
    defining shades of, 226
    outlining with, 225-226
Gray levels, visible for PostScript halftone screen patterns, 236
Grayscale, 208
Greater than (>) operator, in Query Builder, 628
Greater than or equal to (>=) operator, in Query Builder, 628
Grid, 80-82
    changing setting for, 60-62
Grid & Scale Setup dialog box, 55-56, 60, 61
Grid layer, 164

Grid Setup dialog box, 80-81
Grid tool, in CorelQUERY, 625
Group command
    in the Arrange menu, 156-157
    for complex PostScript illustrations, 406
Grouped objects, with the Shape tool, 297
Grouping, objects, 140, 156-158
Grow Inter-Line to Fit settings, 567
Guidelines, 65-67
    in CorelVENTURA, 530
Guides layer, 164
Gutters, 97, 553

H

Hairline icon, 177
Hairline width, 185
Halftone screen angles
    setting, 219
    specifying custom, 419
Halftone screen frequency, selecting, 219
Halftone screen patterns
    and color separation, 421
    filling objects with, 234
    selecting, 218-219
Halftone screen type, selecting, 219
Halftone screens, 218
Hand-sketched look, settings for, 203
Handles, 137
Hanging indent, creating, 565
Hard disk drive, requirements for CorelDRAW! 5, 752-753
Hardware requirements, for CorelDRAW! 5, 752-754
Hardware-specific printing problems, 426-429
Header frames, 527
Header/Footer Insert buttons, 595
Headers, 594-597
Headline, creating a, 497-498
Height scale numeric entry box, 409
Help
    context-sensitive, 13
    context-sensitive in CorelSHOW, 723
Help menu, 12-13
    in CorelMOVE, 692
Help tool, in CorelVENTURA, 536
High-resolution imagesetters, versus 300 dpi printers, 432
High/Low/Open/Close charts, 659-660
HIMEM.SYS, 752
Histograms, 660-661
Hollow box tools, 673
Hollow nodes, 137
Honeycomb Surface format, for 3-D Surface charts, 658
Horizontal alignment, of objects, 161
Horizontal Alignment buttons, in CorelVENTURA, 561-562
Horizontal Bar charts, 653

Index

Horizontal dimension line tool, 55
Horizontal Histogram format, 661
Horizontal Line charts, 655
Horizontal mapping options, for envelopes, 442
Horizontal mirror images, creating, 272
Horizontal ruler, 9, 62
Horizontal scroll bar, 9
Horizontal shift, of characters, 348
Horizontal Shift option, in the Character Attributes dialog box, 345
Horizontal skewing, 283
Horizontal vanishing point, 455
Hot zone, for hyphenation, 126
HP Plotters, printing CorelDRAW! graphics on, 428
HP printers, printing CorelDRAW! graphics on, 428
HPGL Plotter file format, 762, 763
    exporting from CorelCHART, 650
    importing into CorelCHART, 649
HSB color model, 208, 220-221
Hue/Saturation filter, 681
Hyphenation, 126, 127
    selecting, 570
Hyphens, converting to an em dash, 555

I

IBM PIC file format, exporting from CorelCHART, 650
IBM PIF file format, 762, 763
    importing into CorelCHART, 649
.ICB extension, 650, 651, 763
If/After condition, for cues, 702
Image header, including with EPS exports, 773
Image information, transfer of, 365-366
Image menu, in CorelPHOTO-PAINT, 667
Images
    cropping during importing, 761
    fitting to pages, 409-410
    flipping horizontally, 421
    managing the screen display of, 666-667
    retouching, 684-686
    scaling, 408-409
    scaling outlines with, 188-189
    See also Clip-art; Graphics
Imagination (drawing), 434-435
Imaging Options tab, of the Preferences dialog box, 694
Import command, in the File menu, 728, 729
Import command button, in the Two-Color Pattern dialog box, 248
Import Data dialog box, 642
Import dialog box, 765-766
Import file formats, in CorelDRAW! 5, 762-763
Importing
    help for, 649-650, 764
    into CorelDRAW!, 765-768
Impressionism filter, 681
Impressionist filter, 682
Indented margins, setting, 568

Indents, for paragraphs, 607-608
Ink Flow setting, in the Powerline roll-up, 481
Insert menu, in CorelSHOW, 716
Insert New Object dialog box, 616
Insert Object dialog box, 379
Insert Table tool, in CorelVENTURA, 535
Insertion point, 98, 99
Installation methods, 754, 755
Installed Printers list box, 397
"Inter-Character" message, 355
Inter-character spacing, adjusting, 354-356
"Inter-Line" message, 357
Inter-Line setting, 549
Inter-Line space, 565-568
Inter-Line spacing, 607
    adjusting, 357-358
Inter-Paragraph spacing, 567
"Inter-Word" message, 357
Inter-word spacing, adjusting, 354, 356-357
Interactive mode, setting PostScript printers for, 427
Intersection command, 168, 170
Invert filter, 682
Invisible layer, 165
Isometric views, 493

J

Jaggy Despeckle filter, 682
.JFF extension, 649, 650, 762, 763
Join command, in the Node Edit roll-up, 321-323
JPEG Bitmap file format, 762, 763
    exporting from CorelCHART, 650
    importing into CorelCHART, 649
.JPG extension, 649, 650, 762, 763
.JTF extension, 649, 650, 762, 763
Justification, settings for, 549
Justification tool, 536
Justified alignment, of text, 561

K

Kerning, 350-354, 548
    adjusting manually, 548
    multiple characters, 353-354
    single characters, 351-353
Keyboard, moving objects with, 149
Knocked out objects, 419-420
Kodak Photo CD file format, 762
    importing into CorelCHART, 649

L

Labels, adding to charts, 645-647
Landscape orientation, 88
LaserJet mode, switching to, 429
Lasso Mask tool, 679
Lasso Object tool, 672

Lasso tool, 699
Lassoing
    nodes of a word, 343
    objects, 136, 142
Layers, 164-168
    changing the stacking order of, 167-168
    creating, 166
    deleting, 166
    editing, 165-166
    features of, 165-168
    naming, 165
Layers roll-up window, 164
Layers/Objects roll-up, in CorelPHOTO-PAINT, 669
Layout drop-down list box, 544
Layout menu, 11
    in CorelVENTURA, 533
Layout tab, in the Chapter Settings dialog box, 546-547
Leader Character option, 562
Leader spacing, 562
Leadered check box, 562
Leading, 116, 565, 607
Leakproof objects, 208
Leave Original key, 152
"Leave Original" message, 264, 272
Leaves, creating, 337
Left alignment, of text, 105-106
Legend dialog box, 644-645
Legends, adding to charts, 644-645
Leimaker in Moonlight (drawing), 336-337
Lens roll-up, 11
    on the Effects menu, 440, 485-488
Lens types, 487
Less than (<) operator, in Query Builder, 628
Less than or equal to (<=) operator, in Query Builder, 628
Letters. *See* Characters
Library roll-up, in CorelMOVE, 708-709
Light intensity control, in Extrude roll-up, 475
Light Source mode, in the Extrusion roll-up, 466, 475-476
Like operator, in Query Builder, 628
Line art, integrating clip-art with, 496-501
Line breaks, setting in CorelVENTURA, 564
Line Caps options, for the Outline Pen, 181
Line charts, 655
Line end caps, selecting, 190-192
Line endings, selecting all, 179-180
Line Indents options, 565
Line option, for adjusting spacing, 116
Line Percent chart, 655
Line Style attribute, for the Outline Pen, 180-181
Line styles, 192-195
Line tools
    in CorelMOVE, 699
    in CorelPHOTO-PAINT, 673
    in CorelVENTURA, 538
Line Width attribute, for the Outline Pen, 180

Line Width Selector tool, in CorelMOVE, 700
Line widths, adjusting for Outline Pen, 186-187
Linear fountain fills, 237
    defining, 237-241
Lines
    constraining to angles, 41-42
    drawing in Bézier mode, 44-47
    drawing multisegment, 43
    drawing straight, 38-44
    erasing, 43
    erasing portions of, 41
    extending, 41
    finding the beginning of, 179
    joining with curves, 62-65
    selecting with the Shape tool, 295-297
    setting the number of indented, 565
    shaping, 295
Linked objects
    editing, 617
    placing graphics as, 615-616
Linking, 376
    objects, 377-378
Links, updating, 378
List boxes, 15-16
Load Text dialog box, 556, 557
Local Undo tools, 673
Locked layer, 165
Loop button, selecting, 705-706
Loop icon, 704
Loop option, for rotating blends, 461
Loop point, 696
Loop To Here check box, 696
"loose" message, 568
Looser tracking, 568
Lotus 1-2-3 file format, 762
Lotus Graphics file format, importing into CorelCHART, 650
Lotus Pic file format, 762

M

Macintosh computer, printing controlled by, 411
Macintosh PICT file format, 762, 763
    exporting from CorelCHART, 650
    importing into CorelCHART, 650
Magic Wand Object tool, 672
Magic wands, in CorelTRACE, 745-746
Magnification, adjusting, 23-24
Maintain Aspect Ratio check box, 585
Manual tracing
    of bitmap images, 734-738
    combining with AutoTracing, 737-738
Map Nodes button, 463
Map to Sphere filter, 682
Mapping filters, 682-683
Margins, setting indented, 568
Margins tab, in the Frame Settings dialog box, 551

Index

Marquee, 25
    activating, 677
    selecting with, 142-143
Marquee tool, 699
Mask menu, 667
Mask Picker tool, 673
Mask tools, 679
Masking colors, modifying or protecting, 755
Masks, 679-680
Master layer, identifying, 165
Master object, 384
Matching nodes, mapping, 463-464
Matrix/Imapro SCODL file format, exporting from CorelCHART, 650, 763
Maximize button, 8
Maximum filter, 683
Maximum Justification, setting, 549
Median filter, 683
Memory, required for CorelDRAW! 5, 752
Menu bar, 8
    in CorelPHOTO-PAINT, 666-667
Menus, 10-13
    in CorelMOVE, 692-694
    in CorelVENTURA, 530-534
Merge-Back dialog box, 123
Mesh Warp filter, 684
Metafile format, 366
Micrografx file format, 762
    importing into CorelCHART, 650
Microsoft Windows. *See* Windows (program)
Microsoft Word file format, 762
Minimize button, 8
Minimum filter, 683
Minor Heading style tab, 573
Mirror all cels option, 700
Mirror images
    creating, 271-275
    creating diagonal, 273-274
Mirror to Facing Pages command button, 610
Miter corners, 181, 190
Miter Limit setting, 181
Mixing area, for colors, 221
Models, for specifying color, 208
Modes, in CorelSHOW, 717
Mogensen (drawing), 363-364
Mogensen, William, 290-291, 362-363
Monitor, required for CorelDRAW! 5, 753
Moon, creating crescent, 337
Morph Cel option, 700
MOSAIC, importing graphics with, 613-618
Mosaic roll-up, 583, 614
    opening in CorelVENTURA, 535
Mosaic Roll-Up icon, 723
Motion Blur filter, 682
Mouse, required for CorelDRAW! 5, 753
Move Frame With Point command, 697
MultiLayer option, from the Layers roll-up menu, 166

Multilayering, 166-167
Multiple curve segments, converting to straight line segments, 314
Multiple nodes
    adding, 310-311
    deleting, 311-312
    deselecting, 300-301
    making symmetrical, 318-319
    moving, 303-304
    selecting, 300-301
    smoothing, 316-317
    See also Nodes
Multiple Pie chart, 656
Multiple Proportional Pie chart, 656
Multiple Proportional Ring Pie chart, 656
Multiple Ring Pie chart, 656
Multisegment curves, drawing, 49
Multisegment lines, drawing, 43

N

Negative and flipped images, creating, 421-422
Negative images, creating, 421
New Actor dialog box, 697-698
New Animation tab, of the Preferences dialog box, 693
New dialog box, in CorelCHART, 638
New Layer dialog box, 166
New Prop dialog box, 701
New Publication dialog box, 544
    displaying, 535
New tool
    in CorelQUERY, 625
    in CorelVENTURA, 535
New Wave dialog box, 701
Next Page button, in CorelVENTURA, 538
Nib, 181
Nib Shape display box, 181
Nib shapes, varying, 482-483
No alignment, of text, 106-108
No Fill icon, 228
Node Align dialog box, 325
Node Edit roll-up, 483-484
Node Edit roll-up window, 307-325
Node types, changing, 300
Nodes, 45
    adding multiple, 310-311
    adding single, 308-310
    aligning, 323-325
    breaking current, 319
    breaking curves at, 319
    choosing start and end in the Blend roll-up window, 460
    constraining the movement of, 304, 305
    converting curved into smooth, 317
    on a curve, 294, 295, 296-297
    deleting, 311-312
    deselecting multiple, 300-301

determining the number of, 431
editing, 307
hollow, 137
joining, 321-323
making symmetrical, 318-319
mapping, 463
mapping matching, 463-464
moving in 90 degree increments, 304, 305
moving, 301-307
moving multiple, 303-304
moving single, 302-303
selecting multiple, 300-301
selecting for the Shape tool, 297-301
selecting single, 298-300
smoothing, 316-317
splitting into subpaths, 319
types of, 298-299
See also Multiple nodes; Single nodes
Noise filters, 683
Normal Word Spacing, 568
Not equal (<>) operator, in Query Builder, 628
Nudging objects, 149
NUM LOCK key, displaying the status of, 539
Numbering slides, 722
Numeric entry boxes, 14

O

Object Brush Picker tool, 673
Object Linking and Embedding. *See* OLE
Object menu, in CorelPHOTO-PAINT, 667
Object Node Edit Picker tool, in CorelPHOTO-PAINT, 673
Object Picker tools, 677
    in CorelPHOTO-PAINT, 672-673
Object-oriented graphics, 760-761
    importing into CorelDRAW!, 767-768
    versus bitmap graphics, 760-764
Object-oriented graphics formats, exporting to, 772-773
Objects
    aligning, 160-164, 324
    applying PowerLines to, 480-482
    arranging, 153-164
    blending, 459-464
    changing on charts, 651-652
    changing the rotation of, 279-281
    classes of, 19
    cloning, 10, 380-385
    combining, 140
    combining and breaking apart, 157-160
    combining with the Shape tool, 297
    combining to form a curve object, 232
    copying, 367-370
    copying the attributes of, 385-388
    copying between pictures, 369-370
    copying from one layer to another, 166
    copying while moving, 151-153
    copying within a picture, 368-369
    in CorelPHOTO-PAINT, 676-679
    creating with default attributes, 176-182
    cutting and pasting, 370-373
    cutting and pasting between pictures, 374, 372-373
    cutting and pasting within a picture, 371-372
    cycling through, 143-145
    defining outline color attributes for, 209-210
    deselecting, 137, 141, 142
    duplicating, 380-385
    editing Outline Pen attributes for existing, 185-202
    embedding, 379-380
    existing, 210
    extruding, 464-476
    filling all at one time, 384
    filling with PostScript halftone screen patterns, 234-237
    filling with uniform spot color, 229-234
    grouping, 140, 156-158
    jointly selecting, 140
    lassoing, 136, 142
    linking, 377-378
    mirroring with the Transform Roll-up, 274-275
    moving, 145-153
    moving at a 90-degree angle, 147-149
    moving from one layer to another, 166
    moving with the keyboard (nudge), 149
    moving multiple, 147, 148
    moving single, 146-147
    open, 62
    pasting, 367-370
    placing into objects, 440
    positioning with precise measurements, 149-151
    printing selected, 404-406
    reordering superimposed, 153-155
    retaining copies of originals, 264-265
    retaining a copy while rotating, 278-279
    rotating, 275-282
    rotating blended, 460-464
    scaling, 267-271
    selecting, 136-145
    selecting with the Pick tool, 367
    sizing, 259-267
    skewing, 275, 282-288
    spreading the lighter, 420
    transferring from other applications, 376
    transferring to other applications, 375
    transforming, 257-258
    types of, 19
    viewing selected, 29-30
OCR tracing, 745
Octagons format, for 3-D Riser charts, 657
ODBC (Open Database Connectivity) interface, 624
Offset, of a copy, 380
OLE, 366, 376-380
    in CorelCHART, 643
OLE application tools, in CorelSHOW, 718-719

Index

OLE applications, inserting files into CorelSHOW, 719
OLE connections, in CorelSHOW, 714
One-point perspective, 453, 454
Onion skin, 701
Onscreen color palette, 176
Opaque object, 701
Open arcs, creating, 330-331
Open Database Connectivity (ODBC) interface, 624
Open Drawing dialog box, displaying, 71
Open objects, 62
"Open Path" message, 49
Open Path objects, 208
Open paths
    applying extrusions to, 476
    closing, 321
Open tool
    in CorelQUERY, 625
    in CorelVENTURA, 535
Operating system, for CorelDRAW! 5, 754
Operators, in Query Builder, 628
Option buttons, 13, 14
Options menu, in the Painting window, 700
Or relationship, between criteria, 627-628
Order option, of the Arrange menu, 153-155
Order/Group tab, in the Query Builder dialog box, 628, 629
Orientation, of text, 503
Original mapping options, for envelopes, 442
Orphans, controlling, 533
Orthogonal extrusion, 468
OS/2 Bitmap file format, 763
    exporting from CorelCHART, 650
    importing into CorelCHART, 650
Outline color, 174
Outline color attributes
    copying, 227
    defining, 209-210
    setting new, 210-213
Outline Color dialog box, 209-210, 211-212, 213-214
    listing spot colors, 217
Outline filter, 682
Outline Pen, 173-174
    customizing defaults for, 182-183
    defining attributes of, 174
    defining for text, 202
    flyout menus, 184
    hints about, 202-204
    selecting a preset width, 184-185
    using, 174-202
Outline Pen attributes
    editing for existing objects, 185-202
    setting, 179, 215
Outline Pen dialog box, 178, 182-183, 580-581
Outline Pen Dialog Tool icon, 175, 177, 178
Outline Pen flyout menu, 174-175
Outline Pen roll-up icon, 175
Outline Pen styles, customizing, 182-183

Outline Pen tool, for removing box text frame borders, 588
Outline styles, copying, 204
Outline thickness, adjusting, 185
Outline tool, 22
    in CorelCHART, 637
Outline tracing, 744
Outline widths, preset, 184
Outlines
    of an object, 137
    placing behind fill, 182, 187-188
    scaling with the image, 188-189
    tracing around, 744
Output devices, 394-395
    for CorelDRAW! 5, 753
Output mediums, 394
Oval tool, in CorelMOVE, 699
Overtime list box, 100

P

Page breaks, setting, 563
Page controls, 538
Page Layout view, 532
Page Setup dialog box, 89
Page size, for publications design, 602
PageMaker, exporting to, 375
Pages
    displaying entire, 537
    fitting images to, 409-410
    inserting manually, 543
    moving between as chapters, 538
    specifying for printing, 404
    viewing entire, 32-33
Paint Bucket tool, 699
Paint toolbox, 698, 699-700
Paintbrush file format, 763
    exporting from CorelCHART, 650
    importing into CorelCHART, 650
Painting tools, in CorelPHOTO-PAINT, 673
Painting window, in CorelMOVE, 698
Pair Kerning, 548
Palette menu, 212
Palettes, adding colors to Custom, 223-225
Panning, 32-33
PANTONE Process Color, 208
PANTONE Spot Colors, 208, 211
Paragraph attributes, 124
Paragraph dialog box, 124-126
Paragraph mode, 117-120
Paragraph Settings dialog box, 559-574
Paragraph spacing, 125
Paragraph tags, 528
Paragraph text, 21, 97-98
Paragraph Text tool, in CorelSHOW, 717
Paragraphs, 527
    indenting, 607-608

placing side-by-side, 535
Parallel extrusions, and perspective, 468-469
Parallel PostScript printers, 427
Parallel view, of extrusions, 468
Paste, from the Edit menu, 123
Paste command, selecting, 368
Paste Link option, 377-378
Paste Special dialog box, 377
Paste tool, in CorelVENTURA, 535
.PAT extension, 249, 649
Path
    aligning text on, 504
    distance of text from, 504
    fitting text to, 501-511
Path Edit roll-up, in CorelMOVE, 695-697
Path Point Information button, 696
Path Points Distribution button, 697
Path tool, in CorelMOVE, 695-697
Paths, for animated objects, 690-691
Pattern Selector tool, in CorelMOVE, 700
Pause until/for condition, for cues, 702
.PCC extension, 649, 762
.PCD extension, 649, 762
.PCT extension, 650, 762, 763
.PCX extension, 649, 650, 675, 763
PCX format, 728
Pen roll-up, 184-185
    using for outline color, 217-218
Pen shape
    for calligraphic effects, 198-202
    defining a custom, 181
Pen styles, copying, 227
Pencil flyout menu, 44-45
Pencil tool, 20, 37-69
    activating, 736
    in CorelCHART, 646
    in CorelMOVE, 699
    selecting, 20
Percent chart, 655, 656
Perspective, 453
    adding new, 456-457
    clearing, 457-458
    copying, 457, 458
    one- or two-point, 453-455
    and parallel extrusions, 468-469
Perspective effects, creating, 453-458
Perspective filter, 684
Perspective view, of extrusions, 468
.PFB extension, 650, 763
.PIC extension, 650, 762
Pick tool, 21
    activating, 136
    compared to the Shape tool, 293-294
    in CorelCHART, 637
    in CorelMOVE, 694
    in CorelSHOW, 717
    selecting objects with, 367

    for selecting text, 113
Pictographs, 661
Picture frame tag, 590-591
Pie charts, 656
Pie wedges
    creating, 331-332
    creating from circles, 505-506
.PIF extension, 649, 762, 763
Pinch/punch filter, 682
Pixel-based graphics. See Bitmap graphics
Pixelation filter, 682
Pixels, 62, 727, 760
Place Duplicates and Clones settings, 382, 383
Placement drop-down list, 100
Play Forward button, 704
Play Reverse button, 704
Playback controls, in CorelMOVE, 704-705
Playback Options tab, of the Preferences dialog box, 692
.PLT extension, 649, 762, 763
Point Information dialog box, 696
Point size, compared to actual or physical size, 347
Pointers, to source files in, 528
Pointillism filter, 681
Points, 108
    setting the locations of, 696
Polar charts, 658-659
Polygon Object tool, in CorelPHOTO-PAINT, 672
Polygon tool
    in CorelMOVE, 699
    in CorelPHOTO-PAINT, 673
Polygons
    drawing, 44
    drawing in Bézier mode, 46-47
Pop-up Menu tool, in CorelSHOW, 725
Portrait orientation, 88
Position button, in the Transform roll-up, 149-150, 259
Positioning tab, in the Table Settings dialog box, 621, 622
Posterize filter, 684
PostScript controllers, tips about, 426-427
PostScript error handler, downloadable, 429-430
PostScript fills, transferring to other applications, 375
PostScript halftone screen patterns
    filling objects with, 234-237
    outlining, 218-219
PostScript (interpreted) file format, 763
    exporting from CorelCHART, 650
    importing into CorelCHART, 650
PostScript language, internal limits in, 429
PostScript Level 2 printers, 426
PostScript Options dialog box, 218-219, 235
PostScript printers, 753
    complex artwork on, 429-432
    gray levels visible for halftone screen patterns, 236
    running in LaserJet mode, 429
    screen frequency for, 424-425
    setting Flatness for, 423-424

Index

tips about, 426-427
PostScript texture fills, 252-253
PostScript Texture icon, 228
PostScript textures, printing, 430
PostScript Type 1 fonts, 425-426
PowerClip option, on the Effects menu, 440, 488-490
PowerLine roll-up, 11
   on the Effects menu, 440, 480
PowerLines, 479-484
   applying to objects, 480-482
   displaying available, 480
Precision
   improving with the status line, 39-40
   increasing in drawings, 60-62
Preferences dialog box, 84, 382
   in CorelMOVE, 692-694
   in CorelSHOW, 724
Preferences-Curves dialog box, 63-64
   guidelines for setting options in, 735
Presentation tab, in the Preferences dialog box, 724
Presentations
   creating, 714
   moving slides between two, 721
   previewing in CorelSHOW, 724
Preset extrusions, selecting, 467
Preset PowerLines, selecting, 480
Presets roll-up, 12
Pressure lines, 483-484
Preview display box, in the Print Options dialog box, 403
Preview Fountain Steps, in the Preferences dialog box, 254
Preview Fountain Steps settings, 238
Previous Page button, in CorelVENTURA, 538
Print command, selecting, 402
Print dialog box, 400-412
   opening, 414
Print Information buttons, in the Print Options dialog box, 403
Print Manager, disabling, 399-400
Print options, advanced, 412-426
Print Options dialog box, 402-403
Print Quality drop-down list box, 400
Print Setup dialog box, 400, 401
Print To File dialog box, 411-412
Print tool, in CorelVENTURA, 535
Printable layer, 165
Printable page area, 8
   typing text directly in, 103-105
Printer resolution, and gray levels visible for halftone screen patterns, 236
Printer Timeouts settings, customizing, 398-399
Printers
   checking the setup of, 404
   for CorelDRAW! 5, 753
   installing, 396-398
Printers dialog box, 397

Printing
   complex curve objects, 431
   devices, supported by CorelDRAW!, 394-395
   fountain fills, 431
   hardware-specific problems, 426-429
   PostScript textures, 430
   preparation for, 396-400
   process, canceling, 426
   selected objects, 404-406
   to a file, 410-412
.PRN extension, 411
Process color system, 208
   outlining with, 220-225
Process color system (CMYK), generating color separations using, 415, 417
Program Manager window, 5
Prop Information dialog box, 706, 707
Prop tool, in CorelMOVE, 701
Proportional columns, width of, 620-621
Props, 690
   creating libraries of, 708-709
   editing, 706
.PS extension, 650, 763
PS pattern texture fill, 253
Psychedelic filter, 684
Publication Manager dialog box, 530-532
Publication Manager option, in the CorelVENTURA File menu, 529
Publication Operations button, 531
Publications, 528
   adding chapters to, 618-619
   designing in CorelVENTURA, 602-613
   saving, 535
   spacing attributes for, 607
Publications list box, 531
Putty mapping options, for envelopes, 442
Pyramids format, for 3-D Riser charts, 657

Q

Queries
   building, 629
   defining, 623
Query Builder, operators for, 628
Query Builder dialog box, 625, 627-628
Quick Format Roll-up, 536
Quotation marks, converting standard to typographer's, 555

R

Radar charts, 659
Radial fills, offsetting the center of, 243-244
Radial fountain fills, 237
   defining, 241-244
Radial offset, 243
Ranges, of cells, 639

Recent Color Pick-up tool, in CorelMOVE, 700
Records, in tables, 625
Rectangle Picker tool, in CorelPHOTO-PAINT, 672
Rectangle tool, 20, 76-79
    in CorelCHART, 637
    in CorelMOVE, 699
    in CorelPHOTO-PAINT, 673
    in CorelVENTURA, 538
    selecting, 20
Rectangles
    aligning text in, 504
    constraining to squares, 78
    converting to curve objects, 329
    drawing, 76-78
    drawing from any corner, 76-78
    drawing from the center outward, 78
    rounding the corners of, 326-328
Redlake (drawing), 290-291
Registration command, 700
Registration errors, minimizing, 420
Registration marks, 416
    printing, 418
Registration point, defining, 700
Regular format, for Radar charts, 659
Remove Noise filter, 683
Remove Outline tool, 588
Repeat Stretch, from the Edit menu, 287
Repeating frames, 593-594
Resample dialog box, 767
Restore button, 8
Retry command button, 426
Reverse Order command, 154
Rewind button, 706
RGB color model, 208, 220-221
Ribbon bar, 17, 8
    in CorelCHART, 636
    in CorelPHOTO-PAINT, 670-671
    in CorelSHOW, 719-723
Ribbon bar buttons, 17-18
Rich Text file format, importing into CorelCHART, 642
Rich Text Format file format, 762
Right alignment
    of text, 106
    of text in CorelVENTURA, 561
Right mouse button, zooming in with, 27
Ring Pie chart, 656
Ripple filter, 682
.RLE extension, 650, 651, 763
Roll-up menus, in CorelPHOTO-PAINT, 667-669
Roll-up windows, 11, 16
Rotate all cels option, 700
Rotate button
    on the Transform menu, 281-282
    in the Transform roll-up, 259
Rotate roll-up, 281-282
Rotated bitmap images, printing, 767

Rotating
    objects, 275-282
    objects in increments of 15 degrees, 277-278
    retaining a copy while, 278-279
    with Transform roll-up, 281-282
Rotation
    changing for objects, 279-281
    controlling the center of, 461
Round Rectangle tool, in CorelVENTURA, 538
Rounded corners, 181
Rounded line end cap, 191, 192
Rounded line end points, 181
Rounded Rectangle tool, 699
Rows, in tables, 625
.RTF extension, 642, 762
Rulers, 9
    in CorelVENTURA, 529-530
    displaying, 62
    resetting the zero point of, 587
Ruling lines, changing the width of, 581
Ruling Lines dialog box, 554-555
    displaying, 561
Run Screen Show icon
    in CorelSHOW, 720
    on the ribbon bar, 724

S

.SAM extension, 762
Sample Characters display box, 100
SAMPLE.CMV file, 705
SAMPLE.SHW file, 715
Sans serif typefaces, 606
Saturation filter, 681
Save Drawing dialog box, 69-71
Save Options dialog box, in CorelTRACE, 742-743
Save tool
    in CorelQUERY, 625
    in CorelVENTURA, 535
Scale & Mirror option, in the Transform roll-up, 259, 269
Scale & Mirror roll-up, retaining a copy while using, 270
Scale all cels option, 700
Scale with Image setting, in the Powerline roll-up, 481
"Scale" message, 268
Scale numeric entry boxes, 408-409
Scale Path button (=/-), 696
Scale Path dialog box, 696
Scale With Image check box, 182
Scaling
    from the center, 270-271
    images, 408-409
    in increments of 100 percent, 268
    objects, 259, 267-271
Scaling value, in the Print Options dialog box, 408
Scatter charts, 658
Scatter format, for Scatter charts, 658

Index

.SCD extension, 650, 763
Schneider, William, 434-435
SciTex CT Bitmap file format, 763
    importing into CorelCHART, 650
Scitex CTI Bitmap file format, exporting from CorelCHART, 651
Screen
    clearing, 42
    customizing, 22-23
Screen components, 7-10
Screen frequency, for PostScript printers, 424-425
Screen settings, adjusting, 420
Screen shows, displaying, 725
Screen/Menu Help icon, 723
Scroll arrows, 32-33
Scroll bars, 9, 15-16, 32-33
Scroll box, 32
SCROLL LOCK key, displaying the status of in CorelVENTURA, 539
.SCT extension, 650, 651, 763
Select All command, in the Edit menu, 143
Select the Default Database dialog box, 626
Select mode, 21
    for the Pick tool, 136
Select tab, in the Query Builder dialog box, 627-628
Selected Object tool, 23
Selected Objects check box, in the Print dialog box, 405
Selected Text Attributes dialog box, 594, 596
Selected Zoom tool, 29
Selection boxes, 29, 137
Selection tools, in CorelPHOTO-PAINT, 674-676
.SEP extension, 650, 651, 763
Separation sheets, printing, 420
Sequence Effect flyout, 709
Serial number, entering, 755
Serial PostScript printers, 427
Serial printers, installing, 397
Serif typefaces, 606
Set Flatness to setting, 423-424
Settings List drop-down box, 746
Setup dialog box, 404
SETUP program, 754-756
Shaded fill, for extrusions, 475
Shadow, creating, 285
Shape tool, 21-22, 293-294, 536-537
    activating, 297
    combining objects with, 297
    for editing pressure lines, 483-484
    editing text with, 342-344
    selecting objects with, 295-297
    selecting text with, 342-344
Sharp corners, 190
Sharpen filters, 683
SHIFT
    deselecting objects with, 141
    with envelopes, 446-448
    selecting with, 140-142
    for sizing and scaling from the center, 270-271
SHIFT-F4, 24
SHIFT-F11, 229
SHIFT-F12, 213
SHIFT-LEFT/RIGHT ARROW keys, for adjusting kerning, 548
SHIFT-TAB, for cycling through objects, 144, 145
Show Clock icons, 716
Show Color Names, in the Outline Color dialog box, 217
Show Page tool, 23
.SHR extension, 725
Shutter effects, for opening slides, 723
Side-by-Side Bar charts, 653
Side-by-Side Paragraphs button, 564-565
Side-by-Side Paragraphs tool, in CorelVENTURA, 535
Silhouette tracing, 745
Single Arc editing mode, 442, 445
Single arc envelopes, 445
Single curve segments, converting to straight line segments, 313
Single lines, drawing in Bézier mode, 45
Single nodes
    adding, 308-310
    deleting, 311-312
    making symmetrical, 318-319
    moving, 302-303
    selecting, 298-300
    smoothing, 316-317
    See also Nodes
Size button, in the Transform roll-up, 259
Size options, on the Transform roll-up, 265-267
Sizing
    from the center, 270-271
    objects, 259-267
    objects horizontally, 260-262
    objects in increments of 100 percent, 263-264
    objects vertically, 262-265
    with the Transform roll-up, 265-267
Skew, of text, 503
Skew button, in the Transform roll-up, 259
Skew roll-up, 286
Skewed bitmap images, printing, 767
Skewed rectangles, rounding the corners of, 328
Skewing
    in increments of 15 degrees, 284
    objects, 275, 282-288
    retaining a copy while, 284-285
    with the Transform roll-up, 285-286
Slide number icons, in CorelSHOW, 716
Slide Numbering icon, 722
Slide presentations, producing, 713
Slide Sorter View icon, 720-721
Slide sorter view mode, 717
Slide View icon, 720
Slide view mode, 717
Slide/Frame Duration list box, 723

Slides
    assigning the length of time for displaying, 723
    controlling elements and cues for, 722
    displaying in reduced size, 720-721
    modifying the background of, 720
    moving between two presentations, 721
    transition effects for, 722-723
Smear tool group, 684
Smear tools, 673
Smoked Glass filter, 682
Smooth command button, in the Node Edit roll-up, 317
Smooth filter, 684
Smooth nodes, 298
    converting cusped into, 317
    moving the control points of, 305, 306-307
Smoothing button, 697
Snap To Grid, 60
Snap To Guidelines, 60
Snap To Objects, 60
Soften filters, 683-684
Software requirements, for CorelDRAW! 5, 752-754
Solarize filter, 684
Solid fill, for extrusions, 474
Sound icon, 704
Sound tool, in CorelMOVE, 701
Sounds, creating libraries of, 708-709
SPACEBAR, pressing to activate the Pick tool, 136
Spacing
    adjusting inter-character, 354-356
    adjusting inter-line, 354
    adjusting inter-word, 354, 356-357
    adjusting interactively, 354-358
    adjusting for text, 114-117, 118
    options for paragraphs, 125
Spacing attributes, for publications, 607
Spacing tab, in the Paragraph Settings dialog box, 565-568
Speaker notes mode, in CorelSHOW, 717
Speaker Notes View icon, 720
Special characters, entering, 131-132
Special effects, creating, 11, 381
Special filters, 684
Special menu, 12
    in CorelPHOTO-PAINT, 667
Specify Template Destination dialog box, 544-545
Spectral Mapped charts, 660
Speed setting, in the PowerLine roll-up, 481
Spell Check dialog box, 126-128
Spell Check tool, in CorelVENTURA, 535
Spell checker, 534
Spelling checker, 126-128
Spike effect, 683
Spinners, 14
Spot color linear fountain fills, 238-241
    with PostScript halftone screens, 241
Spot color outlines, assigning, 213-214
Spot color radial fountain fills, 242-243
Spot color system, 208
    generating color separations using, 415-416
Spot colors
    filling objects with uniform, 229-234
    outlining with, 210-218
    selecting, 216-217
    translating into CMYK colors, 416
Spray Can tool, in CorelMOVE, 699
Spread, 420
Spread setting, in the Powerline roll-up, 481
SQL, 625
    queries, building, 629
    tab, in the Query Builders dialog box, 629
    tool, in CorelQUERY, 625
Square fountain fills, 237
    defining, 245-246
Square line end cap, 191, 192
Square line end type, 181
Square nodes, 342-343
Squares
    drawing, 78-80
    drawing from any corner, 79-80
    rounding the corners of, 326-328
Stacked Area chart, 656
Stacked Bar chart, 653-654
Stacked Line chart, 655
Stacked Radar format, for Radar charts, 659
Stacking order, of layers, 167-168
Start point, for a line, 40
Status line, 9-10
    in CorelCHART, 637
    for CorelMOVE, 704
    in CorelVENTURA, 538-539
    improving precision with, 39-40
Step Frame Forward button, 704
Steps and rotation controls, in the Blend roll-up window, 460
Stock Market charts, 659-660
Stop button, 704
Story Editor, 611-613
Story Editor view, in CorelVENTURA, 532
Straight Line editing mode, 442, 443-445
Straight line envelopes, 443-445
Straight line segments
    converting curve segments to, 314
    converting single curve segments to, 313
    converting to curve segments, 314-315
Straight Line Threshold option, 735
Straight lines
    drawing, 38-44
    drawing in Bézier mode, 44-47
Straighten Text command, in the Text menu, 352
Stretch attribute, 181
Stretch settings, 200-201, 203
Strikeout list box, 100
Strings, of text, 95
Structured Query Language. *See* SQL

Index

Style list box, 100
Style sheets, 528, 542
    selecting, 543-546
    setting to Read Only, 546
Style Tag drop-down list box, 559
Style tags, 527, 542, 558-575
Styles, 100
    assigning to characters, 346-347
    selecting for fonts, 112-114
Stylized text pictures, creating, 358-360
Stylus, 730
Subpaths
    breaking nodes into, 319
    joining separate, 322
Subscript text, 100
Subscripts, creating, 349
Superimposed objects
    cycling through, 144
    reordering, 153-155
Superscript text, 100
Superscripts, creating, 349
Surface format, for 3-D Surface charts, 658
Surface with Sides format, for 3-D Surface charts, 658
Swirl filter, 682
Symbol library, 130-131
Symbol roll-up, 12
Symmet command button, in the Node Edit roll-up, 318
Symmetrical nodes, 298-299
    moving the control points of, 305, 306-307
Synonyms, finding, 128-129
System requirements, for CorelDRAW! 5, 752-754

T

[T#] code, 590
TAB, for cycling through objects, 143, 144
Table charts, 660, 661
Table menu, 533-534
Table numbers, generating in captions, 590
Table Settings dialog box, 619-621
Tables, 625
    in CorelVENTURA, 619-630
    creating, 535
    creating in CorelVENTURA, 619-623
    importing with CorelQUERY, 623-630
    placing in frames, 619
    width of columns in, 620-621
Tabloid paper size, 407
Tabs, 14-15
    setting in CorelVENTURA, 561-562
Tabs and Returns tool, in CorelVENTURA, 536
Tabs tool, in CorelVENTURA, 535
Tag Base Text tool, in CorelVENTURA, 537
Tagged information, in cells, 639-640
Tags, 527-528
    in CorelCHART, 640
    generated, 591-593
Tags list box, 597
Tags List tool, in CorelVENTURA, 536
Tagwrite Editor, accessing, 534
Tail feathers, adding to lines, 195-196
Targa Bitmap file format, 763
    exporting from CorelCHART, 651
    importing into CorelCHART, 650
.TBL extension, 642
Temporary files, placing, 739
Text
    aligning, 105-108
    aligning on the path, 504
    balancing white space with, 607
    centering within a circle, 230-231
    in columns, 124, 125
    conforming to a shape, 450
    constraining to the nearest baseline, 352
    copying from one layer to another, 166
    creating and duplicating, 443
    defining Outline Pen for, 202
    degree of rotation of, 503
    as a design element, 339
    displaying sample, 100
    distance from the path, 504
    editing attributes of, 339-340
    editing with the Shape tool, 342-344
    entering, 101-105, 498-499
    extracting from CorelDRAW!, 120-123
    fitting to a path, 501-511
    flowing around frames, 579
    formatting in CorelCHART, 643-644
    formatting selected in headers/footers, 594
    importing into CorelDRAW!, 123, 376
    inserting, 96-101
    kerning interactively, 350-354
    merging into CorelDRAW!, 123
    moving from one layer to another, 166
    orientation of, 503
    pasting into CorelDRAW!, 123
    rotating in 90 degree increments, 567
    selecting with the Shape tool, 342-344
    space between the lines of, 565-568
    spell checking, 126-128
    substituting with TypeAssist, 534
    translating into curves, 773
    in two-column format, 125
Text Attributes dialog box, 108-109
Text boxes, 15
Text entry area, moving around in, 102-103
Text files, importing into CorelVENTURA, 555-558
Text mapping options, for envelopes, 442
Text menu, 11-12
Text pictures, creating, 358
Text ribbon, in CorelCHART, 636
Text ribbon bar, in CorelSHOW, 724
Text Roll-Up, 340-341

Text roll-up menu, 104
Text Rotation Angle drop-down list box, 567
Text spacing, adjusting, 118, 114-117
Text strings, 95
    deselecting, 137
    editing attributes for, 340-342
    entering, 15
    selecting, 113
Text tool, 21
    in CorelCHART, 637
    in CorelMOVE, 699
    in CorelPHOTO-PAINT, 673
    in CorelVENTURA, 537
    selecting, 96-97
Texture Fill dialog box, 251, 669, 670
Texture fills, 250-252
Texture icon, 228
Texture numbers, 250
Textured patterns, loading, 755
.TGA extension, 650, 651, 763
Thesaurus, 128-129
Threshold filter, 684
Thumbnail, including, 773
Thumbnail Frame numeric entry box, 693
.TIF extension, 650, 651, 763
TIF files, importing, 729-730
TIF format, 728
TIFF Bitmap file format, 762, 763
    exporting from CorelCHART, 651
    importing into CorelCHART, 650
TIFF Four Color file format, 762
Tight tracking, 570
Tile filter, 682
Tile size, 247
Tiling, 247, 246
    graphics, 406-408
Time On-Screen List, 723
Time So Far, displaying for presentations, 716
Timelines icon, 722
Timelines roll-up, in the View menu in CorelMOVE, 706-708
Timelines window, 722
Timeouts section of the Connect dialog box, 398-399
Tint all cels option, 700
Title bar, 7-8
To Back command, 154, 155
To Curve button, in the Node Edit roll-up, 314-315
To Front command, 154, 155
To Line command, in the Node Edit roll-up, 313, 314
Tone filters, 684
Tone Map filter, 681
Tool ensemble, in CorelPHOTO-PAINT, 671-672
Tool Settings roll-up, in CorelPHOTO-PAINT, 669
Toolbox, 9, 18-23
    in CorelCHART, 636-637
    in CorelMOVE, 694-704
    in CorelSHOW, 716, 717-719

Tools
    in CorelPHOTO-PAINT, 671-674
    creating, 19
Tools menu, in CorelVENTURA, 534
Top alignment, of text, 561
Total Time, displaying for presentations, 716
Trace All command button, in the Batch Files roll-up, 744
Trace menu, 740
Tracing, 738-747
Tracing options, customizing, 744-747
Tracing settings, defining custom, 746-747
Tracking, 568, 607
    adjusting, 84
Transform effects, 437-438, 439
Transform roll-up, 11, 149-150, 258-259
    mirroring objects with, 274-275
    precise scaling with, 269
    rotating with, 281-282
    sizing with, 265-267
    skewing with, 285-286
Transformation, of objects, 257-258
Transformation mode, 21
    for the Pick tool, 136
Transformations, 684
    repeating, 286-288
Transition Effects dialog box, 722
Transition Effects icon, 722-723
Transitions for Prop dialog box, 706, 708
Transmission retry value, 399
Transparency lens type, 487
Transparent areas, apparent fill of, 234
Transparent command, 701
Transparent objects, 701
Trapping, 419
Trim command, 168, 170
TrueType Font file format, 763
TrueType fonts, compared to Type 1 fonts, 425
TRUMATCH Colors, 208
.TTF extension, 763
Turner, Cindy, 336-337
Two Curves editing mode, 442, 446
Two curves envelopes, 446
Two-Color Pattern dialog box, 247
Two-Color Pattern Editor, 248-249
Two-Color Pattern icon, 228
Two-dimensional (2-D) charts, 634-636
Two-point perspective, 453, 454
Two-way arrows, 276
.TXT extension, 642, 762
Type 1 fonts, with PostScript printers, 425-426
Type and Depth mode, in the Extrusion roll-up, 466, 468-471
Type size selection box, 99
Type Size tool, in CorelVENTURA, 536
Type size units drop-down list box, 99

Index

Type sizes
　editing, 347
　selecting, 108-109
Type Style tool, in CorelVENTURA, 536
Type styles
　examples of, 605
　selecting for fonts, 112-114
TypeAssist, 534
Typeface family, 604
Typefaces, 604
　different versions of standard, 606
Typographer's quotes, converting to, 555
Typographical attributes, editing for characters in a text string, 342-344
Typographical text attributes, 340
Typography tab
　in the Chapter Settings dialog box, 547-550
　in the Paragraph Settings dialog box, 568-570

U

Unaligned text, 106-108
Unconstrained editing mode, 442, 448-450
Unconstrained envelopes, 448-450
Underline list box, 100
Undo, 371
Undo tool, in CorelVENTURA, 535
Ungroup command, 156, 157
Uniform Colors, 208
Uniform Fill dialog box, 229, 232
Uniform Fill icon, 228
Unprintable layer, 165
Unsharp Mask filter, 683
User interface, customizing, 10, 22-23

V

Vanishing point
　moving, 470-471
　options for, 469
Vanishing points, 455-456
Variables, placing in headers/footers, 594, 595
.VDA extension, 650, 651, 763
Vector graphics. *See* Object-oriented graphics
Vector images, 130, 246
Ventura, 98
Vertical alignment, of objects, 161
Vertical Alignment buttons, 561
Vertical Bar Bipolar Side-by-Side Bar charts, 654
Vertical Bar charts, 653
Vertical dimension line tool, 55
Vertical Histogram format, 661
Vertical Justification
　settings for, 570
　in tables, 621
Vertical Justification settings, 549
Vertical Line charts, 655
Vertical mapping options, for envelopes, 442
Vertical mirror image, creating, 272
Vertical ruler, 9, 62
Vertical scroll bar, 9
Vertical shift, of characters, 348
Vertical Shift option, in the Character Attributes dialog box, 345
Vertical vanishing point, 455
View, adjusting, 23-30
View menu, 10-11
　in CorelMOVE, 692
　in CorelPHOTO-PAINT, 666-667
　in CorelSHOW, 716
　in CorelTRACE, 740
　in CorelVENTURA, 532
Viewing, at actual size, 28-29
Viewing area, defining, 24-27
Vignette filter, 682
Visible layer, 165
.VST extension, 650, 651, 763

W

Wand, of the AutoTrace pointer, 732
Wave Editor, accessing in CorelMOVE, 701
Waveform curve, drawing, 302-303
Wedges, assigning colors to, 508
Weld command, 168, 169
Wet Paint filter, 683
White, outlining with, 225-226
White space, balancing with text, 607
Widows, controlling, 533
Width scale numeric entry box, 409
Wind filter, 683
Window border, 7
Window menu, 6
　in CorelPHOTO-PAINT, 667
　in CorelSHOW, 716
Windows
　changing the size of, 7
　fitting graphics in, 30-31
Windows program, starting, 5-6
Windows Bitmap file format, 732, 763
　exporting from CorelCHART, 651
　importing into CorelCHART, 650
Windows Clipboard. *See* Clipboard
Windows Metafile file format, 763, 764
　exporting from CorelCHART, 651
　importing into CorelCHART, 650
Windows Print Manager. *See* Print Manager
Windows requirements, for CorelDRAW! 5, 754
Windows swap file, 752
Windows Write, switching to, 121-122
Wireframe mode, 50-51
.WK2 extension, 762
.WK3 extension, 762
.WKS extension, 762

.WMF extension, 650, 651, 763
Woodcut tracing, 745
Word option, for adjusting spacing, 116
Word processor, switching to, 121-122
WordPerfect Graphics file format, 763, 764
    exporting from CorelCHART, 651
Words, placing space between, 568
Work, saving, 69-71
.WPG extension, 651, 763

X

x axis, 634-635
"X scale" message, 263
X-Y charts, 658
X-Y Dual-Axis format, for Scatter charts, 658
X-Y Dual-Axis with Labels format, for Scatter charts, 658
X-Y with Labels format, for Scatter charts, 658
.XLS extension, 642, 649, 762
XYZ Scatter format, for 3-D Scatter charts, 658
XYZ Scatter with Labels format, for 3-D Scatter charts, 658

Y

y axis, 635-636
"Y scale:" message, 262

Z

z axis, 636
Z_BOXTEXT generated tag, 587, 591
Z_CAPTION generated tag, 591, 592, 593
Zero point, resetting for rulers, 587
Z_FNOT# generated tag, 591, 598
Z_FNOT ENTRY generated tag, 591, 598
Z_FOOTER generated tag, 591, 596
Z_HEADER generated tag, 591, 596
Z_INDEX LTR generated tag, 591
Z_INDEX MAIN generated tag, 591
Z_INDEX TITLE generated tag, 591
Z_LABEL CAP generated tag, 591
Z_LABEL FIG generated tag, 591
Z_LABEL TBL generated tag, 591
Zoom Flyout Menu tools, 537
Zoom tool, 22-23
    in CorelCHART, 637
    in CorelPHOTO-PAINT, 673
    in CorelSHOW, 717
    in CorelVENTURA, 535, 536
Zoom-In tool, 23, 24-27
    in CorelVENTURA, 537
Zoom-Out tool, 23, 27-28
    in CorelVENTURA, 537
Z_SEC generated tag, 591
Z_TOC LVL generated tag, 591
Z_TOC TITLE generated tag, 591

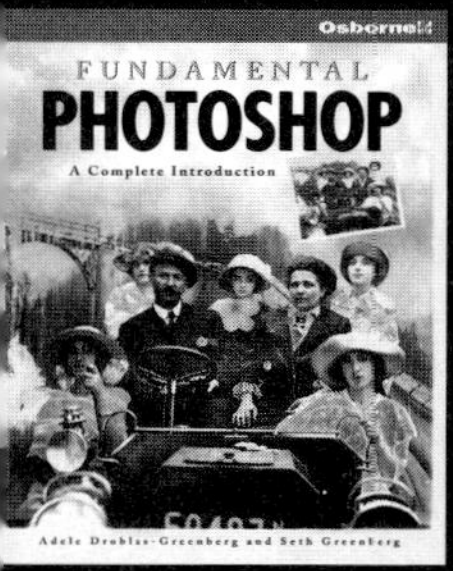

Fundamental Photoshop: A Complete Introduction
by Adele Droblas-Greenberg & Seth Greenberg
$27.95   ISBN: 0-07-881994-6

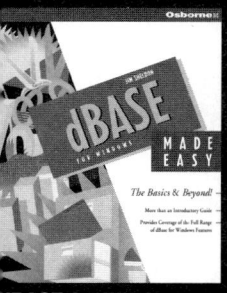

dBASE for Windows Made Easy
by Jim Sheldon
$26.95   ISBN: 0-07-881792-7

The Best Guide To Business Shareware
by Judy Heim, John Haib and Mike Callahan
Includes Two 3.5-Inch Disks
$34.95   ISBN: 0-07-882076-6

The Visual C++ Handbook
by Chris H. Pappas and William H. Murray, III
$29.95   ISBN: 0-07-882056-1

GET WHAT YOU WANT...

Expert Advice & Support 24 Hours A Day

Do you need help with your software?

Why pay up to $25.00 for a single tech support call!

Now, in conjunction with **Corporate Software Inc.**, one of the world's largest providers of tech support (they field more than 200,000 calls a month), Osborne delivers the most authoritative new series of answer books — **The Certified Tech Support** series.

- These books will bail you out of practically any pitfall.
- Find answers to the most frequently asked end-user questions, from the simple to the arcane.
- **Lotus Notes Answers: Certified Tech Support** is the next best thing to having an expert beside your computer.
- Watch for other books in the series.

EXCEL FOR WINDOWS ANSWERS:

From the Data Banks of Corporate Software, One of the World's Largest Providers of Tech Support, Answers to the Most Frequently Asked Questions...From the Simple to the Arcane.

Certified Tech Support

Mary Campbell

Excel for Windows Answers: Certified Tech Support
by Mary Campbell
$16.95
ISBN: 0-07-882054-5

Order Today!

BC640SL

MAKE THE RIGHT Connection

It's what you know that counts. With innovative books from LAN TIMES and Osborne/McGraw-Hill, you'll be the one in demand.

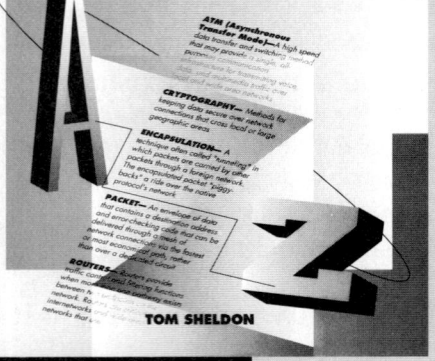

LAN TIMES Encyclopedia of Networking
by Tom Sheldon
An authoritative reference on all networking facets and trends.
$39.95
ISBN: 0-07-881965-2
Available now

LAN TIMES Guide to SQL
by James R. Groff and Paul N. Weinberg
$29.95
ISBN: 0-07-882026-X
Available now

LAN TIMES E-Mail Resource Guide
by Rick Drummond
$29.95
ISBN: 0-07-882052-9
Available June

LAN TIMES Guide to Interoperability
by Frank Hayes and Rick Stout
$29.95
ISBN: 0-07-882043-X
Available July

BC640SL

Revolutionary Information on the Information REVOLUTION

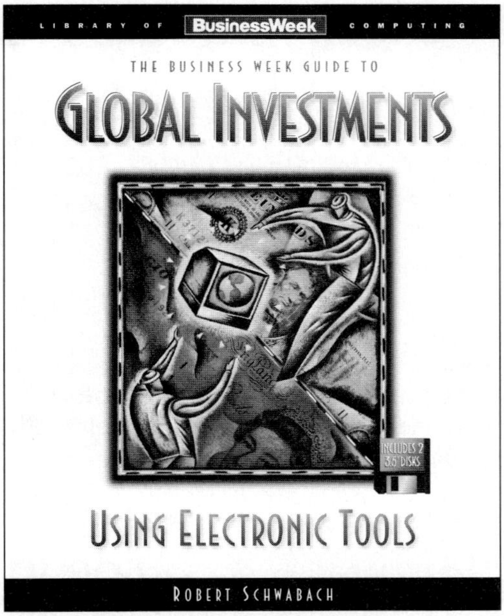

Alluring opportunities abound for the global investor. But avoiding investment land mines can be tricky business. The first release in the Business Week Library of Computing lets you master all the winning strategies. Everything is here — from analyzing and selecting the best companies, to tax planning, using investment software tools, and more. Disks include MetaStock, Windows on Wall Street, and Telescan, the leading investment analysis software.

Business Week's Guide to Global Investments Using Electronic Tools
by Robert Schwabach
Includes 3.5-Inch Disks
$39.95 ISBN: 0-07-882055-3

Business Week's Guide to Multimedia Presentations
Create dynamic presentations that inspire.
by Robert Lindstrom.
Includes One CD-ROM Disk.
$39.95
ISBN: 0-07-882057-X

The Internet Yellow Pages
by Harley Hahn and Rick Stout
$27.95
ISBN: 0-07-882023-5

BYTE's Mac Programmer's Cookbook
by Rob Terrell
Includes One 3.5-Inch Disk.
$29.95
ISBN: 0-07-882062-6

Multimedia: Making It Work, Second Edition
by Tay Vaughan
Includes One CD-ROM Disk
$34.95
ISBN: 0-07-882035-9

BC640SL

When It Comes to CD-ROM...
We Wrote the Book

Everything You Always Wanted to Know About CD-ROMs and More!

This Exclusive Book/CD-ROM Package Includes
- Sound and Clip Art
- Samples of CD-ROM Applications
- Multimedia Authoring Tools

Part buyer's guide, part standards guide, and part troubleshooter, the **BYTE Guide to CD-ROM** discusses all aspects of this proliferating technology so you can take full advantage.

The Internet Complete Reference
by Harley Hahn & Rick Stout
$29.95
ISBN: 0-07-881980-6

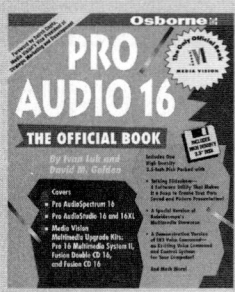

Pro Audio 16: The Official Book
by Ivan Luk and David M. Golden
Includes One 3.5-Inch Disk
$34.95, Book/Disk
ISBN: 0-07-881979-2

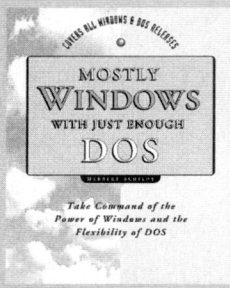

Mostly Windows With Just Enough DOS
by Herbert Schildt
$24.95   ISBN: 0-07-881976-8

Teach Yourself C++, Second Edition
by Herbert Schildt
$24.95
ISBN: 0-07-882025-1

BYTE Guide to CD-ROM
by Michael Nadeau, BYTE Senior Editor
Includes CD-ROM Disk
$39.95
ISBN: 0-07-881982-2

Osborne
Get Answers—Get Osborne
For Accuracy, Quality and Value

BC640SL

Secret Recipes
FOR THE SERIOUS CODE CHEF

No longer underground...the best-kept secrets and profound programming tips have been liberated! You'll find them all in the new BYTE Programmer's Cookbook series – the hottest hacks, facts, and tricks for veterans and rookies alike. These books are accompanied by a CD-ROM or disk packed with code from the books plus utilities and plenty of other software tools you'll relish.

BYTE's Mac Programmer's Cookbook
by Rob Terrell Includes One 3.5-Inch Disk.
$29.95
ISBN: 0-07-882062-6

BYTE's Windows Programmer's Cookbook
by L. John Ribar
Includes One
CD-ROM Disk.
$34.95
ISBN: 0-07-882037-5

BYTE's DOS Programmer's Cookbook
by Craig Menefee, Lenny Bailes and Nick Anis
Includes One
CD-ROM Disk.
$34.95
ISBN: 0-07-882048-0

BYTE's OS/2 Programmer's Cookbook
by Kathy Ivens and Bruce Hallberg
Includes One
CD-ROM Disk.
$34.95
ISBN: 0-07-882039-1

BYTE Guide to CD-ROM
by Michael Nadeau
Includes One
CD-ROM Disk.
$39.95
ISBN: 0-07-881982-2

Yo Unix!

Innovative Books from Open Computing and Osborne/McGraw-Hill

Open Computing's Guide to the Best Free Unix Utilities
by Jim Keough and Remon Lapid
Includes One CD-ROM Disk
$34.95
ISBN: 0-07-882046-4
Available now

Open Computing's Best UNIX Tips Ever
by Kenneth H. Rosen, Richard P. Rosinski, and Douglas A. Host
$29.95
ISBN: 0-07-881924-5
Available now

Open Computing's Unix Unbound
by Harley Hahn
$27.95
ISBN: 0-07-882050-2
Available July

Open Computing's Standard Unix API Functions
by Garrett Long
$39.95
ISBN: 0-07-882051-0
Available July